THE THREE OCCUPIED
UAE ISLANDS
THE TUNBS AND ABU MUSA

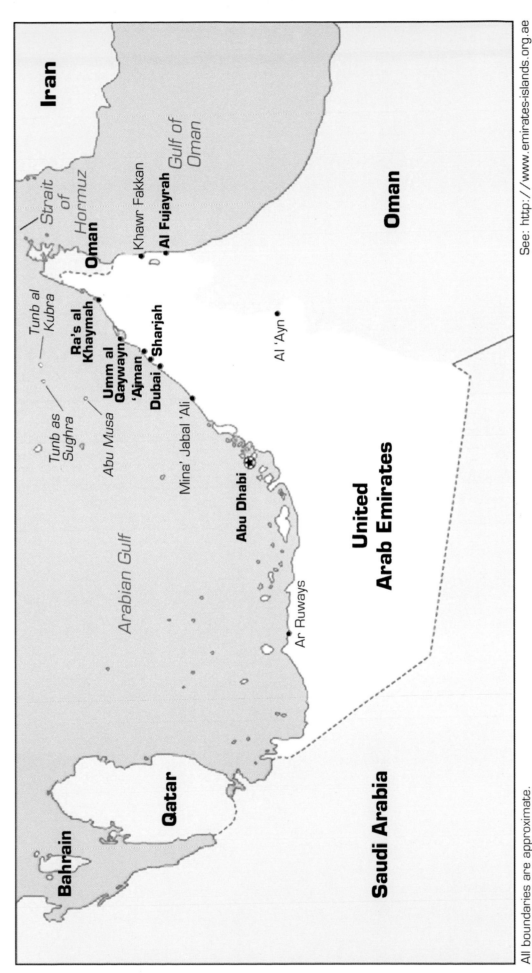

Iran

Strait of Hormuz

Oman

Khawr Fakkan

Al Fujayrah

Gulf of Oman

Tunb al Kubra

Ra's al Khaymah

Umm al Qaywayn

'Ajman

Sharjah

Dubai

Tunb as Sughra

Abu Musa

Al 'Ayn

Mina' Jabal 'Ali

Arabian Gulf

Abu Dhabi

Ar Ruways

United Arab Emirates

Oman

Bahrain

Qatar

Saudi Arabia

See: http://www.emirates-islands.org.ae

All boundaries are approximate.

THE THREE OCCUPIED UAE ISLANDS
THE TUNBS AND ABU MUSA

Thomas R. Mattair

THE EMIRATES CENTER FOR STRATEGIC
STUDIES AND RESEARCH

First published in 2005 by
The Emirates Center for Strategic Studies and Research
PO Box 4567, Abu Dhabi, United Arab Emirates
E-mail: pubdis@ecssr.ae
Website: http://www.ecssr.ae

ISBN 9948-00-765-4 standard hardback edition
ISBN 9948-00-764-6 paperback edition

CONTENTS

══════ ABBREVIATIONS AND ACRONYMS ══════

AAA   anti-aircraft artillery

AIOC   Anglo-Iranian Oil Company

ASW   anti-submarine warfare

APU   Arab Parliamentary Union

AWACS   Airborne Warning and Control Systems

CENTO   Central Treaty Organization

CENTCOM   Central Command (US)

CIA   Central Intelligence Agency

CNN   Cable News Network

DCA   defense cooperation agreement

DIA   Defense Intelligence Agency

EU   European Union

GCC   Gulf Cooperation Council

HH   His Highness

HIM   His Imperial Majesty

HMG   Her Majesty's Government

ICJ   International Court of Justice

IRGC   Iranian Revolutionary Guard Corps

ITLOS   International Tribunal for the Law of the Sea

JCS   Joint Chiefs of Staff

MAAG   Military Assistance Advisory Group

mbpd   million barrels per day

MENA   Middle East News Agency

MoU   Memorandum of Understanding

NIOC   National Iranian Oil Company

NSSM   National Security Study Memorandum

OIC   Organization of the Islamic Conference

PDRY	People's Democratic Republic of Yemen
PFLO	Popular Front for the Liberation of Oman
PFLOAG	Popular Front for the Liberation of the Occupied Arabian Gulf
PFLOAG	Popular Front for the Liberation of Oman and the Arab Gulf
PLO	Palestine Liberation Organization
PNA	Palestinian National Authority
PRC	People's Republic of China
RAF	Royal Air Force
RDF	Rapid Deployment Force
SAM	surface-to-air missile
SDV	swimmer delivery vehicle
SNO	Senior Naval Officer
TOS	Trucial Oman Scouts
UAE	United Arab Emirates
UN	United Nations
UNCLOS	UN Convention on the Law of the Sea
UNESCO	United Nations Educational, Scientific and Cultural Organization
UNSC	United Nations Security Council
USSR	Union of Soviet Socialist Republics
YAR	Yemen Arab Republic
WMD	weapons of mass destruction

FOREWORD

Few disputes have historically heightened tensions among nations as much as those over territory. Of these, the dispute over three small but strategic islands in the Arabian Gulf, namely, Abu Musa and the Greater and Lesser Tunbs has been among the most persistent and recurring in this part of the Middle East. These three islands, belonging to the Trucial States of Sharjah and Ras al-Khaimah and later the United Arab Emirates, have been facing contending claims by Persia and later by Iran under the Pahlavi Dynasty and the Islamic Republic of Iran. Given the strategic location of the islands in the Strait of Hormuz and the wider threats stemming from their occupation by Iran, the security and stability of the Gulf region will remain fragile in the absence of an effective resolution of this dispute and the hopes of bringing about any enduring security architecture will be largely futile.

This study examines the fundamental legal and sovereign rights of the United Arab Emirates in relation to the islands and highlights the issues of power politics that have dominated both regional politics and international relations. The United Arab Emirates is a small and relatively new country situated in the Lower Gulf region, which came into being only in 1971, but one that has already proven that a vibrant and thriving federation in this volatile part of the world is both possible and desirable. At the same time, the seven constituent emirates that make up the UAE have a rich history and tradition based on peaceful relations and open trade routes with all their neighbors. With its small geographic size and its limited population, the UAE has always sought a peaceful and stable regional environment to promote economic and social development, while at the same time clearly rejecting military solutions to the problems of the Gulf. It is this peaceful philosophy that has determined the country's approach to the islands issue and has underlined its efforts, through diplomatic channels, and regional and international forums, to have the sovereignty over the islands restored to its rightful owners, the emirates comprising the UAE federation.

The available historical record provides indisputable and concrete evidence that the three islands of Abu Musa and the two Tunbs belong to the UAE. Yet, Iran has dismissed the weight of such evidence arguing instead that due to their strategic importance, the islands must belong to Iran. Its forcible occupation of the islands on the eve of the formation of the UAE federation, and its refusal to accept any bilateral negotiation, regional mediation or international arbitration to resolve this matter has raised justifiable security concerns in the region regarding Iran's possible hegemonic designs and potential military use of the islands to control or even blockade shipping in the Gulf.

In view of the importance of this issue, Dr. Thomas R. Mattair, a political scientist with training from both Harvard and the University of California at Berkeley, was commissioned by the Emirates Center for Strategic Studies and Research (ECSSR) to carry out meticulous research on the subject. Dr. Mattair was actively assisted in his work by researchers from the ECSSR Strategic Studies section. He brought vast experience to the project, including a deep understanding of the Gulf and a fundamental interest in seeing conflicts of the past resolved. His most significant contribution has been the painstaking efforts to bring together the various source materials available in order to provide as comprehensive a picture as possible. These materials include not only the primary documents and records of the British and American Foreign Service, but also secondary academic studies, legal opinions and extensive interviews with key players and commentators. The result is a work of unprecedented scope and depth which finally brings the full story and historical background of the islands to the attention of policymakers, academics, and interested readers alike.

As an institution dedicated to the promotion of academic research on issues of strategic significance for the UAE and the Gulf region, the ECSSR hopes that the publication of this important in-depth study will provide fresh insight on the issue of the occupied UAE islands and promote a peaceful and just resolution of this dispute by documenting accurately the historical record, legal precedents, political implications and security concerns relating to the islands.

Jamal S. Al-Suwaidi, Ph.D
Director General
ECSSR

INTRODUCTION

The Islands Issue: An Overview

Abu Musa, the Greater Tunb and the Lesser Tunb are three small but strategic islands located along the narrow route through the Arabian Gulf* into the Strait of Hormuz and out into the Gulf of Oman. Much of the Gulf's oil exports and its non-oil imports pass along this route, as do naval vessels entering and exiting the Gulf. In addition, a number of the Gulf's offshore oil and gas fields are located in the vicinity, making the islands uniquely valuable to any power seeking either to protect or to attack this traffic and these fields. Given the strategic location of these islands, it is essential to have an accurate account of the islands' history and to understand their role in the context of the political and security situation in the Arabian Gulf. This comprehensive study attempts to provide such background and to elaborate on the issues of concern. As such, it should serve policymakers, lawyers, officials of international organizations and students of international affairs, as well as anyone concerned with the stability of the Arabian Gulf region.

The book is divided into four major parts. The first focuses on the history of the islands, how they were used, by whom and at what time. The second part covers the legal debates concerning the sovereignty rights of the United Arab Emirates and the contending claims by Iran, and the basis for establishing a right to ownership. It also approaches the islands issue from an overall strategic perspective. Part Three is concerned with the regional repercussions of Iran's presence on the islands and the reaction of the Arab world to the policies of Iran both

---

* Editorial Note: In this book the Gulf has been consistently referred to as the "Arabian Gulf" to reflect accurately the authentic Arabic name "Al Khaleej Al Arabi" rather than the "Persian Gulf" except in quotations, titles of books, documents and other sources, where the names have been retained in their original form purely in the interests of scholarly tradition.

under the Shah and since the establishment of the Islamic Republic. Thereafter, in Part Four, the interests, roles and responsibilities of international organizations and the major states that lead them are reviewed. The study then concludes with an analysis of the strategic importance of peace and stability in the Gulf, both for the region and the world, and the resulting importance of resolving this dispute over the islands. As far as Gulf security is concerned, the islands issue is likely to remain a potentially explosive situation if left unresolved.

Methodology

Painstaking efforts have been made to exhaust all source materials available on matters relating to the islands. Primary documents, secondary academic studies, legal opinions and extensive interviews have been utilized in developing a study intended to shed light on an important but relatively neglected international dispute.

The most important published collection of primary documents used in this research is the second collection of British Government documents in the Arabian Geopolitics series, entitled *The Lower Gulf Islands: Abu Musa and the Tunbs*, edited by P.L. Toye. This collection of six volumes contains three thousand pages of documents from the Public Record Office and the British Library's Oriental and India Office Collections that cover the period from the early 1800s to 1962. Under the 30-year confidentiality rule, when this collection was published in 1993, 1962 was the latest year for which British Government documents were available.

New British Government documents from 1961 to 1965 have also become available and have been consulted in the series entitled *Arabian Boundaries: New Documents*, a collection of ten volumes and five thousand pages edited by Richard Schofield and published between 1993 and 1997. Additional British Government documents have been published and consulted in 2002 in the series entitled *Records of the Emirates: 1966-1971*, a collection of six volumes edited by A.L.P. Burdett. These collections provide the official correspondence, memoranda and agreements among British, Arab, Persian and Iranian officials from the early 1800s to the early 1970s. They are frequently cited in the footnotes to the first section on the history of the islands, so that the reader can easily refer to comprehensive and available collections of the relevant primary material at every point in the historical narrative drawn from these sources. This may prove especially valuable to international lawyers seeking to verify the evidence cited in Part Two on the legal claims of the UAE and contending claims by Iran to these islands.

In addition, thousands of documents covering the years from 1965 to 1973 have been examined after obtaining them from the British Public Record Office, the India Office and Records Library, the Library of Congress in Washington, DC and the National Archives in College Park, Maryland. This material is much harder for the reader to access because it was only declassified between 1997 and January 2004, and has therefore not all been compiled in published volumes. Unfortunately, not all the British Public Record Office documents for the years 1970, 1971 and 1972 were declassified on schedule. Instead, their classification status as "closed" was extended temporarily, in some cases until 2013.

Documents covering Arab League deliberations in 1971 have been obtained from the Arab League's archives, translated and consulted, although they are not available to the public. The unpublished memoirs of Sir Denis Wright, British Ambassador to Iran, as well as the published memoirs of Asadollah Alam, Iranian Prime Minister and later Minister of Court, who engaged in an important dialogue on this issue in the 1960s, have also been consulted.

This primary source material has taken precedence over any secondary literature. A careful reading of these materials has enabled the author to point out the occasional error of fact or misinterpretation in secondary academic and legal studies that have also utilized the same primary sources. Most secondary studies, however, do not focus on the islands. Classic historical studies like J.B. Kelly's *Britain and the Persian Gulf: 1795-1880* barely mention the islands. Moreover, much of the primary material has been declassified so recently that there may be no other secondary source that has already used it. For example, another work by Kelly entitled *Arabia, the Gulf and the West*, a study of the modern era that makes more mention of the islands than his previous work, was published in 1980 and could not benefit from more recently declassified documents. For these reasons, the use of primary source material is absolutely essential.

However, secondary sources are useful in their own right. B.J. Slot's *The Arabs of the Gulf: 1602-1784* is based on a careful examination of Portuguese, French, Dutch and British archival records and is thus an invaluable general history of these years. Muhammad Morsy Abdullah's *The United Arab Emirates: A Modern History* is an excellent general history of the nineteenth and twentieth centuries, making more extensive use of British archival material. A more recent work entitled *Small Islands, Big Politics: The Tonbs and Abu Musa in the Gulf*, edited by Hooshang Amirahmadi, has been helpful in presenting the historical and legal arguments as understood by scholars who are sympathetic to Iran.

The unpublished legal studies entitled *Sharjah's Title to the Island of Abu Musa*, prepared in 1971 by the British and American legal team of Bathurst, Ely and Chance for the Ruler of Sharjah, and *Territorial Sovereignty Over the Tunb Islands*, prepared in 1980 by the American law firm of Vinson and Elkins for the Ruler of Ras al-Khaimah, have been valuable in providing the legal principles and cases that support the UAE's claim to sovereignty over these islands. These studies are referred to in Part Two for the benefit of readers who will not have access to them.

On contemporary developments in the Gulf, including the political impact and strategic significance of this dispute and the importance of resolving it, the literature is more extensive. Here, the reader will find numerous citations and references in the endnotes.

In addition to the printed materials, numerous interviews have also been conducted in the United Arab Emirates, the United States and Great Britain with current and former officials from the UAE Ministry of Foreign Affairs, the US State and Defense Departments, and the British Foreign Office. Several interviews were also conducted with Iranian officials in New York City and Tehran. Scholars, lawyers, oil company executives and others with personal knowledge of and participation in the recent history of the islands have given their valuable time and shared their first-hand knowledge of events to set the record straight and provide necessary clarifications. These interviews are primarily cited in the final chapters of the book.

Throughout the work, a careful effort has been made to standardize the spelling of the most important names and terms cited in this study, particularly Abu Musa, the Greater Tunb and the Lesser Tunb. The historical archives and correspondence mentioned above yield many different spellings of these islands. This does not create a serious problem in the case of Abu Musa, because it is only one island

and spellings such as Bu Musa can be easily recognized. It is a more serious problem in the case of the Tunbs, because these are two islands, the Greater Tunb and the Lesser Tunb. In the archives and correspondence, a spelling like Tanb or Tomb may be used to refer to one or both islands, while a spelling like Tanbs or Tombs may also be used to refer to only one or both islands. In such a case, the entire context has to be examined to determine whether one or both islands are under discussion. Most often, the historical events being described only took place on the larger island, the Greater Tunb. Occasionally the term "Tanb Kubra" is used to refer to the Greater Tunb and the terms "Tanb Sughra" or "Nabiyu Tunb" or "Nabgau" are used to refer to the Lesser Tunb.

In addition, because Persia changed its name to Iran in 1935, the term "Persia" is used for the period before 1935 and the term "Iran" is used for the period after 1935. This is consistent with the terminology employed in official documents and in other secondary studies. It should be noted, however, that "Persia" is a Hellenistic term, and that some Iranian scholars prefer that the term "Iran" be used to cover the period before as well as after 1935. This study utilizes the terms as they have been used historically. Where there might be confusion, the term "Iran/Persia" is used.

The Historical Record

This book begins with a historical section that covers the Islamic era: the early period of European colonialism; the rights of the Arab tribe of the Qawasim to Abu Musa and the Tunbs; the British "protectorate" over the Trucial States of the Arab Coast of the Lower Gulf and the emergence of Iranian claims to the islands; and the British withdrawal from the Gulf and the Iranian occupation of the islands. Also included is a preliminary discussion on the creation of the United Arab Emirates and its quest for a legal resolution of the islands question during its early years, during revolution and wars in the Gulf, during the period of Iranian assertiveness and militarization of the islands, and during the period of growing US military cooperation with the UAE and other GCC states and US warnings to Iran, all of which are topics developed at greater length in subsequent chapters.

From even before the beginning of the Islamic era in the seventh century AD until the era of European colonialism, beginning in 1500, the Gulf coasts and islands were predominantly inhabited by the Arabs, and Arab vessels and Arab sailors dominated trade in the Gulf. The islands of Abu Musa and the Tunbs were part of the island Kingdom of Hormuz, the Arab-ruled trade emporium that flourished from the 1300s to the early 1600s.[1] After the fall of this Kingdom in 1622, the islands of Abu Musa and the Tunbs continued to be possessed and used by the Arabs.

By the early and mid-1700s, it was the Arab tribe of the Qawasim, whose leaders currently rule the UAE emirates of Sharjah and Ras al-Khaimah, and the Arab tribes loyal to and dependent on this family that used and controlled Abu Musa and the Tunbs. By 1720, the Qawasim had established their rule in Ras al-Khaimah, had built a fleet of boats qualifying them as a major naval power in the Gulf, and had begun to develop extensive commercial trade with other ports in the Gulf and beyond. Some of the Qawasim soon migrated from Ras al-Khaimah on the southern coast of the Gulf to Lingeh on the northern coast.

The Qawasim at Lingeh established a state that was independent of the weak Persian central government and one that remained subject to the family's ruler in Ras al-Khaimah on the Arab Coast.[2] During this period, the Qawasim of both coasts inhabited the islands on a seasonal basis. The islands were a source of fresh water and a refuge from bad weather in all seasons. The Qawasim shaikhs would also send their horses and flocks for grazing on the islands during the spring, Qawasim fishing boats would frequent the islands during the summer pearling season and Qawasim fishermen would live there during the winter fishing season.[3]

After Britain accused the Qawasim of piracy, destroyed much of the Qawasim fleet and established itself as the dominant naval and commercial power in the Gulf, close relations between the Qawasim of the two coasts became more difficult. There were quarrels between the Qawasim of the Arab coast and the Qawasim of the Persian coast over the use of these islands. In order to resolve these disputes, the different branches of the family divided the islands for the exclusive use of each branch. By 1835, an agreement was reached whereby the island of Sirri came under the control of the Lingeh Qawasim while the islands of

Abu Musa, Greater Tunb and Sir Abu Nuair fell under the control of the Qawasim of Ras al-Khaimah and Sharjah.[4]

The first known written claim of ownership of these islands by the Qawasim is found in a December 1864 official message from Shaikh Sultan bin Saqr Al-Qasimi, the ruler of the Qawasim of Sharjah and Ras al-Khaimah, to Colonel Pelly, the British Resident. This message instructed Col. Pelly that Abu Musa, the Greater Tunb and Sir Abu Nuair had been governed by Shaikh Sultan bin Saqr's "forefathers" and that they would remain under the Shaikh's rule.[5] This reference to his "forefathers" places the Qawasim in control of the islands in the 1700s at least, if not earlier.

During the 1870s, despite Shaikh Sultan's letter, British officials, misled by their Native Agent in Sharjah, were uncertain as to the ownership of the islands, particularly whether the Qawasim of the Arab Coast or the Qawasim of Lingeh had the stronger claim to the Greater Tunb. However, during 1881 and 1882, in correspondence and talks that took place between British officials and the Qawasim Shaikh Humaid bin Abdullah Al-Qasimi of Ras al-Khaimah, Shaikh Humaid presented letters from two successive Qawasim Shaikhs of Lingeh that were written during the 1870s, acknowledging that the Greater Tunb belonged to the Qawasim of the Arab Coast. In 1884, Shaikh Yusuf of Lingeh wrote the third of these letters acknowledging that the Greater Tunb belonged to the Qawasim of the Arab coast. However, while British officials in the Gulf began to learn of these documents and consequently understand the real patterns of ownership, other British departments maintained the inaccurate view that the Greater Tunb belonged to the Qawasim of Lingeh.[6]

In 1887, Persia seized Lingeh and terminated the Qawasim rule there. They seized Sirri as well and laid claim to the Greater Tunb, advancing the argument that Sirri and the Greater Tunb were dependencies of Lingeh, with the Qawasim of Lingeh being considered Persian vassals during the preceding ten years. The Qawasim of the Arab Coast protested and sought British help. The British opinion was that Sirri and the Greater Tunb had been ruled by the Qawasim of Lingeh, but in their capacity as Qawasim shaikhs, not in their capacity as Persian officials. However, while the British stance on the Greater Tunb was firm, they were more interested in discussions with the Shah over the Persian–Afghan border, and thus acquiesced in the Persian annexation of Sirri.[7]

Persia challenged the sovereignty of the Qawasim over Abu Musa and the Tunbs in March 1904, when Persian customs officials landed on Abu Musa and the Greater Tunb, replaced the Qawasim flags with their own flags, and left guards on the islands. The Ruler of Sharjah protested and was quickly supported by Great Britain, which had prevailed upon the rulers of the Trucial States to enter into "Exclusive Agreements" or "Protectorate Treaties" with Britain in 1892. The Viceroy of India proposed that a British gunboat be sent to lower the Persian flags and remove the Persian guards. The British Foreign Office favored a diplomatic approach and was ultimately successful in persuading Persia to remove its flags and guards from the islands. Persia, however, asserted a right to discuss its claim with Britain and asked that Qawasim flags not be flown until the issue was resolved, a request the British declined. Within days, Qawasim flags were once again flying on the islands. When the British asked Persia for evidence to support its claim, Persia failed to provide any.[8]

In 1923, following the takeover of Persia by Reza Shah Pahlavi, Persia protested the granting of a red oxide concession on Abu Musa by the Shaikh of Sharjah and asserted a claim to Abu Musa and the Greater Tunb. This began a pattern that was to repeat itself over the following years, with the British rejecting each of the Persian claims. During the negotiations for an Anglo–Persian General Treaty between 1929 and 1935 the islands were a subject of dispute. When the British refused to yield on their position, Persia proposed to purchase the Greater Tunb, a proposal that the Ruler of Ras al-Khaimah refused. Later, Persia even proposed to lease the Greater Tunb. In May 1935, the Anglo-Persian negotiations for a treaty broke down, largely over Persian claims to the islands and Britain's refusal to recognize them.[9]

In the two decades after World War II, Iran repeatedly tried to claim the islands, usually after the Ruler of Sharjah or Ras al-Khaimah had granted a concession to exploit red oxide or oil, or during discussions with Britain about maritime boundaries in the Gulf. In 1968, when Britain announced her intention to withdraw from the Gulf, Shah Mohammed Reza Pahlavi of Iran, who was Reza Shah Pahlavi's son and successor, became determined to have Abu Musa and the Tunbs.[10] Under threats by Iran to occupy the islands by force, Sharjah was forced to yield to the circumstances and signed a Memorandum of Understanding (MoU) with Iran under duress in November 1971.

In the MoU, neither Sharjah nor Iran would relinquish its claims to sovereignty over Abu Musa or recognize the claims to sovereignty of the other. While Iranian troops were permitted to land peacefully and take control of the northern half of Abu Musa, Sharjah exercised full jurisdiction over the rest. Iran had never claimed Abu Musa as intensively as the Tunbs, yet it achieved a MoU, largely because Sharjah recognized that the island and its oil resources would be taken by force unless it compromised. These Iranian demands and threats were real enough. On November 30, 1971, after Ras al-Khaimah rejected the Iranian claim to the Tunbs and rejected Iranian offers of compensation made through British mediators, Iran forcibly occupied the islands of the Greater Tunb and the Lesser Tunb.[11]

Meanwhile, on December 2, 1971, the establishment of the United Arab Emirates was officially declared. The UAE's constitution proclaims its sovereignty over all of the territories and waters included within the international borders of its member emirates, including Sharjah and Ras al-Khaimah. Since this date, the UAE has regularly asserted its title to the islands and its desire to resolve the dispute peacefully in accord with international law and custom. On December 9, 1971, when the UN Security Council considered the matter, the UAE's representative maintained its rights and protested Iran's occupation. In the following years, the UAE continued to assert in notes and statements to the Security Council and the General Assembly that the islands were UAE territory.[12] The UAE has also sought a resolution to the issue based on bilateral negotiation, mediation or referral to the International Court of Justice (ICJ). In its attempt to propose a peaceful resolution, the UAE has received wide backing from the Arab as well as the international community.

The Iran–Iraq War from 1980 to 1988 demonstrated the uses to which Iran could put the islands and the challenges this poses to the UAE. Both during and after the war, Iran used Abu Musa and the Tunbs as bases for Iranian armed forces, including the Revolutionary Guard Corps. Specifically, during the "tanker war" years from 1986–88,

Iran launched small boat and helicopter attacks from the islands against shipping in the Gulf and against the UAE's offshore oil installations.[13]

Since 1992, Iran has resumed its war-time violations of the MoU and encroachments on Sharjah's half of Abu Musa. In August 1992, Iran refused entry to 104 residents of Abu Musa, including UAE nationals and Sharjah's governor of the island. The ship carrying the passengers was forced to go back to Sharjah and Iran threatened to sink the vessel if it refused to leave.[14] It was under such hostile conditions that the UAE and Iran held their first round of bilateral negotiations on the islands in Abu Dhabi in September 1992. While the UAE sought to accomplish multiple objectives, including the resolution of the status of the Tunbs and Abu Musa, Iran refused any discussion of the Tunbs and the meeting did not resolve anything.[15] A second round of talks in 1995 also yielded no progress.

Thus, Iran's position on the islands continues to remain a source of concern to the UAE. The fact that Iran has also significantly upgraded its military capabilities on the islands during the 1990s means that the islands case also raises issues of broader international concern. This remains the case in 2005 as no satisfactory solution to the islands case has been found to date.

Legal Debates and Strategic Implications

After the historical discussion, the book examines the question of the rightful ownership of the islands. This includes an evaluation of the legal principles, arguments and evidence supporting the UAE's historical title to the islands, as well as a refutation of Iran's claim based on Iranian violations of international law, the invalidity of the Memorandum of Understanding on Abu Musa, and the flaws in Iran's arguments. The section also includes a review of the accepted means of resolving disputes in international law.

The historical record is clear on the fact that the Qawasim of Sharjah and Ras al-Khaimah possessed and exercised authority over the islands since at least the mid-1700s. This enables them and the UAE to assert their title on the basis of the legal principle of *prescription* or *long and peaceful possession*.[16] The record also shows that the relationship between the Persian Government and the Qawasim Rulers of Lingeh does not establish any basis for an Iranian claim to Abu Musa or the Tunbs. The Rulers of Lingeh never owned or possessed Abu Musa, which belonged to the Rulers of Sharjah. Moreover, the Rulers of Lingeh, although they used the Greater Tunb, consistently acknowledged the Ruler of Ras al-Khaimah as the rightful owner of the Greater Tunb.

Iran only began to assert claims to the Tunbs in the late nineteenth century and to Abu Musa in the early twentieth century. Furthermore, its claims were intermittent and half-hearted, as demonstrated by its lack of response to the British request for evidence supporting the Persian claims in 1904. Most of the claims occurred after the rise of Reza Shah Pahlavi. The Anglo-Persian treaty negotiations from 1929 to 1935 broke down largely because of the islands issue. Overall, it may be observed that Iran primarily asserted its claim to the Greater Tunb, while it considered its claim to Abu Musa to be weaker.

As the legal team of Bathurst, Ely and Chance has argued, the UAE can further claim sovereignty over Abu Musa on the basis of *historical consolidation of title*:

> The most important component of the historical consolidation of title, remains continuous peaceful possession. There can be no doubt but that Sharjah's possession of Abu Musa has been peaceful...Nor can there be doubt that, apart from the fleeting Iranian visits already referred to, Sharjah's possession has been continuous.[17]

The concept also supports Ras al-Khaimah's claim to the Tunbs, inasmuch as its possession was also peaceful and continuous. The UAE's claim is also legally supported by the considerable body of evidence of *recognition* and *acquiescence*. Britain repeatedly declared its recognition of the title of the Qawasim of Sharjah and Ras al-Khaimah. There was also a long period of acquiescence to the *status quo* by Iran.

Meanwhile, Iran's occupation by force of the Greater and Lesser Tunbs constitutes a violation of the twentieth century legal principle requiring states to refrain from the threat or use of force to acquire territory. This includes a violation of the United Nations Charter, particularly Articles 1 and 2, which oblige member states to settle their disputes by peaceful means and to refrain in their relations from the threat or use of force against the territorial integrity or political independence of any state. Iran's actions are also a violation of Article

33 of the Charter, which requires states to employ a wide range of peaceful processes and institutions to resolve disputes.[18]

Furthermore, the MoU on Abu Musa is invalid because Sharjah signed the memorandum under duress, resulting from the threat of force. This abrogated the MoU as a contradiction of contemporary international law prohibiting the threat and the use of force. Indeed, Article 52 of the 1969 Vienna Convention on the Law of Treaties states as follows:

> A treaty is void if its conclusion has been produced by the threat or use of force in violation of the principles of international law embodied in the Charter of the United Nations.[19]

Iran claims a title based on *occupation* of the islands in the 7th century AD, i.e. prior to the Islamic conquests, and intermittently since then, although it produces no evidence of this. It must be noted that short periods of occupation do not constitute a legal basis for title. Iran also claims title based on *geographic proximity* or *contiguity*, but this is not a sufficient or even a valid legal basis for the claim, in addition to the fact that the islands have never been within Iran's territorial waters.

A further Iranian claim is that the islands were ruled by the Lingeh Qawasim, who were acting as Persian officials, and that the residents of Lingeh, Sirri and the Greater Tunb paid taxes to Persia between 1878 and 1887. In fact, however, Abu Musa and the Greater Tunb were not ruled by the Lingeh Qawasim, who were only Persian vassals and later officials for approximately ten years between 1878 and 1887. Moreover, Persia never produced any evidence of taxes paid by the Greater Tunb when the British protested against the Persian occupation of Lingeh and Sirri and against the Persian claims to Sirri and the Greater Tunb. When Persia drove the Qawasim out of Lingeh in 1887, Persia did not control Abu Musa and the Tunbs. Rather, the Qawasim did. There is documentary evidence of the Lingeh Qawasim Shaikhs acknowledging during this time that the Greater Tunb was owned by the Qawasim of the Arab coast.[20]

Finally, Iran claims title on the basis of an 1886 British military map presented by the British Foreign Office to the Shah of Iran in 1888. This map mistakenly portrayed the islands in the same color as the Persian coast. International law does not place much value on maps as evidence, even official maps, particularly when they are clearly contradicted by other evidence, as is the case here. There is considerable evidence, including numerous maps before and after this, showing the islands as belonging to the emirates. Indeed, Qawasim ownership of these islands was explicitly acknowledged by Britain, both before and after this map, in communications with Sharjah and Ras al-Khaimah and Persia/Iran.

International law provides several methods of peacefully resolving disputes between states. Diplomatic means, such as negotiations, good offices, conciliation and mediation have so far failed in this case. These means include direct negotiation in 1992 and mediation by Kuwait, Qatar and Saudi Arabia at various times. Political means, such as resorting to regional and international organizations, have also not produced any result. Although regional organizations have regularly expressed their support for the UAE, Iran has consistently rejected their statements. The pursuit of legal means, such as referring the dispute to the International Court of Justice or to international arbitration, has been suggested by the UAE, only to be rejected by Iran. Despite this record, it is important to peacefully resolve this dispute, as the following discussion will show.

The section then moves on to discuss Iran's motivations for holding the islands and looks in depth how Iranian behavior and policy threatens the security of the UAE and the stability of the Gulf in general. It focuses on Iranian complaints, actions, demands and threats; Iranian military acquisitions and capabilities; contending views about Iranian intentions; regional perspectives indicating how Iran's occupation of the islands threatens to disrupt the stability of the region and engulf it in conflict; and finally, the UAE's policy in dealing with this problem.

In assessing the potential for conflict in the Gulf, some analysts have warned that the Islamic Republic of Iran may disregard "rational" calculations of the outcomes of its behavior and that, therefore, conventional methods of deterrence may not be effective in dealing with potential Iranian threats.[21] Most UAE, British and US officials disagree with such a view. Instead, they argue that Iran is rational and will not provoke an all out war. Thus, Iran will not launch an overt, attributable attack against a GCC state or close the Strait of Hormuz, and would only take selective measures during hostilities, measures that are likely to be retaliatory and proportionate. Rather, what Iran might do is to engage in limited conflict, such as covert, unattributable, deniable aggression, that may damage its adversary without provoking any major response. Iran may, however, engage in unconventional actions, terror and possibly even the use of Weapons of Mass Destruction as a last resort if it is losing a conventional conflict against superior force.[22]

While it is not possible to foresee all of the many scenarios that might lead to the outbreak of hostilities in the Gulf region, it is very important to understand Iranian resentments, capabilities and intentions that could be factors leading to a Gulf conflict involving the islands. Among these considerations one has to include the Iranian resentment over US and GCC support for Iraq during the Iran-Iraq War; the decision by the UAE and other GCC states to permit US military forces to become part of the regional balance; and the existing bilateral security ties with Western powers, all perceived as deliberate efforts to deny Iran its aspiration to play a dominant Gulf role. Iran also blames the United States for allegedly provoking the dispute over the islands, and it has warned the GCC that there will be a bloody conflict if there is any attempt to retake the three islands.[23] This is all the more pertinent in the light of developments in 2002 and 2003 and the inclusion of Iran in the "axis of evil" by the US Administration under George W. Bush.

Following its war with Iraq, Iran embarked on a significant military rearmament program.[24] Most US, UK and UAE officials argue that Iran's capabilities and intentions since the 1990s have included using the islands for naval and air defense of the sea lanes through which most of its oil exports pass, as well as for the defense of its coast and offshore oil fields. They also note that Iran has gone as far as using the islands to engage in offensive actions against international commercial and naval traffic through the sea-lanes, particularly from 1986 to 1988.[25]

In addition, Iran has the potential capability and perhaps the intention to use the islands in a more direct way. This could include deploying battalion-sized forces across the Gulf to support a popular uprising or coup attempt in a Gulf Arab state, or to attack and seize islands or off-shore and on-shore oil facilities. Iran could also use the islands in covert operations to deploy unconventional forces across the Gulf, to supply arms to radical movements across the Gulf, to seize undefended islands, and to sabotage offshore and onshore oil operations, ports, ships, as well as desalination and electrical facilities.[26] Other analysts suggest that Iran wants the islands and a twelve-mile territorial sea around them in order to claim a right to UAE offshore oil and gas fields. There are some who support the assertion that the occupation of the islands is part of a general strategy to intimidate the UAE into investing in Iran's oil and gas sector or to relax Iran's oil production quota.[27]

As early as the UN Security Council discussion in December 1971, Arab states have expressed the view that Iran's occupation of the islands disrupts and threatens the security of the whole Gulf region. Such concerns were validated when Iran used Abu Musa and the Tunbs to launch hit-and-run attacks against international shipping from 1986 to 1988. Particularly from this time onward, the GCC states have been firm in their view that Iran's occupation and fortification of the islands, as well as its naval exercises on and around the islands, constitute a threat to the stability of the UAE and also that of the Gulf and the Middle East at large.

In the face of these potential threats, the UAE is pursuing diplomatic and legal measures to resolve the dispute with its more powerful neighbor. The UAE does not view force as an option and hopes that a policy of peaceful coexistence with Iran will eventually bear fruit. The UAE certainly seeks to develop with the United States and other Western powers a strategy for deterring aggression against and intimidation of the UAE. However, UAE officials indicate that they do not seek a confrontation with Iran and that they do favor bilateral negotiations or recourse to the International Court of Justice to resolve this dispute.[28]

The Political Impact of Iran's Occupation of the Islands

The third part explores the impact of the occupation of the islands by both the Shah's Iran and the Islamic Republic of Iran on relations with the UAE, the GCC, other Arab countries and the Arab League. Included here is a discussion of how Iran's aggression is a major impediment to regional peace, cooperation and stability, and also to engagement in a constructive policy of dialogue and negotiation. Attention is focused on the losses and costs to Iran that stem from this policy.

Iran's occupation of the Tunbs and its landing on Abu Musa on November 30, 1971 led to denunciations and protests throughout the Arab world. Iraq, Algeria, Libya and the People's Democratic Republic of Yemen (PDRY or South Yemen) filed a complaint at the UN Security Council on December 3, 1971. All these states denounced Iran during the subsequent Security Council discussion on December 9, but the Council took no action.[29] On December 6, 1971, when the UAE became a member of the Arab League, the League met in an emergency session to consider the occupation. Due to the concerns of conservative and moderate states, the Arab League passed only a moderate resolution calling on the Arab League's Secretary General to take up the matter. Eventually, fifteen Arab states stated in a letter to the President of the UN Security Council on July 18, 1972 as follows:

> The islands of Abu Musa and the two Tunbs are Arab and constitute an integral part of the United Arab Emirates and of the Arab homeland.[30]

The Iranian behavior incurred indirect costs. For example, while the Shah of Iran's interest in a "Gulf Pact" for security cooperation was never received enthusiastically by Iran's Gulf neighbors, his occupation of the islands made the possibility of such a pact even less likely.[31] Under the Islamic Republic of Iran, Iran's continued violation of the MoU on Abu Musa, its militarization of the three islands, and its rejection of peaceful means to resolve the status of the three islands have galvanized GCC and wider Arab support for the UAE and opposition to Iran. Numerous GCC and Arab League statements expressing support for the UAE and calling the occupation of the islands a violation of UAE sovereignty have underscored such opposition. The consistent message has been that Iran can only improve its relations with the Arabs if it resolves this dispute.[32] The warming of Saudi-Iranian relations in 1999 caused concern in the UAE that Iran might not feel the need to resolve the islands issue, but Saudi Arabia and the other GCC states have pledged to continue pressing Iran on this issue and to limit their relations with Tehran.

Overall, Iran's behavior with regard to the islands has damaged its relationship with the GCC. Any possibility of being included in a Gulf security framework or of loosening military ties between the GCC and the West has certainly been diminished. Iran has also lost out on receiving GCC financial assistance to rebuild and diversify its economy, in particular after the Iran–Iraq war. What the occupation has done is to drive the GCC states closer together at the expense of its northern neighbor. Thus, Reformist President Mohammed Khatami's rapprochement strategy was received with caution and skepticism by GCC member states in the absence of a resolution of the islands dispute.

The International Community and the Dispute

Part Four examines the role and effectiveness of the international community in addressing and resolving the islands issue. The focus here is on the role played by Britain, the United States and, to a lesser extent, by the United Nations and its agencies. The section shows how international public and private statements about the islands dispute have not matched the expressed commitment to the stability of the Gulf region. It also examines the determinants of the international community's responses to regional conflicts and offers an evaluation of international guarantees that purport to ensure the territorial integrity of small states.

Britain, a permanent member of the Security Council and the major power that mediated between Iran and the emirates of Sharjah and Ras al-Khaimah, was generally satisfied with the situation it left behind in the Gulf following its withdrawal in 1971. Britain's major concerns as it withdrew from the Gulf were the future of Bahrain and the establishment of a federation of Arab emirates, not Abu Musa and the Tunbs. Britain did not think that it could leave the Gulf if there was any continuing Iranian claim and threat to Bahrain. Thus, when Iran dropped its claim to Bahrain in 1970, Britain viewed it as a great success.

The Shah's *quid pro quo* for this act and his acceptance of a federation, as he made clear to Britain, was British flexibility on Abu Musa and the Tunbs. The British knew that the Shah would employ force to take the islands. As they were not willing to apply force to defend the Tunbs or Abu Musa, they urged Ras al-Khaimah and Sharjah to compromise with Iran. In the view of some British officials, it was "not a very honorable policy, but it was a practical one." In any case, it constituted a virtual repudiation of over a hundred years of British policy that had entailed publicly and privately asserting and defending the rights of the Qawasim to the islands against Persian and Iranian claims. Sharjah reluctantly accepted a British-mediated MoU on Abu Musa. When Ras al-Khaimah refused to give up its sovereignty for compensation, Britain acquiesced in the Iranian seizure of the Tunbs.[33]

Despite the UN Security Council's decision to take no action in 1971, the UAE continued to assert its sovereignty over the islands to the Secretary General, the Security Council and the General Assembly during the following years. After Iran's violations of the MoU on Abu Musa in 1992, the UAE adopted a more determined policy. On January 2, 1994, after a request by the UAE and the Arab League, UN Secretary General Boutros Boutros Ghali indicated that the UN would play any appropriate role to resolve the dispute. However, when Boutros Ghali sought a meeting in Iran, the Iranians stated that he was not welcome.[34]

In 1995, the attitude of the Security Council was demonstrated when it proposed to list the islands matter as one of the "dead subjects" it intended to drop from its agenda. At the request of the UAE, the issue has been retained on the Security Council agenda, a request that is now renewed annually. While the UAE documents all its protests to Iran for the Security Council, it has not asked for any formal reconsideration of the issue by the Council. Instead, the UAE prefers to exhaust all peaceful avenues for direct bilateral negotiations on the issue and an acceptable negotiated solution. It also hopes that the growing support of the international community in opposing Iran's violation of the UN Charter will help to promote this approach.

Given Iran's refusal to negotiate and rejection of the good offices of the UN Secretary General, the UAE wishes to reserve the option of referring the matter to the binding adjudication power of the International Court of Justice. The UAE has received the diplomatic support of the wider international community in this regard, but Iran has not agreed to refer the matter to the Court and it is necessary for both parties to agree in order for the Court to adjudicate. Moreover, even if Iran were to accept this step, the UAE does not want an ICJ decision that Iran would reject and that would require enforcement. Another possible option would be for the ICJ to issue an advisory opinion on the dispute, a step that would not require the agreement of both parties but would therefore also not be binding on them.

The UAE's call for a peaceful resolution of the islands issue has received support from the GCC, the Arab League, the Non-Aligned Movement, the European Union and from some major powers on the Security Council, particularly the United States and Britain. The UAE is making progress in developing international support. The UAE is patient; it does not want a crisis. Underlying such a strategy is the idea that eventually Iran will realize that it cannot emerge from its isolation and improve its economy until it changes its behavior on the islands case and other issues.

The attitude of the United States, as a permanent member of the Security Council and as the principal guarantor of Gulf security, is important. The US has advised the UAE that confronting Iran at the Security Council could lead Tehran to harden its position. While the US would seek a Security Council resolution to back up US-led military action if Iranian behavior posed an imminent threat to international peace and security, the US does not consider such a resolution absolutely necessary. In addition, the US has not yet seen such a threat materializing. The US would not initiate military action simply to resolve the dispute. Indeed, both US and UAE officials argue that this would only lead to Iranian retaliation against the UAE. However, the US will not allow Iran to interfere with shipping and would consider military options if the UAE and the GCC asked for help in repulsing any Iranian military operations against the UAE.

US officials approve of the UAE's intention to seek a peaceful resolution through bilateral diplomacy, regional mediation or the ICJ. A bilateral negotiated settlement of the issue would be the preferred mechanism. Former Secretary of State Warren Christopher told the GCC Foreign Ministers meeting in Jeddah in March 1995 that the UAE has a "strong claim" to the islands, and this was repeated by the US State Department in 1997. However, the US has never taken an official position on the legal dispute. Overall, it appears that very few, if any, in the US Government can give an informed answer about the legal claims of the UAE and contending claims by Iran. This may also be true of the officials of other major governments and of the UN. One purpose of this book, therefore, is to present the historical record and the legal analysis pertaining to this dispute for the benefit of American policymakers, UN officials and others, and to underline the need to urge Iran to settle this dispute with the UAE.

The British, of course, know the historical record and the legal case very well. Britain's official position is that it supports the UAE's call for bilateral negotiation, regional mediation or for taking the case to the ICJ. However, there are also individual statements of support for the UAE's right to sovereignty and the reversion of the islands to the UAE by members of former British governments, such as former Foreign Secretary Douglas Hurd. Thus, a more informed United States could potentially have an important ally in urging Iran to enter bilateral negotiations with the UAE to resolve this dispute. Like the United States, however, Britain would not entertain a UAE request to use force against Iran to resolve the islands issue.

Conclusion

The book concludes with a discussion about the strategic importance of peace and stability in the Gulf. The Gulf region contains two-thirds of the world's proven reserves of crude oil and 30% of the world's proven reserves of natural gas. The Gulf supplies 30% of the world's daily consumption of oil and this level will increase during the 21st century. Moreover, the Gulf region also has about three-quarters of the world's excess production capacity. Thus, these oil-producing states can respond to any shortage of supply in world markets by increasing production and keeping prices down in this way. Indeed, they did so when Iraqi and Kuwaiti oil were taken off the market in 1990-91. While some of the Gulf's oil is shipped via pipelines, most of it passes through the Strait of Hormuz, a narrow and vulnerable chokepoint.

The United States, as the world's leading power, has crucial national interests in the Gulf that it intends to protect. These include maintaining access to the energy of the region at a reasonable price for itself and its major trading and financial partners, maintaining access to the region's non-oil markets for itself and its major allies and friends, protecting the well-being and security of friendly states in the region against external threats, and containing states and movements that are unfriendly to the US, its friends and their interests throughout the region.[35]

The United States, the UAE, the other GCC states and European states have developed a military presence and a rapid deployment capability that is an effective deterrent against a major attack by Iran or Iraq (under Saddam Hussein) against any GCC state. It is also a credible deterrent against any Iranian effort to interfere with maritime traffic through the sea-lanes of the Gulf. Moreover, this capability and strategy is intended to deter more limited forms of aggression against and intimidation of GCC states, such as encroachments on the UAE's offshore oil fields, sabotage against the UAE or unreasonable political and economic demands against the UAE. A strategy of compellence, i.e. to compel Iran to quit the islands, has not been favored by the UAE, the GCC, the United States or the Europeans.

The first tier of the deterrent is the capability of each GCC state, in this case the UAE. The second tier is the combined capability of the GCC and the third is that of the United States itself. The UAE alone and the GCC countries combined have not deterred Iran from its policies on the islands. Neither has the United States succeeded in preventing Iran from carrying out its policies on the islands. US support for efforts to advance diplomatic or legal means to resolve the contending claims to the islands have not worked so far. However, since the tanker war of 1986-88, Iran has not used its position on the islands to interfere with shipping or to engage in any action against the UAE. Thus, one could argue that the three-tiered deterrent has been effective.

In the end, Iran's potential to destabilize the region, to challenge the basic interests of the UAE, the GCC, the United States, Europe, Japan and their friends, and to produce unforeseen scenarios – and to use the islands in all these cases – cannot be easily dismissed. Thus, it remains a key challenge to strengthen moves to deter Iran and to promote peaceful means of restoring UAE sovereignty over the islands of Abu Musa and the Tunbs.

PART
I

THE HISTORICAL RECORD

CHAPTER
1

From Early History to the
Rule of the Qawasim

A thorough study of the islands of Abu Musa and the two Tunbs necessarily begins with its historical context – to determine when and by whom the islands were inhabited and what their role was in the general history of the region. While the documentation for the early period of this study is not as extensive as one might wish, the documentation for the later period shows that the islands were in the possession of the Arabs since at least the early 1500s, if not before. The historical record leaves no doubt on this point.

In the subsequent pages, a detailed account of the historical record is given. At times, the discussion might appear too minute and repetitive. However, because the dispute over the sovereignty of the islands is critical to the present and future stability of the Gulf, it is important to provide as complete a record as possible and present the case in a clear and concise manner based on the available material. In the light of this discussion, the reader should be able to decide whether or not the evidence is convincing.

This part of the book is divided into four chapters. The first begins with the pre-Islamic and early Islamic period, then focuses on the early period of European colonialism and discusses the rights of the Arab family of the Qawasim to Abu Musa and the Tunbs. It covers the arrival of the British in the region and discusses exchanges between the British and the local residents.

Chapter 2 takes a closer look at the period of the British "protectorate" over the Trucial States of the Arab Coast of the Lower Gulf and carries the discussion into the twentieth century. It reviews in detail the emergence of Iranian claims to the islands and discusses those claims in the light of the historical circumstances that existed in the region.

During the period starting with the announcement in 1968 of the British intention to withdraw from the Gulf, through the Iranian occupation of the islands and ending with the establishment of the United Arab Emirates in 1971, the islands issue took on a broader strategic significance. The third chapter covers the factors that influenced each of these events and attempts to frame the discussion in the context of the historical facts. The fourth chapter then traces the various attempts at resolving the crisis up until the present day and examines the role of the UAE as a federal state and Iran as an Islamic Republic. At the end of this part, the reader should have gained a thorough understanding regarding the position of the islands in the overall history of the region.

The Pre-Islamic and Early Islamic Periods

From the early periods of recorded history, the Gulf was a principal maritime route for commerce between the civilizations of Mesopotamia and Africa, India and the Far East. The historical record does not reveal much about the ancient history of Abu Musa and the Tunbs. It is possible that the islands were first discovered in 3000 BC when the Sumerians and Akkadians, from what is now southern Iraq, engaged in maritime trade with ports in Dilmun (present day Bahrain), Magan (today the United Arab Emirates and Oman), and Melukhkha or the Indus Valley. The islands may also have been discovered by the fishermen and pearlers from Bahrain and the Arab coast who sailed into the Gulf, probably from the time of the Sumerians or earlier.[1]

Darius the Great (521-485 BC) of the Persian Achaemenid Empire (559-330 BC) could have discovered the islands when he sent a fleet from Egypt to Persia, as could the Greek Emperor Alexander the Great (d. 323 BC) when he sent his admiral Nearchus from India into the Gulf to explore the Persian coast, or when Alexander sent Phoenician naval explorers traveling down the Arab coast from Babylon to Cape Musandum. The islands may have been known when the Chaldeans, Arabs, and Persians of the cities of Charax and Apologus along the Tigris River voyaged through the Gulf to trade with India and China during the period of warfare between the Arsacid Parthian Empire (238 BC to 224 AD) and the Roman Empire. They may also have been known when the Persian seafarers of the Persian Sasanian Empire (224-641 AD) made use of the Gulf to trade with Africa, India, and China.[2]

What is clearer is that from the Islamic conquests of Arabia, Mesopotamia, Persia and beyond in the seventh century AD until the era of European colonialism in the early sixteenth century, Arabs inhabited both of the Gulf coasts as well as some of the Gulf's islands. This is regardless of what power exercised *de jure* or *de facto* political authority over the region at any given time.[3] Persia was not an independent political entity during this era. While various Persian, Turk and Mongol governments exercised authority in parts of Persia, they had difficulty maintaining direct contact with the Persian coast of the Gulf or the islands in the Gulf. Moreover, none of these governments possessed any naval power.[4]

Abu Musa and the Tunb islands may have been used or at least passed by on several occasions, including during the campaign in 637 AD, when the Arab Muslims sailed across the Gulf from Julfar, near modern Ras al-Khaimah on the Arab coast, to the island of Qays and the Persian coast to fight against the Sasanians of Persia. It is also possible during the periods when the Ummayid caliphate in Damascus (660-749 AD), the Abbasid caliphate in Baghdad (750-1258 AD) and the Buwayhid dynasty of the Persian emirs in Kirman and Baghdad (945-1055 AD) sent their fleets across the Gulf from harbors like Basra and the island of Qays and Siraf on the Persian coast to the harbor at Julfar to subdue and control Oman.[5]

From the end of the Ummayid caliphate and the early years of the Abbasid caliphate (circa 750 AD) until the era of European colonialism beginning in 1500 AD, Arab vessels and sailors played the leading role in trade through the Gulf to India, China and Africa. While Persians also engaged in this trade, their role was not as dominant as that of the Arabs.[6] After the decline of Basra, it was the port-cities of Siraf, Qays and Old Hormuz that emerged as the major centers of Gulf trade with the outside world from 850 AD onwards. Although located on and along the Persian coast, these places were ruled by Arabs and inhabited by both Arabs and Persians.[7]

The sailors and traders that inhabited these port cities must have known Abu Musa and the Tunbs. Julfar was known to be involved in Gulf trade in 985 AD, when Siraf was the major trade emporium in the Gulf. In all likelihood, vessels sailing between Julfar and Siraf passed the islands.[8] Later, the Arab Banu Qaysar rulers of Qays, the primary trade center from circa 1060 AD to 1225 AD, ruled the neighboring islands and worked an off-shore pearl fishery. Julfar was also known to be engaged in pearling in 1154 AD.[9] Based on this record, it is possible that Abu Musa and the Tunbs may have belonged to the Banu Qaysar of Qays during these years, and may have been used by the pearlers of Qays and Julfar, although the evidence of this is slight.[10]

The Mongol invasions sacked Baghdad and ended the Abbasid caliphate in 1258 AD. These invaders also raided the Gulf's major trade emporium of Old Hormuz in the late 1200s. Following the abandonment of Old Hormuz, its Arab rulers founded and ruled New Hormuz, on the island of Hormuz, in the early 1300s. New Hormuz, as the capital of the Kingdom of Hormuz, soon became the center of trade in the Gulf. This kingdom, with its own fleet and army, ruled much of both shores of the Gulf and most major islands in the Gulf, including Qishm, Larak, Qays and Bahrain, from the early 1300s until the early 1600s.[11]

In 1503, after two hundred years of independence, thirty years after the death of its last great king, and during the internal succession crises of the petty kings who followed, the Kingdom began to pay tribute to Shah Ismail Safavi of Persia (1501–1524), who founded the Persian Safavid dynasty and extended his authority to the province of Fars and its capital Shiraz. The tribute continued briefly until 1515, when the Persians recognized Portuguese sovereignty over the Kingdom.[12] Julfar was inhabited during these centuries and was engaged in trade with New Hormuz, Persia, India and China. Indeed, with its commercial harbor and fleet and its local pearl fisheries nearby, Julfar was the most important possession of New Hormuz on the Arab coast at the beginning of the 1500s.[13] As the Tunbs and Abu Musa were situated just to the west of the transit route between New Hormuz and Julfar, and also along the transit routes in and out of the Gulf, and as they probably served as a haven for pearlers and a source of the fresh water and fish that were vitally important to the island of Hormuz, the islands were very likely valuable parts of the Kingdom of Hormuz prior to the arrival of the Portuguese.[14]

The Era of European Colonialism

The late 1400s and early 1500s marked the beginning of the era of European colonialism in the Gulf. The Portuguese were the first to arrive, and from 1507 onwards, they used their naval force to gain control over the Arab rulers of the island Kingdom of Hormuz, its island dependencies of Qishm and Bahrain, and Julfar. Consequently, they controlled the Strait of Hormuz and the Gulf's major ports, dominating the transit trade through the region for one hundred years.[15] Julfar grew in importance as a commercial harbor during this Portuguese era and it was the site of a Portuguese garrison. In 1518, the Portuguese explorer Duarte Barbosa wrote that Julfar had great navigators and wholesale merchants and that it had a pearl fishery nearby. Merchants from Hormuz came to Julfar to purchase these pearls and export them to India, and he observed that the trade of Julfar brought great revenue to the King of Hormuz. Barbosa also reported that the Greater Tunb was part of the Kingdom of Hormuz.[16] Again, Abu Musa and the Tunbs may have been used by Julfar's pearl fleet and were certainly used by the boats that moved between Hormuz and Julfar and beyond to India and China.

During this Portuguese era, the islands were inhabited by Arabs. They provided fresh water, fruit and sheep to the Kingdom, paid taxes on their trade with the Kingdom and customs duties on Gulf transit trade that passed by the Greater Tunb, and used its warehouses.[17] The Venetian pearl merchant and explorer Gasparo Balbi reported in 1580 that Sharjah and Ras al-Khaimah were used as seasonal villages during the pearling season.[18] The Portuguese explorer Pedro Teixera reported in the early 1600s that Julfar's pearl fleet worked nearby pearl fisheries as well as those off Qatar and Bahrain.[19] During these years, the inhabitants of Julfar, nearby Ras al-Khaimah and Sharjah certainly would have used Abu Musa and the Tunbs during the pearling season.

In 1602, an Arab revolt in Bahrain stripped this important island possession from the Portuguese-controlled and Arab-ruled Kingdom of Hormuz. Bahrain was then ruled by an Arab Sultan on behalf of the Safavid dynasty of Persia under Shah Abbas I the Great (1587-1629). In 1622, the British East India Company fleet enabled the forces of the Safavid Shah Abbas to expel the Portuguese from the island of Qishm and from the island of Hormuz, thus putting an end to that Kingdom after twenty years of challenges from the Persians and various Arab tribes. After a brief occupation, the Safavids abandoned the now pillaged and ruined Hormuz in 1625, except for its fortress, and much of its former trade was subsequently diverted to Bandar Abbas.[20]

Lacking their own navy, the Persians did not command the waters of the Gulf or occupy the Tunbs, Abu Musa or the Arab coast after the fall of the Kingdom of Hormuz. This was the case despite a small Persian garrison at Julfar from 1619 to 1621 and other small garrisons on the coast that were quickly routed by the Portuguese in 1623. Initially, from their base at Muscat, the Portuguese maintained their dominance, exercising authority over many of the Arab ports on both coasts, even after their expulsion from Hormuz. The Persians even paid tribute to the Portuguese for the Persian use of Qishm and shared with the Portuguese the use of and revenue from Bandar Kong, which rivaled Bandar Abbas as a trading port. Indeed, the Greater Tunb island was used after 1622 as a place where boats from the ports of Bahrain, Qatif, Bandar Kong, Qishm and other places came to pay tribute to Portuguese warships.[21] However, the Yarubi of Oman (1624-1741) drove the Portuguese from Julfar in 1632; from Sohar in 1643; from Muscat in 1650; and from Bandar Kong by the end of the century, when the Portuguese lost Basra too, which progressively weakened the Portuguese hold on the Gulf.[22]

The Portuguese were followed by the British, the Dutch and the French, and these European powers competed and fought for the transit trade through the Gulf, with the Dutch emerging as the dominant European presence from the mid-seventeenth century to the mid-eighteenth century, when they abandoned their positions at Basra, Bushire, Bandar Abbas and Kharg Island. Following the Dutch presence, Britain emerged as the primary European power in the late eighteenth century.[23]

It is clear that the islands of Abu Musa and the Tunbs were used by and belonged to the Arabs after the fall of the Kingdom of Hormuz, while Portuguese power was waning and new European powers were emerging. After extensive research in the Portuguese, French, Dutch and British archives, B.J. Slot writes that the islands of the Tunbs and Abu Musa were for the most part uninhabited during this era, but "belonged to the tribes of the Arabian coast," and "seem to have been used by Arabs as places in which to hide when the situation became dangerous for them." He notes that the French explorer Jean de Thevenot wrote that the Greater Tunb had been used as a place where Arab boats went every year after 1622 to pay tribute to the Portuguese fleet.[24] Slot also notes that Dutch sailors exploring the Gulf for sources of water and provisions landed on the Greater Tunb in 1644, where they found people and cows. In 1645, a local pilot employed by a Dutch ship that sighted the island said there was good drinking water on the island, but claimed that it was impossible to get to it because the island was inhabited by snakes.[25] In fact, the island, which had been a source of drinking water during the Kingdom of Hormuz, remained a source during these years, both for the seasonal inhabitants whom the Dutch saw on the island and for Arab boats that were making the one or two-month long trade voyage from Julfar to Basra.[26]

Abu Musa and the Tunbs may have come under the authority of the Yarubi dynasty of Oman after they drove the Portuguese from Julfar in 1632. What is clear is that Abu Musa and the Tunbs were used and controlled by the Arab shaikhs of the Arab coast during this time, particularly by the shaikhs of the Arab tribes that fled from Hormuz and Qishm and the shaikhs of those tribes from the Najd and Oman that settled in the small fishing and pearling villages around Sharjah, Julfar and Ras al-Khaimah and hoped to reclaim Arab dominance of the trade of Hormuz.[27] Among these tribes were the Al-Ali, who inhabited the Ras al-Khaimah area early in the 1600s, and perhaps also the Shihuh.[28] Slot suggests that Sayf bin Ali bin Salih Al-Qasimi, the first known member of the Qawasim tribe, who represented the Yarubi in negotiating an armistice with the Portuguese in 1648, may have been the Shaikh of Sir, the area around Julfar. Thus, a Qawasim leader may in fact have ruled over the tribes that used Abu Musa and the Tunbs at this time.[29]

Meanwhile, the Dutch knew that Julfar was engaged in some trade with Basra in 1646.[30] Ships from Julfar may have taken water from the islands on this long voyage and on any voyages beyond the Gulf. The Dutch were also aware that Julfar was engaged in the pearl trade in the 1650s.[31] In all likelihood, Julfar's pearlers made use of the islands during their pearling season. Indeed, the inhabitants of Julfar, Ras al-Khaimah and Sharjah were probably using Abu Musa and the Tunbs during the pearling season throughout the entire period covered by the reports of Barbosa in 1518, Balbi in 1580 and Teixeira in the early 1600s, as well as through the 1650s and beyond, years after the fall of the Kingdom of Hormuz.

Qawasim Claims to Abu Musa and the Tunbs: From the Early 1700s to the Early 1800s

The period between the early and mid-1700s marked the fall of the Safavid dynasty in Persia and the Yarubi dynasty in Oman, the unification of Oman under the Al Bu Said dynasty and the rise of the Qawasim emirate of Ras al-Khaimah. The acquisition of a fleet of boats meant that the Qawasim would soon play the part of a major naval power in the Gulf. As such, they were able to develop extensive commercial trade with other ports in the area as well as with other countries, particularly India. The Qawasim's rise also involved them in a long struggle against attempted domination by the Al Bu Said. Most significantly, Qawasim use of the islands of Abu Musa and the Tunbs was common during these years.

In the declining years of the Safavid dynasty, the Yarubi raided Bandar Kong in 1714, took Bahrain, Qishm and Larak in 1717, and laid siege to Hormuz in 1717 and 1718. The Yarubi, led by a commander from the Qawasim tribe, Rahma bin Matar bin Rahma bin Mhamet Al-Qasimi, the Amir of Julfar, very likely made use of the islands of Abu Musa and the Tunbs during their expeditions across the Gulf towards the settlements mentioned above. Indeed, in 1719, the Yarubi fleet drew a Portuguese fleet from Bandar Kong to Julfar for a battle and retired afterwards to Qishm, probably passing and using the islands. After the Yarubi took Qishm in 1717, the harbor at Basidu on the western end of Qishm became an important center of trade for Arabs from Bandar Kong, Julfar, Ras al-Khaimah and Muscat, who came to trade and reside there after 1720. Certainly by 1727, some migration from Julfar to Basidu was reported. It is likely that boats from Julfar, Ras al-Khaimah and Muscat stopped on the islands of Abu Musa and the Tunbs on their trips to and from Basidu.[32]

The islands must also have been used on a seasonal basis by pearlers. The Dutch reported that Rahma bin Matar was one of the wealthiest merchants of the Gulf. His boats were very active in the pearling business and must have used the islands during the pearling season. Furthermore, the islands continued to serve as refuge for those fleeing trouble, as they had one hundred years earlier. For example, the Arab Ruler of Basidu, Shaikh Rashid, fleeing from a Portuguese expedition in 1728, attempted unsuccessfully to hide his treasure on the island of Sirri. Shaikh Rashid, who was prominent in Bandar Kong prior to moving to Basidu in 1720, may have been from the Marazik tribe in Bandar Kong and was certainly an ally of Rahma bin Matar.

Both the Marazik tribe and the Huwala in general were Arabs who were part of the Qawasim federation loyal to Rahma bin Matar. They had started moving from the Arab coast to the north coast around Bandar Kong and Basidu as early as the campaigns of the Yarubi and Rahma bin Matar from 1714 to 1720, mostly for its harbors and arable land. Rashid himself may have transferred some of his treasure to Julfar in the face of a challenge from the British East India Company fleet in 1727. Rahma bin Matar reportedly offered Rashid some soldiers for defense against the British, who were concerned about Basidu as a commercial rival to Bandar Abbas. Rahma also sent a fleet to transport Rashid's widow and his treasure from Basidu to Julfar after Rashid's death in 1736.[33] Clearly, by the 1720s, Rahma bin Matar and the Qawasim enjoyed strength not only in Julfar, but also in Basidu, which was ruled by an ally and probably a dependent of the Qawasim leader. There should be no doubt that they made frequent use of the islands during this time.

Under Nadir Shah, who ruled Persia from 1736 to 1747, a Persian fleet largely commanded and manned by Arab sailors captured Bahrain in 1736 and, with assistance from the Dutch fleet in 1737, invaded Julfar and Khor Fakan. In Julfar, Rahma bin Matar was captured and taken prisoner. This Persian fleet, of course, may have used the islands during its voyage across the Gulf. However, in 1738, Arab naval forces defeated the Persians at Muscat and blockaded the Persian garrison in Julfar. In 1740, the Arab sailors of the Persian fleet mutinied, taking most of the ships to Arab ports, and leaving the Persian garrison at Julfar isolated. In 1743, after acquiring a new navy, Persia took Muscat and Sohar, but in 1747 most of the Persian garrison at Julfar joined another mutiny against Nadir Shah and sailed to Bandar Abbas. After Nadir Shah's assassination in 1747, the Al Bu Said expelled the remaining Persian forces from Muscat and their other positions in Oman, and established their new dynasty in 1749.[34]

Julfar was reclaimed by 1749 by Rahma bin Matar and Arab tribes from the Arab and Persian coast that were led by and loyal to him. These included the Banu Ka`ab, the Banu Qitab and the Shihuh. The historical record is clear on the fact that Rahma bin Matar was acting independently of the Al Bu Said. Not only did he refuse to yield his hold on the coast to the Al Bu Said, but he also established an emirate independent of Al Bu Said authority, perhaps moving his base from Julfar to the more defensible Ras al-Khaimah nearby. According to a report by T.F. Van Kniphausen, a Dutch official in the Gulf at the time, Rahma bin Matar also re-established his activity in pearling by 1754, collected revenues from the Za`ab tribe for their pearling activity, and was sending his ships on trading voyages outside the Gulf as far as Mocha on the Red Sea coast of Yemen.[35] Thus, it is natural that he and his dependent tribes would have resumed their use of Abu Musa and the Tunbs as well.

After the death of Nadir Shah in 1747, Persian authority along the Persian coast collapsed. Competition for authority was waged between Mulla Ali Shah, who was the Arab commander of much of Nadir Shah's remaining fleet and also the governor of Bandar Abbas, and the Arab tribe of the Banu Ma'in, who were neither Huwala nor part of the Qawasim federation. From 1751 to 1759, the Qawasim leader Rahma bin Matar supported Mulla Ali Shah, his father-in-law, frequently helping to defend his positions at Bandar Abbas, Hormuz and Qishm against challenges from the Banu Ma'in and the Persian Governor in Lar, Nasir Khan. In 1755, for example, Rahma bin Matar, in alliance with Mulla Ali Shah, conquered the port of Luft on Qishm from the Banu Ma'in and settled the loyal tribe of the Al-Haram there.[36]

At about this time, the Qawasim and the loyal tribe of the Marazik also took control of the trading port of Lingeh on the Persian coast. Indeed, the Dutch official Van Kniphausen, after exploring the coasts, meeting the inhabitants and counting their boats, wrote in his 1756 report that the islands of Farur, the Greater Tunb and the Lesser Tunb belonged to the Marazik tribe of the Huwala, who were inhabitants of Lingeh. He noted that the islands were not inhabited, but served as a shelter in bad times. Van Kniphausen mentioned that although the Huwala along the Persian coast, including the Maraziks of Lingeh, engaged in fishing, pearling and shipping cargo, the local rulers did not collect fees for these activities.[37] Moreover, Carsten Neibuhr, who explored the area from 1761 to 1765 in a Danish expedition, but who also took much of his information from the Kniphausen Report of 1756 and from other Dutch and British sources, reported that Lingeh belonged to the Shaikh of the Qawasim of Ras al-Khaimah and that the Tunbs were uninhabited.[38] These reports suggest that Lingeh and the Tunbs belonged to the Qawasim Shaikh Rahma bin Matar and his dependents in the 1750s and early 1760s, and that the islands were used during the traditional activities of fishing, pearling and shipping.

After Mulla Ali Shah attempted an alliance with Nasir Khan in 1759, Rahma bin Matar seized Bandar Abbas and Hormuz, but soon lost them to the Banu Ma'in and Nasir Khan. Unsuccessful attempts to regain Bandar Abbas and Hormuz by Rahma bin Matar and his brother Rashid bin Matar, who succeeded Rahma after 1760, led to fighting at sea between the Qawasim and Omani fleets. In 1763, the Qawasim were expelled from Lingeh, Shinas and Luft by Karim Khan Zand, who ruled Persia from his capital in Shiraz from 1757 to 1779. In turn, Persian forces were attacked and driven from Lingeh by Omani and Banu Ma'in forces in 1774. Later, after a marriage between the daughter of the Banu Ma'in ruler of Hormuz and the Qawasim ruler Saqr bin Rashid Al-Qasimi, who succeeded Rashid bin Matar in the mid-1770s and ruled until 1803, the Banu Ma'in and the Qawasim became occasional allies. This resulted in the Banu Ma'in inviting the Qawasim to return to Lingeh in 1777 and the Qawasim regaining Qishm in 1779.[39]

It is evident, therefore, that from the 1750s until the 1770s, except for one interlude, the Qawasim again enjoyed strength on both the Persian and the Arab coasts, just as they had in the 1720s and 1730s. From the 1770s onwards, the Qawasim established Lingeh as their major base on the Persian coast, a base that was independent of weak Persian central governments and provincial governments in Fars and that remained subject to the Qawasim tribe's rulers in Ras al-Khaimah. In addition, the Qawasim use of the islands was probably not interrupted during their absence from Lingeh from 1763 to 1777, inasmuch as the islands had been traditionally used by the inhabitants of the Arab coast long before some of the Qawasim moved to the Persian coast.

In fact, from the early to mid-eighteenth century, Abu Musa and the Tunbs, although not permanently inhabited, were used on a seasonal basis by the Arab tribes dependent on and loyal to the Qawasim. The islands were a source of fresh water and a refuge from bad weather and from political trouble in all seasons. The Qawasim shaikhs would send their horses and flocks to graze on the islands during the spring following the rain, while Qawasim boats frequented the islands during the summer pearling season. During the winter fishing season, Qawasim fishermen would live there.[40]

In the latter half of the 1700s, the expanding role of the Qawasim in local trade and transit trade with India aroused the fears of the Al Bu Said of Oman, who desired to dominate this trade. This precipitated decades of conflict in the Gulf between the fleets of the Qawasim and the Al Bu Said. By 1794, the new Al Bu Said ruler Sayyid Sultan bin Ahmed of Muscat, who had just established his authority along the coast while leaving the Imam of Oman in control of the interior, seized Qishm from the Qawasim and leased Bandar Abbas and its dependencies, including the islands of Hormuz and Larak, from Persia. This enabled him to dominate the Strait of Hormuz. He did not, however, take control in Lingeh, which remained under the Qawasim. He soon found a powerful ally against the Qawasim in the form of the British, who sought and received his agreement to stop the French and Dutch trade with Muscat and other ports under his control. This alliance was formalized by a treaty in 1798, and strengthened in 1800 and 1805.[41]

In the early 19th century, the British East India Company argued that British naval expansion into the Gulf was necessary to defeat the Qawasim naval fleet and suppress Qawasim "piracy" against trade in the Gulf, the Arabian Sea and the northern Indian Ocean. His Highness Shaikh Dr. Sultan bin Muhammad Al-Qasimi, the contemporary Ruler of Sharjah and Member of the Supreme Council of the UAE, wrote in 1986 that the British East India Company fabricated a "myth" of Qawasim "piracy" as a means to increase the company's share of Gulf trade with India at the expense of the native Arab traders, including not only their allies in Muscat, but particularly the Qawasim of the lower Gulf.[42] As he notes, even in J.B. Kelly's *Britain and the Persian Gulf: 1795-1880*, which he considers to be an otherwise "imperialistic" account, the author acknowledges that the Qawasim reputation for piracy in the late eighteenth century "was largely earned as a result of incidents arising out of their protracted struggles with successive Al Bu Sa'id rulers of Muscat."[43] Indeed, Francis Warden, the Chief Secretary to the British East India Company's Government of Bombay, which had responsibility for British interests in the Gulf, wrote that "until the year 1796 I was unable to trace a single act of aggression on the part of the Joasmee [i.e. the Qawasim] against the British flag." Following several incidents in 1797, the British Resident at Basra, Samuel Manesty, after demanding and receiving explanations and assurances from the Qawasim Shaikh Saqr bin Rashid, advised the Bombay Government that Shaikh Saqr would prevent incidents like this from happening again.[44]

In 1800, Captain David Seton became the British Resident in Muscat. Seton's views on the Qawasim, their possessions and associations are important. In November and December 1801, during a tour of the Gulf, Seton made the following entries in his journal:

> [Nov] 15th. Off Rumz [Rams, to the northeast of Julfar], the first place belonging to the Beni Joassim [Qawasim], at noon off the Great Tumb, this Island has good anchorage, plenty of fresh water and fish and is capable of cultivation from its Situation between the western extreme of Keshmeh [Qishm] and Ras ul Khimeh [Ras al-Khaimah], every vessel that passes in the Gulph may be seen on this account, the french privateers generally anchor under it, it also has a Pearl fishery carried on by the inhabitants of Julfar Jovill [Jabal] & ca: who assemble to the number of fifty and Sixty and remain on the Island during the Pearl Season from the month of May to October, at present there is nothing but Antelopes on it, the Emam [the Ruler of Muscat] landed from his Ship once and killed 400 another time 200, he thinks of moving his port from Angam [Henjam] to this on account of its more convenient size and Water.

> Julfar, on the Arab Coast is opposite this, and is the Capital of the Beni Joassim [Qawasim], is barren and unproductive except the pearls on the Coast, it was formerly very rich from

trade and formidable at sea from their number of Vessels, but the Eman's of Muscat have humbled them at Sea, and the Wahabee [Wahabbi] by Land have overrun and rendered them tributary, their present Shaickh is called Shaichk Sugger [Saqr bin Rashid].

16th. Off the Lesser Tumb, this is unfrequented probably from want of water. In the Evening off Lengue [Lingeh] and Shinas on the Persian Shore, a brother of Shaichk Sugger of Julfar [Shaikh Saqr's brother Shaikh Qadhib of Lingeh] holds both these places, they are of little consequence…

Dec 7th. Passed between the Island of Moossa [Abu Musa], and Naby Tumb [Lesser Tunb], they are both inhabited…[45]

Seton recognized that the inhabitants of Julfar, or Ras al-Khaimah, the capital of the Qawasim, used and lived on the Greater Tunb. Julfar was poor and had been weakened at sea by the Al Bu Said Ruler of Muscat and subjugated on land by the Wahhabis, a religious-military tribal confederation from central Arabia. Lingeh, meanwhile, was a secondary and subordinate location for the Qawasim. Seton also noted that the Greater Tunb was useful to French "privateers" for its anchorage from the vantage point that it provided inasmuch as shipping in and out of the Gulf passed by the island. He was also aware of the Ruler of Muscat's use of and interest in the Greater Tunb. Inasmuch as Seton had been instructed to thwart French access to the Gulf, French use of a strategically located island in the hands of the Qawasim was undesirable, whereas use of the islands by the British and their allies in Muscat would be desirable.

With regard to the Lesser Tunb, Seton seems to have been mistaken in noting that it was "inhabited." He had already noted that it was "unfrequented." Seton also noted that Abu Musa was inhabited, although it was probably only inhabited on a seasonal basis, similar to the situation on the Greater Tunb. Later on, Seton wrote that most of the islands known to the British, including Abu Musa, had wood, water, antelopes, goats, verdure, and fruit trees, and were "frequented by the inhabitants of the opposite coasts, who are left undisturbed in their possession."[46] The inhabitants of these coasts were largely the Qawasim and their dependents, and they were undisturbed by the Persians in their possession of these islands.

In November 1804, the Ruler of Muscat, Sayyid Sultan bin Ahmad, was killed during a skirmish at Qishm, a development that led to renewed conflict between Muscat and its rivals, the Qawasim and the Banu Ma'in. On December 1, two British merchant vessels, the *Trimmer* and the *Shannon*, were plundered north of Qishm by dhows, which Manesty, Seton and the British captains thought were commanded by Qawasim from Ras al-Khaimah and Lingeh. The account of the captain of the *Trimmer* shows that it fired first, suspecting that the Arab dhows intended piracy. H.H. Shaikh Dr. Sultan writes that while it is possible that the Lingeh Qawasim could have been involved, the Ras al-Khaimah Qawasim were not. Nevertheless, after these incidents, the British prepared to use naval force to assist Muscat against the Qawasim, although not at the port of Lingeh. Indeed, the British Resident in Bushire, William Bruce, reported that the Persian Ambassador claimed that the Qawasim of Lingeh were "subjects of Persia, but this allegiance is very precarious in general, and entirely depended on the state the country was in at the time..."[47] J.B. Kelly added:

> It was some years before Fath 'Ali Shah [the Qajar Shah who ruled Persia from 1797 until 1834] could make his authority felt on the coast of Fars. Only at Bushire was a pretence made of acknowledging the central government by the payment of tribute, and even this was liable to be withheld if the governor-general of Fars [the Shah's son, Prince Husain Ali Mirza] was incapable of enforcing payment.[48]

In an effort to avoid a conflict with the Qawasim that could antagonize both the Persians and the Wahhabis, Seton tried to negotiate a peace between the Banu Ma'in and the Qawasim on the one hand and the British East India Company and Muscat on the other.[49] In February 1806, Seton secured such an agreement only with the Qawasim. It stated that:

> There shall be peace, between the Honble [Honorable] East India Company and Sultan Ben Suggur, Joasmee [the Qawasim Shaikh Sultan bin Saqr] and the whole of his dependants, and Subjects, on the Shores of Arabia and Persia...

The wording indicates that the British considered Shaikh Sultan bin Saqr Al-Qasimi, who had come to power in 1803, to be the Ruler of the Lingeh Qawasim as well as of the Qawasim of the Arab Coast. Indeed, in negotiating this treaty, Seton had written that "the Shaikhs of Lingah, and all other dependants of the Joasim, be obliged to join in this peace."[50]

Later in 1806, a new Ruler of Muscat, Sayyid Said bin Sultan, undertook a series of campaigns against the Qawasim at Ras al-Khaimah and the Banu Ma`in at Qishm. Nevertheless, Seton and other British officials in the Gulf reported throughout the period from 1806 until 1808 that the Qawasim had honored their peace with the British East India Company. It was not until later in 1808 and 1809 that the British accused the Qawasim of various acts of piracy against the *Minerva,* the *Sylph* (which H.H. Shaikh Dr. Sultan ascribes to the Jalahima family of Rahma bin Jabir from Qatar), the *Lively* (off the coast of India, which the Ruler of Muscat attributed to his own subjects), and other shipping off the coast of India. Seton and other British officials thought that the Qawasim had now fallen even more under the domination of the Wahhabis. They were concerned about the possible role of the Qawasim, as instruments of the Wahhabis and possibly as allies of France, in challenging British domination of Gulf trade, particularly if the Qawasim and the Wahhabis controlled Omani ports and if the French gained access to Qawasim ports and islands as well as Omani ports.[51]

Consequently, the British decided to send a naval force to engage the so-called Qawasim "pirates" with the aim of protecting the growing British domination of Gulf trade with India. The British set out to destroy the Qawasim vessels at Ras al-Khaimah, Lingeh and other ports on both shores of the Gulf and the Omani coast. They also wanted to bring the Qawasim ports on the Omani coast and the port of Luft on Qishm island under the Ruler of Muscat's authority. The port of Muscat was to be secured and another treaty prohibiting piracy with the Qawasim was to be obtained. It was also important for the British to identify a defensible island base from which to monitor French movements and command the entrance to the Gulf more effectively against piracy.[52]

Accordingly, in November 1809, a British expeditionary force burned Ras al-Khaimah, its naval stores and dhows, destroyed the Qawasim dhows at Lingeh and at Luft and brought the latter port under the Ruler of Muscat's authority. The following month, with Omani support, the Qawasim fort at Shinas on the Omani coast was destroyed. In January 1810, another British expeditionary force searched for Qawasim dhows, burning them at ports on both coasts of the Gulf. Despite these measures, many Qawasim dhows remained hidden or escaped destruction.

As British officials suspected, Shaikh Sultan bin Saqr had lost control of the situation. In fact, he was no longer in charge even in Ras al-Khaimah, having been deposed by the Wahhabis earlier in 1809. Thus, despite his desire to honor his 1806 peace agreement with the British, he could not do so. The British then concluded that no Qawasim leader could enter into a new treaty, given the extent to which the Wahhabis dominated them. The British invited Persia to participate in attacking Qawasim ports on the Persian coast as well as Ras al-Khaimah and although Persia promised their cooperation, they failed to follow through on their participation with the British expedition. Rather, Persian forces had already attacked Lingeh earlier in the year and held it briefly in an unsuccessful effort to establish authority and collect tribute.[53]

After the *Macaulay* was chased and fired upon in February 1811, the commander of the ship was told in Muscat that the pirates were those who had fled from Ras al-Khaimah during the British siege in 1809 and who had settled at Abu Musa. As this information came from a state that had been long at war with the Qawasim, H.H. Shaikh Dr. Sultan questions whether the Qawasim were the pirates. At least one British official in Bombay believed that Rahma bin Jabir from the Jalahima family of Qatar was the pirate in question. Still, the initial information, which was also reported by other British officials in Bombay, does place the Qawasim from Ras al-Khaimah on Abu Musa in 1811. However, when the British sent a small naval expedition to destroy Qawasim vessels in the Gulf, none were found.[54]

In 1814, British officials blamed the Qawasim of Ras al-Khaimah for seizing ships carrying British passes or flying British flags off the coast of India. Ras al-Khaimah's Ruler Hassan bin Rahma Al-Qasimi denied these allegations. His offer to renew and strengthen the 1806 peace agreement between the Qawasim and the British (negotiated by his uncle Sultan bin Saqr, who was now the Ruler in neighboring Sharjah) was accepted. The new agreement of October 1814 between the Ruler and William Bruce, the British Resident at Bushire, stipulated that the Qawasim would respect British vessels, including those with British passes or flags. Furthermore, British vessels would be allowed into Qawasim ports and Qawasim vessels could visit British ports in India.

Opposition to the agreement came from Bombay officials who sought to prevent armed Qawasim vessels from cruising along the Indian coast, arguing that they could not permit interference by pirates with any ship, whether carrying British flags or not. H.H. Shaikh Dr. Sultan has argued that the British aimed to prevent Qawasim vessels from trading with India. By late 1814 and 1815, Bruce and Bombay officials again accused the Qawasim of more piracy in the Gulf and along the Indian coast, primarily against ships of the Ruler of Muscat. H.H. Shaikh Dr. Sultan states that Indian pirates committed the piracy off the coast of India and that other acts of piracy in and around the Gulf were carried out by Rahma bin Jabir.

In the midst of ongoing Qawasim-Omani engagements, Bruce continued to accuse the Qawasim of piracy in 1816, particularly against the British vessel *Aurora* near the Tunbs. Following his appeal for naval operations against the Qawasim, British ships began to seek and destroy Qawasim vessels in the Gulf from 1817 until 1819. Inasmuch as attacks were launched against other Arab vessels as well, H.H. Shaikh Dr. Sultan has argued that the British were trying to destroy the Arab role in the Gulf trade. Throughout this period, the British were preparing for another major expedition against the Qawasim.[55]

In August 1819, the Qawasim shaikhs from both coasts of the Gulf, including Hassan bin Rahma of Ras al-Khaimah, the deposed Sultan bin Saqr, now at Sharjah, Muhammed bin Qadhib of Lingeh, and representatives of other Gulf tribes like the Bani Yas of Abu Dhabi and the Utub of Bahrain, met in Ras al-Khaimah. Here, they reached an agreement to defend each other and the port of Ras al-Khaimah from a possible British expedition. The tribes were concerned not only about an expedition against piracy, but also about the possible destruction of any Arab role in trade among the Gulf ports. Furthermore, the leaders regarded Ras al-Khaimah as an essential base of Qawasim strength and security. They understood that if Ras al-Khaimah were to fall, Sharjah and Lingeh would become vulnerable.[56] The Qawasim of Lingeh had been allied with the Qawasim of Sharjah since the deposed Sultan bin Saqr had established himself at Sharjah around 1814. Indeed, Sultan bin Saqr had briefly resided in and ruled Lingeh in 1814-1815. However, through this meeting and this agreement, the Qawasim of Sharjah and Lingeh were also emphasizing their link with Ras al-Khaimah, even though the latter was under the influence of the Wahhabis, who had initially deposed Shaikh Sultan.[57]

Meanwhile, the Persians continued to consider the Qawasim of Lingeh to be subjects of Persia. The British, eager to receive the support of the Persian ruler for their expedition against the Qawasim, heeded Persian sensitivities on this issue.[58] Thus, in July 1819, when the British captured a boat belonging to the Qawasim Shaikh of Lingeh, they released it on the orders of the Persian Prince Husain Ali Mirza of Fars, the son of Fath Ali Shah. However, the British did not agree that the Lingeh Qawasim were subjects of Persia. The British view was that Lingeh and the other "pirate" ports had only occasionally paid tribute to the Government of Fars, and then only due to fear of some other power. With this in mind, Britain asked Persia not to offer any protection to the Qawasim and their allies on the Persian coast if they tried to escape British punishment by submitting temporarily to Persian authority.

The British understood that in reality these ports had been independent for many years and that Persia had no real authority or power over them, particularly because it lacked a navy that could establish effective control. Given the British objectives, they were now willing to help Persia establish authority over the Lingeh Qawasim. Nevertheless, when the British encouraged Persia to launch a land attack against the ports of the Qawasim and their allies on the Persian coast as a means of assisting the British naval expedition and as a means of establishing Persian authority, Persia did not cooperate and instead warned the British against such attacks. The argument put forward was that the punishment of pirates on the Persian coast was strictly a Persian responsibility, and they promised to subdue piracy from these ports in the future. Nevertheless, even in the years after the 1819-1820 expedition, these ports remained independent of Persia.[59]

After Hassan bin Rahma sued for peace on terms unacceptable to the British – by offering to respect British vessels but not Indian ones – another expeditionary force, with some assistance from the Ruler of Muscat, arrived at Ras al-Khaimah on November 25, 1819. The town was razed, many Qawasim vessels in the harbor were burned and the rest divided. The expedition also attacked neighboring Qawasim ports on the Arab coast and destroyed Qawasim and other Arab vessels at two ports on the Persian coast, although not at Lingeh. As Kelly has written, although the British thought that the Lingeh Qawasim were engaging in piracy, an attack against them was called off because the expeditionary force could only document one alleged instance of piracy by the Lingeh Qawasim under Sultan bin Saqr in 1815, and only one other act by an allied tribe. Furthermore, Persia had warned against any British attack on ports on the Persian coast.[60] In a memoir published in 1830, Captain G.B. Brucks wrote that many of the best boats of Ras al-Khaimah had been sent to Lingeh and other locations before the British expedition of 1819-1820, had therefore avoided destruction and were soon employed in trade once again by Ras al-Khaimah.[61]

Qawasim Claims to Abu Musa and the Tunbs: From the Early 1800s to the 1880s

In the immediate aftermath of the 1819-1820 expedition, Hassan bin Rahma was deposed and Sultan bin Saqr was reinstated as Shaikh of Ras al-Khaimah. However, as a result of the widespread destruction of Ras al-Khaimah, Sultan bin Saqr maintained his headquarters in Sharjah. The "General Treaty of Peace with the Arab Tribes" of 1820, which prohibited piracy against any vessel, but permitted trade, was imposed upon the reluctant Qawasim, their allies, and the Utoub of Bahrain.[62] In addition, a strong British squadron was initially stationed at Ras al-Khaimah, and thereafter for several years at Qishm. The movements of the Qawasim were monitored and discouraged by this squadron.[63]

While Shaikh Sultan bin Saqr was never linked with piracy, the British did not trust him either. As Kelly writes, this was partly because he did not cooperate with the Ruler of Muscat in attacking Ras al-Khaimah early in 1819. Consequently, immediately after Shaikh Sultan's return to power, the British sought to limit his authority, first by recognizing Ajman and Umm al-Qawain as independent of his rule in 1820, and second by choosing to base a British Residency Native Agent in Sharjah in 1823 to report on him. In the following decades, Shaikh Sultan's ongoing rivalries with the Ruler of Muscat, the Bani Yas federation of Abu Dhabi, Dubai, Ajman and Umm al-Qawain, his growing fleet of boats and the maritime hostilities that grew out of these factors, as well as his intrigues against British efforts to confront Egyptian advances under Mohammed Ali, would feed this British mistrust and would contribute to a British policy of increasing restrictions on the Qawasim.[64]

However, Sultan bin Saqr did try to re-build his authority, revitalize traditional Qawasim activities and restore historical Qawasim relationships. The following quotations from the memoir of Captain G.B. Brucks, based on surveys he conducted from 1825 to 1829 and published in 1830, are revealing about the demographic situation in the region. In Ras al-Khaimah, Brucks wrote:

> At the present time…there are about two thousand four or five hundred inhabitants, of the Joasmee, Shehaheen [Shahouh], Zaal, and Mootarish, and strangers of various tribes…They trade to Bombay and the Malabar Coast during the north-east monsoon, and to the Red Sea; they also take a large share in the pearl fishing.

In Sharjah, he wrote:

> The inhabitants consist of the Joasmees, Al Ali, Shehaheen [Shahouh], and some mixed tribes, and are variously calculated from 2,300 to 5,500 men: but from my own observation, aided by inquiries on the spot, I should think in the pearl season, when most numerous, they may amount to about 3,500 or 3,800.

He added that Sharjah sent several hundred boats to the pearl fishery and that each boat paid a tax to the Shaikh, Sultan bin Saqr. In addition, he noted that they also participated in Gulf trade and in trade with Bombay and the Malabar Coast. On Shaikh Sultan bin Saqr, Captain Brucks wrote that he "pretends great good will towards the English, but is not to be trusted."

About Lingeh, he reported:

> Lingah…has a considerable trade with most parts of Arabia…sends Buggalows and other vessels to India, and takes a very large share in the pearl fishery…It sends thirty boats to the pearl fishery, and employs all those belonging to the opposite coast from Ras-ool-Khyma to Shargah. It imports and exports annually to the amount of near two lakhs of dollars in pearls, and about one-third that amount in grain, dried fruits, and tobacco.

He also reported:

> It contains about seven hundred men of the Joasmee Tribe, of the original people of the Allienny [Al Moainy] Tribe about three hundred, and two hundred and fifty of the Alfarrish [Al Farris] Tribe... The people are mostly Wahabees, and the Shaikh is of the Joasmee Tribe, and nearly related to Sultan bin Sugger, the chief of the tribe, and were always connected with the pirates.

Captain Brucks had little to say about the islands, except that "the Great Tomb...is well stocked with antelopes, and there is good water on it," and that "the anchorage is pretty good to the south-east and west..." Also, there was a safe channel for navigation of about six and a half miles between the island and the port of Basidu on Qishm island.[65] Here it should be added that a British survey of the Arab coast, conducted in the early 1820s by Lieutenants Guy and Houghton, reported that the residents of Ras al-Khaimah were also subjects of Shaikh Sultan bin Saqr of Sharjah and that boats from Ras al-Khaimah engaged in pearl fishing, like boats from Sharjah, also paid tribute to the Shaikh of Sharjah.[66]

The report by Captain Brucks is notable in several ways. It names Sultan bin Saqr of Sharjah as the chief of the Qawasim tribe and its dependents, and mentions that the majority of the family remained at Sharjah and Ras al-Khaimah. The boats from Sharjah, Ras al-Khaimah and Lingeh were again engaged in Gulf trade and trade with India, while the overwhelming majority of the boats sent to the pearl fishery was from Sharjah and Ras al-Khaimah. Lingeh, meanwhile, served as the market for the Qawasim pearl trade. While Brucks had little to say about the islands, his emphasis on Qawasim involvement in pearl fishing and trade would undoubtedly also have involved the continuing Qawasim use of the islands, particularly by the hundreds of boats from Sharjah and Ras al-Khaimah. Seton had already noted the use of the Greater Tunb by pearlers from Sharjah and Ras al-Khaimah in 1801. Traditional Qawasim use of the islands for refuge, water, fishing and grazing livestock was probably continuing as well.

In addition to the trade between the Qawasim of the Arab coast and the Persian coast, the Qawasim Rulers of Lingeh provided boats in support of various campaigns by Sultan bin Saqr, for instance, against the Bani Yas of Abu Dhabi. On occasion, they mediated temporary truces for him throughout the late 1820s, 1830s and 1840s.[67] However, there were also quarrels between the Qawasim of the two coasts over the use of the islands. In order to resolve them, the branches of the family divided the islands for the use of each side. By 1835 or earlier, the island of Sirri was allocated for use by the Lingeh Qawasim, while the islands of Abu Musa, the Greater Tunb and Sir Abu Nuair were allocated to the Qawasim of Ras al-Khaimah and Sharjah.[68] Such a division appears logical in light of the status of Sultan bin Saqr as the chief of the Qawasim tribe, the larger Qawasim population on the Arab coast, the substantially greater number of Qawasim boats from Sharjah and Ras al-Khaimah engaged in the pearl fishery, and the traditional use of these islands by the Qawasim of the Arab coast. As chief of the tribe, Sultan bin Saqr must have made or consented to this arrangement. An agreement between Sultan bin Saqr and his cousin the Shaikh of Lingeh, Muhammad bin Qadhib, would likely have been only an oral agreement.

It is not clear whether the British were privy to this understanding at the time. It is not mentioned in either the joint memoir of Lieutenants Guy and Houghton or the memoir of Captain Brucks, memoirs based on surveys done in the 1820s. In an 1836 publication, James Horsburgh, the hydrographer to the East India Company, reported only about the anchorage off these islands and that these islands were uninhabited.[69] Lieutenant H. H. Whitelock, writing in the *Journal of the Royal Geographical Society* in 1838, also reported that the Greater and Lesser Tunbs were uninhabited and that "the former is well stocked with antelopes, and much resorted to by the officers stationed at Básidóh, for the purpose of hunting. In the winter months the island is well covered with grass, and the water is very good."[70]

Again, Horsburgh and Whitelock were also basing a large part of their publications on surveys done in the 1820s.[71] The agreement is also not mentioned in the historical sketches and other political reports by various officials, such as Lieutenants Samuel Hennell, A.B. Kemball, H.F. Disbrowe, Captain James Felix Jones, and Lieutenant Pelly, which cover the years from 1819 to the 1860s.[72] However, the Qawasim did reach such an oral arrangement among themselves and did refer to this arrangement in numerous written letters from the 1860s onward.

After years of maritime hostilities among various tribes of the coast, particularly between the Qawasim and the Bani Yas of Abu Dhabi in 1834, the British negotiated the Maritime Truce of 1835, which was renewed in successive years until a ten-year truce was agreed upon in 1843. This was followed in 1853 by the Treaty of Maritime Peace in Perpetuity, after which the area, which had been known to the British as the 'Pirate Coast,' became known as the 'Trucial Coast.'

The purpose of these truces and the treaty was to suppress hostilities at sea and permit peaceful trade. It was the British intention to stop piracy, prevent slave trade, curb smuggling in arms and other goods and permit peaceful access to the pearl fisheries during the pearling season.[73] As time passed, the agreements were generally successful in permitting access to the pearl fisheries and trade across the Gulf and to India, and thus received the support of Sultan bin Saqr and the Qawasim, for whom these activities were so important.[74] The relative tranquility certainly permitted the continued traditional usage of the islands by the Qawasim of Sharjah and Ras al-Khaimah.

After the 1835 Maritime Truce, however, the British Assistant Resident Samuel Hennell prohibited Qawasim and Bani Yas warboats from approaching the trade route lying between the Persian coast and the islands of Sirri and Abu Musa at any time of the year, i.e. from crossing a line drawn between these two islands and known as the Hennell Line. The British Resident James Morrison quickly redrew the line from Sha'am on the western side of the Musandam peninsula to a point ten miles to the south of Abu Musa and on to Sir Abu Nuair, explaining that Sirri was a pirate lair and that Abu Musa had the same potential.

The new line would prevent the use of these islands for this purpose, and also prevent Sultan bin Saqr's warboats from sailing around the Musandum peninsula, i.e. through the narrow strait and into the Gulf of Oman. Under such restrictions, he would be unable to challenge both this trade route and the Ruler of Muscat.[75] The new restrictive line prohibited Qawasim warboats from the Arab coast from even approaching Abu Musa and the Tunbs. By the 1860s and 1870s, these developments eventually proved to complicate the ability of Sultan bin Saqr and his successors to defend the right of the Qawasim of Sharjah and Ras al-Khaimah to the traditional usage of Abu Musa and the Greater Tunb against encroachments by adversaries on the Arab coast and the Qawasim of Lingeh.

In 1864, the first edition of the *Persian Gulf Pilot*, compiled by the British Admiralty during the late 1850s and early 1860s, was published. It reported that the Greater Tunb had water and was uninhabited: "at times a few cattle are brought over from the main [i.e. the Persian coast] for pasture, the island being covered with coarse grass and shrubs. There are some wild antelopes on the island."[76] The report mentioned that both the Lesser Tunb (Nabiyu Tumb) and Abu Musa were barren and uninhabited with no water, but that the latter was visited by fishing boats from Sharjah and was near the great pearl bank. Commenting on Lingeh, it stated that it was "one of the most flourishing towns on the Persian coast," with "about 10,000 inhabitants, chiefly of the Joasmí tribe," which was about equal to the population of Sharjah and about double the population of Ras al-Khaimah, although it noted that Lingeh still only sent about 50 boats to the pearl fishery. "The chief of this place, who pays a tribute to the Persian government, has authority over all the places on the coast between Birket Sifleh, and Bostáneh village, with the islands Serí, Nábiyú Farúr, Tumb, Nábiyú Tumb, and Bú Músa."[77]

This British Admiralty view that the Qawasim Ruler of Lingeh had authority over Abu Musa and the Tunbs was probably held because British trade was mainly along the Persian coast, including Lingeh, because the protection of this trade had led the British to prohibit warships of the Qawasim on the Arab coast from sailing to these islands and protecting their rights there, and because cattle from Lingeh were being grazed on the Greater Tunb. Moreover, Sultan bin Saqr was approximately 90 years old in the late 1850s and early 1860s, and his subordinate governors in Lingeh, Sharjah and Ras al-Khaimah were now able to act somewhat independently of him. Furthermore, the authors of the *Persian Gulf Pilot* had incomplete knowledge. They did not note the hundreds of boats Sharjah was still sending to the pearl banks, which must have entailed the continuing use of Abu Musa. They evidently also did not know that Abu Musa was also used for grazing by Sharjah and that, contrary to their report, it had grass and water. They did not seem to know that the Qawasim had agreed in 1835 that Abu Musa and the Greater Tunb were for the use of the Qawasim of Ras al-Khaimah and Sharjah.[78]

Furthermore, although the 1864 *Persian Gulf Pilot* mentioned that the Ruler of Lingeh paid tribute to Persia, this does not mean that Persia actually exercised real authority over Lingeh, the coast or offshore islands. At this time, the port of Lingeh was only nominally under the Persian Governor of Fars and also under the Persian Governor of Bushire in his role of High Admiral of the Seas and Ports. In fact, however, Persia still had no warships. Instead, Lingeh was actually still under independent Qawasim rule in the late 1850s and early 1860s, with Khalifa bin Said Al-Qasimi, the Qawasim ruler in Lingeh, solely responsible for the internal administration, including the collection of taxes and duties and all civil and criminal proceedings.[79] The British Residents Hennell, Kemball and Pelly in the mid-1800s understood that, just as in 1819 and 1820, at the time of the second British expedition against the Qawasim, Persia exercised little or no real authority or control over the Persian coast. This included Lingeh and its environs, as well as the islands off the Persian coast.[80]

The British were concerned about Persia's lack of control over the maritime tribes in ports on the Persian coast. The British therefore wanted to exercise their naval authority in the region in order to protect the truces that had been concluded with the rulers on the Arab shore.[81] They thought that Muhammad Shah, who ruled Persia from 1834 to 1848, would be most unlikely to agree to this, but in 1846, the Governor General of Fars, Husain Khan, approached Resident Hennell to ask the British to coerce the maritime tribes and curb piracy on the Persian coast, only asking that a Persian official accompany any such missions. The British willingly agreed to do so and piracy declined markedly.[82]

Furthermore, in 1850, Mirza Taki Khan, Minister of Defense to Nasr-ed-Din Shah, the Qajar Shah who ruled Persia from 1848 to 1896, conceded to the British that "the power and control of the Government over the people was exceedingly limited." In the following year, Persia granted the British request for its navy to have the right of search and seizure along the Persian coast to curb the slave trade. The only stipulation was that a Persian officer should accompany such missions and any vessels engaged in the slave trade should be turned over to the Governor of Gulf Ports for punishment.[83]

In 1852, the Persian Prime Minister, Mirza Agha Khan, said Persia could do nothing to stop the slave trade at the port of Lingeh. Later in that same year, he authorized the British navy to take coercive action. In 1853, Kemball sent two British cruisers, along with a Persian slave-trade commissioner, to exact fines from the Ruler of Lingeh and others for their participation in the slave trade. In subsequent years, British naval surveillance and operations succeeded in curbing this slave trade. However, the British viewed Persian officials as reluctant to coerce powerful chiefs on the coast and as susceptible to bribes offered by those chiefs. By 1855, Britain was paying a salary to the slave-trade commissioner to overcome these problems.[84] Thus, it was the British navy that actually brought Persian officials to Lingeh and other ports on the Persian coast and helped them to exercise limited authority there. This was the context in which the Qawasim ruler of Lingeh paid fines and tribute to Persia in the late 1850s and early 1860s.

In 1863, one year before the publication of the *Persian Gulf Pilot*, the British Resident Pelly noted that Lingeh's prosperity was growing because British steamers from Bombay could unload goods at the deep harbor at Lingeh, from which they could be shipped by dhow to shallow harbors like Sharjah and Ras al-Khaimah.[85] This growing prosperity led Persia to raise the tribute it received from Lingeh.[86] However, in 1868, when negotiating the renewal of Oman's lease of Bandar Abbas and the islands of Larak, Hormuz and Qishm from Persia, Pelly noted that Persia still had no warship and he expressed his view of the weakness of Persia's claim to these islands off its coast, and presumably to other islands as well. He wrote:

> Were it not for us, the Arabs would plunder her coast and not allow a Persian boat to put to sea. It seems strange that a kingdom so circumstanced along her sole and only ocean seaboard should venture to exclude strangers, or lay claim to sovereignty over islands. The islands, it is true, may in point of distance be nearer to the Persian coast than to the Maskat coast; but channel islands are usually found to belong to a naval and not to a purely military power.[87]

In December 1864, the same year as the *Persian Gulf Pilot* was published, Shaikh Sultan bin Saqr sent an official message to the British Political Resident at Bushire, Colonel Pelly, instructing him that Abu

Musa, the Greater Tunb and Sir Abu Nuair belonged to him and threatening a disturbance at sea if Pelly did not instruct the Ruler of Dubai to stop using Abu Musa:

> Last year I informed you of the interference of the Debai people in regard to Bu Musa island and of their taking their horses and sheep there. This island belongs to me. Tamb, Bu Musa and Sir belong to me from the time of my forefathers. Nobody went there without my permission. But you did not reply to my letter…Finding that you and I were silent, they have taken their sheep this year also…If you will not prevent him [the Chief of Dubai], a disturbance will take place, because I will not give up my right to it, neither will I allow anybody to interfere with it without (my) permission. It is well known from olden times that these islands (i.e. Bu Musa, Tamb and Sir) belong to me. Sirri belongs to the Jowasmis of Lingah, Hinjam to Seyyid Thweini [of Oman] and Farur to the Meraziks [of Abu Dhabi]. If you make inquiries about this (i.e. his statement) you will find it correct.[88]

While Shaikh Sultan bin Saqr had evidently complained to Colonel Pelly a year earlier, Morsy Abdullah writes: "This [1864] letter constituted the first recorded evidence regarding the ownership of these islands among the Qawasim."[89] It is the first written claim that has been found in archival research and it may have been the first time the British were given such precise information (although Seton had written in the early 1800s that the islands were used and possessed by the Qawasim). Inasmuch as Shaikh Sultan was approximately 95 years old in 1864 and had ruled since 1803, his letter's reference to his "forefathers" places the Qawasim of the Arab coast in control of the islands in the early to mid-1700s, at the time of his forefather Rahma bin Matar.

After the death of Sultan bin Saqr in 1866, the Qawasim began to quarrel with each other over borders and islands. This eventually ended with the Greater Tunb being controlled by the Qawasim of Ras al-Khaimah under the rule of Shaikh Humaid bin Abdullah Al-Qasimi, and Abu Musa being controlled by the Qawasim of Sharjah under the rule of Shaikh Salim bin Sultan Al-Qasimi.[90]

In the early 1870s, the reporting of the British Native Agent in Sharjah, Hajji Abd Al-Rahman, to the British Political Residents in Bushire confirmed the claim put forward to the island of Abu Musa by

Shaikh Sultan bin Saqr in 1864 and contradicted the view set forth in the 1864 *Persian Gulf Pilot*. In the autumn of 1871, during the ongoing struggle between the Qawasim Rulers of Sharjah and Ras al-Khaimah, the latter wrote to the British Native Agent that Abu Musa, the Greater Tunb and Sir Abu Nuair were his territory and that he would not permit anyone else to use them for grazing their animals. The British Native Agent advised the British Political Resident at Bushire, Colonel Pelly, that other shaikhs had been warned, "not to send their cattle to the Island of Boo-Moosa, as that Island was for the cattle of the Joasmees and that they had no right even to the other islands." He suggested that Shaikh Humaid bin Abdullah of Ras al-Khaimah should not be permitted to prevent the others from using the islands for grazing and subsequently Shaikh Humaid was so informed.

The Native Agent was naturally trying to prevent the hostilities at sea that would ensue if Shaikh Humaid acted to prevent other shaikhs from grazing their animals on the islands. Moreover, being based at Sharjah, the Native Agent may have favored the claim of Shaikh Salim bin Sultan of Sharjah to Abu Musa. Indeed, on December 27, 1871, when reporting to Colonel Pelly that he had appealed to the Chief of Dubai not to use Abu Musa and that he had narrowly averted maritime hostilities between the Chief of Dubai and the Chief of Sharjah, the Native Agent wrote that "It has been customary from old times for the Chief of Sharjah to send his cattle to that island…" In succeeding years, the sovereignty of the Qawasim over Abu Musa, which was resolved in favor of the Sharjah Qawasim, was infringed by Dubai, Ajman, Umm al-Qaiwain and Lingeh.[91]

In February 1872, Shaikh Salim of Sharjah wrote to British Political Resident Pelly and his successor, Colonel E.C. Ross, with the same complaint, asking for assistance and warning of disturbances at sea. Although the Native Agent again attempted to prevent any infringements of Sharjah's sovereignty, his failure led Shaikh Salim in 1873 to send 50 armed men to Abu Musa, where they fired on ships from Dubai as well as on ships of the Lingeh Qawasim.[92] When Shaikh Salim again asked for British help in preventing other shaikhs from using the island to graze their animals in 1875, Resident Ross asked the Native Agent to determine the ownership of Abu Musa. In his reply, the Agent stated:

The Joasmee chiefs claim the island of Abu Musa and Moonshee Abool Kasim says the island belongs to the Joasmees so that both Sharjah and Ras al-Khaimah chiefs can place their men there.[93]

Notably, he cited the British Native Agent in Lingeh as a source, while at the same time not saying that the Lingeh chiefs could place their men there.

In the spring of 1883, Shaikh Salim of Sharjah was overthrown by his nephew, Shaikh Saqr bin Khalid Al-Qasimi. Following his overthrow, Shaikh Salim chose to live on Abu Musa, where he had previously maintained a house. Shaikh Saqr bin Khalid consented to this arrangement and in the following years continued to send his horses and cattle and other animals to graze on the island in the spring, as had been the historical custom of the Qawasim shaikhs. In 1884, when Shaikh Saqr believed that Shaikh Salim had breached their agreement of 1883, he wrote to British Political Resident Ross, indicating that Abu Musa was a dependency of Sharjah and calling upon the British to persuade Shaikh Salim to honor the agreement. Otherwise, he should be allowed to remove him from the island or to attack him. The British Political Resident warned Shaikh Saqr not to disturb the maritime peace and the two shaikhs soon reached a revised agreement allowing Shaikh Salim to remain on the island.[94]

During the 1870s, despite Shaikh Sultan bin Saqr's 1864 letter, the British Political Residents in Bushire were misinformed by the Native Agent at Sharjah about the ownership of the Greater Tunb, particularly whether the Qawasim of the Arab Coast or the Qawasim of Lingeh had the stronger claim. In the autumn of 1871, when Shaikh Humaid of Ras al-Khaimah wrote his above-mentioned letter to the Native Agent informing the latter about his ownership of the Greater Tunb, Abu Musa and Sir Abu Nuair, Shaikh Humaid also mentioned that Shaikh Khalifa of Lingeh had written a letter that recognized Shaikh Humaid's rights on all the islands and had prevented the Al Bu Sumait from going to the islands. However, in his report to British Political Resident Pelly, the Native Agent only included a copy of Shaikh Humaid's letter in Arabic and it is not clear whether this was ever translated for the Political Resident. In his own accompanying letter to Pelly, which was translated, the Native Agent did not mention the statement by Shaikh Humaid that Shaikh Khalifa of Lingeh had acknowledged Shaikh Humaid's rights on all the islands, including the Greater Tunb.[95]

In November 1872, after Shaikh Humaid sent another message to the Ruler of the Lingeh Qawasim, protesting unauthorized visits to the Greater Tunb by their dependents, the Ruler, Shaikh Khalifa, sent another message acknowledging that the island belonged to the Ras al-Khaimah Qawasim. He wrote:

> ...Your second letter is received. You mention in it about the trip of Albusumait to the Island of [greater] Tunb. Oh my brother, Albusumait are your comrades and they are under your command, but you must prevent such as the Ruler of Dubai, Oman, Umm ul-Qawain and Basidu as they cross over to that place for grass. But Albusumait, as stated, are under your command. Inshallah we shall warn them so as not to harm you. As regards the island, it belongs to you just as it was under the authority of your father. We have nothing to interfere with you about it.[96]

Nevertheless, in February 1873, the new Political Resident, Colonel Ross, asked the British Native Agent in Sharjah "to inquire and report as to whom the Tumb island is supposed to belong." In his report of March 1, the Native Agent, despite his knowledge of Shaikh Khalifa's previous acknowledgment of Shaikh Humaid's rights, wrote that he had already ordered the ruler of the Ras al-Khaimah Qawasim to "keep clear of this island, as I know matters will in the end lead to disturbances at sea between Fars and Arabia for Chief of Ras ul Khymah has no right to the Island unless permitted to go there by consent of Chief of Lingeh." The Native Agent included the Ruler of Ras al-Khaimah's reply to this order in his report, which again stated that the Greater Tunb, Abu Musa and Sir Abu Nuair were under the jurisdiction of the Qawasim of the Arab Coast, while Sirri and the Lesser Tunb (or Nabgau) were under the authority of the Lingeh Qawasim. The Ruler of Ras al-Khaimah wrote:

> I beg to inform you that the island of Tumbs, Boomoosa and Seer are under the authority of the Joasim of Arabistan. The island of Hanjam belongs to the Al Boo Saeed. The islands of Sirree and Nabgau [i.e. the Lesser Tunb] belong to the inhabitants of the Joasim living on the coast of Fars.

This letter repeated the assertions made by Shaikh Sultan bin Saqr in 1864, with the one notable addition being that it also indicated that the Lesser Tunb was under the authority of the Qawasim of Lingeh. The Native Agent, however, advised the Political Resident that Shaikh Humaid's reply was "not suitable."[97]

The Native Agent also told Political Resident Ross that he had ordered the Ruler of Ras al-Khaimah to write an apology to the Ruler of Lingeh and to remove his animals from the Greater Tunb if the apology was not accepted. He later told Ross that the Ruler of Ras al-Khaimah had written this letter. However, Shaikh Humaid's letter did not in fact contain any apology or ask for any permission or recognize any Lingeh claim to the island. The letter did remind Shaikh Khalifa of the previous correspondence with Shaikh Humaid on this matter and it did offer a goodwill gesture:

> We hope that Haji Mohammed Bashir will remind you of the issue of the island of Tunb, when we asked you to recognize our rights over the island and you did not refuse this claim. If you are not satisfied with this situation we can withdraw our horses from the island in spite of our possession of it, just to please you.[98]

In taking this position in favor of the Ruler of Lingeh, the Native Agent was primarily seeking to avoid disturbances at sea. Morsy Abdullah argues that the Native Agent may also have been influenced by his own commercial interests at Lingeh and by an idea that the British would welcome a decision against the Ras al-Khaimah Qawasim. As noted earlier, British commercial interests were centered along the Persian coast and trade was flourishing in the early 1870s, after telegraph lines and postal and steamer services had been established there. Indeed, the supply of Indian goods to the Trucial Coast during this period depended mainly on the port of Lingeh, where the British steamship lines called regularly. Others have argued that the Native Agent may have favored the Lingeh Qawasim because he was himself of Persian origin, or because he was based at Sharjah and had close relations with the Shaikh of Sharjah, who had only recently been engaged in disputes with the Shaikh of Ras al-Khaimah.[99] Since there is no doubt that the Native Agent knew about Shaikh Khalifa's acknowledgment of the rights of Shaikh Humaid, some of these factors may have played a role.

In 1874, Shaikh Khalifah bin Said of the Lingeh Qawasim died and was succeeded by the young Shaikh Ali bin Khalifah Al-Qasimi, who restored friendly relations with the Ras al-Khaimah Qawasim and agreed with Shaikh Humaid's understanding about the Greater Tunb. On January 8, 1877, in response to another request from Shaikh Humaid that the Al Bu Sumait not be permitted to graze their animals on the Greater Tunb, Shaikh Ali bin Khalifah sent the second of three messages from successive Shaikhs of Lingeh to Shaikh Humaid in which he acknowledged:

> I am satisfied that the island of Tanb is a dependency of the Qawasim of Oman, and we have no property there and no interference except with your consent; since I considered the subjects and territories as one, I assumed the authority of giving them permission to go there, but now as you are displeased, and you want they should be prohibited I will prohibit them...[100]

In 1878, however, Shaikh Ali was assassinated by followers of his former guardian Yusuf bin Muhammad, who was then recognized by Persian authorities as Deputy Governor of Lingeh. On June 21, 1879, after renewed disputes over Qawasim islands, British Political Resident Ross asked Hajji Mirza Abu Al-Qasim, the former Native Agent at Lingeh, to study the dependencies of the Trucial Chiefs. On July 16, 1879, Abu Al-Qasim confirmed that Abu Musa was part of Sharjah while the Greater Tunb belonged to Ras al-Khaimah. With regard to the latter, he added "this island is also owned by the Chief of Lingeh in part – as he is also of the tribe of the Joasmee." Abu Al-Qasim's conclusion directly challenged the position on the Greater Tunb taken by the former Native Agent in Sharjah. Ross wrote in the margin at this point "considered Persian," reflecting his or the British view that the Greater Tunb, and perhaps also the Chief of Lingeh, was seen as being Persian. An unidentified person, however, later noted "No," indicating that the island was not Persian, and perhaps also that the Chief of Lingeh, Shaikh Yusuf, who was not of the Qawasim tribe, was not Persian.[101]

In 1881, Shaikh Humaid of Ras al-Khaimah again informed the new British Native Agent in Sharjah, Hajji Abu Al-Qasim, that the Greater Tunb belonged to the Qawasim of the Arab Coast. When

Political Resident Ross maintained the position taken in 1873, Shaikh Humaid showed the new Native Agent the two original letters from the two Qawasim Shaikhs of Lingeh, the letter from Shaikh Khalifa and the letter from Shaikh Ali, which acknowledged that the Greater Tunb belonged to the Qawasim of the Trucial coast. The Native Agent forwarded copies of these letters to Ross in March 1882. This may have been the first time that either Hajji Abu Al-Qasim or Ross learned of the existence of these letters. Shaikh Humaid also wrote to Ross, asking him to check his records and refer to the 1864 letter from Shaikh Sultan bin Saqr to Pelly. In his letter to Ross, Shaikh Humaid expressed his fear about Persian encroachment upon Qawasim rule in Lingeh, especially because Shaikh Yusuf bin Muhammad had become a Persian vassal. In particular, Shaikh Humaid expressed the fear that Persia would claim the Greater Tunb. After receiving these letters, Ross replied to Shaikh Humaid in a way that suggested that he might be reconsidering his view, hoping that "the arrangements about the island of Tunb should continue as of old without alteration and with due respect to the customary rights of all interested."[102]

In 1884, Shaikh Yusuf planted date trees on the Greater Tunb. Shaikh Humaid subsequently destroyed them and sent letters protesting to Shaikh Yusuf and Native Agent Hajji Abu Al-Qasim. On March 29, 1884, Shaikh Yusuf sent the third of three letters by Shaikhs of Lingeh with the following acknowledgment:

> In reality, the island belongs to you the Jowasemis of Oman, and I have kept my hand over it, considering that you are agreeable to my doing so, and that our relations with you are intimate and friendly. But now, when you do not wish my planting date offsets there and the going across of the Busmaithis to cut grass there, God willing, I shall prohibit them and our mutual relations are friendly.[103]

This third letter, however, was not brought to the attention of Political Resident Ross until 1888.

At this point in the historical study, several important facts stand out. First, Abu Musa and the Tunbs were used by Arab inhabitants from both sides of the Gulf for hundreds of years, probably from the days of the Arab Kingdom of Hormuz in the 1400s. Indeed, the islands were continuously used and under the overall authority of the Qawasim

Shaikhs of Ras al-Khaimah and Sharjah from the 1700s. Second, Persia did not use or exercise control over any of these islands, either by itself or through its dependencies. Indeed, Persia never possessed enough strength to establish its authority over any section of the Gulf waters. It also did not put forward specific claims to these islands. As for the Qawasim of Lingeh, although situated on the Persian coast, they were subordinate to the Qawasim of the Arab coast and only paid tribute to Persia temporarily and under the threat from other powers. This was to be the case until the 1880s, when Persia was able to consolidate her rule domestically and thus take a more active interest in Gulf affairs. Third, when the British finally arrived on the scene, they were primarily driven by their interest to protect the trade routes to India and within the Gulf. British antagonism during this period toward the Qawasim and their rights to the islands have to be considered in this context. Nevertheless, even the British did not believe that any of the islands belonged to Persia. When they did make statements on this issue, they generally acknowledged the use of the islands by the Qawasim of Sharjah or Ras al-Khaimah or Lingeh, or, at a minimum, referred to the Arab use of the islands.

CHAPTER
2

The Islands During
the British Protectorate

The previous chapter provided the historical evidence showing how the Qawasim of Ras al-Khaimah, Sharjah and Lingeh were Arabs and how they used and controlled the islands of Abu Musa and the Tunbs from the mid-eighteenth century and possibly earlier. No such record exists in terms of Persian use or control of the islands. With the involvement of the British in Gulf affairs, control over the islands became somewhat more complicated, since an external power began playing a dominant role without necessarily taking into consideration the history and character of the region. During the latter half of the nineteenth century, numerous written letters were made available to the British that clearly showed the Qawasim right to the islands. However, towards the end of the century, Persia became more assertive and attempted to stake its own claim. At this point, Britain began to defend Qawasim rights against Persian claims.

Persian/Iranian Claims from the 1880s until World War II

In 1882, Amin-es-Sultan Aqa Ibrahim was Persian Governor of the Gulf Ports. He paid a fixed annual sum to the Shah for his appointment and his personal revenue was determined by the tribute he could obtain from the ports along the Persian coast. He appointed General Hajji Ahmed Khan as his representative in Bushire and Malik Al-Tujjar as his tax collector. Together, they continued the Qajar effort to gain greater authority over the Persian coast and to exact higher taxes from its ports. After the death of Amin-es-Sultan Aqa Ibrahim circa 1883-

1884, his son, Amin-es-Sultan Mirza Ali Asghar Khan, became the new Governor of Gulf Ports (in addition to being named Prime Minister). His efforts to expand his authority on the Persian coast were made easier by Persia's acquisition in 1885 of two warships from Germany. Shaikh Yusuf, designated by Persia as Deputy Governor of Lingeh after his followers had assassinated the Qawasim Ruler, was himself assassinated in 1885 by the Qawasim Shaikh Qadhib bin Rashid Al-Qasimi, who sought to re-establish independent Qawasim rule in Lingeh and appealed for support to the Qawasim of the Trucial Coast. Later in the year, he was also persuaded to pay tribute and to serve as Persia's Deputy Governor. Thus, Lingeh remained under the nominal jurisdiction of the Governor of Gulf Ports during this time.[1]

In August 1887, Hajji Ahmed Khan visited the Trucial Coast and made an effort to extend Persian authority there. In particular, he tried without success to induce the Shaikhs of Abu Dhabi and Dubai to accept Persian political agents on a similar footing as the British Residency Agents. During the same period, the Ottomans undertook similar attempts to extend their influence over the Trucial Coast, an effort that followed the establishment of their naval presence in the Gulf and their influence over Al-Hasa and Qatar. These challenges posed a threat to the British position in the Gulf and led British Political Resident Ross in December 1887 to obtain a written assurance from the Trucial Shaikhs that they would not correspond with or enter into agreements with any government other than Britain. In addition, they would not permit agents of any other government to reside in the Trucial Shaikhdoms, except with British permission.[2]

However, in September 1887, Persian forces seized Lingeh, imprisoned Shaikh Qadhib, terminated Qawasim authority and occupied Sirri island. The British Residency Agent at Lingeh reported that Persia intended to raise a flagstaff on the Greater Tunb as well. On September 27, British Political Resident Ross, who knew about Hajji Ahmed Khan's visit to the Trucial Coast but had not learned about the Persian's proposals to the Rulers of the Trucial Coast, quickly expressed a new (but still somewhat mistaken) understanding of the issue to Her Majesty's Government of India, which had assumed responsibility for Gulf affairs in 1873 and reported to the India Office in London. He wrote:

> This island [Sirri], as well as the Islands of Tomb, formed
> part of the hereditary estates of the Jowasimee Arab Shaikhs,

but for many years the management, administration, and jurisdiction has by common consent been vested in the Chief Jowasim Shaikh of the Persian Coast, that is to say, the Shaikh of Lingah for the time being. Now the Jowasimee Shaikhs domiciled on the Persian coast have acquired the status of subjects of Persia, and those who have governed Lingah have been subordinate to the Persian authorities, and in fact Persian officials *quá* Lingah. The Persian Government doubtless regards this fact as constituting the islands in question Persian possession, and were it not for the rights of the Arab Shaikhs of the Oman Coast and their joint ownership, the Persian position could not be disputed. As it is, I think it probable that some of the Jowasimee Shaikhs will protest against the islands being annexed by Persia, and may claim the interference of the British Government, or failing that to be allowed to eject the Persian officials.

On October 1, Ross again wrote to the British Government of India that the Persian Government had "no good title" to Sirri and that "with the approval of the Government of India it has been treated as beyond the jurisdiction of Persia proper." He enclosed translations of the earlier letters from Shaikh Khalifa and Shaikh Ali, the Qawasim Rulers of Lingeh, to the Qawasim Shaikh Humaid of Ras al-Khaimah, letters that he had known about since 1882 and that must have influenced the development of his new understanding.[3]

In mid-October of 1887, Shaikh Saqr bin Khalid of Sharjah, the senior chief of the Qawasim, claimed Sirri, the Tunbs and Abu Musa on behalf of the entire Qawasim tribe, i.e. the Lingeh, the Ras al-Khaimah and the Sharjah branches, drawing no distinction between them and their specific claims. He asked that the British bring about the removal of the Persian flag on Sirri and prevent the Persians from raising a flag on the Greater Tunb. As Shaikh Saqr wrote:

> The Island of Sirri, as is known to you, is a dependency of the El-Kowasim tribe and that when our cousins and other relatives were on the Persian mainland, and Lingah was in their hands, there was no difference between us, our affairs and our property were one and the same.

Referring to "the Island of Tomb," he stated "you are aware that those islands belong to the El-Kowasim, in the same way as do the Islands of Seer-bu-Na`eer, Sirri, and Bu-Musa."[4]

Bathurst, Ely and Chance wrote:

> Saqr, writing as head of the Qawasim family, drew no
> distinction between the specific rights of each branch of the
> family to a particular island. Up to that time, these
> distinctions would have been significant only in so far as <u>use</u>,
> <u>jurisdiction</u> or <u>revenue</u> from the island were concerned...
> Qawasim <u>ownership</u> of the island was vested collectively in all
> the members of the family, in the normal manner of tribal
> Arab tenure under which every member held an undivided
> share, subject to the overriding control of the senior member
> of the tribe - in this case Saqr ibn Khalid.[5]

In light of this correspondence, Ross wrote in late October to the
British Government of India and to Sir Arthur Nicolson, the British
Chargé-d'Affaires in Tehran, recommending diplomatic action to
persuade the Persians to lower their flag on Sirri and to refrain from
raising it on the Greater Tunb. In November, the Government of India
instructed Nicolson to seek an explanation for the Persian annexation of
Sirri. Persia's Prime Minister, the Amin-es-Sultan Mirza Ali Asghar
Khan, replied to Nicolson in December that Persia had collected taxes
from Sirri and the Greater Tunb for the past nine years.[6] He was,
however, unable to provide the necessary documents to prove this.

In the first days of 1888, Persia's Prime Minister claimed Sirri and
the Greater Tunb as Persian possessions, again stating that taxes were
levied from them. As proof, he provided five letters written by Shaikh
Yusuf during one month in 1885. After receiving the letters and hearing
the claim, Ross replied to Nicolson and to the Government of India on
January 23 that "these papers do not bear out the Persian claim." The
letters contained only one reference to taxes from Sirri and no reference to
any taxes from either the Greater or the Lesser Tunb. Ross wrote:

> The Persian [Prime] Minister seems to rely on a statement
> made by Shaikh Yusuf that he had 'gone to the Island of Sirri
> to inspect and recover Government (Persian) dues'; but you
> will, I am sure, agree that, in the circumstances of the case,
> this statement could not be accepted as establishing or even
> supporting the Persian claim to possession, nor as sufficient to
> deprive the Joasimi Arab family of their ancient and
> previously recognized rights on that island.

Ross added:

> The Joasimi Shaikhs of Lingah have hitherto been usually
> also Deputy Governors on the part of Persia. These Shaikhs
> were in the habit of exercising certain authority on Sirri

Island and in fact the chief authority, but it was quâ Joasimi Shaikh, and not quâ Persian Governor, that such authority was exercised. The hoisting of the Persian flag would undoubtedly deprive the Arabs of their hereditary rights.[7]

Moreover, Shaikh Saqr of Sharjah again communicated with Ross, arguing that there were no inhabitants on the Greater Tunb from whom Persia could have collected taxes. He requested help from the British in this matter, and sent copies of the letters in which Shaikhs Khalifa, Ali and Yusuf of Lingeh had acknowledged the authority of the Qawasim of the Arab Coast over the Greater Tunb. Ross forwarded Shaikh Saqr's message and the three letters to Nicolson and to the Government of India in February.[8] This may have been the first time that Ross, as well as British officials in Tehran and India, had seen the letter from Shaikh Yusuf to Shaikh Humaid.

In February 1888, Hajji Ahmed Khan again visited the Trucial Coast where he unsuccessfully tried to induce the Shaikh of Umm al-Qawain to fly a Persian flag. In reporting on this to Nicolson and the Government of India, Ross wrote that Hajji Ahmed Khan might also attempt to take Bahrain, in which case, Ross indicated his readiness to use force to stop him. Ross further reported rumors that Persia had promised the island of Hormuz to Russia and that Russian warships would soon be visiting the Gulf at the invitation of Persia. Indeed, Hajji Ahmed Khan had claimed that the Gulf belonged to Persia and that the British had no rights there. Upon receiving this news, Nicolson reported all of the Persian activities of the previous months, including Ross's most recent reports, which concerned him, to the Foreign Office in London.[9]

On March 2, 1888, Nicolson wrote to the Persian Prime Minister:

> I return the papers you were good enough to send me some time ago in regard to Sirri and Tamb Islands. These papers have been very carefully examined and do not bear out the Persian claim.

Days later, again on the instructions of the Government of India, Nicolson asked the Persian Ministry of Foreign Affairs to explain "on what ground the Persian Government have annexed an island [Sirri] which is the property of Joasimee Chiefs who are under British protection..."[10]

Vinson and Elkins write:

> The subsequent exchange of correspondence between Persia and the British concerning the Island of Sirri is a harbinger of

Iran's subsequent arguments concerning ownership of the Tunb Islands and the customary British retort.

The Persian Minister of Foreign Affairs, expressing surprise that he should be asked to present any proof for Persia's claim, replied that Sirri was a dependency of the port of Lingeh and that Lingeh and Sirri were dependencies of Fars. Furthermore, Persia collected taxes from Sirri. He concluded that Persia "will have no necessity to produce new proofs regarding their ownership of the same."[11]

The British Chargé-d'Affaires in Tehran answered that while the Qawasim Rulers of Lingeh exercised "jurisdiction" over Sirri, they had done so as Qawasim shaikhs, not as Persian officials, and asserting the "traditional rights" of the Qawasim shaikhs. He also answered the Persian claim by arguing:

> Possession, if of long standing and undisputed, doubtless carries considerable weight; but this argument would scarcely govern in the present instance.

Upon being pressed again for proofs of ownership, the Persian Government replied in July that because the Lingeh Qawasim Rulers had been Persian governors and rulers of Sirri, no further proof that Sirri was Persian should be necessary.[12]

On 24 April 1888 the British Minister in Tehran, Sir Drummond Wolff, reported to the Government of India and the Foreign Office in London that the Shah had assured him that Persia had no intention of ceding any island to Russia, a possibility that had concerned Ross. Within days, however, Ross learned of a report from Hajji Ahmed Khan to the Persian Prime Minister that had quoted descriptions in the *Persian Gulf Pilot* to support Persian claims to Sirri and the Tunbs. Ross reported to Wolff that the *Persian Gulf Pilot* "is a nautical not a political compilation and statements in it about [the] status of various places cannot be considered authoritative." In response to the argument in Hajji Ahmed Khan's report that the Qawasim Shaikh Salim bin Sultan's "occupation" of Abu Musa, i.e. his residence on Abu Musa, was "without any justification," Ross wrote:

> The claim now put forward to the Island of Bu-Moosa has no justification whatever. Any attempt to assert Persian authority there in a practical form would probably lead to disturbances.[13]

However, as Bathurst, Ely and Chance wrote:

> The report was however an unofficial private document that cannot be interpreted as a claim to Abu Musa. Had the Iranian Government considered there to be any merit in such a claim, no doubt they would have raised the point at that time, instead of referring only to Sirri and Tunb.[14]

Ross had obtained Qawasim letters that eventually led him to a more accurate understanding regarding the ownership of these islands, particularly of the Greater Tunb, and Nicolson had asserted the Qawasim claims and disputed the Persian claims in communications with Persian officials. However, not all British departments had seen these new letters or shared Ross' view of the importance of these islands or of the Persian challenge to Britain in the Gulf.

In 1886, the Intelligence Branch of the British War Office in London had prepared a map of Persia that showed Sirri, the Greater Tunb, the Lesser Tunb and Abu Musa in the same color as Persian territory. In July 1888, during Anglo-Persian discussions about the Persian-Afghan frontier dispute, the British Foreign Office instructed Wolff, its Minister in Tehran, to present this map of Persia to the Shah. Wolff later reported to the Foreign Office that this had produced "certain results which...were hardly contemplated." As the Anglo-Persian communications about Sirri and the Greater Tunb were also taking place in July, the Shah remarked that the map portrayed both islands in the same color as Persia. The Foreign Office considered the Anglo-Persian negotiations then taking place over the Persian-Afghan boundary, which were concluded in 1892, to be more important than the dispute over Sirri and wanted to downplay the latter issue for the sake of the former.[15] Thus, despite Nicolson's earlier communications with the Persian Prime Minister and the Foreign Minister, Sidney Churchill of the British Legation in Tehran tacitly acquiesced in Persia's occupation of Sirri during an audience with the Shah in August 1888, saying that Britain was only acting as the channel for Qawasim complaints.[16]

By 1891, Persian and Ottoman efforts to establish their influence on the Trucial Coast were followed by French efforts to do the same. To counter such challenges and to safeguard the British position in the Gulf, Britain sought to build on the 1887 agreements with the Trucial

Shaikhs and obtain formal treaties with them. Thus, in March 1892, each of the rulers of the Trucial States entered into "Exclusive Agreements" (or Protectorate Treaties) with Britain, promising the following:

> 1st.—That I will on no account enter into any agreement or correspondence with any Power other than the British Government.
>
> 2nd.—That without the assent of the British Government I will not consent to the residence within my territory of the Agent of any other Government.
>
> 3rd.—That I will on no account cede, sell, mortgage or otherwise give for occupation any part of my territory save to the British Government.[17]

In September 1894, the British Minister in Tehran, Conyngham Greene, reminded the Persian Government that it had not refuted the British argument, put forward in 1888, that the Qawasim Rulers of Lingeh had exercised jurisdiction over Sirri as Qawasim shaikhs, not as Persian officials. He therefore requested that the Persians lower their flag on the island. Persia's Prime Minister replied that Persia occupied Sirri on the grounds that it had always been administered from Lingeh, even when there was a non-Qawasim Governor of Lingeh. In this context, however, he only cited the period when Shaikh Yusuf served as a deputy governor, which began in 1883. Nevertheless, the Persian Prime Minister concluded that Persia would never lower its flag. The new British Political Resident, Colonel F.A. Wilson, after considering this Persian reply, wrote as follows:

> ...proof of an alleged long established [Persian] jurisdiction can hardly be found...The conclusion from these historical facts is certainly not that the Joasmees having obtained a footing on the Persian coast, thence derived an authority over outlying islands, but rather that they carried with them to their new settlement a possession in the islands which they already possessed; and the fact that a section of these Arab intruders later acquired the status of Persian subjects, and held their authority on the coast in subordination to the Persian Governments as local Chiefs or Governors, cannot affect any original rights the tribes may have held in common.[18]

Col. Wilson's statement constituted the most accurate assessment of the historical origins of the Qawasim use of and claim to the islands that had yet been made by a British official in the nineteenth century.

Toward the close of the century, the Qawasim began to exercise their sovereignty over the islands in yet another way. In 1898, after Sharjah Ruler Saqr bin Khalid left on a pilgrimage to Mecca, leaving the administration of Sharjah in the hands of his now reconciled uncle Salim bin Sultan, the latter granted the first concession to explore for red oxide in Abu Musa to three Arabs—Hajji Hassan bin Ali bin Samaiyeh, an Arab/Bahraini contractor and British subject from Lingeh, his son Abdullah bin Hassan and Isa bin Abdul Latif, who was the son of the Residency Agent from Sharjah. The agreement was attested to by Abdulrahman bin Faris Kasi of Sharjah, who may have been the former British Native Agent at Sharjah. Hajji Nakhuda Ali Ahmed Saleh Dulash was later made a partner. Shaikh Salim also granted a concession to mine mica to some Arabs who resided at Lingeh, which was now under Persian rule. In the following century, the Qawasim would grant additional economic concessions on Abu Musa and the Tunbs.[19]

Also toward the end of the nineteenth century, on December 13, 1898, the new British Political Resident, Colonel M.J. Meade, sent a report on Sirri to Sir Mortimer Durand, British Minister in Tehran. According to Morsy Abdullah, this report later formed the basis for British official thinking in the 1930s. Meade attributed the problem of Sirri to the gradual assertion of Persian authority over the Qawasim at Lingeh during the nineteenth century, but argued that Persian officials "never actually interfered in the affairs of the place." He stated that the Lingeh Qawasim had dual capacities, eventually exercising authority in Lingeh as Persian officials, but always exercising authority in Sirri as Qawasim shaikhs and arguing that the Qawasim shaikhs on the Arab coast had a claim to Sirri and deserved British support against Persian occupation and usurpation.[20] Despite this assessment, in late 1899 and again in early 1900, the British Government of India and Political Resident Meade warned the Qawasim against any armed effort to retake Lingeh and Sirri.[21]

In 1903, heavy tariffs imposed by Persia at its Gulf ports had led some Lingeh merchants to shift much of their trade to Dubai. They also considered transferring trade to Abu Musa. British Political Resident Colonel C.A. Kemball, anticipating that this might lead to a Persian claim to Abu Musa, recommended that Shaikh Saqr of Sharjah be advised to hoist his flag over Abu Musa. The Government of India, noting that Abu Musa "is in no way dependent on the Persian Government," agreed, and inquired whether the Ras al-Khaimah flag should also be raised over the Greater Tunb. Kemball responded that the claim of the Qawasim of the Arab Coast to the Greater Tunb was even stronger than their claim to Sirri, but that hoisting the Arab flag might lead Persia to seize the island. Under such circumstances, Britain would then have to take forcible measures to assert the rights of the Qawasim. The Government of India proposed that the Arab flag be flown anyway. Shaikh Saqr of Sharjah then raised Arab flags over both Abu Musa and the Greater Tunb, having temporarily inherited the Greater Tunb after the death of Shaikh Humaid of Ras al-Khaimah in 1900.[22]

In March 1904, Persian customs officials lowered the Arab flags on Abu Musa and the Greater Tunb, hoisted their own flags on the two islands and left guards on the islands, thereby challenging Sharjah's sovereignty. Shaikh Saqr of Sharjah protested and was supported by the British Viceroy of India, Lord Curzon, who proposed that a British gunboat lower the Persian flags, re-hoist the Arab flags, and remove the Persian guards. The British Foreign Office also supported Saqr, but agreed with the British Minister in Tehran, Sir Arthur Hardinge, to use a diplomatic approach that succeeded in persuading Persia to remove its flags and guards from the islands. Hardinge learned in his diplomatic efforts that the Persian Prime Minister [i.e. the Mushir-ed-Dowleh], Sultan Abd al-Majid Mirza, considered Persia's claims to Sirri and the Greater Tunb to be "sound," but its claim to Abu Musa to be "more doubtful." Nevertheless, the Persian Prime Minister, on the instructions of Mozaffer-ud-Din Shah, who ruled Persia from 1896 to 1907, stated that the Greater Tunb and Abu Musa were Persian property. He reserved his right to discuss the claims with Britain, and asked that Arab flags not be flown until the issue was resolved. Hardinge declined the latter request and Arab flags were raised on the islands within days. Hardinge also asked the Persian Prime Minister to produce evidence supporting title, which the Persian Government again failed to provide.

The hoisting of the Persian flags is characterized by Morsy Abdullah as "the first official challenge by Persia to the Qawasim's ownership of Abu Musa."[23]

Upon the Persian agreement to lower their flags on the Greater Tunb and Abu Musa in 1904, British Political Resident P.Z. Cox advised the British Government of India that this would be an opportune time to raise the Arab claim to Sirri, a claim which the British had shelved since 1888. The Government of India instructed Hardinge that the passage of time had weakened the Arab claim to Sirri, but that any further Persian claims regarding Abu Musa and the Greater Tunb should be met by a British revival of the Arab claim to Sirri. Hardinge subsequently suggested to the Persian Government that "we might recognize Persia's sovereignty over Sirri in return for an abandonment by Persia of all claims to Tanb and Abumusa, and a pledge that the islet should never be ceded to any Foreign Power [i.e. Russia]." In 1908, Britain protested Persia's granting of a concession to a British company to mine red oxide on Sirri, arguing that it was a disputed island and warning the company to that effect.[24]

The firm British opposition to any Persian claim to Abu Musa and the Tunbs may be attributed to the greater understanding developed by British officials since 1887, but also to the fact that Persian, Ottoman and French challenges to British supremacy in the Gulf were now joined by serious Russian and German challenges.[25] There was a concern that growing Russian political influence in Tehran encouraged Persia to raise tariffs in the Gulf and assert claims to islands in the Gulf. Indeed, Hardinge suspected that the Russian Legation to Tehran had advised the Persian Government to take its 1904 actions on the islands in response to a show of naval force by Lord Curzon, British Viceroy in India, in late 1903. Hardinge also feared that Persia might cede an island to Russia or another foreign naval power.[26]

This British policy was applied again in 1906, when a German businessman from Lingeh, Robert Wonkhaus, purchased from Hajji Hassan bin Ali Samaiyeh, one of the original concessionaires, a share in the red oxide mining concession on Abu Musa that the late Shaikh Salim had granted in 1898. Upon learning of this development, Political Resident Cox became concerned that commercial success might motivate Persia to assert another claim to Abu Musa and, in turn, bolster German steamship trade in the Gulf. Cox thus reminded Sharjah's Shaikh Saqr of his 1892 treaty obligation not to "cede, sell, mortgage or otherwise give for occupation" any of his territory save to the British Government. As it turned out, the agreement with Wonkhaus had initially been made without the knowledge of Shaikh Saqr, who canceled the concession on the grounds that there was no provision for a contract with any new party without his knowledge.[27] Bathurst, Ely and Chance wrote:

> At no time, however, was it ever contended that the island belonged to Iran and no Iranian protest was ever made over the existence of the concession nor at the representations made by both the British and German Governments. The Iranian Government had, however, been reminded privately by the British Minister in 1908 of the 1904 incident, and warned not to renew any claim to the island.[28]

Throughout this era, British officials sent numerous messages to the Rulers of Sharjah and Ras al-Khaimah stating Britain's recognition of their title to Abu Musa and the Tunbs, and conveying such communications to Persia. In 1912, for example, the Ruler of Sharjah, Shaikh Saqr, acting in his capacity as ruler of Ras al-Khaimah, signed an agreement with Britain to establish a lighthouse on the Greater Tunb, with British Political Resident Cox's assurance that "your sovereignty over the Island is recognized." Cox also wrote to Shaikh Saqr that it was advisable that the Sharjah flag should fly on the island, but that "now at all events this island will be preserved for you by the mere presence of the lighthouse." The Persian Government raised this issue with the British in 1912 and again in 1913, noting that Persia contested the ownership of the island. The British told them on both occasions, however, that the ownership of the island was not open to question. Following this, the Persians took no further action.[29]

In 1921, Reza Shah Pahlavi took power in a *coup d'etat* in Persia, establishing a strong central government and a modern army. One of his early accomplishments was to bring border areas like Arabistan (now called Khuzestan) under his control. He also built a strong navy and established control over Persia's coast and islands in order to end smuggling and to raise tax revenues from foreign trade through the Gulf ports. The Anglo-Persian Treaty of 1919 was scrapped and a treaty of friendship with Russia was signed, leading to numerous disagreements between Britain and Reza Shah. Among the issues of contention, the challenge to traditional British privileges on the coast and islands, including access to naval bases, and the continuing Persian claims to Abu Musa, the Tunbs and Bahrain, were some of the most pertinent ones. It was also during Reza Shah's rule that Persia changed its name to Iran.[30]

In the same year as Reza Shah's takeover of Persia, Britain recognized the independence of the emirate of Ras al-Khaimah under Shaikh Sultan bin Salim Al-Qasimi, including its sovereignty over the Tunbs. Abu Musa was to remain under the sovereignty of the emirate of Sharjah, now ruled by Shaikh Khalid bin Ahmad Al-Qasimi. Since this date, Sharjah and Ras al-Khaimah have been separate entities.[31] Following this decision, in December 1922, Shaikh Khalid bin Ahmad granted a five-year concession for red oxide exploration on Abu Musa to a British national. Six months later, in May 1923, Sir Percy Loraine, the British Minister in Tehran, warned the Persian Prime Minister, Mostaufi-ul-Mamalek, that Britain would "take action to uphold" Sharjah's rights to the island against any Persian challenge. However, Zoka-ul-Mulk, the Persian Minister of Foreign Affairs, protested, asserting a Persian claim to sovereignty over both Abu Musa and the Greater Tunb, and pointing to the previous Persian claims made in 1904. The British returned the Persian note of protest and reminded the Persians that "the Persian Government had repudiated, in 1904, an attempt made by its official to place the Persian flag on the islands, had disclaimed it as an unauthorized act, and had ordered him immediately to remove the flag."[32]

Despite the British position, Persian customs officials landed on Abu Musa in 1925 to inspect the red oxide being mined there. Upon hearing the news, the Ruler of Sharjah, now Sultan bin Saqr Al-Qasimi, immediately sent a boat to the island to prevent any Persian action. By the time the boat arrived, the Persian officials had already departed. When the British protested, the Persian Ministry of the Interior reasserted the Persian claim to Abu Musa. The British Minister in Tehran protested to the Persian Minister of Foreign Affairs, threatening "to despatch a ship of war to Abu Musa to uphold the rights of the Sheikh of Sharjah." Following this, Persian Customs Director General M. Molitor instructed the Customs authorities in Bushire "not to take any steps in Abu Musa or Tamb pending reply from Ministry of

Foreign Affairs regarding status of these islands." Persian Minister of the Interior Dadgar then asserted that the Persian Government had "no intention of raising the question of ownership of Abu Musa."[33]

In May 1928, Persian officials detained the wives of Arabs who had fled Hanjam to the Trucial Coast after the murder of a Persian customs official. In July, a Persian customs boat captured a dhow (i.e. a boat) from Dubai in territorial waters off the coast of the Greater Tunb, detaining its passengers and confiscating their possessions. To guard against further incidents, the Trucial Arabs requested British protection. During the ensuing diplomatic crisis, which eventually resulted in the release of the dhow, the Acting Persian Foreign Minister, M. Pakrevan, stated that Persia did not plan to occupy the Greater Tunb and hoped that the issue of disputed sovereignty could be negotiated. However, in response to Britain's official protest and assertion that the Greater Tunb belonged to Shaikh Sultan bin Salim of Ras al-Khaimah, Pakrevan and other Persian officials repeatedly raised a Persian claim to the Greater Tunb and Abu Musa, citing the 1886 British War Office map. They refused recognition of the independence of Ras al-Khaimah and rejected the notion that Britain's protectorate over the Trucial States represented adequate ground for the British protest.

The British Chargé d'Affaires in Tehran, R.C. Parr, wrote to Pakrevan, taking "the greatest exception" to the Persian claims to Abu Musa and the Greater Tunb. He stated:

> His Majesty's Government cannot admit any claim to ownership [of Abu Musa] on the part of the Persian Government...His Majesty's Government [HMG] are unable to admit the claim of the Imperial Government to own this island [of Greater Tunb].

Parr further reasserted that the island of Greater Tunb belonged to the Shaikh of Ras al-Khaimah, that Britain had treaty relations with him and the other shaikhs of the Trucial coast, and he warned Persia not to enter into direct dealings with the shaikhs. Pakrevan was also told that his reference to the 1886 map was "no argument." Britain, while anxious to avoid a showdown, nevertheless proceeded to instruct the Senior Naval Officer (SNO) in the Gulf that Persian occupation of the Greater Tunb and/or Abu Musa should be resisted by force if necessary, but only as a last resort.[34]

In the midst of this episode, on August 24, 1928, British official J.G. Laithwaite of the India Office issued a memorandum on the "Status of the Islands of Tamb, Little Tamb, Abu Musa, and Sirri" that rejected the Persian claims and recognized the Qawasim claims, but acknowledged Britain's tacit acquiescence in Persia's occupation of Sirri since 1887. Unfortunately, the memorandum also repeated the mistaken assertions that "the history and status of these islands is identical" and that "their management, administration and jurisdiction had, however, for many years prior to 1887 by common consent been vested in the chief Jowasimi Sheikh of the Persian coast, viz the Sheikh of Lingah, but in his capacity of Jowasimi Sheikh and not of Persian official..."[35] The fact, of course, is that this had not been true of Abu Musa or the Greater Tunb. At this stage, the British also began to gather all of the original documents they could find bolstering the claims of the Qawasim Shaikhs to the islands, in anticipation of further arguments with Persia over the islands issue.[36]

Indeed, during the 1929-1935 negotiations for an Anglo-Persian general treaty, the islands case did become an issue. In January 1929, the Persian Minister of Court Taimurtash indicated that international arbitration might be the only means of resolving the contending claims to the Greater Tunb and Abu Musa. Later, in August of the same year, after Persia rejected a British draft article regarding the islands, the British Minister in Tehran, Sir Robert Clive, asked Taimurtash if Persia would be prepared to offer money for the islands. Taimurtash rejected the idea. Clive noted that it was his "impression" that Taimurtash would consider withdrawing the Persian claim to Abu Musa, leaving it to Sharjah, if the Persian claim to the Greater Tunb was recognized.[37]

This was followed in April 1930 by a proposal from Taimurtash that the Shaikh of Ras al-Khaimah should be paid to renounce his claim to the Greater Tunb in favor of Persia. Clive reported that Taimurtash was prepared to come to terms on Bahrain and that he again had the "impression" that Taimurtash would drop the Persian claim to Abu Musa. The British referred the Persian proposal on the Greater Tunb to the Ruler of Ras-al Khaimah as well as the Ruler of Sharjah, who both rejected it.[38] When Taimurtash was told by Clive in early October 1930 that Persia must drop its claims to Bahrain, Abu Musa and the Greater Tunb, Taimurtash answered that if Persia renounced its claim to

Bahrain, public opinion would require some territorial concession. He then said that Persia would drop its claim to Abu Musa in order to gain the Greater Tunb. Taimurtash proposed a long lease of the Greater Tunb from the Ruler of Ras al-Khaimah, who could keep his gardens on the island and be exempt from customs duties. Clive initially refused to discuss this and considered general treaty negotiations to have broken down. However, when Taimurtash proposed a 50-year lease of the Greater Tunb, Britain reconsidered, thinking that this might help to secure its desired terms for a lease of Hanjam from Persia, constitute Persian admission of Ras al-Khaimah's sovereignty over the Greater Tunb, and permit the conclusion of a general treaty.[39]

In 1931, the British Political Resident, H.V. Biscoe, conveyed the Persian offer to the ruler of Ras-al Khaimah. By May 1931, Ras al-Khaimah's Shaikh Sultan bin Salim Al-Qasimi signaled his conditional agreement, including the conditions that the Qawasim flag fly over the island, that his representative remain there, that any merchandise imported by him or the island's inhabitants should be free of customs duties, and that Persia refrain from inspecting Arab dhows in Arab waters and from issuing any orders to the island's inhabitants. Due to the British perception that Persia was not serious about concluding a general treaty and that it would not accept any of these conditions for leasing the Greater Tunb, the terms were never communicated to the Persian authorities.[40]

During discussions over the next few years, Persia continued to demand the Greater Tunb and Abu Musa, and Britain continued to refuse. On July 23, 1933, the Head of the Persian Navy, commanding the warship *Palang*, landed on the Greater Tunb, inspected the lighthouse and gave the lighthouse supervisor, a British employee, a certificate indicating that everything was in order. Britain lodged a "vigorous protest" against the landing and the inspection in August. In October 1933, Persian Foreign Minister Bagher Kazemi replied to the British that both the Greater Tunb and Sirri were Persia's *de jure* and *de facto* possession.[41]

It was later rumored that Persian customs officials had landed on the Greater Tunb in March 1934 and had promised to reward the representative of the Shaikh of Ras al-Khaimah if he would lower the shaikh's flag and hoist the Persian flag, an offer he refused. By April 25, the Commanding Officer of the British ship *HMS Lupin*, in conversation with the shaikh's representative on the Greater Tunb, determined that this Persian visit had probably occurred months earlier, and that it may have been the July 1933 visit. However, on April 26, 1934, the Governor, Chief of Police and Director of Customs of Bandar Abbas landed on the Greater Tunb and promised to retain the representative of the Shaikh of Ras al-Khaimah at double his salary if the Greater Tunb became Persian property. Britain did not protest, certain that its rejection of the Persian claim was clearly on the record, and wishing to avoid any needless challenge to Persia while the British navy's use of Henjam and Basidu were in question.[42] Then, on May 4, 1934, the Persian Government asserted that it could not accept any British intervention in Persia's relations with Arab rulers on the opposite shore of the Gulf. A month later, on June 18, 1934, the Persian Majlis (the lower house of the legislature) defined the limit of Persian territorial waters at six miles (with a six-mile contiguous zone). The British refused to recognize more than a three-mile limit.[43]

On August 28, 1934, the Persian warship *Palang* anchored for the night at the Greater Tunb in what was the second visit by a Persian ship to the island that month. The British warned the Persian admiral that the island belonged to the Shaikh of Ras al-Khaimah and that he required advance notification of visits. The British later learned that the *Palang* had searched a Dubai dhow in the territorial waters of the island before anchoring. On September 11, 1934, another Persian warship visited the Greater Tunb and interrogated the Shaikh of Ras al-Khaimah's representative. The captain denied knowledge of the aforementioned British warning, although it was repeated and despite the fact that the two Persian captains had met since the initial warning had been issued.[44]

In late September 1934, the British Minister in Tehran, Sir R. Hoare, conveyed in writing to the Persian Prime Minister, Mohamed Ali Feroughi, the view of the British Secretary of State for Foreign Affairs, Sir John Simon:

> Either the Persian Government wish to invent a fictitious value for their claim in future negotiations; or else they are unwilling to make use of the peaceful and legal methods by which it is open to them to pursue it, and are determined to achieve their object in a manner quite incompatible with their

position as signatories of [the] Covenant of [the] League of
Nations and [the] Kellogg Pact.

Britain would not resume negotiations until the Persian behavior
stopped. The British Minister in Tehran had earlier believed that Persia
might raise its claims to Bahrain, the Greater Tunb and Abu Musa at
the League of Nations, but had concluded that this was not likely. He
also orally conveyed to the Persian Prime Minister, as did the British
Secretary of State to the Persian Minister in London, Hussein Ala, that
any Persian warship found visiting Abu Musa or the Greater Tunb
without proper notification and performing any act of territorial
jurisdiction on the islands or in their territorial waters would be invited
to desist and withdraw. Any failure to comply would be considered
aggression against the respective shaikh and the British ship would
defend the shaikhs' rights, as a last resort by force if necessary. The
Persian Prime Minister told the British Minister in Tehran he "was
almost sure it [the general treaty] would have been concluded had we
[i.e. the British] agreed to [the] proposal for [the] surrender of Tamb
and Abu Musa." The Persian Minister in London informed the British
Foreign Office that Persia regarded the Greater Tunb and Abu Musa as
its own and considered the British policy unfriendly.[45]

As these events were unfolding, Shaikh Sultan bin Salim Al-Qasimi
of Ras al-Khaimah wrote to T.C.W. Fowle, the British Political Resident
in Bushire, on September 3, 1934, asking that Britain lease the Greater
Tunb or permit him to exercise his rights in the matter. In December
1934, the British Navy reported that Shaikh Sultan had removed his
flagstaff and flag from the island. The British also learned that the shaikh
had not paid the salary of his representative on the island. It was rumored
again, as earlier, that Persian authorities were in direct communication
with the shaikh regarding a Persian lease of the island.

The British Residency Agent in Sharjah suggested that the shaikh
had done this in order to attract attention to his desire to be paid rent
for the lighthouse. The Political Agent in Bahrain and Political
Resident Fowle in Bushire suggested that the island should be given to
the Shaikh of Sharjah if the Shaikh of Ras al-Khaimah did not re-hoist
his flag. British Minister Hoare in Tehran and the Government of India
opposed any change in ownership of the Greater Tunb as that might
weaken the British and Arab positions vis-à-vis Persian claims. The

British Foreign Office considered assuming British control over the island. The India Office initially seemed to agree that the British should take the island, but later favored the reversion of the island to Sharjah, the former owner of the island. The British Resident in Bushire recommended that some British payment to the Shaikh of Ras al-Khaimah for the lighthouse be made as an inducement to him to rehoist his flag, before allowing the Shaikh of Sharjah to hoist his flag. Ultimately, the Political Resident in Bushire was instructed to give the shaikh ten days to rehoist his flag, without offering any rent, or the island would be transferred to the Shaikh of Sharjah. This message was conveyed in a note on March 19, 1935.[46]

On March 29, 1935, Shaikh Sultan bin Salim Al-Qasimi wrote to Political Resident Fowle, promising to replace his flag and explaining why it had been removed in the first place and why his representative had left the island. He stated that as long as he had enjoyed an income from pearl-fishing, he had not needed assistance from the British to pay his employees on the island. With the decline of the pearl trade, however, he now required British financial help. Although he had previously, in December 1934, explained this to the British Residency Agent in Sharjah, Isa bin Abd Al-Latif, no support had been provided. On April 3, 1935, Shaikh Sultan complied with the ultimatum from the British Political Resident and rehoisted his flag on the Greater Tunb.[47]

Meanwhile, in January 1935, the Ruler of Sharjah, Shaikh Sultan bin Saqr Al-Qasimi, granted a concession to the Golden Valley Ochre and Oxide Co. Ltd., a British company, to exploit Abu Musa's red oxide.[48] The company agreed to the British Government's conditions "not to sell, lease, or otherwise transfer to persons who were not British subjects any concession or contract which they might obtain..." Persia, reasserting its claim to the island, complained that this was a violation of a purported gentlemen's agreement to continue the *status quo*, which Britain rejected.[49]

In May 1935, Anglo-Persian discussions regarding a general treaty broke down over the Persian claims to the Greater Tunb and Abu Musa and the British refusal to recognize them. This was despite a suggestion by Persian Foreign Minister Kazemi that Persia might recognize the independence of Bahrain and the special relations between Britain and the Trucial Shaikhs in exchange for the two islands, and his assertion that "he was only speaking of sovereignty; the actual ownership of the land of the islands was no doubt vested in various Arab sheikhs and would not be affected." In the meantime, British legal studies continued, in order to provide British representatives at the League of Nations with authoritative policy for any discussions that might take place there.[50]

From 1936 until World War II, there were only a few developments of importance concerning the islands. In 1936, Britain decided that the Golden Valley Ochre Company did not need to pay any import duties on the red oxide from Abu Musa inasmuch as Sharjah and Abu Musa, along with the other Trucial Shaikhdoms, were "territories under His Majesty's protection" in terms of the Import Duties Act of 1932. In 1933, Iran protested the working of this concession. Britain rejected the protest and the India Office advised the Foreign Office that the company should be permitted to accept the invitation of the Shaikh of Ras al-Khaimah to mine for red oxide on the Greater and the Lesser Tunbs, despite the likelihood of additional Iranian protests. In 1937, the Shaikh of Sharjah and the Shaikh of Ras al-Khaimah each granted an oil concession to Petroleum Concessions Ltd. Both the shaikhs and the company regarded the concessions as covering Abu Musa and the Greater and Lesser Tunbs, although the company did not conduct explorations in those islands.

In 1938, in response to a question from the Anglo-Iranian Oil Company (AIOC) as to whether Abu Musa and the Greater and Lesser Tunbs were Iranian or Arab and whether the areas around these islands could be included in the company's oil concession, the Foreign Office advised the company that the islands were Arab. AIOC thus concluded that it could not include these areas within its concession. In 1939, upon learning that the Iranian Ministry of Industry and Mines had negotiated a contract with a Dutch company for mineral exploration in a zone that included Abu Musa and the Greater Tunb, the British Minister in Tehran warned the Dutch Minister in Tehran that the islands were not Iranian and that the company would not be able to work the concession in those areas.[51]

Claims and Proposals in the Early Oil Era

In 1941, Reza Shah Pahlavi was forced to abdicate by Britain and the Soviet Union and was succeeded by his son Mohammed Reza Shah

Pahlavi, who would revive the islands issue in the years after World War II.[52] Following the end of the War, Britain withdrew from India in 1947. Thus, the historic role in the Gulf of the Government of India, the India Office and the Secretary of State for India ended, with the Foreign Office now assuming responsibility for British interests in the Gulf.

Morsy Abdullah has written that while the India Office had practiced a policy of non-interference in the internal affairs of the Trucial States for over a century, the Foreign Office, with a wide understanding of international affairs and local changes in the Gulf, played an active role in reforming the internal affairs of the Gulf, particularly of the Trucial States. With respect to Abu Musa and the Tunbs, Morsy Abdullah wrote :

> [T]he fundamental change in relations between the disputants was in Britain's approach to the problem: she now played an active role as mediator due to her friendship with, and her growing interest in, both Persia [now Iran] and the Arab countries.[53]

However, these new policies of the Foreign Office would unfold gradually, as the following narrative shows.

Official British and US government documents, de-classified as recently as the period 1993 to 2003, shed new light on the years from the late 1940s to the early 1970s, when the British Foreign Office and the United States as a new world power formulated their post-World War II policies in the Gulf. These records show that Iran's claims to Abu Musa and the Tunbs intensified during these years. British and American officials believed that the heightened Iranian interest and commitment could be attributed to the discovery of offshore oil resources, something which Iranian officials eventually acknowledged. In addition to making a spurious diplomatic claim that Britain had acknowledged Persian rights after 1904, Iran also made plans and threats to occupy the islands.

Britain continued to defend the rights of Sharjah and Ras al-Khaimah to the islands, despite Iranian indications that it would yield its claim to Bahrain in exchange for the islands. However, the idea of Ras al-Khaimah selling or leasing the Tunbs to Iran was considered, particularly in the mid-1960s, as the British sought to mediate the negotiation of a median line through the Gulf and as it began to recognize the need to withdraw from the Gulf completely. Meanwhile, the United States was not knowledgeable about the history of the islands and was focused instead on opportunities for American oil companies and the role that Iran could play in containing Soviet advances toward the Gulf region.

In December 1948, the Iranian Ambassador in London reasserted the Iranian claim to the Greater Tunb and Abu Musa. In February 1949, after a brief review, the Foreign Office again made clear that the islands belonged to Ras al-Khaimah and Sharjah respectively, and that both were under the protection of the British Government. At the same time, it stressed that the international situation was too serious for such a disagreement to undermine relations between the two countries with such similar interests, an apparent reference to the threat posed to Iran by the Soviet Union.

This message was repeated by J.H. Le Rougetel, the British Minister in Tehran, to Ali Ashgar Hekmat, Iran's Minister of Foreign Affairs. Iran's Foreign Minister then made reference to "historical records and documents of ownership of those islands held by the Iranian Government." In particular, he claimed that the British Legation in Tehran had allegedly stated in a 1905 note that the Shaikh of Sharjah had hoisted his flag on an island that did not belong to him, and he cited this as evidence that the British opposition to Iran's claim was unjustified. The British Minister replied only that "we had no archives on the subject so old as 1905 and that I would be interested some time to see the note." However, Iran did not produce the note. Indeed, Iran was making a spurious claim that they would often repeat in subsequent years. In fact, as British archives clearly show, the British had energetically defended Sharjah's rights to fly its flags on Abu Musa and the Tunbs in 1904 and 1905 and in the following years.[54]

The British soon became aware of a rumor concerning a formation of Iranian marines on the southern coast that would seek to occupy the Greater Tunb and Abu Musa. When asked about this, Iran's General Ali Razmara, Chief of the General Staff, acknowledged that Iran intended to station small regiments on islands near its coast, but that it would not do so on disputed islands. In a meeting with Le Rougetel, British Minister in Tehran, the Shah stated that a suggestion to place detachments on islands in dispute had been made by the Ministry of Foreign Affairs, but that it had subsequently been rejected. Le Rougetel suspected that this renewed interest in the Gulf and the islands was "a result of the off-shore oil project." When news was received in September that a Persian flag had been hoisted on the Lesser Tunb, the British instructed its Senior Naval Officer in the Gulf to remove it, which he did the following month.[55]

In 1949, after the discovery of oil under the seabed of the Gulf, the six shaikhdoms of Abu Dhabi, Dubai, Sharjah, Ras al-Khaimah, Ajman and Umm al-Qaiwain (Fujairah was not yet recognized as a separate emirate) proclaimed their exclusive jurisdiction and control over their continental shelf, i.e. the seabed and subsoil under the high seas contiguous to their territorial waters. They expressed a willingness to negotiate boundaries with states that made similar claims to their continental shelf. However, they did not think it likely that Iran would be a willing partner in the negotiation of a median line through the Gulf that would be equidistant from either shore through areas that it disputed with them.

In fact, Iran did not claim its continental shelf until 1955.[56] Instead, in February 1951, an Iranian naval vessel landed a party on Abu Musa and asserted that the island was Iranian. Following an investigation into the matter, the British Minister in Tehran again reasserted Sharjah's claim and rejected Iran's claim in a note to the Iranian Foreign Ministry, dated April 26.[57] This took place as Iran, under pressure from Dr. Mohammad Mossadegh's National Front, nationalized the Anglo-Iranian Oil Company, provoking a prolonged crisis that led Iran to break off diplomatic relations with Britain in October 1952.[58]

In March 1953, the British received a warning from Iraq that Iran was considering sending troops to occupy islands in the Strait of Hormuz. When the US Embassy in Tehran asked the Iranian Ministry of Foreign Affairs about this, they were told that a commission was considering the question of the islands, but that it had not yet prepared its report to the Prime Minister. The Ministry of Foreign Affairs also alleged to the Americans that the Arab shaikhs were violating a purported Anglo-Persian agreement dating from the beginning of the century to respect the *status quo* on the islands. This was an invalid interpretation of the relevant Anglo-Persian correspondence. In a subsequent account to the US State Department, the US Embassy interpreted the Iranian statement as follows:

> It is likely that the Mosadeq Government has thus found – or created – another issue, similar to the recurrent charges of British violation of the Iraq-Iranian frontier, which can be utilized for domestic political benefit. This matter could be easily used as a propaganda device to suggest that the British Government is attacking Iran from still another direction.[59]

In order to deter any possible landing, the British sent a naval vessel to Abu Musa. This elicited two formal protests from the Iranian Ministry of Foreign Affairs through the Swiss Legation, the custodian of British affairs in Iran, which charged Britain with a violation of Iran's jurisdiction and of a written "treaty" of 1904 allegedly recognizing the *status quo*. Inasmuch as the second protest, in August 1953, was soon followed by the coup that toppled the Mossadeq government and restored the Shah, the British did not reply.[60]

In 1954, just as Iran was considering a draft bill on its continental shelf, Iranian Foreign Minister Nasrollah Entezam suggested a median line agreement and indicated that Iran might give up its claim to Bahrain in return for the Tunbs and Abu Musa. Iran also continued to misrepresent the Anglo-Persian correspondence of 1904, claiming that in 1904, the Government of the United Kingdom had supposedly reached an agreement with the Iranian Government regarding the aforesaid islands in the Gulf, whereby Iran's rights and the *status quo* in the islands were to be respected and maintained.[61] While the British Foreign Office rejected Iran's claims and proposals, they did consider persuading Ras al-Khaimah to sell or lease the Greater and the Lesser Tunbs, as well as convincing Sharjah to renounce its claim to Sirri in exchange for an Iranian renunciation of its claim to Abu Musa and possibly to Bahrain. Such a deal, the British thought, would conform to the median line between the two coasts.[62]

Upon being told of this idea, Sharjah's Ruler, Shaikh Saqr bin Sultan Al-Qasimi, agreed to drop his claim to Sirri if Iran dropped its claim to Abu Musa, although he was not told that compensation had been proposed for Ras al-Khaimah's Ruler, Shaikh Saqr bin Muhammad Al-Qasimi. The Ruler of Ras al-Khaimah was initially prepared to sell the islands for 50 million rupees, along with the preservation of his oil and mineral rights, the maintenance of the lighthouse, permission for his fishermen to use the island and no Iranian fees, such as customs, with regard to his own subjects. After reflection, however, he decided that a lease of the two Tunbs would be preferable. The British considered his price "ludicrous" and his third condition "unreasonable," and resolved to tell Iran that he was prepared to negotiate without telling Iran what his terms were.[63] It should be noted here that in 1953, Ras al-Khaimah had granted exploration concessions in the Tunbs to the Golden Valley Ochre and Oxide Co. Ltd., but no red oxide discovery had been made on the islands.[64]

In May 1955, these British ideas regarding the islands were conveyed to the Iranian Foreign Minister Entezam by Roger Stevens, the British Minister in Tehran. Entezam seemed to agree that the Iranian claim to Bahrain could not be enforced, but he also thought that domestic opinion would not permit Iran to renounce its claim to Abu Musa. He indicated that he would "touch lightly" on the subject with the Shah, but was not hopeful of a solution.

In August 1955, after Iran claimed sovereignty over its continental shelf, Enezam raised the issue of the islands during a trip to London. He claimed that the issue threatened to harm broader Anglo-Iranian relations since the Majlis and the Iranian people strongly believed that the islands were Iranian. According to the Foreign Minister, there would be a domestic explosion if they realized that Britain claimed them for the Trucial Shaikhs. Entezam did not want to agree to any proposal for arbitration unless Bahrain was included, although he did indicate that Iran would respect the wishes of the people of Bahrain. This led the British to conclude that he considered arbitration as a political inquiry, not a legal process. Entezam promised to provide a book on the history of the islands. Inasmuch as he did not refer to the deal that had been proposed in May, the British decided to propose it again later, through the Iranian Ambassador in London, for the consideration of the Foreign Minister.[65]

In the autumn of 1956, as the British were investigating rumors that Iran had landed or was planning to land officials on Abu Musa, Saudi Arabia and the US informed Britain that Iranian marines had occupied the island of Farsi. US Ambassador in Tehran Selden Chapin reported that the reason for the occupation "was to establish off shore petroleum rights." In October, Ambassador Chapin reported to the State Department that the Iranian Prime Minister, Hussein Ala, had admitted that Iran had occupied Farsi and Arabi and that Ala had added:

> Iran forces would shortly occupy islands of Tunb and Abu Musa if in fact they had not already done so. [The] Prime Minister said he had been surprised at [the] strength [of the] British Ambassador's protest since it seemed odd to him [that the] British should be so zealous [in] taking up [the] Arab cause against Britain's only remaining important friend [in the] Middle East - with whom moreover it [was] bound by [the] Baghdad Pact. Ala alleged [that] Iran had ample documentary proof [of] its sovereignty over [the] islands in question which he promised to furnish me, but admitted action had been precipitated by newly aroused interest in offshore petroleum rights in [the] Gulf.

US Ambassador to Saudi Arabia Carrigan noted that the British Political Resident in Bahrain, Bernard Burrows, "mentioned [the] possibility [of] Iran moves toward Tunb, Nabi Tunb, and Abu Musa Islands and commented such action would be more serious since these islands [were] populated and 'one might say' administered by Sharjah and Ras Al Khaima." Ambassador Chapin reported that Iranian Foreign Minister Haj Aliqoli Ardalan had said that Iran could not back down particularly since it had "undoubted claim" to the islands – and, as he had told the British Ambassador, needed to look ahead fifty years, when perhaps the 'British might no longer be able to restrain Arab States', and take necessary steps to protect its Gulf coast-line and "other interests."[66] In the end, Iran did not carry out its threat to occupy Abu Musa and the Tunbs at that time.

In any case, these events and reports prompted US Secretary of State John Foster Dulles to advise the US Ambassador in Tehran on October 31, 1956 to inform the Iranian Foreign Minister as follows:

> 1) Solution [of] disputes over sovereignty [of the] Persian Gulf islands [is] not repeat not prerequisite to offshore oil operations, which [were] undertaken some time ago [on the] opposite side of [the] Gulf. However, a series of occupations of [the] disputed islands by rival claimants might ultimately create such doubt and insecurity as to

discourage heavy investment required for offshore operations;

2) [The] Department [is] watching [the] situation closely in light [of] its desire that [the] present situation [in the] ME not be worsened by any deterioration in [the] Persian Gulf;

3) While [the] Department does not desire [to] take sides in disputes over sovereignty of [the] islands, [the] US would appreciate being informed as to [the] ultimate objective and scope [of the] Iranian plans, of which [the] occupation [of] Farsi [was] apparently [the] first step;

4) [The] Department has made no representations to other interested states and raises [the] subject with [the] GOI [i.e. the Government of Iran] only because [the] US hopes [the] GOI can clarify [the] situation by providing info on [the] current confused status [of the] islands and [the] scope [of] GOI plans.[67]

In the early months of 1957, the British considered whether the Shaikhs' administration of Abu Musa and the Tunbs could be reinforced in a practical manner as a way to strengthen their legal claims and to deter or respond to any Iranian landing. It was suggested that the Shaikhs' flags, which were flown when visitors were approaching the islands, should be flown permanently. When the Rulers did not act on this advice, the Foreign Office noted:

> [T]he indifference of the Rulers and their local representatives is of course a very long standing problem, but I think that in view of the Iranian seizure of Farsi and Arabi we must give the Rulers of Ras al-Khaimah and Sharjah a more than usually stern warning about the risk of allowing their position to go by default.

It was also proposed that some residents of Ras al-Khaimah might be settled on the Lesser Tunb, but the lack of water on the island discouraged such a step. Instead, the representative of Ras al-Khaimah on the Greater Tunb was encouraged to visit the Lesser Tunb and to fly the Ras al-Khaimah flag there occasionally. In 1958, the British landed the father of the Ruler of Ras al-Khaimah on the island to unveil a brass plaque on a concrete foundation stating the Ras al-Khaimah claim.[68]

Later in 1957, the British also held discussions with the Americans about various Gulf issues, including the rights to the Gulf's waters, the sea-bed, the islands and the problems of off-shore oil concessions. These discussions took into consideration the earlier work done by a joint State Department/Foreign Office team on a median line in the Gulf. While the US proposed that no effort should be made to settle these matters until after the forthcoming UN Conference on the Law of the Sea in 1958, the British suggested that these Gulf issues should be considered on their own and not in relation to other seabed problems. The British favored a joint or parallel approach to the interested parties in the Gulf to elicit their agreement on freezing the *status quo* on the islands pending future negotiations, but the US did not think that such an approach could succeed.[69] However, the two sides did agree in November:

> [T]he basis for a division of the sea-bed in the Persian Gulf between territories of States whose coasts are opposite each other should be a line, every point of which is equidistant from the nearest point or points on the opposite shores of the Persian Gulf, measured from the mean low water mark on the mainland or on islands the mean low water mark of which is in whole or in part within three miles of the mean low water mark of the mainland.

Thus, agreeing on the principle of a median line equidistant from the mainland coastlines or islands within three miles of these coastlines would exclude Sirri, the Tunbs, Abu Musa and Bahrain from consideration in the drawing of a median line.[70]

In December 1958, while Iran and the United States were negotiating the bilateral defense agreement they would sign in March 1959, the US Department of State learned about pending Iranian legislation to amend their 1934 six-mile territorial sea law and unilaterally establish a twelve-mile territorial sea off the Iranian coast and around all islands under Iranian sovereignty. The Department sought a deferral of this decision, pending the second Law of the Sea Conference in 1960, and stressed:

> Narrow territorial seas give maximum freedom of maneuver to free world naval and air forces permitting such forces to be of great effectiveness in neutralizing threats arising from attempts of Communist imperialism [to] extend their jurisdiction by force. This [is] especially true in connection with Iran whose strategic link to [the] US is primarily based on sea and air communications backed up by mobile power of ground force.[71]

Nevertheless, in April 1959, Iran passed the legislation extending her territorial sea to twelve miles.[72]

In December 1959, Shaikh Saqr bin Muhammad Al-Qasimi of Ras al-Khaimah indicated to the British Political Agent in Dubai that part of the sea-bed around the Greater Tunb was his. After a brief investigation into the matter, the legal opinion expressed by the Foreign Office in early 1960, based on Articles 2 and 10 of the 1958 Convention on the Territorial Sea and the Contiguous Zone, was that "there can be no doubt that sovereignty over an island carries with it sovereignty over the seabed and subsoil of the territorial waters surrounding that island." However, the status beyond the territorial waters was considered less clear because the 1958 Convention on the Continental Shelf did not clarify how the location of islands would affect the delimitation of opposite or adjacent continental shelves. Also, there was no agreement on the delimitation of the continental shelf of the Gulf, the whole of which is a continental shelf, between opposite or adjacent states.[73]

In June 1960, the US Navy Hydrographic Office informed the State Department that it had approached the Iranian Government for permission to use Sirri and Abu Musa for a hydrographic survey and that Iran had offered no objection. Upon being informed of this, the British Embassy in Washington told the State Department that Abu Musa belonged to the Ruler of Sharjah. The Embassy subsequently cabled London that the "State Department expressed regret, but explained that this was the first they had heard of the matter" and would therefore be grateful if the Foreign Office could obtain permission from the Ruler of Sharjah. Since the Foreign Office was concerned that Iran might use the US approach as evidence in support of its claim, they asked the US Navy to inform the Iranians that the original inquiry had been made in error. Not only did the US Navy withdraw its request to Iran, but it only landed with surveyors on Abu Musa island in November 1960 after it had received the permission of the Ruler of Sharjah.[74]

On May 18, 1961, a helicopter landed on the Greater Tunb, took photographs of the lighthouse and questioned the inhabitants. It was not until August that the British found out about this visit, including the fact that the landing party had included one Iranian and two Americans, and that this had been followed later by the landing of a boat and another party of Americans. The British concluded that both the helicopter and the boat had been Iranian and that "[t]he presence of

Americans on both visits indicates either the interest of an American oil Company or the employment of American oil experts by the Iranians." In response, the Foreign Office again recommended that the Ruler's flag be flown continuously on the island and he agreed to do so. In September 1961, the Foreign Office also submitted a formal protest to the Iranian Ministry of Foreign Affairs so that Iran could not afterwards point to these landings as acts of sovereignty that supported their claim to the island.

Iran replied later that month by rejecting the claim of Ras al-Khaimah, reasserting its claim and arguing that "[t]he Imperial Government's sovereignty over the Island of Tunb is based on the rules and principles of International Law, and they have never given up their right to it." As far as the British Embassy in Tehran was concerned, the reference to international law was "perhaps a reference to the Median Line principle by which Iran would benefit, since Tunb is considerably nearer the Iranian shore than it is to Ra's al Khaimeh." The Foreign Office disagreed that this was a valid basis for the Iranian claim, but it mistakenly noted that "[i]t is only after sovereignty of the relevant land areas has been determined that median lines can be drawn." The Foreign Office also insisted upon formally rejecting the Iranian Foreign Ministry's reassertion of the Iranian claim to the island, because the failure to do so might prejudice the claim of the Ruler of Ras al-Khaimah. This was done in January 1962 and quickly elicited an Iranian note reasserting Iran's position.[75]

The British Navy visited Abu Musa in October 1961 and found no evidence of any Iranian landing on the island. However, it did report that the Ruler of Sharjah was not represented on the island. This prompted the Foreign Office to recommend in November that a representative be appointed to raise the Sharjah flag, preferably on a continuous basis. The Foreign Office also noted that the same recommendation had been made at the time of the Iranian threat to the island in 1953, and argued:

> [I]t is important that the arrangements then made should not be allowed to lapse since, as you know, continuous administrative actions such as the performance of duties by a headman can be an important factor in supporting a claim to sovereignty in international law. [76]

By 1962, the Shah's concerns about the Gulf ambitions of Egypt under Gamal Abdul Nasser and Iraq under Abdul Karim Qassim had grown to the point that he pledged to the Soviet Union that no foreign power would be permitted to maintain missile bases in Iran. The Shah thought that normalizing relations with the Soviet Union would enable him to concentrate more on Gulf affairs. He also embarked upon his program of domestic socioeconomic reforms, known as the White Revolution, in the hope that that this would persuade the Kennedy administration in the United States to be more forthcoming with economic and military assistance to Iran.[77] The Shah was keen to have British and US help in protecting his interests against radical Arab threats in the Gulf. Due to converging interests, the British were equally enthusiastic to pledge their support. As a result, the dispute over Abu Musa and the Tunbs did not feature as an important item on the agenda of talks held in the spring of 1963 between Iran and Britain, or for that matter between Iran and the United States.

In May 1963, following the visits to Tehran of British Secretary of State for Foreign Affairs Lord Home (Sir Alec Douglas-Home) and US Secretary of State Dean Rusk, the US Embassy in Tehran reported that Lord Home had called Bahrain the only question "on which we and Iran agree to differ." Lord Home is said to have stated:

> You can be assured, Mr. Prime Minister, of the strongest and unqualified support of the British people for all that His Imperial Majesty and you and your Government have been doing in Iran…When a country like Britain, which has nuclear weapons, pledges its support to an ally, it pledges its life.

After consultations with the British Embassy in Tehran, the US Embassy also reported that the Shah had told Lord Home that he was concerned about "the danger from the Arab Federation," i.e. the brief and unsuccessful attempt to establish a federation of Nasser's Egypt and the newly installed Ba'ath governments in Syria and Iraq, and that the Shah had told Lord Home that Mr. Rusk "had promised to study his request for help in strengthening Iranian defenses in the south." Moreover, it was reported:

> [W]ith regard to the Persian Gulf Shaikhdoms and Kuwait, the Shah told Lord Home that his only policy was that the UK should maintain its position in these areas. The Shah was

afraid of their coming under the control of Nasser. Lord Home told the Shah that the desire for unity was very strong among the Arabs and that outside powers could do very little to stop it if the Arabs were determined to bring about this unity. The UK was being very watchful of any indications that the Arabs might seek to impose their will upon non-Arab neighboring states. The UK was very strongly opposed to this kind of activity.[78]

In July 1963, however, British Ambassador to Tehran Sir Dennis Wright reported to the Foreign Office that Iran was reasserting its claims to Sirri, Abu Musa and the Greater Tunb. Writing about a meeting with Iranian Prime Minister Amir Asadollah Alam, Wright reported:

> The prime minister said that one of the islands possessed oil and hinted that this was the reason for the revived Iranian interest. He added, however, that he could assure me that the Iranian Government would not indulge in any adventures which would bring them into conflict with H.M.G. [Her Majesty's Government]; instead they would hope to 'infiltrate' and gain their way through the predominance of the Persian language and culture.

The British Ambassador warned that this "may possibly mean that the Iranians are considering putting ashore clandestinely on the islands with a view to confronting us one day with an overwhelming Persian majority on each island." The Foreign Office noted that John Mecom, an American, had obtained concessions from Sharjah, Ajman, and Umm al-Qaiwain and was exploring the offshore areas of these concessions in the hopes of discovering an oil structure south of Abu Musa. This led to the conclusion that "[t]his increased oil activity may well have revived Iranian interests in the Trucial States and encouraged them to press once more their claims to the three islands under discussion."[79]

Later in July, British Ambassador Wright reported on another meeting with Iranian Prime Minister Alam:

> He repeated that the Iranian intention was to do no more than 'infiltrate' and thereby contribute their [sic] 'Iranization.' In answer to my question he said it was not the intention to put Iranians ashore but merely to provide kerosene and other supplies which they could not get 'from the other side' for the

Iranians already living on the islands. The Prime Minister
hoped that we would turn a blind eye to such activities.

Wright also reported that the Prime Minister inquired about
British shipping interests in the islands inasmuch as he understood that
British tankers and cargo ships passed the islands in large numbers. The
British Ambassador wrote:

> My impression is that the Iranian Government do not want a
> 'showdown' with us on this issue but hope to reach some sort
> of 'gentlemen's agreement' with us not to put any obstacles in
> the way of their peaceful penetration of the islands. Then,
> having done this, my guess (reinforced by an unguarded
> reference by the Prime Minister to a 'second stage') is that
> they will inspire a local demand for Iranian protection.
> Presumably, revival of Iranian interest in these islands is due
> to the belief that they contain oil.

Again, the Foreign Office reached the following conclusion:

> No doubt the activities of the new American oil concessionaires
> have re-awakened Iranian interest in the islands and, with an
> eye toward future negotiations for deciding the limits of their
> own and the Trucial States off-shore concessions, they may
> now have considered it opportune to re-asssert their claims.

In the meantime, the Admiralty reported that the interest of
British shipping was that lights be maintained efficiently, that shipping
might increase as a result of oil developments and that a light on Abu
Musa might have to be added to the light at the Greater Tunb. It also
noted that Iran could not be counted on to maintain the lights
efficiently, and that "calls at Tunb by parties of Iranians are today a
common occurrence."[80]

Upon instructions from the Foreign Office, the acting Rulers of
Sharjah and Ras al-Khaimah were warned about the renewed Iranian
claims and advised to show their sovereignty by flying their flags and
visiting their islands. The Acting Ruler of Sharjah immediately made a
visit to Abu Musa and re-hoisted his flags there. The Royal Navy was
also instructed to maintain the frequency of its patrols in the area and to
plan some future landings on the islands at a time when they would not
be seen as an immediate response to the Iranian démarche. Upon
receiving these instructions in early August, the Political Resident in
Bahrain belatedly reported a complaint made earlier in the year by the

Ruler of Ras al-Khaimah that his flag and flagpole had been pulled down on the Little Tunb in April by an Iranian warship. In response to his request, the British navy had replaced the flagpole in July. The Resident added:

> We did not consider that we would be justified in recommending that a formal complaint be made to the Iranian Government, as there were no firm details (the Ruler's headman of Tunb could not, for example, positively identify the marauders as Persians) and as the incident seemed in any case rather a minor one.[81]

From the outset of this episode in July, British Ambassador Wright told his Iranian interlocutors: "[B]ritain could not surrender sovereignty over islands which belonged to Rulers under our protection; to do so would be regarded as an act of bad faith and undermine our whole position in the Persian Gulf, which I understood to be an Iranian as well as a British interest."

The Foreign Office was determined from the outset that "we should not permit any Iranian activity on Tunb and Abu Musa which would tend to strengthen their position at the expense of the sovereign rights of the two Rulers." Foreign Secretary Lord Home authorized the British Ambassador to remind Iran's Prime Minister that the Shah himself had told Lord Home on April 2 that "all that Iran desired was that we should maintain our position in the Gulf" and to say on behalf of Lord Home that "I do not expect to have His Imperial Majesty's assurances to me questioned by His Ministers unless there is a deliberate change of policy which should be stated plainly," a message that the British Ambassador conveyed.[82]

In their subsequent meetings in late August of 1963, Prime Minister Alam and Foreign Minister Abbas Aram told Ambassador Wright that the Iranian Government "recognized Her Majesty's Government's obligations to the Sheikhs in the Persian Gulf and they respected our unwillingness to forfeit their confidence through failure to protect their interests," but that they "eventually" wanted Iranian "sovereignty" recognized. They also argued:

> [I]t was an Iranian interest that Britain should maintain her position in the Gulf but we would not always be there; since Iran was such an old and true friend of the United Kingdom,

surely it was in our interest to see that the islands became Iranian rather than fell under the rule of unreliable and ungrateful Arabs, whether they be Saudi Arabians or Iraquis [*sic*].

Both Alam and Aram repeated their assurances that "they would not provoke incidents by sending warships to the islands or hoisting Iranian flags there." They asked if Britain would inform the Shaikhs of the Iranian interest and urge them "to negotiate direct with the Iranians, H.M.G. [Her Majesty's Government] acting as an impartial broker." Ambassador Wright, after once more repeating the British positions, rejected this last request, arguing that "it would be our duty to negotiate on their behalf and protect their interests." He advised the Foreign Office that he did not believe the Iranian assurances, a view that was shared in London.[83]

In October 1963, Foreign Minister Aram protested to Ambassador Wright that "The Sheikh" had now begun flying his flag permanently, although he did not indicate whether he was referring to the Ruler of Sharjah flying his flag on Abu Musa or to the Ruler of Ras al-Khaimah flying his flag on the Tunbs or to both. He argued that this seemed to be a response to his recent discussions with the ambassador on the islands and was therefore considered provocative. The Ambassador did not reveal the British recommendations to the Rulers and said only that "The Sheikh" had the right to do so if he wished. The Foreign Minister may have been referring to the Shaikh of Sharjah, because in November Aram had protested the activities of Mecomoil six miles southeast of Abu Musa, including a reconnaissance visit to the island by a company representative and the drilling of a well to a depth of 600 feet. (According to the British Political Agency in Dubai, Mecomoil had actually been drilling 12 miles offshore of Abu Musa to a depth of 6,000 feet.)

The Counsellor of the British Embassy, Mr. Horace Phillips, who thought that the Foreign Minister "was simply going through the motions of a protest," replied "that Abu Musa was inhabited, and under the effective control of the Ruler of Sharja, and that the latter was perfectly within his rights in contracting with an oil company." The Foreign Office subsequently advised him to "say that Abu Musa and its offshore islands [*sic*] are a part of the territory of the Ruler of Sharjah and under his effective control. This change in wording is to make clear that the Ruler not only as a matter of fact controls the island but has, in our view, a right to do so." When the Iranian Prime Minister next complained over the matter, Britain's Ambassador did make the following point:

> H.M.G. regarded Abu Musa as belonging to the Sheikh of Sharjah and saw no reason why he should not grant an oil concession if he so wished.[84]

In November 1963 conversations with the British Ambassador, Iran's Foreign Minister and the Shah both expressed their desire to settle all Anglo-Iranian differences in the Gulf. Ambassador Wright suggested informally to the Shah "that it might be possible for us to agree [to] *de jure* recognition of Iran's sovereignty over Sirri in return for Iran recognizing the Sheikh of Sharjah's sovereignty over Abu Musa and Tonb [*sic*]." The Shah did not accept or reject this suggestion. In subsequent months, despite the recommendation of the Ambassador, Britain did not take up the Shah's offer of a general discussion and settlement of Gulf issues, preferring instead to "agree to disagree." Meanwhile, the Political Agency in Dubai notified the Embassy in Tehran that the two Tunbs did not belong to Sharjah but to Ras al-Khaimah.[85]

Earlier, in September 1963, six months after US Secretary of State Rusk had agreed to study the Shah's request for assistance in strengthening Iranian defenses in the south of Iran, the US Embassy in Tehran reported to the State Department that the Shah was willing to defer acquiring radar stations for the south until the radar stations in the north were fully operational. However, it reported that "in the meantime: he would count on our assurance that if a threat developed, in the Persian Gulf we would give prompt consideration to action to be taken to meet the situation." Moreover, the report stated:

> [T]he Shah said that perhaps Iran does not rpt [i.e repeat] not need torpedo boats in the Persian Gulf but that we should be sure that appropriate vessels in requisite numbers are made available to protect the long coast line, islands, particularly Kharg rpt [i.e. repeat] Kharg, and eventually Bandar Abbas

rpt Bandar Abbas. He hoped that naval requirements would be taken into account in contingency planning for the Gulf.[86]

On October 2, 1963, as the Foreign Office was considering a possible oil concession for Ras al-Khaimah's offshore area, it reasoned that Ras al-Khaimah's continental shelf rights would normally extend up to a hypothetical median line "between the low water lines of the two facing mainlands," i.e. the Iranian shore and the Arab shore. It also reasoned that the Tunbs would fall perhaps ten miles on the Iranian side of this median line, but that Ras al-Khaimah would have rights to the islands themselves and a three mile territorial sea around the islands, leaving the area between the median line and the territorial seas around these islands in an undecided status.[87] On December 31, 1963 a Foreign Office minute suggested the following language as a means of resolving the question of the islands in continental shelf negotiations:

> Each State to have continental shelf rights on its side of the median line; but this provision is without prejudice to the right to owners of islands falling on the other side of the median line to maintain its claim to those islands and to territorial waters not exceeding a breadth of x miles measured from those islands. The inclusion of such provision not to constitute recognition by any other party of the claims of any party to any particular such island or such territorial waters. Any dispute concerning such a title to be submitted to arbitration at the request of either party.[88]

Thus, during the 1950s and 1960s, serious thought was being given to ways in which the numerous boundary issues between the states and emirates in the region could be brought towards some kind of resolution. If agreements could be reached, the regional states and western oil companies could develop the Gulf's oil resources more easily and Britain could feel much more comfortable about eventually leaving the Gulf in an orderly fashion. As it turned out, however, there were no easy solutions. As time passed and Britain increasingly recognized the necessity of its withdrawal from the Gulf and the strategic role that Iran could then play in protecting western interests, Britain became willing to accommodate Iranian interests, even at the expense of Qawasim rights.

CHAPTER 3

British Withdrawal and Iranian Occupation of the Islands

Persia's first official claim to the Greater and Lesser Tunbs was made in the late nineteenth century, and its first official claim to Abu Musa was made in the early twentieth century. When these claims were made, and in the decades that followed, the British consistently and repeatedly asserted to Iran that the islands were the possessions of the Qawasim Rulers of the Arab Coast. When necessary, the British were ready to back up their arguments with military force. During these years, the Iranian claims remained sporadic and intermittent.

Two developments following the end of World War II added impetus to Iran's concern about sovereignty and control. First, with the growing importance of oil and its associated financial benefits, the possession of the islands in the Gulf took on a new significance. On numerous occasions, an Iranian claim or protest could be linked to oil concession agreements being granted or commercial activity being undertaken. Second, the 1960s was a period of growing Iranian power. As the Shah's sense of his increasing strength grew, and as the interest of outside powers such as Britain and the United States in courting Iran took on greater importance, so did the Shah's hegemonic ambitions in the Gulf take on new proportions. As part of his plan, it was important to lay claim to as many of the islands in the Gulf as possible.

The opportunity for the Shah to fulfill many of his ambitions came with the announcement of the British withdrawal from the Gulf. As the self-imposed deadline of November 1971 approached, Britain became increasingly keen to leave a stable and orderly situation in the region, where they had been the predominant power for about one-and-a-half centuries. Satisfying Iran, the regional power deemed capable of defending Western interests in the Gulf, was central to this objective. Up to this point, Britain had staunchly defended the rights of the Rulers of Sharjah and Ras al-Khaimah and reminded the Iranians of their insufficient claims to Abu Musa and the Tunbs. In the end, however, strategic considerations prevailed over legitimate rights as the British succumbed to Iranian demands for these three islands in the Gulf.

Searching for a Settlement

Early in 1964, the British Foreign Office considered whether or not to pursue the Shah's earlier offer to discuss and settle all outstanding issues in the Gulf. It was considered unlikely that Iran would be prepared to yield on its claims to Bahrain, Abu Musa and the Tunbs. A seabed or median line agreement did not seem feasible, nor did the Arab Gulf states appear ready to accept Iranian trade representatives. As far as the Foreign Office was concerned, the Shah was interested in long-term planning for the Gulf "in view of his ambition to step into our shoes if we should ever leave the Gulf." While the possibility of an eventual withdrawal was raised, the Foreign Office asserted that there was "no question" of this under the current [Conservative Party] government and "no question" of discussing such a possibility with the Shah.[1]

British Ambassador Wright in Tehran agreed with these Foreign Office views, particularly that any sign of British withdrawal would be a "severe shock" to the Shah. He noted that the Shah was "very fearful of Arab nationalist encroachment" in the Gulf, and argued that he would therefore "react strongly" to the policy recommended by British Political Resident Sir William Luce to promote "a form of pan-Arabism" and a "federation" of the Trucial States as a means to enhance Gulf stability. "To the Shah's way of thinking," Wright wrote, "any move towards ending the present fragmentation of these States must be regarded as the first step in the by now well-known progress towards independence." He continued:

> [T]he Shah wants to preserve the *status quo* in the Gulf primarily as a bar to infiltration by [Egypt's President] Nasser or anyone else hostile to Iran. Logically he should be content even if this were achieved by some alternative to British paramountcy which is not hostile to Iran -- e.g. British/ Pakistani/American and possibly Iranian-United Kingdom

defensive alliance, or by Arabian Peninsula solidarity on the lines suggested by Luce. However we have to face the fact that the Shah's interest does not lie simply in having British influence remain in the Gulf, but in ensuring that no other influence except Iranian ever replaces it. Any unexplained move towards federation or other manifestations of growing control of their own affairs by the sheikhdoms would immediately rouse his suspicions and might, particularly if he was in domestic difficulties and wanted to divert public attention, provide the cue for him to pick a quarrel with us.

Ambassador Wright therefore recommended that any such moves be thoroughly explained to the Shah beforehand.[2]

The Ambassador also informed Iranian Foreign Minister Aram of Britain's concern that general discussions would end in an impasse, "given among other things the Iranian claim to Bahrain and differences over other islands." Wright assured Aram as follows:

[I]t is Her Majesty's Government's firm intention to maintain the British position in the Persian Gulf. Any political evolution in H.M.G.'s relations with the Gulf States (and some evolution is inevitable) would be designed to make it easier for H.M.G. to maintain the essentials of this position, not as a preparation for abandoning it.

Ambassador Wright reported that the Iranian Foreign Minister was "reasonably satisfied" with his message, but that he wanted to discuss the islands. The Ambassador replied as he had the previous summer:

H.M.G.'s attitude was that they must continue to protect the rights of the Rulers and that any abandonment of these to Iran would result in a loss of confidence in H.M.G.'s ability to protect the Rulers and would thus contribute to the very weakening of the British position in the Gulf which the Iranian Government did not relish. At the same time, in preparation for breaking the news about the Ras al-Khaimah oil concession and inclusion of the Tunb islands in it…I made the point that H.M.G. would be bound, if asked by Rulers to approve their grant of concessions to oil companies, to accede to their requests, even though this might in some cases irritate the Government of Iran.[3]

In his report to the Foreign Office, Wright noted that his "only concern about the question of the seabed was the effect on the position of Tunb islands; and it would surely be illogical, immediately after the grant of an oil concession by Ras al-Khaimah which embraces these islands, to open a discussion with the Iranians which would give them gratuitously the argument of a median line which might favour their claims to the islands." Stewart Crawford of the Foreign Office wrote in the margin that this was "a fallacy," presumably meaning that the British idea of a median line would not bolster Iran's claims to the Tunbs. Wright also reported that the Foreign Minister, the Prime Minister and the Shah were not happy about the British unwillingness to enter into general discussions to settle these outstanding issues in the Gulf, but that they were satisfied with British assurances that Britain intended to stay in the Gulf.[4]

On March 3, 1964, Shaikh Saqr bin Muhammad Al-Qasimi of Ras al-Khaimah granted concessions to explore for oil in his land and sea, including the Tunb islands and a three-mile area around them, to the Union Oil Exploration and Production Company and to the Southern Natural Gas Company. A Foreign Office memorandum considered whether impartial adjudication or arbitration might be suggested to Iran if Iran reacted sharply to this information, but concluded that the Shaikh of Ras al-Khaimah would not agree to such a step and that British interests regarding Sharjah and Bahrain would not be served by such a precedent. Therefore, it should only be considered if Iran itself proposed it. As it turned out, neither Iranian Prime Minister Alam nor Foreign Minister Aram initially protested the concessions.[5] It is worth noting, however, that the confidential memorandum prepared on the subject did raise the following argument:

> From many points of view, arbitration or adjudication would be better than a row with Iran. We have no interest in the islands. We have no great interest in Ras al-Khaimah. The oil companies now in question are American: their fortunes do not worry us. We have an obvious interest in avoiding, where possible, friction with our ally Iran in an area in which she has a direct interest and about the stability of which she is, not unreasonably, concerned.[6]

A different view was expressed in a confidential memorandum in November, which stated that one interest in establishing a median line agreement with Iran "is the straight commercial one of establishing the exact exploration and exploitation areas of concessions in which British companies are interested." The memorandum continued:

> The second interest arises from our responsibility for the external relations of the Protected Shaikhdoms of Bahrain, Qatar and the Trucial States. This requires us to do our best, consistent with correct international practice, to secure those States' offshore interests and, irrespective of the nationality of the companies, the associated interests of companies holding concessions from those Protected Shaikhdoms.[7]

On February 22, 1964, an Iranian Government ship set a light buoy weighing six to ten tons inside the territorial waters of Abu Musa, an act which the British Ambassador in Tehran told the Iranian Prime Minister was "provocative." Inasmuch as both Shaikh Saqr bin Sultan of Sharjah and the British wanted it removed, the latter advised the former to remove it and helped him to do so. The British had concluded that the buoy did not warn of any valid navigational hazard, but rather that it was deliberately intended to assert an Iranian claim to the island, and had indeed been formally publicized in a notice to mariners. The act was seen as part of an expressed Iranian policy of "infiltration."

When the British Ambassador in Tehran informed the Acting Foreign Minister of the buoy's removal, both the latter and the Commander-in-Chief of the Iranian Navy asserted that the initial decision had been taken by the Iranian Ports Administration without their knowledge or approval. In the midst of this episode, the Middle East News Agency (MENA) in Cairo reported inaccurately that Iran had occupied Abu Musa. Later, when writing about the removal of the buoy, MENA and other press outlets in Kuwait and Baghdad continued to refer to this as part of an Iranian occupation of the island as well as to allege that Britain had cooperated with Iran. Anglo-Iranian discussions on how best to return the buoy to Iran proved fruitless through the end of 1964. In the meantime, it became known that Iranian fishermen were paying a tax to the Sharjah Ruler's headman on the island, something the British thought "must invariably weaken their [Iran's] case."[8]

When the Shah repeated his desire for a discussion about the Gulf in an August meeting with the British Ambassador, he suggested that Iran might in the future be in a strong enough position to recognize the independence of Bahrain. Ambassador Wright responded by arguing that it was important "to damp down anti-Iranian propaganda in the Gulf." He stated that "Britain and Iran should not appear to be in collusion in the area," and that Iranian actions "were not always helpful," a clear reference to the buoy incident and subsequent anti-Iranian propaganda. The Ambassador made it clear to the Shah that Britain was "bound to take the side of the Sheikhs, whose interests we protected," and that this would lead to conflict with Iran. "The Shah accepted this and pointed out that although the removal of the buoy had been 'an unfriendly act' on our part, the Iranians had not protested." As far as the Ambassador was concerned, the Shah "still seems to think that one day it will fall to Iran to take over our mantle in the Gulf." After this meeting, Ambassador Wright recommended that the British agree to the Shah's desire for general discussions when he visited London in 1965. He argued that the Shah "may be feeling more than usually vulnerable on the southern flank" and should be "reassured" that Britain was "not yielding further to an Arab pressure."[9]

In their next meeting, in October, the Shah again told Wright he wanted a discussion on the Gulf, arguing that "our interests were identical and that he believed that Iran could help us maintain our position there, or if we left, could help protect the independence of the various sheikhdoms." The British Ambassador reiterated that Britain was "determined to stay," would keep Iran informed of developments, and was "not at the moment pursuing the idea of federating the Sheikhs." However, saying that he "did not think it would be easy for the Iranians to assume our mantle in the Gulf," the Ambassador noted that "[I]f we had to go it would be because we were regarded as Imperialists, no longer acceptable to Arab nationalism, and I did not see that the Iranians, who were likewise not Arabs, would be any more acceptable." The Shah, nevertheless, "indicated that he believed the Iranians could step into our shoes in the Gulf."[10]

In November 1964, the Foreign Office summarized its thinking on the desirability of negotiating a median line between the Trucial States and Iran in a memorandum and also in correspondence to British Ambassador Wright in Tehran and to the British Political Resident in the Gulf, Sir William Luce. In his reply, Luce agreed with the Foreign Office's major recommendation "that we should seek a median line based on equidistance, counting islands within three miles as part of the mainland, and that it is essential to exclude islands outside the three miles in determining the line." His one reservation about proposing such a negotiation to the Shah was that "[I]f the Shah really has it in mind to renounce his claim to Bahrain, perhaps on the occasion of his visit to London in March, we, from our local point of view would prefer nothing to be done in the meantime which might prejudice the possibility of getting this problem out of the way." Ambassador Wright agreed to propose to Iranian Foreign Minister Aram that negotiations for a median line become a part of broader talks on the Gulf to be held in London. He argued:

> [I]n negotiation the Iranians are likely to be very difficult in conceding anything which might prejudice their claim to any of the disputed islands. They will probably treat Bahrain as a special case but I shall be very surprised indeed if the Shah was prepared to concede that Bahrain was not a province of Iran. The fact is, however, that he increasingly regards Bahrain as a millstone and would probably not let the existence of Iran's claim to it upset an otherwise reasonable agreement from his point of view on the median line.[11]

In January of 1965, Ambassador Wright recommended that the British should inform the Shah of plans for "modernising" the British position in the Gulf and for a "federation" of the seven Trucial States. In the light of a report from Iranian Foreign Minister Aram that the Shah was "anxious" to resolve the issue of the islands, the Foreign Office considered reviving the idea of recognizing Iranian *de jure* sovereignty over Sirri in exchange for Iranian recognition of Sharjah's sovereignty over Abu Musa (and also insisting separately on Ras al-Khaimah's sovereignty over the Tunbs). Political Resident Luce thought that the Ruler of Sharjah "would not easily give up all claim to Sirri in exchange for Iranian recognition of his sovereignty over Abu Musa, which he no doubt considers unquestionable." The Political Agent in Dubai agreed, particularly in the light of anti-Iranian sentiment being stirred up in the Gulf by the Arab League. Ambassador Wright equally was convinced that the idea would not be acceptable to the Iranians.[12]

When the Shah visited London in early March, the British Foreign Secretary, Michael Stewart, from the Labour Party, which had come to power in October 1964, explained to him that Britain was trying "to modernize our relationship with the Gulf States in order to make our position there more defensible and thus help preserve stability in the face of hostile Arab pressures." He said that this included an effort to obtain associate membership for Bahrain in specialized UN agencies and asked Iran not to actively oppose this bid. The British also mentioned the possibility of a future grouping of the Trucial States. After the meeting, the Shah agreed on an agenda for talks to be held in April, including technical discussions about a median line as well as discussions about Bahrain's proposed membership in specialized UN agencies. Later in March, Luce argued that the present position of the Trucial States should also be discussed in April to reassure the Shah "that Her Majesty's Government take the threat of Egyptian penetration seriously and are considering ways and means of halting it." He also reported that the Rulers of Bahrain, Qatar and the Trucial States wanted an agreement on a median line.[13]

In April, during meetings in Tehran with Iranian Foreign Minister Aram and his colleagues, the British proposed an agreement that achieved "an equitable division of the continental shelf between Iran and the Gulf States in special treaty relations with the United Kingdom but excluding for the time being the continental shelf in the Gulf of Oman." The agreement was to be "drawn up in such a way as not to prejudice claims to sovereignty over any islands and their surrounding territorial sea" with particular reference to Sirri, Abu Musa and the Tunbs.

Foreign Minister Aram "said that in principle the Iranians were prepared to accept the British proposal for a median line based on 'coast-to-coast' baselines," although he "implied" that Iran would insist on the island of Qishm being considered part of Iran's mainland. When the British argued that Iran should drop its claim to Bahrain, pointing out that Nasser exploited this, Aram stated that this would provoke a nationalist reaction in Iran and that it would even be portrayed by Nasser as a victory for his policies. In a subsequent meeting, the Shah said he wanted to have the median line settled. He also indicated that he would have to vote against Bahrain's membership in any UN agency so as not to surrender Iran's claim. While the Shah said that he had no interest in actually pressing Iran's claim or taking over the island, he insisted that this remain secret to avoid embarrassment at home.[14]

Referring to the idea of a federation among the Trucial States, the British stated during the April meetings that this was a long-term prospect and that it would first be necessary to resolve internal quarrels over borders and to establish some common institutions.[15] In July, after a meeting of the Rulers of Bahrain, Qatar and the Trucial States, Iran's Foreign Minister Aram "reacted badly to the idea of Bahrain's participation in any grouping of Sheikhdoms which might emerge." The Foreign Office instructed the British Embassy to respond that a grouping of the states under British protection would promote evolution and modernization, and would help to keep Egypt and Iraq out of the Gulf. In any case, it was never British policy to exclude Bahrain or Qatar from any discussions concerning a grouping of the Trucial States.[16]

Moreover, when Iran's Ambassador to London, Ardeshir Zahedi, asked that Britain oppose Bahrain's entry into any Gulf group, Foreign Secretary Stewart rejected the idea, explaining that "the moves towards closer cooperation between the nine states, including Bahrain, were a very recent spontaneous move by these states to close their ranks against outside pressures" and that the moves "should be welcome to Iran." Iran's Ambassador replied that "[h]e himself could see the logic of the views I had expressed but public opinion in Iran needed much more education before it could do so. To my surprise, he went on to say that this educative process, [sic] was being pushed ahead so fast now that the problem would cease to be acute in a matter of months, or at most a year. He pleaded that we should keep Bahrain from acting in such a way as to cause the process to go into reverse meanwhile." Foreign Minister Aram, conveying the thinking of the Shah, hinted at an "Anglo-Iranian crisis" over Bahrain and specifically indicated that progress on median line discussions "would become impossible with a Bahrain crisis looming." He let it be known that the Shah was "upset" that the issue of Bahrain's inclusion in a nine-member federation had not been raised in London. Indeed, his Ambassador in London had previously said that the Shah felt "misled."[17]

In response, the Foreign Office cabled the British Embassy in Tehran to inform the Iranians that "at that time such a grouping appeared inconceivable because of the long-standing feuds dividing Bahrain from Qatar and Qatar from Abu Dhabi. The rapid change in this situation is due entirely to reactions on the part of the Rulers themselves to Arab League pressures and the realization that they must close their ranks if the Shaikhly regimes are to survive. The arrangements for the meeting of Rulers in Dubai were made by the Rulers themselves, with Shaikh Rashid of Dubai as the prime mover. There was no British participation in this meeting and we had no control whatsoever over the course it might take." Noting the result of this meeting and the differences among the nine emirates, the Foreign Office cable continued:

> A grouping including Bahrain is therefore no longer imminent and may perhaps never come into being. But we must leave the Iranian Government in no doubt that we consider that such a group is very much in the interests of the Protected States and we could therefore not oppose it if the Rulers wished to embark upon it.

The Foreign Office then proposed a second round of bilateral talks on Gulf issues. Iran's Foreign Minister, on instructions from the Shah, conveyed his acceptance of such discussions in London in September. At the same time, he made it clear that the "measures and organizations" raised since the first round in March were "not acceptable" to Iran.[18]

During a visit of British Minister of State for Foreign Affairs George Thomson to Tehran in September 1965, the Shah was told that British defense commitments would eventually cost "more than we could afford" and that "we had therefore to cut down somewhere," possibly in Aden. British Ambassador Wright later reported on the Shah's reaction:

> He naturally wanted us to stay in Aden and thus be in a position to maintain our existing position in the Persian Gulf; but if we could not afford to do so, it was of the utmost importance to Iran that she be given adequate warning so that she could discuss with us what should be done. He did not like the idea of the Americans taking over responsibility in the Gulf and hinted, as he has done before, that this could be done by Iran.

Wright added that "[t]his is not the moment to speculate on what the Shah might decide to do should we decide to abandon Aden and thus weaken our ability to maintain our position in the Gulf, though it is something we should start thinking about." Sir Roger Allen of the Foreign Office wrote in the margin "I thought Mr. Thomson had put the Shah right on this!" suggesting that Thomson had assured the Shah that a possible withdrawal from Aden would not weaken the British position in the Gulf. Ambassador Wright also argued that the Shah was a valuable ally, and that Britain should take him into her confidence and seek his advice on matters concerning the Gulf.[19]

Towards the end of 1965, the Iranian Foreign Ministry informed the British Foreign Office that Iran would not respond to British proposals for a median line until disputes regarding sovereignty over the islands, particularly Abu Musa and the Tunbs, were resolved.[20] In February 1966, Anglo-Iranian discussions in London did produce an agreed minute on the median line between Qatar and Iran, based on the low water lines of the mainlands. Iran and Britain agreed that the next stage of discussions would take up the issue of sovereignty over the Tunbs. Both sides would collect their respective documentation supporting their arguments and these would then be exchanged. In September 1966, Britain informed Iran that it had prepared these documents and was now ready for this discussion.[21]

Iran was not ready. Then, in October, the Shah suddenly acquiesced in allowing Bahrain to become an associate member of the United Nations Educational, Scientific and Cultural Organization (UNESCO).[22] In December, three months after Britain signaled its readiness to proceed, Iran's Foreign Minister Aram met with Ambassador Wright. Instead of providing or promising documents to support Iran's claim to the Tunbs, as had been agreed in February, Aram argued that the islands were of strategic importance, that the Arab shaikhdoms were weak and unstable, and that the islands would pose a naval threat if they fell into hostile Arab hands. The Foreign Minister also stated that if Britain could hand over the islands this would help Iran abandon its claim to Bahrain, which he called a public opinion problem for Tehran.

Wright disagreed that the islands were of strategic importance and, in any case, Britain was not in a position to hand them over. Remembering that Aram had hinted in August about Iran buying the islands, British Chargé d'Affaires Charles Wiggin asked if Iran would still consider such an option. Aram did not respond to this question. In the light of a possible stalemate over the islands, Wright argued that it might be sensible to discuss the median line without reference to the islands, or at least to discuss the median line between Abu Dhabi and Iran.[23]

In late February and early March 1967, Aram, who had by then become the Iranian Ambassador to London, told several Foreign Office officials, namely Permanent Under-Secretary Sir Paul Gore-Booth, Sir Denis Allen and Minister of State Thomson, that Iran was ready for discussions on the Gulf median line. Since the British thought that Aram had requested meetings at the ministerial level in an effort to obtain concessions on the islands, the Foreign Office informed him that they viewed the Rulers' claims as valid and that, in any case, they were in no position to press them to cede the islands. While they were ready to discuss the islands and exchange documents as agreed, the Foreign Office did not expect an early agreement with Iran. Therefore, they recommended discussing the median line without reference to the islands or considering the subject of the Abu Dhabi-Iran median line instead.[24] Aram seemed to agree, but he cabled Zahedi, now Iran's Foreign Minister, that there was no "give" in the British position. Zahedi then told Wright that there was no point in further talks.[25]

In a subsequent conversation, the Shah told Wright that Britain could count on Iran, but asked rhetorically if Britain could count on the Arabs. He argued that Britain should support Iranian rather than Arab claims to the islands. Aram, meanwhile, repeated that Iran's interest was of a strategic nature. When asked by the Foreign Office's T.F. Brenchley whether this meant that Iran would not consider international arbitration, Aram replied that Iran would indeed not consider it.[26] Meanwhile, Brenchley, Wiggin and Wright also continued to recommend exploring the possibility of the Ruler of Ras al-Khaimah selling or leasing the Tunbs, as well as the possibility of the Ruler of Sharjah, Shaikh Khalid bin Muhammad Al-Qasimi, yielding Sirri for Abu Musa. Stewart Crawford, the Political Resident in the Gulf, indicated that Ras al-Khaimah would not be agreeable. The Political Agent in Dubai, D.A. Roberts, agreed, suggesting it would be political suicide for him to do so, in the light of Arab nationalist complaints about Iranian penetration of Arab Gulf states. While willing to pressure Sharjah on the other issue, Crawford was equally doubtful about being able to convince the Ruler.[27]

In June 1967, Ambassador Aram proposed a solution whereby Sirri and the Tunbs would go to Iran, Abu Musa would go to Sharjah, Qishm would be included in Iran's base line, and the large islands off the shore of Abu Dhabi would not be included in Abu Dhabi's base line. Aram now said that he would urge the Shah to offer compensation for the Tunbs, but thought that Britain might have to provide it instead. He stressed that these were his personal ideas and asked that they not be reported back to Iran.[28] British officials did not think they could advise Sharjah to cede Sirri without a firm commitment on Abu Musa and suspected that the Shah would not approve Aram's ideas about Abu Musa. Furthermore, they thought that Ras al-Khaimah would not readily cede the Tunbs and that a *quid pro quo* for including Qishm in Iran's base line would be necessary.[29] Given these views, Brenchley instead proposed a draft agreement on the Abu Dhabi-Iran median line. Aram seemed to agree that this would be acceptable, but this proposal met with opposition in Iran's Foreign Ministry.[30]

In October, Iran's Prime Minister, Amir Abbas Hoveyda, argued that Iran should have all the islands, and Aram repeated Iran's strategic interest in the islands. However, Aram suggested that it "might be sensible" for Iran to buy the Tunbs.[31] Brenchley thus reiterated to Crawford that they should pursue the idea further, including the possibility of seeking Saudi support for it. Crawford did not favor actually recommending this to Ras al-Khaimah or Saudi Arabia, but noted that Roberts in Dubai could mention that Iran had raised the idea. Ambassador Wright in Tehran questioned whether the Shah would agree to pay compensation, but offered his support to the "Aram Plan" if it was accepted on the other side of the Gulf. Brenchley then issued instructions for Roberts to make this approach to the Ruler of Ras al-Khaimah, although he indicated that Britain would not be willing to pay compensation in case the Shah refused.

Following his meeting with the Ruler of Ras al-Khaimah, Roberts reported that while he thought the Ruler was interested, he was prepared for a long bargaining process. In addition, Shaikh Saqr wanted Iran to officially approach him, probably because this would in effect be an admission of Ras al-Khaimah's sovereignty.[32] In November, Brenchley proposed to Aram a median line agreement without reference to the islands, but Hoveyda and Zahedi argued that the median line could not be settled without reference to the islands. Hoveyda added that an agreement on the Abu Dhabi sector would jeopardize Iran's claim to the islands, while an agreement on the islands would help in regard to Bahrain. Prime Minister Hoveyda further claimed that Iran had correspondence from the former British Government of India offering to buy the islands from Iran, and that this was conclusive proof that Britain recognized the islands as Iranian.[33]

The British Withdrawal from the Gulf

On January 4, 1968, the British Labour Government decided to withdraw its forces from the Gulf by 1971, signaling an endpoint to British control of the foreign and defense policies of the Trucial States. British Minister of State for Foreign Affairs Goronwy Roberts carried this message to the Gulf rulers as well as to the Shah. While subsequent chapters on the legal dimensions of the dispute over the islands, the political and military impact of Iran's occupation, the regional reaction to the dispute, and the international community's role will delve deeply into the years from 1968 to 2003, it is necessary to provide a brief summary of the main historical events of these years both here and in the following chapter.

In conjunction with its decision on withdrawal, Britain intensified its efforts to support the establishment of a federation of Gulf Arab states and to resolve the disputes between Iran and these states over Bahrain, Abu Musa and the Tunbs. Iran, however, immediately pressed the issue of the Tunbs and Abu Musa on the British. On January 8 and 9, 1968, just days after Goronwy Roberts met with the Shah, Iran issued protests to the British Embassy in Tehran and to the Foreign Office in London alleging that Ras al-Khaimah had made an armed landing on the Greater Tunb and had raised the Ras al-Khaimah flag and warning that Iran might be compelled to take action.[34] In response, British Chargé d'Affaires Wiggin handed over a strong Foreign Office note to Foreign Minister Zahedi on January 13, reaffirming Ras al-Khaimah's right to the island and noting that the Ras al-Khaimah flag had flown regularly in the past.[35]

During the course of 1968, the British proposed the package deal suggested by Aram, but learned that it was unacceptable to the Shah, who insisted that he must also have Abu Musa. Then, in early 1969, the Shah publicly indicated a willingness to accept the result of a plebiscite on Bahrain, but insisted soon thereafter that he would not do so without obtaining Abu Musa. In June 1969, the Shah stated publicly that once the Bahrain issue was resolved, he would not continue to oppose a federation.[36] Indeed, Iran would be willing, in cooperation with Saudi Arabia, to protect these Gulf states.[37] In other words, the Shah was now suggesting in public that he would yield on a federation, which the British clearly wanted him to do, if Bahrain was settled, having already indicated in public that he would yield on Bahrain and only the mechanisms for doing so were at issue. However, he was saying in private that he would not yield on Bahrain until he was satisfied on the islands. His real message for the British, then, was that he would not yield on a federation until he was satisfied on the islands. His proposed sequence of events was satisfaction on the islands first, then yielding Bahrain, and then accepting the federation.

In response to British urgings to reach some accommodation with the Shah on the islands, the Ruler of Ras al-Khaimah, Shaikh Saqr, and the Ruler of Sharjah, Shaikh Khalid, each engaged in discussions with the Shah and his officials between 1968 and 1970. Notably, the Shah designated officials from the internal security organization SAVAK, Nematollah Nasiri and Ali Farazian, to conduct these discussions until October 1969, when responsibility was taken over by the Ministry of Foreign Affairs. During an August 1968 meeting in Tehran, the Shah offered Shaikh Saqr an unspecified sum of money in return for Iranian use of the Tunbs.[38] The Shah's officials then presented a draft text that called for Iranian use of the Tunbs for defense purposes and an oral offer of a payment to Ras al-Khaimah of 300,000 pounds sterling. Shaikh Saqr expressed a willingness to consider this. In October 1968, Shaikh Saqr rejected a new Iranian draft text that claimed Iranian sovereignty, and Nasiri and Farazian rejected a draft text carried to Tehran by Ras al-Khaimah Crown Prince Khalid bin Saqr Al-Qasimi that implied Ras al-Khaimah sovereignty. Nasiri did tell Crown Prince Khalid, however, that Ras al-Khaimah could have the proceeds from any oil around the islands.

In early December 1968, Shaikh Saqr told an Iranian emissary that if Iran wished to rent the islands he would lease them to Iran, and stressed that any cooperative arrangement with Iran would have to be seen as honorable in the Arab world. As an adviser to Shaikh Saqr would later explain, Shaikh Saqr thought that Iranian acceptance of a lease arrangement would constitute Tehran's recognition of Ras al-Khaimah sovereignty. However, later in December, in meetings in Tehran between Nasiri and Farazian and Shaikh Saqr's British legal adviser, Richard Weston, the two sides were still not able to agree on the language of an agreement. The Iranians rejected Shaikh Saqr's proposals for compensation, particularly his proposal for annual payments as this could be seen as the equivalent of rent. Negotiations between Ras al-Khaimah and Iran thus broke down by the end of 1968.[39]

When Shaikh Saqr again visited Tehran on December 19, 1969 for talks with the Shah, Prime Minister Hoveyda and Foreign Minister Zahedi, he was still unable to come to an agreement with Iran on the Tunbs. Iran's Minister of Court Asadollah Alam wrote on December 20: "The Sheikh of Ras al-Khaimah is in Tehran at the invitation of our Foreign Minister who hopes to reach agreement on the hand-over of Tunbs. I don't see any chance of a settlement at the moment; the sheikh is too apprehensive, lest he be accused by his fellow Arabs of abandoning Arab land to Iran."[40] Indeed, according to Zahedi and Alam, Shaikh Saqr "had put the Shah's back up" by asserting Ras al-Khaimah's sovereignty, offering a lease to Iran, and offering to accept an Iranian garrison on the Greater Tunb if it was commanded by Ras al-Khaimah officers. Zahedi then stated Iran's position on sovereignty, said Iran could seize the islands and recommended an "amicable accommodation."[41]

According to Shaikh Saqr, Iran gave him a choice between an agreement on an Iranian garrison on the Greater Tunb and the withdrawal of the Ras al-Khaimah police along with agreements on mineral rights and a median line, or an Iranian seizure of the islands. He said Iran dropped the subject of title to the islands when he asserted that he could produce better documentation of his claim that they could of theirs. Shaikh Saqr also said that Iran offered in principle a loan and military equipment and that he had made it clear this would be separate from the issue of the islands. The "impression" of Britain's Political Agent in Dubai, Julian Bullard, was that Shaikh Saqr "thinks it may be possible to find some mutually acceptable solutions," although adding, somewhat sarcastically, "though perhaps not quite on the lines of either of the two Iranian proposals made so far."[42]

Previously, in April 1969, Farazian also visited Sharjah's Shaikh Khalid bin Muhammad Al-Qasimi and told him that Iran wished to establish a military base on Abu Musa for the defense of the area and that therefore the median line should deviate to include Abu Musa on the Iranian side, although Sharjah could retain any oil and minerals. Shaikh Khalid replied that Abu Musa had been an inseparable part of Sharjah for hundreds of years and that he could not enter into talks on the island at this early stage of discussions on the formation of the UAE. If Iran needed a military base in the area, he suggested that it could be established on Sirri.[43]

Later, in January 1970, Shaikh Khalid met in Tehran with the Shah and former foreign minister Aram for talks that included Abu Musa. Shaikh Khalid was seeking a solution that would "guarantee the interest of all parties in maintaining security and stability," but thought that Iran was "using 'the interests of security and protection of sea routes' as a pretext to conceal the aim of imposing its sovereignty on the island." While it was agreed that a joint committee would continue these talks within three months, such meetings did not take place.[44] During these January 1970 talks, Aram told the Shah's Minister of Court Alam that Shaikh Khalid was "a much tougher customer than his counterpart in Ras al-Khaimah..."[45]

Despite Iran's frustration over Abu Musa and the Tunbs at the end of 1969 and the beginning of 1970, a formula for ascertaining the wishes of the inhabitants of Bahrain was announced in early March 1970 after Britain and Iran finally agreed on language and mechanisms that would protect the prestige of both Iran and Bahrain. UN Secretary General U Thant was then invited to appoint a mission of inquiry to determine the "true wishes of the people of Bahrain with respect to the future status of the Islands of Bahrain." A UN mission headed by U Thant's personal representative visited Bahrain from March 29 to April 18 and found that the inhabitants wanted a fully independent, sovereign Arab state. The findings of this mission were announced on May 2, 1970.

Subsequently, on May 11, 1970, the UN Security Council passed a resolution endorsing the independence of Bahrain based on the fact-finding mission conducted by the Secretary General's representative.

Four days later, the Iranian Majlis approved the decision by a vote of 186 to 4, followed by the unanimous approval of the 60-member Iranian Senate on May 18.[46] Britain, which had been concerned that an Iranian occupation of Bahrain would upset Gulf security, was pleased with this outcome. The Shah of Iran abandoned Iran's claim to Bahrain, thinking it would enhance his case on Abu Musa and the Tunbs. He also communicated his expectation to the British that they must pressure the Arabs to this end.[47]

The Shah's public claims, offers, rationalizations, demands and threats regarding the islands began in April and May 1970, in the period before, during and after the UN findings on Bahrain were announced. The Shah said in the April 13 issue of the Iranian newspaper *Kayhan International* that he would provide economic assistance to Ras al-Khaimah and Sharjah after an agreement on the islands. He gave an interview to *The Times* of London on April 14 in which he explained the historical and strategic reasons for Iran's claim; this interview was evidently not published until May 11, one week after the UN findings on Bahrain were announced, on the very day the UN Security Council unanimously approved these findings, and three days before the Iranian parliament voted to approve them. In May 1970, the Shah threatened to use force against the Occidental Petroleum Company, which had a concession from Umm al-Qawain, if it did not cease drilling operations off the coast of Abu Musa. Britain quickly instructed the American company to stop. In October 1970, Iran repeated its opposition to a federation of Arab emirates unless the islands issue was resolved in line with Iranian interests, and in February and June 1971, the Shah threatened to occupy the three islands by force if an acceptable settlement was not reached.[48]

Throughout 1970 and 1971, as the date of British withdrawal neared, British representative Sir William Luce conducted discussions with Iran, Sharjah and Ras al-Khaimah over the issue of the islands. In these discussions, Britain no longer acted as a representative or negotiator on behalf of its protectorates Sharjah and Ras al-Khaimah, but rather as a provider of its "good offices" between them and Iran, carrying proposals and messages back and forth. For various reasons, the British clearly sought to use their influence with Sharjah and Ras al-Khaimah to achieve a compromise with Iran regarding the islands. They were impressed with the Shah's willingness to give up his claim to Bahrain, knew that Iran would oppose the union of nine favored by Britain unless Iranian aspirations on the islands were satisfied, and regarded both Bahrain and the union to be more important than Abu Musa and the Tunbs. Furthermore, Iran was increasingly viewed as an anti-radical, anti-Soviet actor capable of taking on the role of regional policeman.[49]

In May and June 1971, Luce strongly urged the Rulers of Sharjah and Ras al-Khaimah to accept the Shah's proposals that Iran take over the islands based on compensation provided to the emirates, saying that Tehran would delay asserting sovereignty over the islands for two years. Luce warned that if Sharjah did not negotiate, Iran would seize Abu Musa and would not support the newly emerging Federation. Moreover, he warned, if Ras al-Khaimah did not accept the Shah's proposal, Iran would seize the Tunbs. Despite these warnings, the two rulers continued to reject the exchange of sovereignty for compensation.[50]

During these years, there were several Arab efforts to mediate and to preserve Arab sovereignty over the islands. Saudi Arabia proposed in April 1970, for example, that a joint Iranian-Arab garrison might be placed on the islands, and Kuwait suggested in August 1971 that the islands be de-militarized.[51] Iranian Foreign Minister Abbas Ali Khalatbari explained Iran's response to such proposals by stating that Iran's "sovereignty over the islands was not negotiable." Not only did Iran "insist on her right to the islands when the British left the Gulf..." she also "rejected Arab suggestions that Abu Musa and the Tunbs should be leased to Iran when Britain left the area."[52]

The Shah gradually let it be known that there would be little compromise. In a meeting with Sir Alec Douglas-Home, the Foreign and Commonwealth Secretary, and the Shah in July 1970, the latter made it clear that "with the Bahrain question out of the way it was necessary that the islands revert to Iran." He went on to state that "if the Rulers did not come to terms 'we are going to take those islands.'" As far as the Shah was concerned, the islands were a "sine qua non."[53] In an audience with Luce in September, the Shah repeated his threat of occupation in addition to letting Luce know that he saw "no distinction between the Tunbs and Abu Musa."[54]

As the date for the British withdrawal approached, the position of the Shah hardened. In another meeting with Luce in Tehran in May 1971, the Shah made it clear that the Ruler's forces must leave the islands before the formation of the UAE, that sovereignty was Iran's and that he was only considering putting the issue of sovereignty in abeyance for a two-year period so to enable "everyone to forget about the whole thing."[55] Finally, in late September 1971, the Shah again demanded that Britain turn over the islands, declaring:

> Those islands, Abu Musa and Greater and Lesser Tunb, are ours! We need them. We shall have them. No power on earth will stop us...I have a war fleet, Phantom aircraft and brigades of paratroopers. I could defy Britain and occupy the islands militarily.[56]

Ras al-Khaimah's Shaikh Saqr, however, remained unwilling to yield sovereignty for financial compensation, although he indicated that he would still be willing to lease the islands. He also remained concerned that any agreement be seen as honorable in the Arab world and was counting on Arab and particularly Iraqi support for his refusal to yield Arab sovereignty to Iran.[57] Moreover, Shaikh Saqr did not want to join the emerging UAE on an unequal footing with Abu Dhabi and Dubai, particularly while he still hoped that the discovery of oil could put him on an equal footing.[58] Thus, in late September 1971, Shaikh Saqr communicated with the US State Department, requesting that the United States recognize Ras al-Khaimah as an independent state, establish diplomatic relations with it, and support its admission to the UN. He also offered the United States a military base in Ras al-Khaimah.[59]

Despite negative answers from the State Department, Shaikh Saqr continued to resist the Shah's threats and Luce's warnings throughout October. Shaikh Saqr informed Luce of his rejection of the Shah's proposal on October 30 and then immediately revealed this to the public:

> William Luce proposed to us that we should surrender the two islands for an annual payment by Iran of 1.5 million pounds sterling, in installments over nine years, in addition to 50% of the oil and minerals that may be produced from the two islands in future; but we have rejected this offer, and we are not prepared to bargain over the sale of our islands.[60]

Shaikh Khalid of Sharjah also publicly rejected the Shah's proposal for surrendering sovereignty in exchange for financial compensation on October 30:

> Sharjah flatly rejects the conditions proposed by Luce in connection with the Island of Abu Musa. We regard them as an infringement of Sharjah's sovereignty, which we will never give up.[61]

However, Luce had discovered that Shaikh Khalid would be willing to consider a compromise on Abu Musa that could include the stationing of an Iranian garrison on part of the island. Thus, Luce had been conveying messages between Shaikh Khalid and the Shah and was negotiating agreements enabling Iran to garrison the heights in the north of the island while leaving Sharjah the village, the palm gardens, the well and the ancestral burial site in the south of the island.[62] In publicly rejecting the formula of yielding sovereignty for compensation on October 30, Shaikh Khalid had not revealed that progress was being made on a compromise. Shaikh Khalid may have been attempting to buy time in the court of public opinion while he continued seeking the better deal that a compromise would provide, especially because the Ruler of Ras al-Khaimah had publicly revealed his rejection of the proposal to yield sovereignty over the Tunbs for compensation.[63]

The ultimate outcome of these discussions concerning Abu Musa was that on November 29, 1971, the Ruler of Sharjah announced agreement on a Memorandum of Understanding (MoU) in which neither Sharjah nor Iran relinquished its claims to sovereignty over Abu Musa or recognized the claims to sovereignty of the other. Iranian troops were permitted to land peacefully on and occupy the northern half of Abu Musa, exercise full jurisdiction and fly the Iranian flag over their military headquarters. Sharjah would exercise full jurisdiction over the rest of the island and fly the Sharjah flag over its police post. Iran and Sharjah recognized the island's territorial waters as extending for twelve nautical miles, with Iranian and Sharjah nationals allowed to fish in the island's waters.

Petroleum exploitation on the island and in the seabed and subsoil of its territorial waters would be conducted by the Buttes Gas and Oil Company, which would pay half of any future governmental oil revenues to Sharjah and the other half to Iran. Furthermore, a financial assistance agreement between Iran and Sharjah would be signed in which Iran agreed to provide 1.5 million pounds in economic aid per annum to Sharjah until Sharjah's share of any future oil revenues, to be split evenly between Iran and Sharjah, reached 3 million pounds.[64] Although Britain and Iran had reached another arrangement whereby Iran would provide some revenues to Umm al-Qaiwain, this was never implemented.[65]

The result was that while Persia/Iran had never claimed Abu Musa as intensively as it had the Tunbs, it nevertheless achieved a MoU on Abu Musa and occupied the island in accordance with it on November 30. However, Sharjah thought that it had little choice. Given Iran's warning that it would not recognize the UAE and would oppose its formation unless a satisfactory resolution of the islands issue was reached, Sharjah's desire to join a successful UAE, Iran's threat to occupy the islands by force, British warnings that it could not defend Sharjah against Iranian use of force, and the failure of Arab mediation efforts, Sharjah felt compelled to yield to these pressures and sign the MoU under duress.[66]

During this time, the Ruler of Sharjah had worried not only about the Shah using force but also about criticism from Arab nationalists.[67] Shaikh Khalid had written in advance to Arab rulers that he would seek a compromise and that the alternative was that the island would be taken by force. Although he sought the advice of his fellow Arab rulers, only four replied, offering statements of support, while the others raised no objections. Upon signature, Shaikh Khalid lodged the agreement with the Arab League.[68]

Towards the end of 1971, it became clear that the Shah's threats were serious. On November 30, after Ras al-Khaimah had rejected the latest British-mediated proposal that Iran take the Tunbs in exchange for compensation, Iran forcibly occupied both islands. The Iranians arrived on the Greater Tunb in great force and the Ras al-Khaimah police resisted. In the end, there was one Ras al-Khaimah and three Iranian fatalities, and the police station and a primary school were destroyed. Fearing for their safety, the citizens of the island fled by small boats to Ras al-Khaimah, leaving behind their property and possessions. Iranian forces occupied the Lesser Tunb with less difficulty as the island was inhabited at the time by only one fisherman and his son. On the same day as the occupation, Ras al-Khaimah formally submitted a protest to the Arab League and the UN Security Council.[69]

Furthermore, it became clear at the end of 1971 and the beginning of 1972 that the Sharjah Ruler's concerns about Arab criticism were reasonable. News of Iran's occupation of the Tunbs and the MoU on Abu Musa led to riots in the emirates, particularly in Ras al-Khaimah and Sharjah. Shaikh Saqr bin Muhammad bin Saqr Al-Qasimi, who was the brother of Sharjah's ruler, and who had received the Iranian landing party on Abu Musa, was shot and wounded.[70] The following month, in January 1972, Shaikh Khalid was himself assassinated by forces under the former Ruler of Sharjah, Shaikh Saqr bin Sultan, who had been deposed and exiled by the British in 1965 for his pan-Arab sympathies. Shaikh Saqr bin Sultan's return to Sharjah and his effort to regain control, which quickly failed, was financed by Iraq, which had strenuously condemned the Iranian occupation of the three islands and had broken diplomatic relations with Britain. During his effort, Shaikh Saqr bin Sultan called upon the population of Sharjah to help him avenge the "traitorous" transfer of Abu Musa to Iran.[71]

Thus, as Britain withdrew from the Gulf on December 1, 1971, it had not fully achieved its goal of leaving behind an orderly situation. While it had helped Bahrain to obtain independence, and while it had helped the Trucial States to prepare for federation, it had also left behind the seeds of a continuing dispute over Abu Musa and the Tunbs.

CHAPTER
4

The Islands since the Formation
of the United Arab Emirates

On December 2, 1971, just days after Iran's landings on the Tunbs and Abu Musa, the United Arab Emirates (UAE) was declared a sovereign state. The UAE's constitution proclaims its sovereignty over all of the territories and waters included within the international borders of its member emirates, namely Abu Dhabi, Dubai, Sharjah, Ajman, Umm al-Qawain, Fujairah and Ras al-Khaimah, although Ras al-Khaimah did not join the federation until early February 1972. As such, the issue of sovereignty over Abu Musa and the Greater and Lesser Tunbs took on a new character, with the dispute no longer being between Iran and the emirates of Sharjah and Ras al-Khaimah, but between Iran and the UAE, two fully independent states. In addition, the dispute over the islands assumed a broader significance in the following years, particularly by the 1980s, as it became clear that the Iranian military presence on the islands could threaten the security and stability of the Gulf region. Far from being an isolated and unimportant legal case, Iran's presence on Abu Musa and the Tunbs began to take on international strategic significance.

From the moment of its creation, the UAE sought to resolve the islands dispute in a peaceful and amicable manner. While it has steadfastly maintained its right to sovereignty over all three islands, it has also offered Iran opportunities to reach a negotiated solution, either by direct talks or by mediation, or to submit the case for international legal review, for example by the International Court of Justice (ICJ) in the Netherlands. The UAE has also made use of regional and international organizations such as the Arab League and the United Nations to press its case. However, Iran has rebuffed the UAE's efforts. Whether under the Shah or under the Islamic Republic after 1979, Iran has continued to deny the UAE its lawful and sovereign rights to the islands. Moreover, Iran has tried throughout the 1990s and early 2000s to create a *fait accompli* with regard to the islands by expanding its presence into the southern zone of Abu Musa, in violation of the MoU with Sharjah, and creating institutional and administrative processes to consolidate Iranian control over Abu Musa and the Tunbs. The result has been that the islands case today represents a major stumbling block towards a more stable Arabian Gulf security environment.

The Early Years of the United Arab Emirates

From its inception, the UAE asserted its title to the islands and its desire to resolve the dispute peacefully in accordance with international law and custom. Within days after the Iranian landings on the Tunbs and Abu Musa, the newly formed UAE began to underline its own case. A statement issued by the Supreme Council of the Federation on December 2, 1971 declared:

> The Federation condemns the principle of the use of force and it regrets that Iran has recently occupied part of the Arab nation and it therefore deems it necessary to honour legal rights and to discuss possible repercussions which might ensue because of disputes between nations. Such discussions should be conducted in ways which are internationally recognized.[1]

On the same day, a UAE delegation headed by Ahmed Khalifa Al-Suwaidi visited Ras al-Khaimah's Shaikh Saqr, who submitted a letter to the rulers of the six emirates comprising the newly formed UAE, in which he seemed to drop his previous conditions about equality of representation and make recovery of the islands his only condition for joining the new federation. This letter stated Ras al-Khaimah's willingness to join the UAE "without restrictions or conditions except one condition, and this is that the State should set in motion effective measures to defend, by all kinds of means, the islands which have been seized, and the State should adopt and consider this matter as a corner-stone of its policy."[2] Among the measures and means that Shaikh Saqr mentioned in the letter were the denial of political, economic and cultural relations with Iran and the deportation of Iranians who had spent less than five years in the emirates and who had not become nationals of any emirate.[3] He was also reported to seek the use of force to liberate the islands.[4]

Days later, on December 5, His Highness (HH) Shaikh Zayed bin Sultan Al-Nahyan, the President of the new UAE and the Ruler of Abu Dhabi, carefully going beyond the condemnation of the principle of the use of force in the statement issued by the Supreme Council of the Federation on December 2, said: "We condemn the aggression by a neighboring and friendly state." However, he added: "We are waiting for the Arab states' practical support to assist us in regaining our rights." He said that the UAE accepted Ras al-Khaimah's call for "returning the islands to Arabism" as its condition for joining the federation. He said the UAE and its Arab brothers would try to raise the subject at the international level and that the UAE would adhere to the Arab League decision about the islands.[5] Thus, the federal government of the newly formed UAE put the issue into an Arab context, referring to the islands as "part of the Arab nation," stressing the need for "practical support" from other Arab states, and indicating that it would accept the Arab League approach. However, little practical Arab support came forth and without such support the UAE could do little to satisfy Ras al-Khaimah. Still, the UAE did delay the establishment of diplomatic relations with Iran for eleven months.

On December 6, 1971, the day the UAE became a member of the Arab League, the organization met in an emergency session to consider the occupation. Ras al-Khaimah and Iraq proposed severe measures to be taken against Iran, including the breaking of diplomatic, economic and cultural relations with Iran and even Britain. Saudi Arabia, Jordan and Egypt, now under President Anwar Sadat, although critical of the Iranian behavior, preferred a more moderate approach that would not alienate Iran. For these states, Iranian power represented an important element in checking Iraqi and South Yemeni ambitions in the region. They also appreciated Iran's gestures in dropping its claim to Bahrain and supporting them on the Arab-Israeli conflict. As a result, the Arab League passed a tempered resolution (2865), calling on the League's Secretary General to take up the matter. An Arab League delegation subsequently visited the Gulf, reporting that the emirates were interested in a peaceful settlement of the issue and that they wanted the League to undertake negotiations to that end. However, Iran was not willing to accept Arab League mediation and subsequent Saudi Arabian communications with Iran also failed.[6]

On December 9, 1971, the day of the UAE's admission to the United Nations, the UN Security Council considered the matter after a complaint filed earlier by Iraq, Algeria, the Libyan Arab Republic and the People's Democratic Republic of Yemen (the PDRY or South Yemen). These four states denounced Iran in their statements to the Council, while Iran claimed that the islands had always belonged to it, and Britain argued that the arrangements that had been reached offered a reasonable basis for security. The UAE protested Iran's use of force to resolve the territorial dispute. Based on the argument put forward by Somalia's representative that to recommend recourse to Chapter VI, Article 36 of the Charter would be precipitate, and that debate should be deferred until a third party could seek an appropriate resolution, the President of the Security Council, noting that there were no objections, so ordered it.[7]

On December 20, 1971, Shaikh Zayed wrote to Shaikh Saqr to acknowledge the concerns expressed by the latter in his December 3 letter and to encourage Shaikh Saqr to join and work with the federation in order to address the islands issue. Shaikh Zayed wrote:

> We want to assure Your Highness that we appreciate your deep patriotic and noble feelings with regard to the aggression which took place on a beloved part of our nation, and we certainly share these feelings…The points to which you have referred in your letter have attracted our most intense concern, and your presence in the Federation will enable us all to deal with these points in order to preserve the existence and security of the Federation and to repel all aggression from its territory.[8]

Shaikh Saqr replied on December 23, expressing his intention to join the federation and adhere to the constitution, and writing:

> Your statement has given us the reassurance that our State will not forsake our Arabian islands which were usurped by Iran on 30 November 1971, and that it will make every effort to restore the islands to the Arabian fold.[9]

However, Ras al-Khaimah would not formally join the federation for another two months. It was not until weeks later, on February 10, 1972, that Shaikh Saqr bin Muhammad Al-Qasimi of Ras al-Khaimah, seeing no alternative, and having failed to discover oil in commercial quantities, asked to join the UAE without any preconditions. On the following day, Ras al-Khaimah was admitted to the UAE federation.[10]

On January 24, 1972, prior to Ras al-Khaimah's accession, HH Shaikh Khalid of Sharjah was assassinated during a failed coup attempt led by his cousin Shaikh Saqr bin Sultan, who had been deposed as Ruler of Sharjah and exiled by the British in 1965.[11] During his interrogation in Abu Dhabi, Shaikh Saqr bin Sultan said that he had originally planned to lead a coup after the withdrawal of the British, but that he had abandoned the plan until he learned that Shaikh Khalid was partitioning Abu Musa with Iran. He had also expected that popular dissatisfaction with the MoU and its provisions to share Abu Musa's offshore oil with Iran would provide support for the coup and stated that he had intended to abrogate the MoU after seizing power.[12] Indeed, Shaikh Saqr bin Sultan's failed coup was financed and armed by Iraq, the leading Arab opponent of Iran's presence on the islands. He had set sail on his journey by dhow from Iraq's port of Basra and called upon the population of Sharjah during the coup to help him avenge the "traitorous" transfer of Abu Musa to Iran.[13] Others, however, have argued that the coup and assassination were perhaps not entirely due to the MoU on Abu Musa.[14]

Months after the initial Arab League and UN Security Council meetings, when it was evident that third party mediation could not resolve this issue, the UAE and fourteen other Arab states wrote in a July 18, 1972 letter to the President of the UN Security Council that "the islands of Abu Musa and the two Tunbs are Arab and constitute an integral part of the United Arab Emirates and of the Arab homeland."[15] In succeeding years, the UAE continued to assert its rights at various regional and international meetings. On October 5, 1972, the UAE reaffirmed its sovereignty over the islands in a statement read to the 27th session of the UN General Assembly. This was reaffirmed in a statement to the UN Security Council on February 20, 1974 and before the UN Special Political Committee on November 19, 1974.[16]

As noted earlier, from the first days after the Iranian occupation of the islands, Shaikh Zayed and the federal authority of the newly formed UAE had put the issue into an Arab and international context.[17] However, the UAE received only limited support from the Arab League, as evidenced by the moderate Arab League resolution of December 1971, the tame Arab League resolution of July 1972 and the cautious mediation efforts after these resolutions. Moreover, British and US satisfaction with the situation continued to make it difficult for the UAE to garner meaningful support in the UN, particularly in the Security Council.

Shaikh Zayed recognized that the UAE's prospects for success would be limited by the unwillingness of conservative Arab states, as well as Britain and the United States, to challenge Iran. In addition, the overall inability of the federal government of the UAE to confront Iran may also be attributed to some reasons unique to the UAE. As Shaikh Zayed said in June 1972, the UAE sought a resolution of the islands issue "without resorting to what may harm the interests of the two countries or lead them into armed conflict."[18] First, Abu Dhabi, the largest and wealthiest of the emirates, could not confront Iran inasmuch as it not only viewed Iran as a counterweight to radical Arab states and forces, but also viewed Iran as a counterweight to Saudi Arabia, which was making territorial demands on Abu Dhabi and refusing to recognize the new UAE until those demands were met.[19] Second, the UAE needed to focus its energies on nation-building as there existed important differences and historic rivalries among the various emirates. For example, Dubai valued its trade with Iran and traditionally even viewed Iran as a "protector" against the power of Saudi Arabia. Moreover, Sharjah had some benefits under the MoU with Iran. Furthermore, Ras al-Khaimah viewed Saudi Arabia as a "protector" against the power of Iran.[20]

Thus, Abu Dhabi sought the recognition and support of both Iran and Saudi Arabia for the UAE as a nation-state, not as a collection of individual emirates, and sought the influence these two states could exercise on certain emirates to join and stay in the federation.[21] Confronting Iran and not deferring to Saudi Arabia would not have been helpful to this strategy. Finally, on November 30, 1971, Iran did not officially use force against the UAE, which had not yet been declared, or against Sharjah, which was about to become a member of the UAE and which signed a MoU under pressure, but rather used force against Ras al-Khaimah, an emirate which was declining to join the

UAE and was still under a British umbrella. Indeed, Iran actually recognized the UAE on December 4, 1971, although the UAE delayed diplomatic relations until November 1972.[22]

In December 1975, UAE President Shaikh Zayed visited Iran. While he may have discussed the issue of the islands with the Shah, he did not refer to it in public statements made during the trip and the issue was not mentioned in the joint communiqué issued at the end of the visit. This trip was intended to be an important part of the effort to normalize relations between the UAE and Iran, an effort that had involved numerous bilateral meetings over the previous two years. The Dhofar rebellion remained an ongoing concern of both states at the time of Shaikh Zayed's visit and Iran's military support to Oman since 1973 was valued by the UAE. Moreover, Shaikh Zayed wanted the Shah's support for the UAE federal authority rather than for individual emirates like Dubai.

At the same time, the resolution of the border dispute with Saudi Arabia in 1974 meant that the UAE no longer needed Iran to balance Saudi Arabia and brought the UAE into a closer relationship with Saudi Arabia. This was reflected in the UAE joining Saudi opposition to Iran's general plans for a formal Gulf collective security pact in 1976. Both Saudi Arabia and the UAE viewed Iranian proposals as designed to promote Iranian hegemony, and the UAE also considered it necessary to resolve bilateral issues, such as the islands issue, prior to any such pact.[23] Iran's conservative Arab Gulf neighbors had never received the Shah's earlier interest in a "Gulf Pact" in 1968 with enthusiasm, but the occupation of the islands in 1971 had further undermined any possibility of such a pact.[24] In November 1977, however, the UAE and Saudi Arabia did cooperate with Iran in issuing an alert of possible terrorist attacks to tanker captains transiting the Strait of Hormuz and warning them not to stop for any vessel in distress.[25]

In October 1975, the Crown Prince of Ras al-Khaimah, HH Shaikh Khalid bin Saqr Al-Qasimi, visited Iran. During this visit and a subsequent visit in October 1978, the Crown Prince met with the Shah, the Prime Minister and the Chief of the Intelligence Service, asserted that the Tunbs belonged to Ras al-Khaimah and called for peaceful negotiations to resolve the dispute.[26] Ras al-Khaimah may have thought that it had no choice but to make such a direct approach. However,

Iran, facing no serious Arab pressure, did not respond positively. In April 1976, HH Shaikh Saqr of Ras al-Khaimah appealed to Ahmed Khalifa Al-Suwaidi, the UAE Minister of Foreign Affairs, to seek a peaceful return of the islands and if this effort failed, to raise the matter again at the upcoming session of the UN or submit the matter to the ICJ. This appeal was conveyed in a letter in which Shaikh Saqr set forth a comprehensive legal argument for Ras al-Khaimah's territorial claim.[27] Shaikh Zayed visited Iran in November 1977, but again the islands issue was not emphasized.[28]

Revolution and War in the Gulf

In 1979, a popular revolution in Iran overthrew the Shah and installed an Islamic Republic under the Ayatollah Ruhollah Khomeini. The UAE was concerned about the revolutionary upheaval that took place, but quickly recognized the revolutionary Islamic regime that took power in February 1979 and forged "correct" relations with the new regime. The UAE was keen to avoid any threat from the new regime, particularly in view of the potential appeal that this new regime might have with the considerable Iranian Shi'a population in some of the emirates, such as Dubai.[29] Moreover, differences in 1979 between Abu Dhabi on the one hand and Dubai and Ras al-Khaimah on the other hand over the powers of the UAE federal government could have offered Iran's new regime an opportunity for meddling. Kuwait and Saudi Arabia, however, were instrumental in helping the emirates find a compromise in order to maintain Gulf security in the face of what they also perceived to be a new and dangerous threat from Iran.[30]

Initially, there was some cautious optimism in the region that the new government might refrain from the hegemonic policies of its predecessor. Indeed, UAE officials were hopeful that Iran's new regime might cooperate in resolving the dispute over the islands.[31] In fact, Palestine Liberation Organization (PLO) Chairman Yasser Arafat carried a message from Ayatollah Khomeini to Shaikh Zayed in February 1979 expressing appreciation for the UAE's attitude toward the revolution and an interest in stronger relations with the UAE. It also expressed an intention to abandon the expansionism of the Shah's regime and make a comprehensive review of all of his expansionist measures and agreements.[32] Moreover, in late May 1979, while on a visit to the UAE, Shaikh Sadeq Khalkhali, the first head of Tehran's revolutionary courts and a close associate of Ayatollah Khomeini, told the UAE's Emirates News Agency (WAM) that Iran might be ready to review the status of the islands.[33]

However, these hopes were dashed quickly when the revolutionary Islamic regime began to wage a propaganda war against Iraq and the conservative regimes of the Arab Gulf, and when it became clear that there would be no difference in the Iranian position on the islands. In March 1979, the Iranian Foreign Ministry said that Iranian troops would not be withdrawn from the islands. In June, the Iranian Deputy Prime Minister asserted that the islands were Iran's "property" and Iranian Foreign Minister, Ibrahim Yazdi, denied that Iran might be ready to return the islands.[34]

Despite these statements, Shaikh Saqr of Ras al-Khaimah wrote to Ayatollah Khomeini in November 1979, reviewing the Shah's actions on the islands, appealing to Khomeini's sense of Islamic brotherhood, and asking that his "rational government...correct the misdeeds of the previous regime and...restore justice." Khomeini did not answer the letter.[35] When asked about the islands in April 1980, Iran's new Foreign Minister, Sadegh Qotbzadeh, said "Iran will not cede a single inch of its territory." He added later in the month that the Arabs could not claim the islands and that all the Arab states of the Gulf had historically been part of Iran.[36] In a message sent to the UN Secretary General on May 26, 1980, Qotbzadeh restated his position that the three islands had always been an integral part of Iran. He claimed that when the British forces withdrew from the Gulf in 1971, Iran merely regained its "sovereignty" over them.[37]

The entire region would soon be thrown into turmoil with the outbreak of the Iran-Iraq War in September 1980. Just prior to the war, the UAE had once again reasserted its sovereignty over the islands in a note to the UN Secretary General on August 18, 1980. This was a response to the statements of Qotbzadeh and followed Iraqi and Saudi statements of support for the UAE. Indeed, the note from the UAE's Minister of State for Foreign Affairs, Rashid Abdullah Al-Nuaimi, expressed the UAE's regret that the Islamic Republic of Iran intended to continue the Shah's expansionist policy. However, the UAE note called for a peaceful dialogue with Iran to regain the islands.[38]

After the outbreak of the war, in order to receive Arab support for its cause, Iraq quickly made the return of the islands a condition for peace. Iran responded that it would never relinquish them. Subsequently, on December 1, the UAE again asserted its sovereignty in another note to the UN Secretary General. This note also rebutted a claim by Iran's President Abol Hassan Bani Sadr that the Shah had paid "certain sheikhs" to keep quiet about the Shah's takeover of the islands.[39]

In early January 1981, Shaikh Zayed said that the islands were "part and parcel of the UAE and its possession"; that the UAE's "permanent and fixed attitude" regarding the islands "springs from its rights to these islands"; and that the UAE had confirmed this during and after the Shah's reign and would continue to do so. However, the UAE's method for doing so would be "to present legal evidence and through joint consultation and mutual understanding so that each gets his due and the Arab entitlement reverts to its people."[40] This was repeated in May 1981, when Shaikh Zayed said: "These islands are part of the UAE and belong to it. We hope to be able to solve our differences with Iran with understanding and dialogue based on logic." At the same time, he made it clear that the UAE "supports every effort to stop this war [between Iraq and Iran] and end its grave losses for these two Muslim countries as well as for us all."[41]

In May 1981, largely in response to the Iranian revolution and the outbreak of the Iran-Iraq War, the UAE, Qatar, Bahrain, Kuwait, Saudi Arabia and Oman joined together to establish the Gulf Cooperation Council (GCC). In terms of the war itself, the UAE remained formally neutral, although it did provide political and economic support to Iraq, which it saw as a counterweight to Iran. The UAE did, however, maintain diplomatic relations with Iran throughout the war and even mediated between the two warring sides.[42]

The war demonstrated the uses to which Iran can put the islands and the challenges this can pose, not only to the UAE, but also to international shipping. Both during and after the hostilities, Abu Musa and the Tunbs served as bases for regular Iranian Armed Forces and for the naval branch of the Iranian Revolutionary Guard Corps. During the "tanker war" years of 1986-88, Iran launched small boat and helicopter attacks from the islands against shipping in the Gulf and against some of the UAE's offshore oil installations.[43] From 1983 onwards, Iranian forces conducted regular patrols into Sharjah's zone on the island, and in 1987, Iranian forces briefly occupied Sharjah's zone on the island during an abortive coup attempt in Sharjah, withdrawing to the Iranian zone only after it became clear that the coup did not succeed.[44] The UAE supported the West's tanker re-flagging operation as an attempt to protect shipping, and it also worked for a ceasefire resolution in the Security Council.[45] However, given the difficulty of resolving the war itself during its eight-year course, the UAE certainly had no practical opportunity to seek a resolution of the contending legal claims to these islands during these years.

Despite the end of the Iran-Iraq War in 1988, peace did not last long in the Gulf. On August 2, 1990, Iraq invaded Kuwait. The UAE immediately joined the worldwide condemnation of the invasion, which it also considered a direct threat to itself, inasmuch as Iraqi President Saddam Hussein had been complaining about alleged overproduction of oil by the UAE just prior to his move against Kuwait. As part of the coalition to expel Iraq from Kuwaiti territory, the UAE participated in the buildup of forces and in the actual liberation campaign. UAE Air Force planes played an active role in the initial air campaign and UAE military contingents were part of the first group to enter Kuwait during the ground war in late February 1991. Following the war, the US and European military presence became an integral part of the western security arrangements with various GCC member states. Despite its official neutrality during the war, Iran denounced the UAE and other GCC states for permitting western military forces to increase their presence in the region during and after Desert Shield and Desert Storm. Iran has since pressured these states to cut their ties with the US and Western European militaries.[46]

Renewed Assertiveness of the Islamic Republic of Iran

In 1992, Iran resumed its war-time violations of the MoU on Abu Musa with further encroachments on Sharjah's southern half of the island. It sought to impose restrictions on third-country citizens (i.e. non-UAE citizens) disembarking at Abu Musa's best pier, which is in the Iranian zone, and seeking to transit to the UAE's zone on Abu Musa, by requiring that they secure Iranian entry permits.[47] In March 1992, Iran's President Hashemi Rafsanjani visited the island, leading to speculation that he, a "pragmatic" leader interested in better relations with the GCC states, must have known and approved of the Iranian measures that soon followed.

In April 1992, Iran refused entry to a group of non-UAE citizens, primarily Indian, Pakistani and Filipino laborers and Egyptian teachers. It also seized a desalination plant and school belonging to the UAE. Iran's foreign minister, Ali Akbar Velayati, on a visit to Kuwait on April 19, 1992, argued that Iran continued to recognize the validity of the 1971 MoU on Abu Musa. However, he claimed, without merit, that the 1971 MoU did not permit foreigners on the island. Iran also began to make claims that it had not received a fair share of the revenue from the island's offshore oil production. When the UAE Foreign Ministry denounced Iran's measures as a violation of the MoU, Iran relented and permitted this group of non-UAE citizens to enter.[48]

One potential reason for the Iranian actions in April was that Iran staged its biggest amphibious exercise since the end of the Iran-Iraq War from April 25 until May 4, 1992 in the vicinity of the islands. The exercise practiced blocking the Strait of Hormuz to an outside military power and launching attacks against enemy coastal positions. It covered 10,000 square miles of ocean and involved 45 surface ships, 150 small craft and an unknown number of military aircraft.[49] Iran would stage many more such exercises in the following years. While the United States and the UAE have the technical means to observe such exercises, Iran may have wanted to remove potential human observers from Abu Musa.

Within months, the situation would escalate even further. On August 24, 1992, Iran refused entry to 104 residents of Abu Musa, including Sharjah's governor of the island, UAE nationals, as well as Palestinians, Syrians, Egyptians and Jordanians. Many of them were teachers returning from summer vacation. Iranian authorities did not allow the passengers to disembark and threatened to sink the ship if it did not immediately return to Sharjah.[50] This was the most serious violation of the existing MoU to that date and was vigorously protested by the UAE on September 1.[51] While Iran relented somewhat by allowing 20 UAE nationals from Sharjah and Sharjah's governor to disembark on September 3, the others were not allowed to return.[52]

As the UAE adopted a determined policy of asserting its rights and seeking a peaceful resolution of the dispute with Iran, significant regional support for the UAE was forthcoming. In September 1992, the GCC foreign ministers, the Damascus Declaration foreign ministers (i.e. the foreign ministers of the GCC and Egypt and Syria), and the Arab League foreign ministers all issued statements denouncing the Iranian occupation of the three islands and supporting the UAE's rights to these islands.[53] This pattern would repeat itself over the coming years as both regional and international backing for the position of the UAE became consolidated.

On September 27 and 28, 1992, the UAE and Iran held their first round of bilateral negotiations on the islands in Abu Dhabi. The UAE favored an agenda that would include a comprehensive discussion of all three islands. It sought an end to the Iranian military occupation of the Tunbs, reconfirmation of the Iranian commitment to the MoU regarding Abu Musa, non-interference by Iran in the UAE's exercise of its sovereignty/jurisdiction in its area on Abu Musa, cancellation of all arrangements and undertakings which adversely impact UAE nationals, non-UAE residents and UAE government institutions on Abu Musa, and the finding of a suitable framework for a decisive resolution of the issue of sovereignty over Abu Musa.

However, Iran would only discuss the status of the MoU with regard to Abu Musa. It refused to consider the status of the Tunb islands or to refer the islands issue to the International Court of Justice.[54] Thus, the talks broke down without any agreement on an agenda. One UAE delegation member has argued that Iran sought to portray itself as willing to hold discussions because the dispute was complicating its relations with Saudi Arabia, but that Iran had no intention of conducting serious negotiations. Indeed, at one point, the Iranian delegation argued that the islands were not important as long as the UAE and Iran had good bilateral relations. Clearly, Iran meant that the islands should not be important to the UAE.[55]

Two days later, on September 30, 1992, in a speech before the UN General Assembly, Rashid Abdullah Al-Nuaimi, in his capacity as the UAE Minister of Foreign Affairs, said:

> The Iranian authorities have undertaken a number of illegal
> measures and arrangements with regard to the island of Abu

Musa. These measures violate the Memorandum of Understanding of 1971. My country has expressed its rejection of these measures as being a clear violation of the sovereignty and territorial integrity of the Emirates as well as the principle of good neighbourliness. They also contradict the original provisions and spirit of the Memorandum of Understanding which demand justice and equivalency of treatment; taking into consideration that this Memo was signed under duress which according to international law makes it null and void.

The latest Iranian measures are aimed at assuming control of the island of Abu Musa and tacitly annexing it to Iran, just as the Iranian Government did in 1971 when it militarily occupied the two islands of the Lesser and Greater Tunbs which belong to the United Arab Emirates. Because of the nature of these measures, tension is bound to increase in the area and security and stability will be endangered, since these actions are incompatible with the principle of coexistence, good neighbourliness and the traditional relations which exist between the two countries.[56]

Iranian statements during this period appear somewhat contradictory. In September, just after the GCC, the Damascus Declaration states and the Arab League had supported the UAE, and just days before the bilateral talks were set to begin, Iran asserted full sovereignty over Abu Musa. Nevertheless, also in September, despite Iran's assertion of sovereignty and Iran's violations of the MoU, the head of the Iranian negotiating team with the UAE, Ambassador Mustafa Haeri Foumani, reiterated that Iran recognized the continuity and validity of the 1971 MoU on Abu Musa. Then, following the breakdown of the bilateral talks and Rashid Abdullah's statement at the UN, Foumani claimed: "No Iranian would allow himself to negotiate with others on the sovereignty of his own land."[57]

In effect, what Iran conveyed by these statements was that it would discuss administrative measures on Abu Musa, but would not discuss issues of sovereignty over Abu Musa or the Tunbs. Iran's definition of the problem, which avoids any consideration of the issue of sovereignty over Abu Musa and any consideration of the Tunbs at all, has remained the Iranian position since 1992 and has been completely at variance with the UAE, GCC and Arab League definition.

Iran's Militarization of the Islands

On October 23, 1992, the London-based Saudi newspaper *Al-Sharq Al-Awsat* reported that Iran had established eight missile launching sites on Abu Musa to be used to launch Chinese-made Silkworm anti-shipping missiles and modified North-Korean-made Scud-B surface-to-surface missiles. UAE and Western official sources had doubted that Iran would place Scuds, which were already deployed on Iran's shore and have a sufficient range to hit the UAE, on an exposed island such as Abu Musa. However, these sources confirmed that Iran had built launching sites for anti-ship missiles and, indeed, has had them on the island since the Iran-Iraq war in the 1980s. More importantly, they also suggested that Iran may have already brought anti-ship missiles to the island.[58]

Developments like these began to form a pattern in which Iran would not only attempt to bring the island increasingly under its control, but also to unilaterally use the island's strategic significance as a means to extend its own power throughout the Gulf region. This would in turn lead UAE, GCC and Western defense officials to scrutinize potential Iranian capabilities and to issue some pointed warnings to Iran.

In December 1992, the annual GCC summit publicly supported the UAE on the issue of the islands, calling for negotiations, stressing the sovereignty of the UAE, rejecting Iran's occupation and particularly denouncing Iran's behavior on Abu Musa as a threat to the development of friendly GCC-Iranian relations and to security and stability in the region.[59] The Iranian media reported President Rafsanjani as responding that the GCC would have to cross "a sea of blood" to reach the islands.[60] In that same month, Iran deployed additional Iranian Revolutionary Guard Corps forces in the islands and declared that it was willing to defend the islands against any attack. It also reminded its Gulf Arab neighbors that it was willing to fight for eighty years against Iraq.[61]

Despite the numerous Iranian violations of the MoU, as well as the Iranian military exercises and deployments, Rashid Abdullah, UAE foreign minister and chairman of the GCC foreign ministers committee, said at the 4th GCC-EC joint ministerial meeting that the GCC states believe that Iran can play a positive role in achieving regional security and stability. His comments came at the same time as Iranian Foreign Minister Velayati was paying official visits to the six GCC states. Once again, however, the GCC was rebuffed on the islands issue. Not only did Velayati's visit fail to resolve the issue, but on May 12, 1993, Iran promulgated a law entitled *Act on the Marine Areas of Iran in the Persian Gulf and Oman Sea*, which claimed that Iran had sovereignty over Abu Musa and the Tunbs.[62]

Nevertheless, the UAE continued to propose various peaceful means of resolving the dispute. On the occasion of its 22nd National Day in December 1993, UAE President Shaikh Zayed bin Sultan Al-Nahyan called on Iran to enter a direct dialogue aimed at the return of the islands to the UAE.[63] Shortly after Shaikh Zayed's remarks, the UAE officially asked the UN Secretary-General to use his good offices to mediate. On January 2, 1994, the Secretary General, Boutros Boutros Ghali, stated that the UN would play any appropriate role in resolving the dispute over the island. Iran, however, refused to receive him to discuss the matter.[64]

Then, on March 20, 1994, in an interview with the London-based newspaper *Al-Hayat*, Shaikh Zayed stressed that the dispute should be referred to the International Court of Justice.[65] These UAE suggestions were reiterated on October 5, 1994, in an address before the 49th session of the UN General Assembly by the UAE Foreign Minister.[66] Again, on December 2, 1994, in an address marking the 23rd anniversary of the establishment of the UAE, Shaikh Zayed urged Iran to enter into an objective and constructive dialogue or to accept international arbitration to resolve the dispute over the islands.[67]

Despite these proposals from the UAE, Iranian behavior still did not change. In June 1994, Iranian President Rafsanjani himself rejected the proposal to refer the issue to an international court. In addition, from the fall of 1994 through early 1995, Iran once again significantly increased its Revolutionary Guard forces and its military assets on Abu Musa. This included the stationing and upgrading of fast-attack boats, helicopters, tanks, anti-aircraft artillery and surface-to-air missiles. With the completion of the anti-shipping missile launchers on the island, missiles could now be brought quickly to the island from the Iranian mainland. Similar fortifications took place on the Tunbs.[68] On December 29, 1994, Iran inaugurated an air route linking Bandar Abbas to Abu Musa, where a lengthened runway could accommodate landings by cargo planes carrying military supplies and personnel.[69]

In February and March 1995, numerous US officials warned of the potential threat posed by these Iranian military deployments on and around Abu Musa. General John Shalikashvili, Chairman of the Joint Chiefs of Staff, argued that Iranian deployments were indicative of the fact that Tehran might be seeking the capability to interdict traffic in the Strait of Hormuz.[70] US Secretary of Defense William Perry also highlighted these developments, particularly 6,000 military personnel on Abu Musa and the Tunbs, SA-6 surface-to-air missile batteries on Abu Musa, chemical weapons on Abu Musa, including 155 mm artillery shells, and anti-ship missiles on Iran's coast. While he did not mention it, there were SA-6 surface-to-air missile batteries on the Tunbs as well. He called these forces a threat to shipping and called for greater military cooperation between the GCC states and the United States. Initially, some believed that the Iranian deployments were a response to the build-up of US forces in the Gulf in the fall of 1994 to deter threatening moves by Saddam Hussein's Iraq toward Kuwait. However, the Iranian deployments continued even in the winter and spring of 1995, after the US had already began to significantly reduce its forces.[71]

As a result of events like the Iraqi invasion of Kuwait and the growing potential Iranian military threat to the UAE due to Tehran's militarization of the islands, the UAE entered into defensive military arrangements with major military powers. These included a military cooperation protocol with Russia, signed on January 4, 1993, a defense cooperation agreement (DCA) with the United States dated July 25, 1994, a military cooperation accord with France in January 1995, and finally a MoU on defense matters with Britain, concluded in late 1996.[72] As a UAE Foreign Ministry official explained, the UAE wanted the deterrence or defense against a major attack on the UAE or international shipping that such arrangements provide. He noted, however, that these defensive arrangements did not motivate Iran to resolve the islands dispute, and recognized that the UAE would have to continue building international diplomatic support for a peaceful resolution of the dispute.[73]

Thus, the UAE continued its diplomatic approach. On October 4, 1995, in an address to the 50th session of the UN General Assembly, the UAE Foreign Minister again called for "direct, unconditional, bilateral negotiations" or referral of the issue to the ICJ. He noted that GCC states had supported this approach and protested that Iran continued to take illegal measures to consolidate its occupation.[74] On October 23, UAE Deputy Prime Minister HH Shaikh Sultan bin Zayed Al-Nahyan addressed the UN General Assembly on the occasion of the UN's 50th anniversary and argued that Iran's occupation of the three islands was a direct threat to the UAE and the security of the region.[75] Significantly, the UAE received diplomatic backing from one of its major allies in 1995 when US Secretary of State Warren Christopher said that the UAE had a strong claim to the islands and supported the UAE's efforts to resolve this issue with Iran peacefully.[76]

In mid-November 1995, following an invitation to Iran and the UAE by the foreign minister of Qatar, Shaikh Hamad bin Jassim bin Jabir Al-Thani, a second round of bilateral talks between the UAE and Iran was held in Doha, Qatar. The letter of invitation called for agreement on an agenda for bilateral negotiations. In response, the UAE submitted a proposed agenda covering, first, the Iranian occupation of the Tunbs, second, Iranian compliance with the MoU on Abu Musa, third, the issue of sovereignty over Abu Musa, and fourth, submission of the disputes to the ICJ if bilateral negotiations failed. Iran, which had consistently been unwilling to consider the first, third or fourth issues, rejected the UAE proposal and the meeting failed to produce any agreement.[77]

Both parties indicated a willingness to talk again in the future, but Khalifa Shahin Al-Marri, the head of the UAE delegation, argued that Iran's refusal to agree to an agenda was a rebuff of the good offices of Qatar.[78] In an interview, Khalifa Shahin Al-Marri said that Iran argued that their basis for accepting the letter of invitation from Qatar was another letter from Shaikh Zayed to Rafsanjani, in which Shaikh Zayed had called for a meeting of the foreign ministers of the two countries, and that their only purpose in accepting the invitation from Qatar was to prepare the protocol for a meeting of the foreign ministers. The UAE answered that they should prepare for a meeting of their foreign ministers by preparing an agenda for the meeting and the Iranians refused.[79]

In the aftermath, the UAE continued to receive declarations of support from Arab leaders. This time, however, these statements began to reflect increasing anxiety. The GCC summit in December 1995, for example, expressed "concern" about Iranian behavior on the islands and "regret" that Iran had rebuffed UAE calls for a peaceful resolution of the dispute.[80] In June 1996, the GCC Ministerial Council argued that Iran's policy and behavior jeopardized the security and the stability of the region.[81] A month later, in July, the foreign ministers of the Damascus Declaration states voiced their "great concern" over Iran's occupation of the islands, calling on Iran to "end its occupation" and to accept peaceful means of resolving the dispute over the islands. The ministers "affirm[ed] that the security and stability of the UAE, and the protection and preservation of its independence and territorial integrity and its support, is considered an integral part of the security of the Arab Gulf countries and Arab national security..."[82] This was followed by the next GCC summit in December 1996, which expressed its "extreme concern over the deployment by the Islamic Republic of Iran of land-to-land missiles in the Arab Gulf, including its deployment of missiles on the three occupied islands," calling this "a matter which poses a direct threat [to] the Council's states and their vital installations."[83]

Despite the heightened concern about the islands during these years, the UN Security Council prepared in 1996 to delete a number of items from its agenda, including the islands matter.[84] However, when the UAE submitted a formal request to keep the issue on the Security Council agenda, this was accepted. The UAE now annually renews its request and as such the islands issue is a permanent feature of the agenda. The UAE also documents all its protests to Iran for the Security Council. However, an official at the UAE Ministry of Foreign Affairs notes that the UAE still has not asked for any formal reconsideration of the issue by the Security Council. While the UAE wants to exhaust all avenues for getting direct negotiations on the issue, it does not see the need to go that far.[85]

The election of the reformist-minded cleric Mohammed Khatami to Iran's presidency in May 1997 was greeted with guarded optimism throughout the region. In one of his first statements following the election, Khatami called for the opening of a new chapter in Arab-Iranian relations. Regional states hoped that the ascendance of reformists at the expense of conservatives in Iran would mean that cooperation on a host of issues, non-interference by Iran in the domestic affairs of other states, and Iranian willingness to find peaceful settlements of disputes would now be possible. Shaikh Saqr of Ras al-Khaimah quickly wrote to President-elect Khatami on May 26, congratulating him on his victory, expressing the hope for improved relations and explaining how Iran's occupation of the islands fostered tension. However, within days, and despite calling for increased dialogue and cooperation, Khatami publicly stated that "the islands belong to Iran."[86]

Thus, even under a more moderate leadership, there was no hint of flexibility concerning the prospects of a negotiated solution of the islands issue. The result was that while regional leaders affirmed their readiness to build cordial relations with Iran on the basis of good neighborliness, they stressed the importance of resolving the islands issue before this could be done. This was the message conveyed by the foreign ministers of the Damascus Declaration states at their June 1997 meeting, by the GCC Council of Foreign Ministers in September 1997 and by the Arab League during the same month.[87] However, when Iran's new foreign minister, Kamal Kharrazi, toured the GCC states in November 1997, he carried with him Iran's message of improved relations, but did not bring new proposals regarding the islands.[88]

At the 8th summit of the Organization of the Islamic Conference (OIC), which was held in Tehran in December 1997, Iran was again urged to reach a peaceful settlement with the UAE, either through negotiation or by submitting the case to the International Court of Justice.[89] At a later press conference in Tehran, Iran's President Khatami responded by saying "We have said this elsewhere, and we are saying it emphatically now, that we are ready to go there." However, he rejected third party mediation, saying "our dispute over the islands does not need the interference of outsiders."[90]

GCC leaders also appealed to Iran at the 18th summit meeting of the GCC later in December 1997. The communiqué issued at the end of the summit "expressed its regret over Iran's continuous failure to respond positively to sincere and serious calls by the UAE and regional and international bodies to settle the dispute through peaceful means." It also read:

The GCC leaders also reviewed recent statements by Iranian President Khatami in which he expressed his desire to meet with President His Highness Sheikh Zayed and listened to Sheikh Zayed's welcome for Khatami's approach. They welcomed any meeting between the two countries' leaders and reaffirmed the UAE's sovereignty over the three islands and their full support for peaceful means adopted by the UAE to restore its sovereignty over the islands.[91]

As the summit was concluding, the then Chief of Staff of the UAE Armed Forces, HH Lt. General Shaikh Mohammed bin Zayed Al-Nahyan, also called President Khatami's statements "positive and encouraging" and said that bilateral talks could be held in the coming weeks. However, he noted that "the UAE did not observe any positive and concrete act yet by Iran to solve the issue of the islands." Indeed, Iranian Foreign Ministry spokesman Mahmoud Mohammadi was quoted as saying that the islands "are Iranian" and as calling upon the GCC "to persuade the UAE to hold bilateral talks with Iran."[92] In the end, Khatami did not meet with Shaikh Zayed.

In May 1998, Iranian Foreign Minister Kharrazi visited the UAE, meeting with Shaikh Zayed and other officials. While the visit took place in a cordial atmosphere, Kharrazi again did not make any new proposals about the islands.[93] On the eve of Kharrazi's visit, the head of the Iranian Foreign Ministry's Arab Department, Dr. Mohammed Al-Sadr, again expressed Iran's narrow definition of the dispute, saying, "The problem that is facing us is that of Abu Mousa and the mechanics of implementation of the 1971 memorandum of understanding." He added: "We believe that it could be solved and there is no obstacle that could prevent us from reaching a solution."[94] This definition of the problem avoids consideration of the issue of sovereignty over Abu Musa and avoids any consideration of the Tunbs at all. It is not responsive to UAE, GCC and Arab League concerns.

The GCC summit in December 1998 called upon Iran to respond to appeals for a peaceful resolution of the dispute in a way that would bring credibility to statements by Khatami and other Iranians. The GCC summit also welcomed efforts by UN Secretary General Kofi Annan to promote bilateral negotiations.[95] Iranian military exercises in the waters around the three islands and on the islands themselves in December 1998 and February 1999 caused deep concern to the UAE, the GCC and the Arab League, all of which protested.[96] Furthermore, in February 1999, Iran opened a new municipal building and an educational institution on Abu Musa. The UAE protested to the Arab League about Iranian attempts to strengthen its occupation of the three islands, and asked in a message to Secretary General Dr. Ismet Abdel Magid that Iran's occupation of the three UAE islands should be placed on the agenda of the March meeting of the Arab League Foreign Ministers. In its own protest to Iran, the UAE wrote that it "considers this action illegal and all previous actions implemented by successive Iranian governments on the island of Abu Musa as unjustified provocation that does not give any legal rights to Iran over the island." Copies were sent to the GCC, the Arab League and the UN.[97]

During a press conference after the GCC meeting, UAE Foreign Minister Rashid Abdullah, when asked whether the UAE had asked the GCC to delay rapprochement with Iran, expressed the UAE's understanding of the importance of relations with Iran for GCC states, saying:

> We are working to change Iran's policies and not for breaking ties or stopping dealing with it. We want to use these relations to serve stability, cooperation, common interests and to resolve problems in the region.

Indeed, when asked if the GCC had taken precautionary steps after Iran's military exercises, Rashid Abdullah said, "We view these exercises as dangerous and provocative and we don't like on our part to be accused of escalating the situation and adding more risks in the region."[98]

In December 1998, when Kofi Annan became the first UN Secretary General to attend a GCC summit, he revealed that he had proposed that the UAE and Iran hold preparatory talks for negotiations on the islands. Annan said that Shaikh Zayed and Kamal Kharrazi had both responded positively.[99] The Secretary-General also reportedly proposed to Shaikh Zayed that he was willing "to mediate between his country and Iran if bilateral negotiations failed" and was said to have discussed the possibility of arbitration with Kharrazi. Shaikh Zayed had called on Iran one week earlier to accept "constructive dialogue, or recourse to adjudication" by the ICJ. Kharrazi welcomed the proposal for direct talks, but said that Annan had not proposed mediation to him.[100]

In the following months, however, the UAE and Iran did not move closer toward negotiations and Kofi Annan did not mediate. Indeed, Iranian construction on Abu Musa and the use of both Abu Musa and the Tunbs in military exercises led Arab League Secretary General Ismet Abdel Magid to write to Secretary General Annan and the Security Council President in March 1999, asking the Security Council again to keep the issue of Iran's occupation of the islands on the Security Council agenda until the islands were returned to the UAE.[101]

In June 1999, after Khatami's May visit to Saudi Arabia signaled that Saudi-Iranian relations were becoming even warmer, the UAE became concerned that Iran would not feel pressed to resolve the islands issue unless closer relations were made a prerequisite for resolving the islands dispute. The result was that critical comments were exchanged between the UAE and Saudi Arabia. After this, however, Saudi Arabia and the other GCC states offered assurances that they would continue to support the UAE on this issue. Indeed, a tripartite committee composed of representatives of Saudi Arabia, Oman and Qatar was created in order to promote bilateral negotiations between the UAE and Iran on the islands.[102]

In mid-July, after Saudi officials briefed Iranian Foreign Minister Kharrazi on the tripartite committee's meeting, and after Qatari officials briefed HH Shaikh Hamdan bin Zayed Al-Nahyan, the UAE's Minister of State for Foreign Affairs, Shaikh Hamdan stated: "We are ready to visit Iran, but on what basis? And what would be the agenda of the talks to be conducted?" He noted that "Iran is currently not responding to, if we do not say refusing, the positive stance of the AGCC ministerial council which set up the [tripartite] commission."[103] An Iranian Foreign Ministry spokesman responded that Iran welcomed negotiations, but again rejected any "preconditions."[104]

Days later, after an Iranian Foreign Ministry spokesman said that the islands were "inseparable from Iranian territory," the then Abu Dhabi Crown Prince HH Shaikh Khalifa bin Zayed Al-Nahyan said: "We ask Iran to see reason, by ending the occupation of the three islands, so that historic, religious, and trade ties can be consolidated between the two countries."[105] UAE Foreign Minister Rashid Abdullah then told the 54th session of the UN General Assembly on September 22, 1999 that Iran threatened regional and international security and stability by carrying out military maneuvers and changing the demographic and historic character of the three islands.[106] Within days, Iran launched its Unity-7 (Vahdat-7) air and naval exercises from the lower Gulf through the Strait of Hormuz and into the Gulf of Oman. For the first time, all three of Iran's Kilo-class submarines participated in the exercises.[107] As these Iranian exercises were ending, the GCC launched naval exercises code-named Solidarity-6 in Qatar's waters, exercises that included the participation of frogmen.[108]

In late January 2000, Shaikh Zayed stressed the UAE's "clear policies to end Iran's occupation of the three UAE islands of Abu Mousa and the Greater and Lesser Tunbs by peaceful means." Welcoming the GCC tripartite committee's efforts to prepare for negotiations between the UAE and Iran, he said: "We are hoping that Iran will respond positively to these efforts."[109] When the reformists decisively defeated the conservatives in Iran's February 2000 parliamentary elections, Shaikh Zayed and GCC officials congratulated President Khatami, expressing the hope that this election would facilitate better relations between Iran and the UAE and the GCC.[110]

UAE Minister of Information and Culture HH Shaikh Abdullah bin Zayed Al-Nahyan was more critical, saying: "We hope that after the results of the Iranian elections the [tripartite] committee will move more quickly and that it will be welcomed by Iran. We sincerely hope that the committee will approach Iran for a solution despite the Iranian refusal to receive its members under different pretexts."[111] As Iran began new naval exercises involving its submarines in the Gulf, Oman's foreign minister said that the tripartite committee "will soon start contacts with Iran now [that] the parliamentary elections are over..."[112] As Iran's naval exercises were ending, UAE Deputy Prime Minister HH Shaikh Sultan bin Zayed Al-Nahyan called on Iran to resolve the islands dispute for the sake of regional cooperation and stability.[113]

Ultimately, however, the tripartite committee did not succeed in eliciting a positive response from Iran. At the GCC summit held in December 2000, the committee reported that Iran would not cooperate and in response the summit declared that the mandate of the committee was "finished."[114] In March 2001, the UAE lodged protests with Iran and the UN over Iran's claims to the islands, its construction of housing for the settlement of Iranians on the islands, and the visit to the islands by members of the Iranian parliament's national security and foreign policy committee. Iran responded by lodging a protest with the UAE over the UAE's claims to the islands.[115] In May 2001, Shaikh Hamdan bin Zayed had an inconclusive discussion about the islands with Kharrazi on the sidelines of an OIC meeting in Doha, Qatar.[116] Then, in July 2001, Shaikh Hamdan traveled to Iran to congratulate Khatami on his election to a second term and to discuss the islands. Khatami said "This visit opens new horizons for relations between the two countries," but again no progress was made on the islands issue.[117]

On the 30th anniversary of Iran's occupation of the islands, Ras al-Khaimah Deputy Ruler Shaikh Khalid bin Saqr Al-Qasimi and the UAE Federal National Council stressed the UAE's continuing commitment to recover the three islands and called upon Iran to accept peaceful means of resolving the dispute.[118] The GCC summit in late December 2001 noted the contacts between the UAE and Iran, reaffirmed its support for the UAE's efforts to restore its sovereignty, repeated its unconditional rejection of Iranian claims and measures, and again called on Iran to take the matter to the ICJ.[119]

In February 2002, Shaikh Zayed, Shaikh Sultan and Shaikh Hamdan received Mohammed Ali Abtahi, Iranian Vice President for Legal and Parliamentary Affairs, for talks in Abu Dhabi.[120] In May 2002, Shaikh Hamdan traveled to Iran again and held discussions with Abtahi, Kharazzi and Khatami. He also delivered a letter from Shaikh Zayed to Khatami, which included an invitation for Khatami to visit the UAE. It was reported that Khatami accepted the invitation and that he would likely make the visit in December 2002.[121] Tajeddin Abdulhaq reported in *Al-Sharq Al-Awsat* on June 10 that the UAE and Iran had agreed to remove the islands dispute from the media spotlight and to avoid the issue in international forums, while ongoing bilateral contacts would attempt to achieve a mutually acceptable solution.[122]

Subsequent remarks by a number of UAE officials indicated that progress on agreement had not yet been attained. In early September 2002, Ras al-Khaimah's Shaikh Khalid called on Iran "to return those islands to their normal status."[123] On September 20, Rashid Abdullah's remarks to the 57th session of the UN General Assembly reiterated the UAE's call for Iran to resolve the islands dispute through bilateral negotiations or at the ICJ, and reaffirmed:

> The UAE has complete sovereignty over our three islands, including their air space, regional waters, continental shelf and the economic region related to the three islands, which are an integral part of the UAE.[124]

In early October, Shaikh Zayed told Egypt's *Al-Ahram* that he hoped for serious bilateral negotiation with Iran on this issue, clearly suggesting that substantive agreement had not yet been reached.[125]

Shaikh Hamdan told the Kuwaiti paper *Al-Siyassah* in early December that he had found "great understanding" by the Iranian leaders and that he was "looking forward to a lasting settlement of all outstanding issues to serve the interests of both sides as this will reflect positively on all countries of the region...I am optimistic about such a settlement and my optimism has strong reasons and justifications."[126] However, Khatami did not make the trip to the UAE in December 2002 or in the months thereafter, and no agreement was announced or implemented. Instead, Iran's Deputy Foreign Minister for Arab-African Affairs, Mohammed Sadr, traveled to Abu Dhabi in mid-January 2003 to meet with Shaikh Khalifa and Shaikh Hamdan and to deliver a message from Khatami to Shaikh Zayed.[127] The message appeared to include no new proposal or forward movement.

As of early 2003, Iran's position on the islands remains a source of concern to the UAE and the Arab world, as well as to other external powers. The election of a new president in Iran and his re-election in 2001, had not led to any real progress on the islands issue. Iran has publicly expressed a willingness to negotiate, but no progress has been made in private meetings like those held during Kamal Kharrazi's visit to the UAE in May 1998 or Shaikh Hamdan's visits to Tehran in July 2001 and May 2002. Indeed, Iran's militarization of the islands and the conducting of military exercises around the islands have continued.

In conclusion, the historical record affirms the rightful title of Sharjah and Ras al-Khaimah, and now the UAE, to Abu Musa and the Tunbs. When the British arrived in the Gulf and engaged in a confrontation with the Qawasim in the early 1800s, they did not have much knowledge or sympathy for this issue. However, by the time Persia first made its claims to the islands in the late 1800s and early 1900s, the British understood that these claims were not valid. Indeed, the British defended the Arab rights to these islands into the post-

World War II era. Later, when Britain recognized the strategic importance of Iran, and particularly the role the Shah could play after a British withdrawal from the Gulf, Britain sought ways and means to satisfy Iranian interests in the islands. As Britain's 1971 withdrawal neared, this realization led to British pressure on Sharjah and Ras al-Khaimah to heed Iranian threats and to accommodate Iranian demands. This eventually resulted in the MoU on Abu Musa and the Iranian seizure of the Tunbs. While radical Arab states called for punitive measures against Iran and Britain, conservative Arab states, also recognizing Iran's strategic importance, sought a mediated resolution of the dispute. However, Iran remained unreceptive to all such efforts.

When the Iranian revolution swept the Shah from power in 1979 and was followed by war with Iraq from 1980 to 1988, it became clear that Iran's control of the islands was not a strategic advantage, but a threat. Iran used the islands to attack international shipping during these years, something that it could do again in the future. When Iran consolidated its administrative grip on the islands in the early 1990s, the UAE intensified its calls for a diplomatic or legal resolution of this dispute and was supported by its GCC partners, the Arab world and, subsequently, by the United States and Britain. Iran reacted with threats, with increased fortification of the islands, with extensive military exercises around and on the islands, and with a rigid unwillingness to discuss anything more than the MoU on Abu Musa. This has been the case even under the reformist President Khatami.

Inasmuch as strategic considerations have taken precedence over historical and legal rights, and inasmuch as these strategic considerations have backfired with the Iranian Revolution, it is appropriate to emphasize the legal arguments that flow from the historical record. This will be the focus of the next chapter.

PART
II

LEGAL AND STRATEGIC
PERSPECTIVES

A Legal Perspective
on the Islands Issue

Following a detailed examination of the historical record, a closer look at the legal conclusions that may be drawn from this record is warranted. This entails a consideration of the legal evidence that has been provided by the UAE and by Iran in light of the international legal principles and cases that are most applicable in deciding contending claims to sovereignty. It also includes an evaluation of the behavior of the UAE and Iran, and whether such behavior is in conformity with or in violation of international law. Finally, this chapter examines the methods and procedures available under international law for the resolution of such disputes.[1]

It should be pointed out that the constitution of the United Arab Emirates, a fully independent sovereign federal state established on December 2, 1971, states that the federal government or "Union" is responsible for foreign policy, security and defense. The constitution further notes that "the Union shall exercise sovereignty in matters assigned to it, in accordance with this Constitution, over all territory and territorial waters laying within the international boundaries of the individual Emirates," adding that "the member Emirates shall exercise sovereignty over their own territories and territorial waters in all matters which are not within the jurisdiction of the Union as assigned in this Constitution." Both Sharjah and Ras al-Khaimah agreed that the new federal state would have the ultimate responsibility for asserting, negotiating and defending their rights to Abu Musa and the Tunbs, although it is accepted that consultations should precede the conclusion of any agreement or treaty that affects the two emirates. Also, the individual emirates retain the rights to their own natural resources and wealth on and around the islands.[2]

The UAE's Legal Claim

The basic international legal principles upon which territorial sovereignty has generally been acquired and claimed are: *prescription* or *title founded on long and peaceful possession*; *historical consolidation of title*; *accretion*; *contiguity*; *cession*; *occupation*; and *conquest*.[3] The basic rulings of cases like the 1928 *Island of Palmas Case* (United States v. The Netherlands); the 1933 *Legal Status of Eastern Greenland Case* (Denmark v. Norway); the 1953 *Minquiers and Ecrehos Case* (France v. United Kingdom); and the 1975 *Western Sahara Case* (Morocco v. Spain) explain the weight and acceptability of each of these principles. These principles and cases will thus be considered at appropriate points in evaluating the legal claims of the UAE and opposing claims by Iran to Abu Musa and the Tunb islands.

Sharjah and Ras al-Khaimah have presented considerable documentary legal evidence supporting their respective titles since the first known written claim of the Qawasim Ruler Sultan bin Saqr in 1864. A report prepared by the Anglo-American legal team of M.E. Bathurst, Northcutt Ely and the firm Coward Chance in 1971 entitled *Sharjah's Title To The Island Of Abu Musa*, which was commissioned by the Ruler of Sharjah, presented numerous official documents establishing the legal claim of Sharjah to Abu Musa. In addition, hundreds of documents in a 1980 report, entitled *Territorial Sovereignty Over the Tunb Islands*, prepared by the Houston, Texas law firm of Vinson and Elkins, and commissioned by the Ruler of Ras al-Khaimah, similarly established the legal claim of Ras al-Khaimah to the Tunbs. The report included eighteen documents that the Ruler submitted to the Arab League in 1971. These and many other supporting documents are also found in the Arabian Geopolitics Series *The Lower Gulf Islands: Abu Musa and the Tunbs*. Taken together, they provide legal evidence of the use, presence, administration and display of authority of the Qawasim of Sharjah and Ras al-Khaimah on Abu Musa and the Tunbs from the early and mid-1700s onwards.[4]

Prescription

As the historical evidence shows, the Qawasim of Sharjah and Ras al-Khaimah used, possessed and exercised authority over Abu Musa and the Tunbs in a peaceful manner since the early and mid-1700s. This enables them and the UAE to claim their legal title to the islands on the basis of the principle of *prescription* or *title founded on long and peaceful possession*. As J. Brierly wrote in *The Law of Nations*, "long possession may operate either to confirm the existence of a title the precise origin of which cannot be shown or to extinguish the prior title of another sovereign."[5]

While there is no deed or treaty to show the precise origin of the Qawasim title to the islands, this title does date from the early and mid-1700s. In 1864, the paramount Ruler of the Qawasim tribe, Shaikh Sultan bin Saqr (1803-1866), who had earlier been based in Ras al-Khaimah and who was now based in Sharjah, asserted in his letter to British Political Resident Pelly that Abu Musa and the Greater Tunb had belonged to his family for generations. This would date the use and possession of the islands by the Qawasim tribe and the tribes that were loyal to them from the early and mid-1700s, when the Qawasim military commander Rahma bin Matar established his hold in and around Ras al-Khaimah and then later in and around Lingeh.

Between 1801 and 1809, the British recognized Shaikh Sultan bin Saqr to be the ruler of his dependents and subjects on both the Arab and Persian coasts. The British knew that the inhabitants of these coasts were undisturbed in their use and possession of these islands, and particularly that pearlers from Ras al-Khaimah used the Greater Tunb. There is also evidence available showing that the islands were used by and belonged to the tribes of the Arab coast long before the early and mid-1700s, at least from the early and mid-1600s. Indeed, it may have been the Qawasim who ruled these tribes during this time. Even earlier, the Greater Tunb was inhabited by Arabs and part of the Arab-ruled Kingdom of Hormuz in the early 1500s and probably in the 1400s. As a result, even if there were any prior Persian title, it would have been extinguished by such long possession by Arabs. However, as this chapter will show, there was no prior Persian title to be extinguished.

The Qawasim use and possession of the islands was peaceful and uninterrupted from the mid-1700s, after Nadir Shah's brief presence on the Arab coast, until 1971. There was some quarreling among the Qawasim about the use of these islands, but by at least 1835, this was resolved by an agreement to apportion the islands for the use of different branches of the family and their dependents. Abu Musa and the Greater Tunb were allocated to the paramount branch of the family at Sharjah and Ras al-Khaimah with Sirri designated for the subordinate branch of the family at Lingeh.[6]

When Ras al-Khaimah split from Sharjah in 1868, the Greater Tunb went to Ras al-Khaimah and Abu Musa went to Sharjah. There were some infringements of Sharjah's authority on Abu Musa in the 1870s by tribes from other emirates as well as from Lingeh, but this did not break the chain of possession. Ras al-Khaimah's authority on the Greater Tunb was also encroached upon by dependents of the Lingeh Qawasim in the 1870s and 1880s, but this was resolved peacefully. Episodic challenges by Persia/Iran to Ras al-Khaimah's authority over the Tunbs and also to Sharjah's authority over Abu Musa only occurred from 1887 until 1971, but these were infrequent, brief and ineffective.

In particular, the evidence makes it clear that before, during and after the years from 1878 until 1887, when the Qawasim Rulers of Lingeh acted as Persian officials, Abu Musa was subject to the sovereignty of the Ruler of Sharjah, not the Ruler of Lingeh. Coward Chance and Associates wrote in 1971:

> It is wrong to assume or suggest that the case of Tunb (which seems to have been subject to some form of joint administration from Ras al-Khaimah and Lingeh) and the case of Sirri (which was occupied by Persian forces in 1887) are the same as that of Abu Musa, which has always been in the exclusive possession and administration of the Ruler of Sharjah in his own right.[7]

This quotation demonstrates that the evidence on the Tunbs is not quite as clear as the evidence on Abu Musa. However, careful examination of the evidence shows that the Greater Tunb was also before, during and after the period from 1878 to 1887 subject to the sovereignty of the Qawasim Rulers of the Arab Coast. By the agreement reached before 1835, the Greater Tunb was reserved for the possession and administration of the Ruler of Sharjah and Ras al-Khaimah, along with Abu Musa and Sir Abu Nuair. This is established by the letter from Shaikh Sultan bin Saqr to British Political Resident Pelly in 1864. Shaikh Sultan, who with his son Shaikh Khalid bin Sultan actually ruled Lingeh in the mid-1850s, consented to the use of the Greater Tunb for the grazing of animals by dependents of the Qawasim of Lingeh. When Shaikh Sultan died and the Greater Tunb passed to the Ruler of Ras al-Khaimah, the new ruler reasserted the right of the Qawasim of the Arab Coast to the Greater Tunb and demanded an end to the use of the island by the dependents of the Lingeh Qawasim.

The Ruler of Ras al-Khaimah's right to prohibit others from using the island and the status of the island as his territory was acknowledged by three successive Rulers of Lingeh in three letters to him. Two of these letters were written before the Qawasim rulers of Lingeh became officials of Persia in 1878 and one of them was written afterwards.[8] In this context, Vinson and Elkins wrote that "although the Lingah shaikhs may have administered some of the affairs concerning Great Tunb, (i.e. the use of the island for grazing animals) they did so with the knowledge and consent of the rulers of the Trucial Coast Qawasim, the primary owners of the island as paramount shaikhs of the Qawasim family."[9]

In *The Law of Nations*, Brierly has written that "Possession of territory consists in the exercise or display of state authority in or in regard to the territory in question." Indeed, as he notes, the ruling of the *Island of Palmas Case* recognized the title of the Netherlands to that island based on its "continuous and peaceful display of State authority." Similarly, the *Eastern Greenland Case* recognized the title of Denmark to Greenland based on "the peaceful and continuous display of State authority over the island."[10]

There is evidence of a significant display of state authority by the Qawasim Rulers of Sharjah and Ras al-Khaimah over Abu Musa and the Tunbs. These Rulers historically collected fees for the economic activities carried out by the residents of the islands, such as pearl diving, fishing and herding. Pearlers and others using the islands paid fees to the paramount Qawasim Rulers in Sharjah and Ras al-Khaimah in the early 1800s and almost certainly from the time of the Qawasim Ruler Rahma bin Matar in the 1700s. Indeed, pearlers operating from Julfar in the mid-1600s may have used the islands and must have paid fees to the Arab shaikhs of Julfar. Moreover, merchants on the Greater Tunb paid taxes and trading vessels using the island paid customs duties to the

Arab rulers of the Kingdom of Hormuz in the early 1500s and probably even earlier.

The Rulers of Sharjah and Ras al-Khaimah also lodged complaints to British officials responsible for the foreign affairs of the Trucial States when their rights to the islands were challenged in the 1860s, 1870s and 1880s. On one occasion, the Ruler of Sharjah fired on boats unauthorized to use Abu Musa. The laws, regulations and customs of Sharjah and Ras al-Khaimah were followed on the islands, and the residents of the islands were subjects and citizens of the two emirates. Upon advice from the British and in order to substantiate his claim, the Ruler of Sharjah raised the Qawasim flag over Abu Musa in 1903, as well as over the Greater Tunb, which he had temporarily inherited after the death of the Ruler of Ras al-Khaimah in 1900. When Persia lowered the Qawasim flags on these islands and raised its own in 1904, the Ruler of Sharjah protested sharply. Qawasim flags were immediately restored after Persia was persuaded by the British to lower its flags.

The Rulers and their representatives were generally present on the islands since the 1800s and must have made periodic visits long before this time. Shaikh Salim bin Sultan of Sharjah maintained a house on Abu Musa in the 1870s and retired to it when he was overthrown in 1883. Representatives of the Rulers raised flags on Abu Musa and the Tunbs in 1903 and 1904 and regularly thereafter. They also typically resided on the islands in the 1900s.

The Rulers also granted economic concessions on the islands to third parties. In 1898, Shaikh Salim, acting as the representative of his successor, Shaikh Saqr bin Khalid, granted a concession to mine for red oxide on Abu Musa. Subsequent Rulers of Sharjah also granted red oxide mining concessions on Abu Musa in 1923 and 1935. Concessions were given to explore for oil and gas on Abu Musa and in its territorial waters to the Petroleum Company, Inc. in 1937, to the Mecomoil Company in 1962 and to the Buttes Gas and Oil Company in 1970. In 1912, Shaikh Khalid of Sharjah, who was ruling Ras al-Khaimah too, granted permission for the building of a lighthouse on the Greater Tunb. Rulers of Ras al-Khaimah also granted concessions in and around the Tunbs to third parties, notably a red oxide concession in 1953 and oil and gas concessions in 1964.

The Rulers of Sharjah and Ral al-Khaimah collected revenues for the working of these concessions. They also established public utilities such as schools on the islands of Abu Musa and Greater Tunb. The Lesser Tunb had no such utilities because of its small size, the lack of fresh water resources and the paucity of inhabitants. However, this island was under the supervision of Ras al-Khaimah's representative on the Greater Tunb, who made periodic visits to the Lesser Tunb.[11]

The recognition of the sovereignty of the Qawasim of Sharjah and Ras al-Khaimah over Abu Musa and the Tunbs by British officials constitutes further evidence in support of the emirates' historical possession of these islands. From the early 1800s, the British considered the paramount Qawasim Ruler, then based at Ras al-Khaimah and later based in Sharjah, to be the ruler of his dependents and subjects on both the Arab and Persian coasts and it was recognized that these dependents, especially those on the Arab coast, used the islands. Sharjah's right to Abu Musa was frequently asserted, defended and exercised on behalf of the Qawasim of Sharjah by British officials from the late 1860s and early 1870s until 1971. British officials knew that the Ruler of Sharjah had traditionally used Abu Musa and consistently defended Sharjah's title against challenges by other emirates and later by Persia/Iran.

Moreover, Ras al-Khaimah's right to the Tunbs was similarly defended on behalf of the Qawasim of Ras al-Khaimah by British officials from the 1880s until 1971. Initially, after the British naval expedition against the Qawasim of Ras al-Khaimah in 1819 and 1820, and following the British prohibitions against Qawasim warboats from Ras al-Khaimah and Sharjah approaching Abu Musa and the Tunbs after 1835-1836, the British Admiralty mistakenly thought in the late 1850s and early 1860s that the Ruler of Lingeh had authority over the Greater Tunb. During the 1860s and 1870s, British officials in the Gulf were also misinformed by a Native Agent that the Greater Tunb was under the authority of the Lingeh Qawasim. However, British officials began to believe in the 1880s that the island was co-owned and jointly administered by the Lingeh Qawasim and the Ras al-Khaimah Qawasim and they asserted the Qawasim family title to the Greater Tunb against Persian claims from 1887 onwards, following the occupation of Lingeh by Persia. Indeed, the British argued that the Lingeh Qawasim had administered Sirri and the Greater Tunb as members of the Qawasim tribe, not as Persian officials.

British recognition continued in the twentieth century. The British involvement in the flags incidents of 1903 and 1904 has already been mentioned. In 1908, the British recognized the Lesser Tunb as belonging to Sharjah, which still had temporary authority over Ras al-Khaimah. During Anglo-German legal proceedings from 1907 to 1914, the British defended the right of the Ruler of Sharjah to cancel the share in the Abu Musa red oxide concession purchased by German businessman Robert Wonkhaus. When the Ruler of Sharjah agreed to the building of a lighthouse on the Greater Tunb in 1912, the British assured him that "your sovereignty over the Island is recognized."

In 1921, when Ras al-Khaimah re-established its independence from Sharjah, the British recognized the sovereignty of Ras al-Khaimah over the Tunbs and the sovereignty of Sharjah over Abu Musa. They advised the Ruler of Ras al-Khaimah to continue flying his flag over the Greater Tunb in early 1935 and again in 1957 and 1963. In 1949, after learning that a Persian flag had been raised on the Lesser Tunb, the British removed it. They assisted in erecting a plaque on the Lesser Tunb stating the Ras al-Khaimah title in 1958 and advised that the Ruler's representative on the Greater Tunb visit the island periodically and fly the flag over the island. They also helped to replace the Ras al-Khaimah flag on the Lesser Tunb after it was pulled down by the Iranians in 1963. The British advised the Ruler of Sharjah to continue flying his flag over Abu Musa in 1957 and 1963, and they helped to remove an Iranian light buoy from the waters of Abu Musa in 1964.

The British protested Persian behavior whenever necessary, even threatening to use naval force to defend the rights of the Rulers of Sharjah and Ras al-Khaimah in 1925, 1928 and 1934. They defended Qawasim rights whenever necessary, rejecting Persian claims to the islands during the negotiations for a general Anglo-Persian treaty from 1929 to 1935 and also after World War II, particularly during the early and mid-1960s, when Britain repeatedly asserted Sharjah's and Ras al-Khaimah's sovereignty over the islands.

It may also be argued that acquiescence in the sovereignty of the Sharjah and Ras al-Khaimah Qawasim over Abu Musa and the Tunbs constitutes evidence in support of Sharjah's and Ras al-Khaimah's historic possession of these islands. Persia acquiesced to the *status quo* on these islands from the mid-eighteenth century until the late nineteenth and early twentieth century, i.e. for about one hundred and fifty years. Persia had no navy and had little authority on its coast during this time, and therefore no ability to press any claim. Nevertheless, Persia did not make any specific claim to these islands during this time. Aside from a general claim to all of the islands in the entire Gulf in 1840, Persia did not begin to assert any specific right to the Tunbs until the late nineteenth century or to Abu Musa until the early twentieth century, and its assertions over the following decades were relatively infrequent.

Persian claims to the Greater Tunb were not made until 1888, after Persia had raised its flag on Sirri the previous year. Persia also made claims in 1904 during the flags incident and in the context of the Anglo-Persian negotiations for a general treaty from 1928-1935. The British refusal to recognize Persia's claims to the islands was in fact a major reason for the breakdown of the talks.[12] Following World War II, Iranian assertions of a right to the Tunbs became more frequent, although these claims were never accepted by the British.

Persia's first assertion of a claim to Abu Musa did not occur until the 1904 flags incident. During the Anglo-Persian negotiations from 1928 to 1935, Persia again declared a right to Abu Musa, although it became apparent that it considered this claim to be weaker than the claim to the Greater Tunb. Just as in the case of the Greater Tunb, the claims to Abu Musa increased in frequency throughout the post-World War II years.[13] Iran's more frequent claims to these islands, however, should be seen in the context of the exploration for and discovery of oil in the Gulf, as the Rulers of Sharjah and Ras al-Khaimah were granting concessions for oil exploration on and around the islands, and as questions about maritime boundaries in the Gulf were being considered.

It is most significant that Persia/Iran has not been able to produce good legal evidence to support its claims. The letters Persia produced in the case of the Greater Tunb after the 1887 incident on Sirri provide no evidence of Persian officials collecting any taxes from the Greater Tunb and no evidence of any other kind. When the British requested supporting documentation after the 1904 flag incidents, Persia did not respond. Instead, in the late 1940s and 1950s, Iran repeatedly misrepresented the outcome of the 1904 incident as "evidence" in its favor. Subsequent

Iranian promises to provide documents to the British and the Americans during the 1950s and 1960s were not kept. Iran did not even present documents at the UN Security Council discussion in December 1971, except to refer to maps that will be discussed below. All in all, Persia/Iran has generally taken a dismissive attitude to requests for evidence during the past one hundred years.

Furthermore, Persia/Iran protested relatively infrequently and ineffectively to the display of state authority on Abu Musa and the Tunbs by Sharjah and Ras al-Khaimah during the entire period from 1904 until 1970. While Persia did lower the Qawasim flags on Abu Musa and the Greater Tunb in 1904 and raised its own, the action was soon reversed and the Persians withdrew. The same sequence of events occurred in the case of the Ras al-Khaimah flag on the Lesser Tunb in 1963. Bathurst, Ely and Chance wrote in 1971 that their research had not revealed any protest made by Iran at the working of the mineral concessions in and around Abu Musa other than one made in 1970.

Official British Foreign Office and US State Department documents made available since the release of their study do show a record of additional protests, but these were still infrequent and ineffective. There is no record of a Persian protest about the 1898 red oxide concession on Abu Musa, but Persia protested the red oxide concessions granted by the Ruler of Sharjah in 1923 and in 1935, the activities of the oil concessionaire off the coast of Abu Musa in 1963 and the oil and gas concession activities off the coast of Abu Musa by the Occidental Company in 1970. In the case of the Tunbs, there was substantially less concession activity and, as a result, less protest by Persia. Persia raised the issue of the lighthouse on the Greater Tunb in 1912, noting that the island was contested, but took no formal action. There is no record of an Iranian protest at the Ruler of Ras al-Khaimah's granting of a red oxide concession in 1953 or to oil concessions granted to the Union Oil Exploration and Production Company and the Southern Natural Gas Company in 1964.

Vinson and Elkins have argued that "Persia's infrequent and indecisive protests to the British about such state activity [by Ras al-Khaimah on the Tunbs] do not nullify the value of Ras al-Khaimah's acts as manifestations of sovereignty, although such protests arguably may have served to prevent Persia's claim from lapsing by tacit abandonment."[14] Furthermore, they write:

An argument can be advanced, however, that Persia's diplomatic protests were insufficient to overcome the presumption of Persia's tacit acquiescence in Ras al-Khaimah's display of state activity on the Islands. Arguably, other action such as reference of the matter to international adjudication should have been taken by Persia in an attempt to resolve the dispute. The failure to take such action when such action was called for should have a detrimental effect on Persia's legal position and may provide evidence of non-existence of sovereignty due to acquiescence in or admission of the validity of Ras al-Khaimah's claim to the Islands.[15]

Persia's protests regarding Abu Musa's display of state authority were slightly more frequent, but they were similarly ineffective. While these protests may have prevented Persia's claim to Abu Musa from lapsing, they may also be insufficient to overcome the presumption of Persian acquiescence in Sharjah's display of state activity on Abu Musa, again due in part to Persia's failure to submit the matter to international adjudication or arbitration.[16]

Persia/Iran has also contradicted its claims and protests through its own conduct, in particular, by offering periodically to buy or lease the Tunbs from Ras al-Khaimah. Persia submitted a proposal through the British in 1930 to the Ruler of Ras al-Khaimah to lease the Greater Tunb for a period of fifty years. In 1934, the British heard rumors of direct Persian offers to buy or lease the Greater Tunb. In an interview, the Ruler of Ras al-Khaimah has said that the Shah made direct offers to him of financial inducements for the Tunbs in private meetings in Tehran in the years before Sir William Luce began his shuttling in 1970-1971.[17] The Shah also offered financial compensation to Sharjah for Abu Musa and to Ras al-Khaimah for the Tunbs in April 1970 and again in 1971.

These proposals suggest that Persia/Iran recognized the strength of the claims of Sharjah and Ras al-Khaimah while considering its own claims to be weak. In turn, these Persian/Iranian offers may warrant the application of the principle of *estoppel*, which stipulates that if a party, by words or deeds, makes a "conclusive admission" that contradicts its claims, then it should be stopped or precluded or barred from continuing to make its claims.[18]

Historical Consolidation of Title

In addition to the legal principle of *prescription*, the UAE can also claim sovereignty over the three islands on the basis of *historical consolidation of title*, a concept and approach advocated by former Judge and President of both the Permanent Court of International Justice and the International Court of Justice Charles de Visscher. The concept of the historical consolidation of title usefully encompasses the various factors which create an historic title, i.e. a title that, in the words of Y.Z. Blum's *Historic Titles in International Law*, is "the outcome of a lengthy process comprising a long series of acts, omissions and patterns of behavior which, in their entirety, and through their cumulative effect, bring such a title into being and <u>consolidate</u> it into a title valid in international law." Blum adds that such title is distinguished from others such as cession or conquest, which "rest on an instantaneous act having an immediate effect."[19]

Robert Jennings wrote in *The Acquisition of Territory in International Law* that de Visscher's work is important because it provides "a penetrating and illuminating observation of the way Courts actually tackle questions of title to territorial sovereignty."[20] Judge de Visscher himself wrote in *Theory and Reality in Public International Law*:

> This consolidation, which may have practical importance for territories not yet finally organized under a State regime as well as for certain stretches of sea-like bays, is not subject to the conditions specifically required in other modes of acquiring territories. Proven long use, which is its foundation, merely represents a complex of interests and relations which in themselves have the effect of attaching a territory or an expanse of sea to a given State. It is these interests and relations, varying from one case to another, and not the passage of a fixed term, unknown in any event to international law, that are taken into direct account by the Judge to decide <u>in concreto</u> on the existence or non-existence of a consolidation by historic titles...
>
> In this respect such consolidation differs from acquisitive prescription properly so-called, as also in the fact that it can apply to territories that could not be proved to have belonged formerly to another State. It differs from occupation in that it

can be admitted in relation to certain parts of the sea as well as on land. Finally, it is distinguished from international recognition - and this is the point of most practical importance - by the fact that it can be held to be accomplished not only by acquiescence so-called, acquiescence in which the time factor can have no part, but more easily by a sufficiently prolonged absence of opposition either, in the case of land, on the part of the States interested in disputing possession or, in maritime waters, on the part of the generality of States.[21]

Bathurst, Ely and Chance argue in their legal opinion that this concept is relevant in the case of Abu Musa. It can also be argued that it applies to the Tunbs islands. A closer examination will show why.

The island of Abu Musa was "not yet finally organized under a State regime" during the early stage of possession by the Qawasim of Ras al-Khaimah and Sharjah, although, as Bathurst, Ely and Chance argue, in the later stage Sharjah was a sovereign state.[22] Certainly "proven long use" has been documented and can be said to have attached the island to Sharjah. Indeed, Bathurst, Ely and Chance wrote:

> The most important component of the historical consolidation of title remains continuous peaceful possession. There can be no doubt but that Sharjah's possession of Abu Musa has been peaceful...Nor can there be doubt that, apart from the fleeting Iranian visits already alluded to, Sharjah's possession has been continuous.[23]

Moreover, the island had not "belonged" to and had not been steadily governed by Persia. As such, the Qawasim title was not acquired from Persia prior to the peaceful exercise of authority by the Qawasim in the early to mid-eighteenth century. Instead, there was a "prolonged absence of opposition" by Persia and any other neighboring state to the exercise of sovereignty by the Qawasim. This was certainly true from the mid-eighteenth century until the early twentieth century, when there was virtually no opposition at all. Indeed, Persian behavior could be called "acquiescence." From the early twentieth century, Persian opposition was infrequent and ineffective. Bathurst, Ely and Chance wrote in 1971:

> The de facto position is that Sharjah occupies and administers the island and Iran has never done so, the only Iranian

167

visitations to the island in 1904, 1925 and perhaps in 1964 being short-lived and subsequently either repudiated or denied by Iran.[24]

It should be added here that Iran landed a naval party on Abu Musa in 1951, but not in 1964.

Similar facts and arguments make this concept pertinent in the case of the Tunbs. The Tunbs also were not "finally organized under a state regime" during the early stage of possession by the Qawasim of Ras al-Khaimah and Sharjah, although Ras al-Khaimah was a sovereign state during the later stage. "Proven long use" attached the Tunbs to Ras al-Khaimah with Ras al-Khaimah's possession being peaceful and continuous, despite the rare visits and intermittent claims by Iran. The Tunbs had not "belonged" to or been steadily governed by Persia before the peaceful exercise of authority by the Qawasim in the early to mid-eighteenth century. There was "acquiescence" or at least a "prolonged absence of opposition" by Persia to this exercise of authority by the Qawasim from the mid-eighteenth century until the late nineteenth/early twentieth century. Persian/Iranian opposition in the twentieth century was infrequent and ineffective. Prior to 1971, Ras al-Khaimah occupied and administered the Tunb islands. Persia's only visits to the Greater Tunb took place in 1904, 1933 and 1934, with a possible Iranian visit in 1961, and Iran's only visits to the Lesser Tunb occurred in 1949 and 1963.

As previously stated, possession involves the display of state authority. The *Island of Palmas* case and the *Eastern Greenland* case should be considered on this point. Judge Huber wrote in the *Island of Palmas* case:

> Manifestations of territorial sovereignty assume, it is true, different forms, according to conditions of time and place. Although continuous in principle, sovereignty cannot be exercised in fact at every moment on every point of a territory. The intermittence and discontinuity compatible with the maintenance of the right necessarily differ according as inhabited or uninhabited regions are involved, or regions enclosed within territories in which sovereignty is incontestably displayed, or again regions accessible from, for instance the high seas.

As a result, he ruled in favor of the Netherlands, although he observed: "The acts of indirect or direct display of Netherlands sovereignty at Palmas (or Miangas), especially in the 18th and early 19th centuries are not numerous, and there are considerable gaps in the evidence of continuous display." Judge Huber ruled this way partly because of "the consideration that the manifestations of sovereignty over a small and distant island, inhabited only by natives, cannot be expected to be frequent..."[25]

Similarly, when the Permanent Court of Justice ruled in favor of Denmark over Norway in the *Eastern Greenland* case, the Court noted:

> It is impossible to read the records of the decisions in cases as to territorial sovereignty without observing that in many cases the tribunal has been satisfied with very little in the way of the actual exercise of sovereign rights, provided that the other state could not make out a superior claim. This is particularly true in the case of claims to sovereignty over areas in thinly populated or unsettled countries.[26]

Quoting Sir Humphrey Waldock's "Disputed Sovereignty in the Falkland Islands Dependencies," Bathurst, Ely and Chance wrote in 1971:

> In assessing Sharjah's assertion of actual authority over Abu Musa, one must remember that, as with the occupation of sparsely inhabited territory when it is taken into sovereignty, a state, in order to keep its claim to sovereignty alive, is not necessarily 'required to maintain even a single official permanently on the spot. It is enough if the state displays the functions of a state in a manner corresponding to the circumstances of the territory, assumes the responsibility to exercise local administration and does so in fact as and when occasion demands.'[27]

They further argue:

> Sharjah's long-continued possession of Abu Musa more than satisfies these requirements for, in the circumstances of that island, there can be little doubt that the title of Sharjah was (to use the words of Hall, *International Law*, 6th edition, p. 103) 'kept alive by repeated local acts showing an intention of continual claim.' Iran on the other hand is unable to show anything more than a momentary possession and that not peaceable.[28]

The circumstances of the islands were such that Abu Musa and the two Tunbs were sparsely inhabited from the fall of the Arab-ruled

Kingdom of Hormuz in the early seventeenth century until the late nineteenth century, and generally on a seasonal basis. They remained sparsely inhabited during the twentieth century, although now on a year-long basis. Sharjah and Ras al-Khaimah have each displayed the functions of a state in a manner corresponding to the circumstances of the islands. They have assumed the responsibility to exercise local administration, and have done so in fact as and when occasion has demanded. Their title has been kept alive by repeated local acts showing the intention of continual claim. Iran, meanwhile, has not been able to show anything other than momentary possession that was not peaceable.

For example, Sharjah displayed the functions of a state by collecting dues from pearlers that used the islands from at least the 1820s, when Sharjah became the seat of Qawasim authority. Sharjah repeatedly protested the use of Abu Musa by Dubai and Lingeh in the 1860s and 1870s, requesting British assistance so as not to have to disturb the peace at sea, and actually firing on boats from Dubai and Lingeh in 1873. Sharjah granted economic concessions on and around Abu Musa from as early as 1898 through the 1960s. Sharjah flew its flag on Abu Musa in 1903, protested when it was lowered by Persia in 1904, and raised its flag again when the crisis was over. Moreover, Sharjah kept officials on Abu Musa from as early as 1904.

Ras al-Khaimah collected revenues from pearlers using the Greater Tunb in the early years of the 1800s and probably even earlier, in the 1700s, when the emirate was the seat of Qawasim authority. Ras al-Khaimah repeatedly protested the use of the Greater Tunb by dependents of the Qawasim of Lingeh in the 1870s and 1880s and requested British assistance during these years. When it had temporary authority over Ras al-Khaimah, Sharjah raised the Qawasim flag over the Greater Tunb in 1903, protested when it was lowered by Persia in 1904, and raised the flag again in the same year.

Sharjah also reached an agreement with Britain for a lighthouse on the Greater Tunb in 1912. While Ras al-Khaimah did lower its flag on the Greater Tunb in 1934, this was only done in order to pressure Britain to pay rent for the lighthouse, and the flag was raised again in 1935. Ras al-Khaimah granted economic concessions on and around the Tunbs from 1937 through the 1960s. Sharjah and Ras al-Khaimah kept officials on the Greater Tunb from as early as 1904. Ras al-Khaimah also erected a plaque on the Lesser Tunb in 1958. The island was under the supervision of the representative of Ras al-Khaimah on the Greater Tunb, who made periodic visits to the Lesser Tunb.

Moreover, as noted earlier, the laws, regulations and customs of Sharjah and Ras al-Khaimah were followed on the islands, and the residents of the islands were subjects and citizens of the two emirates. Abu Musa and the Greater Tunb had public utilities that belonged to the emirates of Sharjah and Ras al-Khaimah, although the Lesser Tunb did not. Even if all this were regarded as very little in the way of the actual exercise of sovereign rights, Iran cannot make out a superior claim. Iran has not provided any evidence that would substantiate the exercise of sovereignty, e.g. the collection of taxes, on the islands.[29]

Robert Jennings has written in *The Acquisition of Territory in International Law* that the concept of historic consolidation involves a shift in which factors like recognition, acquiescence and estoppel are not only evidence of sovereign possession of territory by a state, but are "themselves decisive ingredients in the process of creating title."[30] Thus, Britain's repeated assertions and consistent defense of the rightful title of the Qawasim of Sharjah and Ras al-Khaimah to Abu Musa and the Tunbs are more than evidence, and constituted part of the process of consolidating that title.

Similarly, the long period of acquiescence to the *status quo* by Persia, the pattern of infrequent and ineffective Persian protests, and the failure of Persia to submit the matter to international arbitration or adjudication are not just evidence, but also part of the process of consolidating the title of Sharjah and Ras al-Khaimah to the islands. The same can be said of the Persian/Iranian financial offers for the islands. To put this point in the vocabulary of Y.Z. Blum, in the fabric of "acts, omissions, and patterns of behavior" that created and consolidated the title of Sharjah and Ras al-Khaimah to the islands, it is important to note the telling acts by Persia in offering to lease the Greater Tunb in 1930 and by Iran in offering financial compensation for Abu Musa and the Tunbs in the late 1960s, 1970 and 1971; the glaring omissions by Persia and Iran in failing to submit the dispute over these islands to international arbitration or adjudication and the refusal of all requests by the UAE to do so; and even the pattern of infrequent and ineffective claims and protests.

Iran's Presence on the Islands

Before looking at how these same legal principles and others apply to the Iranian claims, it is relevant here to look at the legal nature of Iran's actions in 1971, including its occupation of the Tunb islands and the Memorandum of Understanding signed with Sharjah concerning Abu Musa.

Iran's Use of Force and International Law

Iran's occupation by force of the Greater and Lesser Tunbs on November 30, 1971 clearly constitutes a violation of the twentieth century legal principle requiring states to refrain from the threat or use of force to acquire territory. It is a violation of the United Nations Charter, particularly Article 1, paragraph 1, and Article 2, paragraphs 3 and 4, which oblige members of the United Nations to "settle their international disputes by peaceful means in such a manner that international peace and security, and justice, are not endangered" and to "refrain in their international relations from the threat or use of force against the territorial integrity or political independence of any state, or in any other manner inconsistent with the Purposes of the United Nations." It is also a violation of Article 33 of the Charter, which states:

> The parties to any dispute, the continuance of which is likely to endanger the maintenance of international peace and security, shall, first of all, seek a solution by negotiation, enquiry, mediation, conciliation, arbitration, judicial settlement, resort to regional agencies or arrangements, or other peaceful means of their own choice.[31]

The threat and use of force to acquire rights and privileges is also prohibited by General Assembly resolution 2625 of 1970, entitled "Declaration On Principles Of International Law Concerning Friendly Relations and Co-operation Among States in Accordance with the Charter of the United Nations" and by General Assembly Resolution 3314 of 1974, entitled "Definition of Aggression."[32] Resolution 2625 proclaims: "Every State has the duty to refrain from the threat or use of force to violate the existing international boundaries of another State or as a means of solving international disputes, including territorial disputes and problems concerning frontiers of States." The resolution also states:

> The territory of a State shall not be the object of military occupation resulting from the use of force in contravention of the provisions of the Charter. The territory of a State shall not be the object of acquisition by another State resulting from the threat or use of force. No territorial acquisition resulting from the threat or use of force shall be recognized as legal.[33]

Resolution 3314 declares: "Aggression is the use of armed force by a State against the sovereignty, territorial integrity or political independence of another State, or in any other manner inconsistent with the Charter of the United Nations, as set out in this Definition." In an explanatory note, the resolution pronounces: "In this Definition the term 'State': (a) Is used without prejudice to questions of recognition or to whether a State is a Member of the United Nations; (b) Includes the concept of a 'group of States' where appropriate."[34]

Taking all of these documents into consideration, Iran's occupation by force of the Greater and Lesser Tunbs thus constitutes a violation of its obligation to employ peaceful measures; an aggression; and a violation of the legal principle of the inviolability of the territorial integrity of states, as well as a violation of the legal principle of the finality and stability of borders.

Moreover, Iran has acted in contravention of the legal obligations of an occupying power, as defined in the 1949 Geneva Convention Relative to the Protection of Civilian Persons in Time of War. These obligations include the prohibition of deporting the native population and of importing the population of the occupier. Article 49 of this convention states: "Individual or mass forcible transfers, as well as deportations of protected persons from occupied territory to the territory of the Occupying Power or to that of any other country, occupied or not, are prohibited, regardless of their motive." Furthermore: "The Occupying Power shall not deport or transfer parts of its own civilian population into the territory it occupies."[35]

Affidavits from inhabitants on the Greater Tunb testify that the inhabitants were forced to leave in 1971, and other inhabitants recall that they fled in fear.[36] Inasmuch as Iran regards the Israeli occupation of the West Bank and the Gaza Strip as illegal, and particularly the mass expulsions of Palestinians in 1948 and 1967 and the individual and mass deportations of Palestinians since 1967, as well as the settlement of Israelis in the territories occupied in 1967, Iran cannot claim legal justification for its own occupation of these islands, its own treatment of the civilian populations on these islands, and the settlement of its own population on these islands.

Indeed, Iran's forcible occupation of the Greater Tunb violates the principle of self-determination expressed in the UN Charter and in General Assembly Resolution 2625. A UN plebiscite or fact-finding mission could have ascertained the wishes of the population. The eviction and flight of the Arab inhabitants of the island in 1971 makes that impractical now. Moreover, the migration of 2,000 Iranian workers to Abu Musa since 1971, the Iranian military personnel on the island and Iran's pressure against the Arab residents of Abu Musa since 1992, which has intimidated and reduced this population, would also make it difficult to have any meaningful exercise of self-determination on Abu Musa.[37] The outcome of an exercise of self-determination on the Greater Tunb or on Abu Musa in 1971 would not have been difficult to predict. The inhabitants of both islands were primarily Arabs, with Arabic as their mother tongue and family and commercial ties with the Arab coast. They belonged to prominent Arab tribes and extended families in the UAE, such as the tribes of the Al-Sudan, Al-Boumheir, Banu Hammad, Al-Shawames, Banu Tamim and many others, and owed their allegiance to the Rulers of Sharjah and Ras al-Khaimah.[38]

The Memorandum of Understanding on Abu Musa

Iran also violated legal principles prohibiting the threat of force in obtaining the November 1971 Memorandum of Understanding (MoU) with Sharjah regarding Abu Musa. The basic terms of the agreement are: "Neither Iran nor Sharjah will give up its claim to Abu Musa nor recognize the other's claim." Referring to the Iranian arrival on the northern half of the island, the MoU states: "Within the agreed areas occupied by Iranian troops, Iran will have full jurisdiction..." while the MoU's language on Sharjah's presence on the island is that "Sharjah will retain full jurisdiction over the remainder of the island."[39] Thus, the MoU is essentially an interim arrangement between a state that came to occupy part of the island and a state that was already on the island and retained its position on a part of it. Sharjah exercised all aspects of sovereignty over the remainder of the island during the ensuing years, including flying its flag and the flag of the UAE, as well as providing public services. This was done despite the numerous Iranian encroachments on Sharjah's zone, which began in 1983, as outlined in Chapter 6.

The record clearly shows that Sharjah signed the MoU with Iran under duress, which makes it an invalid document. In February, June and August 1971, the Shah explicitly threatened to occupy the islands by force unless a resolution satisfactory to Iran was reached. The Shah's threat was also conveyed by Sir William Luce, who told the Rulers of Sharjah and Ras al-Khaimah in June 1971 that the Shah would seize Abu Musa and the Tunbs by force. Luce added that Britain's remaining force in the Gulf would not be adequate to stop such action.[40] The Ruler of Sharjah, Shaikh Khalid bin Muhammad, clearly recognized that the island and its oil resources would be taken by force unless he compromised. Indeed, he said so in a letter sent in August 1971 to other Arab rulers.[41] He was right to take the Iranian threat seriously, as shown in the forcible occupation of the Greater and the Lesser Tunbs in late November 1971. The Ruler of Sharjah felt that he had little choice but to acquiesce to the Shah's demand for a solution acceptable to Iran.

Soon after agreeing to the MoU in mid-November 1971, Shaikh Khalid explained:

> I had spent about two years collecting documents proving that the island is Arab territory, and that it belongs to Sharjah. I had asked a team of jurists to prepare legal documents and papers. These were presented to the Iranian Government. However, the logic of force and threat allowed no room for reason and legitimate proofs…Several factors contributed to the delicacy of the situation, combining to form significant pressure: Britain had threatened not to maintain the status quo on the island; Iran insisted that the island was Iranian, and that they would seize it by force; unfavorable economic conditions placed Sharjah in an awkward situation and weakened its position, severely affecting its manoeuverability; other powers came to support Iran…Thus, after consultations with brothers, I deemed it appropriate to seek a formula that would freeze the problem politically, while dealing with it economically. Hence came the said Agreement.[42]

Taking these events and facts under consideration, it is clear that the MoU is null and void *ab initio* due to a "defect of substance" relating to one signatory, namely the Ruler of Sharjah, who signed the MoU under threat of force and duress. This abrogated the MoU as a contradiction of contemporary international law prohibiting the threat and the use of force and means that the legal status of the island is that of military occupation.[43] Indeed, Article 52 of the 1969 Vienna Convention on the Law of Treaties states: "A treaty is void if its conclusion has been procured by the threat or use of force in violation of the principles of international law embodied in the Charter of the United Nations."[44]

In spite of this, Sharjah and the UAE have adhered to the terms of the MoU. Notably, in July 1992, following Iran's violations of the MoU, the Supreme Council of the UAE, which is comprised of the seven rulers of the constituent emirates, declared that agreements concluded by individual emirates with neighboring states would be considered agreements between the UAE and the neighboring states.[45] Even so, UAE Foreign Minister Rashid Abdullah argued in a speech before the UN General Assembly on September 30, 1992 that "this Memo was signed under duress which according to international law makes it null and void."[46] On the surface, the two statements appear to be in contradiction with one another. Upon further examination, however, the position of the UAE with regard to the invalidity of the MoU has been consistent.

The Supreme Council of the UAE issued its July 1992 declaration because it found that Iran wanted to conduct its discussions about the MoU solely with Sharjah. Yet, with the establishment of the UAE, the dispute over Abu Musa had become a federal issue. Thus, it was natural for the Supreme Council to assert the authority of the UAE federal government and negotiate directly with Iran. The declaration does not specifically refer to the MoU itself as an international agreement and certainly does not accept it as a legally binding commitment. Rather, the declaration was a political signal with the intent to remind Iran of the proper negotiation channels. It is still the position of the UAE that the MoU is null and void because it was signed under duress, as stated in September 1992.[47]

There are, of course, those who would argue that the MoU is a valid document that adheres to accepted legal principles. In 1974, Bahraini legal scholar Husain Albaharna wrote in his *The Arabian Gulf States: Their Legal and Political Status and their International Problems* that "it seems doubtful that the Agreement on Abu Musa…can easily be questioned under international law." He noted in particular that the MoU had been accepted in official letters exchanged between Sharjah and Iran through the channel of the British Government.[48] Albaharna argued in a December 1997 interview that this correspondence shows voluntary negotiation. He also noted that Sharjah was in need of money and accepted financial compensation from Iran until oil was discovered and oil revenues were shared. Furthermore, he dismissed the threat to use force as a fact of power politics and not evidence of duress.[49]

Albaharna's line of argument, however, falls short in several respects. He mistakenly indicated that it was only the British who warned the Rulers of Sharjah and Ras al-Khaimah about force, not the Shah, noting only that Luce informed the Rulers that Britain could not protect them against the use of force by Iran. However, more importantly, to argue that the threat of force does not constitute duress is to reject contemporary international law and to revert to an earlier era, when the threat and use of force was acceptable as a means of inducing one party to sign an agreement.[50] Despite his personal opinion, however, Albaharna argued in 1974 that the UAE had not at the time of his writing announced its position toward the MoU "and it remains doubtful, therefore, whether the UAE has legally succeeded to the obligations under the said Agreement."[51]

In addition, the MoU can be questioned on other grounds. The Iraqi representative to the UN Security Council discussion on the islands on December 9, 1971 questioned the validity of the MoU on Abu Musa, not only because it was signed under duress, but also because it was entered into while Britain was responsible for the territorial integrity of the Trucial States, on the basis of agreements concluded between 1820 and 1922, particularly the 1892 Exclusive Agreement between Sharjah and Britain.[52] It may be recalled that in that agreement, the Ruler of Sharjah promised as follows:

> 1st.- That I will on no account enter into any agreement or correspondence with any Power other than the British Government.

2nd.- That without the assent of the British Government I will not consent to the residence within my territory of the Agent of any other Government.

3rd.- That I will on no account cede, sell, mortgage or otherwise give for occupation any part of my territory save to the British Government.[53]

The Iraqi representative argued that the MoU was null and void because the 1892 Exclusive Agreement prohibited Sharjah from entering into any agreement with any power other than Britain and prohibited Sharjah from disposing of, e.g. "giving for occupation," any of its territory save to Britain. Based on the language of this agreement, this line of argument appears to be valid. The Iraqi representative also argued that Britain had failed to honor its treaty obligation to protect the territory of Ras al-Khaimah from Iranian occupation.[54] It may similarly be argued that Britain failed to honor its treaty obligation to protect the territory of Sharjah from Iranian occupation. Britain clearly knew that Iran would use force to take Abu Musa and the Tunbs. Sir William Luce warned the Rulers of Sharjah and Ras al-Khaimah of this in June 1971.[55]

One British legal source who has advised the Ruler of Sharjah argued in an October 1997 interview that the 1892 Exclusive Agreement with Sharjah did not invalidate the MoU of November 1971 because Britain itself participated in and confirmed the agreement. He further said that the Exclusive Agreements operated on the basis of keeping any other power out of the emirates unless the British approved. The argument about British participation, however, is not strictly in conformity with the first article of the 1892 agreement, while the second article of the agreement only refers to British approval of the residence of a representative of another power within an emirate and not British approval of the occupation by another power of part of the territory of an emirate. Indeed, while this legal source noted that the Shaikhs promised in the Exclusive Agreements not to cede territory to foreigners, he did not note that the Shaikhs also promised in the third article not to "give for occupation" any of their territory to foreigners. Moreover, he acknowledged that the British sometimes "ignored" the fact that a Ruler could not alienate territory and that the British themselves sometimes estranged a Ruler's territory without his consent, e.g. alienating Somali land in the Ogaden by the 1897 treaty with Ethiopia.

Nevertheless, the fact that the British "ignored" the terms of agreements in other cases does not mean it was legal to do so in the case of Sharjah and Abu Musa.[56] Julian Walker, who was a member of William Luce's team, argued in another October 1997 interview that Sharjah did not dispose of its territory because it did not abandon its claim to sovereignty. Even this, however, is not strictly in conformity with the language and meaning of the third article.[57]

The same legal source mentioned above also argued that the Exclusive Agreements imposed no obligations on the British, despite the fact that they came to be described as defence or foreign relations or protectorate treaties.[58] While the Iraqi representative to the UN Security Council discussion acknowledged that "the responsibility of the United Kingdom Government to protect the territorial integrity of the States was not explicitly mentioned in so many words," he also maintained:

> The British Government may dispute the point of whether a legal protectorate situation exists here, but the terms of the agreements of March 1892, particularly articles 1 and 3, prove beyond any shadow of doubt Britain's responsibility for the territorial integrity of each and every one of the Trucial States.[59]

Technically, the British obligation to protect or defend the territorial integrity of the Trucial States emanated not from the language of its agreements with the Trucial States, particularly the Exclusive Agreements of 1892, but rather from traditional practice. As J.B. Kelly has written in *Britain and the Persian Gulf: 1795-1880*, the 1853 Treaty of Maritime Peace in Perpetuity "made no provision for the defence of the Trucial Shaikhdoms against aggression from an outside power by sea. On the other hand, it had by now become an accepted fact that responsibility to defend the Trucial Shaikhdoms from such aggression devolved upon the British Government from the Trucial System." Indeed, Kelly notes that British Political Resident Kemball assured the Ruler of Dubai that the British "would protect them from attack by sea."[60] This responsibility was also expressed in the address made to the Trucial Chiefs by the British Viceroy of India, Lord Curzon, in 1903, particularly his assurance that Britain would "adhere to the policy of guardianship and protection which has given you peace and guaranteed your rights for the best part of a century."[61]

In fact, the British accepted and fulfilled this obligation by explicitly warning Persia that Britain would use naval force to defend the rights of the Rulers of Sharjah and Ras al-Khaimah to the islands in 1925, 1928 and 1934. British officials also categorically told Iranian officials that Sharjah and Ras al-Khaimah were under British "protection" during the 1960s. Based on this, it is clear that the British abandoned their traditional practice of protecting the territorial integrity of the emirates on the eve of the termination of the British treaty relations with the emirates on December 1, 1971.

Not only was the MoU obtained in violation of international law, but Iran has openly, repeatedly and systematically violated its terms since the early 1980s, as specified in a complaint issued by the UAE Ministry of Foreign Affairs in 1992. Among these violations, Iran has built roads, an airport, civilian and military facilities, and agricultural projects in Sharjah's zone, in addition to constantly interfering with construction and other business activities by local residents. Iran has further instituted measures that compel residents of Sharjah's zone to enter and exit through an Iranian point of entry, as well as requiring new employees to acquire an Iranian entry permit. Other residents and workers have been physically prevented from disembarking.

Other transgressions include interfering with the police in the Sharjah zone, linking the administration of the Iranian zone of the island to the province of Bandar Abbas, trying to link the municipal services in the Sharjah zone to both the services in the Iranian zone and the Bandar Abbas province, and interfering with Sharjah fishermen in the territorial waters of the island. One aspect of particular concern has been the building in Sharjah's zone of anti-ship missile-launching sites that threaten Gulf shipping and the territorial security of the UAE proper.[62] Despite all this, Iran continues to assert the continuity and validity of the MoU, as reiterated by its foreign minister on a visit to Kuwait on April 19, 1992 and by the head of Iran's negotiating team, Ambassador Mustafa Haeri, in September 1992.

Iran's claim to acknowledge the continuity and validity of the MoU and its concurrent engagement in behavior that violates the same agreement may be based on a letter written on November 25, 1971 by

Iran's Foreign Minister Khalatbari. In this letter, Khalatbari wrote that "Iran's acceptance of the arrangements relating to Abu Musa...is given on the understanding that nothing in the said arrangements shall be taken as restricting the freedom of Iran to take any measures in the Island of Abu Musa which in its opinion would be necessary to safeguard the security of the Island or of the Iranian forces." In this context, however, it has to be said that Iran's understanding does not form part of the MoU. Indeed, Khalatbari's letter was only written after Sharjah and Iran had already submitted letters to the British Foreign Office accepting the terms of the MoU. The British Foreign Office conveyed this new letter containing Iran's understanding to Sharjah, but neither the Foreign Office nor Sharjah actually accepted Iran's understanding as part of the agreement.[63]

Iran's Legal Case

It has already been shown that the UAE can base its claim to the islands of Abu Musa and the Greater and Lesser Tunbs on the legal principles of *prescription* as well as *historical consolidation of title*. In addition, it is also clear that in occupying the two Tunbs and in obtaining the MoU regarding Abu Musa in 1971, Iran violated the principles of international law. At this point, it is appropriate to look at the Iranian claims to the islands in order to be able to make an objective assessment of the validity of those claims. At the outset, it should be noted that while Iran claims rights to Abu Musa and the Tunbs on the basis of several legal principles, it does not provide much evidence. Moreover, its consistent rejection of international adjudication or arbitration raises questions as to how confident Iran is regarding its claims.

Prescription, Historical Consolidation of Title and Occupation

Iran first claims title based on an alleged long historical possession. The Shah said in October 1971: "What we are demanding is what has always belonged to our country throughout history...It is perfectly natural and reasonable that, now that imperialism is withdrawing, Iran should regain what has always been its possession historically."[64] Under the Islamic Republic, Foreign Minister Qotbzadeh made the same argument in May 1980, saying that "the three islands have always been an integral part of Iran. When the British forces withdrew from the Gulf in 1971, Iran regained its sovereignty over them. Iran did nothing more than restore sovereignty over territories that had fallen under foreign domination."[65]

However, Persian/Iranian governments have not presented documentary legal evidence of this claimed historic possession. Iranian scholars have claimed that Persia possessed the islands prior to the 7th century AD, i.e. prior to the Islamic conquests and during successive historical periods since then, for example before the era of the Portuguese naval presence in the Gulf and then again before the period of the British naval presence. However, these scholars have not presented convincing documentary evidence to substantiate their line of argument.[66] As a result, there is no publicly available legal evidence of long and peaceful use and possession of the islands and display of Persian state authority on the islands to support an Iranian claim on the basis of *prescription*, *long and peaceful possession* or *historical consolidation of title*.

Iranian scholars and others sympathetic to Iran argue that Persia repeatedly established and lost control of the islands during the medieval period and the period of European colonialism. However, *occupation* of territory for short periods of time does not constitute a legal basis for title. In order for occupation to be a valid legal basis for sovereignty, the territory occupied must be *res nullius*, i.e. territory owned by no one; the occupation must lead to the establishment of sovereignty and the sovereignty must be continuously and peacefully displayed. In the *Western Sahara Case*, the opinion rendered argued that "territories inhabited by tribes or peoples having a social and political organization were not regarded as *terra nullius*." The Western Sahara was not *terra nullius* because "at the time of colonization Western Sahara was inhabited by people which, if nomadic, were socially and politically organized in tribes and under chiefs competent to represent them."[67]

As Brierly wrote in *The Law of Nations*, "in the *Island of Palmas* case M. Huber emphasized that proof of an original taking of possession is not enough and that possession must be maintained by display of State authority."[68] The record shows that the islands of Abu Musa and the Tunbs were not *res nullius* territory, that Iran never established sovereignty over the islands, and that Iran certainly never continuously or peacefully established or displayed sovereignty and/or state authority on the islands. Thus, Iran has not met any of the three conditions necessary for *occupation* to be a valid basis for a claim.

Indeed, the facts do not even support Iranian claims of Persian possession or occupation of the islands at specific points in time. Persia did not possess or occupy the islands prior to the Portuguese presence in the Gulf. The islands were part of the Arab-ruled Kingdom of Hormuz at this time.[69] Persia also did not possess or occupy the islands prior to an alleged British usurpation and occupation of the islands in approximately 1820, when Britain allegedly turned *de facto* administration over to Sharjah and Ras al-Khaimah with Persia too weak to defend its title.[70] Dutch and French and British archives provide documentary evidence of Arab use and ownership of the islands for most of the period, from the gradual collapse of Portuguese power in the Gulf in the early 1600s to the progressive establishment of British power in the late 1700s and early 1800s. The islands belonged to the Arabs of the Arab coast and were used by them and, with permission, by the Arabs of the Persian coast.

The Qawasim exercised naval and administrative power in the Gulf and on the islands from the early and mid-1700s. On numerous occasions at the beginning of the nineteenth century, Qawasim possession was recognized by the British, including in 1801, when they noted that the Greater Tunb was used by pearlers from Ras al-Khaimah, and in 1806, when the Qawasim Ruler of Ras al-Khaimah was recognized as the ruler of the Qawasim and their dependents on both shores of the Gulf. In 1809, the British noted that the inhabitants of the two coasts frequented these islands and were undisturbed in their possession of these islands. Two years later, in 1811, the British noted that Abu Musa was a base for so-called Qawasim "pirates" from Ras al-Khaimah.

Moreover, there is no record of any British usurpation or occupation of the islands after 1820, although it was reported in 1838 that British officers from Basidu did hunt wild antelope on the Greater Tunb, nor is there any evidence of Britain turning the *de facto* administration of the islands over to the Qawasim after 1820. Indeed, the Qawasim constituted the very power the British were trying to suppress at that time. British officers reported again in 1835 that Abu Musa was a potential pirate lair, and this led to a British prohibition on Qawasim warboats from even approaching Abu Musa and the Tunbs.

However, Britain did not occupy the islands, have any claim to them or dispose of them.

The Shah made the following claim in 1971: "The islands were ours, but some eighty years ago Britain interfered with the exercise of our sovereignty and grabbed them and subsequently claimed them for her wards, Sharjah and Ras al-Khaimah," can also not be substantiated.[71] Persia did not possess, occupy or exercise sovereignty over Abu Musa and the Tunbs in 1887 or 1888, and was unable to produce any evidence of ownership when asked to do so by Britain at that time. Persia's only "exercise of our sovereignty" was to raise its flag over Sirri in 1887 and then to briefly raise its flags over Abu Musa and the Greater Tunb in 1904. Britain had already advised the Rulers of Sharjah and Ras al-Khaimah to raise their flags on the islands in 1903 in order to underline their traditional use and possession of the islands. This did not constitute grabbing the islands from Persia. Instead, following Persia's lowering of the Sharjah and Ras al-Khaimah flags and the raising of its own in 1904, and Britain's successful pressure on Persia to reverse its action, Britain did in fact prevent Persia from grabbing the islands from Sharjah and Ras al-Khaimah. Once again, Persia was not able to produce evidence of ownership when Britain asked for such proof in 1904.

Iran has also claimed title on the basis that the islands were allegedly ruled by the Lingeh Qawasim, and that they were administering them as Persian officials, i.e. on the basis of a vicarious display of state authority.[72] Nevertheless, the evidence is clear that Abu Musa and the Greater Tunb were not ruled by the Lingeh Qawasim. It is true that the Greater Tunb was used by dependents of the Lingeh Qawasim for grazing their animals. Nevertheless, letters written by successive Rulers of the Lingeh Qawasim in the 1870s and 1880s acknowledge that the Greater Tunb was owned by the paramount Rulers of the Qawasim tribe, who were based on the Trucial Coast, and that the dependents of the Lingeh Qawasim only used the Greater Tunb with the consent of these paramount Rulers. The British had erroneously believed at one stage that the Lingeh Qawasim had a claim to the islands, but even they concluded that this claim was based on their Qawasim identity and not on their status as Persian officials. More importantly, the British were unaware of the correspondence from the Lingeh Qawasim acknowledging the title of the Trucial Coast Qawasim over the Greater Tunb until the early 1880s.[73]

One particular Iranian claim is that the residents of Lingeh, Sirri and the Greater Tunb paid taxes to Persia between 1878 and 1887.[74] Although Persia promised to do so, it never actually produced any evidence to substantiate such a claim regarding the Greater Tunb. The letters that Persia did provide reveal only a reference to one instance of taxes paid by Sirri and certainly nothing regarding the Greater Tunb. Furthermore, the British thought that even this one reference to taxes paid to Persia from Sirri was insufficient to support the Persian claim or deprive the Qawasim of their rights to that island.

The Bathurst, Ely and Chance report in 1971 correctly asserted: "It is clear that, whatever the relationship between the Iranian Government and the Ruler of Lingeh may have been, it would afford no basis for an Iranian claim to Abu Musa, for the reason that the Ruler of Lingeh never owned or possessed Abu Musa; it belonged to the Ruler of Sharjah."[75] It also seems clear that any relationship between the Persian Government and the Ruler of Lingeh affords no basis for an Iranian claim to the Tunbs. Successive Rulers of Lingeh acknowledged in writing that, although they used the Greater Tunb, they recognized that the island belonged to the Ruler of Ras al-Khaimah. While the Lesser Tunb may have been allocated for use to the Lingeh Qawasim in 1835, it remained subject to the paramount branch of the Qawasim tribe in Sharjah and then later to the Ruler of Ras al-Khaimah.

The Issue of Maps as Evidence

The evidence that Iran has emphasized in support of its claims are some British maps of the late eighteenth and nineteenth century, particularly an 1886 British War Office map presented by the British Foreign Office to the Shah of Iran in 1888, a map which erroneously portrayed Sirri, the Tunbs and Abu Musa in the same color as the Persian coast. Upon receiving this map in 1888, Nasr-ed-Din Shah of the Qajar dynasty cited it as evidence against British arguments on behalf of the Qawasim right to Sirri, noting that both Sirri and the Greater Tunb were depicted in the same color as Persia. Shah Mohammed Reza Pahlavi also cited this map in February 1971, claiming: "These islands are our property, and we have British Admiralty maps and other documents which prove this." Iran's representative to the UN Security Council deliberations in December 1971 even argued that these maps constituted British recognition of an Iranian title.[76]

Before considering this specific evidence in more detail, it is important to consider the general issue of maps in international law. In a comprehensive 1963 article on maps in cases such as the islands case, G. Weissberg wrote:

> In determining the location of a boundary, international as well as national tribunals have in the past been reluctant to place much evidentiary value on maps, regardless of their number or designation. Such a tendency has been particularly noticeable whenever the map described territory of which the authors have had little knowledge, is geographically inaccurate, or is sketched in order to promote a country's claim. Even official maps, that is those issued or approved by a governmental agency, have been treated with considerable reserve.[77]

The *Minquiers and Ecrehos* case and the *Island of Palmas* case may be cited to similar effect. In the former, after France and the United Kingdom emphasized the cartographic evidence, the International Court of Justice (ICJ) ruling did not comment upon this evidence. One judge wrote that "maps do not constitute a sufficiently important contribution to enable a decision to be based on them."[78] In the latter case, Judge Huber wrote that maps could be "methods of indirect proof, not of the exercise of sovereignty, but of its existence in law..." However, he did add: "If the arbitrator is satisfied as to the existence of legally relevant facts which contradict the statements of cartographers whose sources of information are not known, he can attach no weight to the maps, however numerous and generally appreciated they may be."[79]

The maps cited by Iran in the case of Abu Musa and the Tunbs were drawn by mapmakers who lacked adequate knowledge and may have been biased. As a result, the maps were inaccurate and therefore do not in any way constitute indirect proof of the existence of Persian sovereignty. Furthermore, the maps were and are contradicted by a substantial body of other legally relevant evidence. It should be noted, for example, that most British and other European maps and charts of the nineteenth century and earlier centuries did not, either through coloring or text, designate the islands as belonging either to Persia or to the Trucial Coast. As for the rest, some maps designated the islands as belonging to Persia while others showed the islands as belonging to the Trucial Coast.[80]

The 1886 British War Office map cited by Iran was based on a map drawn in 1876 by Captain St. John of the British Royal Engineers. While the 1876 map did not present the islands or Iran in any color, it could have been misinterpreted by the War Office mapmakers, causing them to designate the islands as Persian, simply because the map was titled "Persia" and named the islands. It should also be noted that the 1876 map was based solely on "original authorities," such as other previously published maps, charts and commentaries and not on any personal visit to the Gulf or any specific, primary research about the ownership of the islands. Thus, it could have easily repeated the errors of previously published works.[81]

Indeed, there is the possibility that both the 1886 and the 1876 maps may have been based on the *Persian Gulf Pilot*, a British Admiralty hydrographic survey that was compiled in the late 1850s and then published in 1864. This was a navigational commentary based on a hydrographic chart rather than a map, and it mistakenly indicated that Sirri, Farur, the Greater Tunb, the Lesser Tunb and Abu Musa were under the authority of the Ruler of Lingeh, noting that he paid tribute to the Persian Government. While the authors visited the Gulf and did some specific, primary research, their knowledge was incomplete. They did not know, for example, that Abu Musa was used for grazing and had grass and water.

In turn, the *Persian Gulf Pilot*'s error about the ownership of the islands may have been based on a reference to a map drawn up in 1853 for internal British reference at the time of the Treaty of Maritime Peace in Perpetuity, to illustrate the line beyond which armed boats from the Trucial Coast could not cross. This map reflected British Resident James Morrison's significant re-drawing of the Hennell line, which was drawn soon after the first maritime truce in 1835, and showed the line running to the south of Abu Musa.[82] This line, however, only indicated that armed boats from the Trucial Coast could not approach Abu Musa and the Tunbs, and not that these islands were under the authority of the Ruler of the Lingeh Qawasim or that they were under the sovereignty of Persia. Moreover, the line was meant in large part to protect British trade, which was concentrated along the Persian coast, particularly at Lingeh. During this period, the British still did not trust the Qawasim of the Trucial Coast, whom they had militarily suppressed in 1809 and again in 1819-1820. Such economic and political facts may have influenced mapmakers at the time.

The 1886 and 1876 maps may also have been based on maps such as one published by Sidney Hall circa 1860, which erroneously portrayed the islands in the same color as the Persian province of Laristan, or a map of Persia in 1831 published by G. Long in 1852, which also mistakenly portrayed the islands in the color of Persia. In fact, all of these maps may have been based on an 1832 map prepared by the private London cartographer, A. Arrowsmith, which mistakenly colored Abu Musa and the Tunbs in the same color as Persia. The errors in these maps could also have been the simple result of mis-coloring by the printers, which was a frequent occurrence at the time.

Similarly, the same economic and political considerations just mentioned could have played a role. Prior to this time, most British and other European maps and charts of the early 1800s and of previous centuries did not give any indication of the ownership of the islands. They also demonstrated greater knowledge of the northern coast and islands than of the southern coast and its islands. Lieutenant G.B. Brucks, who conducted surveys from 1825 to 1829, attempted to chart the safest passage through the Gulf and the Strait of Hormuz, a passage that was known to lie in the northern part of the Gulf, between the Greater Tunb and Qishm and between Sirri and Nabiyu Farur. Since his survey ship visited the islands from a base on the northern coast, this may explain why he listed these islands in his 1831 chart of the northern coast from Bushire to Basidu. This could also be the reason why one copy of his 1832 chart of the Gulf of Persia portrays Abu Musa and the Greater Tunb in the same color as Persia. Another copy of this same chart is not colored, suggesting that the coloring was done at a later date and not when the original chart was published.

Prior to Brucks, British surveys such as those by Captain R. Taylor were intended primarily to prepare for attacks against Qawasim "pirate" ports on the southern coast and therefore it can be assumed that they reflected such bias. Considerations such as these could certainly have led mapmakers like Arrowsmith in 1832 to associate the islands with the Persian coast in their coloring. However, it needs to be repeated that most British and other European maps of the early, mid- and late 1800s did not designate the islands as belonging to either Persia or the Arabs.[83]

The value of these maps as evidence supporting an Iranian claim is thus undermined by the inaccuracies in the maps and the reliance on previous sources that were themselves inaccurate rather than based on primary research. Their significance is also undermined by the fact that British commercial interests were focused on the Persian coast and that the British exerted an extensive effort to suppress the Qawasim of the Arab Coast. These issues may have collectively influenced and biased those British surveyors and mapmakers who did do some primary research.

Furthermore, the value of these maps for Iran is undermined by a large body of contradictory evidence. First, there are other maps before the 1870s and after the 1890s that show these islands as being Arab islands. Some British maps of the 1700s indicate that the islands are connected to the Arab coast, while some German maps of the 1800s indicate that the islands are connected to Arab-ruled parts of the Persian coast. In 1825, the British mapmaker Arrowsmith published a map that portrayed the Tunbs in the same color as Persia, but portrayed Abu Musa in the same color as the Arab coast, thus demonstrating that he later altered this in his 1832 map. German and French cartographers from the 1840s to the 1870s produced maps portraying the islands as belonging to the Arab coast. In 1864, for example, the eminent German cartographer H. Kiepert produced a map that colored the Tunbs as possessions of Oman and designated Abu Musa as belonging to the Qawasim of the Arab coast. British, German, and French maps of the twentieth century have generally shown Abu Musa and the Tunbs as Arab.[84]

Even more important than the maps themselves is the fact that British officials based in the Gulf eventually received enough contradictory evidence in the form of correspondence from the Qawasim Rulers of the Trucial Coast and of Lingeh to understand that the assertions made in the *Persian Gulf Pilot* and the coloring in the 1886 War Office map were inaccurate. British officials explicitly and repeatedly recognized the authority of Sharjah and Ras al-Khaimah over the islands before the map was given as a gift to the Shah in 1888 as well as in succeeding years. Overall, the very few official and semi-official maps cited by Iran cannot even be considered as containing indirect, supplementary, secondary or hearsay legal evidence. Certainly, these maps do not independently constitute an adequate or sufficient basis for a claim, nor do they represent a British recognition of a claim. Furthermore, the inaccurate 1832 Arrowsmith map, which may have been consulted by official British cartographers, seems to have been a private map, and private maps generally have less legal weight than official maps.

Indeed, with respect to the Iranian claim that these maps constitute British recognition of Iran's claim, the British Chargé in Tehran told the Persian Acting Foreign Minister in 1928 that Persia's reference to the 1886 map given to the Shah in July 1888 was "no argument" and explicitly rejected Persia's claim to the islands. The Foreign Office agreed:

> The Persian argument...proves nothing. It certainly does not prove that His Majesty's Government recognized Persian ownership at that date. On the contrary, the Legation had only recently reminded the Persian Government of the rights of the Arab Sheikhs, as will be seen from Sir A. Nicolson's letter of March 2, 1888 to the Ameen es Sultan and the Legation memorandum of March 19 1888...

The March 2, 1888 letter from Nicolson, who had been the British Chargé in Tehran at that time, said: "I return the papers you were good enough to send me some time ago in regard to Sirri and Tamb islands. These papers do not bear out the Persian claim."[85] Moreover, after the Shah noted in 1888 that the islands were portrayed in the same color as Persia, the British Minister in Tehran, Sir Drummond Wolff, wrote to the Foreign Office that the gift of the map had "certain results which were hardly contemplated," indicating that it had not been the British intention to recognize the Persian claim.[86]

Acquisitive Prescription, Cession and Conquest

Considering the above discussion, it is clear that the evidence does not support Iran's claim to the islands based on the two dominant legal principles applicable in cases involving territorial disputes, i.e. *prescription* and *historical consolidation of title*. The weakness of the Iranian claims is also evident when one broadens the scope and considers other legal principles that are applied in cases such as this. Certainly, Iran cannot claim title to the islands on the basis of *acquisitive prescription*, i.e. the laying of hands on territory under another state's sovereignty or the exercise of sovereignty over it for a long uninterrupted period without opposition or protest by the other state, since Iran has not met any of the necessary conditions.[87]

First, Iran's acquisition of the islands in 1971 was not effected through the sovereign parties, namely Ras al-Khaimah and Sharjah. Ras al-Khaimah refused to enter into an agreement with Iran. Sharjah, in its MoU with Iran, expressly did not recognize the Iranian claim to sovereignty over Abu Musa. Second, the acquisition was not peaceful. The MoU with Sharjah was obtained under duress using the threat of force, while the Tunbs were in fact forcibly occupied, leading to skirmishes with Ras al-Khaimah and subsequent fatalities. Third, the acquisition has not lasted a sufficient length of time. Fifty years is generally considered a necessary period of time, but Iran has only occupied the islands for thirty-two years. Fourth, the sovereign party, namely the UAE, has not submitted through acquiescence, or lack of protest or opposition to the acquisition. Instead, the UAE has repeatedly and consistently protested Iranian behavior from 1971 until the present day. While all four of the above conditions would have to be met if Iran were to have a valid claim under acquisitive prescription, the fact is that not even one of these conditions has been fulfilled.

Iran also cannot claim the islands on the basis of *cession*, i.e. the transfer of sovereignty from one state to another by an agreement. The sovereign powers have not ceded, transferred or relinquished their sovereignty by any agreements with Iran. The Lingeh Qawasim did not make any agreement ceding sovereignty to Persia when they became Persian officials or when Persia drove them from Lingeh in 1887. Indeed, the first condition that must be met for cession to be a valid legal act is that the ceding state must actually have sovereignty, which the Lingeh Qawasim did not possess. They may have had co-ownership to family/tribal property, but only as a subordinate branch of the family. They did not cede this possible co-ownership, not even in the case of Sirri, which had been allocated for their use. Under Arab tribal law they would have had no right to do so. According to Vinson and Elkins, doing so would have been "invalid as an <u>ultra</u> <u>vires</u> act. Apparently, common tribal property could not be alienated by the administering sheikh without the concurrence of the entire tribe."[88] The Rulers of the Qawasim tribe in Sharjah and Ras al-Khaimah did not cede sovereignty to Persia, and under Arab tribal law it is doubtful that even they could have lawfully done so.

Vinson and Elkins write:

> ...if an argument alleging cession of the [Tunb] Islands to Persia is advanced, the most that Iran could legally claim is acquisition of the undivided co-interests in the Islands held by the Lingeh Qawasim. Even assuming *arguendo* that Persia validly could have acquired by cession the co-interests to the Islands of the Lingeh sheikhs, an assumption that is quite improbable, Persia, by its seizure of the Island of Sirri, arguably partitioned unilaterally its co-interests in the four Qawasim islands in the Gulf, leaving the islands of the Great and Little Tunb and Abu Musa to the Trucial Coast Qawasim. Such a de facto partition arguably may have reflected the appropriate share acquired by Persia of the undivided interest in the four islands. After such a partition, Persia would have had no remaining interest in the Tunb islands or Abu Musa.[89]

More importantly, Iran would still have to produce evidence of an agreement, which it has been unable to do.

The same applies for the year 1971. Britain did not cede sovereignty over the three islands to Iran since it never had any sovereignty to cede. The Ruler of Ras al-Khaimah did not cede the Tunbs to Iran. In fact, he rejected any agreement with Iran, ultimately leading to the occupation of the Tunbs by force. Finally, the Ruler of Sharjah did not cede Abu Musa to Iran. Instead, he explicitly did not relinquish his claim to sovereignty and did not recognize an Iranian claim to sovereignty in his 1971 MoU on Abu Musa with Iran. Even if the Ruler of Ras al-Khaimah or the Ruler of Sharjah had ceded sovereignty to Iran in 1971, this would not have any binding legal effect inasmuch as it would have been done under the explicit and illegal threat of force by the Shah of Iran.

Iran cannot claim title to the Tunbs by citing the principle of *conquest* and noting that Persia drove the Qawasim from Lingeh in 1887. While conquest is illegal in contemporary international law, it was not illegal in traditional international law and meant that force could be used to terminate the legal existence of a state or to annex part of a state's territory. However, as Vinson and Elkins write:

> Although naked conquest was not illegal in traditional international law and was recognized as a valid means of acquiring sovereignty over territory, three elements had to be necessary: (i) actual possession of the territory based on force; (ii) an announcement of intention to retain the subjugated territory; and (iii) ability to retain possession. There is no evidence of which we are aware that indicates that Persia possessed the islands by force, announced an intention to retain them, or in fact did retain them. Furthermore, without a treaty of cession, the conquest of mainland Lingeh would not, under international law, support a vicarious claim to the islands.[90]

Clearly, the evidence permits substantially more definitive statements than those made by Vinson and Elkins. In fact, Persia clearly did not conquer or possess Abu Musa and the Tunb islands, neither did it announce an intention to retain possession of them, nor demonstrate an ability to retain them. Instead, the Qawasim continued to possess these islands even after Persia drove the Qawasim from Lingeh.

Claims on the basis of conquest in 1971 would certainly be invalid because this accepted principle of traditional international law has been expressly prohibited in contemporary international law as made clear in the UN Charter, in numerous treaties and conventions, and in UN General Assembly resolutions, as noted in an earlier section of this chapter.

Contiguity

Iran has attempted to claim title to the Tunbs based on *contiguity*, or the geographic proximity of the islands to Iran's mainland. In his remarks to the UN Security Council in 1971, Iran's representative said that "the Greater Tunb lies only seventeen miles from the Iranian mainland and the Lesser Tunb twenty-two miles off-shore. On the other hand, both islands lie almost fifty miles away from Ras El-Khaimeh on the other side of the Persian Gulf."[91]

Contiguity, however, is not a sufficient basis for a claim to sovereignty. If an effective display of sovereignty over territory can be demonstrated, then geographic proximity may help to determine the extent of the territory where sovereignty pertains. Iran, however, cannot demonstrate any effective display of sovereignty over these islands prior to occupying them by force in 1971. In addition, when another state can demonstrate an effective display of sovereignty, as Ras al-Khaimah and Sharjah can, even if only by isolated acts, then geographic proximity carries little or no weight.[92] Moreover, the islands have never been within Iran's territorial waters. As Judge Huber wrote in the *Island of Palmas* case:

> Although States have in certain circumstances maintained that islands relatively close to their shores belonged to them in virtue of their geographical situation, it is impossible to show the existence of a rule of positive international law to the effect that islands situated outside territorial waters should belong to a State from the mere fact that its territory forms the *terra firma* (nearest continent or island of considerable size).[93]

It should also be remembered that while the Tunbs are closer to Iran than to Ras al-Khaimah, Abu Musa is closer to Sharjah than to Iran. A hypothetical median line would therefore place the Tunbs on the Iranian and Abu Musa on the UAE side of the line. Indeed, Northcutt Ely stated in an ICJ deposition in 1992 that during the November 1971 negotiations over the Buttes Gas and Oil concession off Abu Musa, Luce said that the outcome of his mediation would essentially be a median line settlement: Abu Musa was on the Arabian side and the Tunbs were on the Iranian side.[94] However, the 1971 MoU was not really based on a median line inasmuch as it gave Iran a foothold on an island that lay on the Arab side of a median line. Agreement on a median line would also not be a legal basis for Iranian sovereignty over the Tunbs and would not undermine the sovereignty of Ras al-Khaimah and the UAE over these islands.

Geopolitical and Strategic Significance

Finally, Tehran has claimed the islands on the basis of their geopolitical and strategic significance for Iran, i.e. that Iranian control of the islands is necessary since they command the entrance to the Gulf. The Shah suggested that if the islands fell into the hands of radical Arab forces, these forces could attack and disrupt the oil tanker traffic of Iran and its consumers. On the other hand, he argued, Iranian control of the islands could help Iran to act as a guarantor of security in the Gulf.[95]

This argument, however, cannot be considered a valid legal basis for a claim to title over the islands. Rather, it is a political claim. It is similar to an Israeli claim to the Golan Heights for its strategic significance to Israel. As a political claim, it was challenged at the time by Arab states, which made the strategic argument that Iran's occupation of the islands could threaten Arab oil tanker traffic on their only route to the high seas.[96] This Iranian political claim was of a very transitory character. Indeed, Iran itself confirmed the reasonableness of Arab concerns when it used the islands to attack shipping during the Iran-Iraq War in the 1980s.

Iranian Acts and Omissions

Based on existing legal principles as well as international legal standards regarding the use and/or threat of force, Iran does not have a valid claim to the islands of Abu Musa, the Greater Tunb and the Lesser Tunb. In addition, there are also several acts and omissions by Persia/Iran that arguably are not consistent with and may even contradict Iran's claim of sovereignty. For example, as Vinson and Elkins write:

> The failure of Iran, and the earlier failure of Persia, to make proposals for arbitration or adjudication of the question of ownership of the Tunb islands is an omission that points to the possibility that in fact neither Iran nor Persia was confident that its claim to the Islands would be upheld. The failure also may evidence the non-existence of Iranian sovereignty over the Islands or constitute an admission of the validity or strength of Ras al-Khaimah's claim.

They note: "The failure to take such action when such action was called for should have a detrimental effect on Persia's legal position and may provide evidence of non-existence of sovereignty due to acquiescence in or admission of the validity of Ras al-Khaimah's claim to the islands." Furthermore, "The attempts of Persia and later Iran to purchase the

Tunb Islands from the Ruler of Ras al-Khaimah buttress this last argument. Such offers arguably would not have been made by a state convinced of its own claim to sovereignty over the involved territory." Indeed, Vinson and Elkins state:

> The 1934 Persian offer and the 1971 Iranian offer to purchase or lease the islands from Ras al-Khaimah constitute tacit acknowledgments that Ras al-Khaimah possessed sovereignty over the islands. Indeed, depending upon the particular wording of any written evidence concerning the offers, it may be possible to establish that such offers constituted direct admissions of Ras al-Khaimah's sovereignty over the islands. Documentary evidence of these offers therefore should be developed and closely studied.[97]

Similarly, Iran's failure to propose arbitration or adjudication as well as Iran's offer of compensation for Abu Musa may arguably constitute at least tacit acknowledgment and possibly direct admission of Sharjah's sovereignty over the island. In addition, Vinson and Elkins write:

> The failure of Iran to act in accordance with international law following the refusal of His Highness Sheikh Saqr to sell the Islands also should be detrimental to Iran's claim. Instead of referring the matter to the International Court of Justice or the United Nations, Iran chose to use military force to enforce its claim. Such a use of force clearly violates international law. It could be argued that Iran's possibly illegal acts reflect its recognition of the weakness of its legal claim to the Islands.[98]

Furthermore, any argument by Iran that Sharjah and Ras al-Khaimah did not constitute independent sovereign states in 1971 and that they were therefore not protected by international law, would not hold. Shaikh Fahim bin Sultan Al-Qasimi, who has served as the head of the Legal Department at the UAE Ministry of Foreign Affairs and as the Secretary General of the GCC, has argued that any such argument could be countered by pointing out that the British, by acquiring exclusive rights over the external relations of the Trucial States in the 1892 Exclusive Agreements, had prevented the emirates from becoming fully independent sovereign states until the actual British departure from the Gulf at the end of 1971.[99] Such an Iranian argument could also be rebutted by noting that "Under international law, a state is an entity that has a defined territory and a permanent population, under the control of its own government, and that engages in, or has the capacity to engage in, formal relations with other such entities."[100]

Sharjah and Ras al-Khaimah certainly each had a defined territory and permanent population under the control of its own government in 1971.[101] Iran would therefore have to argue that the emirates of Sharjah and Ras al-Khaimah did not engage in or lacked the capacity to engage in foreign relations in 1971. However, Iran itself attempted to negotiate directly with these emirates. The Shah negotiated with the Ruler of Ras al-Khaimah in the late 1960s and with the Ruler of Sharjah in 1970. Thus, Iran's behavior is indicative of its belief that the emirates had the capacity to engage in foreign relations and that Iran and the emirates did in fact engage in foreign relations with each other.

Moreover, in international law, "An entity which has the capacity to conduct foreign relations does not cease to be a state because it voluntarily turns over to another state some or all control of its foreign relations." Indeed, "'Protectorates' or 'Protected States' predominantly of the colonial era involved agreements by local rulers conferring authority over foreign affairs or other matters on an external state, usually an 'imperial power.'" The result was that "In the last three decades a large number of newly 'independent' states have been admitted [to the UN] without question although they have often been heavily dependent in actuality on other powers for security and economic viability."[102]

Based on these excerpts, it can be argued that Ras al-Khaimah met the criteria of statehood, in particular engaging in formal relations with other states by at least 1806, when Shaikh Sultan bin Saqr entered into a treaty with David Seton, the British Resident in Muscat. In 1814, the Governor General of India wrote to the Governor of Bombay that Qawasim "piracy" might be justification for civilized states to attack the Qawasim on the grounds of self-defense, "but whether it be or be not so on general grounds, the British Government has deprived itself of the right of acting upon it, since by taking engagements from the Joasmees to respect its own trade it has to that extent recognized them as a power capable of maintaining the ordinary international relations with other states."[103] This line of argument also holds in relation to the fact that

Sharjah and Ras al-Khaimah did not cease to be states in 1892 when they entered into the "Exclusive Agreements" with Britain.

Finally, upon or prior to the termination of their treaty relations with Britain at the end of 1971, Sharjah and Ras al-Khaimah could possibly have been admitted to the UN. Ras al-Khaimah was a state when its territory was taken by force, and Sharjah was a state when the MoU was obtained from it under duress. At the very least, Sharjah and Ras al-Khaimah were "dependent states" or entities that possessed international "personality."

Iran had even threatened to withhold its recognition of the United Arab Emirates and to disrupt and prevent the establishment of the United Arab Emirates unless a satisfactory resolution of the islands issue was reached. The likelihood of Iran making good on its threat delayed the declaration of the UAE as a fully independent sovereign state, the UAE's admission to the UN, and Iran's recognition of the UAE from July 1971 to December 1971. However, the weight of legal authority and state practice is that a state is a state if it meets the criteria for statehood and that recognition by other states is not essential in "constituting" its statehood, but is merely "declaratory" of its statehood. Even those who argue that recognition is essential also argue that states have an obligation to recognize entities that meet the criteria of statehood or at least to treat these entities as states, i.e. not deny these entities their rights.[104] Iran thus had an obligation to recognize or treat Sharjah and Ras al-Khaimah as states, "dependent states," or entities with international "personality," rather than deny them their rights.

The Concept of the Critical Date

UAE Ministry of Foreign Affairs official Khalifa Shahin Al-Marri, who became UAE Ambassador to Iran in 1999, has argued that nothing Iran has done since 1971 can support their claim to the islands since their use of force and threat of force in 1971 were illegal. He also states that no change in international law since 1971 would be relevant since the case was "crystallized" in 1971.[105] In the *Minquiers and Ecrehos* case, the International Court of Justice considered the notion of a "critical date," i.e. the date on which a dispute is considered to "crystallize." After this date, the acts of either state are not determinative of sovereignty, so that one or both parties cannot try to improve their position after that date. The ICJ held as follows:

> A dispute as to sovereignty over the groups did not arise before the years 1886 and 1888, when France for the first time claimed sovereignty over the [islands of] Ecrehos and Minquiers respectively. But in view of the special circumstances of the present case, subsequent acts should also be considered by the Court, unless the measure in question was taken with a view to improving the legal position of the Party concerned. In many respects [United Kingdom] activity in regard to these groups had developed gradually long before the dispute as to sovereignty arose, and it has since continued without interruption and in a similar manner. In such circumstances there would be no justification for ruling out all events which during this continued development occurred after the years 1886 and 1888 respectively...[106]

The Court therefore did consider displays of state activity by the United Kingdom after the "critical date." Contemporary practice is to consider all acts of both states, but different evidentiary value is placed on them depending upon when they occurred.[107]

In the case of the islands, the ICJ might decide that the "critical dates" on which this case "crystallized" may not have been 1971, but either in 1888, when Persia claimed the Greater Tunb or in 1903/04 when Persia lowered the Qawasim flags flying over Abu Musa and the Greater Tunb and raised its own. If so, the displays of state authority by Ras al-Khaimah and Sharjah on the Tunbs after 1888 and after 1903-1904 and by Sharjah on Abu Musa after 1903-1904 would be considered by the ICJ and would have significant evidentiary value because they were displays of state authority that were continuing from the period prior to the critical date. The claims, protests and visits by Persia and Iran to these islands would also be considered, but these would have less evidentiary value since they would likely be seen as efforts to improve Persia's/Iran's legal case inasmuch as they were not continuations of prior behavior. If the critical date were determined to be 1971, the continuing displays of state activity by Sharjah and the UAE before and after the 1971 MoU on Abu Musa would be taken into consideration by the ICJ and would have significant evidentiary value. The activities of Iran on Abu Musa after the 1971 MoU would also be considered.

However, due to the fact that the MoU was obtained under duress, Iran's activities on the northern half of the island would have less evidentiary value than Sharjah's activities on its half of the island. Those Iranian activities following Iran's encroachment on Sharjah's half of the island in violation of the MoU would have no evidentiary value. Iran's activities on the Greater and Lesser Tunb since its occupation of the islands in 1971 would also be taken into consideration, but because these islands were obtained illegally, Iran's behavior again would have no evidentiary value.

Finally, Judge Huber noted in the *Island of Palmas Case*:

> Both parties are also agreed that a juridical fact must be appreciated in the light of the law contemporary with it, and not of the law in force at the time when a dispute in regard to it arises or fails to be settled. The effect of discovery [of the island] by Spain is therefore to be determined by the rules of international law in force in the first half of the 16th century.[108]

Nevertheless, Judge Huber ruled that discovery alone was not sufficient, but that it must be followed by some display of state authority prior to the critical date, i.e. when Spain ceded territories to the United States in the Treaty of Paris in 1898. He found that there was no evidence of such a display of state authority, and that the discovery had no effect. Thus, he ruled in favor of the Netherlands.[109] As a result, even if Iran could provide evidence that Persia had ever discovered, conquered or occupied the islands during some previous historical era when a different standard of international law applied, which is not the case, Iran would still need to show evidence of some display of state authority prior to the critical dates of 1888, 1903-1904 or 1971.

International Law and Conflict Resolution

In addition to the principles and cases concerning sovereignty, international law provides numerous methods of peacefully resolving disputes between states, as set forth in Article 33 of the UN Charter. Diplomatic means, such as negotiations, good offices, mediation, conciliation and inquiries are all applicable measures that have relevance in the case of the islands. Unfortunately, up to this point, none of these approaches have proven successful. Britain, for example, offered its "good offices" and acted as a "mediator" in 1970 and 1971. Saudi Arabia and Kuwait tried to play mediatory roles in those same years. The UAE attempted direct, bilateral negotiations in 1992 and 1995, the latter when Qatar offered its good offices and brought the UAE and Iran together. In the end, these meetings produced no progress. Still, as far as the UAE is concerned, direct bilateral negotiations remains its preferred means to settle the islands dispute.

Political means, such as resorting to regional and international organizations, have also failed. Regional organizations, such as the Gulf Cooperation Council, the Damascus Declaration states, and the Arab League, have regularly expressed their support for the UAE and for a peaceful solution to the dispute. The UAE reasons that such support may eventually influence Iran to enter into a serious bilateral dialogue. In the spring of 1999, a GCC tripartite committee composed of Saudi Arabia, Qatar and Oman was formed to promote bilateral negotiations between the UAE and Iran. However, the committee made no headway and concluded its efforts at the end of 2000. On numerous occasions, Iran simply refused to meet with committee members.

International organizations, including the United Nations, have been less involved. At the outset in 1971, the UN Security Council heard a discussion of the issue, but decided at the time not to invoke Article 36 as a means to "recommend appropriate procedures or methods of adjustment." The UN Secretary General agreed to a UAE request to use his good offices to mediate the dispute, but his request for a meeting in Iran in 1994 was rebuffed. The dispute remains on the agenda of the Security Council, at the request of the UAE, but the Council has still taken no action.

Legal means, such as referring a dispute to the International Court of Justice (ICJ) for adjudication, in accordance with Article 36 of the UN Charter and in accordance with the Statute of the ICJ in the Hague, is another means that the UAE has recommended. Kuwait recommended this option to Iran in 1971 and the UAE has called for such a step ever since. Having territorial disputes referred to the ICJ for judgment certainly has its precedents. In 1953, the *Minquiers and Ecrehos* case was decided by the ICJ. The dispute between Bahrain and Qatar over the Hawar islands went before the ICJ in May 2000, and the ICJ rendered a judgment in March 2001. As a matter of procedure, it is generally necessary for both parties to consent to have such a case heard by the ICJ.

Iran, however, has consistently refused to refer this dispute to ICJ jurisdiction. Even in the unlikely event that Tehran would agree, it is not clear that it would comply with a final and binding judgment rendered by the Court. Under the enforcement proceedings in Article 94 of the UN Charter, the UAE would then have to consider recourse to the Security Council in order to give effect to the judgment. In 1979 and 1980, for example, Iran refused to appear before the Court or to accept the Court's decision in the *Case Concerning United States Diplomatic and Consular Staff in Tehran* (United States of America v. Iran).[110] Indeed, UAE official Khalifa Shahin Al-Marri has suggested that "even if the parties were to agree to go to the ICJ, the ICJ will not reach a judgment until they think there is a mutual understanding and that their decision will be implemented. They do not want the Security Council to implement the decision against the will of one of the parties."[111]

Arbitration by an arbitrator or arbitrators drawn from the Permanent Court of Arbitration may be more expeditious and private and afford the disputants more control over the selection of judges and procedures than recourse to the ICJ. This was the means by which the *Island of Palmas Case* was settled in 1928. It is the means by which the Yemen-Eritrea case concerning the Hanish islands was decided in 1998. The UAE has called for arbitration, but here again, the consent of both parties is necessary. This consent is being withheld by Iran. Since there are no formal enforcement proceedings for decisions of arbitral tribunals comparable to the enforcement proceedings for judgments of the ICJ referred to in Article 94 of the UN Charter, it is not clear that Iran would accept such a decision.[112]

There is no language in the already negotiated 1971 MoU on Abu Musa that allows for further negotiation of details or commits the parties to submit disagreements about the MoU to adjudication or arbitration. Despite this, and notwithstanding Iran's previous rejections of adjudication and arbitration, Husain Albaharna has suggested that the UAE could only call for voluntary arbitration of the dispute over Abu Musa on the basis of the MoU, which Iran recognizes as a legal document and according to which problems of administration on the island should be settled.[113] However, it is doubtful that Iran would agree to this.

Iran's attitude toward adjudication and arbitration may be based on the basic procedures involved. Bathurst, Ely and Chance write:

> Arbitral tribunals and the International Court of Justice have adopted in cases such as this the method of examination of each side's basis of claim, and of the evidence in support of it, followed by a comparison of the relevant weight and merit of the claims as thus reviewed, and determination in favour of one of them as being the better.[114]

The fact that Iran has not consented to adjudication or arbitration indicates that it has doubts whether its case could withstand such procedures.

It can be noted here that arbitration has been determined to be the preferred means to be employed in default of any other means at the UN Conference on the Law of the Sea. Annex VI of the 1982 Convention on the Law of the Sea (UNCLOS) called for the establishment of the International Tribunal for the Law of the Sea (ITLOS) as a standing tribunal to arbitrate maritime boundaries or the maritime dimensions of a mixed land and sea boundary dispute. ITLOS was actually established in 1996 and began to consider its first case at the end of 1997.

> ITLOS, except for the Sea-Bed Disputes Chamber open only to States Parties to UNCLOS (Annex VI, article 20(1), is limited in principle to disputes arising out of the interpretation or application of the 1982 Law of the Sea Convention and related instruments and other applications submitted to it in accordance with the Convention (Annex VI, article 21)...For ITLOS, both the Council and the Assembly of ISBA [i.e. International Sea-Bed Authority] may request an advisory opinion from the Sea-Bed Disputes Chamber on legal questions arising in the course of their activities.[115]

This may be a vehicle for reaching agreement on a delimitation of the continental shelf between the UAE and Iran.

Finally, according to Article 96 of the UN Charter, "The General Assembly or the Security Council may request the International Court of Justice to give an advisory opinion on any legal question." Indeed, "[four] other organs of the United Nations and [fifteen] specialized agencies, which may at any time be so authorized by the General Assembly, may also request advisory opinions of the Court on legal questions arising within the scope of their activities."[116] The Court's 1975 opinion on the *Western Sahara Case* seems to indicate that if the Court has sufficient evidence and if it does not violate the propriety of the Court, the Court may render advisory opinions even when one or more of the parties to the dispute does not consent.[117] In the light of Iran's unwillingness to give its consent to adjudication or arbitration, this may be a legal option worth considering. While an advisory opinion is non-binding, the General Assembly could adopt the recommendation and seek to have the Security Council do the same.

In conclusion, a careful historical and legal analysis shows that Sharjah's claim to Abu Musa and Ras al-Khaimah's claim to the Tunbs are based on valid legal principles and compelling evidence. Iran, meanwhile, has not produced evidence to support its claims and has instead engaged in behavior that contradicts its claims, including illegal actions. The UAE's claims would be likely to succeed at an international tribunal, and this may explain Iran's unwillingness to submit the issue to such a tribunal. The UAE is aware of the difficulties involved in taking the legal route and therefore continues to prefer direct bilateral negotiations. This, however, requires a great deal of patience since Iran is the stronger power.

Occupation and Regional Instability

The dispute between the United Arab Emirates and Iran over Abu Musa and the Tunb islands has a direct bearing on the regional stability of the Gulf region. This stems partly from the strategic location of these islands. Abu Musa and the Tunbs lie along the two traffic lanes used by the world's merchant ships to navigate the shallow waters of the Gulf just inside the Strait of Hormuz. The Tunbs lie directly between the two traffic lanes. The westbound traffic lane from the direction of the Strait of Hormuz into the Gulf runs to the north of the Tunbs and then on to the north of the island of Forur. The eastbound traffic lane from the Gulf heading towards the Strait of Hormuz runs to the south of the Tunbs, making a northeast turn in the direction of the Strait of Hormuz at a point just south of the Greater Tunb. Sirri and Abu Musa lie a few miles to the south of the eastbound traffic lane. The use of these navigation channels is designed to ensure that merchant ships stay in sufficiently deep waters and that they avoid collisions and congestion.[1]

Most of the Gulf's oil exports are shipped by tankers through the Gulf and the Strait of Hormuz. By the late 1970s, Gulf states were exporting about 18 million barrels per day (mbpd) through this channel, nine-tenths of their production and almost one-third of the total world production of 60 mbpd.[2] When attacks on shipping during the Iran-Iraq War demonstrated the vulnerability of this route, pipeline capacities were expanded to serve as an alternative route to world markets.[3] By 2002, oil exports through the Gulf and the Strait had declined to about 13 mbpd, equivalent to two-thirds of regional production and a little over one-sixth of the total world production of about 74.5 mbpd.[4] Nevertheless, the traffic lanes through the Gulf and near the islands are destined to be the route for much of the Gulf's oil exports for the foreseeable future.

In addition to oil, tankers carried 21 billion cubic meters of Gulf liquefied natural gas exports in 1999 through this route, virtually all of the Gulf's exports of natural gas.[5] The Gulf states' growing imports of general cargo are also shipped through the Strait of Hormuz to Gulf ports. In 1980, twelve million tons of imports, thirty percent of the Gulf states' total imports, entered the Gulf this way. By 1998, 40 million tons of imports passed through this route on their way to UAE ports alone.[6] In general, it may be noted that the islands lying along these lanes are strategically located for monitoring, safeguarding or interfering with this important commerce in oil, gas and general cargo.

Moreover, Abu Musa, the Greater Tunb and the Lesser Tunb are located within relatively close range of the UAE's offshore oil and gas fields. The Mubarak oil field lies within the territorial waters of Abu Musa. The Fateh and Rashid oil fields are within close range of Abu Musa, as are the Sharjah and Umm al-Qaiwain gas fields. The Baih oil field as well as the Bukha, West Bukha and Saleh gas fields are within easy range of the Tunbs.[7] Their location makes the islands a potential platform for seizing, attacking or sabotaging the UAE's oil and gas fields.

Since 1971, when Imperial Iran seized the Tunbs from Ras al-Khaimah by force and successfully demanded that Sharjah acquiesce in an Iranian military presence on Abu Musa, Iran has controlled all the islands lying along these traffic lanes and close to these oil and gas fields. In 1986-1988, during the final years of the Iran-Iraq War, the Islamic Republic of Iran used its positions on Abu Musa and the Tunbs to launch attacks on shipping in the Gulf and oil platforms in the Mubarak offshore oil field, thus demonstrating how the control and use of these strategic islands can threaten the stability of this region.[8]

Since then, and particularly since 1992, Iran has violated its agreement with Sharjah on Abu Musa. It has fortified the islands, including Sharjah's zone, with advanced weaponry, and developed its potential capability to use the islands in order to interfere more effectively with maritime traffic and attack oil fields.[9] Iran has also rejected negotiation with the UAE about sovereignty over the three islands, as well as international adjudication and arbitration. Iran's past use of Abu

Musa and the Tunbs, as well as its growing military capabilities on all three islands and the Iranian mainland, represents a source of concern, not only to the UAE, but also to the GCC, the United States and all consumers of Gulf oil and gas. In addition, Iran's intentions, which are considerably more difficult to fathom, have to be seriously considered.

Iranian Motivations, Rationality and the Possibility of Conflict

In order to put the discussion into a proper context, it is important at the outset to mention briefly the motivations underlying the Iranian actions towards the islands. In 1971, Shah Mohammed Reza Pahlavi expressed the nationalist argument that the islands were the historic possessions of Iran. He claimed that the British had interfered with Iran's exercise of sovereignty and argued that it was important to recover them as British imperialism was withdrawing from the Gulf. Iranian officials had already argued in the 1960s that Iranian domestic opinion and national pride required the recovery of the islands. The Shah also advanced the strategic argument that Iranian control of the islands was important in guarding the vitally important sea-lanes through the Strait of Hormuz. Furthermore, Iran's Prime Minister Amir Abbas Hoveyda indicated an economic motivation when he expressed an Iranian interest in offshore oil locations surrounding the islands. These nationalist, strategic and economic arguments were powerful enough for Iran to oppose the federation of Trucial shaikhdoms during the 1960s until December 1971.

The Islamic Republic of Iran has shared all these motivations with the Shah's Iran. It views the islands as historic possessions recovered after years of foreign domination and argues that national pride will not permit any compromise over them. The islands are considered important in terms of the naval and air defense of the sea-lanes through the Strait of Hormuz, as well as for interfering with the shipping of other powers through those same sea-lanes. Moreover, the Islamic Republic of Iran continues to enjoy half of the revenue from the Mubarak oil field offshore of Abu Musa as agreed in the 1971 MoU.

The Islamic Republic has also had Islamic motivations that were not shared by the Shah's Iran, particularly a motivation to export its revolution and bring about changes in the governments and societies of the conservative states of the Lower Gulf. Islamic Iran's ideological challenge to Saddam Hussein's regime in Iraq contributed to the 1980–1988 Iran-Iraq War and Iran's use of the islands during the subsequent tanker war. Hooshang Amirahmadi, a scholar known for his sympathetic understanding of Iran, has noted these Islamic motivations in *Small Islands, Big Politics*, writing that revolutionary Iran's efforts to export its Islamic revolution and its anti-Western posture galvanized the GCC states to form their organization in 1981 in order to support Iraq during its war with Iran, and continued to underline their perception of the threat that exists vis-à-vis their larger northern neighbor. Nevertheless, he seems to stress nationalist motivations when he writes:

> …the small Persian Gulf monarchies consider Iran's rearmament program threatening…In this vein, the islands dispute reflects the UAE's fear of Iran's potential threat to its security. To some extent, the UAE's concerns are justified. When a territorial dispute has become embedded in nationalistic fervor between states in the region, a military confrontation has often followed, sometimes years later.[10]

Thus, while Amirahmadi argues that more recently a new pragmatism has emerged in Iran, that the previous commitment to export Iran's revolutionary ideology to the Gulf Arab states has therefore waned, and that Iran has learned from Desert Storm that attacking a Gulf Arab shaikhdom would be a major blunder, he also notes that the islands issue is a nationalist issue that could lead to conflict. "In Iran today," he writes, "the islands dispute has indeed become a national issue, making it impossible for the Iranian government to negotiate any concession."[11]

Moreover, Iran remains an Islamic state, and this influences its views about the importance of these islands. First, radical elements survive alongside pragmatic forces in Iran, and these radicals may still take opportunities to promote change and undermine regimes in Gulf Arab states. Second, Iran is at the very least committed to defending its Islamic character and is concerned that the United States is opposed to Iran because of its Islamic character. As Iran's Foreign Minister Kamal Kharrazi said in an interview in September 1994, when serving as Iran's Ambassador to the United Nations, US officials "claim that they do not have any quarrel with Iran's Islamic character, but in fact I think the problem is that our system is an independent, new model of living

Islamically, governing a state in an Islamic way and doing everything with Islamic values."[12] Iranian radicals and pragmatists alike fear that the United States will seize the islands and use them against Iran in order to undermine its Islamic regime.[13]

All of these Islamic and nationalist motivations underline the possibility of conflict. Indeed, there are many ways, short of a large-scale attack, that the Islamic Republic of Iran could use its occupation of the islands and its military capabilities on them to pressure, intimidate and damage the UAE. This could include attempting to force the UAE to help re-build the Iranian economy and/or to undermine UAE military ties with the United States. Iran could use the islands to launch commando operations against the UAE or its offshore oil fields or even to seize its offshore oil fields and, of course, to interfere with commercial shipping. Moreover, there are many ways that Iran could use the islands to interfere with US naval access to or presence in the Gulf.

A closely related issue that concerns analysts and officials who must assess the challenge posed by the Islamic Republic of Iran is whether Iran should be considered a rational or irrational actor. On the one hand, the possibility has been raised that the Iranian regime may not be rational and that it may therefore start a major conflict with the GCC states and the major Western powers despite the lessons, constraints, vulnerabilities and risks that would make it likely that Iran would suffer "massive costs."[14]

Some argue that the Iranian Revolutionary Guard Corps (IRGC) is not a professional military force, and that it may therefore disregard objective criteria and rational calculations of the outcomes of its behavior, acting instead on irrational or politically inspired motives to export the Islamic revolution. Thus, the Revolutionary Guard may undertake military action against the GCC that "is certain to fail" and costly to Iran, especially in the face of the US military presence, but that nevertheless imposes costs on the UAE, other GCC states and the United States. The examples of the Iranian attack on the US navy on April 18, 1988 and the military fortification of Abu Musa in the 1990s are cited as examples in this regard.[15] Others argue that Iran's deeply factional political system allows for the possibility that autonomous centers of power may emerge that will act on their own ideological convictions rather than on responsible calculations.[16]

Many others disagree with these assumptions. While acknowledging that Islamic Iran may want to be perceived as "crazy" because of the deterrent value associated with such recognition, a UAE official argues that in fact Iran knows exactly how far to go, and does not want to provoke a Western military response by attacking a GCC state. Therefore, instead of risking an all-out war against the US Fifth Fleet, Iran would carefully select its targets to show only that it is not weak and that it can take selective measures.[17]

Officers and analysts on the staff of the Joint Chiefs of Staff, at the US Defense Intelligence Agency (DIA) and in the US Navy say that while the US military plans for Iranian irrationality, Iran's behavior is often rational. They argue that Supreme Religious Leader Ayatollah Ali Khamene'i controls the regular armed forces and the Revolutionary Guard forces and that there is a deliberate and accountable decision-making process in place. Since the end of the Iran-Iraq War, there simply is not much evidence of behavior that can be called "irrational." Furthermore, they argue, since the US military can react even before Iran completes any provocation, Iranian assets on the islands could be destroyed the first time that Tehran carries out any provocative act.[18] A former commander of US Central Command (CENTCOM) in the 1990s says he never thought there would be a head-on US collision with Iran. Instead, it was always more likely that Iran would engage in asymmetrical responses, such as the bombing of the Khobar Towers in Saudi Arabia, rather than any direct response to the United States.[19]

One former diplomat in the UAE has stated that the virtual annexation and militarization of Abu Musa and the Tunbs demonstrate that the Iranians are "paranoid" and consider themselves a "beleaguered" race. This, however, does not mean that they are "stupid" and that they will launch just any type of military adventure.[20] Their paranoia, according to another diplomat, makes them operate on assumptions that are not correct, but again this does not mean that they will engage in irrational behavior. When the *USS Vincennes* mistakenly shot down an Iranian commercial aircraft flying over the Strait of Hormuz in July 1988, killing its 290 civilian passengers, Iran wrongly assumed that this was a deliberate US decision. This, however, caused Iran to be more rather than less cautious. The US military might displayed in 1990-1991 in Desert Shield/Desert Storm and in the campaign that toppled the regime of Saddam Hussein in 2003, have also made Iran more cautious. While Iran is unlikely to be reckless, it is possible that paranoia may result in miscalculations.[21]

Whether Iran is rational or irrational, there is general agreement that the country poses an extremely dangerous threat. For example, instead of choosing major conflict with considerable costs, Iran may choose limited, unattributable or deniable acts of aggression that cause damage to its adversary and that would be "less likely to trigger Western response or any coherent reaction by the Gulf states." Iran may also choose threats, pressure and intimidation to achieve its objectives. Thus, Iran may make rational calculations that harm the GCC and the West.[22] Moreover, Iran may engage in unconventional actions, terror and the use of weapons of mass destruction (WMD) as last resorts if it thinks that it is losing a conventional conflict against a superior force.[23] Under conditions where Iran perceives that its existence is threatened, seemingly irrational behavior like the use of unconventional actions, terror and WMD becomes defensive and "rational."[24]

What is clear in this debate is that the dispute over such strategically located islands could lead to or at least play a role in a future conflict. As a result, Iran's future behavior in the Gulf and on the islands is a subject of concern to analysts and officials. Thus, a closer examination of Iranian complaints, behavior, capabilities and intentions is merited, as is a consideration of the UAE responses to this problem.

Iranian Complaints, Demands, Threats and Actions

While basically pro-Western in orientation, the Shah did harbor certain resentments regarding the history of British intervention in Iran, which had included the forced abdication of his father in 1941. He also resented what he considered a history of unfair advantages enjoyed by Western oil firms in Iran and of inadequate western financial and military support to Iran.[25] What particularly aggravated the Shah was the history of British policy in the Gulf, which he viewed as having frustrated Iranian national ambitions, specifically regarding British support for the claims of Sharjah and Ras al-Khaimah to Abu Musa and the Tunbs. In June 1971, the Shah alleged: "The islands were ours: but some eighty years ago Britain interfered with the exercise of our sovereignty and grabbed them and subsequently claimed them for its wards, Sharjah and Ras al-Khaimah."[26] When Britain first announced its decision to pull out from the Gulf, the Shah demanded that Iran control Abu Musa and the Tunbs after the withdrawal. He threatened to seize the islands by force and to withhold recognition to the emerging United Arab Emirates if he did not get his way. In the end, Iran did obtain a negotiated MoU with Sharjah on Abu Musa, which permitted Iranian forces to occupy the northern half of the island in November 1971, and its military forces occupied the Tunbs by force in the same month.

The rulers of the Islamic Republic of Iran harbor more serious complaints regarding the history of major power intervention in the area, particularly regarding the history of US policy toward Iran, including US involvement in the coup that overthrew Prime Minister Mohammed Mosaddegh and restored the Shah to power in 1953.[27] In January 1979, after his return to Iran from exile, Ayatollah Rouhollah Khomeini expressed some of this feeling of ill-treatment:

> As for our own oil, it was given away to America and the others. It is true that America paid for the supplies it received, but that money was spent buying arms and establishing military bases for America. In other words, first we gave them our oil, and then we established military bases for them. America, as a result of its cunning (to which that man [the Shah] was also a party), thus benefited doubly from us. It exported weapons to Iran that our army was unable to use so that American advisers and experts had to come in order to make use of them. If the Shah's rule had (God forbid) lasted a few years longer, he would have exhausted our oil reserves in just the same way that he destroyed our agriculture.[28]

These resentments would increase throughout the 1980s and would be directed not only against the United States, but also against other major powers and the GCC. Primarily, this was due to support for Baghdad during the 1980–1988 Iran–Iraq War, a war in which Iraq invaded Iran and eventually used chemical weapons against it. The United States provided weapons and intelligence to Iraq and led an international arms embargo against Iran for much of the time after 1983. Saudi Arabia and Kuwait alone provided $50 to $60 billion to the Iraqi effort by the end of the war. Particularly damaging were Iraqi air force attacks against Iranian oil installations and Iranian shipping, particularly oil tankers carrying Iranian oil in the Lower Gulf, since Iran had no pipelines through neighboring countries and depended on the Gulf shipping lanes for its oil exports.[29] In response to these challenges, Speaker of the Majlis Akbar Hashemi Rafsanjani argued in October 1983:

> ...world arrogance does not wish the war to end, and all its noise is aimed at preventing an end to the war. When the United Nations, America, the Soviet Union, the West, and the region's reaction say that there must be peace, they lie. They precipitated the war to overthrow the Islamic Republic and to bring another shah to power so that he would protect the southern potentates. They intended to shape Saddam in this way, but their calculations went wrong...[30]

Iran warned producers and consumers of Arab oil that it would close the Strait of Hormuz if Iran could not export oil through it and told the GCC states not to support Iraq. In June 1984, for example, President Ali Khamene'i said:

> If you find that after all the help you have given it, Iraq refuses to listen to you [about halting attacks on oil tankers], then stop helping it. Stop making available your ports, your money, your propaganda. Get out of this war...we have nothing against you. If you continue, then we will have the right to act with firmness against all who oppose us...We do not want to fight Saudi Arabia, Qatar, Bahrain and others...but this is on condition that they do not get mixed up in this war.[31]

In November 1986, Iraqi air force attacks disabled the Iranian pumping facilities at its offshore Sassan (now named Salman) oil field on Iran's side of a shared UAE-Iran oil reservoir. When the UAE continued pumping oil from the UAE's Abu Al Bu Khoosh field on the UAE side despite Iranian protests, Iran attacked the UAE facilities.[32] Indeed, during the "tanker war" from 1986 to 1988, Iran attacked UAE off-shore oil fields, stopped and searched, and attacked "neutral" commercial shipping going to and coming from Kuwaiti and Saudi ports, as well as ports in the Lower Gulf. It also laid mines in the Gulf. Iran used its offshore oil platforms as well as Abu Musa and the Tunbs as bases for many of these attacks. Iran even launched eight Silkworm anti-ship missiles against Kuwaiti targets, hitting three of them, including the US-flagged Kuwaiti oil tanker, the *Sea Isle City*, in October 1987.[33]

The re-flagging and escorting of Kuwaiti and other oil and gas tankers by the United States and other major powers during the "tanker war" was particularly upsetting to Iran. In May 1987, Rafsanjani expressed the view that "the collusion between the United States and the USSR over the Persian Gulf is a conspiracy against Iran…This latest move, and the use of the superpowers' flag to allow passage of ships off Iran's shores is a flagrant intervention and disgrace."[34] This was followed by more direct confrontations. US naval forces retaliated against Iranian mine-laying in September and October 1987, and after an Iranian mine struck and damaged the USS *Samuel B. Roberts*, a US Navy destroyer, in April 1988. Iran fired on US naval forces in October 1987, April 1988 and July 1988, ultimately leading to US retaliation and serious Iranian losses.

In the case of the retaliatory US attacks in October 1987 and April 1988 against Iranian offshore oil platforms used to coordinate and conduct attacks against shipping, Iran has filed a suit against the United States at the International Court of Justice.[35] Iran is also deeply aggrieved by the shooting down of an Iranian civilian Airbus on a flight from Iran to Dubai by the USS *Vincennes* in July 1988, resulting in the death of all 290 passengers, believing that it was not an accident, but rather, as Rafsanjani called it, "a calculated plot." Following the incident, Tehran Radio said that "the criminal United States should know that the unlawfully shed blood in the disaster will be avenged in the same blood-spattered sky over the Persian Gulf."[36]

In general, Iran blames the major powers, particularly the United States, for the war itself and for the military defeat, economic destruction and political isolation that Iran found itself in at the end of the conflict. After discussing the damages suffered by Iran during this war, for example, President Rafsanjani told participants at the December 1994 seminar in Tehran on *Horizons for Cooperation in the Persian Gulf and the Oman Sea*: "It is a terrible experience for an aggressor country (such as the US) to force its dictates on the region…For instance, in Iraq's war against Iran, the countries from outside the region benefited from the sale of arms and imposed their desires."[37]

Tehran is particularly upset that the United States characterizes Iran as a threat to the GCC states and promotes arms sales to these states, thereby frustrating Iranian efforts to persuade the GCC states to join Iran in a Gulf security system that excludes foreign powers. In a 1994 interview, Iran's Ambassador to the UN Kamal Kharrazi said: "If Americans claim that this [Iranian] military expenditure is to threaten the states in the Persian Gulf, that is a baseless accusation. I think they make this claim to sell more arms to other states, and so far they have been successful." He continued: "We have tried our best to convince the southern states of the Persian Gulf that eventually we have to get together and come up with a security plan. But it seems that they are under pressure from outside powers, especially the United States."[38] Foreign Minister Ali Akbar Velayati stated that Iran was "a target for hostile propaganda of world imperialism," that "western interests are the enemies of the Islamic Republic," and that "the problems of the Persian Gulf are the result of western powers trying to loot the natural resources of the Persian Gulf." As far as Velayati was concerned, Iran was "trying to promote ties with its Persian Gulf neighbors to nullify the goals of its western enemies."[39]

As already noted, these criticisms are not limited solely to the US. Iran is highly critical of the GCC states, including the UAE, for permitting the US and other foreign military forces to increase their presence in the Gulf during and after the Iran–Iraq War, following Desert Shield and Desert Storm, and during mobilizations for military action against Iraq in 1994, 1998 and 2002–2003. This includes the financing of this presence, the purchasing of billions of dollars of conventional weapons from the United States and other major power vendors, and the developing of bilateral security ties with the United States, France and Britain, all of which are viewed as an effort to prevent Iran from exercising its rightful role in the Gulf. Iran has asked the GCC states to cut these ties.

In early 1993, President Rafsanjani criticized individual GCC states for their security agreements with the United States, saying "we are opposed to these pacts and believe that any military presence of the Westerners in the region is a factor disturbing peace and stability."[40] In his 1994 interview, Kharrazi echoed such sentiments and said: "It is a danger to Iran's national security and is not in the interest of the region to have so many forces here. How long do the Americans want to stay and protect these small countries? It costs a lot, and the small nations have to pay for it."[41] Notably, however, Iran has been relatively frank about how it views its rightful role in the Gulf vis-à-vis the GCC states. President Rafsanjani explained Iran's view in 1995: "We believe the littoral states in the Persian Gulf are the true owners of this area, and they have the responsibility to maintain security and peace there. Half of the coastline belongs to Iran, so Iran alone has the same amount of rights and responsibilities as all those countries put together."[42]

Iran's resentments go even further and are also directed at the United Nations Security Council for not condemning Iraq's 1980 invasion of Iran, for apathy regarding Iraqi missile and chemical weapons attacks against Iranian cities, for resolutions that Iran regarded as biased against Iran, and for engineering the secession of Iranian territory to Iraq after the cease-fire.[43] On June 24, 1987, for example, one month before the passing of Security Council Resolution 598, which called for a cease-fire and for an impartial body to investigate who started the war, and which Iran eventually accepted in July 1988, Prime Minister Mir-Hosain Musavi said that until the UN took action to "change its direction and expose the aggressor, condemn the aggressor, and suggest a way of trying the aggressor...a resolution by the Security Council will be considered worthless."[44]

Iran's Supreme Religious Leader, Ayatollah Khamene'i, expressed many of these ideas in his speech to the Organization of the Islamic Conference (OIC) held in Tehran in December 1997. He said:

> For eighteen years now, the political designers of arrogance are breathing their poisonous breath to make our neighbors in the Persian Gulf fearful of Islamic Iran...I declare that Islamic Iran poses no threat to any Islamic country...Right now, the presence of foreign warships and more importantly the US military muscle flexing in the Persian Gulf, which is an Islamic sea and an important source of energy for the entire world, [means that the region] is faced with insecurity. A powerful Organization of the Islamic Conference can...use the medium of Islamic power and dignity to force the alien forces to dispense with this intervention and...eliminate the pretexts for this presence [in the region.] The organization can, when needed,

deploy forces from the Islamic countries to preserve and safeguard peace and security in this area.[45]

Even Mohammed Khatami, the reformist cleric who became President of Iran in 1997, and who it was hoped would usher in a new era of relations between Iran and the outside world, expressed similar views during the OIC meeting. In his speech to the delegates, Khatami spoke of "the efforts of American politicians to impose their will on others," and called on Muslim nations to "valiantly resist all kinds of expansionism" and shape a new world based on pluralism. He continued:

> In the sensitive and strategic region of the Persian Gulf, the regional states themselves should undertake to preserve security and peace. In our view, the presence of foreign forces and armada in this sensitive area serves, not only as a source of tension and insecurity, but also of tragic environmental consequences...The Islamic Republic of Iran, while emphasizing cooperation among states in the Persian Gulf region for the preservation of regional peace and stability, considers the conclusion of collective defense-security arrangements for the Persian Gulf an assured step towards the establishment of lasting security in the region and towards the defense of the common interests and concerns of all the countries and nations concerned.[46]

Obviously, Tehran also resents the US policy of containment of Iran, including unilateral US economic sanctions on Iran and US efforts to persuade other states to join in these sanctions, viewing this as a continuing effort to reduce Iranian revenues and to keep it underdeveloped, in debt and isolated.[47]

Due to all these factors, Iran is highly distrustful of US offers for an authoritative dialogue. Rafsanjani said in 1995:

> Unfortunately, because of the behavior of the United States, there is not much trust in this country for the United States. It may be presumed in Iran that the United States has ulterior motives for this proposal [for an authoritative dialogue.] That is why we have said that the United States should, for once at least, prove its good intentions, so the road can be paved. I told them, for example, that as a show of good will, they can free our assets that have been illegally frozen in the United States.[48]

In December 1997, the new Iranian President, Mohammed Khatami, did call for a "thoughtful dialogue" with the United States, followed by an interview with the Cable News Network (CNN) on January 7, 1998, in which he explained his wish for an "exchange of professors, writers, scholars, artists, journalists, and tourists..."[49] However, Ayatollah Khamene'i insisted: "Talks with the US [Government] have no benefit for us and are harmful to us."[50] Khatami himself argued in a May 24, 1999 interview with the Qatar-based *Al-Jazeera* satellite television channel that any improvement in relations with Washington was conditional on a change in US policies and actions, stressing that US efforts to dictate and impose its policies by force should cease.[51]

Iranian suspicion and animosity toward the United States have been extended to the dispute over the islands. Specifically, Iran resents the United States for allegedly provoking the dispute between the UAE and Iran over Abu Musa and the Tunbs. Iranian President Rafsanjani said in 1992 that the UAE's position on the islands was part of a US "conspiracy...to justify its illegitimate presence in the Gulf."[52] Ayatollah Khamene'i stated at the same time that "the propaganda surrounding the Iranian island of Abu Musa is part of a conspiracy by the enemies of the Ummah [i.e. the Islamic brotherhood] to divide Iran from its neighbors," and particularly blamed the United States and Britain.[53] In 1995, President Rafsanjani again attributed this dispute to "foreign instigation, coming mainly from the US. They want to use this as a pretext to assert their military presence in the Persian Gulf."[54]

Whatever the case or motivation, Islamic Iran has warned that it will defend the islands with force against any attempt to re-take them. President Rafsanjani warned the GCC in December 1992 in most emphatic terms that "to reach those islands one has to cross a sea of blood."[55] Iran declared in that same month that it is willing to defend the islands against any attack and reminded its Gulf Arab neighbors that it was willing to fight for eighty years against Iraq.[56] Since President Khatami's election in 1997, Iran has been indicating that it wants more conciliatory relations with the Gulf Arabs. However, in his first news conference as President-elect, Khatami asserted that "the islands belong to Iran," and asserted that the dispute "should be settled through friendly and open dialogue" between Iran and the UAE. He further argued that "the intervention of other governments and powers would not be in the interest of either of us."[57] Since that time, Iranian officials have continued to insist that "the problem that is facing us is that of Abu Mousa and the mechanics of implementation of the 1971 memorandum of understanding."[58]

Clearly, Iran's manifold complaints against the United States, other major Western powers and the GCC states could lead it to perceptions and calculations that could in turn lead to the use of these islands in a wide range of defensive and offensive military operations. In order to consider this more fully, it is useful to examine Iran's military capabilities, particularly its capabilities on and around the islands. Thereafter, a much deeper re-examination of Iran's motivations or intentions will be warranted.

Iran's Military Acquisitions and Capabilities

Iranian ambitions in the Gulf are backed by a long history of military acquisitions and capabilities that seek to underline Iran's predominant position in the region. While Iran's security predicament is a factor behind its armament program, it is nevertheless a fact that the scale and scope of Iranian arms purchases are being viewed as a direct threat to the Arab Gulf states. Many of the systems are offensive in nature and Iran has also attempted to gain an unconventional weapons capability. In terms of ballistic missiles, Iran is in a position to launch attacks against the entire coast of the southern Gulf. Thus, the issue is not that Iran has the right to defend and arm itself, but that its armament program goes beyond what would normally be considered a reasonable deterrent posture. A particular concern, given Iran's other military capabilities, are the Iranian military forces positioned on the islands, which may again be used to interfere with Gulf shipping and/or to harass the UAE.

The Shah's Iran embarked on a major program of military modernization in anticipation of Britain's withdrawal from the Gulf. By the early 1970s, Iran had the only effective naval force in the Gulf. It had bases at Bushire and Bandar Abbas, conducted regular military exercises with the air force and army in the waters and islands of the Gulf, and had the capability to patrol all of Iran's coastal waters, its islands and much of the northwestern Indian Ocean. In November 1970, Iran's offensive power was demonstrated in a military exercise that included all three armed services near the island of Farur, to the west of the Tunbs. One year later, Iranian helicopters and hovercraft seized the

Tunbs and landed forces on Abu Musa. Thereafter, the Shah was in a position to fortify the islands.[59]

Under the Islamic Republic, Iran has attempted to re-build and expand its military capabilities after the significant losses of its equipment during the 1980-1988 Iran-Iraq War. Initially, particular attention was focused on building up the Iranian Air Force. This included the acquisition of Russian-made Sukhoi-24 ground attack strike fighters equipped with long-range fuel tanks and capable of being refueled in flight by an aircraft such as the US-made F-14, which, along with US-made F-4s and F-5s, forms part of Iran's older inventory. Not only does the Sukhoi-24 have the potential capability to strike any point target in Iraq and the southern Gulf states, but the version acquired by Iran, the Sukhoi-24 MK (Fencer-D), can also deliver air-to-surface missiles and chemical, biological and nuclear weapons.[60] This and other purchases led one analyst to observe: "It is clear from Iran's imports that it is seeking to obtain first-line air defense and long-range strike fighters and to rebuild a high-technology air force that can provide both effective air defense and the ability to strike deep into Iraq, the southern Gulf states, and any other neighboring power."[61]

Iran's ballistic missile capability and its pursuit of a weapons of mass destruction (WMD) program is another concern. Iranian purchases of missile systems include the Chinese-made CSS-7 and CSS-8 (with ranges of 300 km and 150 km respectively) and Scud-B and Scud-C missiles from North Korea (with ranges of 290-310 km and 550 km respectively). In July 1998, Iran test-fired the Shahab-3 intermediate-range ballistic missile, based on the North Korean No-Dong model, with a range of 1,300 km, a test repeated in July and September 2000. Some of these tests were only partially successful, but in early May 2002 Iran conducted a successful test flight of the Shahab-3 missile, thus bringing Israel and US troops in the region within Iran's range.[62] A final delivery test was conducted in June 2003.[63]

Iran is also reportedly developing the Shahab-4, with a range of over 2000 km, based on the Soviet SS-4 Sandel intermediate-range missile. This would bring some of southeastern Europe within Iran's range.[64] Iran does not yet have sophisticated long-range targeting capability and ballistic missile systems with the accuracy to attack point targets. However, Iran clearly has obtained the capability to launch ballistic missile attacks against large area targets such as cities along much of the coast of the southern Gulf. Thus, Iranian ballistic missiles carrying conventional warheads pose a major threat as weapons of terror that could arouse popular fear and intimidate the Gulf Arab states.[65]

Indeed, these ballistic missile developments may also advance Iran's weapons of mass destruction capabilities, and the obvious terror and intimidation this could arouse.[66] It may be noted here that the Revolutionary Guard's land forces operate Iran's ballistic missile forces, have offensive and defensive chemical warfare capabilities, and are reportedly involved in the development and management of Iran's chemical, biological and nuclear weapons programs.[67] With foreign assistance, some of it from China, Iran has produced chemical weapons, including blister agents like sulfur mustard gas and blood agents like hydrogen cyanide, phosgene gas and chlorine gas. Iranian forces used these in bombs and artillery shells during the Iran–Iraq war after being attacked with chemical weapons by Iraq. Iran may also be producing chemical weapons like the nerve agents Sarin and Tabun.[68] Furthermore, Iran appears to be trying to develop biological weapons, including toxins and diseases like anthrax and foot and mouth disease. Iran may acquire biological weapons capabilities similar to its chemical weapons capabilities, enhancing its intimidation and deterrence capabilities.[69]

Finally, Iran may also be trying to develop a nuclear weapons capability. In addition to Russia's agreement to complete two 1,200 megawatt light water nuclear reactors in Bushire, originally started by German firms during the Shah's regime, there have also been numerous reports about Iranian attempts to acquire enriched uranium from foreign sources or seeking assistance to produce weapons-grade uranium and plutonium themselves.[70] In June 2002, Russia announced plans to build five additional nuclear reactors for Iran. In August, it was reported that Iran was constructing two or more facilities for fabricating and processing nuclear fuel. One of these was a large centrifuge facility for uranium enrichment. Another was a heavy water plant. In December 2002, satellite photographs confirmed the construction of new facilities, and in February 2003 Iran announced that it was mining its own uranium deposits for nuclear fuel.[71] If it were to acquire a working nuclear weapon and the capability to deliver it, Iran would be able to destroy any hardened target, any area target or any city in the Middle East.[72]

These developments certainly give cause for anxiety. Of more immediate concern, however, are Iranian acquisitions of missiles and other military hardware that provide the Islamic Republic with the capability to interdict shipping in the Gulf. On its own shore, Iran has surface-to-surface anti-ship cruise missile batteries with Chinese CSSC-2 (HY-1) Silkworm and CSSC-3 (HY-2) Seersucker cruise missiles, Chinese CSS-N-4 (C-801) Sardine-1 cruise missiles and the more capable and reliable CSSC-8 (C-802) Sardine-2 cruise missiles, and Russian SS-N-22 Sunburn cruise missiles. These missiles are operated by the naval branch of the Revolutionary Guard and easily have the range to cover shipping through the Strait of Hormuz, which is only 39 km wide at its narrowest point. In addition, Iran has test-fired C-801 and C-802 missiles from ship and aircraft launching platforms and therefore may be able to extend the range of its ability to attack shipping in the Gulf.[73]

Iran has also added to its surface navy, which includes frigates and corvettes, by acquiring Chinese-supplied Houdong-class fast attack boats and Chinese-supplied missile patrol boats for the naval branch of the Revolutionary Guard.[74] These new Houdong-class fast attack boats are reportedly armed with the C-802 anti-ship missile with a 120 km range, as are Iran's older Combattante II Kaman-class fast attack boats.[75] These naval craft can be used to defend against the re-taking of islands like Abu Musa and the Tunbs and in defense of Iranian shipping and oil and gas facilities in the Gulf. These craft can also be used in offensive operations against commercial and naval shipping, islands, oil and gas facilities, ports and coastal targets of other states.

Moreover, the ship-based platforms for these anti-ship missiles, like air-based platforms, would provide Iran not only with the ability to conduct operations over a greater range of area, but also to do so with more mobility. These platforms would be harder to target than Iran's shore-based anti-ship missile batteries. These naval craft could be joined in these missions by the fast patrol/interdiction/interceptor boats of the Revolutionary Guard's naval branch, such as the Swedish-built Boghammer fast interceptors, with a range of 926 km, as well as Boston

Whalers, both of which played a role in attacking shipping during the 1986-88 "tanker war."[76]

Between 1992 and 1997, Iran took delivery of three Russian-made diesel-electric powered Kilo-class submarines equipped with torpedoes, mines and surface-to-air missiles.[77] These are operated by the regular navy and the naval branch of the Revolutionary Guard.[78] According to *Jane's Fighting Ships*, "The northern Gulf of Oman and the few deep water parts of the Persian Gulf are notoriously bad areas for anti-submarine warfare. These submarines will be vulnerable to attack when alongside in harbor but pose a severe threat to merchant shipping either with torpedoes or mines."[79]

In June 1999, US Navy Rear Admiral Malcolm Fages, the director of submarine warfare operations, said that by 2005 Iranian anti-ship cruise missiles, mines and diesel submarines could threaten and possibly deny access to the Gulf by the US Navy.[80] Indeed, the primary purpose of the Iranian submarines may eventually be to serve as barriers to shipping traffic, e.g. other submarines, surface warships, oil tankers or LNG tankers. This may be the case outside the Strait of Hormuz in the Gulf of Oman, where deep water allows better sound propagation for detecting their targets at a longer distance and where the Iranian submarines are closer to their home base at Bandar Abbas and their operational and logistical support.[81]

Iran also has a small number of midget submarines, three of its own make and three of North Korean design. These submarines can release mines from inside the hull, allow divers to exit and attach mines to a target and then re-enter, or allow divers to exit and swim to a target shore for commando operations.[82] Iran also has about six swimmer delivery vehicles (SDVs).[83] These are submersible vehicles that can carry one or two frogmen and a payload of mines from a mother ship, such as a submarine or even a fishing vessel, to a target, such as an oil rig, ship's hull, port or coast, and then back to the mother ship.[84]

Iran also has mine-laying and mine-sweeping surface vessels. Considering all its mine-laying capabilities, Iran could lay mines in the Gulf's tanker lanes, in the approaches to the Strait of Hormuz, in the Strait itself or in the Gulf of Oman, where sweeping and defensive coverage would be harder than inside the Gulf. Mining these waters would enable Iran to intimidate, harass and disable shipping. The use of mining as well as land-based, ship-based and air-based anti-ship missiles, commando raids and submarine torpedoes would enable Iran to mount diverse attacks against shipping that would be difficult to counter-attack.[85] Mines alone, or even the threat to lay mines, could be enough to deter tankers from entering these waters. Mines, anti-ship missiles and submarines could also be enough to keep US aircraft carriers from venturing into trouble.

Iran's surface navy includes amphibious craft that allow Iran to deploy 30-50 tanks and 800-1,200 troops in an amphibious assault. Thus, Iran has the potential capability to deploy battalion-sized forces across the Gulf to support a popular uprising, a civil war or a coup attempt in a small Gulf Arab state, or to seize or attack islands or off-shore oil facilities. Iran could use its amphibious forces in covert operations to deploy unconventional forces, to supply arms to radical movements in the Gulf, to smuggle a chemical weapon across the Gulf, to seize undefended islands and to sabotage off-shore oil operations, ships, ports and desalination facilities, particularly if it achieved surprise and/or operated at night.[86]

Operations such as these could be carried out by elite Revolutionary Guard land forces capable of performing special forces, commando, infiltration, terrorism and unconventional warfare missions. Revolutionary Guard naval forces are also capable of performing wide-ranging unconventional warfare missions. These IRGC naval forces have naval artillery divers, mine-laying units, scuba equipment and an underwater combat center based at Bandar Abbas.[87]

Knowledge about Iranian amphibious capabilities is partly based on observation. Iran conducts regular land, sea and air military exercises in the Gulf, including missile, amphibious and unconventional warfare training. During these exercises the regular army, navy and air forces operate jointly with the Revolutionary Guard land, navy and air force units. One major exercise in 1992, named Victory 3, practiced blocking the Strait of Hormuz to an outside military power, mining waters and "amphibious operations and the deployment of marines on enemy shores," including "ground combat units penetrating into the depths of the hypothetical enemy's coastal positions."[88] In numerous exercises held from March 1995 onwards, Iran has continued to practice blockades of the Strait of Hormuz, interdiction of traffic, deployment of land-based

SS-N-22 Sunburn and HY-2 Seersucker anti-ship missile batteries, testing of anti-ship missiles, including the C-802, submarine warfare, electronic warfare, seizing islands and oil fields, sabotaging ports, covert landings with midget submarines and attacking coastal targets.[89]

A UAE military source notes that in recent years Abu Musa and the Tunbs have figured in these Iranian exercises. The command post on Abu Musa has coordinated forces located there with forces at the Tunbs and Sirri. Air defense radars on the islands have been tested, and special forces have landed and taken off from the islands on small boats.[90] These activities have taken place during exercises such as the "Fateh-77" or "Victor-77" exercises held in February and March 1999.[91] Indeed, Iran has also brought Houdong-class fast attack boats armed with C-802 missiles to Abu Musa during these exercises and during patrols. As far as the UAE is concerned, the size of the Iranian forces and scale of the exercises at Abu Musa, only 50 km away from the UAE mainland and 20 km away from UAE oilfields, has to be considered a potential threat, since Iran is quite capable of bringing forces from Abu Musa to the UAE mainland.[92]

Overall, it can be said that the United States and several GCC states regard the general Iranian military buildup as a serious threat. In a 1995 publication entitled *United States Security Strategy for the Middle East*, the US Department of Defense cited Iran's acquisition of conventional weapons and its military build-up on the disputed islands as evidence that Iran "is actively seeking the capability to menace merchant ships moving in and out of the Gulf" and "is assertively flexing its muscles vis-à-vis its smaller Gulf neighbors."[93]

Since that time, the concerns over Iran's intentions and its growing ability to interfere with shipping in the Gulf as well as to block the Strait of Hormuz have not been allayed. As Secretary of Defense William Cohen said in June 1997: "Iran's words and actions suggest that it wants to be able to intimidate its neighbors and to interrupt commerce in the Gulf."[94] Clearly, as US officials have argued, and as Iran's military exercises have demonstrated, Iran's occupation and militarization of the islands could play a key role in many of these operations, thus warranting scrutiny of Iran's military assets on these islands.

Iran's Military Assets on Abu Musa and the Tunbs

There is relatively widespread agreement that Iran has certain kinds of military assets on Abu Musa and the Tunb islands, including small, company-size numbers of personnel. Eyewitness and news reports indicate that the Iranian military presence on Abu Musa had grown from just over one hundred in 1992 to several thousand in early 1995, largely Revolutionary Guard naval forces.[95] A US Navy Intelligence source indicated in September 1997 that Abu Musa had 2000 Iranian military personnel, the Greater Tunb had 1100 and the Lesser Tunb had 300 Iranian military personnel.[96] According to a UAE military source in May 1999, there is a regular and a Revolutionary Guard marine brigade on Abu Musa, a Revolutionary Guard marine brigade on the Greater Tunb, and a Revolutionary Guard marine battalion on the Lesser Tunb. He noted that these marine forces are offensive in character, not defensive.[97]

In terms of military hardware, Iran has had limited numbers of short-range defensive anti-aircraft artillery (AAA), surface-to-air missiles (SAMs) and radar stations on Abu Musa and the Greater Tunb since the Iran–Iraq War. These weapons are capable of tactical, close-in defense of the islands, but they are not comparable to the larger, more potent systems like the SA-5s at Bandar Abbas with a range of 250 km.[98] In the fall of 1994, Iran deployed 155 mm artillery and Russian-made SA-6 surface-to-air missiles on Abu Musa. The SA-6, with a maximum range of 24 to 40 km, is also a short-range defensive missile. In February 1995, Iran also deployed older versions of the US-made Improved Hawk (IHawk) surface-to-air missiles to Abu Musa, another 40 km short-range defensive missile developed during the 1970s.[99] There are also SA-6 surface-to-air missile sites on the Greater Tunb.[100]

Prior to 1992, there was a pier, an airstrip, helicopters and a desalination plant on the island of Abu Musa.[101] Since then, there has been major construction, in addition to the deployment of older heavy tanks, artillery and missiles. The analyst Anthony Cordesman writes that by February 1995 "Iran had lengthened the runway on Abu Musa so that it could accept larger military cargo aircraft, built a new pier inside the breakwater, constructed a new command bunker, deployed IHawk missiles south of the runway, and established a new desalination plant."[102] Plans for a regular air service from Bandar Abbas to Abu Musa raised concerns in the UAE that this would facilitate the movement of military and civilian personnel and the supplying and stockpiling of the island with military and other supplies.[103] There is also a pier and an airstrip on the Greater Tunb.[104]

Some of these military assets on Abu Musa were made public in the March 8, 2000 issue of *Jane's Defence Weekly*, which published the first commercially-released 1 meter resolution satellite image of Abu Musa, an image taken by the IKONOS satellite on October 29, 1999 while orbiting at a height of 423 miles or 680 km. This image shows a 4 km long airstrip, running east to west along the length of the island and capable of handling medium-transport and fighter aircraft, a concrete pier and a ramp for roll-on and roll-off landings near a breakwater on the western end of the island. The satellite image also reveals what appears to be a desalination facility to the east of the port area and residential accommodation in the north for officers, soldiers and construction workers.

Other features that can be identified include an apparent command bunker near the residential area, which is cut into the side of a hill and could later be filled in for concealment and protection, and a series of revetments cut into a hillside in the northeast, which could serve as multiple entry and exit points for an underground storage facility. It shows another series of revetments in the northeast that could also indicate a storage facility. In addition, there are a series of revetments in the southeast of the island that face the beach and contain armored vehicles, possibly tanks and/or self-propelled guns such as AAA or SAMs.[105]

In general, *Jane's Defence Weekly* was struck by "the lack of major military infrastructure and fortification" and wrote that "there is little visible evidence of surface-to-air batteries and their tracking radar." It concluded that the image "could refute many of the claims made by the UAE and the USA." However, the magazine acknowledged that "Gauging capabilities is difficult with only one image, and careful photo reconnaissance would be needed over a period of months to gain a more accurate picture."[106]

In fact, an accurate picture would actually require looking at photo reconnaissance obtained over the past fifteen to twenty years of military developments on the island from the early years of the Iran–Iraq

War in the beginning of the 1980s. The image released in March 2000 is unable to show any bunker or depot that had already been built and concealed or the assets stored inside those depots. For example, Iran's SA-6 and IHawk surface-to-air missiles, launchers and radars may have been in storage when this photo was taken. This may also be true of AAA and anti-ship missile systems and tanks.[107] Moreover, this image is not a high-resolution image. It does not show assets on the island that have already been identified in higher resolution images that are not commercially available.

Classified evidence from May 1999 of Iranian military developments on Abu Musa include military assets such as barracks, troops, bunkers, storage depots, tanks, artillery, surface-to-air missile sites and anti-ship missile sites on both the northern half of Abu Musa assigned to Iran, and the southern half of Abu Musa assigned to Sharjah. On Abu Musa, there is a network of underground bunkers stretching around the circumference of the island, i.e. including the southern zone allocated to Sharjah. These bunkers are linked to each other for easy troop movements between them and are equipped with machine guns. There is a second ring of bunkers behind this, followed by a third ring of tanks. This network of bunkers is underground and covered with sand.

At the time this evidence was obtained, the building on the network was continuing, as attested by the presence of portable bunkers above ground, next to holes dug for them and near mounds of sand intended to cover them over. There are also land mines scattered throughout these rings of defense. Furthermore, there are anti-aircraft artillery sites in the center of the island and surface-to-air missile sites and anti-ship missile sites in the southeast of the island, i.e. in Sharjah's zone. The airstrip runs the entire length of the island, east to west.[108]

Nevertheless, there remain significant differences of opinion, also among UAE and US officials, regarding other military assets that Iran may or may not have on the islands. On October 23, 1992, the London-based Saudi newspaper *Al-Sharq Al-Awsat* reported that Iran had set up eight missile launching sites on Abu Musa. The paper reported that these were to be used to launch Chinese-made Silkworm anti-shipping missiles and modified North Korean-made Scud-B surface-to-surface missiles. UAE Brig. Gen. Mohammed Al-Kaabi wrote in 1994:

Since these are very different sorts of weapons there is some
reason to doubt the story; Western sources [in 1994] only
confirm surface-to-air missile sites on Abu Musa, though
Iranian opposition sources have also said Silkworms will be
based there. Militarily the Island could be a potent site for
Silkworms, which are used against shipping.[109]

Another UAE official argues that the Iranians do have Silkworms,
Scuds and short-range chemical weapons on Abu Musa and the Tunbs,
and that these weapons can reach all vital installations in the UAE.[110]
While US intelligence analysts agree that Iran has the capability to
deploy the long-range strategic Scuds on the islands, they also point out
that Iran does not need to move Scuds off the mainland in order to hit
the emirates.[111] Evidence provided by a UAE military source does not
show Scuds on the islands, although they could possibly be in storage.[112]

US Secretary of Defense William Perry spoke publicly in the
spring of 1995 about Iranian deployment of chemical weapons on Abu
Musa, including 155 mm shells, and called this "very threatening."
Cordesman writes that some US experts feel that Secretary Perry
confused the deployment of poison gas with the deployment of non-
lethal agents. He notes instead that Iran seems to have deployed small
stocks of non-lethal CS gas (i.e. Civil Service gas, or tear gas) on the
island.[113] Again, evidence provided by a UAE military source does not
actually show such weapons, but they could be in storage.[114]

There are reports that Iran deployed CSSC-3 (HY-2) Seersucker
anti-ship missiles on Abu Musa in the fall of 1994, and that an anti-
ship missile site for launching the CSSC-3 was built on the south side
of Abu Musa in February 1995. The Seersucker missile, an advanced
modification of the Silkworm with a range of 150 km, would be capable
of hitting the UAE's major ports, including those to the south and west
of Abu Dhabi. It should be noted here that Dubai's Jebel Ali port is
where US naval forces in the UAE are concentrated. It has also been
reported that Iran may have deployed Silkworms and Seersuckers on the
island of Sirri, to the west of Abu Musa, which would add even more to
its potential range for attacks on shipping and ports.[115] A UAE military
source has verified that there are anti-ship Seersucker missiles on Sirri.[116]

A US official has stated that there were launchers for surface-to-
air missiles and for Silkworm anti-ship missiles on Abu Musa as early as

the tanker war of 1986-88. He also recalls that there were concealed storage bunkers for these weapons, although it was never verified that these bunkers were stocked with missiles or that these launchers were loaded with missiles. Indeed, the official admits that the US never had a picture of a Silkworm on the island and could never confirm the presence of such a missile. As he pointed out, there was and is no surveillance capable of looking underground and the US therefore has to be looking at the right time to see any offloading of missiles before they are stored in a bunker. There also was and is no constant surveillance and the US can only see an offloading of missiles when an orbiting reconnaissance satellite is in the right position.[117]

Analysts from the US defense community say that Iran does have the capability to deploy Silkworms and Seersuckers as well as C-801 and C-802 anti-ship cruise missiles on the islands. These analysts showed evidence to the author of this study that designates an Iranian anti-ship cruise missile site on the southern half of Abu Musa. Silkworms and Seersuckers (and C-801s and C-802s) are mobile and can be constantly moved on and off the islands. Anti-ship missiles are hard to detect because they can be relatively easily and quickly transported from the mainland and stored in underground bunkers on the islands. They would also be deployed in a mobile mode. Iran could hide them on ships below deck, transport them to the islands, offload them in minutes at night and put them in buildings or in underground storage depots. The inhabitants of the islands would not know and satellite reconnaissance might not detect the movement. Since these weapons are short-range tactical weapons that can already hit shipping from the mainland, it is suggested that Iran would only deploy these weapons on the islands in an extreme case, because they also rely on shipping through the Gulf and the Strait of Hormuz.[118]

A UAE military source has reported, however, that Iran has brought C-801s to the Greater Tunb, where there also is an anti-ship missile launching site.[119] Clearly, deployment on the islands would give Iran the capability to increase the range of its attacks against shipping and UAE ports well beyond its range of attacks from the mainland. Even if one were to put military issues aside, there still exists a political reason for deploying the missiles on the islands in that Iran does not actually have to attack shipping but can simply alarm shipping and insurance companies with its potential to attack shipping.[120]

The foregoing discussion indicates that it is difficult to verify whether Iran had Silkworms or the CSSC-3 Seersucker variant of the Silkworm on Abu Musa in the fall of 1994, or whether they have been stored or deployed on the island since then. The same applies to the C-801s or C-802s on the Greater Tunb or on Abu Musa. However, it is clear that Iran has the capability to move these weapons to these islands, to store them and to deploy them.

Finally, since the Iran–Iraq war, Iran has had fast interdiction boats, such as the Boghammers and the Boston Whalers, based at Bandar Abbas but operating out of Abu Musa and the Tunbs.[121] One US official indicates that other fast attack boats were also calling at Abu Musa during the war, perhaps the Kaman-class Combattante fast attack boats, and that they were armed with Styx missiles (a Soviet-made surface-to-surface anti-ship missile comparable to the Chinese-made Silkworm).[122]

These kinds of naval assets not only give Iran some capability to defend the islands, but also the capability to interfere with shipping by laying mines and attacking vessels with recoilless rifles, machine guns, multi-grenade and multi-rocket launchers, and anti-ship missiles. When operating from Abu Musa and the Tunbs, they can also threaten operations at oil and gas fields in the Gulf. If Iran's Houdong-class fast attack boats armed with C-802s were to operate from the islands, it could significantly extend their range of attacks with these 120 km range anti-ship missiles. According to a UAE military source, Iran has brought the Houdong-class fast attack boats armed with the C-802s to Abu Musa and the Tunbs during patrols and military exercises.[123]

Some US intelligence analysts say the islands give Iran primarily defensive capabilities, but very little power projection capability. However, as Iran could use the islands for mining and to interdict shipping, the islands do provide forward staging capabilities. Along with Iranian military assets on the mainland, the islands give Iran the additional capability to close the strait and permit greater range to interfere with shipping and attack oil and gas facilities to the west of the strait. Still, there is a cost/benefit ratio for Iran to consider, as Iranian military assets on the islands are even more vulnerable than their military assets on the mainland. The terrain is susceptible to US air and sea interdiction, with little risk to US forces. In fact, the Iranians are aware of just how vulnerable their forces are on the islands, including those on Sirri and Qishm. The result is that Iran is constrained from being too aggressive.[124]

Inasmuch as Iran's ship-based C-802s are now reported to have an over-the-horizon range of 120 km, it would seem that the shore-based C-802s would also have that range. Deployment on the islands would extend their range even further. One should also consider that in a complex and confused conflict scenario, Iran might be able to launch more than one anti-ship missile from the islands before the islands were neutralized. Moreover, if the islands were used in mine-laying operations, the mines would do damage even after the islands have been neutralized. Iran could also launch amphibious or covert operations from the islands against the UAE or other targets on the southern coast before the islands were neutralized. Finally, and importantly, the islands could provide these diverse forward staging, power projection military advantages to the Iranians if, as during the 1986-1988 tanker war, the US decided for political and legal reasons not to make Abu Musa and the Tunbs targets for the US military.

The Iranians argue that their country's re-armament is essentially a rebuilding effort after the devastation of the Iran–Iraq War and that it is a defensive response to the perceived dangers on all of Iran's borders, particularly the threat of the US military presence in the Gulf. They argue that Iranian defense expenditures involve a smaller percentage of GNP than the military expenditures of Iran's neighbors in the Gulf, particularly Saudi Arabia, and that they are not intended to threaten Iran's Gulf Arab neighbors.[125]

The question remains whether the Iranian buildup is only meant to deter conflict and to defend Iran, whether the military development is part of a spiraling "arms race" in the Gulf that could inadvertently provoke the very conflict it is meant to deter, or whether Iranian actions are meant to intimidate, threaten and prepare for aggression. Some officials from the UAE, other GCC states and the United States think that Iran has hegemonic ambitions, but not offensive intentions. Nevertheless, US and UAE planners have to be prepared for the possibility that the intent behind the Iranian military rebuilding is to commit aggression or at least to intimidate and threaten GCC states. They cannot rely on speculation about Iranian intentions, but must depend on the hard realities of Iranian capabilities. Many observers argued, right up to the last minute in the summer of 1990, that Iraq had no intention to invade Kuwait. Moreover, intentions can change. Nevertheless, the more that can be understood of Iranian intentions, the better.

Contending Arguments About Iran's Intentions

Contending arguments about Imperial Iran's intentions in occupying the islands in 1971 focus on domestic, nationalistic, economic and strategic factors. A former aide to British mediator Sir William Luce recalls that the Shah told Luce that he had lost some domestic credibility in yielding Iran's claim to Bahrain in 1970 and thought he ought to be compensated for this with the islands.[126] Indeed, the Shah had claimed in the 1960s that surrendering Iran's claim to Bahrain would provoke a nationalist reaction and embarrass the regime. He had therefore sought recognition of Iran's claim to the islands before yielding Iran's claim to Bahrain.

Others have argued that while the domestic nationalist reaction, which turned out to be rather mild, was a consideration, the Shah was fundamentally using Bahrain as a bargaining chip to obtain the three islands.[127] Beyond the issue of domestic credibility, some have reported that Iranian officials actually believed their own argument that Iran had historical claims to the islands, despite their inability to produce documentation.[128] The Shah himself often made the nationalist argument that the islands were rightfully Iran's and insisted that he was determined to "restore" them to Iran. In a meeting with William Luce at Niavaran Palace on May 4, 1971, the Shah is said to have stated that "he could not preside over an auction of Iranian territory" and claimed that the islands were Iranian.[129] Similarly, in January 1972, he tried to justify taking the islands on the alleged basis that "historic facts and documents prove that these islands belong to us. We are not here to watch the annexation of a part of our territory to please no matter which country."[130]

Others have argued that Iran wanted the islands for the potential oil reserves around them.[131] The possibility of discoveries around the islands was certainly a factor in the Shah's thinking. As early as 1956, Iranian Prime Minister Hussein Ala acknowledged that Iran intended to occupy Abu Musa and the Tunb islands partly because of Iranian interest in offshore petroleum rights in the Gulf. In 1959, Iran established a twelve-mile territorial sea around islands under its sovereignty, so as to extend its claim to the oil resources around them. Prime Minister Asadollah Alam confirmed in 1963 that Iran's interest in the islands stemmed from the belief that one of them had offshore oil reserves.

Mecomoil had expectations of discovering oil off the coast of Abu Musa at that very time. Through the 1960s and 1970s, Mecomoil, the Buttes Gas and Oil Company and Occidental Petroleum Company were exploring in the area off Abu Musa, and the Union Oil Exploration and Production Company and the Southern Natural Gas Company had concessions to explore around the Tunbs.[132]

Thus, the islands held potential economic value to the Shah, who wanted to restore the Iranian superiority in oil production that had been lost during the international embargo of Iranian oil following the Mosaddegh government's 1951 nationalization of the Anglo-Iranian Oil Company. At that time, Saudi Arabia, Kuwait and Iraq had emerged as major producers and competitors. In the 1960s, oil provided 50% of the Iranian government's revenue and 75% of its hard currency, while concessions in the Gulf accounted for one-eighth of Iran's oil production and constituted Iran's most profitable deals with oil companies.[133]

There is also general agreement that the Shah sought Iranian hegemony in the Gulf. As early as 1964 and 1965, the Shah indicated to the British that Iran could take over the British role in the Gulf and expressed his opposition to the United States moving in to replace the British. In the wake of the British announcement in 1968 that Britain would withdraw its forces from the Gulf in 1971, the Shah initially expressed some ambivalent interest in regional defense cooperation among the littoral states. Nevertheless, he intended and prepared for Iran to become the principal guardian of the Gulf, even discouraging any US and certainly any Soviet military bases inside the Gulf.[134]

A number of analysts have pointed to the Shah's argument that the three islands were of strategic importance and that Iran must control them as they lay at the entrance to the Strait of Hormuz. After all, this was the route through which not only most of Iran's oil and gas exports and its vital imports passed, but also most Gulf oil flowed to its Western consumers.[135] Referring to the islands on October 23, 1971, the Shah expressed concern about "the possibility of certain strategic positions falling into the wrong hands: a small group of men using a boat and a bazooka could threaten navigation in the waterway."[136] Speaking specifically about Abu Musa in January 1972, he explained "our forces were sent to the island to take up positions on strategic heights there so that they could ensure the stability of the region."[137]

The Shah had also previously expressed his concern about the brand of radical pan-Arab nationalism being championed in Yemen's civil war and in the Gulf by Egypt's President Gamal Abdul Nasser, who had asserted the Arab character of Bahrain, Abu Musa, the Tunbs and the Gulf. The Shah told British Foreign Secretary Lord Home in 1963 that he feared that the shaikhdoms would come under Nasser's control, and he complained to his Majlis in 1964 about Nasser's "conspiracy," "subversive plans" and "aggressive and imperialist policy" in the Gulf. This fear, however, receded after Egypt's defeat by Israel in the 1967 war and Egypt's subsequent withdrawal from Yemen and from Gulf affairs.[138]

The Shah next expressed his concern that the rebellion in the Dhofar province of Oman, a rebellion supported by the Marxist-Leninist People's Democratic Republic of Yemen (PDRY), i.e. South Yemen, as well as by Baathist Iraq, might spread throughout the Gulf region. South Yemen and the rebels, known as the Popular Front for the Liberation of the Occupied Arabian Gulf and later as the Popular Front for the Liberation of Oman and the Arab Gulf (PFLOAG), had pledged to "liberate" the Arab Gulf states under British protection. The Shah was concerned that PFLOAG, South Yemen or other subversives might seize the emirates and the islands and interfere with oil traffic. In July 1971, for example, he commented on the islands: "Their geographic position can make them issues of tremendous military value," adding that "Only the other day the South Yemenis issued a communiqué vowing to bring revolution to the whole region of the Persian Gulf."[139]

After taking control of the islands at the end of 1971, the Shah became more concerned about the growing presence of the Soviet navy in the Arabian Sea and the Indian Ocean, including the increasing Soviet naval visits to Iraqi ports and Soviet arms deliveries to Iraq. Thus, he began to extend Iran's line of defense from the north of the Gulf through the Lower Gulf and the islands and out into the Gulf of Oman.[140]

Others have argued that Iran's motives were "imperialistic" and "expansionist," that its historical claims were "propaganda," that Iran was "not motivated by considerations of stability and security in the area," and that it would use the islands to interfere with the shipping of others. The Iraqi representative at the UN Security Council debate on Iran's occupation of the islands in December 1971 made these arguments, stressing that the three islands and the Strait of Hormuz constituted the economic lifeline of the Arab states of the Gulf, their only navigable outlet through the shallow Gulf to the high seas. He warned that Iran could use its military build-up and its position on the islands to threaten this lifeline and to bring pressure on the Arab states that depended on it. The Kuwaiti representative at this debate also expressed this concern. Similarly, the PDRY representative warned that Iran intended to use the islands to intervene in Oman and to destroy the Dhofar revolution.[141]

Two other examples of contending arguments may be offered. The historian J.B. Kelly has argued that Iranian positions on the islands of Sirri, Qishm, Henjam and Larak could have been sufficient to afford Iran strategic protection of the sea-lanes, and that Abu Musa and the Tunbs were thus not necessary for this purpose. Instead, he argues, a claim to any oil discoveries around the islands was Iran's real intention.[142] The historian and political scientist R.K. Ramazani, on the other hand, has accepted the Shah's arguments about the strategic importance of the islands in protecting the sea-lanes and the threat posed by radical forces, and has argued that "the real interest of Iran was more politico-strategic than territorial-historical."[143]

Overall, it appears that the Shah's intentions in occupying these three islands included, in the following order of importance, all of the strategic, economic, nationalist and domestic arguments that he and his top officials advanced. This also included the unstated strategic motives of having the capability to interfere with others' commerce and to intervene in Dhofar or elsewhere on the Arabian Peninsula.

Contending arguments about Islamic Iran's intentions in occupying and militarizing the islands since the early 1980s have focused on the same domestic, nationalistic, economic and strategic factors as put forward under the Shah, along with Islamic motives to export the revolution or to defend it. A UAE official has argued that since Islamic Iran has had to give up land in settling border disputes with Iraq and other neighbors, Iran might become more determined to hold onto the islands, especially when it still has outstanding border disputes with Afghanistan and Pakistan and may not want to set any more precedents about giving up territory.[144] This official also contends that, particularly since 1992, the islands issue has become a vehicle for regime legitimacy and popular mobilization that is enmeshed in Iranian feelings of isolation and resentment (see the above discussion about Iranian resentments).[145]

Another UAE official asserts that Iran has unwisely made the islands issue a nationalist problem. The islands issue figures in the people's minds and national pride and is entangled in domestic Iranian politics. This has complicated the issue and made it harder to compromise. Despite the changing demographics and politics in Iran, with a younger population voting for domestic reform and an end to international isolation, he does not think this issue of national pride will recede and improve the prospects for negotiation.[146]

While serving as Iran's Ambassador to the UN in 1994, Kamal Kharrazi, Iran's current Foreign Minister, expressed this widespread sense of a valid claim when he said: "We have documents that show these islands have been part of Iranian territory for centuries."[147] Other pragmatic officials of the Islamic Republic have told this author that the people believe the islands are Iranian and the regime could therefore not compromise on them.[148]

There is also the economic argument. Since Iran's proven oil reserves of 47.9 billion barrels will be depleted long before the 452.4 billion barrels of the GCC, some analysts argue that Islamic Iran claims sovereignty over the islands and an exclusive right to a twelve mile belt of territorial water around each island in order to present a legal and physical challenge to the UAE's sovereign rights to offshore oil and gas fields in these waters. This includes the Mubarak fields off the coast of Abu Musa and any other fields that might yet be discovered within twelve miles of Abu Musa or the Tunbs, where exploration continued in 1999.[149]

The UAE's then President, the late H.H. Shaikh Zayed bin Sultan Al-Nahyan reportedly expressed concern that this is a motive.[150] Indeed, one Iranian scholar has described the oil from the Mubarak field as the "best-quality oil produced in the Persian Gulf."[151] Furthermore, a quarrel over the Mubarak field was cited by Iran as justification for its April 1992 action on Abu Musa, when it claimed that it had not received its fair share of the revenue from the field.[152] However, a former British official in the Trucial States says this is probably not a motive, noting that Iran has long shared the revenue from the Mubarak oil field with Sharjah.[153] Nevertheless, it is precisely Iran's continuing claim to and occupation of these islands that enables it to have this revenue.[154]

Most US, British and Arab officials and analysts argue that the Islamic Republic of Iran, like the Shah's Iran, seeks hegemony in the Gulf, and that Islamic Iran is frustrated that its ambitions to reassert a *Pax Iranica* have been foiled by the *Pax Americana*. A UAE official argues that Islamic Iran maintains the Imperial Iranian attitude toward the Gulf region and the islands which it regards as Iranian "property." He contends that they have always thought in terms of hegemony because of their history, size and population, and that they think these factors entitle them to a dominant regional role beyond their borders. Indeed, they believe Iran's oil, economic and developmental needs should be given priority over the needs of others.

Certainly, the Iranian position that the presence of foreign military powers in the Gulf is a stumbling block to Iran exercising its desired regional role has been consistent since the time of Reza Shah. Similarly, Iranian jargon regarding the Arab states reveals a negative attitude toward both the foreign military powers and their GCC partners. By not referring to the UAE and the other GCC states by their internationally recognized names, but rather as "shaikhdoms" or "the groups or peoples of the southern coast of the Persian Gulf," Iran is attempting to de-legitimize these states and to suggest that these states are under the effective control of foreign powers. Iran is taking this approach instead of arguing the merits of the case relating to the UAE's claim to the islands.[155]

A former US official in the region also argues along these lines when he says that Islamic Iran considers itself the rightful hegemon of the Gulf and views the new Arab states as small and weak states that should look up to Iran as the regional power. Thus, the Iranians, knowing that the UAE made concessions on territory to Saudi Arabia in the 1970s, mistakenly thought that Shaikh Zayed would tolerate the virtual annexation of Abu Musa in 1992.[156] A former US CENTCOM commander has argued that Iran thought it could just slip this islands issue by the UAE in 1992, but then got caught with a UAE response that it thinks is uncharacteristic.[157] In this view, Iran's motivations have to be seen as hegemonic and opportunistic. In the view of another analyst, Iran's military build-up on the islands in the 1990s, and particularly since 1994, has been intended as a rebuff to the GCC states for supporting the UAE's claim to the islands and as a signal of Iran's determination to keep them.[158]

Most US and British officials do think that Islamic Iran's intentions regarding the islands since the early 1980s, like Imperial Iran's intentions in the 1970s, have included naval and air defense of the sea lanes through which most of Iran's oil and gas exports pass, as well as defense of Iranian off-shore oil facilities.[159] Indeed, in October 1982, Iran reinforced its garrisons on Farsi, Sirri and Larak, as well as its artillery and anti-aircraft assets on the Greater Tunb and Qishm, in anticipation of the threat posed to Iranian shipping and facilities in the Lower Gulf by Iraq's acquisition of French-made Super Etendard strike aircraft armed with Exocet air-to-surface missiles.[160] One US defense official, however, argues that naval and air defense of Iran's shipping and oil installations is a motive, but not the primary motive for occupying and fortifying the islands, and that their military assets on their mainland coast can provide these defensive capabilities.[161]

There is also general agreement that Islamic Iran's intentions on the islands have included the ability to interfere with others' shipping through the sea lanes of the lower Gulf.[162] Certainly, Iran demonstrated this intention during the Iran-Iraq War. Iraqi commercial shipping through the Gulf virtually ceased during this war because Iraq used Jordanian, Saudi and Turkish export routes and pipelines. However, there was considerable shipping through the Gulf by GCC states that were supportive of Iraq, and from 1984 to 1988 this shipping was subjected to Iranian attacks. From 1986 to 1988, there were numerous Iranian attacks in the southwestern Gulf off the coast of the UAE and toward the Strait of Hormuz against commercial shipping going to and from Kuwaiti and Saudi ports.

Many of these attacks were launched from Abu Musa by helicopters and Boghammer and Boston Whaler boats strafing ships with machine guns and rocket propelled grenades. Indeed, an official at the Department of State Legal Department argues that Abu Musa may have staged more attacks against shipping during the tanker war than Iran's offshore oil platforms did. During this period, 200 ships were attacked by Iran, with about one-third of these attacked by Iran's small motorboats. A substantial number of these, perhaps one-third to one-half, were probably launched from Abu Musa, given the location of the attacks. This is based on intelligence from merchant captains and eyewitnesses servicing oil installations who saw small boats moored at the harbor at Abu Musa. There were also helicopter attacks launched from these islands. The Greater Tunb was not reported to be an active base for these operations, but in fact there are recorded incidents of the Greater Tunb also being a base for some of these operations.[163]

Iran, however, needs to export through the Gulf, so the question arises as to why Iran would interfere with traffic, particularly when the US military presence and retaliatory capability is so much greater than in 1986-1988? One former US diplomat argues that there is no reason for Iran to interfere with others except for defensive reasons during a war, and even then not while Western navies are there.[164] However, as in the 1980s, if their oil facilities and shipping are attacked again and their exports through the Gulf are reduced, or conceivably if their nuclear facilities are hit in a pre-emptive attack, Iran may want to be able to use Abu Musa and the Tunbs to counter-attack. Judging from their military assets on the islands and their military exercises on and around the islands, Iran may at least want to use the islands to interfere with shipping more effectively than during the Iran–Iraq War, even with the greater presence of the US military in the Gulf.

In a possible scenario in which their exports are embargoed, or their shipping is blockaded or actually halted by bombing, Iran may even want to be able to use the islands in an attempt to shut the strait. While these options sound defensive on the surface, Iran may provoke the conflict that leads to these scenarios. Furthermore, use of the islands to interfere with commercial shipping could be part of an offensive Iranian operation, particularly if US military forces were reduced or withdrawn. Moreover, the mere threat to interfere with traffic or to close the strait would cause Lloyd's of London to increase its insurance rates and discourage some shipping from entering the Gulf, as happened during the Iran-Iraq war. Actual interference with traffic could also result in higher oil and gas prices.

In addition, Iran's behavior on the islands may be a reaction against the US military presence in the area, which Iran thinks is directed against them. A UAE official argues that Iran's violation of the 1971 Memorandum of Understanding on Abu Musa in 1992 and ever since then has been motivated partly by a desire to send a political signal expressing Iran's displeasure at its exclusion from the developing Gulf security system after the Desert Shield and Desert Storm military operations. The damage inflicted on Iraq's military and industrial capability in Desert Storm and the restrictions imposed on Iraq's sovereignty in the aftermath created a military imbalance in the Gulf that Iran could have exploited in its favor. Iran wanted to warn its Gulf Arab neighbors not to go too far in inviting US military, especially naval, power into the Gulf to redress the imbalance. This official views President Rafsanjani's visit to Abu Musa in March 1992 and the escalation of nationalist rhetoric about the islands, including Rafsanjani's own December 1992 warning about a "sea of blood," to be signs of Iran's unhappiness with the military arrangements being contemplated and made between the GCC and the United States.[165]

A high-ranking US official in the Clinton administration stated in December 1994 that Iran thinks that the United States is using Iraq as an excuse to bolster its military forces in the Gulf and also believes that the real reason for the US military presence is to attack Iran, including dislodging Iran from the islands.[166] Another US analyst argues that fortification of the islands became even more important to Iran after the United States rushed additional forces to the Gulf in October 1994 to deter a new Iraqi threat to Kuwait, as Iran thought the US was planning to attack it over a pretext such as its occupation of the islands. As part of this view, Iran considers the islands a strategic asset, as elements of a layered defense against US naval forces, and fears that the United States wants to capture the islands and deprive Iran of these defensive positions.

Indeed, Iran thinks its national interest requires the islands for defense against the United States. Iran's militarization of the islands and its naval exercises are meant to send a message that they are prepared to defend the islands, their coast, their ports and their mainland.[167] This rationale could have been on the minds of Iranian officials during the deployment of US military forces to the Gulf area in 2002-2003 in preparation for US military action against Iraq, a deployment that was denounced by Rafsanjani, Khatami and Khamenei.[168]

Iran may thus want the ability to use its anti-ship missile and other capabilities on the islands, as well as its capabilities on the mainland, to attack US naval vessels in Gulf waters or in Gulf ports, such as Dubai's Jebel Ali, if it thinks its self-defense requires this. A former US CENTCOM commander agrees that Iran appears to be preparing and training for a US-UAE attempt to seize the islands. According to a UAE official, Iranian leaders think in conspiracy terms and fear that the United States will seize the islands and use them against Iran. Moreover, when it has attempted to project its power and influence outside the Gulf and into the Indian Ocean, Iran has viewed the islands as part of a marine defense line running from the islands of Hormuz to Larak to Qishm to Henjam to the Greater Tunb to Abu Musa. In light of Iran's acquisition of submarines and the logic of their use in the Gulf of Oman, where they could be used in an attempt to deny Western naval access through the Strait of Hormuz and into the Gulf, Iran now considers the islands as part of such a marine defense line.[169]

US intelligence analysts argue, therefore, that Iran pursues multiple objectives with regard to the occupation of the islands: to reduce or end the Western military presence in the Gulf, to reassert itself as the premier military force in the Gulf, to protect its shipping and to monitor and threaten others' commercial shipping in the Gulf, to control foreign naval access both to the Gulf and the Gulf of Oman, to engage foreign navies inside the Gulf and in the Gulf of Oman, and to control the islands, not only for these aspects of regional hegemony, but also for regime survival.[170] With this in mind, one US official argues, Iran claims sovereignty over the islands and an exclusive right to a twelve-mile belt of territorial water around each island in order to bring much of the Gulf's traffic lanes within Iranian territorial waters.

Iran has not only asserted its twelve-mile territorial water limits around the islands, but has also passed legislation prohibiting the passage of warships through its territorial waters without prior authorization. The United States, however, demands the right of innocent passage of warships through territorial waters (that is, passage that is not prejudicial to the security of the coastal state) without prior authorization. Indeed, the US Navy travels through waters claimed as Iranian territorial waters in order to show Iran that the US considers them international waters and has done so past Abu Musa.[171]

The possibility of Iranian offensive intentions must also be considered. One regional analyst suggests that Iran is not likely to launch an overt and attributable military attack against GCC states because of its painful experience in the Iran–Iraq War and its observation of Desert Shield and Desert Storm. Iranian military leaders would advise the country's political leadership to refrain from any action that would produce a reaction from the GCC–Western coalition. At the same time, however, a weakening of the Western commitment to the GCC might embolden Iran to move against the GCC or to destabilize it from within. However, since Iran is aware of the devastating consequences for its own military as a result of a counter-attack by the GCC and its security partners, an overt attack against the GCC "is for the immediate future effectively deterred." In this sense at least, Iran is rational. Moreover, it is suggested that military leaders regard the political leadership as the ultimate decision-makers.[172]

A UAE official underscores the point that Iran understands that the United States would not tolerate an Iranian attack against the UAE or other GCC states. Iran cannot go too far in using the islands to make a foreign policy point or to externalize domestic problems because, being concerned about its economy, it cannot afford to suffer the kinds of economic consequences that Iraq has suffered since 1990. Even moves against the UAE's oil fields, this official believes, would produce a US reaction that would set Iran back a decade.[173]

The past few years have shown that Iran is interested in breaking out of its regional and international isolation. The recent rapprochement with certain Arab Gulf states and the establishment of closer political ties with all European states are achievements that Iran would not want to endanger. While ties with the United States remain strained, there have also been hints that both sides may have sought ways to establish some sort of dialogue. Thus, it does not seem likely that Iran would initiate a confrontation in the Gulf at a time when it is seeking to overcome past suspicions. As one former British official has indicated, Iran wants to dominate its neighbors, but does not want to physically occupy them, and the islands are not necessary for domination.[174]

Instead, Iran is seen as seeking to project its growing military power and its demographic and geographic strength to increase its leverage over the GCC states. This may include intimidating the GCC into making financial investments in Iran's badly needed economic reconstruction and diversification, as well as giving Iran more leverage when it comes to the oil policy of OPEC or at least of the Gulf.[175] More specifically, Iran may want the islands as part of any strategy to threaten and intimidate and exercise leverage over the UAE.[176]

However, a former aide to Sir William Luce disagrees that these are motives for fortifying the islands, arguing that the sheer size and strength of Iran is sufficient to intimidate the Arab states without needing the offshore islands to do so. Moreover, after Khatami's election, Iran has been making it clear that it wants more conciliatory relations with the Gulf Arabs.[177] A US official notes that Iran used the 1992 negotiations with the UAE over the islands as an opportunity to seek UAE support for raising Iran's oil quota.[178] In early 1999, Iran did agree with Saudi Arabia on OPEC production cuts, but this was in order to stop a slide in prices, and in March 2000 Iran opposed OPEC production increases because these were intended to stop a dramatic increase in prices.[179] Iran may need to boost its production at a future date and it may want to use the islands as leverage to offset any Arab opposition at that time.

Still, there are a number of scenarios that could result in an Iranian attack against UAE targets, either overt and attributable or covert and unattributable. Iranian failure to gain GCC cooperation as envisioned under the recent rapprochement initiatives, as well as rising domestic tensions inside Iran, could influence Iranian military moves regionally, perhaps including some foreign adventure to distract attention from foreign policy failure or to counter domestic opposition. Iran could also respond to an unexpected opportunity or challenge.

In this context, Cordesman has written:

> Iran and Iraq [under Saddam Hussein] face fewer constraints in using force to intimidate and conduct more limited attacks than they do in using force to fight large-scale conflict...Iran seems far more likely to use force, or threaten to use force in spite of its military weaknesses, in a wide range of other contingencies.

In addition to the possibilities listed above, internal unrest in one of the Arab Gulf states, an air or naval clash in the Gulf over oil rights or shipping lanes, disputes over off-shore or on-shore oil or gas fields, as well as a military challenge to Iran's control over Abu Musa and the Tunbs could provide other scenarios.[180] Given the continuing presence of Western military forces in the Gulf at the present time, Iran would more likely resort to covert and unattributable actions that might not lead to a Western military reaction. However, at some point in the future, there could also be a weakening of the Western commitment to the GCC, in turn emboldening Iran to move against the GCC or to destabilize it from within.[181]

In addition, there is the possibility of using the islands for covert sabotage of UAE oil and gas fields, its ports, as well as UAE, US and other naval vessels in those ports. Most UAE oil fields are further west, but the Mubarak oil field, the Baih, Fateh and Rashid oil fields and the Bukha, West Bukha, Saleh, Sharjah and Umm al-Qaiwain gas fields are all within relatively close range of the islands. It is not entirely clear what the US would do in case such an attack was covert and unattributable.[182] Thus, the question is whether Iran could successfully carry out an operation in such a manner. The Revolutionary Guard's underwater commando units, midget submarines and swimmer delivery vehicles could possibly be for such a purpose.

While Iran's presence on the islands and their militarization provides the country with the range of overt and covert military capabilities noted above, some analysts will argue that this is a byproduct of Iran's presence and buildup, rather than any outright intention. Such a view is supported by a UAE official, who doubts that Iran is deliberately increasing its military capabilities on the islands for the day when it can take some offensive action. He argues that the Iranians are probably preparing for a worst-case scenario, in which there is a military effort to seize the islands from them, particularly because the islands are perceived as part of Iran's marine defense line. However, this official has no doubt that Iran would use its capabilities on the islands in a crisis, possibly occupying more land or oil fields. This by itself is sufficient cause for concern from the UAE perspective.[183]

The review provided here demonstrates that there is significant disagreement among officials and analysts about Iran's intentions regarding the islands. However, Iran's past use of the islands, its resentments, its capabilities and the arguments that Iran may again seek to use the islands in a wide range of overt and covert operations against shipping, oil and gas fields, foreign navies and perhaps even the UAE itself, are plausible indications of the potential security threat posed by Iran's continued occupation and militarization of the islands.

The UAE's Response

The UAE is a small, wealthy state with a combined armed forces strength of some 64,500, which includes 59,000 in the army, 1,500 in the navy, and 4,000 in the air force. The UAE is well aware of the asymmetry of power between itself and Iran, which has over 300,000 personnel in its armed forces. As a result, the UAE is developing an air force with offensive and defensive capabilities to counter possible Iranian hostilities. UAE naval assets are also being developed, and they will have a growing ability to complicate any Iranian attempts to disrupt oil and gas and shipping activities in the Gulf. UAE ground forces are also being upgraded.[184]

The UAE participation in the GCC collective security framework is another factor that partially redresses this asymmetry of power with Iran. In July 2001, the UAE ratified the joint defense treaty that had been accepted at the December 2000 GCC summit in Bahrain. The agreement stipulates that an attack on any member would be considered an attack on all. The signatories also agreed to pool their resources, expand their Peninsula Shield joint defense force and equip it with an early warning system and a communication network.[185] Already in March 2001, the $160 million *Hizam al-Taawun* (Zone of Cooperation) project became operational, linking the military headquarters and radar systems of the six GCC states. This allows for instantaneous military communications and a consolidated air picture of the region.[186] The UAE also regularly participates in joint GCC military exercises.

Meanwhile, the UAE regards its security relationships with the United States and other Western powers as very important to redress the existing asymmetry of power with Iran. The UAE is well aware that there is no regional framework or world power that has deterred Iran from its policy of occupation and fortification of Abu Musa and the Tunbs. The UAE does have confidence, however, that its security relationships with its Western partners, and particularly with the United

States, deter Iran from overt and attributable direct attacks against the UAE, and perhaps from lesser challenges as well.[187]

The UAE pursues diplomatic and legal measures to resolve the islands dispute with its more powerful neighbor. It knows that it cannot resort to force to eject Iran and reclaim the islands, and it certainly does not seek the use of force by the United States or its other security partners to eject Iran from the islands. The UAE knows that Iran will always be its large neighbor to the north and hopes that a policy of peaceful coexistence, diplomacy, and trade will eventually bear fruit.[188] As has already been mentioned, the UAE has attempted negotiation with Iran in 1992 and 1995, and continues to call for negotiations or the referral of the case to the International Court of Justice (ICJ). The UAE also patiently supported the efforts of the GCC's tripartite committee to promote bilateral negotiations in 1999 and 2000. In the meantime, the Ruler of Sharjah continues to deal directly with Iran on the issue of Abu Musa. Sharjah is particularly keen to avoid confrontation with Iran and is more inclined toward dialogue with Tehran. Indeed, the Mubarak oil field shared with Iran is one of Sharjah's few sources of revenue.[189]

However, after the threat posed by Iran during the Iran–Iraq War, Iraq's invasion of Kuwait in 1990 and Iran's increased fortification of Abu Musa and the Tunbs in the 1990s, the UAE has looked to the United States and Europe to bolster its security against foreign threats through bilateral security relationships, joint military exercises and the acquisition of modern weaponry.[190] If necessary, the UAE would also seek emergency assistance from its security partners, as for example, in defending shipping against Iranian attacks in 1987–1988, in liberating Kuwait from Iraq in 1990, and in deterring Iraq from invading Kuwait again in 1994. The UAE signed a Defense Cooperation Agreement (DCA) with the United States in 1994, which allows US ships to dock in UAE ports, permits US access to UAE air facilities and allows the United States to deploy military personnel and equipment in the UAE in time of crisis.[191] The UAE also signed a defense cooperation agreement with France in 1995 and a MoU on defense cooperation with Britain in 1996. More recently, it has been developing defense relations with Germany.[192]

Among the most significant and most recent arms agreements between the UAE and the United States was the UAE's decision in May 1998 to acquire 80 US-made F-16 jet fighters.[193] In the spring of

1999, the United States reportedly agreed to supply the aircraft with electronic warfare software codes that the UAE had requested. The aircraft will also be equipped with a wide range of air-to-air, air-to-ground and air-to-ship missiles, and high speed anti-radiation missiles.[194] Following the signature in May 2000, delivery of the first batch of F-16s was made in May 2005 and the last batch of aircraft is expected to be delivered by 2007.[195] This agreement may also permit the United States to base US aircraft and pre-position equipment at the airbase being expanded for the F-16s.[196] The UAE also began negotiation with France in 1998 to acquire 30 Mirage 2000-9s and to modernize its 33 Mirage 2000s, a deal that was finalized in late 2002.[197]

Furthermore, the UAE has ordered maritime patrol aircraft and helicopters with anti-surface ship and anti-submarine warfare (ASW) capabilities and also helicopters with ground attack capability.[198] It took delivery of 2 Dutch Kortenaer-class frigates for its navy in 1997 and 1998, and purchased US-made Harpoon anti-ship missiles for these frigates, as well as US-made anti-aircraft missiles. Future planning includes the purchasing of more advanced frigates, large patrol craft, mine hunters, submarines and corvettes. UAE naval forces will also be trained in defense against nuclear, biological and chemical warfare.[199]

Furthermore, in February 2002, the UAE confirmed that it has ordered twelve amphibious assault craft, three large landing craft for transporting heavy equipment and six Baynunah missile-armed patrol craft. The UAE commissioned the first of the twelve amphibious assault craft in February 2003.[200] Deliveries of French-made Leclerc battle tanks began in the mid-1990s, with the last tank scheduled to arrive in 2003.[201] Finally, the UAE's inventory includes Scud-B ballistic missiles and it plans to acquire air-launched cruise missiles, particularly the Matra BAe Dynamics "Black Shaheen" cruise missiles, with a range of 400 km, for its fleet of Mirage 2000 aircraft.[202] All of these developments should improve the UAE's ability to defend its mainland, coast, ports, offshore oil and gas facilities, shipping, and islands against Iranian attacks. The F-16 may even enable the UAE to neutralize Iranian forces on Abu Musa and the Tunbs.

The UAE seeks to develop, together with the US and other major Western powers, a strategy for deterring unconventional and conventional attacks against the UAE, as well as more limited forms of aggression against and intimidation of the country. However, UAE officials stress that they do not seek a confrontation with Iran and do not want the use of force by the US. A UAE official agrees that the US arguments about Iran's growing capabilities and the need to deter Iran are valid. He argues, however, that the use of force by the UAE and/or the US to liberate the islands is not an option so far. The UAE does not need or seek a confrontation with Iran and does not want the islands dispute to figure in US-Iranian relations.[203] Aware that US military action could trigger an Iranian response against the UAE, the UAE wants to be consulted "and have a say" about the use of US force in the Gulf.[204]

According to US officials, the UAE appears satisfied with US policy. The UAE does not want the United States to be too vocal about the islands, because Iran could then accuse the UAE of being a "stooge" of the United States and Iran could provoke and "justify" conflict. While Bahrain tried to get the United States involved in the Hawar islands dispute with Qatar, the UAE has no such intention with regard to the Abu Musa and Tunbs dispute. Indeed, the UAE thinks that US involvement might stiffen Iranian resolve.[205] However, while the UAE calls for negotiation, adjudication or arbitration, it also seeks diplomatic support from many sources for its claims and for its advocacy of diplomacy and law. The UAE has received such support from the GCC, the Damascus Group, the Arab League, Britain, the European Union and the United States. Furthermore, the UAE annually requests that the issue remain on the UN Security Council agenda, and the UAE documents its protests to Iran for the Council. However, the UAE has not yet sought a Security Council resolution on the issue.[206]

In essence, the UAE has adopted a patient policy of modernizing its military, forging regional and bilateral security agreements, and advocating a peaceful diplomatic or legal resolution of this dispute while marshalling international support for its position. Given Iran's past use of the islands as bases for military attacks, the many Iranian political resentments toward the West and the GCC states, the diverse Iranian military capabilities on the mainland and the islands, the wide range of probable and possible motivations and intentions discussed above, and the very clear possibility of Iran again using these strategically located islands against the UAE and international shipping, the UAE's concerns are justified and its response remains prudent.

PART
III

REGIONAL REPERCUSSIONS

CHAPTER
7

The Arab World's Reaction
to the Shah's Occupation

Arab views of the islands issue developed gradually during the late 1960s and early 1970s. Late in December 1968, after the breakdown of negotiations with Iran, Ras al-Khaimah's Crown Prince Khalid had disappointing meetings in Riyadh with the leaders of Saudi Arabia, the largest Arab state on the Arabian peninsula and the most important of the conservative Arab states. Iranian officials had told him in October that Saudi Arabia had agreed on a median line that would leave the Tunbs on the Iranian side. In Riyadh, King Faisal bin Abdulaziz Al-Saud stressed the importance of finding a solution and advised Ras al-Khaimah against "forcing" anything on the Shah. He also asked whether Shaikh Saqr, Ras al-Khaimah's Ruler, could give Iran one of the Tunbs and keep the other.

This suggestion was somewhat similar to the compromise that Saudi Arabia had made with Iran in October, in which the Saudi-Iranian median line was drawn in a way that gave the island of Farsi to Iran and gave the island of Arabi to Saudi Arabia. Prince Nayaf bin Abdulaziz Al-Saud, King Faisal's Counselor on Gulf and Oman affairs, said that the Tunbs were part of a complex of problems that should be settled together and in agreement with the other emirates. British officials later wondered if this was an implicit suggestion that the Tunbs might go to Iran while Abu Musa would remain with Sharjah.[1]

In addition, however, Saudi Arabia was considering the status of Bahrain. Saudi Chief of Intelligence Kamal Adham told British officials that Iran had asked King Faisal in late 1968 or early 1969 to help persuade Sharjah and Ras al-Khaimah to give up the islands and Faisal had replied that he could only consider this after Iran had shown goodwill towards Bahrain. Adham said that he himself had assured the Iranians that if Iran cooperated on Bahrain, Saudi Arabia would help Iran obtain satisfaction on the Tunbs, although it is not clear whether he had explained to the Iranians what he meant by this.[2] Moreover, British officials reported in 1968 that Kuwait's Crown Prince Shaikh Jabir al Ahmad al Jabir Al-Sabah and Defense Minister Shaikh Saad al Abdullah al Salim Al-Sabah were resigned and philosophical about Iran taking over Abu Musa and the Tunbs, although they would defend Arab rights in public, and that Bahrain's Emir Shaikh Issa bin Salman Al-Khalifa reacted favorably to a proposed deal in which Iran would drop its claim to Bahrain, in exchange for gaining Abu Musa and the Tunbs and paying for them.[3]

In July 1970, after Iran had agreed to an independent Bahrain, Saudi Arabia's Ambassador in London said that King Faisal had advised Shaikh Saqr to make the best arrangement with Iran he could, obtaining as much aid and financial assistance as possible. Faisal reportedly said that "Saudi Arabia would not fight for the islands and it was only realistic to make concessions over particular problems with an eye to the wider interest."[4] In September 1970, however, Crown Prince Khalid and his adviser Tawfiq Abu Khader were given a message from King Faisal that if any agreement were reached with Iran over the Tunbs, the agreement should clearly state that sovereignty remained with Ras al-Khaimah.[5]

Meanwhile, in June 1970, Shaikh Saqr had meetings with officials in Iraq, the center of radical Arab nationalism in the Gulf. Shortly before his trip, Iraq had conveyed a warning to British Ambassador Sir Denis Wright in Tehran through the Soviet Ambassador in Iran that Britain would "be ill-advised to contemplate an Iranian takeover in the islands."[6] When Shaikh Saqr arrived in Baghdad, Iraqi President Ahmad Hassan Al-Bakr and other officials told him that Iraq strongly opposed any agreement, whether a sale or a lease, that would allow Iran on the Tunbs, arguing that imports and exports through the Strait of Hormuz were "a matter of life and death" for Iraq, and offering military, economic and technical assistance to Ras al-Khaimah.[7]

In December 1970, Sharjah's Ruler, Shaikh Khalid, received Hassan Sabri Al-Khuli, a personal representative of Egypt's President

Anwar Sadat. Al-Khuli told Shaikh Khalid that Egypt could give Sharjah only moral support. Nasser had recently died, Egypt was pre-occupied with Israel, and Egypt could not be involved in the Gulf, he said.[8] In March 1971, however, Al-Khuli told British officials in Cairo and Bahrain that Britain and Iran would lose the Arab goodwill that had been generated by their positions on the Arab-Israeli conflict if Iran occupied the islands by force with British acquiescence.[9]

Conservative Saudi Arabia and Kuwait did make some attempts to mediate between the emirates, Iran and Britain in 1970 and 1971, but their suggestions were rejected by Iran. The first suggestion, made by Saudi Arabia to Iranian Prime Minister and Foreign Minister Ardashir Zahedi in April 1970, just prior to the Bahrain settlement, was that if security rather than sovereignty was the Iranian concern, a joint Iranian-Arab garrison should be stationed on the islands.[10] In July, soon after the Bahrain issue was settled, Zahedi told the Saudis that Iran would be willing to use force to take the islands and that Iran would respond to any call for an International Court of Justice ruling on the islands by re-opening the issue of Bahrain. King Faisal responded that "he considered that the islands were Arab, and that the question should not be pressed now."[11]

In August, King Faisal told British mediator Sir William Luce "that it was essential that the Arab sovereignty of the islands should be assured." He also argued that the Shah did not need garrisons on the Tunbs since he could place them on Qishm and he said that he had told this to Zahedi.[12] When King Faisal met with Zahedi in October in Geneva, Zahedi sought Faisal's help in promoting Iran's proposals of financial compensation to Sharjah and Ras al-Khaimah in return for sovereignty over the islands. This met with Faisal's refusal. Days later, US Assistant Secretary of State Joseph Sisco asked Saudi Arabia's Acting Foreign Minister Omar Al-Saqqaf if Saudi Arabia could encourage Sharjah and Ras al-Khaimah to reach an arrangement with Iran. Al-Saqqaf explained that Saudi Arabia could not support "bargaining over Arab rights to [the] islands."[13] Another Saudi suggestion made to Iran was that Iran lease the islands but recognize Arab sovereignty over them.[14] King Faisal visited Iran in June 1971 "and tried to do something, but he achieved nothing new."[15]

In August 1970, Kuwait's Crown Prince, Shaikh Jabir al Ahmad al Jabir Al-Sabah, told Luce that a union of Arab emirates should be established before any agreement with Iran over the islands, but that Kuwait would not object if such a union then entered into an agreement permitting the stationing of Iranian troops on the islands.[16] In November, however, Kuwait's Foreign Minister, Shaikh Sabah al Ahmad al Jabir Al-Sabah, told Luce that Kuwait did not agree to Iranian troops on the islands and would advise the Ruler of Sharjah against this. Indeed, Shaikh Sabah implored Britain not to proceed with this proposal, arguing that it would be opposed throughout the Arab world.[17]

Later in November, Saudi Arabia's Prince Nayaf visited Kuwait's Shaikh Sabah and the two agreed that the islands must remain Arab and that they could not accept any Iranian occupation of the islands. They agreed to establish a joint committee to achieve this and to make an arrangement with Iran that would satisfy Iran and ensure that no one would place troops on the islands.[18] Finally, on August 11, 1971, with time running out, Kuwait's Foreign Minister Shaikh Sabah met with the Shah in Tehran and made this last suggestion, namely that the islands should be de-militarized, that Iran and the emirates should have no military presence on them, and that the sovereignty of the emirates over the islands should not be questioned. As with the other Arab proposals, the Shah also rejected this one.[19]

Shaikh Khalid of Sharjah sent messages on August 18, 1971 to the rulers of all the Arab states and to the Secretary-General of the Arab League, Abdul Khaliq Hassouneh, informing them about Iran's positions and seeking their advice and support. On August 23, he sent these Arab leaders a lengthy and detailed memorandum explaining Sharjah's claim to Abu Musa, including the history of the dispute with Iran over the island, Sharjah's rejection of the Iranian claim, Iran's threats to use force, Iran's refusal to negotiate on the issue of sovereignty or to submit the question to international arbitration or the United Nations, and Iran's proposals for financial compensation to Sharjah and for sharing oil revenues with Sharjah in exchange for Iranian sovereignty over Abu Musa. This memorandum drew in part on the research and analysis that Shaikh Khalid had requested from the Anglo-American legal team of Bathurst, Ely, and Chance and that had been presented to him in a preliminary or "Interim Report" on July 23. This Anglo-American report supported Sharjah's claim on the basis of prescription and refuted Iran's claim, as did the numerous historical documents, many of them official British records that Shaikh Khalid included with his memorandum. The memorandum also provided details of British mediator Sir William Luce's communications during his mediation.[20]

Shaikh Khalid's communication stated that Sharjah would not agree to Iranian sovereignty over the island, but that Sharjah was "prepared to negotiate with Iran towards the achievement of a peaceful solution which will satisfy both sides without harming their national interests." It further stated:

> Sharjah considers that the problem of Abu Musa in its present and future dimensions is a problem affecting not Sharjah alone, but all the Arab states and peoples, since the defense of the island is a national defense of Arab territory threatened with occupation. Sharjah appreciates that it is not appropriate at this stage to request its Arab brothers to use force against Iran to prevent it from occupying the island. However, we hope that all the Arab states will support us in our position and will attempt to bring pressure on Iran by all possible means to persuade it to change its stand, and that they will not permit Iran to act freely in occupying the island by force.[21]

In addition to being concerned about the Shah's threat to use force, Shaikh Khalid was also concerned about the reaction of radical Arab nationalists if he were to yield Arab sovereignty to the Shah. Indeed, he feared assassination by Arab nationalists.[22] Shaikh Khalid also understood from earlier communications with Arab leaders that they were not prepared to use force to defend the islands against Iran and that they favored a peaceful solution.[23] Thus, he was disappointed when only four governments answered his August 1971 correspondence and his proposal for a compromise. Moreover, while these four endorsed the idea of a peaceful solution in which Sharjah did not abandon its sovereignty over the island, they advised only "restraint" and "a commitment to wisdom" in achieving such a solution.[24] As he later said, "I turned to the Arab states, who advised me to be wise. But wise how? I took it that it was for Sharjah to act alone. There was no one to give support."[25]

Under these circumstances, as he later explained, he was influenced by the Shah's threats to occupy Abu Musa by force, the prospect of the loss of the entire island and all of its future oil revenues, the Shah's obstruction of the emerging UAE, which Shaikh Khalid wanted to join, and British warnings that Britain would not defend the islands and that Sharjah must satisfy the Shah. Thus he searched for a compromise solution.[26]

One Arab leader who did attempt to support Shaikh Khalid was the Ruler of Abu Dhabi, H.H. Shaikh Zayed bin Sultan Al-Nahyan, who was destined to become the first president of the emerging UAE. During a visit to London in mid-June 1971 to discuss this emerging federation of seven emirates, Shaikh Zayed said that he did not think a federation could do much by itself to resolve the islands issue, but that it could be helpful to enlist the support of the independent Arab states in negotiations with Iran.[27] Nevertheless, in September and October 1971 meetings with British mediator Sir William Luce, Shaikh Zayed made it clear that if Britain "sells out Abu Musa" the emerging UAE would not cooperate with Britain. He also made it clear in these meetings that he was determined that Sharjah should not yield sovereignty over Abu Musa, but that he was amenable to a Sharjah compromise proposal for an Iranian garrison on a part of Abu Musa.[28] Shaikh Zayed had sent Abu Dhabi's Minister for Cabinet Affairs Ahmad Khalifa Al-Suwaidi to Tehran to try to persuade the Shah to abandon the threat of force and to postpone negotiations until the establishment of the UAE. Shaikh Zayed, however, knew from this meeting that the Shah could not be persuaded to do either.[29]

Although willing to consider the idea of leasing the islands, Shaikh Saqr of Ras al-Khaimah was unwilling to yield sovereignty for financial compensation. He also remained concerned that any agreement be seen as honorable in the Arab world and was counting on Arab and particularly Iraqi support for his refusal to yield Arab sovereignty to Iran. In his public rejection of the Shah's proposals on October 30, 1971, Shaikh Saqr stated:

> The two islands do not belong to Ras al-Khaimah alone, but to the entire Arab nation. Responsibility lies on the shoulders of the Arab states one and all, and every Arab State has a right to the islands in the same way as Ras al-Khaimah to any Arab land.[30]

Shaikh Khalid also courted Arab support when he publicly rejected the Shah's proposals for surrendering sovereignty in exchange for compensation on October 30: "We regard them as an infringement of Sharjah's sovereignty, which we will never give up. Nor will we relinquish one inch of Arabian soil, which is the property of the entire Arab nation."[31]

Meanwhile, Ahmad Khalifa Al-Suwaidi continued Shaikh Zayed's efforts, writing to Egypt's Foreign Minister Mahmoud Riyad and Kuwait's Foreign Minister Shaikh Sabah on November 4, warning them about the threat that Iran's claims to the islands posed to the establishment of an independent UAE and seeking their support. Egypt, then a moderate state under President Anwar Sadat and the dominant state in the Arab League, and Kuwait, which had already been mediating between the emirates and Iran, were potentially important allies. Al-Suwaidi argued that the emirates were not prepared to give up their legitimate territory and that this dispute should concern all Arabs. He argued that the emirates were not capable of defending their rights alone, but with the support of Arab states "the just solution can be obtained."[32] Days later Kuwait's Foreign Minister met with the Iranian Chargé d'Affaires in Kuwait and said that it was essential to solve the crisis by peaceful means. Kuwait was interested in maintaining good relations with Iran, he said, but it was necessary to recognize the just Arab rights on the islands. Kuwait could never agree to relinquish them. He also prepared to discuss this crisis with the Kuwaiti Council of Ministers and to provide the Council with the memoranda that Kuwait had received on the issue.[33]

In light of these events and communications, the Council of Foreign Ministers of the Arab League discussed the issue of the islands on November 12 and 13, 1971. Iraq pressed at this meeting for a resolution denouncing Iran's threat to use force to occupy the islands, but could not persuade the other members, who argued that Arab mediation and Secretary-General Hassouneh, an Egyptian, should try to resolve the issue.[34] The Council then instructed Hassouneh on November 14 to inform the ambassadors of Iran and Britain in Cairo that the Arab League members were unanimous in their assertion of the Arab character of the islands, that the Arab states that had previously contacted the Iranian and British governments on this issue had been advised to continue these contacts, and that the Arab League itself would continue to pursue the matter.[35]

When the Assistant Secretary-General for Political Affairs, Muhammad Saleem Alyafi, then met with the British Ambassador to Egypt on November 23, he conveyed these Arab League points and also argued that the Arab League's view was that Britain had the responsibility to maintain Arab sovereignty over the three islands.[36] In his meeting with the Iranian Chargé d'Affaires in Cairo on the same day, Alyafi spoke of "the friendly atmosphere" of the Arab League meeting and the "practical" character of the memorandum submitted by Iraq. He stressed the "unanimous desire" for good relations and the avoidance of any dispute with Iran, and the "hope" that Iran would arrive at a peaceful solution with Sharjah and Ras al-Khaimah. Moreover, Alyafi mentioned the special desire to avoid any dispute with Iran at a time when the Arab nation faced "a fatal battle" with Israel.[37] Tunisia's Foreign Minister Muhammad Al-Masmoudi also made a trip to the region and returned with the impression that a peaceful solution through negotiation was still possible.[38] However, these meetings did not persuade Britain and Iran or accurately gauge Iran's intentions.

Ahmad Khalifa Al-Suwaidi wrote to the Egyptian Foreign Minister again on November 18, stating that the position of Shaikh Zayed of Abu Dhabi was that the islands should not be surrendered. He also informed Shaikh Khalid and the other shaikhs of Sharjah, who were now negotiating a compromise with Iran, that this was the Abu Dhabi policy and advised them to adhere to it.[39] Sharjah's Shaikh Khalid had written to Saudi Arabia's King Faisal seeking his mediation with Iran in reaching a peaceful solution. However, King Faisal left the matter in Shaikh Khalid's hands, replying on November 19, 1971:

> With reference to your allusion to the position of the Iranian government regarding the subject of Abu Musa island, we still contend that the door of dialogue between you and the Iranian government should be left open. We also share with you the opinion that this subject should be kept secret, and distant from any external influences until you reach a satisfactory result with God's all powerful will.[40]

Having received so little Arab support, Shaikh Khalid of Sharjah saw no other possibility than to agree to the Memorandum of Understanding on November 23, a compromise more favorable than the Shah's earlier proposal. The MoU did not require Shaikh Khalid to concede Sharjah's sovereignty over Abu Musa or to recognize Iranian sovereignty over the island, and it limited the Iranian presence on the island to only the northern half of the island and maintained the Sharjah presence on the southern half of the island. The agreement also provided for 1.5 million pounds sterling of annual Iranian aid to Sharjah until such time as Sharjah began to earn 3 million pounds sterling annually from a 50% share of the island's future oil revenues. Shaikh Khalid did not publicly announce the MoU or notify the Arab League about it until November 29.[41]

In the meantime, however, the Legal Department of the Arab League, responding to the earlier correspondence and documents sent by Shaikh Khalid and the instructions of the Secretariat-General, had prepared a memorandum on Abu Musa. This memorandum, dated November 28, 1971, five days after the conclusion of the MoU and one day prior to its announcement, reviewed the various means of acquiring territory in international law and stressed that Sharjah had a strong claim to Abu Musa on the basis of prescription. It also rejected Iran's legal claims to Abu Musa and criticized Iran for its threat to use force as a violation of international law, arguing that Iran should instead rely upon negotiation or arbitration to resolve the issue.

The memorandum made it clear that Sharjah, the UAE and the Arab states would have the right to raise the issue at the Security Council or the General Assembly if Iran were to use force.[42] The report did not make any reference to the MoU and appeared to have been written without knowledge that the MoU was about to be concluded. It would probably not have been a sufficiently strong Arab League response to offset the pressure that Sharjah faced, even had it been written and released earlier. Indeed, Assistant Secretary General Alyafi, when told about the MoU and its provisions during a visit by the British Ambassador to Egypt on November 29, the day the MoU was publicly announced, predicted that it would cause future problems.[43]

Meanwhile, on November 20, Shaikh Saqr wrote to the Arab League Secretary General, informing him of Iran's threat to take the Tunbs by force, referring to documents that proved Ras al-Khaimah's uninterrupted possession of the islands since 1750, noting that Iran had no proof of previous possession, and appealing to the Arab League "to take appropriate measures to deal with the Iranian threats" and to help

Ras al-Khaimah bring the issue before international public opinion, the Security Council, the United Nations, and the members of the Arab League.[44] In late November, Shaikh Saqr wrote to the rulers of all the Arab states and to the Arab League Secretary-General, expressing his regret that Sharjah had agreed to the MoU on Abu Musa and asking for Arab mediation with Iran for the sake of "preserving Arab rights and securing the permanent sovereignty of Ras Al-Khaimah over the said two islands" of the Greater and Lesser Tunbs. Furthermore, he would welcome "any form of action duly adopted by Arab states to the extent of determining effective Arab presence on the said two islands with the intention of preserving their Arab roots." Shaikh Saqr requested that the matter be discussed at the next meeting of the Arab League Council and also wrote to United Nations Secretary General U Thant, asking for his help in preventing Iran from carrying out its threats to use force to resolve this issue.[45]

No appeal for Arab help and no Arab communication with Iran or Britain, however, was sufficient to stop Iran from occupying the Tunbs by force on November 30, 1971. Immediately, Shaikh Saqr sent a cable to all Arab rulers protesting the Iranian occupation and appealing to them "to take immediate and effective measures to repulse the aggressors," "to unite in support of Arab rights," "to shoulder your full national responsibilities before God and history," and "to submit the call to the United Nations, the Security Council, and the League of Arab States."[46] He also sent a message to the Secretary-General of the Arab League, appealing for his defense of "the Arabian heritage and Arab lands," and calling upon him to inform all Arab leaders "so that they may take urgent action to deter the aggressor and raise the issue at the United Nations, the Security Council and the Council of the Arab League."[47]

Shaikh Saqr also informed British Prime Minister Edward Heath and called upon Britain to carry out its "duty to protect our subjects and our lands from any external aggression." He wrote: "We strongly protest at the British silence, and demand that speedy measures be taken to withdraw the Iranian forces from the islands..."[48] In another letter to the President and Members of the Security Council, Shaikh Saqr appealed for a Security Council resolution calling upon Iran to withdraw from the islands and he challenged Iran to take its claim to the Security

Council, the General Assembly or the International Court of Justice.[49] Finally, he wrote to the UN Secretary General and to the US, Soviet, British, French and PRC Ambassadors to the UN, appealing that they "take urgent measures in the name of humanity and in pursuance of the noble objectives for which the United Nations Organization was established."[50]

News of Iran's occupation of the Tunbs and landing on Abu Musa led to demonstrations in all of the emirates, particularly in Ras al-Khaimah, Sharjah and Abu Dhabi, where Iranian property was attacked, as well as in Baghdad, Kuwait, Damascus, Tripoli and Beirut. Shaikh Khalid's brother, who had received the Iranian forces landing on Abu Musa, was shot and wounded on December 2, although he did recover.[51]

The official reaction to the events was also immediate, with Shaikh Saqr receiving expressions of support and/or Arab governments issuing public protests against Iran and Britain. Shaikh Khalid of Sharjah condemned and rejected Iran's occupation of the Tunbs. Shaikh Zayed of Abu Dhabi said: "We have evidence which proves that the islands are Arabian, but we will not try to snatch back these islands in an unbrotherly manner." He added:

> A human being has to respect another's right, and in this case it is the right of a nation and a right of a State which cannot be forsaken or relinquished. We do not want discord with our neighbors. Our reluctance to have any confrontation is the only thing that has made us pursue our rights in a courteous fashion, so that no enemy can take advantage of us.[52]

Other conservative Gulf Arab leaders also crafted reserved rhetoric and responses. Kuwait's parliament drafted a resolution on November 30 calling upon the government to break diplomatic relations with Iran, Britain and the United States. While the government did not heed these calls, Kuwait's Emir, Shaikh Sabah al Salim Al-Sabah, cabled Shaikh Saqr on December 1 to assure him of Kuwait's "readiness to stand by the side of our Arab brothers in whatever steps and actions they agree to take to safeguard the rights of the Arabs." Kuwait did lodge protests with Iran and also with Britain for failing to honor its treaty commitments to the emirates and for "connivance" with the Iranian occupation. Indeed, the Kuwaiti Foreign Ministry refused to allow the new Iranian Ambassador to meet with the Emir to present his credentials in early December, which resulted in this post remaining vacant during most of 1972.

Saudi Arabia issued an official statement in a Radio Riyadh broadcast on December 1 which said: "The Saudi Arabian Kingdom was caught by surprise by the action of Iran in using force to occupy the Arab islands and, indeed, did not expect Iran to undertake such action. It hopes that Iran will reconsider this position as assurance for the area's future and stability." Bahrain's Emir Shaikh Issa bin Salman also expressed "surprise" and the hope that Iran would "reconsider" in a cable to Shaikh Saqr. Qatar's Emir Shaikh Ahmad bin Ali Al-Thani noted that Qatar had publicly "condemned this regrettable act" and he promised that Qatar "will do everything in its power, jointly with the rest of the Arab states, to restore rights to their owners." On December 4, the Rulers of Saudi Arabia, Bahrain and Qatar warned that any other efforts by Iran to extend its influence in the Gulf would be prevented.[53]

Responses from the other more moderate Arab governments were also relatively reserved. Egypt's President Anwar Sadat counseled "prudence and understanding" in a cable to Shaikh Saqr. Egypt issued a public statement on December 1 that expressed "surprise" at Iran's military actions and called the Iranian occupation of the islands a "contradiction" of the UN Charter and of Arab-Iranian friendship. It argued that Britain would continue to be responsible for defending the Arab islands until they were returned to their owners and that Egypt could not recognize any agreement made under circumstances of military pressure and occupation. Tunisia, Jordan and Yemen each expressed "regret" over the Iranian occupation on December 2, with Yemen's President Abdul Rahman Al-Iryani promising that Yemen would support "Ras al-Khaimah's right to recover its stolen possessions and occupied land."[54]

Radical Arab nationalist governments and movements made the strongest protests. Iraqi President Ahmad Hassan Al-Bakr cabled Shaikh Saqr, declaring that "we will stand with you side by side until our Arabian islands are liberated from usurping aggressors." Iraq broke diplomatic relations with Iran and Britain on the same day as the occupation and publicly accused them of "collusion in the flagrant aggression mounted by Iranian forces against the three islands in the

Arabian Gulf." It also called upon Arab ambassadors in Baghdad to discuss "joint Arab retaliatory action" against Iranian aggression.

Syria's President Hafiz Al-Assad condemned the Iranian occupation, calling it a colonialist plot between Britain and Iran against the Arab homeland. The People's Democratic Republic of Yemen (PDRY) and Algeria echoed these sentiments. On December 5, Libya's Revolutionary Command Council Chairman Muammar Qadhafi cabled Shaikh Saqr and argued that Britain was "primarily responsible" for the Iranian occupation, having demonstrated "its attributes of imperialist domination, hatred for the Arabs, betrayal of pledges, and scorn for international law." He regretted that Iran had "connived" with Britain as its "obedient servant." The Palestine Liberation Organization (PLO) compared Iran's occupation of the islands with Zionist aggression against Palestine and argued that the Arab nation had to restore any Arab land usurped by aggressors.[55]

On December 1, Arab League Assistant Secretary General Alyafi told the British Ambassador in Cairo that he was "surprised and astonished" by the news of the seizure of the Tunbs, and lamented that "If only we had persevered in our contacts with Iran and Britain and used quiet diplomacy to reach an agreement..." He said the Arab League regarded Britain as "fully responsible for Iran's conduct; it should have protected the territories of Ras al-Khaimah" and called on Britain "to reject this occupation in any shape or form, to condemn it, to demand the withdrawal of Iranian forces, and to confirm that those islands are Arabian." He also argued that the islands were of strategic importance and would enable Iran to control the Gulf.[56] In a meeting with the Iranian Chargé d'Affaires, Alyafi referred to documents that proved the Arab character of the islands and called Iran's behavior an aggression that violated Arab-Iranian friendship and the UN Charter. He offered to work with Iran in achieving a peaceful solution, but Iran would then have to withdraw from the islands and resume negotiations.[57] Alyafi relayed a similar message to Iran's Ambassador in Cairo.[58]

Alyafi later noted that his arguments regarding all three islands had been prepared in a memorandum by the Legal Department of the Arab League on the basis of documents provided by Ras al-Khaimah and Sharjah.[59] In addition to its November 28 report, the Arab League had also prepared a 'complementary memorandum' following the events of the week. This second document argued that Ras al-Khaimah had a strong claim to the two Tunbs on the basis of prescription, rejected Iran's claims to the two islands and criticized Iran's use of its armed forces to occupy all three islands as a violation of international law. Furthermore, it argued that Ras al-Khaimah, Sharjah and the Arab states had the right to bring the issue before the Security Council and the General Assembly, and rejected the MoU on Abu Musa as being legally void on the basis that it had been obtained by threat and pressure.[60]

On December 6, 1971, the Arab League met in an emergency session to consider the occupation. Iraq had already withheld recognition of the new UAE and now opposed its membership in the Arab League and the UN until several conditions were met: that Sharjah issue a statement annulling the MoU on Abu Musa; that the UAE denounce Iran's occupation of the three islands; that the UAE should refrain from establishing diplomatic relations with Iran until the islands were returned; and that the UAE should encourage Arab immigration to the UAE and give equal treatment to all Arab citizens wishing to emigrate to the UAE. Iraq may not have been aware that the UAE's first President Shaikh Zayed had already condemned Iran's aggression one day earlier. Although Iraq called upon other member states to take the same position, a large majority, with only the PDRY and Saudi Arabia opposing UAE membership for different reasons, admitted the UAE to the League.[61]

With procedural matters resolved, the meeting moved to the issue at hand. The head of Ras al-Khaimah's delegation, Shaikh Abdul Aziz Al-Qasimi, the Director of the Ruler's Court, argued that Iran had committed aggression against the entire Arab world and appealed to the member states to break diplomatic, commercial and cultural relations with Iran, to raise the issue at the Security Council or the ICJ, and to stir international public opinion through the Arab media. In making his case, he distributed historical documents demonstrating Ras al-Khaimah's continuous and undisturbed sovereignty over the Tunbs and substantiating Ras al-Khaimah's title to the islands. These documents included the correspondence from the former Qawasim Shaikhs of Lingeh and the British representatives in the Gulf, as well as the concession agreements from British firms and oil-companies. He also declared that Ras al-Khaimah did not acknowledge or approve the MoU on Abu Musa.

The Legal Adviser to Sharjah, Yosri Al-Dowaik, a member of the UAE delegation, rejected Iran's use of force to occupy the Tunbs, but explained that Sharjah's MoU on Abu Musa had been negotiated after encouragement from Arab states to find a peaceful solution that preserved Sharjah's sovereignty, which the MoU did. Iraq, which had already submitted the issue to the UN Security Council on December 3, then presented a proposal to condemn Iranian aggression, to request an immediate Iranian withdrawal from the islands, to sever diplomatic relations with both Iran and Britain, and to take a united Arab stand at the United Nations.[62]

When the session reconvened on December 7, Egypt, Saudi Arabia, Kuwait, Tunisia, and even Jordan and radical Syria counseled a moderate response. As a result, the Arab League reaction was restrained.[63] The League passed resolution 2865, which stated that the League resolved:

> First: To confirm that the three islands of Abu Musa, the Greater Tunb and the Lesser Tunb are purely Arab and that they are part of the Arab homeland by history and international law and legitimacy, and that their Arab owners have sovereignty over them.
>
> Second: To denounce this occupation of a part of the Arab land by force, which threatens security and stability in the region and contradicts the UN Charter, the Arab League Charter, and international treaties.
>
> Third: To hold Britain responsible for abandoning its international obligations and to condemn it for not honoring its obligations.
>
> Fourth: That Iran, by this occupation, endangers Arab-Iranian friendship and relations. In order to avoid this, the Council requests the Arab League's Secretary General to initiate communications at the highest level in order for Iran to reconsider its position.
>
> Fifth: That the Secretary General shall report on his communications to the next meeting of the League's Council of Foreign Ministers.[64]

The resolution stopped short of calling for the breaking of diplomatic relations with Iran and Britain and did not even explicitly call for Iranian withdrawal from the islands. Not even the PDRY, Libya and Algeria fought for the tabled Iraqi proposals. In terms of the text itself, the resolution carefully denounced "this occupation" rather than

"Iran's occupation." Saudi Arabia and others, including even Syria, argued that denouncing "Iran's occupation" would produce an Iranian reaction that would serve to undermine efforts by the Secretary-General or other Arab officials to communicate with Iran. However, even the call for the Secretary-General to "initiate communications" was deliberately vague. Hassouneh, noting that Iran had already refused Arab League mediation, preferred to initiate communications with those Arab heads of state who enjoyed close relations with the Shah, particularly the heads of state of Kuwait, Saudi Arabia and Tunisia, and that these Arab heads of state should take the responsibility for communications with the Shah.

Kuwait and Saudi Arabia were reluctant to communicate with Iran again. Instead, they wanted the Secretary-General to communicate with Arab states prior to him communicating with the Shah. Iraq, the PDRY and Libya recorded their reservations over this call, largely because they thought it would be futile and also because their call for the drafting of a joint Arab plan of action to recover the islands was voted down.[65] Later that day, Libya announced the withdrawal of its foreign reserves from Britain and nationalized the British Petroleum Company's assets in Libya.[66]

Iran's actions and Shaikh Saqr's appeals had led Iraq, joined by Algeria, Libya and the PDRY, to file a complaint at the UN Security Council on December 3, 1971. Kuwait and Somalia joined these states in participating in the debate on December 9, as did Iran, the UAE and the UK. Syria, a member of the Security Council, did not participate. The reasons for the strong reactions of Iraq and the other radical Arab nationalist states to the Iranian behavior are explained well in the extensive formal statements made by their representatives at this session.[67]

Iraq denounced Iran's "covetous and expansionist policies" and the "collusion" between Iran, the UK and the United States. Iraq accused them of an "imperialistic" effort to fill an alleged power vacuum left by the British withdrawal from the Gulf and of seeking to counter Soviet and Arab radical moves in the Gulf by bequeathing Britain's colonial role to Iran, in violation of Britain's treaty obligations to protect the emirates. Iraq rebutted Iran's historical claims and legal arguments for sovereignty over the islands, as well as the legal validity of the MoU on Abu Musa, and rejected arguments that Iran alone should be selected to fill a power vacuum. Noting major arms sales to Iran, it rebutted Iran's strategic arguments about promoting security and stability in the area, arguing that Iran would now control the only outlet to the high seas for the commerce of Iraq and the other Gulf Arab states, and that Iran would use this control to threaten and pressure these states. Iraq also noted that since 1969, Iran had been repudiating the 1937 treaty that had acknowledged Iraqi sovereignty over the Shatt al-Arab river up to the Iranian shore, and Iran had been claiming equal sovereignty over the river and building up its forces along the river, Iraq's only outlet to the Gulf. Iraq called on the Security Council to uphold the relevant principles of international law enshrined in the UN Charter, particularly enjoining the threat or use of force, and to ensure the withdrawal of Iran's forces from the islands, lest the states of the region conclude that the use of force is the only way to defend their rights, with the region and the world thus subjected to the danger of war.[68]

Algeria denounced Iran's "bellicose imperialism," condemned its "annexationist policies," criticized Britain for not protecting the territory of Ras al-Khaimah and Sharjah, and argued that the Security Council should condemn Iran's use of force. The PDRY argued that the islands were "extensions of the Arab mainland" and expressed the fear that Iran's invasion of the islands was a prelude to an invasion of the mainland, particularly to "destroy the revolution" in the Dhofar province of Oman. It also held Britain, which it denounced for its imperialism and exploitation in the region, responsible for Iran's "illegal act of aggression," and called for Iran's immediate withdrawal. The PDRY further accused the rulers of Ras al-Khaimah and Sharjah of "collaborating" with Iran and Britain, and vowed that the Popular Front for the Liberation of the Occupied Arabian Gulf would "liberate" the whole Gulf area. Libya, denouncing "imperialism in all its forms—old, new, or emerging," strongly condemned Iranian military aggression and occupation, as well as British "connivance" and violation of its own treaty obligations and the UN Charter. Libya expressed "diminishing faith" in the Security Council's willingness to hold major powers and their allies accountable, and argued that it nationalized British Petroleum Company assets in Libya and withdrew Libyan deposits from British banks on December 7 "because imperialists understand only the language of their own self-interest." [69]

Kuwait, the one conservative Arab state to speak, recalled its diplomatic efforts to dissuade Iran from using force, including meetings between Kuwait's and Iran's Foreign Ministers and meetings with the Shah. Kuwait "deplored" Iran's behavior, its disruption and threat to the security of the Gulf, and its violation of the UN Charter. It severely condemned Britain, arguing that Sir William Luce pressured Sharjah and Ras al-Khaimah to abrogate their territorial integrity when Britain had an obligation to protect their territorial integrity. Kuwait also demanded a Security Council resolution calling for Iran's immediate withdrawal.[70]

The UAE, which had just been admitted as a Member of the UN on the morning of this discussion, noted that it had been advised to delay its declaration of independence and application for membership in the UN because of Iranian threats to disrupt and prevent the establishment of the UAE. The UAE noted that Iran had refused to negotiate with a fully independent and equal state and member of the UN, but had insisted on a settlement prior to the independence of the UAE. Furthermore, Iran had refused negotiation or arbitration or recourse to the ICJ or the Security Council because it had no evidence to back up its claims to the islands. The UAE expressed the hope that Iran would agree to settle the issue in a way that restored friendship and avoided enmity.[71]

Iran denied it had any expansionist ambitions against anyone's territory, but warned that interference by any outside power would endanger peace and security in the region. It protested the use of the term "Arabian Gulf" during the discussions and argued that the riparian states should cooperate. As far as Iran was concerned, Sharjah was satisfied with the MoU. Iran claimed that the three islands were Iranian, although offering no evidence of its claim to Abu Musa and only providing British maps, an unnamed encyclopedia, Iran's protests over the years, and the islands' geographical proximity to Iran as arguments for its claim to the Tunbs.[72]

In the end, Somalia argued that it would be precipitate to recommend recourse under Chapter VI, Article 36 of the Charter, which would enable the Security Council to "recommend appropriate procedures or methods of adoption." Somalia recommended deferring the matter so that diplomatic efforts by third parties friendly to both the complainants and Iran might be given a chance. This call for third-party diplomacy was similar to the call contained in Arab League Resolution 2865. The President of the Security Council, noting that there were no objections to Somalia's recommendation, ordered such a deferral.[73]

Reaction and initiatives in the Arab world continued as the Arab League and the UN Security Council meetings took place and through the following weeks and months. Iraq's Oil Minister, Saadoun Hamadi, and Syria's Deputy Prime Minister and Foreign Minister, Abdul Haleem Khaddam, visited Shaikh Saqr in Ras al-Khaimah in early December to convey their support, although Syria did not back Iraq's positions in the Arab League and Security Council meetings. Libya's Premier and Vice-Chairman of the Revolutionary Command Council, Major Abd-al Salam Jaloud, also visited Ras al-Khaimah and argued that diplomatic, commercial and cultural relations with Iran should be severed, that Iranian communities be expelled and that Shiites be removed from key positions. Libya would be ready to send a military force to face Iranian ambitions and to organize commando forces to disturb the Iranian presence on the islands, he claimed.[74] Ras al-Khaimah's Crown Prince Khalid then visited Tripoli on December 10, where Colonel Qadhafi told him that Libya would support efforts ·to recover the Tunbs, but advised Ras al-Khaimah to join and work within the UAE to achieve this.[75] An Iraqi delegation also visited Shaikh Khalid in Sharjah in early December and criticized him for the MoU. Shaikh Khalid's reply, which he made public in *An Nahar*, was: "Your radio service described me as an agent and traitor because I signed an agreement with Iran but you kept silent when I asked for your help and the help of all the Arabs."[76]

On December 11, the Kuwaiti parliament, returning to its draft resolution of November 30, unanimously passed resolutions calling for Kuwait to break diplomatic and economic relations with Iran, Britain and the United States and to impose a wide range of economic and cultural sanctions against these states, including nationalization of oil assets, the use of oil as a weapon, withdrawal of Kuwaiti funds from Britain, termination of Iranian immigration to Kuwait, deportation of illegal Iranian immigrants, military conscription, the formation of a combined Arab defense force, and even support for national liberation movements in the Gulf. *Middle East Economic Survey* noted that the parliamentary debate was characterized by "exceedingly bitter invective" against these three states and demonstrated the extent to which Kuwaiti public opinion had been "inflamed" by the situation. Again, the Kuwaiti Government did not heed these calls.[77]

On December 14, 1971, Arab League Assistant Secretary-General Alyafi began a visit to the Gulf, pursuant to Arab League Resolution 2865's call for the Secretary General to "initiate communications." Alyafi visited Abu Dhabi, Dubai, Ras al-Khaimah, Sharjah, Bahrain, Qatar and Oman. His subsequent report for the Arab League's Council of Foreign Ministers, submitted upon his return to Cairo in early January 1972, reviewed the opinions of the rulers and noted "that all the rulers were not inclined to escalate the dispute with Iran into a real conflict and simply wanted an amicable settlement." He further wrote "that all of them favoured an initiative by the Arab League to make contacts with Iran, affirming that they would commit themselves to any decision by the League" and "that the ruler of Ras Al-Khaimah welcomed a settlement with Iran on the basis of leasing the two islands of the Greater and the Lesser Tunbs."[78]

Although Saudi Arabia and Kuwait were not on Alyafi's itinerary, the Secretary-General asked them, as well as Tunisia, Jordan and Morocco, to take responsibility for mediating with Iran. While Saudi Arabia's King Faisal conveyed a willingness to mediate, Kuwait informed the Secretary-General that its potential value as a mediator with Iran was very weak in light of its dispute with Iran and Iranian media attacks on Kuwait.[79] Jordan declined because of its preoccupation with Arab-Israeli affairs, but stated that it did not mind making a personal communication to the Shah.[80]

In late December, toward the end of the Assistant Secretary-General's visit, Shaikh Saqr also appealed to Saudi Arabia, Kuwait, Morocco and Tunisia to attempt to make diplomatic contacts with Iran in order to persuade Iran to withdraw. Alyafi reported on January 3 that Saudi Arabia, Tunisia and Morocco were all in touch with Iran on the issue. These states had expressed their reservations about denouncing the occupation of the islands in Arab League Resolution 2865, and indeed Morocco had attached its formal reservation to the resolution itself, largely because this could undermine any Arab mediation.[81] Nevertheless, the contacts made by these individual states were not successful. Moreover, Iran remained unwilling to accept official Arab League mediation. Meanwhile, Iraq, which had broken diplomatic relations with Iran and the UK on November 30, 1971 and had argued that Arab mediation would be futile, expelled 60,000 Iranians at the end of December 1971. Iraq also nationalized the British Iraq Petroleum Company concession on June 1, 1972.[82]

On July 17, 1972 the Arab League's efforts ended in a bland letter to the President of the UN Security Council, in which fifteen Arab member states of the Arab League and of the UN, stretching from North Africa to the Gulf, stated only that "the Islands of Abu Musa and the two Tunbs are Arab and constitute an integral part of the United Arab Emirates and of the Arab homeland."[83] Ali Humaidan, who was then the UAE's delegate at the UN, explained: "In a meeting of the Arab group of states at the United Nations, Iraq proposed that Arab ambassadors from the region send a signed letter to the Chairman of the Security Council ascertaining that the islands were Arab territory and formed an integral part of the wider Arab world. The UAE delegate to the United Nations [i.e. Humaidan] suggested rewording the proposal to state that the islands were an integral part of the United Arab Emirates."[84]

Notably, Saudi Arabia and Jordan were not signatories to this letter. Jordan's King Hussein was attempting to mediate a normalization of relations between Iran and the UAE at the time, and would do so again in September, while Saudi Arabia had also made private communications to Iran about the islands in January 1972 and would continue to do so in the future. Both may have reasoned that their signature could disrupt these efforts.[85] Indeed, Shaikh Saqr of Ras al-Khaimah says that when meeting King Faisal in 1972, King Faisal asserted that "not an inch of the islands should be surrendered. Maybe we are not in a position to get them back by force, but one day we will bring them back to their rightful fold."[86] When Iranian Foreign Minister Khalatbari visited Riyadh in July 1973, King Faisal "raised the islands issue, which he insisted should be settled in a manner acceptable to the Arab shaykhdoms," but Khalatbari answered that Iran would not permit anyone to lay claim to what Tehran perceived as "her lands." The Shah then wrote to Faisal that "no Iranian, even a traitor to his country, could be found now or in the future who would cede an inch of national territory."[87]

An Analysis of the Early Arab Reaction

The conservative states of Saudi Arabia and Jordan and moderate Egypt under Sadat were reluctant to confront Iran over Abu Musa and the Tunbs. Their reluctance may be attributed in part to their perception that Iran under the Shah was a counterweight to the radical Arab socialist Baath regime in Iraq, which harbored territorial designs on Kuwait and political designs for leadership throughout the Gulf region and the Arab world. Indeed, even earlier, when Iraq under Abdul Karim Qassim had asserted a claim to Kuwait soon after Kuwait's achievement of independence in 1961, Saudi Arabia, Jordan and even Egypt under Nasser had all committed military forces to an Arab League force sent to join British forces to defend Kuwait.[88]

Nasser's Egypt, normally critical of Gulf shaikhdoms like Kuwait as agents of "feudalism" and "imperialism," acted in this case out of its traditional geopolitical rivalry with Iraq. The Baath government that came to power in Iraq in 1968 also adopted a threatening posture toward Kuwait. In March 1973, it would occupy a Kuwaiti military post, and between 1973 and 1976 it laid claim to the Kuwaiti islands of Bubiyan and Warba near the Iraqi port of Umm Qasr, prompting Saudi Arabia to send military forces to assist Kuwait again in 1973.[89] From 1968 to 1975, the Iraqi Baath regime supported the PFLOAG and other followers in the Gulf that were revolutionary threats to the continued rule of the conservative Gulf Arab regimes.[90] Iraq also financed and supported the coup attempt that took the life of the Ruler of Sharjah in January 1972.

Saudi Arabia, Jordan and Sadat's Egypt also viewed Iran as a counterweight to communist challenges posed by the radical People's Democratic Republic of Yemen, which had come to power after the British withdrawal from Aden in 1967, and to the radical Popular Front for the Liberation of the Occupied Arabian Gulf. The latter group, with PDRY support, was leading a rebellion in the Dhofar province of Oman and seeking to overthrow "the imperialists and their lackeys – the feudal rulers," not only in Oman but throughout the Arab Gulf. Both the PDRY and PFLOAG were receiving military assistance from the People's Republic of China, the Soviet Union, East Germany and Cuba. King Faisal offered financial assistance to Sultan Qaboos in December 1971 and again in late 1972, and Jordan lent military forces in 1975.

It was the deployment of the Shah's military forces from 1973 to 1978 that made the real difference in defeating the PFLOAG, renamed the Popular Front for the Liberation of Oman (PFLO) in 1974 to reflect its now more narrow goals. In addition, the Shah had diplomatic successes in bringing about an end to PRC support for the insurgents in 1973 and, through the Algiers Accord of 1975, an end to Iraqi support.

After the PDRY changed its policy and had a rapprochement with Saudi Arabia in 1976, Saudi Arabia mediated a cease-fire between the PDRY and Oman in 1976.[91] Indeed, during the civil war in North Yemen from 1962 to 1967, Saudi Arabia and Jordan had also found Iran to be supportive to the royalist forces supported by Saudi Arabia and Jordan against the republican forces supported by Nasser's Egypt.[92]

Of course, Saudi Arabia, with the second longest Gulf coastline, had misgivings and apprehensions about the Shah's aspirations to dominate the Gulf and about his growing military power, including the Iranian military presence in Dhofar, i.e. on the peninsula itself. These issues disposed Saudi Arabia to be concerned about the islands. Nevertheless, Saudi Arabia still viewed the Shah's Iran as a counterweight to the ideological and military challenges posed by Iraq, the PDRY and PFLOAG. The Shah and his foreign ministers cultivated Saudi Arabia's goodwill through arguments about the need for cooperation against radicalism in the area, in an effort to mute Saudi Arabia's criticism of Iran's occupation of the islands.[93] Thus, as Saudi Acting Foreign Minister Al-Saqqaf told the US Ambassador to Saudi Arabia in early December 1971, Iran's actions on the islands had fostered Arab bitterness, but Saudi Arabia's moderate response was based on its recognition that Saudi-Iranian harmony was vital to Saudi interests and regional security.[94]

Indeed, in 1968, Saudi Arabia and Iran had resolved disputes over their median line in the Gulf including the islands, oil fields and oil concessions in the area. Iran had recognized Saudi Arabia's claim to Arabi, although Farsi went to Iran. Moreover, the Shah had given up Iran's claim to Bahrain, accepting the wishes expressed by the Bahraini population in May 1970 to be independent, and accepting Bahrain's proclamation of independence in August 1971. For Saudi Arabia, which had taken a strong stand in support of Bahrain's Arabism and independence in discussions with Iran, this was an important achievement.[95]

Saudi Arabia also sought Iranian cooperation on oil issues, or at least to limit contention on these issues. On this, they were less successful, with Iran raising production at a time when Saudi Arabia wanted to keep production low as a form of pressure on Western oil consumers that supported Israel. Again, after the 1973 Arab-Israeli war, Saudi Arabia and other major Arab oil producers imposed an oil embargo on Western oil consumers that supported Israel, and supplemented it with production cutbacks, but Iran did not participate or cooperate. After Arab production cutbacks enabled OPEC, at Iranian and Venezuelan urging, to raise prices to a level that threatened to disrupt Western economies, Saudi Arabia sought to stabilize and reduce these prices and to elicit Iran's cooperation, but Iran resisted again. It was not until 1977 that agreement over oil policy was reached.[96]

The fact that Saudi Arabia was also engaged in border disputes with Abu Dhabi may have influenced the Saudi decision to withhold its full support to the new United Arab Emirates over the issue of the islands. Initially, Saudi Arabia, along with Kuwait, supported the idea of a proposed nine-member Federation of Arab Emirates during the years of negotiation from 1968 to 1971, in part because they came to share the British view that such a union could promote security in the Gulf after the British withdrawal and because they saw such a federation as a potential bulwark against the spread of any radical Arab movement in the Gulf area, such as the PFLOAG, and against the infiltration of radical forces into the Gulf area from the outside.[97]

In May 1968, King Faisal had said that Saudi Arabia supported the Federation of Arab Emirates "unconditionally."[98] Nevertheless, when Shaikh Zayed visited King Faisal in May 1970 to express his concern about the threat posed by the PFLOAG and his desire for Saudi Arabia's help in containing this threat, King Faisal warned Shaikh Zayed that Saudi Arabia would not recognize the nine-member Federation of Arab Emirates unless Saudi claims in eastern Arabia were recognized. King Faisal also demanded that the Abu Dhabi Petroleum Company cease its operations in territory claimed by Saudi Arabia and threatened to use force to stop the company if Shaikh Zayed did not do it.[99] When the UAE was established in 1971, Saudi Arabia refused to extend recognition to or establish diplomatic relations with the new six-member federation. It subsequently also opposed its admission to the Arab League. It was not until Saudi Arabia received a corridor to the Gulf between Qatar and Abu Dhabi, through the area of Khor al-Udaid, and most of the territory covering the Shaiba/Zararah oil field, in exchange for renouncing its claim to the Buraimi/al-Ain region, that the border dispute was settled in July 1974 with Saudi Arabia subsequently recognizing the UAE.[100]

The Gulf Arab states of Bahrain, Qatar and Oman were similarly reluctant to confront Iran. These states also viewed Iran as a counterweight to Iraq, the PDRY and PFLOAG. This was particularly true of Oman, which was the most directly threatened by the PFLOAG.[101] Moreover, Iran had quickly recognized the independence of Bahrain in August and of Qatar in September 1970, established diplomatic relations with them and announced that it would support their membership in the UN.[102] Iran had also supported Oman's admission to the UN in October 1971.[103]

These were achievements that Bahrain, Qatar and Oman did not want to disturb. There were also territorial agreements in place that these Gulf States did not want to place in jeopardy. These included Bahrain's new maritime boundary with Iran, as well as Qatar's 1969 agreement with Iran on their maritime boundary and its 1965 land boundary agreement with Saudi Arabia. Meanwhile, Oman was keen to achieve a maritime boundary with Iran and did so in 1974. Other factors included unresolved territorial issues between the UAE and Oman, as well as the fact that lingering resentments remained between Qatar and Abu Dhabi over the settlement in the 1960s of its maritime borders and disputed islands in which three of four disputed islands went to Qatar and the fourth went to Abu Dhabi.[104] Finally, all three states may have been deferring to their more powerful neighbor Saudi Arabia.[105]

Among the conservative Arab Gulf states, Kuwait, which had sought to mediate a settlement of the dispute only months before Iran's occupation, was the most forceful in deploring Iran's occupation of the islands. Kuwait's initial efforts to mediate and its subsequent criticism of Iran may be attributed to its vulnerability and concern that Iran should not take actions that would provoke a more aggressive policy in the Gulf by radical Iraq or that would provoke radical domestic elements in Kuwait. At the same time, Kuwait shared with Saudi Arabia and the other conservative Gulf Arab states the perception that Iran was an important bulwark against radical Arab forces and trends in the Gulf, and that Iran should therefore not be alienated.

To be sure, Iran's power and ambition made Kuwait uneasy.[106] Indeed, after the occupation, when Kuwait issued a joint communiqué with Iraq stating that the islands were Arab, Iranian newspapers expressed concern that Kuwait was adopting a pro-Iraqi policy and warned that this would harm Kuwait's interests.[107] In 1973, however, when Iraq clashed with Kuwait, Iran offered military aid to Kuwait.[108] Other issues of concern to Kuwait were its 1965 maritime boundary agreement with Iran and the fact that Kuwait had lent its good offices to resolve the issue of Bahrain. The Kuwaiti representative to the Security Council discussions in December 1971 noted that his government "cherished" the Shah's decision on Bahrain.[109]

Outside the Gulf, Egypt's reluctance to confront Iran may be attributed in particular to Cairo's preoccupation with the Arab-Israeli conflict. Nasser's Egypt had broken diplomatic relations with the Shah's Iran, in part because of Tehran's *de facto* recognition of and oil sales to Israel. Egypt's relations with Iran had improved somewhat after the former's defeat in the 1967 war, when it lost the Sinai peninsula to Israel. Egypt's preoccupation with regaining the lost Sinai led to the country's subsequent withdrawal from North Yemen, where it had supported republican forces, and also resulted in Egypt's diminishing involvement in Gulf affairs.

Iran now supported Arab demands for Israeli withdrawal from the territories occupied by Israel in 1967, and Arab demands for a Palestinian national home. Furthermore, Iran now opposed Israeli policy on Jerusalem. As a result, Nasser and the Shah restored diplomatic relations in August 1970, just before Nasser's unexpected death.[110] Sadat wanted to preserve and develop this rapprochement, seeing the Shah's support as important in his effort to resolve the Arab-Israeli conflict either by enlisting US diplomacy or by eventual war.[111] In exchange, Iran asked for and received Egypt's abstention from involvement in the Gulf and, in particular, Egypt's neutrality on the issue of the islands.[112] Sadat was also keen on a rapprochement with Saudi Arabia and good relations with Jordan, thinking they would be crucial in his strategy toward Israel, and thus may have wanted to support their cautious policy on the islands.[113] In fact, Ali Humaidan reports that Sadat once referred to the islands as "'a few rocks that did not warrant all that fuss."[114]

Immediately following the Iranian occupation of the islands, Shaikh Zayed had put the issue into an Arab context, referring to the islands as "part of the Arab nation" and expressing the need for "practical support" from other Arab states. However, the UAE received only limited support from the Arab League, as evidenced by the moderate

Arab League resolution of December 1971, the tame Arab League resolution of July 1972 and the cautious mediation efforts after these resolutions. The UAE realized that Saudi Arabia and the other conservative Arab states did not want to confront Iran, that the Arab League was not united on the issue, and that the Security Council was not prepared to make any recommendations.[115]

Under these circumstances, there was not much the UAE could do to resolve the issue. Moreover, the UAE was understandably skeptical about declarations of support from the radical Arab states.[116] Iraq initially withheld recognition of the new UAE and opposed its membership in the Arab League and the UN, insisting that the UAE meet several Iraqi demands regarding Iran's occupation of the islands and regarding Arab immigration to the UAE. Soon thereafter, Iraq supported the coup against the Shaikh of Sharjah. In addition, Iraq was a supporter of the PDRY and the PFLOAG. The PDRY also voted against membership for the UAE in the Arab League and the UN. At the UN Security Council meeting, the PDRY called the rulers collaborators and vowed that the PFLOAG, which the PDRY supported, would liberate the entire Arab Gulf, which would presumably include the UAE along with Saudi Arabia and the other conservative states in the area. Algeria and Libya were too geographically remote to threaten the UAE or to offer more than rhetorical support, even though Libya's rhetoric did threaten military action against Iran.

The UAE's relations with Saudi Arabia were finally normalized in 1974, when their border dispute was resolved and Saudi Arabia recognized the UAE. In April 1975 Saudi Arabia expressed a commitment to defend the UAE against any threat.[117] In 1976, Saudi Arabia supported the forces favoring greater unity of the federation under the continued leadership of Shaikh Zayed, as opposed to the forces favoring decentralization. Later in 1976 a Saudi-UAE security agreement was signed.[118] The UAE was a supporter of Saudi Arabia's regional policies and OPEC policies during these years.[119] This, however, would have enabled Saudi Arabia to pressure the UAE not to press the islands issue during these years.

In addition, other states retreated on the issue, with Iraq not even raising the islands issue from 1975 to 1979. In March 1975, Iraq's then Vice President Saddam Hussein and the Shah of Iran had reached a temporary rapprochement with the conclusion of the Algiers Accord.

This accord acknowledged the middle of the navigable channel of the Shatt al-Arab, i.e. the *thalweg*, as the border between the two countries, a surprising concession for Iraq to make. In return, however, the Shah terminated his support for the Kurdish insurgency in the north of Iraq, which enabled Iraq to quickly rout the insurgents.[120] Moreover, Iraq agreed to accept the *status quo* in the Gulf region.[121]

According to *Al-Azminah Al-Arabiah*, a secret side agreement was concluded between the Shah and Saddam Hussein when they concluded the Algiers Accord. In this secret side agreement, Iraq agreed to freeze its demand for the liberation of Abu Musa and the Greater and Lesser Tunbs.[122] Having been forced to make such a painful concession on the Shatt al-Arab, Iraq certainly was in no position to make demands regarding these islands over the next four years.

Overall, during the 1970s, divisions and disagreements within the Arab world meant that it was not able to thwart Iranian designs on the islands or to bring about an end to Iran's occupation of the islands. As the 1971 date for British withdrawal from the Gulf and the Shah's deadline for gaining control over Abu Musa and the Tunbs approached, Sharjah and Ras al-Khaimah sought support from the Arab world. The response was limited and unsuccessful.

In the aftermath of Iran's occupation of the islands, the Arab response was more pronounced, but no more successful. This may be attributed to Iran's military superiority over the Arabs, to Arab pre-occupation with the Arab-Israeli conflict and to divisions in the Arab world between "radical," socialist, pan-Arab, pro-Soviet states and "conservative," monarchical, pro-American states, particularly their differing views regarding Iran's role in the region. The radicals viewed Iran as a threat, but the conservatives warily viewed Iran as a potential security partner that could not be aggressively challenged and alienated over the islands dispute.[123]

Thus, throughout this decade, the UAE had no choice but to work within these practical constraints in asserting its rights. During the 1980s and the early 1990s, different constraints would operate on the Arab world.

The Arab World's Reaction to the Conduct of the Islamic Republic of Iran

The issue of Abu Musa and the Tunbs was briefly revived as an Arab issue at the beginning of the 1980s. With Iran in revolutionary turmoil and Egypt ostracized after its separate peace agreement with Israel in March 1979, Iraq again tried to exert leadership in the Gulf region. Baathist Iraq, an early target of Ayatollah Khomeini's fiercest criticism, now saw an opportunity to redress the 1975 Algiers Agreement on the Shatt al-Arab and formally threatened to abrogate the agreement in October 1979.[1] Iraq also sought to generate Arab support by once again raising the islands issue. In April 1980, as tensions and clashes intensified along the Iraq-Iran border and conflict appeared increasingly likely, Iraq's Foreign Minister Saadoun Hammadi wrote a letter to UN Secretary-General Kurt Waldheim, noting that Iran's President Abolhassan Bani Sadr had recently stated that Iran would not return the islands, stating that Iraq had never recognized the illegitimate Iranian occupation of the islands, and again calling on Iran to withdraw from the islands.[2] In May, Iraq cited Iran's retention of the islands as evidence of its expansionism in a memorandum to the Islamic Conference.[3]

Iraq's reassertion of Arab claims to Abu Musa and the Tunbs was made in part for many of the same reasons its representative had articulated during the 1971 Security Council discussion, particularly Iraq's concern that Iran could use these islands to threaten the only outlet to the high seas for Iraq and other Gulf Arab states. However, Iraq's claims may also partly have been an effort to capitalize on an Arab grievance to rationalize Iraq's own agenda with Iran, particularly to regain control over the Shatt al-Arab and areas in Khuzestan, and to win support from the UAE and others for these objectives and for the impending war with Iran. While the UAE and other Gulf states, such as Saudi Arabia and Kuwait, were now beginning to view Iraq as a potential counterweight to Iran, they continued to be skeptical about Iraq's support on the islands, for the same reasons that prompted skepticism in 1971, namely the potential threat that radical Iraq could still pose to them.

Iraq was not the only Arab state, however, to call for the return of the islands to the UAE. In June 1980, at the Algiers OPEC conference, Saudi Arabia also expressed its full support for the UAE's demand to regain sovereignty over the islands.[4] This statement followed the public remarks of Iran's President Bani Sadr and Foreign Minister Qotbzadeh that Iran would never return the islands, and reflected the Saudi concern that the islands in the hands of the revolutionary regime in Iran constituted a threat. In addition, it is unlikely that Saudi Arabia was ready to accept Iraq's championing of this issue. The UAE was encouraged by this Saudi statement of support, coming as it did from a defender of the conservative *status quo* that had not offered strong support on the issue in the 1970s. Indeed, with the fall of the Shah, Saudi Arabia emerged as the most reliable defender of the Gulf Arab states like the UAE.

With the actual outbreak of the Iran–Iraq War in September 1980, Iraq continued to raise the islands issue in order to garner support for its actions. When Iraq demanded the return of the islands to their Arab owners as a condition for peace, Iran again responded that it would never relinquish them.[5] The *Financial Times* of October 2, 1980 reported that the Iraqis had sent a small force of men and helicopters to the UAE to bomb and recapture the three occupied islands. However, as the *Daily Telegraph* noted on October 3, Shaikh Zayed was personally against the use of force to restore the islands.[6] The UAE, along with Saudi Arabia, Britain and the United States, did not want to see the geographical scope of the war expanded to the Lower Gulf. This would prove to be a prudent path to follow, because Ayatollah Khomeini, Islamic Republican Party leader Hojat Al-Islam Muhammad Ali Khamene'i, and President Bani Sadr all issued warnings in early October

1980 to the shaikhs and emirates that supported Iraq. Bani Sadr, in particular, warned that Iran would bomb oil installations of the Gulf states supporting Iraq. Other officials indicated that Iran might mine the Strait of Hormuz.[7]

As these events were unfolding, Ras al-Khaimah's Shaikh Saqr visited Iraq's President Saddam Hussein, a visit which signaled Ras al-Khaimah's support for Iraq's war effort and Iraq's demand on the islands. Shaikh Saqr acknowledged on October 1, however, that the issue of Iran's occupation of the three islands was the responsibility of the federal government and he noted on October 2 that the federal government had previously requested the return of the islands. "Our request is simple," he said. "The Emirates want to see the islands restored to their rightful owners – in this case the Emirates – as soon as possible..."[8]

On May 25, 1981, the UAE joined Saudi Arabia, Kuwait, Bahrain, Qatar and Oman to establish the Gulf Cooperation Council (GCC). This was largely in response to the Iranian revolution, and particularly the inclination of the revolutionary Iranian regime to export its revolution to the conservative Arab regimes of the Gulf, the Soviet invasion of Afghanistan, which brought the Soviet military closer to the "warm waters" of the Gulf, and the outbreak of the Iran-Iraq War, which threatened to widen and destabilize the entire Gulf region.[9] The GCC was meant to promote coordination on the foreign and security policies, as well as the economic and social policies of its six member states.

The conservative Gulf states remained concerned about the ambitions and behavior of the radical Arab socialist Baath regime in Iraq, but they were even more concerned about the ambitions and behavior of the militant Islamic revolutionary regime in Iran. This became all the more important as Iran under Khomeini began to wage a propaganda war against the regimes of the Arab Gulf, even questioning the legitimacy of the Saudi regime's Islamic credentials. The result was that the Gulf states, while formally maintaining non-belligerent status during the war, provided support to radical Iraq. Saudi Arabia and Kuwait alone may have contributed as much as $50 to $60 billion over the course of the entire war.[10] On the other hand, Dubai continued its important trade relations with Iran and Sharjah continued to share the revenue from the Mubarak oil field with Iran throughout the war.[11]

During and after the spring of 1982, when Iraqi forces were pushed back from their positions in Iran's southern province of Khuzestan, particularly when Iran recaptured its main port city of Khoramshahr in May 1982, and when it appeared that the war could be a long one, the UAE's efforts to maintain neutrality sometimes elicited the criticism of Iraq.[12] The UAE, however, was quite aware of the disruptive potential of Iran with regard to its security and stability.

Indeed, Iranian pressure was increasing. Bahrain had already been the victim of an aborted Iran-backed coup attempt in 1981 and Saudi Arabia experienced Iranian disturbances during the annual Hajj in 1981 and 1982. Kuwait would later see Iran-backed agitation in the Shi'a community, the bombings of foreign embassies in 1983 and an attempted assassination of the Emir in 1985.[13] Furthermore, after Iran recovered Khoramshahr in May 1982, Tehran pressured Dubai and other emirates to try to limit Abu Dhabi's recent move towards greater defense cooperation with Saudi Arabia and the other GCC states. Such Iranian pressure persuaded Kuwait not to sign a bilateral security agreement with Saudi Arabia, although the UAE and the other GCC member states proceeded to do so.[14]

At the same time as Iraqi forces were pushed back from their positions in Khuzestan and as Iraq sought a negotiated end to the fighting, the UAE offered to use its neutral status to act as a mediator. Shaikh Zayed told Iran's Foreign Minister Ali Velayati during the latter's visit to Abu Dhabi in early May that if Iran wanted the UAE's help for a peaceful settlement "then we are ready." He also informed all the GCC states that the UAE and Algeria were prepared to conduct mediation between Iran and Iraq.[15] Iraq was so keen for a negotiated solution that it even gave up its demands regarding the Shatt al-Arab and the islands of Abu Musa and the Tunbs. However, Iran, not trusting Baghdad's calls for negotiations and sensing an opportunity to defeat Iraq, end Saddam Hussein's rule and promote the Islamic revolution in the heart of the Arab world, was not interested in negotiation or mediation at this time. As a result, it did not heed the UAE's many appeals to end the war in 1982.[16] This hardened Iranian position also precluded any opportunity for the UAE to make demands regarding the islands at this time.

In May 1983, as Iraq was defending its own territory against Iranian assaults, the UAE and Kuwait began to mediate on behalf of the GCC. They were concerned with arranging a cease-fire lest Iraqi control of the Shi'a-inhabited south of Iraq collapse and be replaced by Iranian control there. During one round of this mediation, Iran said it would consider a cease-fire if the mediators could persuade Iraq to cease its air attacks against Iranian oil and shipping installations, such as those at Kharg Island.[17] Iraq, however, continued its air campaign throughout 1983. In late September and early October, Khomeini and Velayati responded by threatening to close the Strait of Hormuz and by actually reinforcing Iran's garrisons on Larak, Henjam, Sirri and Farsi islands, while increasing artillery and anti-aircraft emplacements on Qeshm and the Greater Tunb. The UAE warned Iran against closing the strait, while expressing the belief that Iran would not act on its threat. The UAE's careful language came as it once again expressed a willingness to mediate between the belligerents.[18]

Iraq intensified and widened its air campaign in 1984 and Iran retaliated with attacks against the shipping of Iraq's GCC supporters, particularly Kuwait and Saudi Arabia. UAE mediation continued during the tanker war years of 1984-1985, while the GCC was successfully pressing for UN Security Council Resolution 552 of June 1, 1984, which condemned the attacks on neutral shipping to and from Kuwaiti and Saudi ports and demanded an end to them, although not mentioning Iran by name. While an exchange of visits between the foreign ministers of Saudi Arabia and Iran took place in 1985, the situation actually worsened. As Joseph Twinam has written:

> ...the prospects for improving relations with Iran, to say nothing of hopes for ending the conflict, soon faded, particularly with respect to Saudi Arabia and Kuwait. In the aftermath of Iranian provocations – the riots in Mecca during the hajj [especially in 1986 and 1987] and various terrorist acts against both states – Saudi Arabia and Kuwait became in the last years of the war the most hard-line of the Gulf Council governments in their attitudes toward Iran.[19]

Moreover, Iraqi attacks on Iranian shipping and Iranian attacks on neutral shipping, including on Saudi and Kuwaiti shipping off the UAE coast, escalated during 1986 and 1987. Furthermore, in February 1986 Iranian forces crossed the Shatt al-Arab and seized the Iraqi port on the Fao peninsula, putting Iranian forces within striking distance of Kuwait and Saudi Arabia. Saudi Arabia finally broke diplomatic relations with Iran in April 1988.[20]

The last years of the war demonstrated the uses to which Iran could put the islands and the challenge this could pose to the UAE, the other GCC states and the West. During the war, Iran used Abu Musa in particular and also the Tunbs as bases for regular Iranian Armed Forces and for the naval branch of the Iranian Revolutionary Guard Corps. From 1986 to 1988, the islands became bases for launching helicopter attacks and small boat attacks against shipping in the Gulf and for inflicting some damage on the UAE's offshore oil installations. For example, the Saudi tanker *Al-Nisr Al-Arabi* was attacked off the coast of Dubai by Iranian helicopters from Abu Musa in May 1986, the Cypriot bulk carrier *August Star* was wrecked off the coast of the Dubai port, Mina Jebel Ali on October 5, 1986 by an Iranian helicopter attack from Abu Musa and the US-operated tanker *Grand Wisdom* was crippled off the coast of Jebel Ali by speedboats from Abu Musa on November 6, 1987.[21] As Martin S. Navias and E.R. Hooton have reported:

> The vast majority of attacks [against neutral shipping] were conducted by the Pasdaran [i.e. the Revolutionary Guards]...by 1987 the Pasdaran had 20,000 men with two major naval bases, at Abu Musa and Farsi Island. Distributed evenly between them was the force of Boghammer Marin small boats which operated in patrols of three or four from forward bases at Kharg, the Reshadat (formerly Rostam) oil platform, Larak, Sirri, the Tunbs, Qeshm, Henjam, Al Karan...the majority [of these attacks in late 1987] were off the western coast of the UAE whereas those upon the *Diamond Marine* and *Petroship B* were actually in the Straits of Hormuz, the attackers using a base established upon the Tunbs.[22]

The UAE, along with Saudi Arabia, Kuwait and the other GCC states, welcomed and supported the US re-flagging and escorting of Kuwaiti shipping, as well as the US military strikes against the Iranian naval assets used in attacking Gulf shipping during 1987 and 1988. The UAE, meanwhile, allowed the use of its ports, naval repair facilities, airfields and airspace by the United States on a case-by-case basis.[23] As a member of the UN Security Council (UNSC) in 1986 and 1987, the

UAE also worked for the cease-fire resolutions passed in the Security Council during those years, including Resolution 598 of July 1987, which Iraq accepted in 1987 and Iran accepted only in July 1988.[24]

While maintaining sovereignty over the islands throughout the war, the UAE and its GCC partners were mostly preoccupied with the larger issues of the war. It was not considered prudent to try to take the islands by force in the fall of 1980 or at any other time during the eight-year war. One could also not expect a diplomatic resolution of the contending claims to these islands while open hostilities continued. Thus, diplomatic efforts were focused instead on arranging a cease-fire. Even from 1986 to 1988, when Iran was using Abu Musa and the Tunbs to attack Gulf shipping, the UAE and the other GCC states were more concerned with the problem of overcoming Iranian resistance to UNSC Resolution 598. Adding the issue of the islands to the diplomatic agenda, particularly during that final year, would not have been fruitful.

A diplomatic resolution of the islands issue in the aftermath of the Iran-Iraq war was also unlikely. When Iran finally accepted UNSC Resolution 598 in July 1988, after a full year of resisting it, Iraq demanded the abrogation of the 1975 Algiers Accord on the Shatt al-Arab, but did not make demands regarding the islands. Then, on August 2, 1990, after two years of unsuccessful efforts to reach an Iran–Iraq peace agreement, Iraq invaded Kuwait. In order to free itself for this new war, Iraq subsequently announced that it would accept the Iranian conditions for peace, including the reconfirmation of the Algiers Accord, although this was never formally implemented. Clearly, as it plunged into this new war, Iraq was in no position to make any demands to Iran about Abu Musa and the Tunbs.

A few words should be said about the role of the Arab League during the Iran–Iraq War and during the war over Kuwait. The Arab League had generally reflected a certain degree of Arab unity and cooperation, particularly on issues of liberation from Western imperialism. However, the League had also generally been constrained by a considerable degree of inter-Arab competition and conflict. Competing and shifting interests of various member states hampered the organization's ability to agree on and advance policies throughout the 1950s, 1960s and 1970s, as for example on Iran's occupation of the islands in 1971.

The League was seriously weakened when Egypt signed a separate peace agreement with Israel in March 1979, which led to Egypt being ostracized by most of the Arab world. As a result, regular meetings of the League were not even held between 1982 and 1985. When it did meet in 1985, there was a deep split between a group led by Jordan and the PLO, which favored negotiations with Israel, and a group led by Syria, which opposed such negotiations. Thus, throughout most of the Iran–Iraq War, the UAE and the other GCC states could not count on substantial support from the League, certainly not on the issue of the islands. It was not until November 1987 that the GCC states and Jordan's King Hussein were able to orchestrate an Arab summit conference in Amman to address the Iran–Iraq War. This Arab summit expressed its support for Iraq's territorial integrity and condemned Iran for resisting international demands to end the fighting, thus providing the GCC with wider Arab support for the GCC positions taken during the war.[25]

The Arab League's weakness was demonstrated again following Iraq's invasion of Kuwait, when the PLO, Jordan, Yemen and the Sudan refused to condemn Iraq, and with Libya and Iraq remaining absent. The UAE, which had also been privately and publicly threatened by Iraq, as well as the other GCC states, recognized that it could not count on the League as an organization or on Pan-Arabism as an ideology to help with the invasion of Kuwait, much less the issue of the islands. Egypt rehabilitated itself with the GCC, however, and Syria also gained favor with the GCC when both states committed military forces to Desert Shield and Desert Storm, and pledged in the March 6, 1991 Damascus Declaration to continue their cooperation for security with the six GCC states, although their forces were soon withdrawn from the Gulf.[26] Instead, the GCC states realized that they could not depend on their own military capabilities or the military capabilities of the Arab world to ensure their short to medium-term security. This could only be achieved through relations with Western military powers, particularly the United States.[27]

Iraq had emerged from the eight-year long Iran–Iraq War with some prestige in the Arab world, largely because it had withstood Iranian offensives for years and finally inflicted heavy losses on the Iranians. However, Iraq squandered this prestige when it invaded Kuwait, was defeated in Desert Storm, and was subsequently subjected to international sanctions and isolation.[28] Indeed, the UAE, Saudi Arabia and the other GCC states condemned Iraq, cooperated with Western military action against Iraq and supported sanctions against Iraq.[29] Iraq's diminished regional status consequently enabled Iran to improve its status in the region. Following a pragmatic line laid down by President Rafsanjani, Iran slowly began to emerge from its isolation.[30]

Even before Desert Storm began, the GCC Supreme Council's "Closing Statement" at the end of the December 1990 GCC Eleventh Summit in Doha, Qatar welcomed "the wish of the Islamic Republic in Iran to improve and develop its relations with all the states of the Gulf Cooperation Council," although it stressed "the importance of working seriously and realistically to solve the outstanding differences between Iran and member states" and stressed the GCC's "wish to establish distinct relations with Iran on the basis of good neighbourliness and non-interference in internal affairs and respect for sovereignty, independence and peaceful coexistence derived from the interconnections of religion and heritage which connect states of the region."[31]

Even Kuwait and Saudi Arabia, the most direct victims of Iranian provocations and attacks during the Iran-Iraq War, indicated a willingness to consider some steps towards reconciliation. During Iraq's occupation of Kuwait, Kuwaiti Foreign Minister Shaikh Sabah visited Tehran and apologized for Kuwait's previous support to Iraq during the Iran–Iraq War. Kuwait clearly needed Iran's cooperation during the crisis. Saudi Arabia wanted to normalize its relations with Iran for the sake of a stable Gulf environment in which Iranian ambitions might be moderated while Iraqi ambitions were thwarted.

Saudi Arabia's Crown Prince Abdullah bin Abdulaziz Al-Saud met President Rafsanjani in Senegal in December 1990 and Saudi Arabia and Iran restored diplomatic relations in March 1991. The two sides subsequently agreed on the number of Iranian pilgrims that would be allowed to travel to Mecca to perform the Hajj. This was followed by the visit of President Rafsanjani to King Fahd bin Abdulaziz Al-Saud in Riyadh in April 1991 and the visit of Saudi Foreign Minister Prince Saud al-Faisal Al-Saud to Tehran in June 1991. Meanwhile, Qatar's Foreign Minister, Mubarak Al-Khatir, said at a meeting of GCC foreign ministers in May 1991 that Iran was a friendly state and should play a role in the region's security.[32]

In June 1991, the GCC foreign ministers issued a communiqué looking forward to cooperation with Iran. GCC foreign ministers also met with the Iranian Foreign Minister in September 1991 and together promised "respect for sovereignty and territorial integrity, inviolability of internationally recognized boundaries, peaceful settlement of disputes, non-resort to force or the threat of force – and non-interference in the internal affairs of each other." The closing statement of the Supreme Council's Twelfth GCC Summit in December 1991 in Kuwait expressed "its satisfaction about the positive and concrete development of relations" with Iran and expressed "its desire to push forward bilateral relations."[33]

However, Iran's violation of the MoU on Abu Musa in 1992 severely undermined the efforts that Rafsanjani was making to improve relations between 1989 and 1992. A UAE Ministry of Foreign Affairs spokesman reacted to Iran's actions in August by saying that the Iranian actions reflected negatively on UAE-Iranian relations at a time when the UAE wished to establish good neighborly relations and cooperation with Iran.[34] On September 1, 1992, GCC Assistant Secretary-General Saif Al-Maskri said that Iran's actions would have "extremely negative" repercussions on GCC-Iranian relations, fostering distrust and tension. He expressed the serious concern and disappointment of the GCC, particularly because Iran's actions had come after a period of improvement in relations, and he expressed the GCC's hope that Iran would reconsider its policy.[35]

In the aftermath of Iran's violations of the MoU, the UAE began to receive important regional diplomatic support. The most important source for the UAE was from the GCC. On September 9, 1992, the GCC Council of Foreign Ministers issued a strongly worded communiqué that expressed their "deep denunciation of the procedures taken by Iran on the island since this represents a violation of the sovereignty and territorial integrity of one of the GCC states and undermines the security and stability of the region." The communiqué requested that Iran respect the MoU with Sharjah "with particular emphasis on the fact that the island of Abu Musa has become the responsibility of the government of the UAE since the federation was declared." It also made the following statement regarding Iran's behavior:

> [It] violates the declared interest in boosting bilateral relations...violates the principles of relations between the GCC states and Iran and bilateral agreements to maintain relations based on respect for the principles of international law: independence, sovereignty, and territorial integrity; non-interference in internal affairs; rejecting the use of force or threat of force; and solving disputes through peaceful means.

Expressing "complete support for the UAE and its complete sovereignty over the island of Abu Musa and complete support for all measures taken by the UAE to affirm its sovereignty over the island," the communiqué also expressed its "categorical rejection" of Iran's continued occupation of the Tunbs.[36]

On September 10, 1992, the foreign ministers of the Damascus Declaration states (the GCC, Egypt and Syria) issued a statement of support for the UAE that was very similar to the GCC Ministers statement. This expressed "strong denunciation of the unnecessary measures taken on the island that violate the sovereignty and integrity of the regional territories of the UAE and violate the principles of international law which call for respect for independence, sovereignty, and territorial integrity and solving disputes through peaceful means." The foreign ministers requested Iran to honor its MoU with Sharjah and also rejected Iran's continued occupation of the Tunbs.[37]

Iran's violations of the MoU on Abu Musa also occasioned a restoration of unity among the Council of Ministers of Foreign Affairs of the Arab League, which passed Resolution 5223/98/3 on September 13, 1992, stating their support for the UAE's "full sovereignty" over the three islands and "denouncing" Iran's occupation as "illegal." The Arab League offered "unqualified support" for all UAE measures to assert its sovereignty and to bring the matter of Iranian violations, which were deemed to "most seriously endanger the security and stability of the region," before the UN and called upon Iran to "respect" its pacts and covenants with the UAE and the UAE's sovereignty over the islands. It also asked the Arab League's Secretary General, Dr. Ismet Abdel Magid, to take up the matter. This resolution was also circulated as an official document of the UN General Assembly.[38]

It is noteworthy that Syria criticized Iran's position on the islands, despite their common interests in containing Iraq and in supporting

Hezbollah's resistance to the Israeli occupation of southern Lebanon. Indeed, Syria's endorsement of the UAE, GCC, Damascus Declaration and Arab League position on the islands was a bitter pill for Iran, as was Syria's participation in the Madrid peace process with Israel. Syria's view of Gulf security and stability included containment of Iraq, but did not include Iran challenging the UAE and the GCC.

Nevertheless, Syria's close relations with Iran, its endorsement of UAE rights and its interest in Gulf stability made Syria both willing and capable of mediating between the UAE and Iran.[39] Syria's President Hafiz Al-Assad met with Egypt's President Hosni Mubarak on September 16 and they agreed that Iran should be persuaded to follow a policy that would not escalate the problem further.[40] After President Assad met with Shaikh Zayed, Syrian Foreign Minister Farouk Al-Sharaa held meetings with both UAE Foreign Minister Rashid Abdulla Al-Nuaimi and Iranian Foreign Minister Ali Velayati respectively. While not resolving the dispute, he at least elicited an agreement that Iran would enter into direct talks with the UAE.[41]

Egypt's endorsement of the above declarations on the islands was also a cause for concern to Iran, particularly when Egypt's commitment to contain Iraq was joined with a promise to support the UAE against "Persian expansionism."[42] Egypt and Syria had withdrawn their troops from the Gulf in May and June 1992 respectively. Nevertheless, Egypt's statements of support were followed in December 1992 by Egyptian President Mubarak's shuttle diplomacy between Riyadh and Doha to arrange an agreement for the demarcation of their border and by another high profile visit to the Gulf in May 1993.[43] Egypt and Syria thus appeared to be committed to being diplomatic players in Gulf affairs, even if not military ones. Moreover, Iraq argued in mid-September 1992 that it was the only regional state capable of protecting the islands from Iran.[44] Once again, the unresolved conflict had given Iraq an opportunity to promote its own agenda, this time to argue for its early reintegration into the regional and world systems, barely two years after it had invaded Kuwait.

Following the failure of the 1992 bilateral negotiations on the islands between the UAE and Iran, the other GCC states and a number of other Arab states made public statements supporting the UAE position. Saudi Arabia's Foreign Minister Prince Saud Al-Faisal told the

47th session of the UN General Assembly that Saudi Arabia had learned "with grave concern of the failure of the UAE's efforts to reach a peaceful and amicable solution with Iran for the restoration of its sovereignty over the Island of Abu Musa, Greater Tonb, and Lesser Tonb." He expressed Saudi Arabia's "support for the UAE and its quest to cancel the measures taken unilaterally by Iran in order to solve this problem by negotiation and arbitration in conformity with international law and legitimacy."[45] Saud Al-Faisal's public statement was very significant due to the preeminent role of Saudi Arabia in the GCC and because Saudi Arabia did not allow the "thaw" in its relations with Iran to stand in the way of its support for the UAE on this issue. As such, Saudi Arabia showed its support for the GCC's security compact without allowing Iraq to use the issue to its advantage.[46]

During the same UN session, Oman's Minister Responsible for Foreign Affairs, Yusuf bin Alawi bin Abdullah, noted that "the United Arab Emirates announced the failure of its efforts with the Islamic Republic of Iran during the year to reach an amicable understanding on its rights of sovereignty over Three Islands in the Gulf, namely, Abu Musa, Greater Tonb, and Lesser Tonb," and said that this caused Oman to be "gravely concerned over the potential negative developments of this situation." He called on Iran, "to which we are connected with links of friendship, neighbourliness, and mutual interests diligently to seek peaceful means to resolve this dispute in a manner that will safeguard the rights of all concerned and the mutual interests of the member states of the Cooperation Council."[47] Oman's willingness to speak out on the three islands was also significant since Oman shared responsibility with Iran in the Strait of Hormuz, had agreed with Iran on their maritime boundary and had the closest relations with Iran of any of the six GCC states.[48]

Kuwait, Qatar and Bahrain used more careful language in their comments to this session of the General Assembly, each of them referring only to Abu Musa, but clearly expressing their support for the UAE.[49] Kuwait, still reeling from its invasion by Iraq, viewed Iran as an important counterweight to Iraq. Moreover, Kuwait had suffered a barrage of Iranian protests when it signed a defense cooperation agreement with the United States in September 1991 and therefore may not have wanted to antagonize Iran any further.[50]

Qatar, considering the tensions with Saudi Arabia in 1991 and 1992 regarding their 1965 border agreement and the flare-up of this issue at the Khafus border post in September 1992, may also not have wanted to alienate Iran, which it has viewed as a potential balancer to Saudi Arabia. The 1991 and 1992 discussion between Qatar and Iran about resolving their dispute over the North Dome off-shore gas field (called the South Pars field by Iran) may have played an additional role.[51] Bahrain is simply so close to Iran and so vulnerable to Iranian influence over its Shi'a population that it cannot afford to openly antagonize Iran. Nevertheless, all three states supported and would continue to support the UAE position on all three islands by passing official GCC statements.[52]

Egypt's Foreign Minister Amr Mousa alluded to all three islands and to Egypt's interest in the Gulf, saying, "In the Gulf region, which is a part of the Middle East, we witness another tension at its eastern boundaries, reflected in Iran's occupation of Arabian islands, Abu Musa being the latest." He called on Iran to "restore the situation to the *status quo ante*."[53] The Libyan, Tunisian and Jordanian foreign ministers also expressed their countries' support for the UAE's position on the three islands in their speeches to this session of the UN General Assembly.[54] Mousa spoke out again on October 1 in a speech to the National Press Club in Washington, DC, saying "Iran tried to play on the tension that has been prevalent in the region since the Iraqi invasion of Kuwait and began to take actions and measures that made up the current crisis on the island of Abu Musa." He argued that "Egyptian support for the UAE in its present conflict with Iran emerged from a constant attitude that has nothing to do with the present disputes between Cairo and Tehran," disputes that centered around Egypt's conviction that Iran supported extremist anti-government elements inside Egypt.[55]

The Thirteenth GCC Summit of the Supreme Council, held in Abu Dhabi in December 1992, provided further support for the UAE on the issue of the three islands. The GCC summit first issued "The Abu Dhabi Declaration," which was directed at Iran's behavior. After the failure of the bilateral negotiations in September, this declaration stressed the GCC's "adoption of the principle of dialogue and negotiation as a basic means of solving disputes among states," as well as the sovereignty of the UAE over the three islands, calling them "an integral part of the State of the United Arab Emirates." It also underlined the

GCC's "complete rejection of the continuing occupation by the Islamic Republic of Iran of these islands."[56]

In addition, in its closing statement, the GCC's Supreme Council denounced Iran's behavior, "which represents [a] violation of the sovereignty and territorial integrity of the State of the United Arab Emirates and rocks security and stability in the region." It expressed "its extreme regret and great concern about the unjustified Iranian measures which upset the declared wish to develop relations between the two sides," stressing that "the development of relations between the two sides are connected with strengthening trust and to what the Islamic Republic of Iran undertakes in measures compatible with its commitment to good neighbourliness and respect for sovereignty and territorial integrity of the region's states, and non-interference in internal affairs."

The closing statement noted that "the continuation of Iranian occupation of the three islands and the measures taken by the Islamic Republic of Iran on the island of Abu Musa represent a violation of these principles and the declared wish to develop relations between the two sides" and requested Iran "to cancel and remove all measures taken on the island of Abu Musa and the ending of its occupation of the islands of Tonb al-Kubra and Tonb al-Sughra both of which belong to the State of the United Arab Emirates." It also stressed the GCC's "complete solidarity with and absolute backing of the State of the United Arab Emirates, and [that the GCC] supports all measures and peaceful means which it sees appropriate to recover its sovereignty on its three islands and this is in reliance on international legitimacy and based on the principle of collective security."[57]

The GCC's statements elicited a quick and violent outburst by Iran's President Rafsanjani, who answered that "Iran is surely stronger than the likes of you...to reach those islands one has to cross a sea of blood...we consider this claim as totally invalid."[58] As already stated earlier, Iran deployed additional Iranian Revolutionary Guard Corps forces to the islands and declared that it is willing to defend the islands against any attack. It also reminded its Gulf Arab neighbors that it was willing to fight for eighty years against Iraq.[59] Iran's aggressive reaction to the GCC statement provided the background for another statement of support for the UAE from the Arab League on April 19, 1993.[60]

Egypt's President Mubarak also strongly criticized Iranian behavior and ambitions in the Gulf and throughout the entire region.[61]

Meanwhile, Saudi Arabia tried to maintain the "thaw" in Saudi-Iranian relations. In October 1993, Saudi Arabia supported Rafsanjani's earlier appeal for a higher Iranian oil production quota, and officially endorsed Iranian and Kuwaiti production increases and a freeze of Saudi and UAE production levels at the subsequent OPEC meeting in Vienna on October 4. Saudi Arabia's understanding was that Iran, in return for this, would now be willing to resolve the islands dispute peacefully through bilateral negotiations with the UAE. Moreover, Iran's Foreign Minister Velayati announced on October 7, 1993 in Qatar that King Fahd had accepted an official invitation to visit Iran.

Saleh Al-Mani has written: "This seemed to be the zenith of the honeymoon and the two countries were almost on the verge of an historic compromise that would settle almost all major issues of contention." However, a visit by King Fahd did not take place, in part due to protests and media criticism by hard-liners in Iran that offended the Saudis. The Iranian government also would not agree to discuss all three islands in bilateral negotiations with the UAE, which led the UAE's Minister of State for Foreign Affairs, Shaikh Hamdan bin Zayed, to cancel a planned visit to Tehran which dismayed the Saudis. Saudi Arabia concluded that Iran had misread Saudi Arabia's conciliatory policies towards the country as a sign of Saudi weakness. It therefore decided to adopt a tough approach toward Iran, an approach that was demonstrated during the May 1994 pilgrimage season, when Saudi Arabia decreased the number of Iranian pilgrims permitted to attend the Hajj.[62]

At the 48th session of the UN General Assembly on October 4, 1993, UAE Foreign Minister Rashid Abdullah again called on Iran to engage in direct discussions on all three islands. Kuwait now issued a statement of support for the UAE position on all three islands. Bahrain and Qatar issued somewhat more careful statements, calling for "the removal of all outstanding questions" concerning the three islands.[63] Thus, only five months after the Iranian press reported improving relations with Kuwait following Velayati's May 1993 visit to Kuwait, the same press now criticized Kuwait for its support for the UAE.[64]

Richard Schofield has written that since the 1992 summit in Abu Dhabi, GCC summit statements have dealt with the immediate concerns of the host state. To support this observation, he notes that the 1994 summit in Manama, Bahrain focused on Hawar and the shoals and, because Oman's borders were resolved, the 1995 summit in Muscat did not focus on territorial problems.[65] Thus, it may be a measure of the unusual importance of the dispute over Abu Musa and the Tunbs to the GCC states that the issue has figured prominently in all closing statements of GCC summits since 1992.

Indeed, the Supreme Council of the GCC issued a closing statement at the end of the Fourteenth Summit in December 1993 in Riyadh, reaffirming the GCC's "complete solidarity with and absolute backing for the State of the United Arab Emirates and its support of all peaceful measures and means it sees appropriate to recover its sovereignty over the three islands based on the principles of international legitimacy." The statement called upon Iran "to respond positively" to Shaikh Zayed's call for "direct dialogue" with Iran "in connection with the occupation of the islands," a call that was made by Shaikh Zayed at the UAE's National Day celebration on December 2. The communiqué also welcomed an Iranian government statement made during the GCC summit meeting, hoping "that it would be an indication for canceling all measures and arrangements carried out by Iran on the island of Abu Musa and ending the occupation of the two islands of Tonb al-Kubra and Tonb al-Sughra," and reaffirming:

> the development of relations with the Islamic Republic of Iran is connected to the strengthening of trust and with what Iran carries out in measures compatible with its commitment to the principles of good neighbourliness and the respect of sovereignty and territorial integrity of the region's states and non-interference in their internal affairs.[66]

After the failure of Saudi Arabia's effort to use its good offices during the fall of 1993, the failure of the appeal made to Iran during Saudi Arabia's hosting of the GCC summit in December 1993, and just prior to a revised agreement on the Saudi-UAE border in the summer of 1994, King Fahd of Saudi Arabia reportedly took a personal interest in promoting proposals for peacefully returning the islands to the UAE during the early summer of 1994.[67] At the meeting of GCC foreign ministers in April 1994, Saudi Prince Saud Al-Faisal also called upon Iran to return the islands to the UAE and to observe "mutual respect and non-interference in the domestic affairs of states" as a basis for "constructive cooperation."[68]

Iran responded, however, by rejecting Saudi "interference" and by repeating the warnings it had issued in December 1992.[69] Kuwait's Foreign Minister Shaikh Sabah, explaining the problem between the GCC and Iran in language that publicly expressed Kuwait's solidarity with the GCC, noted in July 1994 that "the dialogue proposed by Iran concerns only one island, Abu Musa, and we really want the dialogue to concern all three islands."[70]

Meanwhile, after assuming office as the new Secretary-General of the GCC in December 1993, Shaikh Fahim bin Sultan Al-Qasimi, a UAE national from the Qawasim tribe of Ras al-Khaimah, advanced the argument that the islands dispute should be referred to the ICJ in The Hague or referred to impartial third-party arbitration.[71] In the light of the failure of bilateral negotiation and third party mediation and good offices from 1992 through 1994, and in view of the statement of the new GCC Secretary-General, which echoed statements by Shaikh Zayed and Shaikh Hamdan bin Zayed and Rashid Abdullah, the GCC's Ministerial Council issued a communiqué at the end of its September 1994 meeting, calling upon Iran to refer the matter to the ICJ.[72] In November 1994, the Omani Minister Responsible for Foreign Affairs shed light on this call to refer the dispute to the ICJ when he publicly expressed skepticism about the prospects for successful mediation.[73] The closing statement of the GCC Supreme Council's Fifteenth Summit in Manama, Bahrain in December 1994 also urged referral of the issue to the ICJ:

> The Supreme Council, while appreciating the efforts exerted by the State of the United Arab Emirates to solve this dispute bilaterally, and in view of the lack of any indication of serious desire on the part of Iran to discuss the ending of its occupation of the three islands, Tonb al-Kubra, Tonb al-Sughra and Abu Musa, the Council calls on Iran to accept the referral of this dispute to the World High Court of Justice [i.e. the ICJ]...[74]

On March 12, 1995, the foreign ministers of the GCC issued another joint communiqué that again "expressed their deep appreciation of the UAE's efforts to peacefully resolve the issue of the Iranian occupation of the three islands" and "urged the Islamic Republic of Iran to respond positively to the initiative of the UAE and to agree to refer this dispute to the ICJ."[75]

The foreign ministers of the Damascus Declaration states expressed a small shift in this position in their statement in July 1995, which read:

> The ministers renewed their support and backing to the UAE's sovereignty over its three islands, and urged Iran to hold direct talks with the UAE on the status of these islands at the earliest opportunity. Meanwhile, they backed the UAE's call for referring the issue to the International Court of Justice if no agreement is reached through dialogue.[76]

Richard Schofield has argued that this renewed call for direct talks prior to taking the issue to the ICJ may have been linked to the 1994 Manama GCC summit decision to seek a bilateral settlement of the Bahrain-Qatar dispute before seeking an ICJ settlement. At this summit, the GCC was hesitant to condone the ICJ's consideration of the Hawar and shoals dispute, particularly because the host state, Bahrain, was reluctant. Thus, a call to refer the Abu Musa and Tunbs dispute to the ICJ only after bilateral efforts to solve it were exhausted was more consistent with the directives given by the GCC Supreme Council for states to solve their territorial disputes on a bilateral basis.[77]

The renewed call for direct talks may also have been linked to a growing concern in the UAE that, while the UAE would have an excellent chance of having its title to Abu Musa confirmed by the ICJ, there also existed the possibility that in light of recent ICJ decisions on territorial disputes that have attempted to satisfy both parties, the ICJ might make an essentially political decision to award the Tunbs to Iran in order to not leave Iran feeling entirely dissatisfied.[78] The Damascus Declaration statement may also have been linked to increasing concern about the Iranian militarization of the islands in late 1994 and in 1995, as well as a desire to reach a resolution faster than would be possible through the ICJ.

In September 1995, the GCC foreign ministers and then the Arab League foreign ministers again expressed their support for the UAE on the issue of the three islands.[79] This was just prior to a second round of direct bilateral negotiations held between the UAE and Iran in Doha, Qatar in November 1995, following an invitation to Iran and the

UAE by the Foreign Minister of Qatar, Shaikh Hamad bin Jassim bin Jabir Al-Thani. Those talks failed when the Iranians refused to consider the UAE agenda for the talks. In the aftermath of this breakdown, the GCC argued that the UAE had entered into the talks in good faith, therefore following the directives issued at the 1994 GCC summit in Manama, and that the UAE had been rebuffed once again by Iranian intransigence.[80]

The closing statement issued at the end of the GCC summit in Muscat, Oman in December 1995 expressed "great regret for the lack of an Iranian positive response to the repeated, serious and sincere calls made by the State of the United Arab Emirates to reach a peaceful resolution to this question." It also voiced "concern" about Iran "carrying out measures aimed at perpetuating its occupation of the three islands" and reaffirmed "complete support for and absolute backing of all the measures and peaceful means being undertaken by the Emirates to recover its sovereignty over the three islands." In closing, it again called on Iran "to accept the referral of this dispute to the World Court of Justice [i.e. the ICJ]."[81]

On June 2, 1996, the Ministerial Council of the GCC reaffirmed its resolute support for the UAE and for any peaceful methods it adopted to restore its sovereignty over the three islands, including referring the dispute to the ICJ. It noted that Iran was continuing to consolidate its occupation of the islands and argued that Iran's insistence on continuing its illegal occupation by force was provocative and a violation of the sovereignty and the rights of the UAE. Moreover, the Ministerial Council argued that Iran's policy and behavior jeopardized the security and the stability of the region.[82] New GCC Secretary-General Jamil Al-Hujailan, a Saudi Arabian, underlined that Iran's behavior on the islands was contrary to good neighborly relations.[83]

On July 14, 1996, in the final communiqué released at the end of their meeting in Muscat, the foreign ministers of the Damascus Declaration states expressed their "great concern" over Iran's occupation of the islands, noting "the continuous, serious and honest calls and initiatives" to Iran from the UAE, the GCC, the Damascus Declaration states, and the Arab League, and reaffirming "their support and absolute backing to all peaceful means, methods and measures that the UAE takes to restore its sovereignty over these islands." The statement called on Iran to "end its occupation of the three islands and desist from exercising *de facto* policy by force and effecting the implementation of any unilateral measures in the three islands" and "to follow peaceful means to solve the dispute over these islands in accordance with the principles, rules and regulations of international law and to accept the referral of the issue to the International Court of Justice." The ministers also affirmed that "the security and stability of the UAE, and the protection and preservation of its independence and territorial integrity and its support, is considered an integral part of the security of the Arab Gulf countries and Arab national security."[84]

The closing statement of the Seventeenth GCC Supreme Council Summit in December 1996 in Doha said that the Council, while noting Iran's continuing measures aimed at "the perpetuation of its occupation of the three islands" and "creating a fait accompli by force," reiterated its "extreme regret for the continuation of the Islamic Republic of Iran avoiding responding positively to the repeated serious and sincere calls" for a peaceful solution issued by the UAE, the GCC, the Damascus Declaration states, the Arab League and the Arab summit. It continued:

> The Supreme Council, while stressing again the sovereignty of the State of the United Arab Emirates over the three islands, Tonb al-Kubra, Tonb al-Sughra and Abu Musa, and the Council's absolute support for all the measures and peaceful means being undertaken by the Emirates to recover its sovereignty over these three islands, reiterates its call to the Iranian government to end its occupation of the three islands and to desist from pursuing a policy of creating a fait accompli by force and to stop carrying out any measures unilaterally and to cancel any measures and to remove any installations established unilaterally on the three islands, and to pursue peaceful means to solve the dispute over the islands in accordance with the principles and rules of international law, including the acceptance of the referral [of] the question to the International Court of Justice.

The statement also expressed "extreme concern over the deployment by the Islamic Republic of Iran of land-to-land missiles in the Arab Gulf, including its deployment of missiles on the three occupied islands," which it called "a matter which poses a direct threat [to] the Council's states and their vital installations."[85]

The foreign ministers of the Damascus Declaration states responded positively to the election of the reformist cleric Mohammed Khatami to Iran's presidency and his call for a new chapter in Arab-Iranian relations. In the final communiqué issued at the end of their June 1997 meeting, these foreign ministers affirmed their readiness to build cordial relations with Iran on the basis of good neighborliness, but nevertheless stressed the importance of resolving the islands issue before this could be done.[86]

In early August 1997, after the inauguration of President Khatami, GCC Secretary-General Jamil Al-Hujailan was quoted by the London-based *Al-Sharq Al-Awsat* as saying "I can't say there is a danger coming out of Iran. I don't believe in this…Iran knows well its interests in the region. It is a big neighboring country and we are fully anxious in maintaining good relations based on good intentions…It's impossible for me to say that Iran forms a danger for the GCC." Al-Hujailan said the GCC did not want US-Iranian relations to remain strained because that had a negative impact on Gulf stability. "Iran is a big and strong neighbor. Iran represents a major factor behind stability in the region. Agreeing with Iran and deepening its conviction on the need to cooperate with the GCC is important to the stability in the region."[87] Al-Hujailan, a Saudi, was reflecting the fact that Saudi-Iranian relations and GCC-Iranian relations were beginning to thaw again after Khatami's election. This statement did not, however, mean that there would be any quick relaxation of the policy of the GCC or Saudi Arabia toward Iran's occupation of the islands.

In September 1997, for example, the GCC Council of Foreign Ministers welcomed President Khatami's calls for a new relationship with Iran, but again warned that Iran would have to settle the islands dispute with the UAE.[88] Arab League Secretary-General Ismet Abdel Magid and the Arab League foreign ministers meeting in Cairo in the same month also noted the calls by the new Iranian leadership for improved relations, but called on Iran to respond to the UAE's calls for peaceful means to end the Iranian occupation. They reaffirmed support for the UAE's sovereignty over the three islands, rejected all Iranian measures to assert its control over these islands, and appealed to the UN to keep the issue of this dispute on its agenda.[89] Saudi Arabia's Foreign Minister Saud Al-Faisal supported the UAE's position on the islands at the UN General Assembly session in the fall of 1997. In November, Iran's new Foreign Minister, Kamal Kharrazi, toured the GCC states with the general message of improved relations, but he did not bring serious proposals regarding the islands.[90]

On the eve of the Eighth Summit of the Organization of the Islamic Conference (OIC), held in Tehran in December 1997, Arab League Secretary-General Abdel Magid sent an open letter to President Khatami calling for a peaceful settlement of the islands issue with the UAE through international arbitration, and later said that he would attempt to persuade Iranian officials during the summit to reach a peaceful settlement of the issue with the UAE.[91] In Abdel Magid's speech to the summit, he referred to the constitution of the OIC and to the speech earlier in the day by Khatami, both of which called for the peaceful settlement of disputes between members, and appealed to Iran to respond to the UAE's calls for a peaceful settlement of the islands dispute.[92] He was joined in this effort by the head of the UAE delegation, Foreign Minister Rashid Abdullah, who called for a peaceful settlement of the dispute in his formal speech on December 10.

Abdel Magid would later characterize his discussions with Iranian leaders at the OIC summit as "encouraging," saying that the new Iranian government's attitude towards a peaceful resolution of the dispute seemed "positive."[93] Indeed, in a press conference in Tehran soon after the OIC summit, President Khatami replied to a question about visiting the UAE to negotiate on the islands by saying, "We have said this elsewhere, and we are saying it emphatically now, that we are ready to go there." He rejected any third party mediation, however, stating "our dispute over the islands does not need the interference of outsiders."[94]

In the aftermath of the OIC summit, at the Eighteenth GCC summit meeting in Kuwait in December 1997, some GCC leaders again thought it necessary - and also possible - to appeal to Iran's new leaders. The summit's host, Kuwait's Emir Shaikh Jabir al Ahmed Al-Sabah, while saying that Iran's new leaders sought closer relations with the Gulf Arab states, nevertheless called on Iran to "respond positively to repeated calls to follow means to resolve the current dispute over the UAE's three islands in accordance with international law, to enable us to open a new chapter in our relations."

Bahrain's Shaikh Issa bin Salman Al-Khalifa argued that "there are outstanding problems, including Iran's occupation of three UAE islands, and I don't think we can talk of any security partnership [with Iran] unless we overcome all these issues." Shaikh Issa's willingness to speak publicly came after Bahrain's 1996 accusations of Iranian involvement in political unrest and a coup conspiracy in Bahrain. Indeed, the GCC summit was expected to consider increasing GCC defense cooperation, which has been based on the brigade-strength Peninsula Shield force, and which has envisioned a coastal defense system, by integrating the command, control, communications and intelligence systems of the member states, in a first step to establish a region-wide air defense shield.[95]

The closing statement issued at the end of the 1997 GCC summit reflected the continuing concern of the Supreme Council, which "reiterated its deep regret over the continued failure on the part of the Islamic Republic of Iran to respond favourably to the repeated, earnest and sincere calls by the United Arab Emirates as well as regional and international organizations, organs and groups to resolve this dispute peacefully." The statement noted that the GCC leaders reviewed recent statements by Iranian President Khatami in which he expressed his desire to meet with President His Highness Shaikh Zayed, listened to Shaikh Zayed's "welcoming reaction" and "welcomed any leadership encounter between the two countries."

The communiqué reaffirmed the UAE's sovereignty over the three islands and full support for all peaceful means adopted by the UAE to restore its sovereignty over the islands. It reiterated its demand that Iran end its occupation of the three islands, cease its practice of imposing a policy of *fait accompli* by force, stop building new facilities on the islands designed to change the demographic character of the islands, reverse all measures and dismantle all installations unilaterally made, and pursue peaceful measures to resolve the dispute in accordance with international law, including referral of the case to the ICJ.[96]

In February 1998, former Iranian President Rafsanjani, on a two-week visit to Saudi Arabia that also included a stop in Bahrain, said that Iran was willing to negotiate bilaterally with the UAE to find a solution to the issue. He requested, however, that the UAE should send a delegation to Iran inasmuch as former Foreign Minister Velayati had already visited the UAE.[97] In the aftermath of Rafsanjani's visit to Saudi Arabia, and on the eve of a meeting of GCC foreign ministers in Saudi Arabia in March, GCC Secretary-General Al-Hujailan could only say "Our wish to cooperate with Iran is one of the basic principles of the GCC. We hope that this GCC stand towards Iran would make the Islamic Republic of Iran respond to efforts to resolve the problem of the three UAE islands occupied by Iran peacefully through negotiations or by going to the International Court of Justice."[98]

The statement issued at the end of the March GCC foreign ministers meeting expressed "deep regret" that Iran had not responded positively to UAE and GCC calls for a peaceful resolution of the dispute, reiterated support for UAE sovereignty over the islands, and "demanded that the Iranian government end its occupation of the three islands and...stop the policy of introducing facts on the ground."[99] In May 1998, Iran's Foreign Minister Kharrazi again visited the UAE, but again did not bring new proposals regarding the islands.[100]

During preparations for the Nineteenth GCC summit in Abu Dhabi in December 1998, GCC Secretary-General Al-Hujailan again stated "We hope that the Iranian leadership will respond to the calls of the GCC states to end its occupation of the three UAE islands and to resolve the dispute peacefully."[101] However, days before the summit opened, an Iranian Foreign Ministry spokesman said that "Iran looks forward to settling all issues within the framework of the 1971 accord" on Abu Musa and reaffirmed Iranian sovereignty over the three islands, a position that was certain to elicit a negative response from the GCC states.[102] Moreover, Iran began naval exercises in the approaches to the Strait of Hormuz with regular navy and Revolutionary Guard naval units in the days before the summit opened.[103] These naval exercises ranged over an area from the Strait of Hormuz into the territorial waters around Abu Musa and the Tunbs.[104]

Although he had found the attitude of the new Iranian government toward a peaceful resolution of the islands dispute to be positive at the 1997 OIC summit in Tehran, Arab League Secretary-General Magid again called upon Iran to heed the UAE's efforts to find a peaceful solution through negotiation and the ICJ.[105] Kofi Annan, the first UN Secretary General to attend a GCC summit, revealed that he had proposed that the UAE and Iran hold preparatory talks for negotiations on the islands and that Shaikh Zayed and Kamal Kharrazi had both responded positively.[106] Kofi Annan reportedly proposed to Shaikh Zayed that he was willing "to mediate between his country and Iran if bilateral negotiations failed." Indeed, Shaikh Zayed had called on Iran one week earlier to accept "constructive dialogue, or recourse to adjudication" by the ICJ. Kharrazi welcomed the proposal for direct talks, but said that Annan had not proposed mediation to him.[107]

The final communiqué issued at the end of the 1998 GCC summit "noted the continuation of unacceptable Iranian claims designed to perpetuate the occupation." It also stressed:

> ...the necessity for Iran to respond to the serious and sincere calls from the UAE, the GCC countries, the countries of the Damascus Declaration, the Arab League and from international and regional organizations for this dispute to be brought peacefully to an end in such a way as will add credibility to the positive indications from the government of President Mohammed Khatami, in order to build mutual confidence, to develop cooperation and to maintain security and peace in the region.

The statement "reaffirmed the UAE's sovereignty over the three islands of Greater and Lesser Tunb and Abu Musa and expressed its full support for all steps and peaceful means it may take to restore its sovereignty over the islands. It called on the Iranian Government to end its occupation of the three islands, to refrain from imposing *fait accompli*, to remove all installations it has constructed unilaterally and to adopt peaceful means in resolving the dispute, in accordance with the principles and rules of international law, including referral of the issue to the International Court of Justice in The Hague." It also "welcomed the efforts being made by Annan to devise a framework for negotiations between the UAE and Iran that can resolve the current dispute on the three islands," and "called on him to continue his efforts and to sponsor the negotiations," and "urged the Iranian government to respond seriously to the secretary general's efforts, in order to help towards the establishment of security and stability in the region."[108]

Following the opening by Iran of a new municipal building and an educational institution on Abu Musa in February 1999, the UAE protested to the Arab League and asked Secretary-General Magid that Iran's occupation of the three UAE islands be placed on the agenda of the March meeting of the Arab League Foreign Ministers. The Secretary-General made a statement to *Al-Hayat*, once again rejecting Iranian actions on the three islands and urging Iranian officials to respond to the UAE endeavors calling for a diplomatic solution, including referring the issue to the ICJ.[109] GCC Secretary-General Al-Hujailan warned that if Iran "persists in occupying these islands and consolidating its occupation, it will not be in the interests of relations between the GCC and Iran." He also said "A favorable response from Iran to UAE calls to resolve this conflict through direct negotiations or the International Court of Justice would go a long way toward a strengthening of relations."[110]

Even as Al-Hujailan spoke, Iran began new nine-day naval exercises, the "Fateh-77" or "Victor-77" exercises, involving eleven warships, two submarines, eight helicopters, three diving units, ten special operations units and the air force, in an area stretching from the Strait of Hormuz to the islands of Abu Musa and the Tunbs.[111] The Arab League expressed "extreme concern" about these Iranian exercises, warning that they could have "negative repercussions" on relations with the Gulf Arabs. At the same time, the six air forces of the GCC states began their annual joint aerial exercises, named "Standard of Justice 99." Meanwhile, Iran answered UAE, GCC and Arab League protests by repeating its claim to sovereignty over the three islands and its readiness "to continue constructive negotiations with the UAE on the basis of the 1971 agreements and without preconditions," i.e. to negotiate about implementation of the MoU on Abu Musa, but not about the Tunbs and not about sovereignty.[112]

The UAE then lodged another protest at the Arab League. The UAE Ambassador in Cairo explained: "The UAE views all past and future actions by Iran on the islands as undue provocations," and urged Iran to resolve the dispute through bilateral negotiations or international arbitration.[113] Abdel Magid declared that "Iran's behavior towards the Arabs is incompatible with Arab policies towards the Islamic republic. Arab countries are committed to good relations with Iran and, therefore, Iran must reciprocate that." Reacting to Arab League criticism, an Iranian Foreign Ministry official said that Iran's military "maneuvers are essentially a use of Iran's reserve forces to defend Iran's territorial integrity." He added that the Arab League should "encourage the UAE to adopt a realistic position in regards to Iran and negotiate with the Islamic Republic instead of hurling accusations."[114]

Seeing the Iranian military maneuvers as a severe provocation and threat, the UAE called an emergency meeting of the GCC Ministerial Council in Abu Dhabi to discuss Iran's new violations and military exercises.[115] On the eve of the emergency GCC meeting, Saudi Foreign Minister Prince Saud Al-Faisal traveled to Oman to meet with Omani Minister Responsible for Foreign Affairs Yusuf bin Alawi bin Abdullah and said that "I wish to see Iran respond favorably to the calls by UAE President His Highness Sheikh Zayed bin Sultan al Nahyan to negotiate on the issue of the islands." He said the GCC states were avoiding any provocation and were trying to resolve all problems through negotiations, that the islands dispute was the most important problem to be resolved, and that all problems could be resolved through goodwill. He also stated that the islands dispute had been discussed during Iranian Foreign Minister Kharrazi's just concluded visit to Saudi Arabia, that he had told Kharrazi that Saudi Arabia wanted the dispute resolved "in a direct manner," that Kharrazi had "expressed his country's desire to settle issues peacefully" and that "we await the deeds."

Kharrazi had also met with King Fahd and Crown Prince Abdullah and the two countries called for OPEC oil production cutbacks. Kuwaiti Foreign Minister Shaikh Sabah al Ahmad Al-Sabah said "If there is no agreement for direct talks, then there is the International Court of Justice...and I hope that this issue is sent to the court." He expressed the hope that the ICJ would resolve the dispute, "which is not in the interest of Iran and does not benefit the region."[116]

The Saudi Foreign Minister's trip to meet the Omani Minister Responsible for Foreign Affairs on the eve of this GCC meeting may have been an effort to coordinate in advance in order to make sure that the GCC support for the UAE would not undermine Saudi Arabia's bilateral relations with Iran at an important moment. Saudi Arabia wanted Iran to adhere to agreed oil production cuts aimed at supporting falling oil prices so that further cuts could be agreed upon at an OPEC meeting in Vienna in late March, thus cutting the surplus supply of oil in the world market and allowing oil prices to rise. Saudi Arabia also wanted Iranian good behavior during the upcoming Hajj later in March. Saudi Arabia and Kuwait both wanted Iranian cooperation in containing

Iraq, which had been calling for the overthrow of these two regimes, because of their support for the US military operations against Iraq from December 1998 through March 1999.

Saudi Arabia also expected a visit from Iranian President Khatami later in March. Oman shared the Saudi interest in having Iranian cooperation on oil production and pricing, had no dispute of its own with Iran, and was moving closer to a partial border agreement with the UAE, an agreement that was actually reached and signed on May 1, 1999. Thus, it would prove to be a potentially valuable partner in a Saudi effort to promote a response that did not alienate Iran. However, despite all these considerations, Saudi Arabia endorsed a very strongly worded GCC statement, as did Oman.

The statement issued at the end of the emergency GCC meeting in Abu Dhabi in early March 1999 declared: "The ministerial council condemns these Iranian military maneuvers being held by Iran on the three UAE islands...and in its [the UAE's] territorial waters." It demanded that Iran "immediately call a halt to its provocative acts that threaten security and stability in the Arab Gulf, raise extreme concern, and do not help to build confidence," calling the maneuvers a "violation of the UAE's sovereignty and an attempt by Iran to secure its occupation of the three islands." The ministerial council reaffirmed its rejection of Iran's occupation of the three islands, reaffirmed the sovereignty of the UAE over the islands, and again called on Iran to end its occupation. It stressed the "true desire" and the "true initiatives" of the UAE, the GCC, and the Arab world to build good relations with Iran, and noted as follows:

> ...all these initiatives were met by Iran with more dedication to the occupation and obvious violation of the territorial sovereignty of the UAE, even increasing this by declaring the three islands as military areas with repeated marine and air training over the territorial waters of the UAE, which raises the highest concern of the GCC and is a contradiction between Iran's words and actions.[117]

It called again for Iran to translate its declared interest in improved relations with the GCC into practical steps by responding to the calls of the UAE, the GCC, the Damascus Declaration states, the Arab League, regional and international organizations, and the UN Secretary

General to resolve the dispute over the three islands through direct negotiations or through the ICJ. It said the ministerial council was commissioning UAE Foreign Minister Rashid Abdullah and GCC Secretary-General Al-Hujailan to communicate with friendly states and regional and international organizations with the following mission:

> ...to explain the seriousness of the situation in the region in the presence of the Iranian armament programme, especially in the areas of missiles and weapons of mass destruction, which is more extensive than Iran's legitimate defence requirements and represents a source of great concern for the GCC states and threatens the regional security and stability of the Arabian Gulf.[118]

This was a very strong statement of support for the UAE. UAE observers noted, however, that Kuwait and Qatar did not send their foreign ministers to attend the meeting, sending lower level officials instead. Kuwait certainly wanted Iran to balance the threat from Iraq and to cooperate on oil production and prices at a time when both issues were of such critical importance. Moreover, Kuwait's Crown Prince and Prime Minister, Shaikh Saad al Abdullah al Salam Al-Sabah, was scheduled to make an official visit to Iran only days after the emergency meeting.[119] Qatar, usually careful to avoid antagonizing either Iran or Saudi Arabia, and also wanting Iran's cooperation to boost oil prices, may have sent a lower level official for similar reasons.[120]

Iran's Foreign Ministry rejected the GCC statement as "provocative," calling it "blatant interference in Iran's internal affairs." It argued that "these maneuvers not only do not threaten the security of the region but will also lead to the strengthening of security and stability in the region." It added: "It is astonishing that these unreal claims against Iran are made at a time when regional countries were themselves engaged in carrying out maneuvers." Finally, it claimed that the three islands were an "inseparable, integral part" of Iran and again proposed bilateral talks with the UAE on the basis of the 1971 agreement.[121]

At a regularly scheduled GCC Ministerial Council meeting in Riyadh in mid-March, GCC foreign ministers issued another forceful statement saying that they were "following-up the continued unacceptable Iranian allegations about the three islands and the provocative military maneuvers in the territorial waters of the UAE and the opening of an

Iranian municipality and educational complex on the island of Abu Musa for the purpose of consolidating the occupation and imposing a status quo." The statement again asked Iran to translate President Khatami's public statements that Iran sought better relations with the GCC states, by heeding the many regional and international actors that had called upon Iran to enter into negotiations with the UAE or resort to the ICJ to resolve the dispute over the three islands.

It also reaffirmed the UAE's sovereignty over the islands, expressed "unequivocal support" for the UAE's peaceful efforts to restore its sovereignty, and called again on Iran to end its occupation, "and to stop a forced *fait accompli* and building of Iranian establishments on the islands with the aim of changing their demographic nature, and to cancel all measures and to remove all establishments already built unilaterally on the three islands." Regarding Iran's recent military maneuvers near the UAE islands and in UAE territorial waters, it called on Iran "to stop the provocations which are flagrant violations of the sovereignty of the UAE and pose a serious threat to regional security and stability and jeopardize regional and international navigation in the Gulf." The statement reiterated the belief that "confidence can only be built by Iran taking practical and credible steps to solve outstanding problems" between the GCC states and Iran, specifically naming the islands dispute.[122]

Days later, at a mid-March Arab League meeting, Secretary-General Abdel Magid said: "We are closely watching the latest developments on the UAE islands and we hope that Iran would respond to the repeated calls made by the UAE to settle the dispute through peaceful means or resorting to the International Court of Justice."[123] While Syrian sources indicated that Syria offered to mediate between the UAE and Iran, as it had already attempted in 1992, UAE sources said that this offer was not made.[124]

The communiqué issued at the end of the meeting affirmed the UAE's sovereignty over the three islands and full support for all peaceful efforts to restore the UAE's sovereignty. It denounced the Iranian occupation of the three islands, its attempts to consolidate its occupation and violate UAE sovereignty and the Iranian military maneuvers including the islands. It called on Iran to stop its provocations, which undermined confidence and jeopardized security and stability in the region, to end its occupation of the islands and its imposition of a *status quo* by force, to stop building installations on the islands with the intention of changing their demographic structure, and to cancel all installations and measures already built unilaterally. The statement further said Iran should translate its declared interest in improving relations with the Arab states into practical, tangible steps by responding to the many Arab calls for settling the dispute by peaceful means through direct negotiations or the ICJ. It also stated the decision to inform the UN of the importance of keeping the issue on the Security Council agenda until Iran ended its occupation and the UAE regained its full sovereignty over the islands.[125]

Secretary-General Abdel Magid said after the meeting: "There will not be good Arab-Iranian relations should Iran continue its occupation of the three UAE islands. Once this occupation is terminated, relations will be good."[126] Within a week, Abdel Magid wrote to UN Secretary-General Annan and the President of the UN Security Council, asking the Security Council to consider Iran's occupation of the islands, condemning Iran's recent military exercises near the islands, and calling for an end to Iran's policy of creating *fait accompli* on the islands. Indeed, he continued to stress these points during the following weeks.[127]

In the aftermath of these strong GCC and Arab League statements, the Iranian English language daily *Tehran Times* reported that President Khatami was canceling his planned trip to Saudi Arabia because of what Tehran viewed as "Riyadh's wrong stance on the three Iranian islands." Within a week, however, the Islamic Republic News Agency (IRNA) was reporting that Khatami was very pleased with Saudi-Iranian cooperation on oil and would go ahead with his trip to Saudi Arabia.[128] Moreover, the planned visit of Saudi Defense Minister Prince Sultan bin Abdulaziz Al-Saud to Iran in April to discuss regional stability was postponed until May.[129] However, Saudi Foreign Minister Prince Saud Al-Faisal visited Tehran in mid-April for talks with Khatami and Kharrazi on bilateral ties and OPEC issues, and Qatar's Foreign Minister Shaikh Hamad also visited Khatami in Tehran.[130]

When Prince Sultan visited Tehran in early May, Iranian Defense Minister Ali Shamkhani called for discussions on a regional security plan and Iranian President Khatami called for a military alliance with Saudi Arabia. Prince Sultan responded by saying: "The question of military cooperation is not easy between two countries whose relations were cut for years and which have now made a good start. We should start with economic, social and cultural cooperation." He did agree, however, to exchange defense attachés.[131] Meanwhile, Bahrain's Foreign Minister Shaikh Mohammed bin Mubarak Al-Khalifa also made a visit to Iran to discuss bilateral and regional issues, signaling an improvement that had begun even prior to the death of Shaikh Issa and the succession of the new Emir, Shaikh Hamad bin Issa Al-Khalifa, in March 1999.[132]

On May 10, 1999 in the aftermath of these Saudi, Qatari and Bahraini visits to Tehran and on the eve of Khatami's planned visit to Saudi Arabia, GCC rulers met in Jeddah for the first of their planned biannual consultative summits. Although no communiqué was issued, Saudi Prince Sultan said after the meeting that the GCC members "welcomed and accepted" improved relations with Iran and thought this would contribute to regional "security and stability." He repeated that it was too early for any security pact between Saudi Arabia and Iran, saying there were too many unresolved issues, including the dispute over Abu Musa and the Tunbs. A UAE delegate also said: "We welcome improved relations between Iran and the GCC. We think it will help, not hinder, our quest for a resolution in the dispute over the islands with Iran." During the following week, Bahraini and Kuwaiti officials linked improvement of ties with Iran to resolution of the islands dispute.[133]

When Iranian President Khatami visited Saudi Arabia in mid-May, Saudi King Fahd hailed the opportunity for better relations. Saudi Prince Saud Al-Faisal called for confidence-building through the resolution of outstanding problems and said: "The results of the visit…will have a positive impact on the whole region, with the two countries able to play a key role in resolving conflicts in the region." The Saudi paper *Al-Riyadh* reported that Saudi officials discussed Abu Musa and the Tunbs with Khatami, but one Saudi official later said that Khatami "does not seem to be able to make Iran's position more flexible or to offer concessions on this issue for the time being."[134] During Khatami's subsequent visit to Qatar for talks on strengthening cooperation, he denied that Iran was an occupying power on the islands, claimed that Iran had evidence proving its right to the islands, and asserted that the dispute with the UAE was only a "misunderstanding."[135]

Towards the end of the trip, the Arab League Secretary-General called for Khatami to respond to the UAE's calls for a settlement of the dispute.[136] The following week, Khatami also had bilateral talks with Oman's Foreign Minister in Tehran. Moreover, despite Khatami's private and public inflexibility on the islands, Saudi Crown Prince Abdullah still maintained: "By clearing the path for our brothers in Iran, we can contribute to a settlement of the outstanding problems, notably that of the three UAE islands." Furthermore, he said: "Iran has the right to develop its military capabilities to ensure its security without harming or damaging the rights of others." This was a defensible statement, but one that could understandably raise questions in the UAE.[137]

In the aftermath of Khatami's trip, UAE Foreign Minister Rashid Abdullah criticized the efforts of some unnamed individual GCC members to improve bilateral ties with Iran, saying "this individualism is harmful to the collective work and to the UAE islands issue," and arguing that "Iran has exploited these [bilateral] visits to further its own interests. Now we see the Iranian forces having a free hand to do whatever they want in the islands."

While he did not mention Saudi Arabia by name, the UAE was concerned that the willingness of Saudi Arabia, the most powerful member of the GCC, to have a rapprochement with Iran, in the absence of progress on the islands issue, was undermining the GCC's basic security compact and encouraging other GCC states to follow the Saudi lead. This prompted the UAE to voice unusually blunt public criticism of its GCC partners. Rashid Abdullah even warned that the UAE would reconsider its GCC obligations if individual members ignored their own duty to link improving ties with Iran to a solution of the islands dispute. He expressed concern that Iran had seen that GCC states had given up on the UAE's interest in the islands in their efforts to improve ties with Iran and saw this as isolation of the UAE.[138]

Saudi Prince Sultan rejected these arguments as "not true in any way."[139] After meeting in Abu Dhabi with President HH Shaikh Zayed, Minister of State for Foreign Affairs HH Shaikh Hamdan bin Zayed, and Defense Minister HH General Shaikh Muhammad bin Rashid Al-Maktoum, GCC Secretary-General Al-Hujailan argued that the UAE's GCC neighbors were "seeking to use the improvement in relations with Iran to help find a settlement" to the islands dispute.[140] Qatar's Foreign

Minister Shaikh Hamad stated: "All the GCC countries, including Saudi Arabia, support the UAE."[141] At the same time, Oman's Foreign Minister Yusuf Al- Alawi said after meeting with Shaikh Hamdan that the UAE "does not only have the right for reproof but has more than that."[142]

GCC foreign ministers who met in Riyadh in mid-June did not resolve the disagreement, with Saudi Arabia now insisting that criticism of Iran's occupation be toned down in the final communiqué. A UAE official repeated that the UAE had "an open option" to quit the GCC and said: "We are certainly going to look at our GCC membership if we do not see any commitment from the others to resolve our issue over the islands."[143] Bahrain and Jordan then issued a joint communiqué supporting the UAE, Egypt's Foreign Minister Amr Mousa said that the UAE's concern was "very logical," and GCC Secretary-General Al-Hujailan began shuttling to GCC capitals to end this public row.[144]

By June 19, Qatar's Emir Shaikh Hamad mediated an end to the disagreement between the UAE and Saudi Arabia, meeting in Abu Dhabi with Shaikh Zayed and then accompanying Shaikh Hamdan bin Zayed and others to Riyadh for meetings with King Fahd, Crown Prince Abdullah, Prince Sultan and Prince Saud Al-Faisal. The UAE's Shaikh Hamdan bin Zayed and Saudi Prince Saud Al-Faisal both said after these meetings that the two countries now shared a "unity of views." The UAE received Saudi agreement for a GCC resolution linking closer ties with Iran to Iranian willingness to negotiate over the three islands, and the UAE joined Saudi Arabia in reaffirming the importance of the GCC.[145] Qatar's mediation reflected its improving relations with the UAE after the first meeting in May 1999 of a joint committee to promote bilateral cooperation.[146] During the following weeks, the UAE received numerous expressions of support from Bahrain, Oman, the Arab League, the Arab Parliamentary Union and the Palestinian National Authority (PNA).[147]

In early July, the meeting of GCC foreign ministers in Jeddah released a statement saying they had decided to form a tripartite committee composed of Saudi Arabia, Qatar and Oman charged with "working out a mechanism for direct negotiations between the UAE and Iran to settle the question of UAE islands occupied by Iran." The committee was to submit its recommendations to the GCC by May

2000. Its composition could be seen as an attempt to group together the most powerful member and those with the best relations with Iran, in order to maximize the committee's influence.[148]

The GCC statement also called for "good relations [with Iran] on the principles of good neighborliness, non-interference, and solutions to conflicts through dialogue and peaceful means." It welcomed "the positive policies expressed by Iranian President Mohammad Khatami during his visit to Saudi Arabia and Qatar," notably Tehran's readiness to hold direct talks with Abu Dhabi.[149] The Arab League General Secretariat issued a statement supporting the GCC statement and calling on Iran to respond to the position of the Arab countries and interact positively with the GCC's tripartite committee.[150]

Saudi Prince Sultan also visited Shaikh Zayed in Abu Dhabi and expressed the hope that Iran would respond to the tripartite committee, but an Iranian Foreign Ministry spokesman said "there is no need for third country mediation," including the tripartite committee.[151] Again, Iran's position was to engage in direct talks only on the "misunderstanding" concerning Abu Musa. As the tripartite committee was meeting for the first time in Jeddah, Prince Sultan said in Kuwait that Iran should resolve the dispute over the three islands as "the basis for improved cooperation with the GCC."[152]

In mid-September 1999, Arab League foreign ministers, going beyond what GCC foreign ministers were prepared to say, issued a strong statement expressing their support for the UAE's peaceful efforts to end Iranian occupation of the UAE islands of Abu Musa and the Tunbs, and denouncing Iranian measures to perpetuate its occupation by holding military maneuvers on the islands. It further called on Iran to end its occupation, to end its policy of *fait accompli*, to remove all installations it had built on the islands in order to change their demographic structure, and to accept peaceful means for resolving the dispute, including referring the dispute to the ICJ.[153]

In early November, UAE Foreign Minister Rashid Abdullah stated that the GCC tripartite committee had not yet informed the UAE of "any steps or progress," and other UAE officials indicated they would query the tripartite committee at an upcoming GCC foreign ministers meeting to prepare an agenda for the annual GCC summit.

Saudi Prince Saud Al-Faisal told the GCC foreign ministers meeting that there was "marked progress" in GCC relations with Iran, but noted that "there are still some problems that needed to be resolved in order to get relations back to their proper places and these include the issue of the three UAE islands being occupied by Iran."

Prince Saud's comments indicated that the committee still did not have much progress to report.[154] Nevertheless, when the GCC summit was held in late November 1999 in Riyadh, the rulers issued a communiqué that made only lenient reference to Iran's occupation of the UAE's islands, without actually criticizing Iranian behavior. GCC rulers thought that condemnation of Iran would undermine Khatami's reforms and bolster his hard-line critics, and the UAE agreed to be patient while the tripartite committee continued its efforts.[155]

On April 8, 2000, as GCC foreign ministers met in Jeddah, an Omani official noted that the UAE was not satisfied with the "ambiguous role" of the GCC's tripartite committee and had a "particular sensitivity" about the lack of activity by the committee. In his opening statement, Saudi Prince Saud Al-Faisal called on Iran to cooperate with the committee, while in their final statement, the foreign ministers "expressed hope that the Islamic Republic of Iran would respond to these serious and well-intentioned efforts." Prince Saud revealed afterwards: "There is a letter from the (GCC) council states [to Iran] and we are awaiting a reply to it.[156]

As he was preparing for the GCC's second annual consultative summit, GCC Secretary-General Al-Hujailan expressed hope that Iran would respond positively to the tripartite committee.[157] On the eve of a visit to Saudi Arabia by the then Abu Dhabi Crown Prince HH Shaikh Khalifa bin Zayed Al-Nahyan, Chief of Staff of the UAE Armed Forces HH Lt. General Shaikh Mohammed bin Zayed Al-Nahyan, Minister of State for Foreign Affairs HH Shaikh Hamdan bin Zayed Al-Nahyan and Minister of Foreign Affairs Rashid Abdullah Al-Nuaimi, a Saudi Foreign Ministry official called the islands dispute "the only stumbling block which mars relations between the GCC and Iran."[158] When Iran's Defense Minister Shamkhani arrived in Riyadh days later and raised the subject of a regional defense pact, Saudi officials replied again that such a pact was premature before Iran resolved its dispute with the UAE over the islands. Saudi Prince Sultan said: "Any direct cooperation with Iran to guarantee the protection of the Gulf is quite inadmissible."[159]

At the GCC consultative summit in Muscat in late April, the tripartite committee presented its first report on its efforts. While having little concrete progress to report, the final statement "called on the members of the tripartite committee to continue their efforts and expressed hope the Iranian government will cooperate with the committee's noble cause."[160] The GCC foreign ministers meeting in early June issued a similar statement calling for Iran to "respond" to the tripartite committee. Saudi Foreign Minister Prince Saud Al-Faisal said "The work of the committee is continuing and we look to cooperation from Iran in the efforts exerted by the committee."[161] On the following day, the Damascus Declaration states issued a statement welcoming the efforts of the tripartite committee and urged Iran to accept a peaceful solution that would end its occupation of the islands.[162] In the meantime, however, Iran was able to secure a bilateral agreement on fighting organized crime with Oman, was reportedly on the verge of securing similar agreements with Saudi Arabia and Kuwait, and also secured agreement on a sea link with Bahrain and an air link with Oman.[163]

In early September 2000, GCC foreign ministers again called on Iran to respond to the efforts of the committee, and Saudi Prince Saud Al-Faisal revealed that the committee had asked to be received in Iran to discuss the islands issue.[164] At the UN Millenium summit in early October, the UAE delegation called on Iran to resolve the islands dispute peacefully as "the only way to enhance bilateral relations between the two countries and between all the countries of the region." Moreover, Algerian President Abdelaziz Bouteflika was expected to discuss the issue with Iranian Foreign Minister Kharrazi during the summit.[165]

The tripartite committee finally reported to the GCC summit held in December 2000 that Iran would not cooperate with it, and the summit concluded that the mandate of the committee was "finished." The final communiqué of the summit asked the Ministerial Council "to examine all the available peaceful means, which lead to regaining the legitimate rights of the UAE to its three islands – Tunb al-Kubra, Tunb al-Sughra, and Abu Musa – which are still occupied by the Islamic Republic of Iran."

The summit's communiqué also returned to the kind of critical language that had characterized the communiqués in previous years and that had been omitted in the 1999 communiqué. It rejected Iranian claims, Iranian occupation and Iranian measures on and around the islands, including Iranian military maneuvers like the naval maneuvers that Iran had conducted in the Strait of Hormuz and the Gulf of Oman in October and November 2000, and said: "All these measures threaten security and stability in the region and increase tension in it. Consequently, this threatens international peace and security." It again asked Iran to refer the dispute to the ICJ. Soon thereafter, Saudi Arabia's Prince Saud Al-Faisal said: "One party, Iran, has declined to allow an opportunity for direct negotiations. The ICJ is the best means to end the dispute if direct negotiations could not be held." Iranian Foreign Minister Kharrazi said that Iran was prepared to discuss Abu Musa under the terms of the 1971 MoU, but that it was the turn of the UAE Foreign Minister to visit Iran for such discussions.[166]

In February 2001, the Arab Parliamentary Union (APU) issued a statement declaring: "The council expresses full support to the UAE initiatives to regain its three islands occupied by the Islamic Republic of Iran."[167] In mid-March, the Arab League foreign ministers called on Iran to end its occupation of the three islands. Also in mid-March, the GCC foreign ministers said the dispute was a source of "instability in the region" and called on Iran to stop its "military manoeuvers in the three occupied islands and in the territorial waters of the UAE." It also demanded that Iran stop building houses for the settlement of Iranians on the islands.[168] The final communiqué of the Arab League summit in Amman later in March reaffirmed the UAE's sovereignty over the islands and called on Iran "to end its occupation of the three Arab islands and stop the policy of imposing a status quo by force on these islands, including the establishment of facilities to settle Iranians on these islands."[169]

Despite its support for the UAE, Saudi Arabia signed a security cooperation accord with Iran in mid-April, one that would fight crime, terrorism and drug trafficking. However, the accord did not include and was not likely to lead to any military defense agreement with Iran, which again had conducted naval exercises in the Gulf in March and April.[170] The meeting of the GCC foreign ministers in Jeddah in early June again criticized "Iran's rejection of the many peace initiatives advanced to resolve the issue of the three islands," its construction of housing on the islands, and the "provocation" of its military exercises on the islands, and called on Iran to submit the issue to the ICJ.[171] In December 2001, at the end of a year in which Shaikh Hamdan had met with Kharrazi and Khatami, the GCC summit communiqué noted these contacts, supported the UAE's sovereignty over the islands and its peaceful efforts to find a settlement of the dispute, and rejected Iranian claims and measures, declaring: "As these claims are void and unjustifiable they do not affect the UAE's legitimate rights over the three islands." Once again, the communiqué called upon Iran to take the issue to the ICJ.[172]

In January 2002, the new GCC Secretary General, Abdul Rahman bin Hamad Al-Ateyya, who had been Qatar's Deputy Foreign Minister, urged a settlement of the dispute, saying: "Resolving this problem will contribute to the improvement of the atmosphere of stability and cooperation between the two sides."[173] In mid-March, the Arab League foreign ministers "expressed the hope that Iran revise its position rejecting reaching a peaceful settlement of the conflict over the islands" and condemned "Iran's building homes on these three islands to house Iranians, as well as military manoeuvers" in the region.

Also in mid-March, the GCC foreign ministers "expressed full support for all measures taken by the UAE to regain its sovereignty over the three islands by peaceful means," rejected "all Iranian claims and measures in the three islands, which are null and void and do not detract from the UAE's rights to the islands," and urged Iran to go to the ICJ.[174] Later in March, the Arab League summit held in Beirut supported the UAE's sovereignty, called on Iran to end its occupation and called on Iran to go to the ICJ. It also asked Secretary General Amr Mousa to study the issue and present a report to the Arab League summit to be held in Manama in March 2003.[175]

A GCC consultative summit held in late May hailed Shaikh Hamdan's May visit to Iran. GCC foreign ministers also met soon after

Hamdan's trip to Tehran and issued a communiqué on June 8 that "reaffirmed its adherence to the consistent stand taken by the GCC States in support of the right of the United Arab Emirates to sovereignty over its three islands." It noted UAE-Iranian contacts and hoped that Shaikh Hamdan's visit to Iran and President Khatami's expected visit to the UAE "would lead to positive steps conducive to strengthening the relations between the two neighboring countries, and would strengthen the ties of friendship, deepen the existing cooperation between the GCC States and the Islamic Republic of Iran and place security and stability in the region on a sound footing."[176]

It was reported in *Al-Sharq Al-Awsat* on June 10 that the UAE and Iran had agreed to remove the islands dispute from the media spotlight and avoid the issue in international forums, while ongoing bilateral contacts would attempt to achieve a mutually acceptable solution. The paper also reported substantive concessions by Iran on all three islands.[177] However, on July 2, the Saudi paper *Al-Watan* reported Iranian sources as indicating that any agreement would be based on the Abu Musa MoU, with Iran retaining control over the Tunbs.[178] In subsequent months UAE officials suggested that substantive agreement still had not been achieved.[179] GCC foreign ministers, after reaffirming the UAE's full sovereignty over the three islands in early September, "hoped that the two countries would manage to find a peaceful solution that would put an end to the occupation of the three islands by the Islamic Republic of Iran."[180] Days later, Arab League foreign ministers supported the UAE position in stronger terms, saying in a communiqué: "The ministers reject the continued Iranian occupation of the UAE islands and backs the UAE's full sovereignty over them as part and parcel of the UAE territory." The communiqué denounced Iranian military manoeuvers, saying: "These measures represent a violation of the UAE's sovereignty and do not help build mutual confidence, threaten regional security and stability, and put regional and international navigation in the Gulf at risk."[181]

The GCC summit in Doha in December 2002 denounced Iran's occupation of the three islands, expressed the hope that the direct contacts taking place between the UAE and Iran "will lead to concrete positive steps that could contribute to enhancing the bilateral relations between the two states, and develop cooperation between the GCC states and the Islamic Republic of Iran, and further consolidate the security and stability of the region." It reasserted "its firm stance in supporting the full right of the United Arab Emirates to regain its sovereignty over its three islands, its territorial waters, airspace, the continental shelf and the economic zone of the three islands as an integral part of the United Arab Emirates." It again tasked the Ministerial Council with responsibility to exert all peaceful efforts to help the UAE regain the islands.[182]

Despite the emergence of some reformist leaders in Iran, and despite the new efforts of the GCC tripartite committee, Iranian policy on the three islands remains the same. The support of the Damascus Declaration states, the Arab League and particularly the GCC will therefore continue to be important for the UAE. Shaikh Saqr of Ras al-Khaimah said in an April 1998 interview: "Arab support is overwhelming; there is no softness."[183] However, only a year later, in June 1999, UAE dissatisfaction with Saudi support led to a public row. To conclude, other UAE and GCC views on the extent of Arab support should be considered.

A former Secretary-General of the GCC has argued that on the official level, the GCC has been very supportive of the UAE's position on the islands, although some member states do have different tactics. The UAE does not want to develop special relations with Iran, nor does it want its GCC partners to develop special relations with Iran so as to show dissatisfaction with Iran's occupation of the islands. Oman and Qatar, however, have traditionally had their own reasons for closer relations with Iran and have argued that these closer relations might enable them to persuade Iran to change its position on the islands. It is not easy to know what the other GCC partners are thinking, he said, but they have been committed to the UAE's position.[184]

A former aide to the above mentioned GCC Secretary-General, who is now an official in the UAE Ministry of Foreign Affairs, has also argued that the GCC speaks with one voice on the islands and that its statements of support for the UAE have real weight. The Omani and Qatari foreign ministers have joined all the other foreign ministers in endorsing GCC joint and summit communiqués. Kuwait has been more obsessed with Iraq than with Iran, but it will not stand idly by if Iran takes action against the UAE[185]

Another UAE official stresses that the importance of the GCC's support for the UAE's position on the islands is the role it may play in inducing Iran to negotiate. This official, however, while noting that Qatar does support the UAE on the islands, has questioned the depth of its support. He has argued that there has been some difference between the collective support of the GCC and the support of individual members of the GCC, and that Iran has not thought that it has been confronting a solid GCC wall on this issue. Iran has been getting occasional signs that the wall is not solid, for example from Qatar.[186]

All six of the GCC states do not, of course, have identical policies towards Iran. The differences that exist in the policies of these six states may be attributed to different geostrategic considerations, different security priorities and different bilateral relations.[187] Saudi Arabia's reasons for agreeing to a thaw with Iran and Bahrain's reasons for not antagonizing Iran have already been mentioned. It should be noted, however, that all of the GCC states that have tried to use their relatively closer bilateral relations with Iran in an effort to persuade Iran to respond to UAE and GCC appeals regarding the islands have failed in this effort, including GCC heavyweight Saudi Arabia in 1999 and 2000. This is also reflected in the failure of the GCC's tripartite committee in 1999 and 2000. Nevertheless, it is important to stress that one consideration that does and should unite them in supporting the UAE is that each GCC state is a potential target of Iranian ambitions and each state could thus in future need the kind of GCC support that the UAE now needs.

The UAE Foreign Ministry official who previously served as an aide to the former GCC Secretary General has argued that, generally speaking, Iran's words and deeds led to its isolation in the region throughout most of the 1980s and 1990s. Iran has engaged in a rhetoric of supremacy, preached to Gulf Arabs about their friends and enemies, and played the role of "big brother." This has made cooperation with Iran difficult for the GCC states. More specifically, Iran's behavior on the islands since 1992 has aroused the suspicions of all the GCC states, to varying degrees, about the intentions of a rearming Iran at a time when Iraq cannot be a balancer. The GCC states have been suspicious of periodic Iranian calls for a regional security system that excludes external actors. They have been particularly concerned about the role of hard-line radicals in Tehran, even after the election of a reformist president.[188]

Former GCC Secretary-General Abdullah Bishara argues that Iran's behavior on the islands has meant that the GCC has been unwilling to engage in collective GCC-Iran talks on a large agenda of trade, investment and security issues. Moreover, he argues that Iran will not have such talks and cooperation with the GCC as a collective entity until the islands issue is resolved, and expresses the concern that resolution of the issue is unlikely as long as moderates such as President Khatami and Foreign Minister Kharrazi are not the real authorities in the making of Iran's foreign policy, and real authority remains in the hands of hard-liners instead. Thus, Iran has to settle for bilateral talks with individual members of the GCC, who limit these talks to their own bilateral concerns in the absence of resolution of the islands issue.[189]

Iran's behavior on the islands since 1992 has been seen as part of a larger strategy of intimidation of the UAE and the GCC, particularly in the framework of its military re-armament and its military exercises in the Gulf, and has contributed to a number of developments that were not desired by Iran. It has brought the GCC states into a closer embrace, provided a continuing rationale for the involvement of Egypt and Syria in Gulf affairs and brought about a renewed unity within the Arab League. Furthermore, the GCC as a group and its individual member states have been driven to a greater degree of reliance on US and other Western military forces. Iran has further alienated the United States, therefore providing yet another rationale for a tougher US containment policy.

Any possibility of Iran being included in a Gulf security framework, always a remote possibility at best, has been diminished, as has the possibility of persuading GCC countries to loosen their military ties with the West. Indeed, while the GCC does not welcome this, Iran's behavior on the islands may also increase the possibility of future conflict with the United States and the physical punishment this would entail for Iran. The real possibility of receiving GCC financial assistance to rebuild and diversify Iran's economy after the Iran–Iraq war has been weakened. The same can be said for receiving technical and economic assistance and investment from the United States. Finally, the diminished role and stature of Iraq and Iran, and the enhanced role of the United States, has permitted the GCC states to respond to Iran's behavior on the islands by offering more support to the UAE on the islands than was possible in the 1970s and 1980s.

While individual GCC members had responded to the overtures of reformist leaders in Iran by repairing and restoring some bilateral ties and entering into some bilateral agreements, there is still a limit to what Iran can expect as long as it occupies and fortifies the islands, uses them in military exercises and insists on limiting negotiations to implementation of the MoU on Abu Musa. Individual GCC members appear to be proceeding cautiously, and Iran's aspirations may still be frustrated in the absence of a resolution of its dispute with the UAE, especially if this dispute were to escalate.

PART
IV

INTERNATIONAL CONCERNS

The International Community and the Islands Dispute in the 1960s

The next three chapters will examine the role and effectiveness of the international community in addressing and resolving the islands issue. The main focus is on the actions and policies of Great Britain and the United States, and to a lesser extent, the United Nations and its agencies. Based on the historical record, it is clear that international public and private statements about the islands dispute have not matched the expressed commitment to the stability of the Gulf region.

Britain was generally satisfied with the situation it left behind in the Gulf. Its main concerns as it withdrew from the Gulf were the future of Bahrain and the establishment of a federation of Arab emirates, not Abu Musa and the Tunbs. Having achieved those objectives, Britain acquiesced in the use of force by the Shah of Iran to take the islands. In the view of some British officials, it was "not a very honorable policy, but it was a practical one."[1] Moreover, it had the support of the United States. In any case, it constituted a virtual repudiation of over a hundred years of British policy of both publicly and privately asserting and defending the rights of the Qawasim to the islands against Persian and Iranian claims.

The Record of the Major Powers

In early 1968, when the British Labour Government decided to withdraw from the Gulf by 1971, they had learned much from their discussions with Iran during the 1950s and 1960s. Iran had proposed giving up Bahrain in exchange for Abu Musa and the Tunbs as early as 1954 and indicated that it was amenable to a political inquiry regarding Bahrain in 1955. Britain had countered by proposing that Iran give up Bahrain as well as Abu Musa for the Tunbs and Sirri. Ras al-Khaimah had considered a sale of the Tunbs, but had preferred a lease in 1954. Thus, the general elements of a package deal appeared to be in place in the mid-1950s.[2]

Almost a decade later, in early 1964, the Foreign Office did not think Iran was prepared to yield its claims to Bahrain, Abu Musa and the Tunbs. However, the Shah stated later in 1964 that Iran might yield on Bahrain in the future. Both the British Political Resident Sir William Luce and the British Ambassador to Tehran Sir Denis Wright shared the opinion that the Shah might be flexible on Bahrain, possibly in a package deal regarding a median line and Abu Musa and the Tunbs. Britain and Iran subsequently had several rounds of talks pertaining to the continental shelf in the Gulf and other Gulf matters.

During the first round, in April 1965, the Shah said that he had no intention of pressing his claim to Bahrain or taking over the island, but that he had to oppose Bahrain's admission to UN agencies for domestic reasons. In the summer of 1965, after learning that Bahrain might be part of a federation and an Arab Gulf currency, Iran said median line discussions would be impossible with a Bahrain crisis looming. After an inconclusive second round of talks in September 1965, Iran said it would not negotiate on a median line until Abu Musa and the Tunbs were resolved.[3] During the third round, in February 1966, when Britain signed an agreed minute with Iran regarding the delineation of a median line between Iran and Qatar, it was agreed that the subject of the Tunbs should be given priority in subsequent discussions.

However, Iran was again not prepared to provide any documents concerning the basis of its claim to ownership of these islands.[4] Indeed, Iranian Ambassador to Britain Abbas Aram told the Foreign Office in early 1967 that because Iran's interest in the islands was strategic, she could not risk any international process such as arbitration in case she did not win.[5] In June 1967, Ambassador Aram suggested informally that Abu Musa might go to Sharjah, with Sirri and the Tunbs going to Iran, and with compensation being given to Ras al-Khaimah, as part of a median line agreement.[6] When Britain and Iran held informal talks on the continental shelf in the Gulf in late November 1967 in London, however, Britain proposed resolving the median line without prejudice to the islands.[7]

Nevertheless, the British Political Agent in Dubai, D.A. Roberts, approached Shaikh Saqr of Ras al-Khaimah in December 1967 about a sale of the Tunbs. While reporting that he thought the Ruler was interested, Roberts also stated that the Ruler was prepared for a long bargaining process and that he also wanted Iran to approach him officially, probably because this would in effect admit his sovereignty.[8] On January 3, 1968 Aram met with officials in London and proposed common exploitation of disputed islands and seabeds. The British, however, had doubts about Iranian sincerity.[9]

Declassified official British records show that in 1968, after the decision to withdraw, the British presented the diplomatic and legal case for Ras al-Khaimah's sovereignty over the Tunbs in conversation with the Iranians. However, they were ambivalent about it and once again invited Iran to document its contending case. The British wanted Ras al-Khaimah to sell the Tunbs and Iran to buy them, and sought Saudi support in achieving this as part of the package deal informally and unofficially proposed in June 1967 by Iran's Ambassador Aram. Moreover, in the aftermath of Iranian naval moves around the Tunbs and veiled threats of force, the British decided not to defend the islands. Instead, the British would "bluff" the Shah that they were willing to defend the islands until their withdrawal and "hint" that they would not oppose Iranian action after their withdrawal in order to promote a negotiated compromise solution. After repeated arguments from British officials in the Gulf, the Foreign Office agreed to defend Abu Musa under certain circumstances, but only because they believed that Iran did not want Abu Musa anyway.[10]

By May 1968, the British explicitly accepted a median line package deal in which Iran would get Sirri and the Tunbs and yield its claims to Bahrain and Abu Musa, although they knew the Shah did not really want Bahrain and thought he might not be so determined with regard to Abu Musa. In June, the British proposed this specific package deal to the Shah as well as to King Faisal, believing that agreement between Iran and Saudi Arabia was the key to promoting this deal and to fostering stability in the Gulf. However, the British did not propose the deal to the Rulers of Ras al-Khaimah and Sharjah. The British soon learned that the proposed terms were not acceptable to the Shah, who demanded Abu Musa in addition to the Tunbs. He also opposed a federation of emirates unless the Bahrain issue was resolved in a face-saving way and Iran acquired Abu Musa and the Tunbs. Thus, the British had to reconsider their strategy for resolving these issues.

Following the announcement on January 4, 1968 of an intended British withdrawal, Minister of State for Foreign Affairs Goronwy Roberts embarked on a tour of the Gulf. During his meeting with the Shah on January 7, the Shah stressed the importance of settling quickly the problem of "the little islands" and a discussion regarding the Tunbs ensued. Roberts expressed sympathy for the Iranian case on the islands and proposed the demilitarization of the Tunbs. The Shah, however, said this idea was unacceptable, arguing that Iran could not give up the right to militarize what it considered its own territory.

T.F. Brenchley of the British Foreign Office noted that legal experts in the Foreign Office thought that the Ruler of Ras al-Khaimah had a strong legal claim to the Tunbs, which other Arab states would be bound to support. He expressed the fear that if the problem were not settled amicably it would undermine prospects for Arab-Iranian cooperation. The Shah retorted that he was not prepared to lose any more territory, that if the Arabs did not like it they would have to "lump it," and that although Iran wanted cooperation, it was strong enough to go forward alone if need be. Indeed, it soon became clear that the more the British searched for a compromise, the more determined the Shah became to proceed alone if necessary.[11]

On January 8 and 9, Roberts met with the rulers of Kuwait, Bahrain, Qatar and the Trucial States. The rulers were shocked to learn of Britain's withdrawal plan only one month after Roberts had traveled to the region to assure them that Britain would stay as long as necessary to assure peace and stability. Abu Dhabi's Shaikh Zayed told Roberts he could make a financial contribution to support the continuation of the British presence, and the rulers of Qatar, Bahrain and Dubai soon made similar offers, but after some consideration the British did not accept these offers. When asked if withdrawal would mean the end of the treaty relations, the British answered only that the Gulf Rulers should come together and build a new security grouping for themselves, but by April the British notified the Rulers that treaty relations would indeed end with the withdrawal.[12]

On January 10, Roberts met with Saudi Arabia's King Faisal bin Abdul Aziz Al-Saud, who expressed concern that Iran was making claims on some Arab lands. Roberts said that the Shah had assured him that he had no intention of interfering in Bahrain, but that he could not declare this in public because of domestic Iranian opinion. When discussing the Shah's interest in the Tunbs, Roberts concluded that Faisal considered the issue unimportant, and he then expressed this opinion himself. Faisal did express support for a federation of the emirates of the Gulf.[13] Later, Saudi Arabia also offered to help pay for a continued British military presence and Kuwait hinted that it might do so.[14]

British Secretary of State for Foreign Affairs George Brown carried the message of British withdrawal from the Gulf to the United States on January 11. President Lyndon Johnson and Secretary of State Dean Rusk asked Britain to continue to maintain its bases in the Gulf and to reconsider and postpone its withdrawal. Despite Anglo-American commercial competition in the area, the US thought that the British military and political presence safeguarded the flow of oil and the stability of conservative regimes in the face of radical Arab and Soviet threats. Thus, British withdrawal would leave a vacuum in which Western interests would be threatened.[15]

The US would continue to maintain a small and symbolic naval and air presence (MIDEASTFOR) in Bahrain, which had started in 1949, in order to demonstrate US interest in the Gulf.[16] However, the Johnson administration, deeply involved in an increasingly unpopular war in Vietnam, did not intend for the US to replace the British presence and assume the British role in the Gulf. Undersecretary of State Eugene Rostow suggested on January 19 that the US should instead rely on security groupings, including Iran, Turkey, Pakistan, Kuwait and Saudi Arabia, to fill the vacuum left by the British withdrawal. Ultimately, the US did agree with Britain on a "two-pillar" policy under which both would provide military sales and training primarily to Iran and secondarily to Saudi Arabia in a bid to have these two Gulf states promote stability and Western interests in the Gulf region.[17] The US also quietly supported British efforts to encourage the establishment of a nine-member federation, as well as British moves to resolve the disputes over Bahrain, Abu Musa and the Tunbs.[18]

The Soviet Union welcomed the British withdrawal decision. Indeed, it had long been a Soviet objective to reduce Western imperialist influence in the Gulf. Responding to a report in the Tehran newspaper *Ittilaat* that Roberts had proposed joint defense arrangements including Iran, Kuwait, Saudi Arabia and the Lower Gulf shaikhdoms, the Soviet news agency Tass wrote on January 8 that the idea of a "joint defense system of Persian Gulf countries" was an attempt to maintain British influence and predicted that this would not have the support of the Arab world. On March 3, Tass reported that a recent visit to Iran by US and British officials was an attempt "to impose" a "so-called joint defense system" for "neocolonialist purposes," including the defense of "capitalist oil monopolies" and challenges "against the security of the USSR's southern boundaries." It warned that the Soviet Union "resolutely opposes the new attempts by aggressive circles of the U.S.A. and Britain to interfere in the affairs of countries in the Persian Gulf region and to dictate their will to them."[19]

Subsequently, Soviet naval vessels made the first of many visits to Gulf waters to the Iraqi port of Umm al-Qasr on May 12, clearly demonstrating the Soviet interest in extending its influence in the Gulf in the wake of the British withdrawal decision.[20] The Soviet Union, wanting to build relations not only with radical and even conservative Gulf Arab states but also with Iran, did not express its views on the disputes over Bahrain or Abu Musa and the Tunbs. However, it opposed a federation of the Gulf Arab emirates as another British effort to maintain its influence and warned that it would fail.[21]

As British officials were informing Gulf and American officials of Britain's decision to withdraw from the Gulf, Iran pressed the issue of the Tunbs and Abu Musa on the British. On January 8 and 9, 1968, just days after Roberts met with the Shah, and just as Iranian Foreign Minister Ardishir Zahedi had warned in that meeting, Iran issued protests to the British Embassy in Tehran and to the Foreign Office in London, alleging that Ras al-Khaimah had made an armed landing on the Greater Tunb and had raised the Ras al-Khaimah flag and warning that Iran might be compelled to take action.[22] The Commander of British Forces in the Gulf noted that the Ras al-Khaimah flag had flown for years. He also reported that an Iranian frigate in the area of the island had trained its guns on British reconnaissance aircraft, but that no Iranians were found to have landed on the Greater Tunb and that the frigate soon left the area.[23]

Nevertheless, in response to these developments, British Chargé d'Affaires in Tehran Charles Wiggin handed over a strong Foreign Office note to Foreign Minister Zahedi on January 13, reaffirming Ras al-Khaimah's right to the island and noting that the Ras al-Khaimah flag had flown regularly in the past. Iran was reminded about the 1966 agreement to exchange documents regarding the Ras al-Khaimah and Iranian claims to the islands. The note also rejected the Iranian claim, called on Iran not to take any unilateral action, and protested the Iranian action in sending a naval vessel into the territorial waters of the islands. Zahedi answered by stating that talks on the Tunbs could not resume until the flag was taken down and he again threatened action.[24] Moreover, on January 15 the Iranian Embassy in London protested that a British aircraft had made harassing flights over an Iranian naval vessel "in the coastal waters of Iran" in the Gulf and threatened that the vessel would take "such action as considered necessary" if it occurred again, even though Wiggin had already explained to Zahedi on January 13 that these were only British reconnaissance aircraft.[25]

On January 15, Iranian Ambassador Aram met with British Minister of State Roberts. Aram said that in view of the British intention to withdraw from the Gulf, Iran wanted the Ras al-Khaimah flag taken down. Roberts emphasized that there had been no change in Britain's position on sovereignty, that Britain had treaty obligations to Ras al-Khaimah, and that Britain defended Ras al-Khaimah's right to fly its flag. He noted that Britain and Iran had agreed in early 1966 to discuss the Tunbs and that Britain had been willing to discuss the issue for the past two years. However, Roberts said that until Iran submitted its documentation and proved its case, Britain would not betray Ras al-Khaimah's trust. He expressed concern that Iran had sent a warship to the area and urged Iran not to take any unilateral action to change the *status quo*. He also handed over the British note of January 13 answering the Iranian protest of January 9. Aram acknowledged that Ras al-Khaimah had a claim to the Tunbs, but argued that Ras al-Khaimah could not protect the islands. Roberts noted that the islands would be vital in a future security system and again suggested that perhaps demilitarization was the answer. This, however, was not acceptable, according to Aram.[26]

On January 17, the Foreign Office noted that the Political Resident in Bahrain, Sir Stewart Crawford, had recommended placing a Trucial Oman Scouts (TOS) presence on the Tunbs as a measure to pre-empt any Iranian landing while Chargé d'Affaires Wiggin in Tehran had recommended against it. The Foreign Office acknowledged that this would reassure Rulers shocked by the announcement of British withdrawal, but argued that it would offend the Iranians and thus jeopardize British overflight and staging rights. In addition, it would raise questions as to how and when to withdraw the Trucial Oman Scouts, who could not defend the islands after British withdrawal, and undermine the previously floated idea that the Shah might buy the islands. Thus, the Foreign Office not only opposed Crawford's recommendations, but even considered "whether we should not go further to placate the Iranians and suggest to the Political Resident that the offending flag might be replaced by some less obtrusive symbol of Ras al-Khaimah sovereignty."[27]

On January 18, the Foreign Office informed Crawford of its rejection. It also advised Crawford to raise again with the Ruler of Ras al-Khaimah the idea of selling the islands "now that he knows the date beyond which he will no longer be able to count on our protection." Finally, despite having defended Ras al-Khaimah's right to fly its flag in the January 15 meeting with Aram, and clearly with a desire to "placate" Iran, the Foreign Office wrote that "it would clearly be a help if we could devise some less conspicuous symbol of the Ruler's sovereignty than the flying of the flag in its present position, provided that this could be put across without suggesting to the Ruler that we were weakening in support of his claim," and asked Crawford for ideas on how to achieve this objective.[28]

On January 23, Political Resident Crawford cabled the Foreign Office to say that since King Faisal was not informed about the islands, he should be briefed prior to the Shah's upcoming visit to Saudi Arabia. Otherwise, he might be led to agree with the Shah.[29] The Foreign Office replied by providing the Embassy in Jeddah with a proposed briefing for King Faisal regarding Iranian claims to Bahrain, Sirri, Abu

Musa and the Tunbs. This included arguments for and against Iran's claims, with the Foreign Office expressing its rejection of Iran's claims.[30]

At the same time, the Foreign Office also provided the Embassy with "Talking Points" for the briefing of the Saudis on the islands and median line negotiations. Here, it suggested informing the Saudis that the British would consider the sale of the Tunbs a "convenient solution," in keeping with the informal and perhaps unofficial proposal by Iran's Ambassador Aram in June 1967 that Sirri should go to Iran with Abu Musa going to Sharjah and the Tunbs going to Iran with the Ruler of Ras al-Khaimah being compensated for them.[31]

Crawford advised the Foreign Office on February 1 that the Ambassador in Jeddah should not inform the Saudis that Britain thought the sale of the Tunbs to Iran would be a "convenient solution." He argued that in the aftermath of the announcement of the British withdrawal it would jolt the confidence of the rulers for Britain to support the disposing of Arab territory to Iran.[32] On the same day, however, the Shah cancelled his state visit to Saudi Arabia, and British efforts to enlist Saudi help with Iran had to be postponed.[33]

On February 1, Political Resident Crawford recommended against any further British approach to Ras al-Khaimah about a sale of the Tunbs, arguing that any further initiative should be made by Iran.[34] Crawford also recommended against departing from the *status quo* and asking Ras al-Khaimah to lower its flag.[35] In a cable dated February 3, Crawford argued that if Britain failed to thwart the Shah from military action against the Tunbs by getting there first "we should have proved to the Arabs that the nationalist accusation that we were conniving at an Iranian advance in the Gulf was justified."[36] If an Iranian occupation of either island appeared to be imminent, Crawford argued again that he should take the pre-emptive action of putting a TOS troop on the island in question.[37] A February 5 cable from the Commander of British Forces in the Gulf agreed with Crawford, although it recognized that this might prejudice the use of the overflight route provided by the Central Treaty Organization (CENTO), an alliance of Britain, the United States, Turkey, Iran and Pakistan.[38]

A February 7 Foreign Office memo to Crawford saw "little future in swapping statements of claim [with Iran] and the legal and historical arguments which would ensue" and also expressed doubt "that the

Iranians are in a position to produce a dossier in support of their claim." It agreed with Crawford that Britain could not depart from the *status quo* and press Ras al-Khaimah to take down the flag. However, the memo noted that non-militarization of the islands was not acceptable to Iran and that joint militarization under Iranian sovereignty was not acceptable to the Arabs. Thus, it argued that the package deal proposed earlier by Aram would be a good deal, since otherwise the Shah would seize the Tunbs, and possibly Abu Musa, when Britain left the Gulf. The memo also suggested compensating Ras al-Khaimah with extra seabed by not accepting Iran's demand that Qishm be its baseline. Finally, it noted that if a union were formed, the cession of the Tunbs would be offset somewhat by the retention of Abu Musa. The memo made no reference to Bahrain as a part of this package deal.[39]

A memo written by the Foreign Office's Arabian Department on February 9 recommended against any preemptive military presence on the islands to deter Iran or any military effort to evict Iran if it took the islands, instead arguing solely for a diplomatic response. In support of its argument, it cited the agreement of both the Eastern Department and the Defence Department of the Foreign Office, as well as the Ministry of Defence. The memo expressed the idea that if Britain sought assurance from the Shah that Iran would take no military action prior to the British withdrawal, then this "might hint to the Shah that we would be less concerned about his taking the islands after our withdrawal from the Gulf." Although it questioned whether the Shah could be relied on to keep such an approach to himself, it recommended, in effect, that British Ambassador Wright should bluff about the British reaction to any Iranian military move before British withdrawal and hint about the reaction after withdrawal. The Shah should be urged to respect the *status quo* on the following ground:

> ...that so long as Ras al-Khaimah and Sharjah are under H.M.G.'s protection we would be obliged to react strongly to an Iranian attempt to occupy either the Tunbs or Abu Musa. If the Shah asked about the position after our withdrawal he should be told that while H.M.G. would no longer be directly concerned we should nevertheless have to condemn publicly any forcible action against the islands...

Foreign Secretary Brown agreed that Britain should take no military action if Iran seized the islands.[40] Thus, a Foreign Office memo to Crawford on February 14 rejected his request for authority to pre-empt Iran by moving TOS troops to the islands, arguing that a pre-emptive British military presence on the islands might not deter Iran and might therefore result in real conflict with Iran.[41]

Crawford replied on February 17 that he hoped that Ambassador Wright would remind the Shah that Britain had agreements to protect the Trucial States, that the Prime Minister had stated that Britain would honor these obligations, and that the Shah should therefore not take any action on the islands that would lead the Rulers to ask for this British protection and lead to confrontation between Iran and Britain. However, he also argued that he was not persuaded that a pre-emptive use of the TOS would lead to conflict with Iran and that in the event of an imminent Iranian action against an island he would still be bound to recommend this.[42]

On February 22, a Foreign Office memo to Crawford noted that the Secretary of State had not only decided against any pre-emptive action, but had also decided that in the event of an Iranian occupation of the islands, "HMG [i.e. Her Majesty's Government] should confine their defence of the Rulers' rights to diplomatic action and should not attempt to evict the Iranians by force." The memo extended the policy to Abu Musa as well as the Tunbs, and argued that this was necessary to avoid the consequences of a conflict with Iran. It noted that Wright would strongly urge the Shah to maintain the *status quo* and said that "We do not intend to give the Iranians any reason to believe that we shall not back Sharjah's and Ras al-Khaimah's rights all the way," but also called this a "bluff" that Iran probably would not call.[43]

On March 25 and 26, 1968, new Secretary of State for Foreign Affairs Michael Stewart, Political Resident Crawford, Ambassador Wright and other officials held discussions on the Gulf at the Foreign Office. Wright thought that the Arabists like Crawford were "uncompromising over Iranian aspirations," but that he [Wright] made "some progress in ensuring that Iranian interests and claims were not just brushed aside as unreasonable."[44] The meeting ended with Stewart calling for an examination of possible solutions to the conflicting claims to the islands.[45] At the same time, the Foreign Office noted Wright's report that the Shah had apparently instructed Foreign Minister Zahedi to provide Britain with Iranian documentation on the islands. The

Foreign Office argued that if Iran did not provide this documentation, it should renew its suggestion to Iran that it do so as soon as the Foreign Office had completed its review of possible solutions. It also noted, clearly in response to the Iranian charge that Britain was planning to relinquish Iranian land it had previously taken by force:

> There is no historical basis for the allegation that we 'usurped' the islands by force and guile or otherwise. The disputed islands were already occupied by Arabs owing allegiance to the Rulers' (Arab) predecessors when we concluded our various treaties with these states.[46]

On April 6, British Ambassador Wright met the Shah. The Shah showed interest in a comprehensive settlement of the median line along the entire length of the Gulf and including all the islands, and said that he would be willing to talk to Kuwait and Saudi Arabia about it. The British idea of such a settlement was that Sirri and the Tunbs would go to Iran, while Abu Musa and Bahrain would go to the Arabs, although it is not clear that Wright was explicit about this in the meeting. The Shah, however, did hint at a somewhat different package deal. In a review of the meeting, a Foreign Office memo from May 21 noted as follows:

> It has been proposed (from the United States by Mr. Rostow in 1968, and from Iran by Mr. Aram in 1955 and Mr. Entesam in 1954) that if we were to hand over the smaller islands (including Abu Musa) to Iran, the Iranians would drop their claim to Bahrain. The Shah has now (April 1968) hinted to H.M. Ambassador in Tehran that a deal on these lines might provide a hopeful framework for a settlement.

In addition, Zahedi had said that settlement of the islands issue was a prerequisite to the median line discussions. During the meeting with the Ambassador, the Shah also proposed a plebiscite on Bahrain.[47] Thus, despite Iranian protests regarding Saudi support for Bahrain and regarding the latter's participation in a federation, the Shah was still signaling in private that he was willing to give up Bahrain for the Tunbs and Abu Musa in a package deal. Moreover, the deal had been put forward by as high ranking a US official as Undersecretary of State Rostow.[48]

On April 5, the day before Wright's meeting with the Shah, Crawford had cabled the Foreign Office and cautioned that discussing solutions to the islands dispute with the Shah might lead him to expect British cooperation in acquiring the islands. Crawford had also warned that any eventual discussions with the Rulers of Ras al-Khaimah and Sharjah about solutions might arouse their concern and lead them to pressure Britain for commitments to defend the islands, particularly if the discussions also stirred up the concerns of the wider Arab world about Britain conceding Arab land.[49]

In another cable the same day, Crawford once again made the case for placing a British military presence on the islands. Acknowledging the objections of the Foreign Office, however, he now recommended that Britain should develop a contingency plan that would allow British forces to quickly garrison Abu Musa if Iran moved to occupy the Tunbs. This would demonstrate the British readiness to protect Arab territory, enable Britain to better preserve her interests in the Arab world, while at the same time only necessitating a diplomatic response to the occupation of the Tunbs.[50]

Crawford's recommendation proved persuasive to the Foreign Office. Beginning on April 9, the Foreign Office, the Secretary of State for Foreign Affairs and the Secretary of State for Defense all approved and the Commander of British Forces in the Gulf was instructed to develop such a plan.[51] Still, on April 18 the Foreign Office cabled Crawford to defend the logic of discussing solutions to the islands dispute with Iran. They also noted that Secretary of State Stewart had let Ambassador Aram know that Britain was seeking a way out of the impasse.[52]

Meanwhile, the British Ambassador to Kuwait, Geoffrey Arthur, had been questioned by Kuwait's Crown Prince Shaikh Jabir al Ahmad al Jabir Al-Sabah and Defense Minister Shaikh Saad al Abdullah al Salim Al-Sabah about the Tunbs and Abu Musa. When asked by Shaikh Jabir if Iran would take the islands when Britain left the Gulf, Arthur had answered that he thought Iran would do so. Arthur reported that he thought they were both privately resigned and philosophical about Iran taking over the Gulf and the islands, but that they could be expected to defend Arab rights in public.[53] The Foreign Office cabled Arthur on April 25 and recommended avoiding any publicity about the Iranian claims to the islands. On April 29, Crawford also warned that if Iranian claims were brought to the attention of the Rulers of Ras al-

Khaimah and Sharjah, they might seek assurances from Britain about protection against Iranian action. Arthur agreed, but said that he had only been answering direct questions from the Kuwaiti officials.[54]

On April 29, Iranian Ambassador Aram met with Foreign Office officials and spoke about the Shah's determination to have the Tunbs and Abu Musa, partly for strategic reasons but even more for political reasons. Aram said the Shah suggested that the British purchase them from the two Rulers and transfer them to Iran. The British replied that they would consider the possibility of purchase as well as all other possible solutions during their review of the subject, but that they were not optimistic about finding a solution. Aram repeated that the Shah was amenable to a referendum on Bahrain and that he wanted better relations with Saudi Arabia. The British urged Iran to seek improved relations with Saudi Arabia. Aram then asked for British help in convincing the Rulers to satisfy Iran's claims to the islands and to persuade Saudi Arabia to reach an understanding with Iran.[55]

On May 1, Sir Denis Allen of the Foreign Office reported on another conversation with Ambassador Aram, who said the Shah may "do nothing" regarding Bahrain if he got satisfaction on the issue of the Tunbs and Abu Musa. Allen advised Aram that Iran's ability to get this deal would depend on establishing relations of confidence and goodwill with the Gulf Arabs, particularly with Saudi Arabia. Aram asked the Foreign Office to persuade the Rulers, but Allen replied that this would be difficult.[56]

In these two meetings, Aram conveyed the Shah's determination to have not only the Tunbs but also Abu Musa, contrary to what the Ambassador had said informally and unofficially in June 1967. The British were leaving the Gulf for financial reasons and did not really reply to the proposal that Britain purchase the Tunbs and Abu Musa. Indeed, they replied that they were not optimistic about any solution, although they actually thought that Ras al-Khaimah might accept a deal in which Iran bought the islands. Aram had gone beyond the Shah's hint of April 6 and made an explicit linkage and trade-off proposal of Bahrain for the Tunbs and Abu Musa. In response, the Foreign Office only said that its success would depend on Iranian relations with the Gulf Arabs. Thus, Britain seemed to be trying to line up Iranian-Saudi agreement and then have the Iranians approach the Rulers, while at the same time keeping the Rulers in the dark until that time.

In the meantime, on April 26, the US-sponsored Central Treaty Organization (CENTO) had met and stressed the urgent need for the Arab emirates of the Gulf, which had not formed their federation as proposed on March 30, to resolve their differences and to reach agreement with Iran on arrangements for safeguarding the flow of oil supplies to the West.[57] Soon afterwards, the United States and Britain became concerned about the visit to the Gulf by units of the Soviet navy.[58]

When the Shah visited Washington in June 1968 to request US military sales to Iran, a joint communiqué noted that the Shah "reaffirmed Iran's determination to sustain an adequate modern defense force to ensure Iran's national security, and the President expressed the desire of the United States to continue cooperating with Iran to this end." The United States had agreed in November 1967 to supply Iran with two squadrons of F-4 Phantom jet fighters and other weapons financed by $250 million in easy credit loans. Now, in June 1968, the United States began to deliver the Phantoms.[59] Thus, broader geopolitical and strategic concerns began to override the question of right and justice as related to the islands.

British Compromise Proposals

On May 21, the Foreign Office produced its comprehensive memorandum on the possible solutions to the islands disputes. Coming just one week after the Soviet naval visit to Iraq, the memo noted at the start:

> Our objective is stability in the area to ensure security for our investments and commercial interests, and to prevent Soviet penetration. The greatest danger to stability is an Arab/Iranian confrontation, whether before or after our departure. It is therefore greatly in our interest to bring about a settlement of the questions in dispute, as the basis for a system of security in the Gulf. Otherwise we may in effect be forced into a political choice between our economic interests in Iran and those in Arab territory, the later collectively being the larger.[60]

Before reviewing possible solutions, the memo stated:

> Until recently the Iranians have not seriously pressed their claims to Abu Musa, but they now put it on the same basis as their claim to the Tunbs. Judging from the Shah's recent discussions with Sir Denis Wright [on April 6] this could be

a bargaining position concealing flexibility on Abu Musa: on the other hand there has been no dissent from Zahedi's recent line that the Iranians' determination not to compromise their position on the islands explains their unwillingness to negotiate on the median line.

It also mentioned the Shah's private assurances that while he did not intend to press Iran's claim to Bahrain, he needed an honorable way out of the dispute, such as a plebiscite, in order to disarm the nationalists in Iran.[61]

In terms of solutions, the memo considered the isolated sale of the Tunbs as being unlikely. An overall package deal for a median line for the entire Gulf, with islands and oil fields allocated according to which side of the median line they were on, was also thought to be difficult to achieve, particularly given the disputes among Iran, Iraq and Kuwait. Instead, the memo recommended energetically pursuing a "reduced overall package" deal involving a median line along the Saudi-Iranian border, including the sector opposite Bahrain, with the median line extending into the Lower Gulf between the Trucial States and Iran, again with islands and oil fields allocated according to which side of the median line they were on. This would give Bahrain and Abu Musa to the Arabs and give Sirri and the Tunbs to Iran. To make its case, it noted as follows:

> The difficulty of the unfair distribution of profit and loss to the Rulers would be greatly reduced if it were possible to regard the Union of Arab Emirates as a single entity in which the profit and loss would be absorbed. Though the Shah may not at present be prepared to recognize this, the effective inclusion of Bahrain in the Union might help both sides: the Arab side by counter-balancing any concession over the Tunbs or the seabed, and the Iranians by providing greater appearance of a comprehensive settlement in which an Iranian concession over Bahrain could be subsumed with credit to Iran. Even if it were possible to treat the Union as a unit for the purpose of negotiating a median line there would still, however, have to be an element of sweetener for the principal real loser, the Ruler of Ras al-Khaimah. The sweetener might be in terms of cash payment and/or seabed concession.

The memo also mentioned a similar but more limited package deal, which would not include the Saudi-Iranian border, including the area opposite Bahrain, but thought it less likely to succeed. On the idea of an Iranian concession of Bahrain in return for Arab surrender of the Tunbs and Abu Musa, as suggested by the Shah on April 6, the memo noted that it did not think the Rulers would agree to this, but that this might be a possibility if there was compensation for the Tunbs. In addition, "Iranian acquisition of the Tunbs and Sharjah's retention of Abu Musa" was viewed as being extremely difficult.[62]

Other ideas included the demilitarization of the Tunbs, which the memo thought was worth pursuing, condominium, which it thought unlikely and Iran paying rent for military bases on the Tunbs, which it thought slightly more realistic than the condominium idea. On the possibility of British acquiescence to Iran's seizure of the islands, it noted that failing compromise, "we must make it clear to the Shah that we cannot wash our hands of the problem while we are present, and leave any indication of indifference after 1971 to the most tacit implication, not a clear understanding. It would not be wise to enter into such an understanding with the Iranians, as to do so would restrict our freedom to have unilateral recourse to the United Nations."[63]

The memo also considered third party settlement, i.e. arbitration and reference to the ICJ, but thought that the acceptance of both parties could not be obtained. Conciliation and mediation, which were deemed reasonable, and recourse to the UN, which was thought to be a possible way of forestalling Iranian action before British withdrawal, were considered too. Finally, a plebiscite for Bahrain was mentioned.[64]

On May 30, the Foreign Office issued instructions and background for British Ambassador Wright in Tehran regarding the islands disputes and included a copy of the above May 21 memo. Wright was asked to help get Iran and the Arab States including Saudi Arabia into direct discussions, inasmuch as this would make it obvious to Ras al-Khaimah and Sharjah that British responsibility was declining and reduce their practical claim for British defense of the islands in the event of an Iranian attack. Such discussions might also persuade all of them, particularly the Shah, of the necessity of a compromise to avoid endangering the stability of the region and its freedom from penetration by Great Powers. "We ourselves would aim not to play too leading a role on behalf of the Rulers in any actual negotiation," Wright was advised.[65]

As the instructions noted, the Arabs, including Saudi Arabia and Kuwait, demanded that Britain fulfill its duty under its protection treaties before leaving, particularly regarding Bahrain but also the islands. Meanwhile, Iran wanted to involve Britain in pressing its claim to the islands before the Arab states became independent and their title was consolidated. Thus, Britain should be the broker of the negotiations, but not a principal or a plenipotentiary.[66]

Wright's instructions said that he should try to convince the Shah of the dangers of direct action to enforce his claims and of the necessity for him to make concessions in negotiations. Britain should also make an effort to convince Ras al-Khaimah and Sharjah that Iran had an arguable case and try to get Ras al-Khaimah to give up the Tunbs for cash or as part of a "package deal which would establish a median line and within which Iran would give up its claim to Bahrain and Abu Musa, provided that the Ruler of Sharjah gave up his claim to Sirri." The instructions made it clear that this "reduced overall package deal" was the most attractive solution and therefore the British objective. "It would give the Shah the Tunbs and get him off the hook over Bahrain…" The limited package deal was the next best solution, although "the Rulers would be more isolated and therefore more fearful of making concessions" and it "would not…provide cover for an Iranian concession over Bahrain." Sale of the Tunbs would be "satisfactory" but "unlikely." Demilitarization of the Tunbs should be pursued with the Shah. Other solutions and procedures could be mentioned but not advocated. An agreement between the Shah and King Faisal on their common interest in a settlement as the basis for stability and freedom from foreign encroachment in the area was considered a prerequisite for a settlement and the British should try to persuade them of this.[67]

The May 30 instructions as well as the May 21 memo that was attached to it are explicit evidence that Britain accepted the linkage and trade-off of Sirri and the Tunbs for Bahrain and Abu Musa in a package deal that would also include a median line and preferably also a federation. Clearly, the Shah's preferred package deal differed from the British one in that the Shah wanted Abu Musa for Iran and the British wanted it for the Arabs. Nevertheless, the British wanted to reduce the

346

claim that both Ras al-Khaimah and Sharjah would have for British defense of the islands, even though they had recently agreed to garrison Abu Musa in the event of an imminent attack by Iran. The instructions also provide clear evidence that the British would seek to minimize British responsibility in negotiating such a compromise, and that it would try to promote the compromise through direct negotiations supported by major Gulf Arab parties. Subsequent memos show that the British actually presented the package deal proposals to the Shah and to King Faisal, but not to the Rulers of Ras al-Khaimah and Sharjah.

On June 2, Ambassador Wright conveyed the British proposals to the Shah. Wright emphasized that Britain could not force the rulers to accept Iran's claims and could only lend its good offices to a compromise that was fair to the rulers. He stated that agreement between Iran and Saudi Arabia was essential to a compromise, that Britain wanted the Shah to discuss these proposals with King Faisal, and that "if King Faisal agreed with the Shah's views and was prepared to put them to the rulers we for our part would do our best to persuade the rulers to accept them." The Shah agreed to discuss these ideas with King Faisal in the future. He also concurred with an approach in which Britain would be a broker but not a principal.[68]

The Shah preferred the overall package deal for a median line through the entire Gulf, although he recognized that there would be difficulties with Iraq and Kuwait. He continued to insist, however, not only on Iran's claims to the Tunbs but also to Abu Musa, although he would agree to a median line that left Abu Musa on the Arab side. He also persisted in his opposition to British support for a federation of nine and was adamant on a plebiscite for Bahrain before he would give up his claim.

In his reports to the Foreign Office, Wright indicated that the Shah's insistence on Abu Musa might be a "bargaining counter." He also noted, however, that the Shah had hinted that he might eventually have to occupy the islands even at the risk of conflict with Britain. On June 4, Wright discussed British proposals with Deputy Foreign Minister Amin Khosrow Afshar, who disliked the overall package because it involved Iraq and who preferred the reduced package. Wright told him that if the Shah insisted on Abu Musa, a compromise package deal would be impossible.[69]

On June 6, British Chargé d'Affaires in Jeddah James Craig conveyed to the Foreign Office his concern that the British attitude was designed to "placate" the Shah. He noted that British proposals already envisaged Iran gaining the Tunbs although not Abu Musa and wondered if there would not be further British concessions, asking "have we not already surrendered a large part of our position?" Despite this, the Foreign Office instructed him to present these proposals to King Faisal, being careful to stress that Britain was acting on behalf of sovereign states and had no authority to promote these proposals without the agreement of these independent states, an argument that was not entirely forthright inasmuch as the Trucial States did not even know of the existence of these proposals. Furthermore, Craig was to solicit King Faisal's views on a plebiscite for Bahrain and indicate that Britain did not think this idea should be ruled out.[70]

During a meeting with Foreign Minister Omar Al-Saqqaf in mid-June, Craig conveyed the British proposals, stating that these had been made to the Shah, and requesting that Faisal discuss them with the Shah. He listed the idea of an Iranian renunciation of Bahrain in return for the Tunbs and Abu Musa as a potential compromise proposal. However, Craig also indicated that Britain would support the Rulers gaining their "full rights."[71]

Upon reading the reports of the meeting between Craig and Al-Saqqaf, Ambassador Wright pointed out that the phrase "full rights" could be interpreted to mean the Rulers would retain all their islands. He also said that the trade-off of Bahrain for both Abu Musa and the Tunbs was an idea that the British memo of May 21 had rejected and that therefore Wright had not mentioned it to the Shah. Subsequently, Craig was instructed to tell the Saudis that the phrase "full rights" did not mean the Arabs would not have to compromise and that the option of trading Bahrain for both Abu Musa and the Tunbs had been rejected. While King Faisal agreed on an effort for a comprehensive settlement and to discuss this with the Shah, he also said a union of all the Protected States was a prerequisite to a comprehensive negotiation.[72]

Crawford then suggested that if the Gulf Rulers learned of these discussions through Saudi channels, misunderstandings could occur. In order to reduce any damage from a possible Saudi leak to Ras al-Khaimah, he advised the Foreign Office that it should inform the

Saudis of the British view regarding the strength of Ras al-Khaimah's legal claim to the Tunbs and of the need for a *quid pro quo* if the Tunbs were to be relinquished. The Foreign Office, however, rejected this advice and argued that there might actually be some tactical advantage if the Rulers heard through Saudi channels that some compromise formula might be necessary. Crawford was thus told to brief the Rulers only if they received "garbled versions."[73]

Meanwhile, the British had briefed the State Department on the British proposals as well as on Wright's meeting with the Shah. The British asked the United States to encourage the Shah and King Faisal to cooperate in general terms, but not to recommend any proposal, and the United States agreed to this.[74] On June 3, the Shah had met with King Faisal at the Jeddah airport while on his way to the United States, thus starting a new chapter in their relations after the Shah had cancelled his February visit to Saudi Arabia.[75]

Nevertheless, it was clear that important differences remained between the two sides. King Faisal had announced Saudi Arabia's support for a federation of emirates on May 22 while the Shah had expressed Iran's opposition to the same on May 24.[76] Their June 3 meeting did not resolve this difference and the Shah did not even inform the King of the British proposals on a median line and the islands during their brief meeting.[77] After being briefed by Craig in mid-June, King Faisal told the British that a federation was a prerequisite to the negotiations and the packages the British proposed, but on July 8 Iran's Foreign Ministry again expressed opposition to a federation. Moreover, Foreign Minister Zahedi explained that the Iranian objection to a federation was based not only on Iran's claim to Bahrain but also on Iran's claim to other islands, namely the Tunbs and Abu Musa.[78] As a result, the most fundamental difference in the British and Iranian ideas about a package deal remained.

The May 30 instructions to Wright and May 21 review of possible solutions were contained in a "Comprehensive Memorandum By Arabian and Eastern Departments: Islands and the Median Line in the Persian Gulf" produced by the Foreign Office. A brief overview at the beginning acknowledged that "Britain is responsible for the protection and external relations of the Arab Protected States," argued that Iran was alarmed about its security after the British withdrawal, had no confidence in the Arabs to thwart radicalism and communism, and faced domestic opposition to giving up Iranian claims. It recognized that the Shah privately understood that he must drop the claim to Bahrain in a face-saving way, but noted that he was obdurate about the Tunbs and perhaps for tactical reasons obdurate about Abu Musa.[79]

The overview also acknowledged that Britain knew the Shah was thinking about seizing the islands before the British left rather than after. Furthermore, it argued that the Arab Protected States were not yet convinced of the need for unity, were not yet chastened into reconsidering their claims, and were still depending on Britain to impose a solution. Nevertheless, Britain must continue to try to promote comprehensive negotiations towards a settlement, which would depend on the littoral states and not on Britain. This included a Saudi-Iranian agreement on a compromise settlement, even though these two states were mutually suspicious and reserved toward each other. The overview concluded by arguing again that Britain should aim for the reduced overall package deal.[80]

On July 1, T. F. Brenchley of the British Foreign Office reviewed British proposals with Ambassador Aram, who preferred the reduced overall package deal, which would include Qatar and Ras al-Khaimah. On July 11, Deputy Foreign Minister Afshar told Wright that Abu Musa was the main problem in reaching agreement and that Iran could give up Bahrain more easily. Wright insisted that Britain could not agree to Iran acquiring Abu Musa, which would fall on the Arab side of a median line. He said Britain could not be sure of persuading Ras al-Khaimah to surrender the Tunbs, but at least there would be some logic to this as the Tunbs would be on the Iranian side of a median line. Afshar warned Wright that the Shah did not like the proposal for settling the islands issue on the basis of a median line. On the issue of the federation, Afshar said that Iran would not be concerned once the Bahrain issue was resolved. Until that time, however, Iran would continue to oppose it.[81]

In late July, *The Times* of London reported the possibility of an offer to recognize Iran's claims to the Tunbs as well as Abu Musa in order for Iran to drop its opposition to a federation of Gulf Arab states and its claim to Bahrain. The report stated that Saudi Arabia supported this idea. The Foreign Office was concerned that this story would make it difficult for King Faisal to negotiate with the Shah and that it would elicit resistance from the concerned Trucial Rulers. Thus, the Foreign Office denied at a press conference that it had made this proposal. At the same time, the Foreign Office went beyond the truth in claiming that "We cannot make proposals about territory that does not belong to us, and therefore we have not done so."[82]

As these statements were being issued, Wright met with Iranian Minister of Court Asadollah Alam to propose a meeting with the Shah and stated that Iran's insistence on Abu Musa would dash hopes for a compromise package deal. Wright dismissed Alam's argument that Abu Musa and the Tunbs were of strategic significance or were a matter of prestige for Iran. Wright did tell Alam, however, as he had told Afshar, and as Brenchley had told Aram, that King Faisal had not rejected the idea of ceding the Tunbs to Iran, but thought that this must be done in the context of a nine-member union.[83]

On July 28, T.J. Clark of the British Political Agency in Dubai informed the Ruler of Ras al-Khaimah about the story in *The Times* article and the subsequent British denial. The Ruler's response was that any decision regarding the Tunbs was his and not that of a federation. Clark understood the implication to be that the Tunbs "could not be used as a bargaining factor for Iran's recognition of the UAE with Bahrain in it."[84] On the same day, Anthony Parsons of the British Political Agency in Bahrain reported that the Ruler of Bahrain's reaction to the story was that he would be happy with a deal in which Abu Musa and the Tunbs went to Iran and the Shah dropped his claim to Bahrain; that the members of the federation could argue to the Rulers of Sharjah and Ras al-Khaimah that they must make sacrifices for the good of the federation; and that the Shah could alleviate the sacrifice by paying for the islands. When Parsons indicated that this reaction was predictable, one British official wrote in the margin, with apparent relief and satisfaction, "The Gulf was predicting a few months ago that any idea of parting with one iota of sacred Arab territory would set the whole Arab world against us beginning with the other Gulf rulers!"[85]

On July 31, the Foreign Office wrote to Wright that he should tell the Shah that Britain could not recommend to the Arabs that they surrender Abu Musa, but cautioned:

> We should not however wish you to go so far as to tell the Shah that his insistence on having Abu Musa destroys all prospect of a negotiated settlement since the basis of your approach is that the present problems must be settle [*sic*] by negotiation between the Iranians and Arabs and we do not want the Shah to be able to claim that we are setting limits to the possibilities of negotiation between them, as distinct from what we are prepared to use our good offices to put to the Arabs.

Furthermore, Wright was told that he could volunteer to the Shah that a treaty of friendship between Britain and a federation would contain no commitments for British protection of the federation.[86] The meeting between Wright and the Shah on August 5, however, ended in deadlock. Wright wrote:

> None of the proposals I put to him were acceptable. He was uncompromising on the islands and insisted that there must be a plebiscite or referendum in Bahrain before he would abandon the Iranian claim. He was unimpressed by my argument that a testing of opinion among people who had never voted in their lives in this way was impractical and, in any case, would be unacceptable to the Ruler.[87]

Clearly, the Shah was insisting on Abu Musa as well as the Tunbs.

During the summer and fall, the Shah invited a number of shaikhs from the Trucial coast as well as Qatar to visit Tehran to discuss the future of the Gulf. These were not the comprehensive negotiations that the British had hoped for, but at least they were the kind of direct discussions the British wanted. Before the Ruler of Ras al-Khaimah visited Tehran from August 15 to 25, Clark advised him not to reach an agreement without consulting Britain and warned him that the Shah would object to any proposal to lease the islands because it would imply that they did not belong to Iran. Clark also asked if Shaikh Saqr would consider relinquishing the Tunbs in exchange for Iranian recognition of a federation including Bahrain, and Saqr said no.[88] During the discussions in Tehran, the Shah and his officials proposed to provide compensation to Ras al-Khaimah in exchange for Iranian use of the Tunbs, not raising the issue of sovereignty, and Shaikh Saqr expressed a willingness to consider this proposal.[89]

A September 10 Foreign Office memo considered this visit to be the first step toward negotiation over the Tunbs. As such, it recommended accepting the advice of Ambassador Wright and the Acting Political Resident in Bahrain, Michael S. Weir, for Britain to encourage the two states to continue direct negotiations over the Tunbs without becoming involved, even if it undermined any future prospect for getting Iranian agreement on a package deal that preserved Sharjah's sovereignty over Abu Musa.[90] Wright's recommendation and Foreign Secretary Stewart's subsequent approval for Wright and Weir to encourage bilateral negotiation between Iran and Ras al-Khaimah for a bilateral agreement between these two states must have been made in light of the Shah's August 5 rejection of Wright's proposals of package deals leaving Abu Musa with Sharjah. Moreover, Wright argued in a July 1999 interview that at this point Britain had also decided not to link Bahrain with the islands.[91]

In mid-October, Wright argued to Afshar that Iran should not take any action on the Tunbs without a written agreement with Ras al-Khaimah.[92] At the same time, the British learned that Iran had submitted new language to Shaikh Saqr stressing Iranian sovereignty over the Tunbs, that Saqr had refused to sign this and that Saqr was considering sending a counter-draft that stressed Ras al-Khaimah's sovereignty and offered a lease to Iran. British Political Agent Julian Bullard in Dubai was able to convince Shaikh Saqr not to mention Ras al-Khaimah sovereignty in his counter-draft.

Wright also advised Iran to find language that did not press Shaikh Saqr to recognize Iranian sovereignty. However, when Ras al-Khaimah Crown Prince Shaikh Khalid carried Ras al-Khaimah's counter-draft to Iran in late October, SAVAK officials demanded that he sign the Iranian draft, telling him that Iran had reached agreement with Britain and Saudi Arabia over a median line that left the Tunbs on Iran's side. Wright advised Iran against pressuring Ras al-Khaimah, that Ras al-Khaimah was within its rights to uphold its sovereignty, and that Iran should use carrots rather than sticks to persuade Ras al-Khaimah. Bullard replied to Shaikh Saqr that Britain had not reached agreement with Iran on a median line and on the islands, and that Britain still recognized Ras al-Khaimah's sovereignty over the islands.[93]

While it was true that Britain had not actually reached agreement with Iran on a median line and on the islands, Britain had certainly proposed to Iran a package deal involving a median line agreement that gave Abu Musa to the Arabs and the Tunbs to Iran, with compensation to Ras al-Khaimah. Britain had also made this proposal to the Saudis and had asked for and received agreement from both the Shah and King Faisal that they would discuss this. The British had not revealed to Ras al-Khaimah that such a package proposal was being discussed, thus keeping Ras al-Khaimah unaware of the role that Britain was playing behind the scenes.

Indeed, when the Shah visited Saudi Arabia in November, following the October 24 signing of a Saudi-Iranian median line agreement, the Foreign Office instructed its Embassy in Riyadh to ask the Saudis to propose to the Shah a median line with the Trucial States that would be based on the mainland coast as its baseline. For fear that the information that this would leave Sirri and the Tunbs on the Iranian side and Bahrain and Abu Musa on the Arab side would be leaked to Ras al-Khaimah, "the implications" regarding the islands were made orally instead of in writing. Crawford commented that Britain could now find itself "in a very false position" with Ras al-Khaimah and recommended that it should be King Faisal and not the British who should persuade Ras al-Khaimah to accept such a package deal.[94]

In December 1968, British Ambassador Wright suggested to Abbas Massoudi, the Iranian senator, publisher and confidant of the Shah, that the UN might sound out public opinion in Bahrain as an alternative to a plebiscite or referendum. Two days later, Massoudi told Wright that the Shah liked this new idea. The Foreign Office then instructed Wright to propose this officially to the Shah, which he did on Christmas Eve. The Shah again responded positively to the idea but stated that it would take him some time to prepare Iranian public opinion.

Wright has recalled that he was therefore surprised when on January 5, 1969 the Shah announced publicly that he would not use force to reclaim Bahrain and that he would accept the will of the inhabitants of the island if this will was internationally recognized.[95] Certainly Wright's new idea resonated with the Shah. However, the Shah also must have reasoned after his November state visits to Saudi

Arabia and Kuwait that he could gain more support from these two states, and from Britain, even on acquiring Abu Musa as well as the Tunbs, if he publicly expressed his willingness to yield his claim to Bahrain.[96]

Thus, as 1968 ended and 1969 began, the British had proposed to the Shah direct negotiations with the Arabs and a package deal. To the Ruler of Ras al-Khaimah, the British had proposed direct negotiations with the Shah, but had not revealed the proposals on package deals. After initially expressing interest in the British proposal for a package deal, the Shah had rejected it, the main dispute being over Abu Musa. The Shah and a number of Arab leaders had then started direct bilateral negotiations, during which the Shah had a somewhat encouraging discussion regarding compensation for the Tunbs with the Ruler of Ras al-Khaimah and had reached a median line agreement with King Faisal.

The British then decided to support continuing direct bilateral negotiations between Ras al-Khaimah and Iran, even if this undermined the apparently dim prospects for a package deal including Abu Musa for Sharjah. However, negotiations between Ras al-Khaimah and Iran soon became deadlocked. As a result, the British appealed to Saudi Arabia to help persuade Iran to agree to a median line agreement that would give the Tunbs to Iran, but leave Abu Musa to the Arabs and persuade Ras al-Khaimah to accept this, thus in essence reviving the idea of a package deal. The Shah then publicly indicated a willingness to yield Bahrain, which had been the major concession the British expected of him with or without a package deal.

By February, the British indicated to the Shah that they had tried to persuade Ras al-Khaimah to reach an agreement with Iran on the Tunbs, which had been the major concession that the British expected of the Arabs with or without a package deal. They may have even conveyed the idea that Ras al-Khaimah would agree. However, Iran soon indicated that it would not go through with a deal on Bahrain unless it got Abu Musa too. Gradually, the Shah became angry with Britain, which was not promoting the package deal that Iran wanted, despite the Shah's public flexibility on Bahrain. He thus increased the pressure on Britain. Up to this point, Britain had been reluctant to concede Abu Musa to Iran. However, by April the British proposed that Sharjah also engage in direct discussions with Iran, and by July the

British offered assurances to the Shah that they were also trying to persuade Sharjah to reach an agreement with Iran on Abu Musa.

Change in British Compromise Proposals

On January 31, on the eve of a visit to the United States by Ras al-Khaimah's Crown Prince Khalid, the British Embassy in Washington asked the State Department to encourage Ras al-Khaimah to come to an early agreement with Iran over the Tunbs and to join a union of nine emirates. It also let the State Department know that Undersecretary Rostow's proposed package deal giving Bahrain to the Arabs and Abu Musa and the Tunbs to Iran would be unacceptable to Sharjah. During their meeting on February 12, the State Department did encourage Ras al-Khaimah to settle the Tunbs issue with Iran, as well as expressing support for a eventual federation of nine.[97]

Late in January, Deputy Foreign Minister Afshar argued that Iran "could not lose" Abu Musa. Wright answered that Iran could yield its claim to Abu Musa in the context of a median line agreement giving Sirri and the Tunbs to Iran, thus reviving the idea of a package deal with Iran. The British Ambassador argued that "the Arab world would not tolerate the surrender to Iran of all the islands, apart from Bahrain, in dispute." When Afshar hinted that Iran had recently uncovered evidence that strengthened its legal claim to Abu Musa, Wright answered only that if its case was that good, Iran should take it to the ICJ.[98] In February, when Aram asked Foreign Office officials to support a package deal giving Abu Musa and the Tunbs to Iran so that the Shah "could show that he could gain something in exchange for Bahrain," the Foreign Office repeated its position on Abu Musa.[99] Days later, Iran formally protested against claims to sovereignty over Abu Musa made by Sharjah's Shaikh Khalid, but Britain waited until June to formally respond and then only delivered a mild note that once again repeated Britain's position.[100]

During 1969 and 1970, Ambassador Wright held a number of important meetings with the Shah's Minister of Court Amir Assadollah Alam. The published diaries of Alam, the unpublished memoirs of Wright, and Wright's recollections in a July 1999 interview with the author can be compared along with British Foreign Office documents declassified in January 2000 and January 2001 in order to construct the record and import of these meetings. Alam recalls one conversation with Wright in Tehran on February 17, 1969:

> As for Bahrain, negotiations are already under way with a view to implementing HIM's [His Imperial Majesty's] wishes. In strict confidence he [Wright] told me that the Islands of Tunbs are certain to be handed over to Iran. The British have warned the Sheikh of Ras al-Khaimah that the islands lie on our side of the median line and that, unless he comes to some sort of understanding with us, we shall simply take them, legally or if needs be by force. The Sheikh is prepared to make a deal. I then asked about the island of Abu Musa. The Ambassador replied that it lies below the median line. I told him that we are sufficiently powerful to disregard the line. We joked for a while. More seriously he expressed concern that our policy in the Gulf may lead to trouble with the Arabs. 'To hell with it,' I said. 'What have the Arabs ever done for us? If only they would stop all this nonsense, agree to pay for the defence of the Gulf, and let us get on with the work.' The Ambassador questioned the extent to which the Arabs will allow us a free hand. After all they persist in describing it as the 'Arabian' Gulf. I replied that we are prepared to draw up a fifty years defence agreement with them, and that all in all it will be much the same as the agreement they once had with the British...[101]

On February 20, the British Embassy in Tehran reported that in this same meeting Alam had insisted on the Tunbs while indicating that a deal could be made on Abu Musa. Meanwhile, Britain hoped to settle the issue of Bahrain before dealing with the islands. In the July 1999 interview, Sir Denis Wright said he doubts that he would have been so explicit about the Tunbs as recounted by Alam. He also did not recall any evidence that the Ruler of Ras al-Khaimah had been prepared to make a deal satisfactory to Iran.[102] Nevertheless, Alam's account does reflect the British proposal for the Tunbs going to Iran, its efforts to persuade the Ruler of Ras al-Khaimah, the acknowledgment and even resignation that Iran might use force to take the Tunbs, British reluctance to concede Abu Musa to Iran, and its concern that Iranian policy on the islands might undermine prospects for Arab-Iranian cooperation.

Alam writes about another meeting with Wright on March 19, 1969:

> The British Ambassador met me in the afternoon. We discussed Bahrain and the Gulf islands which he was keen to present as two distinct issues. He told me that Tunbs will be easy for us to recover but not Abu Musa, which lies too close to the Arabian peninsula. I replied that this didn't alter Iran's rights nor entitle the Arabs to hold on to Iranian territory; territory which HIM will never abandon. The ambassador suggested that a solution to the problem of Bahrain will almost certainly encourage the establishment of a Federation of Arab Emirates, at which stage Iran might well occupy Abu Musa in the interests of joint security in the Gulf. We can depend on support from the British, should this happen.[103]

Again, Wright does not think he was so explicit on the Tunbs.[104] Alam's version, however, again reflects the British interest in resolution of the Bahrain problem and the establishment of a federation, as well as the preference for Iran gaining the Tunbs. Alam's version of Wright's statement that Iran might "occupy" Abu Musa is not entirely clear from this quotation, but Wright's idea would later be explained as Iranian occupation of Abu Musa under Sharjah's sovereignty. It does appear from Alam's version that the British were trying to move away from the idea of a package deal linking Bahrain with the islands, while still trying to suggest ways of satisfying Iran on the islands, even on Abu Musa.

According to Wright's recollections:

> At one point, on March 19, 1969 to be precise, the Minister of Court intervened on instructions from the Shah to tell me that a satisfactory settlement of the Iranian claim to Abu Musa and the Tunbs would need to be part of any Bahrain settlement. I told him that no such link had ever been contemplated and would be unacceptable to HMG since the islands were nothing to do with Bahrain. I heard little more of this last minute attempt to strike a bargain over Bahrain.[105]

Elsewhere he notes that "I had to reject an Iranian proposal that agreement on Bahrain must be subject to agreement on the islands…"[106] In fact, however, although the British no longer favored this, they had earlier contemplated and even proposed to the Shah and King Faisal a link between Bahrain and the Tunbs. Moreover, Wright heard more of this bargain within days.

On March 21, Alam wrote that the Shah "told me of...his disappointment at the British attitude towards the islands, especially Abu Musa which he was sure he'd bagged after his declaration on Bahrain."[107] Two days later, Alam states:

> ...The British Ambassador called. I told him we can reach no settlement on Bahrain until we know the fate of Tunbs and Abu Musa. In that case, he declared, we have all been wasting our time. 'So be it,' I said. He then suggested we approach the Sheikh of Sharjah as we did the Sheikh of Ras al-Khaimah. A deal might be struck and the British would back us.

Despite Wright's rejection of Alam's insistence on linking Bahrain with the islands, Alam nevertheless wrote: "The ambassador seemed more inclined than he was the other day to link any solution for Bahrain to proposals over the islands. He hinted that if Iran were to back the creation of an Arab Federation in the Emirates, then we might well be called upon to occupy the islands on the Federation's behalf, without any fear of a backlash from the Arabs."[108]

The British were being careful about linkage and any package deal. First, Bahrain was more important to them and they wanted it settled first. Indeed, the British saw this as a key to the establishment of a nine-member federation, one that would include Bahrain. They did not want to promise to deliver the Tunbs or to conform to Iranian *desiderata* on the sequence of implementing a package deal whereby Iran would first get satisfaction on the islands and then yield Bahrain. The British reference to Iran occupying the islands on behalf of the federation suggests that Iran would get a security presence but not sovereignty and appears to refer to the Tunbs as well as Abu Musa. Britain wanted these outcomes to emerge from direct negotiations between Iran and Sharjah, Ras al-Khaimah and Saudi Arabia without Britain explicitly agreeing to them or even promoting them to the emirates.

On April 5, after SAVAK official Ali Farazian had visited Sharjah and told Shaikh Khalid that Iran wanted to put a military base on Abu Musa, to which Khalid had replied that he could not enter into negotiations, British Foreign Secretary Michael Stewart advised Crawford and Bullard to tell Shaikh Khalid that while Britain recognized Sharjah's sovereignty over Abu Musa, Britain would not be able to uphold

Sharjah's claim after 1971 and had "no objection" to Khalid discussing the island with Iran. Crawford replied that any early discussion would be unlikely to give Iran what it wanted and could complicate matters. The Embassy in Tehran informed SAVAK head Nematollah Nasiri that if Khalid refused to discuss the subject it was not on British advice. Bullard spoke to Khalid as instructed. By doing so, Britain's Labour Government was signaling to Shaikh Khalid that he should not rely on the recent comments of Conservative Party leader Edward Heath, who had said during a March and April tour of the Gulf that Britain should remain in the Gulf.[109]

Alam's April 30, 1969 diary reads:

> I reported the comments of the British ambassador [at a meeting with Alam on April 29], who tells me that the delay in negotiations with Bahrain springs from the Sheikh's reluctance to allow the UN Secretary-General U Thant to send a fact-finding mission to the island at the invitation of Britain and Iran. This has come as a real surprise. According to HIM, 'We shall accept no compromise on Bahrain until the status of Abu Musa and Tunbs has been clarified.' I told him that I had already made this point clear to the ambassador, but HIM instructed me to make it doubly clear.[110]

On May 27, 1969, Alam met Foreign Secretary Stewart. Alam's version of his argument and Stewart's reply is as follows:

> [F]aced with HIM's magnanimity and vision in negotiations over Bahrain and the creation of a Federation of Arab Emirates, the British continue to drag their feet in respect to restoring our islands of Tunbs and Abu Musa. As I told him, he must be well aware that Britain had gained unlawful possession of these islands and handed them as blighted inheritance to the Sheikhs of Sharjah and Ras al-Khaimah whom his government now supports against Iran. We can see no sense in this policy, since Iran is set to become the Emirates' sole protector once the British withdraw. He thought for a while before delivering the following reply. Its wisdom disarms me: 'You are absolutely correct in all you say. Britain cannot simply disregard the concerns of the Arab world, but I tell you in all good faith that I consider it our duty to ensure that the islands are restored to Iran.[111]

Wright gives another version of the conversation: "Stewart explained that the islands were not ours to give away and could not be part and parcel of a Bahrain settlement, but he promised to do what he could to deliver them – going, I thought, rather further in this direction than was wise. I wrote in my diary 'The Stewart visit was a success – he is perhaps over-sold on Iran and her islands claims, etc.'"[112] Stewart himself wrote that he had "made it quite clear to the Iranians that the settlement of Bahrain was both indispensable to progress in the Gulf and our essential first requirement." He also wrote: "I think we shall be able to resist their [Iranian] conditions about a package involving Bahrain and the Lesser Islands." Nevertheless, and even though he called Iranian claims to sovereignty over these islands "dubious," he subsequently suggested that Britain should press the Rulers on the islands:

> I recognize that we cannot...deliver a concession by the Rulers and I reiterated this in Tehran. Nevertheless, they cannot serve either our interest or their own by standing on our support of their sovereignty hitherto, even though...we have repeatedly reaffirmed it within the last year to the Iranians in the case of Abu Musa.[113]

Alam's version suggests that Stewart supported the Iranian view regarding Abu Musa and the Tunbs, although the Foreign Office knew that Alam's version of the historical record was not accurate and Stewart himself wrote that Iran's claims were "dubious." It also indicates that the Foreign Secretary went so far as to say that the British considered it their "duty" to "restore" the islands to Iran. Even Wright's version states that Stewart said he would do what he could to "deliver" them, but that this could not be linked in any package deal including Bahrain. All three versions suggest that Stewart was now willing to help Iran get satisfaction on Abu Musa and the Tunbs.

In April 1968, Stewart had approved of the plan to garrison Abu Musa in the event of an Iranian occupation of the Tunbs, but this was designed only to prevent forcible occupation of Abu Musa before the British withdrawal and certainly envisioned acquiescence in forcible occupation of the Tunbs before British withdrawal. While the British were already on record as favoring Iran's acquisition of the Tunbs, they had resisted Iranian claims to Abu Musa. Although Wright's ideas on delivering the Tunbs and Abu Musa meant promoting an Iranian occupation of the islands on behalf of and therefore perhaps under the sovereignty of an Arab federation, it would soon become clear that Stewart's ideas on the three islands were more favorable to Iran.

Nevertheless, Stewart's remarks did not entirely satisfy the Shah, to whom Alam reported his discussions on May 28: "He ordered me to let the British know that a satisfactory response to our demands over the islands remains a pre-condition of any future settlement over Bahrain..."[114] On May 31, however, when Afshar argued to Wright that the Iranian public would be dismayed if Abu Musa and the Tunbs were "surrendered" in addition to Bahrain, Wright held to the position that a package deal including Bahrain was not possible and that the best deal on the islands would be Sirri and the Tunbs for Iran and Abu Musa for the Arabs.[115]

In the meantime, Stewart's remarks raised questions for Weir in Bahrain, who asked on May 30 for confirmation that Britain's position on Abu Musa had not changed.[116] The Foreign Office, however, was now considering "how to put into effect the commitment to the Iranians to renew pressure on the Rulers of Ras al-Khaimah and Sharjah to take an initiative over negotiations with the Iranians with a view to meeting Iranian demands over Abu Musa and the Tunbs." The Foreign Office noted that Britain had an interest in "appeasing" Iran, but was concerned that too much pressure on the Rulers would undermine British influence on the formation of the UAE. Additionally, it was concerned that anything that undermined the Rulers' authority would complicate Britain's withdrawal, and therefore recommended pressing the Rulers to enter into median line negotiations with the Shah. The Foreign Office speculated that Britain and Sharjah might even earn "grudging respect" from the Shah if Sharjah expressed willingness to discuss the median line and refused to discuss Abu Musa.[117]

Nevertheless, Stewart instructed Crawford and Bullard in a telegram on June 13 to argue to both Rulers that there was "a chance that they could secure their material interests (i.e. the mineral rights, and equitable median line (with none of the islands carrying an effect on the construction of the median line) and possibly some financial benefits as well). In return, they would have to be prepared to lease the islands or permit the Iranians to establish joint military facilities, or perhaps contemplate some form of joint sovereignty with Iran." He argued that such negotiations "could yield the Rulers two important benefits which would greatly exceed the value of the islands themselves: Iranian agreement to equitable division of the exploitation of the sea bed (which in purely economic terms could be very important over any oil which may lie around the median zone) and amicable relations with their powerful neighbor, Iran, in the future." Thus, both Sharjah and Ras al-Khaimah should initiate median line negotiations with Iran, discuss the islands in this context, and be prepared to accept the outcome Stewart outlined, even if it meant joint sovereignty.[118] The answer to Weir's question, then, was that Stewart was indeed changing Britain's position on Abu Musa.

Crawford's reply to Stewart on June 19 recommended delaying this approach to the Rulers until after Britain and Iran reached agreement over the procedures to be followed in resolving the future of Bahrain. Otherwise, he argued, an early initiative by the Rulers would encourage the Shah to link progress on Bahrain to his demands on the islands. Wright responded that, despite everything the Shah had said, he did not think the Shah would make progress on Bahrain conditional on the islands. Instead, the Shah might become suspicious if there were no approach from the Rulers and that this in itself could affect progress on Bahrain. Stewart considered these arguments and renewed his instructions to Crawford to make an early approach to the Rulers. When Bullard did so on June 26, Shaikh Saqr calmly said he had already offered a lease and a military base to Iran but had been refused. Shaikh Khalid insisted that Abu Musa belonged to the people of Sharjah and the Arabian peninsula and was not his to lease or give away.[119]

For the next few months, the British struggled to persuade either the Rulers or the Iranians to initiate contact with the other. In early July, as these efforts were underway, Wright informed Afshar that Britain had encouraged both Rulers to reach agreements on the islands satisfactory to both sides and that the Iranians should assure the Rulers that they would be reasonable and generous. Afshar argued that the islands could not be "abandoned," hinted at Iranian occupation of the islands after 1971, and "expressed concern that the example of Bahrain 'getting its independence' might encourage the rulers to intransigence." Wright repeated that Britain had encouraged the Rulers to reach agreement with Iran before British withdrawal and that Britain would continue to do so. Bullard subsequently encouraged Shaikh Saqr in mid-July, and Goronwy Roberts encouraged Sharjah's Shaikh Khalid during Khalid's late-July visit to London.[120] Alam then wrote on August 8 that according to Wright: "Firstly, Michael Stewart has badgered the

Sheikhs of Ras al-Khaimah and Sharjah into agreeing to some sort of arrangement with us over the islands of Tunbs and Abu Musa. Next, negotiations for a plebiscite in Bahrain are making satisfactory headway."[121]

On September 12, Afshar visited the Foreign Office in London and indicated that he had only learned of the strength of Iran's claims to the islands during the past year. He referred to documents allegedly showing that Iran had sovereignty until sixty years earlier, i.e. the early 1900s, argued that Iranian sovereignty had only been frustrated by British threats of force, and referred to maps supposedly showing Iranian sovereignty. The Foreign Office answered that it did not agree that Iran's case was strong and noted that it had previously offered to exchange documentation. Afshar said exchanging documentation would be "inappropriate" since the parties were not going to the ICJ. Once again, Iran was not producing any documents. On September 15, Afshar told the Foreign Office that the Iranian Foreign Ministry had decided to contact both Rulers "urgently" and invite them to Iran.[122]

At the same time, the Shah publicly insisted that he would not recognize a federation including Bahrain or an independent Bahrain and that Iran would leave the UN if the UN admitted Bahrain. Some have interpreted these remarks as a warning that Britain must stay involved in the bargaining over the procedures for determining Bahrain's will and that Iran would not accept any unilateral British decision to grant independence to Bahrain.[123] However, the Shah was also using the Bahrain issue to pressure the British on the islands and he was in a strong position to do so.

On July 25, US President Richard Nixon had articulated the Nixon Doctrine, which called upon the US's Asian friends, including South Vietnam, to take greater responsibility for their own defense. This doctrine would also be applied in the Gulf, where the Nixon administration viewed Iran as capable of playing an important role in defending its own as well as the West's interests.[124] After the Shah's October 21-23 visit to Washington, the United States and Britain subsequently agreed to a one billion dollar defense program in which the United States would sell Phantoms and Britain would sell tanks and naval units to Iran.[125]

Alam's account of a November 9 conversation about the islands with the British Ambassador indicates that Wright was now more explicit about Abu Musa and the Tunbs and that the Iranians were not satisfied: "'We are bound', said the ambassador, 'by our commitments to the Sheikhs of Sharjah and Ras al-Khaimah, but we will nevertheless encourage them to reach some sort of accommodation with Iran, provided always that you confine yourselves to an occupation based on mutual agreement or a lease, and do not insist on pressing a claim to occupy the islands by legal right.'" Alam answered, "This makes no sense; go about it any other way, and we face a new confrontation with the Arabs..."[126] Wright's report to the Foreign Office on this meeting notes that he told Alam "that so long as the Iranians insisted on the rulers recognizing Iranian sovereignty over the islands I could see no chance of a solution."[127]

The Foreign Office then developed the formula that Iran, Ras al-Khaimah and Sharjah would state publicly that they were convinced of their respective sovereignty over the islands and that they agreed to differ over this issue. In that context, Iran would establish garrisons on the islands for some years, benefits from any mineral rights would be shared, and Iran would contribute financially to the development of Ras al-Khaimah and Sharjah. On November 19, Wright proposed this formula to the Shah, although he omitted the point about Iran making financial contributions to the development of the two shaikhdoms. The Shah said a solution might be possible along these lines, but asked Britain not to weaken Iran's bargaining position by revealing to the Rulers the extent to which Iran would compromise on sovereignty. Stewart was encouraged and suggested that Bullard inform the Rulers that there was flexibility in the Shah's positions without going into too much detail.

Crawford, however, answered that Wright had now weakened the Rulers' bargaining positions by not making any distinction between Abu Musa and the Tunbs, by undercutting Iran's earlier proposal that the two emirates should have all the mineral rights, and by not mentioning Iranian financial contributions to the development of the two emirates. He cautioned that Iranian garrisons should not be established until after the British withdrawal, and advised that Iran should be told of the distinction between Abu Musa and the Tunbs as well as the need for financial assistance to the Rulers and recognition of the Rulers' rights on the islands, e.g. the flying of their flags. Crawford said that he wanted to be able to tell the Rulers that Britain had proposed to Iran "that a practical solution should be sought under which none of the parties would have to renounce their claims," and that Britain had warned Iran that it would have to offer financial compensation, including the "apportionment" of mineral resources.[128]

With Wright on leave, Donald Murray at the Embassy in Tehran responded that it was too early to discuss details of proposals, the timing of garrisons, or the idea of financial compensation with the Rulers. Evan Luard at the Foreign Office in London disagreed, arguing that the point about financial compensation should be made to Iran and that the Rulers should be told the details of the proposals as suggested by Crawford. However, after advice from Anthony Acland and Donald McCarthy at the Foreign Office, Stewart instructed Crawford on November 27 to say only that "[t]he islands came up in discussion" between Wright and the Shah, and not to go into details about sovereignty, garrisons, or mineral rights, but to suggest that there was some Iranian flexibility. Stewart also instructed Crawford to note that Britain had made the point to Iran about financial compensation in earlier conversations.[129] Stewart did not want the Rulers to know that Britain had proposed a formula to Iran, that the Shah was considering an agreement to disagree on sovereignty, or that the British had undercut the Shah's previous offer on mineral rights. In essence, the Rulers were to go blind into these meetings with the Shah.

In December, Bullard spoke as instructed to the Rulers. Murray suggested to Iranian Foreign Ministry Under-Secretary Abbas Ali Khalatbari that Iran should at the right time offer financial contributions to the development of the shaikhdoms, to which Khalatbari quickly agreed, noting that Iran had already expressed this willingness. Meanwhile, Murray had advised Alam that "[i]f...the Iranians intended to explore the possibilities of a solution on the basis of putting aside the sovereignty issue, they would need to put this over with a lot of careful explaining." In a subsequent meeting, however, Khalatbari said that Foreign Minister Zahedi had talked to the Shah and that "there could be no question of putting in doubt the Iranian rights of sovereignty over the Tunbs and no question of not mentioning sovereignty at all." Murray recorded his response as follows:

> I said the best course of all would be not to talk about sovereignty but the Iranian position was understandable and I would not question it. This was all a matter of tactful handling.

> If the Iranians intended to tell Ras al-Khaimah that they were convinced of their sovereignty they must expect him to do the same and the essential aim should be for both sides to say their piece in a way which would allow amicable agreement to disagree so that there could then be rational discussion of practical requirements of the situation.[130]

It appears from Khalatbari's remarks that Iran did not intend to offer the idea on sovereignty discussed by Wright and the Shah. Indeed, when Ras al-Khaimah's Shaikh Saqr visited Tehran in December 1969, and when Sharjah's Shaikh Khalid visited Tehran in January, 1970, the Iranians did not make this compromise proposal on sovereignty. Instead, Iran and the two Rulers pressed their respective claims to sovereignty and negotiations broke down. The Rulers proposed that Iran exchange documents with them supporting their respective claims, but during the early months of 1970 Iran did not respond.[131]

On April 29, 1970, days before Ras al-Khaimah's Shaikh Saqr was to visit the Foreign Office in London, the Political Director of Iran's Foreign Ministry, Manuchehr Zelli, summoned Wright and expressed the hope that Britain would take this opportunity to pressure Ras al-Khaimah to settle the Tunbs issue with Iran. Wright answered that "If [a] settlement was to be reached we believed that [the] question of sovereignty must be blurred." Zelli said sovereignty was "not negotiable," and Wright answered that "if sovereignty was not negotiable I saw no possibility of settlement except through force." Wright asked Zelli to consider how the Rulers could possibly survive Arab propaganda attacks if they yielded sovereignty and argued that "if [the] Iranian interest in the islands was strategic there was no reason to make an issue of sovereignty."

Wright then reminded him that Sharjah's Shaikh Khalid was waiting for an Iranian answer to the suggestion made by Khalid in January that Sharjah and Iran should exchange documents supporting their respective claims. When Zelli answered that Iran had no intention of exchanging documents, Wright told him, "I deplored this given that I was always being told that Iran had irrefutable proof in support of their claims."[132] Upon learning this from Wright, the Foreign Office concluded that "It therefore seems likely that the Iranians will also refuse to exchange documents with the Ruler of Ras al-Khaimah, but this is not yet entirely clear."[133]

When Shaikh Saqr met with British officials on May 6, Peter Hayman of the Foreign Office stressed British support for a union of nine and the importance of Ras al-Khaimah reaching an agreement with Iran over the Tunbs before British withdrawal, suggesting that the latter would generate Iranian goodwill toward a union, facilitate agreement on a median line between Iran and the Trucial States, and promote stability in the Gulf. Hayman also stated Britain's opposition to any unilateral effort by Ras al-Khaimah to extend its territorial sea to twelve miles, particularly around the Tunbs. Hayman told Saqr that Britain could only play the role of an "honest broker" on the question of the Tunbs. However, Hayman and his colleagues did not share details about British proposals to Iran or Iranian reactions to them. However, Saqr knew Iran's positions. In reporting to Bullard on Hayman's conversation with Saqr, the Foreign Office's M.A. Holding wrote: "Saqr is determined not to negotiate on the question of sovereignty over the islands…he would prefer the Iranians to take the islands by force rather than renounce his sovereignty as part of a deal."[134]

In the meantime, Britain and Iran had agreed in March on a formula for ascertaining the wishes of the people of Bahrain and in April a UN fact-finding mission found that the people of Bahrain wanted a fully independent, sovereign Arab state. Alam complained to Wright on April 19 that the "stalwart approach" Britain expected from Iran "requires us to solve the Bahrain question before that of the Tunbs and Abu Musa, whilst meanwhile the Sheikhs of Sharjah and Ras al-Khaimah mock us behind our backs."[135]

This tends to support the argument that once the Shah had yielded on Bahrain, he needed to save face by acquiring the islands. Years later, however, Alinaghi Alikhani, who edited and translated Alam's diaries into English, wrote that "the Iranian public reacted favourably [to the outcome on Bahrain], contrary to the Shah's fears."[136] This raises doubt about whether the Shah really had to "climb down" and "lose face" and then "save face" through a public success in being "compensated" with the islands. At the same time, US Assistant Secretary of State Joseph Sisco asked King Faisal about Saudi-Iranian cooperation to promote stability in the Gulf. Faisal answered that he understood the need for this, but that Iranian claims to Arab territory made this difficult, although a beginning had now been made. The

British understood this to mean that Iranian claims to the islands made cooperation difficult, although the resolution of the Bahrain issue was a beginning.[137]

On May 22, 1970, the Shah conveyed a demand through Alam to British Ambassador Wright that Sharjah and Umm al-Quwain should not drill for oil in a twelve-mile territorial sea offshore of Abu Musa. The Shah threatened to use force to stop drilling, and even to use force against Britain if it supported the Shaikhs. Britain quickly complied with the Shah's demand. Alam wrote:

> The [British] ambassador pleaded with me to discourage any confrontation over Abu Musa; if needs be Iran should lodge a written protest. At the same time he would do all within his power to prevent drilling around the island, although Occidental Petroleum has already been granted a concession there...”[138]

Sir Denis Wright has explained that if the Shah had used force to stop this drilling, the Rulers would have asked Britain to defend their rights under the protection treaties, and that Britain wished to avoid such an escalation of the situation.[139] This may have been especially true only one month before the upcoming general election in the UK. Wright wrote to the Foreign Office on May 28:

> Although the Bahrain exercise went off so well I suspect that the Shah is suffering some second thoughts now that he is face to face with the trickier problem of the other disputed islands and realizes he is not going to get them on a plate...Some of his anger may be simulated; in other words a deliberate tactic to force our hands on the islands.”[140]

However, inasmuch as the British did not act in the spirit of their early 1968 decision to defend Abu Musa, this can be seen as another point at which the British acquiesced on the islands issue. In fact, they acted in a way that was consistent with Stewart's intention to satisfy the Shah. Moreover, they signaled to the Shah that they were responsive to threats.

Nevertheless, despite the drilling ban imposed by the British, Iran was not satisfied. Alam writes on May 29, 1970 that he told Ambassador Wright as follows:

> HIM feels that Britain hasn't budged an inch over the islands...With regard to the islands I warned him that his

country would forfeit all credibility if there were no new initiative soon. Why, he [Wright] asked, were we so insistent on the question of legal sovereignty over the islands. Far simpler for us just to occupy them. Solve the issue in one fell swoop. A typically British suggestion, but a suggestion with which I just happen to agree.

Alam does not explain what Wright meant by occupation here, and Wright does not believe he used this language, but Wright had said on November 9, 1969 that he meant occupation by agreement or lease. On May 30, Alam writes that the Shah planned to cause difficulty for the federation of emirates by forcing every member to conclude and finance separate defense arrangements with Iran. However, Alam had also asked at his May 29 meeting with Wright that Britain help Iran get a 100 million pound loan from Kuwait so Iran could make military and other purchases from Britain. "The Shah is a man of insight," Alam writes, "and knows full well when to throw yet another card onto the bargaining table."[141] Clearly the Shah, who was not satisfied with Britain in the aftermath of the Bahrain outcome, was not only threatening force and planning obstruction, but was also dangling a reward.

In early June, Bullard learned that Ras al-Khaimah's Shaikh Saqr had accepted an invitation to visit Iraq. Bullard told Saqr that "the visit would annoy Saqr's real friends, damage the U.A.E. and entangle him in dealings with Iraq from which he would not be able to escape. The Iraqi philosophy of Baathism and revolution was quite contrary to Saqr's interests." Bullard recommended that Crawford orchestrate cautionary advice from other Rulers and Crawford did so, recommending that the Rulers be told that "a visit would be likely to give offense to the Iranians, and, in view of the recent propaganda about a possible deal over the Tunbs, to reduce Saqr's freedom of manoeuvre on that problem."

Crawford also instructed Bullard to continue trying to dissuade Saqr from going and Bullard tried, but without success. Crawford concluded that "we must reconcile ourselves to Saqr paying this visit and doing the best we can to discourage him from embarrassing initiatives or statements." Indeed, Bullard had expressed concern that "it may even be that the Iraqis have offered to put a garrison on the islands before the Shah does so." He thus elicited a promise from Saqr not to discuss the details of his discussions with Iran on the islands. He was relieved to report after the trip that "Iraq has not yet argued that she must occupy the islands herself lest they fall into hostile hands."[142]

On June 9, as Shaikh Saqr was preparing his trip to Baghdad, Alam writes that he complained to Wright about the shaikhs traveling in the Arab world and spreading "misunderstanding" about the islands and that Britain was not lending a hand to Iran: "'Again I tell you, the islands will be ours come what may.' 'And I tell you', he [Wright] said, 'that we shall answer force with force to defend the islands.'" After Alam's "tirade," the British Ambassador "confessed that he's been so upset over the past fortnight that he's had difficulty sleeping. 'I'm at a loss to know what I should tell you, or what I should report to London', he said, 'and for that matter London is at its wits' end knowing what to say to the Sheikhs. We're all of us in the soup.' He confided one final point before leaving: 'Following representations from Iraq, the Soviet ambassador came to tell me that I'd be ill-advised to contemplate an Iranian takeover in the islands. So much, you see, for the friendship between Iran and her so-called comrades in the North!'"[143]

This exchange reveals that the British were still trying to prevent a forcible take-over of the islands by Iran before the British withdrawal. This was British bluffing, however, because a decision had already been made in 1968 not to defend the Tunbs and the British had just weeks earlier imposed the ban on drilling around Abu Musa in the face of an Iranian threat to use force in part so that they would not be called upon to honor the protection treaties.[144]

Thus, when Iran put forward some ideas about joint occupation, the British embraced them. Alam writes of Ambassador Wright on June 19, the day after the Labour party lost the election in Britain to the Conservatives:

> He admitted that he had been unable to dissuade the Sheikh of Ras al-Khaimah from traveling to Baghdad. 'But we are pressing him [the Ruler of Ras al-Khaimah] and the Sheikh of Sharjah to accept a solution to the problem of the islands in line with the Iranian proposal for joint occupation. We have stressed to them that this is a rare opportunity, a genuine prospect of a settlement thanks to the magnanimity of Iran.' Like HIM the ambassador is convinced that the British withdrawal from the Gulf has already gone too far to be reversed.[145]

Several years later, in 1974, when addressing the question of whether or not Britain and Iran had agreed to a package deal by which Iran would yield on Bahrain in exchange for the islands, Chubin and Zabih wrote:

> Although Iran sought to obtain the return [*sic*] of the islands as part of a package deal in which it relinquished its claim to Bahrayn, no formal or explicit agreement on such a *quid pro quo* was reached. Nevertheless, it was the Iranian government's understanding that in the wake of the goodwill created by the Bahrayn settlement, Britain would not actively oppose Iran's claim to the islands, and might even bring its influence to bear on the relevant shaykhdoms on behalf of Iran's claim.[146]

Actually, the historical record shows that Britain's Labour Government had proposed a package deal, although it did not include Abu Musa for Iran, and although there had been no formal or explicit agreement on it between Britain and Iran. The British had tried to persuade the Ruler of Ras al-Khaimah to give up the Tunbs, but had not succeeded. They then discouraged Iran from thinking in terms of a package deal including Bahrain.

Indeed, Britain had revised its thinking about the islands and had thought of Iranian occupation of the Tunbs and also Abu Musa on behalf of a federation and through a lease or some other form of mutual agreement. Following this, they had thought of joint sovereignty or an arrangement in which the parties agreed to disagree about sovereignty. However, after accepting Bahrain's independence in May 1970, Iran pressed even harder for the islands. As Sir Denis Wright noted, the euphoria over the Bahrain settlement did not last for long.[147] In his words, "...the Shah believed that, unless he kept up the pressure, he stood little chance of acquiring the islands peacefully, no matter which party won the impending elections in the United Kingdom."[148]

The International Community and the Islands Dispute in the 1970s

When the Conservatives gained power in the United Kingdom on June 18, 1970, they continued to criticize the Labour Party's decision to withdraw from the Gulf, as they had done while in opposition and during the campaign. The new Secretary of State for Foreign Affairs, Sir Alec Douglas-Home, told the House of Commons on July 6 that Britain might maintain small units and maintenance bases in the Gulf, would work to help resolve the many local disputes that he said had been unleashed by the Labour decision, and would consult with the Gulf leaders on how to contribute to stability in the area. However, he did not promise to reverse the Labour decision.[1]

On July 10, Douglas-Home consulted with the Shah, who had already publicly called on the new Conservative government led by Prime Minister Edward Heath to implement the withdrawal decision.[2] Alam writes that the Shah was "delighted" by this meeting.[3] Indeed, Wright notes that after this meeting, Douglas-Home "came back feeling, I think, that HMG must do more than hitherto to put pressure on the Sheikhs over the islands." He also writes:

> I flew back to Tehran the following day feeling that my journey had been worthwhile and that the Foreign Office were taking 'a very sensible line' on the Gulf (i.e. on the need for withdrawal and the need to accommodate the Shah over the islands), though I doubt whether my view was shared by those in charge of Arab interests.[4]

Actually, even Crawford, who had protested the withdrawal decision in 1968, and other British officials in Arab capitals now agreed with

Wright and many Foreign Office officials in London that the process of withdrawal had gone too far to be reversed.[5] Moreover, in the following weeks, Iran, Saudi Arabia and Kuwait all said they wanted the British to withdraw, although Shaikh Rashid bin Saeed Al-Maktoum of Dubai argued that all of the smaller emirates wanted the British to remain.[6]

As time would tell, the Conservative policy on withdrawal and also on federation would be no different from the Labour policy, while its policy on Abu Musa and the Tunbs would be more accommodating to Iranian demands than the Labour policy had been. Moreover, the Conservatives would receive support for their policy on Abu Musa and the Tunbs from the US State Department.[7]

At the end of July 1970, Douglas-Home appointed former Aden Governor and later Bahrain Political Resident Sir William Luce to consult with Gulf leaders and to report on Britain's options in the Gulf. Luce had published his views on the subject of Britain's role in the Gulf after retiring in 1966, well before the Labour Government's 1968 decision to withdraw from the Gulf. He had written in 1967 that Britain had a continuing interest in maintaining the peace and security of the inherently unstable Gulf, particularly because of the importance of its oil to the West. As far as Luce was concerned, there was no single Gulf power friendly to Western oil interests that could fill the vacuum that would be left by an early British withdrawal. It was also important, in his view, to achieve Saudi-Iranian agreement on the territorial inviolability of the Gulf states, a union of the small emirates supported by the leadership of Saudi Arabia, and a reconciliation between Saudi Arabia and Oman.

Furthermore, the timing of Britain's eventual withdrawal from the Gulf should not be made unilaterally or arbitrarily, although Luce recognized that Britain would eventually have to withdraw. Thus, he had argued that Britain should strive "to terminate honourably our special treaty relationship with the Gulf states and to withdraw without undue risk to the peace and stability of the region." Two years later, in October 1969, after the Labour Government's decision to withdraw, Luce argued that any hesitation about withdrawing on schedule would reduce the incentive for the emirates to federate. Nevertheless, he also warned against leaving the area "wide open to uncontested Russian influence" and therefore advocated offering assurances of support to an Arab federation and the deployment of a British naval force in the Indian Ocean that would pay frequent visits to the Gulf.[8]

On his departure for the Gulf on August 19, Luce said he would have "wide-ranging discussions with Gulf leaders on the best mutually-acceptable security arrangements for the area."[9] He learned in these discussions that Saudi Arabia, Kuwait, Qatar, Oman, Iraq and Nasser's Egypt wanted Britain to withdraw on schedule, but most of the smaller emirates wanted the British to remain. He also heard that there was general support among these states for a union of nine, although Bahrain expressed interest in independence.[10]

Luce also focused on the islands issue. When he met with King Faisal on August 22, Luce explained: "H.M.G. was proposing that the Ruler of Ras al-Khaimah should reach an agreement with the Iranians over the stationing of an Iranian garrison on the Tunbs; the preamble to the agreement would probably contain a formula stating that the agreement was without prejudice to the views of the parties concerning sovereignty over the islands." Luce told Kamal Adham later that day that he was "disappointed" with Faisal's rejection of these ideas and said that Britain was "convinced" that the Shah "was not to be shaken in his determination to get satisfaction soon."[11]

Luce also discussed this in the following weeks with Kuwait's Acting Emir Shaikh Jabir, Bahrain's Emir Shaikh Issa, Abu Dhabi's Shaikh Zayed, Dubai's Shaikh Rashid, Sharjah's Shaikh Khalid and Ras al-Khaimah's Shaikh Saqr. Luce argued to Shaikh Saqr that the "without prejudice" formula "would allow the question of sovereignty to remain undisturbed; i.e. both sides would continue, as they did now, to claim sovereignty over the Tunbs." Luce doubted that the Shah would be willing to ask permission in writing to station a garrison on the Tunbs, as Saqr wanted him to do, and argued that "the insertion of the 'without prejudice' formula would safeguard Ras al-Khaimah's claim to sovereignty; the fact of Iran signing an agreement would to some extent strengthen Ras al-Khaimah's position." Finally, he asked Ras al-Khaimah to consider a package deal with a "without prejudice" formula.[12]

In mid-September, Luce met with the Shah, Prime Minister Hoveyda, and Foreign Minister Zahedi. Zahedi told reporters Iran had again stressed its opposition to any British military presence in the Gulf after 1971.[13] Duncan Slater, Luce's aide, adds that the Shah also said there could be no federation until he was satisfied on the islands.[14]

Before leaving Tehran for Cairo on September 22, Luce said Britain was not insisting on the establishment of the federation as a condition for the withdrawal of British forces but that it was "trying very hard indeed" to speed up its formation.[15] After concluding his tour of the Gulf, Luce submitted a preliminary recommendation for withdrawal on schedule and the stationing of a naval force in the vicinity, essentially what he had previously advocated in his publications.[16]

After Luce returned to London and reported on his mission, Foreign Secretary Douglas-Home stressed to Iranian and American officials the importance of a Saudi role in resolving the islands issue. Meeting Zahedi in New York on September 25, Douglas-Home asked if King Faisal was "still unwilling to recommend that the rulers should come to terms with Iran," and Zahedi answered that King Faisal and the Emir of Kuwait had said that the issue was not important to them.[17] On October 16, Douglas-Home told the Shah's confidante Abbas Massoudi that "a main difficulty would disappear if King Faisal would tell the Rulers that progress must be made." Britain was "doing what we could, but the Rulers were concerned about Arab opinion…Agreement could be reached with King Faisal's help. He could do it if he would."[18] Thus on October 20, Douglas-Home told US Secretary of State William Rogers and US Assistant Secretary of State Joseph Sisco:

> The main trouble [in achieving a union of nine] was that King Faisal would not use his influence to promote this, or to persuade the two Shaikhdoms to reach a reasonable accommodation over the Gulf islands. Anything which the US Government could do tactfully to persuade Faisal to play a helpful role would be useful. A solution of the islands problem was the key to securing Iranian backing for the UAE.[19]

Moreover, when Prime Minister Edward Heath visited the UN from October 19 to 24, he recommended to Iran that it continue to urge Saudi Arabia and other Arab friends, perhaps even the new regime in Egypt after Nasser's death, to encourage Ras al-Khaimah and Sharjah to reach an agreement with Iran over the islands based on joint Arab/Iranian garrisons on the islands, while leaving the question of sovereignty in abeyance.[20]

In the meantime, Luce visited the Gulf again from October 13 to 19 for discussions in Bahrain, Kuwait and Qatar. His main purpose on this trip was to promote the nine-member federation, but on this matter he did not succeed. First, Qatar was opposed to Bahraini inclusion in a federation.[21] Second, his meetings in Bahrain made it clear that Bahrain itself was keen on independence.[22] Meanwhile, Iran formally notified Britain and the shaikhdoms that it would not recognize or support a federation until it gained the islands.[23] A British official subsequently expressed pessimism about the nine-member federation to the American Consul in Dhahran.[24]

By late September, British efforts conducted by Sir Gawain Bell to mediate the dispute over oil operations in Abu Musa's offshore waters had not produced any results. Over the following months, the US State Department remained neutral in this dispute, which involved two American companies, the Occidental Oil Company and the Buttes Gas and Oil Company, and deferred to Britain's mediation of the dispute.[25] In late October, for example, the State Department declined a request from Buttes representatives to persuade Britain to submit the matter to binding arbitration.

The State Department was influenced in part by Iran's position on the issue. They advised the Buttes representatives that a State Department official had been told in Tehran that Iran unequivocally asserted sovereignty over Abu Musa and the Tunbs and the necessity for Iran to control these islands, although Iran would be generous to the Shaikhs, flexible about the modalities of control and would "fuzz" the question of sovereignty.[26] It was not until April 1971 that Douglas-Home decided that Sir Gawain Bell's mediation had run its course and recommended arbitration of the disputed claims between Sharjah and Umm al-Qaiwain (and Ajman).[27]

Responding to British and Iranian requests, the State Department supported British and Iranian efforts to persuade Ras al-Khaimah and Sharjah to reach an agreement with Iran over the islands, particularly by appealing to Saudi Arabia for help. On October 23, the US Embassy in Tehran provided the State Department with an account by Iranian Acting Foreign Minister Abbas Ali Khalatbari of an October 17 meeting in Geneva between Iranian Foreign Minister Zahedi and Saudi Arabian King Faisal in which Khalatbari claimed that Faisal said the islands dispute "was none of his affair." The memo noted: "Recalling Khalatbari's request to Ambassador [Douglas] MacArthur [II] that

USG [i.e. the US Government] send emissary to Faisal in support of Zahedi's efforts (Ref A), I informed him that while USG had not been able to arrange for such a person Ambassador Thacher had registered with Saudi For[eign] Ministry strong US interest in Saudi-Iranian cooperation in Gulf and had asked that Faisal be informed of our views. (Ref B)."[28]

On October 26, six days after hearing Douglas-Home's request for US help with Saudi Arabia, US Assistant Secretary of State Sisco asked Saudi Acting Foreign Minister Al-Saqqaf if Saudi Arabia could encourage the Shaikhs of Sharjah and Ras al-Khaimah to reach an arrangement with Iran. As noted previously, Al-Saqqaf replied that Saudi Arabia could not say even this much because this would mean that Saudi Arabia supported bargaining over Arab rights to the islands.[29]

The British also kept the Americans informed about continuing British efforts. On November 6, 1970, a State Department telegram reported that the new British Political Resident Sir Geoffrey Arthur, who had replaced Crawford in October, had urged the Rulers of Ras al-Khaimah and Sharjah on November 3 to promptly settle the Tunbs and Abu Musa disputes with Iran. Arthur told Shaikh Saqr of Ras al-Khaimah on November 3 that if the Tunbs issue was not resolved there would be no Federation of Arab Emirates, Iran would seize the islands when Britain withdrew, and Ras al-Khaimah could not expect help from Britain or anyone else. "Saqr could no longer afford to consider [the] Iranian claim on historic or legal grounds; it was [a] practical political problem requiring urgent solution."[30] The British message to Saqr was that Ras al-Khaimah's historical and legal rights were not going to stop Britain from pressuring Ras al-Khaimah to satisfy Iran. Arthur may have made the same arguments to Sharjah's Ruler. Indeed, *Al-Rai Al-Aam* and *Kayhan International* both reported on November 9 that Iran would use force to take the islands if its claims were not satisfied. *Kayhan* reported that the Shah had conveyed this warning to both Sharjah and Ras al-Khaimah through Britain and Saudi Arabia.[31]

The "solution" that Iran had proposed and that Britain and the United States seemed to accept at this time was an Iranian garrison on the islands, compensation to Ras al-Khaimah and Sharjah, and "fuzzing" of the issue of sovereignty. This, however, did not prevent the British Political Agent in Dubai, Mr. Julian Bullard, from writing to

Sharjah's Shaikh Khalid on November 8, 1970 as follows: "In the view of Her Britannic Majesty's Government, sovereignty over Abu Musa is vested in Sharjah and in no other state."[32]

Sir William Luce also said at about this same time:

> The British Government did not seize Abu Musa from the Iranians and hand it over to Sharjah at the time of its entry into the Gulf. The British Government has since its entry into the Gulf considered Abu Musa to be Arab, and according to old documents in possession of the British Government the island was Arab.[33]

In November, the British engaged in joint naval exercises with the United States and Iran in the northern Gulf of Oman.[34] These exercises demonstrated the US interest in the Gulf, particularly in light of the increasing Soviet visits to the region.[35] They also underlined the British and US idea that Iran was the regional power best able to play a regional defense role. Significantly, Iran itself engaged in the same month in naval, air and army exercises near the island of Farur, just to the west of the Tunbs and Abu Musa, thus stressing their determination about playing that role.[36] The US also decided in November that it would maintain the small MIDEASTFOR presence at Bahrain.[37]

Also in November, during Anglo-American talks on the Middle East in Washington, Assistant Secretary of State Sisco expressed support for British efforts to promote a union of nine and resolve outstanding problems in the Gulf, and promised American support with Iran.[38] The British Ambassador in Kuwait asked Kuwait to try to persuade Ras al-Khaimah and Sharjah to reach an agreement on the islands with Iran: "I stressed in particular the danger that Iran would block any moves toward a federation until this problem was settled. I also stressed that no transfer of sovereignty was proposed."[39]

At the same time, the British hoped that Anglo-Saudi talks in London in December would provide "an excellent opportunity...to explain the problems of union and the relevance of the islands dispute and demonstrate that Saudi policy on both issues could be an important factor in avoiding the instability which the King says he fears."[40] Douglas-Home met with Saudi Prince Fahd prior to these talks and expressed the hope "that Saudi Arabia also would actively support the union [of nine] and would co-operate in helping to solve the problems of the Gulf in the interests of stability and peace, which he believed she shared."[41] Al-Saqqaf agreed that the islands could be on the agenda of the talks, but said that there had been no change in the Saudi position on this issue and indicated that for the Saudis the main concern would be the union of emirates.[42] At the same time, Wright told the Shah and Alam that the Saudis and Kuwaitis would not be helpful in resolving the islands issue and that this would not be the main issue for discussion at the upcoming Anglo-Saudi talks.[43] When these talks were held from December 8 to 14, the Saudis agreed on the importance of a union but vigorously pressed their territorial claims against Abu Dhabi. In January 1971, the Foreign Office pressed Shaikh Zayed to yield to the Saudi demands.[44]

By early December, Luce had produced a report outlining his recommendations on British policy in the Gulf, namely, that British military withdrawal should be implemented on schedule, that British protection and exclusive agreements should be terminated, that a British naval force in the Indian Ocean should periodically visit the Gulf, and that small British naval, air and land contingents should be available for training of, liaison with and secondment to a union's military forces. He wrote that the islands dispute was "urgent," that it could lead to "an Iranian/Arab confrontation," and that it could obstruct the formation of a union of emirates, but that "it is hardly conceivable that it could be in British interests to come into conflict with Iran over the islands…"

Thus, although he recommended a treaty of friendship with a union that would entail an offer of consultation in the case of emergency, he also recommended:

> If the islands and the Saudi/Abu Dhabi disputes were still
> unsettled, we would probably either have to exclude in advance
> from the field of consultation any threats to peace arising from
> them, or recognize that consultation would not be allowed to
> lead us into conflict with Iran or Saudi Arabia.

In the event that no union could be formed before British withdrawal, he recommended against any British protection or friendship agreements with Sharjah, Ras al-Khaimah, Ajman, Umm al-Qawain and Fujairah. Among his reasons for this, he wrote: "If a solution of the islands problem had not already been found, the prolongation of our protection over Ras al-Khaimah and Sharjah could lead to serious difficulties with Iran." He hoped that communicating this decision to these five emirates might encourage them to agree to a union.[45] Douglas-Home and Heath agreed with the report, as did the Defence and Overseas Policy Committee, but a decision was made not to publicize its contents until the Ministry of Defence and the Foreign and Commonwealth Office had worked out the practical implications of the report and until Luce had the opportunity to inform the Gulf Rulers and their neighbors of the report's recommendations.[46]

Even so, London's *Daily Telegraph* wrote on December 14 that the Conservative government had "decided to adhere to the much-criticized Labour plan for a military withdrawal from the Gulf by the end of 1971, on the advice of Sir William Luce...who made a tour of the area and found that there were considerable difficulties in a reversal of policy." The paper noted that the Foreign Office had made no statement on the issue but that in well-informed circles it was taken for granted that the Conservatives will adhere to the withdrawal plan and timetable. In the light of the now certain withdrawal, a London *Times* article on December 16 advocated that the emirates make concessions to Saudi Arabia and Iran. The *Daily Telegraph* also reported on the same day that Douglas-Home wrote to the nine rulers that their "continued inability to decide on a federal structure now seriously threatened international credibility of its future success."[47]

On December 17, Douglas-Home shared the thinking in Luce's report with Rogers and Sisco, stressed the difficulty of achieving a union, in part because of the islands dispute, and asked for continuing American support with Iran and Saudi Arabia, which Rogers pledged.[48] On December 18, Prime Minister Heath briefed President Nixon on Luce's report.[49] Soon afterwards, on December 27, Zahedi warned that Iran would never abandon its rights to the islands and that unless these rights were recognized there could be no peace and security in the Gulf or in the Strait of Hormuz. In such a case, the creation of a federation or any other measure for the stability of the area would serve no purpose.[50] In early January 1971, Luce himself briefed Rogers and other State Department officials in Washington on his report.[51]

Concurrently with its intention to withdraw from the Gulf, Britain's Conservative government at the end of 1970 also wanted to promote a federation of nine, or at least a federation of seven if Bahrain and Qatar did not join. Britain also wanted to accommodate the Shah on the islands and to urge the Rulers of Ras al-Khaimah and Sharjah to do the same. At the same time, without immediate tangible progress on achieving its objectives, British statements became more blunt. Indeed, Political Resident Arthur warned the Rulers that Britain would not stop Iran from using force to take the islands after the British withdrawal.

This led to Alam's observation on December 31, 1970: "Apparently the British are doing their utmost to secure the islands of Tunbs and Abu Musa on our behalf..."[52] On the other hand, Sir Denis Wright has written: "For my part, I kept reminding the Iranians that any attempt to take the islands while our treaties with the rulers were in force would mean hostilities between us."[53] This was bluffing, however, and certainly did not signal to Iran that there would be hostilities if the Iranians took the islands when the treaties with the rulers were no longer in force.

Luce's Mediation and the US Role

As 1971 began to unfold and the deadline for withdrawal approached, British efforts to promote a federation and accommodate Iran on the islands intensified. Luce went to the Gulf again from January 26 to February 14, 1971. The *Daily Telegraph* wrote on January 29: "Britain will stand by her decision to withdraw all forces from the Gulf by the end of this year...Sir William Luce...is on a tour of the nine Gulf Shaikhdoms to tell the Rulers of this decision. The run-down of forces has begun, and it will now be accelerated."[54] Indeed, the purpose of this trip was to inform Gulf leaders that Douglas-Home would soon announce the decision to withdraw from the Gulf and encourage them to resolve all of the differences standing in the way of a federation as well as between the emirates and their larger neighbors.[55]

After visiting Saudi Arabia, Kuwait, Bahrain, Qatar and the seven Trucial States, Luce arrived in Tehran on February 11 and told reporters that the idea of the nine-member Federation of Arab Emirates had not failed. Britain, Saudi Arabia and Kuwait were doing everything in their power to bring it about and differences among the Rulers had been narrowed. He added that he did not agree with the idea of a smaller union.[56]

On the other hand, Luce and Sir Denis Wright had tried unsuccessfully to persuade Kuwait's Foreign Minister to encourage the Rulers of Sharjah and Ras al-Khaimah to reach agreement with Iran over the islands.[57] It was precisely the islands issue that topped the agenda during Luce's meetings with the Shah and Zahedi. The Shah told Luce to do whatever was necessary to persuade the Rulers to satisfy him.[58] On February 19, only days after Luce's departure from Tehran, the Shah threatened to use force to recover the islands.[59] Following a long session with the Shah after this threat, Wright wrote:

> The Shah is determined to have them [the islands] by force if we can't arrange some settlement with the sheikhs concerned before we leave the Gulf. This looks almost impossible despite all our efforts: on Saturday it was clear that the Shah's attitude had hardened so that the sort of compromise settlement we were trying for is not going to work. Our hope now is that he won't seize the islands while we are still bound by our treaty obligation to the Sheikhs to defend them — if he does we'll be in a state of war with our Persian ally![60]

A State Department telegram of February 19 also considered the Shah's statement to be a hardening of his attitude compared to his previous willingness to consider joint garrisoning and a fuzzing of sovereignty. It expressed concern that seizing the islands would strain Iran's relations with moderate Arabs, and thus undermine US interests. It also considered discouraging the Shah from his proposed action inasmuch as this could weaken his leadership role. While the telegram indicated that Iran and Ras al-Khaimah were making progress in exploring a deal, it also argued that "we do not believe it possible for any Gulf Ruler to reach agreement which would surrender sovereignty over these islands. Thus, unless there is to be forcible seizure with attendant adverse repercussions for Iran in Peninsula and Arab world generally, some compromise not involving surrender of sovereignty must be sought."[61]

The US considered whether to make a compromise proposal of a joint Iranian-Ras al-Khaimah defense of the Tunbs as well as Iranian support for Ras al-Khaimah's coastal defenses and a delimitation of the continental shelf without reference to the islands.[62] The understanding of the importance of sovereignty over the islands to the Rulers of Ras al-

Khaimah and Sharjah made the telegram quite remarkable. It is not clear, however, whether the proposal in the telegram was ever communicated to the Shah and the Rulers.

On March 1, 1971, Foreign Secretary Douglas-Home announced to the House of Commons that British military forces would be withdrawn from the Gulf by the end of the year and that a treaty of friendship had been offered to the nine emirates to replace the protection treaties that would be terminated at the end of the year. Douglas-Home implied that acceptance of the proposed friendship treaty depended on the successful formation of the federation. When asked by a former Defence Secretary, Duncan Sandys, for an assurance that British forces would not be withdrawn until the federation was established, the Foreign Secretary replied, "If the union were not formed, of course, I would come back to the House."[63] Iran welcomed the statement and said it would cooperate with the emirates in safeguarding the Gulf's security. However, Zahedi also said in an interview published in the *Daily Telegraph* on March 11 that he hoped Britain would "hand over" Abu Musa and the Tunbs and that if they were not yielded peacefully "it would be necessary to use force."[64]

Meanwhile, the US stated publicly that it did not intend to replace the British presence in the Gulf or increase military supplies to Iran or Saudi Arabia.[65] While the first part of this announcement was broadly consistent with earlier statements, the second was not entirely accurate. Indeed, the Nixon doctrine envisioned US support for friendly regional powers. The United States had in fact already increased its military supplies to Iran and Saudi Arabia.

Nixon had made a number of policy choices in the latter part of 1970 following a review of US policy in the Gulf, which included the sale of military items to Iran and Saudi Arabia. During 1971 and 1972, the administration was developing a National Security Study Memorandum (NSSM) in order to determine how to implement Nixon's policy choices.[66] Even in 1971, however, after advice from the US Military Assistance Advisory Group (MAAG) in Iran, Tehran adopted a five-year modernization program for its armed forces. US arms sales to Iran's air force, army, and navy accelerated in 1971 and 1972 and in February 1973, a $2 billion arms deal with the United

States was announced.[67] A similar development could be observed with regard to Saudi Arabia.[68]

In April 1971, the US Consul General in Dhahran, Lee Dinsmore, reported to the State Department that Mustafa Zayn, who was an advisor to Shaikh Khalid, informed him that Shaikh Khalid was willing to give the Shah a 99-year lease to Abu Musa. Zayn warned that an Iranian seizure of the islands would inflame Arab opinion against Iran and that the United States would be viewed as Iran's strongest supporter. On the other hand, the US could enjoy much of the credit if a successful compromise could be enacted, similar to what had happened after the resolution of the Bahrain issue.[69] Both this lease formula and warning fit in with US thinking on the subject.[70] It is not clear that the United States acted on this information although US Secretary of State Rogers and Douglas-Home met in April and discussed the islands.[71] Sir William Luce may have made this lease suggestion to Iran during this time, but by now it seemed only a faint hope as far as the British were concerned.[72]

Indeed, on April 17, Sir Denis Wright was given new compromise proposals by the Shah, which he then conveyed to Luce. The basic proposal as Wright reported it was that Iran would occupy the islands, the police forces of the shaikhdoms would withdraw from the islands within a week or two after the establishment of a federation, and the Shah would fuzz the issue of sovereignty for two or three years after the establishment of the federation.[73] Wright was retiring, and this was his farewell meeting with the Shah. He wrote in his memoirs: "I brought up the United Arab Emirates and the islands and on the latter felt I moved HIM quite a bit and got him to agree not to force the sovereignty issue for the time being. Maybe this will provide a way out."[74] After leaving Tehran, Wright toured the Gulf and, joined by Julian Walker, who had replaced Bullard as the Political Agent in Dubai, "had meetings with the Rulers of Ras al-Khaimah and Sharjah, when I did my best to persuade them to come to terms with the Shah over the islands (the Shah was ready to share any income from oil with them) rather than have him seize them by force."[75]

William Luce met the Shah on May 4, 1971. According to US records, in discussing the proposals the Shah had made to Wright, the Shah insisted that Iran should establish a military presence on the islands and that the shaikhdoms withdraw their police forces from the islands before, not after, the establishment of the federation of Gulf states. Luce argued that demanding the withdrawal of their police forces before the creation of the federation would not offer the shaikhs much incentive to accept the compromise. However, Luce considered it positive that the Shah said Britain could count on Iran recognizing the federation if Iran could put its troops on the islands before the federation was established. Iran would also offer generous aid to and cooperation with the shaikhdoms once their police were withdrawn and even more assistance to the two shaikhdoms after two years if they left the issue of sovereignty dormant during this time, including 49% of the oil revenues from fields in areas claimed by Sharjah.

Luce referred to keeping the sovereignty issue in abeyance several times in his discussion with the Shah, but the Shah countered him, claiming that Iran's sovereignty was clear and saying that Iran was only willing to not make an issue of it during the first two years. Luce then suggested that no official statement or act be made at the time of Iranian annexation of the islands, even after the two-year period passed, as such an act might re-open and re-invigorate the issue. The Shah also said he was prepared to enter into a defense agreement with the federation, perhaps a Gulf arrangement like CENTO for stability and cooperation in the Gulf, and that this might even include the exchange of a token Iranian force on federation territory and a token federation force on Iranian territory.[76]

From the reading of the US State Department telegram, Luce appeared receptive to these ideas and was working with the Shah to refine them. Nevertheless, on May 8, Iran turned up the heat on Britain by protesting the flights of RAF planes over islands in the Gulf, including Abu Musa and the Tunbs, and the alleged harassment of Iranian naval vessels near these islands. Iran stated that their warships in the Gulf had been given orders to fire on British planes if this happened again. Britain replied that its planes were not harassing Iranian vessels, but were only conducting reconnaissance missions and were not equipped for attack.[77] Indeed, in mid-May, the British Ministry of Defence approved a plan to defend the islands, not against any Iranian takeover, but rather against any possible takeover by Arab guerrillas who might seek to establish themselves on the islands in order to pre-empt an Iranian takeover, or even to evict any such Arab guerrilla force from the islands. The plan rationalized that this was so that Iran might not be tempted to pre-empt any possible Arab guerrilla move.[78] Moreover, the British signed a £100 million contract to sell Chieftain tanks to Iran in May, yet another demonstration of its support for Iran.[79]

After meeting with the Shah, Luce conveyed the Shah's proposals to Sharjah's Shaikh Khalid.[80] On May 12, Northcutt Ely, the American legal adviser to the Ruler of Sharjah, informed the State Department that Shaikh Khalid was unhappy with the Shah's 49/51% oil revenue-sharing idea but still receptive to a general compromise. Shaikh Khalid had been angry to learn, however, that Britain had lifted its ban on oil drilling offshore of Abu Musa pending Iranian approval. This approval, which had earlier been given to Occidental and which the National Iranian Oil Company (NIOC) had offered to Buttes as well, but was now delayed by Iran for both oil companies.[81] Luce also visited Ras al-Khaimah on May 8 and conveyed the Shah's proposals to Shaikh Saqr, adding that the Shah would oppose the federation if the proposals were not accepted. Saqr replied that the British should work to establish the federation instead of trying to please the Shah on something to which he had no right.[82]

At this point, the United States conveyed to Britain the seriousness of its interest in a resolution of the islands dispute. During a lengthy discussion between State Department officials and British Embassy officials in Washington on May 16, the British said the Rulers of Sharjah and Ras al-Khaimah had not indicated whether they could accept the proposals from the Shah conveyed by Luce. Nevertheless, they were pursuing a hard line with both of them. The Americans "pressed" the seriousness with which they viewed the continued drift on the issue, saying that the Shah's security and financial proposals were the best deal the two Rulers could get. US officials "urged" the British to consider all possible sovereignty proposals, including the idea that the Shah would be sovereign but that the Rulers would be property owners, an idea that Robert Jennings, another legal advisor to Sharjah, had made to Iranian Ambassador Afshar and that Sharjah legal advisor Ely had made to the Shaikh of Sharjah.

The British said that the Rulers cared more about sovereignty than about the practical benefits being offered. Nevertheless, they also suggested that because of anxiety over the Arab reaction to any compromise on sovereignty, face-saving considerations and inertia, the Rulers might feel that Iran's seizure of the islands was the best way out of the dilemma. The Americans "impressed" on the British the US willingness to test the Shah's flexibility on the sovereignty issue but their view that this would be doomed to fail unless the British first, brought the shaikhs to accept the Shah's financial and garrisoning arrangements, and second, brought them to adopt flexible positions on sovereignty.[83] It should also be noted that the US seemed to approve of the Shah's proposal regarding the garrisoning of Iranian forces in the federation and federation forces in Iran. Indeed, this proposal went one step further than the February 1971 US idea that Iran might play a role in the defense of the Trucial Coast.

On June 3, Luce met at a gathering in Dubai with the Rulers of Sharjah and Ras al-Khaimah and a group of notables from both emirates, where he advised them to negotiate and reach a compromise with the Shah. After again conveying the Shah's "suitable" proposals regarding compensation to the emirates, Luce warned the Rulers that the Shah would use force to occupy the islands before the end of the year and that the British would not defend the islands in the event of an Iranian occupation.[84] Most of this British message became public when *Al-Khaleej* reported Luce's comments on June 5.[85] Kelly writes that the Shah "refused to treat with Ras al-Khaimah over the Tunbs." However, the accounts by Wright, the State Department, the Ras al-Khaimah Ruler's Court and the British Foreign Office indicate that Wright and Luce were conveying the Shah's compromise proposals, including offers of compensation, to Ras al-Khaimah as well as to Sharjah.[86] Indeed, on June 19, Douglas-Home instructed the Political Agent in Dubai to continue to try to persuade both rulers to accept the Shah's proposals.[87]

Taryam writes that Luce pressed the Ruler of Sharjah harder than the Ruler of Ras al-Khaimah because Shaikh Saqr rejected negotiations and because the Shah was not persistent in his claims.[88] This is also not supported by the evidence. Not only did Luce put tremendous pressure on Shaikh Saqr, but the Shah had also been quite persistent in his demands on Saqr. As far as the Ruler of Ras al-Khaimah was concerned, he rejected ceding sovereignty rather than the idea of negotiations. However, inasmuch as the British considered Sharjah's legal claim to

Abu Musa to be stronger than Ras al-Khaimah's legal claim to the Tunbs, Luce may have thought it necessary to put somewhat more pressure on the Ruler of Sharjah.[89] On June 24, the Shah again threatened force if the islands were not "restored" to Iran.[90] This did not discourage the US from conducting special forces exercises with Iran from July 1 to July 15.[91]

On July 18, 1971, the six emirates of Abu Dhabi, Dubai, Sharjah, Ajman, Umm al-Qawain and Fujairah agreed on a provisional constitution for a federation to be called the United Arab Emirates. Britain and the United States welcomed this development.[92] However, Britain, which wanted the federation established successfully before withdrawal, also remained apprehensive that it might flounder due to Iranian opposition if the islands issue was not resolved to Iran's satisfaction. Indeed, because of Iranian opposition the six emirates delayed declaring the federation.[93] It became clear that Britain would have to continue to work to resolve the islands issue and remove the reason for Iranian opposition to the federation before the British withdrawal:

> ...Britain sought to achieve a compromise agreement [on the islands] before its scheduled withdrawal, conscious that it would bear much of the odium whether there was an agreement or not, but preferring this to the inauguration of a new era with Iran-Arab hostilities.[94]

On July 29, 1971, the US Embassy in London forwarded to the Department of State the conclusions of a legal study conducted by the British law firm Coward Chance for the Ruler of Sharjah. The embassy noted that a longer study, including historical documentation, would later be provided.[95] This study made a very convincing historical and legal case for Sharjah's sovereignty over Abu Musa based on Sharjah's long possession and use of Abu Musa, or what is called "prescriptive title" in international law.[96] In the following months, however, this knowledge did not change the favorable US attitude about the Shah's proposals on the islands.

Indeed, in a September 13, 1971 letter from US Secretary of State Rogers to UK Foreign Secretary Douglas-Home, Rogers stated that the Americans had received a message from the Shah saying that the terms he had agreed to were the furthest he could go in being accommodating.

Rogers himself thought the terms that Luce had negotiated with the Shah were as good as the shaikhs could expect. Furthermore, the US would inform the Shah of their confidence that the British would make every effort to bring this promising opportunity for a settlement to a successful conclusion.[97]

The basic thrust of the letter was to encourage Britain to secure the agreement of the shaikhs for the sake of cooperation and security in the Gulf. The letter repeatedly described the terms as those Luce had negotiated rather than terms that the Shah had conveyed to Luce. This was at a stage when the terms were that Sharjah and Ras al-Khaimah should yield sovereignty in exchange for financial compensation, i.e. before Sharjah succeeded in getting a better deal, one involving partition and avoiding acknowledgement of any Iranian sovereignty. As a result, Duncan Slater has noted that he thought "the Americans were 100% behind the Shah."[98]

In the meantime, on September 7, Luce met with Shaikh Saqr and Crown Prince Khalid in Ras al-Khaimah, conveying tough new proposals from Ambassador Afshar that Ras al-Khaimah and Sharjah should issue public communiqués relinquishing the islands, in return for which the Shah would provide financial assistance to the two shaikhdoms. Luce said that he had been unable to obtain better conditions and that the Shah would take the islands by force if agreement was not reached. "Time is short," he said, "and [British] protection will come to an end; this is the last opportunity."

Shaikh Saqr replied that this was a matter for all the Arabs. When Walker met with Shaikh Saqr and Crown Prince Khalid on September 9 to ask their response, Saqr again called on the British to help the federation come into being and obtain recognition from the UN, arguing that Iran would then be powerless to take the islands. Walker argued that Iran would not allow the federation to come into being before resolving the issue of the islands and might do something "regrettable" adding "It is difficult to ignore the Iranians, because we are concerned over the Iranians' relations with the region and its security."

When Luce visited again on September 12, he received the same response from Shaikh Saqr about the need to consult with the Arab states and the elders of Ras al-Khaimah and that Britain was responsible for the protection of the islands. Luce did not comment on the question of British protection, but replied that Ras al-Khaimah had already consulted the Arab states, which had not been able or willing to help. Furthermore, Iran would not provide compensation if Ras al-Khaimah raised the issue with the Arab League or the UN. In a subsequent meeting on September 14, Geoffrey Arthur warned that if Iran occupied the islands and established a median line, Ras al-Khaimah would forfeit much of its territorial waters, while Walker argued that Iranian forces might even land at Ras al-Khaimah. Throughout the conversation, however, Shaikh Saqr continued to reject the proposals and to argue that the Arab states would support him.[99]

On September 18, Luce asked if Ras al-Khaimah could offer any new proposals to Iran. Shaikh Saqr said that if Iran recognized Ras al-Khaimah's sovereignty they could then discuss the other matters. Luce indicated that the Shah would not accept this but might agree to increased aid. He also said he did not believe that there was any oil on or around the Tunbs, a point which Saqr disputed. Crown Prince Khalid asked Luce to propose a lease to Iran, but was told that the Shah had already rejected this. Iran also rejected arbitration, with Saqr saying that Ras al-Khaimah accepted such a move.

On the question of the position of Saudi Arabia, Egypt and Kuwait, Luce argued that they did not object to a settlement while Saqr insisted that they did not favor concessions. Luce said that the Shah "knows that these proposals are stronger, and previous proposals were better. But, for certain, they will not change their thinking, and there is no hope that it will change." When Saqr expressed hope that someone stronger than the Shah would intervene, Luce was concerned that he meant the Russians or the Chinese. Once again, Shaikh Saqr repeatedly rejected the Shah's proposals throughout this conversation.[100]

On September 21, a British Embassy official in Washington briefed the State Department's Richard Murphy and Joseph Twinam about Luce's meetings with the Rulers on September 18 and 19. The Department's telegram on this briefing reported:

> Luce on own initiative took sounding re acceptability of possible counter proposal to Iran under which median line agreement would give Tunbs outright to Iran and allow Iranian garrison on Abu Musa. Ras al-Khaimah Ruler [sic] did not rpt not categorically refuse this solution but asked for more time to consider it.

Murphy and Twinam must have meant to refer to Sharjah's Ruler, not Ras al-Khaimah's Ruler, because Ras al-Khaimah's Ruler had categorically rejected relinquishing the Tunbs and because the evidence does not show that Luce had made this proposal to him. It is also possible that the State Department was given confused information by the British Embassy. The telegram reported on the counter-proposals put forward by Sharjah's Ruler, which marked the beginning of the Memorandum of Understanding on Abu Musa. It also noted that Luce considered any US approach to the shaikhs as unhelpful and possibly even harmful as the shaikhs might view it as a "put-up-job" by London.[101]

On September 28, British official Anthony Parsons briefed Sisco about Luce's mediation and revealed that the British were in the "final and most desperate stage" in their efforts to resolve the islands dispute. Luce had "absolutely busted himself" in his meetings with the shaikhs to sell them on the Luce-Afshar proposals but had made no "progress." He said that Ras al-Khaimah had showed "marginal flexibility" to these proposals (to yield sovereignty for financial compensation), but Shaikh Khalid of Sharjah had "dug in his heels" because he feared assassination. In fact, however, Ras al-Khaimah's Ruler had categorically refused and Sharjah's Ruler had offered counter-proposals.

Parsons said that Luce would now propose to the Shah a median line agreement in which Ras al-Khaimah would give up the Tunbs in return for compensation, and Sharjah would agree to an Iranian garrison on Abu Musa. He also said the British were confident they could put pressure on Shaikh Saqr to get him to acquiesce over the Tunbs. At the same time, he mentioned that the British were concerned about the reaction of Gulf Arabs to the appearance of selling out Arab rights on Abu Musa and any instability which such a move could foster. Therefore, the British considered the median line counterproposals as a "reasonable proposition," especially considering the fact that if the Shah was concerned about the possibility of a "row" with the Arabs over the islands, these counterproposals were not "hopeless."

In case the Shah rejected the counterproposals, the British were prepared for a "stormy period" in their relations with Iran, including Iranian cancellation of CENTO overflights, but Parsons thought this would be temporary and preferable to loss of influence with Gulf Arabs, which might be permanent. Sisco said the counterproposal was "logically not unreasonable" and that the United States would be willing to follow-up British efforts to persuade the Shah "at least to [the] extent of urging [the] Shah not to reject [the] counterproposal out of hand."[102]

Another version of this meeting between Luce and Sharjah's Ruler was provided to the State Department by Buttes Gas and Oil Company officials Boreta, Ely and Kuchel. They said that Shaikh Khalid had told them that Luce had pressured him to accept the Luce-Afshar proposals; that Luce had threatened Shaikh Khalid, saying, "you know what we can do to you"; and that Shaikh Khalid had refused, replying, "the days of slavery are over." Only then did Luce agree to carry Shaikh Khalid's counter-proposals to the Shah, they said.[103]

Luce was scheduled to deliver Sharjah's counterproposals to the Shah on October 2. Days before this, the Shah again demanded that Britain turn over the islands, warning that Britain could not stop him from using his military forces to take the islands.[104] At the same time, after meeting with the new British Ambassador to Tehran, Peter Ramsbotham, US Ambassador to Tehran Douglas MacArthur II reported to Washington that while he thought the Shah might give more on the length of time he was willing to fuzz on sovereignty, he would be adamant in rejecting any counterproposal that would involve trappings of sovereignty for the shaikhs, such as the flying of their flags, after the establishment of the Iranian presence on the islands. In the event that Iran was "obliged" to seize the islands after the British withdrawal and radical Arabs were to "exploit" the issue and take it to the UN, MacArthur thought the Shah would blame the British and make life difficult for them in Iran and throughout the Gulf.

Thus, it was very important for the British to achieve a settlement before their withdrawal, even if it was at the expense of their present relations with the shaikhs, particularly with Sharjah, which MacArthur understood to be "more negative" than Ras al-Khaimah.[105] On October 5, while Luce was still in Iran, and despite MacArthur's views, the United States nevertheless urged the Shah to seek a negotiated settlement of the dispute.[106] Indeed, Sisco had told Parsons that Shaikh Khalid's ideas were reasonable and that the United States would try to persuade the Shah not to reject them.

In late October and early November, Luce was shuttling again. On November 2, 1971 the State Department received a briefing from British Embassy officials noting that Luce had presented proposals from the Shah regarding Abu Musa to the Ruler of Sharjah. Ely thought Luce had made progress in moving the Iranian position toward a compromise solution and promised to help Luce persuade Sharjah to make a reasonable response. However, Ely sought a non-aggression pact to prevent Iran from eventually annexing areas of Abu Musa designated to Sharjah and warned that the Shah's insistence on getting other shaikhs to provide a written disclaimer of the federation's interest in Abu Musa would be difficult.

Shaikh Khalid told Luce the Shah's new terms were "better," but also raised the same concerns that Ely had mentioned. Khalid made counterproposals, and after meeting with Sharjah notables, made further revisions to these counterproposals, including more area for Sharjah, a well, a possible oil loading facility and Khalid's grandfather's grave, as well as a 50/50 oil revenue split, with Iran compensating Umm al-Qawain and Ajman out of its 50%. He insisted that both sides recognize each others' decrees on a twelve-mile territorial sea, and that the inhabitants of Abu Musa would have fishing rights around the island. Khalid also insisted on a written agreement and on making a public statement about the agreement before the Iranian landing.[107]

Luce now informed the Ruler of Ras al-Khaimah about the compromise proposals concerning Abu Musa, again advising him to accept the previous proposals on the Tunbs and warning him that the Shah would take the islands by force. Saqr again rejected ceding sovereignty for compensation. When Saqr pointed out that the Shah had given up Bahrain and asked why he would not give up the islands, Luce answered: "He [the Shah] gave up Bahrain in order to obtain the islands." Luce continued: "The Shah gave up Bahrain, but the people did not approve. It will not be possible to give up the islands."

When Luce argued that the proposals concerning Abu Musa and the Tunbs were in "the public interest of the region," Saqr replied that Ras al-Khaimah and Iran should submit their evidence to a tribunal. Luce replied that the British had tried to persuade the Shah to do this, "but he refused — because agreement to submit the case to an international tribunal would be tantamount to recognition of Ras al-Khaimah's sovereignty – which he does not accept."[108] In the course of the meeting, Luce conveyed numerous Iranian arguments that were not valid, namely, that the Iranian people did not approve of the Shah yielding Bahrain, that taking the islands issue to the ICJ was tantamount to recognizing Ras al-Khaimah's sovereignty, and that the Shah's proposals were in the region's interest. He also conveyed the Shah's threat to invade the islands.

On November 8, Ely provided the State Department with the proposed terms of the MoU and asked the Americans not to reveal to the British that he had done so.[109] On November 12, the British briefed the State Department on Luce's talks in Tehran and indicated that the Shah was being flexible in working out the remaining details of the MoU on Abu Musa and that the British were now optimistic.[110]

On November 8, Ras al-Khaimah Crown Prince Khalid and advisor Toufiq Abu Khadir met with Assistant Secretary Sisco and Deputy Assistant Secretary of State Rodger Davies. The Crown Prince asked for US recognition, diplomatic relations and assistance, including US good offices to settle the dispute with Iran over the Tunbs. He again offered a military base to the United States. Sisco said the United States would study the Ras al-Khaimah requests but he repeated US support for the largest possible federation for the sake of the stability of the area after the British withdrawal and said the United States was disappointed that a federation of nine had not materialized.

In response to Sisco's questions, Abu Khadir indicated that Ras al-Khaimah would end its treaty relationship with Britain by January 1, 1972 (which means that Ras al-Khaimah did not understand how little time it had left). While Britain had offered treaties of friendship to other emirates or to the federation, it had refused to enter into one with Ras al-Khaimah (which must have been British pressure on Ras al-Khaimah to join the federation). Thus, Ras al-Khaimah needed US protection. The Crown Prince's advisor indicated that Ras al-Khaimah would have no problem with Iranian troops on the islands as long as Ras al-Khaimah's sovereignty was recognized. Sisco replied that the United States was concerned that the islands dispute could be an element of instability. He asked whether there had been any discussion about setting aside the sovereignty issue for some time and stressed that some pragmatic solution that would meet the interests of both sides must be possible.[111]

On November 11, Consul General Dinsmore in Dhahran argued against satisfying the Ras al-Khaimah requests. He argued that relations with the federation, the riparian states and the wider Arab world would be undermined by recognizing "a non-viable principality," and that establishing a military base there would seem a US effort to "revive a world which no longer exists." The "only reasonable future" for Ras al-Khaimah was to join the federation.[112]

On November 11, Crown Prince Khalid and Abu Khadir met with Deputy Assistant Secretary Davies, after having met with Ambassador to the UN George H.W. Bush, Chairman of the Senate Foreign Relations Committee William J. Fulbright, Congressman Hale Boggs and Deputy Assistant Secretary of Defense James Noyes, all of whom had referred Ras al-Khaimah back to the State Department's Near East Affairs bureau for an answer. Davies told Shaikh Khalid that the United States was concerned about the possible consequences of Ras al-Khaimah going it alone and thought any lack of cohesion or unity among the Gulf states "could tempt outsiders to fish in muddy waters."

He asked Ras al-Khaimah to reconsider and to consult with its Trucial neighbors, Saudi Arabia, Kuwait and the UK, emphasizing that the United States hoped that problems regarding the islands and the federation could be ironed out or minimized. "As Davies had discussed with Shaykh Khalid and his father as early as the mid-60s, USG continues to think some form of union is necessary to assure secure future of Gulf shaykhdoms." In reply to questions, Davies said the US would answer later about Ras al-Khaimah independence, but that the US recognized the British treaties with the emirates and that it was the British role to resolve the islands dispute. The United States could only offer indirect encouragement to all parties to reach an amicable solution.

On the very same day, November 11, however, the US Embassy in Beirut was instructed to tell the Crown Prince if he passed through Beirut that the US could not give assurances of recognition or support to an independent Ras al-Khaimah and to urge Ras al-Khaimah to resolve the territorial problems and other issues preventing it from joining the federation. US Consul General Dinsmore was also instructed to convey this message if the Crown Prince did not pass through Beirut.[113] On November 17, Dinsmore speculated that Ras al-Khaimah might offer itself as a military base to another power in order to establish independence from the federation. He referred twice to the "Wawasim" and said they were "pirates" whom the British were forced to subdue before concluding treaties with them.[114] These misspellings of "Qawasim" may have been typographical errors, but they suggest that the US historical knowledge was not very deep. The United States was gently discouraging Ras al-Khaimah, but at the same time perhaps misleading them that any real reconsideration of their requests would really be undertaken.

On November 17, after departing Tehran and traveling to the Trucial States, Luce said "Iran and Britain have sorted out their differences over the Tumbs and Abu Musa. The shaikhs can now form their federation."[115] What he meant was that on Abu Musa, Iran and Britain had agreed along with Sharjah on the MoU.[116] However, Ras al-Khaimah was not party to any agreement on the Tunbs. Instead, Britain clearly understood that Iran would take the Tunbs by force, and Iran clearly understood that Britain would not defend them. In return for all of this, Iran was now prepared to permit the federation to go forward.

After Sharjah accepted the MoU in mid-November, Kelly writes:

> Only the question of Ras al-Khaimah and the Tunbs remained, and on this, after some delicate manoeuvring at Tehran, a tacit understanding emerged that the British, for their part, would not oppose a Persian occupation of the islets, while the shah, on his side, would take no step to effect an occupation until after the abrogation of the British treaties with Ras al-Khaimah on December 1, when the British government would be under no requirement whatever to assist the shaikhdom. Moreover, since Ras al-Khaimah was not a member of the UAE, the federal rulers would have no legal obligation to support Shaikh Saqr in resisting any Persian move to occupy the Tunbs.[117]

The British had had no intention of opposing an Iranian occupation of the Tunbs since early 1968 and had previously communicated this to Ras al-Khaimah. Now, it was also communicated to Iran. Iranian senator and *Ittilaat* editor Abbas Massoudi later provided support for this assertion of a tacit understanding that Iran would take the islands only after the British withdrawal and indicated that Iran violated this understanding: "...the negotiations between Iran and Britain concluded that Iran could regain its islands after the British withdrawal. But Iran wished to regain its islands at the time of the British presence, it did so a day before the British departure."[118]

Chubin and Zabih have argued that Iran reasoned that military action after the termination of Britain's protection treaties would be action against an Arab state, namely Ras al-Khaimah. In addition, unilateral action to take the islands after the establishment of the UAE and its admission to the Arab League and the UN would be more complicated. Thus, Iran preferred to act before the British departure so as to portray this as a dispute between Iran and Britain.[119] Indeed, Julian Walker has said: "By landing his forces on the islands before the creation of the UAE the Shah gave himself the opportunity of abandoning his previous hostility to the creation of that new state. Had he sent his forces to the Islands after December 2, 1971, peaceful coexistence between the UAE and Iran would have been rendered almost impossible."[120] Meanwhile, Glen Balfour-Paul has written:

> It is also uncertain whether the British knew in advance of the Shah's chosen timing. The fact that the Ruler of Sharjah announced his Abu Musa Agreement on 29 November and had a welcoming party ready on the island when the Iranian troops landed the following day, implies that he had been forewarned of the timing of the Abu Musa landing. If, as seems likely, the British were aware that the Shah would occupy the Tunbs the same day, they may have calculated that the timing would now make little difference: even if the Shah considerately waited until Britain's defence obligations had been terminated, critics in the outside world would in any case hold Britain up to execration and doubtless to charges of duplicity.[121]

During the last days before Iran's forced landing on the Tunbs, Ras al-Khaimah was still requesting and the United States was still declining a special relationship. On November 27, 1971, US Consul General Dinsmore conveyed a letter from Ras al-Khaimah's Crown Prince Khalid to Sisco repeating his requests to the United States. Dinsmore recommended delivering an "unequivocal" rejection before British Political Agent Walker made one last effort to persuade Shaikh Saqr to join the federation, hoping that this would help the British effort.[122] On the same day, November 27, Sisco replied to the letter from Crown Prince Khalid as follows: "I urge that Ras al-Khaimah not take decisions now that might set it unilaterally on a course away from future cooperation with her neighbors, and that you reconsider the possibilities of joining with other Gulf states in the coming months."[123]

On November 30, 1971, Dinsmore reported that he had delivered Sisco's letter to Shaikh Saqr on November 29. Saqr insisted he would not join the federation and that the terms of the federation's constitution "forced" him to establish independence. Dinsmore argued that Ras al-Khaimah could best influence the formation of the federation from within and that he was sure they could still find a way to associate with the federation. From remarks gathered by Shaikh Saqr and his advisor, the Consul suggested that there might be some possibility of some future adherence to the federation.[124]

Big Power Reactions to the Iranian Occupation

On November 30, 1971, one day before the termination of Britain's special treaty relations with Sharjah and Ras al-Khaimah, Iran landed on Abu Musa pursuant to its MoU with Sharjah and made a forced landing on the Tunbs. As the *Middle East Economic Survey* observed on December 3:

> ...the timing of the invasion, just one day before the
> cancellation of the protection treaty with Britain, left Britain
> in technical default of its defense obligations vis-à-vis Ras al-
> Khaimah and therefore subject to Arab opprobrium on this
> account – all of which contributed to a thoroughly inglorious
> ending to Britain's century-old presence in the Gulf.[125]

Indeed, on the day of the Iranian landing on the Tunbs, the British aircraft carrier *HMS Eagle* and cruiser *HMS Albion* were in the Gulf of Oman. However, they did not attempt to stop Iran, which deployed not only troop-carrying hovercraft and helicopters but also destroyers and Phantom jets in its military action.[126]

During the first week of December, Foreign Office officials such as Arthur, Walker and Douglas-Home expressed regret for the loss of life, but carefully noted that Britain had warned Ras al-Khaimah of the Shah's intention to occupy the islands by force.[127] The Foreign Office also said on December 1 that Iraq's severing of diplomatic relations with Britain for conniving with Iran in the seizure of the Tunbs was unjustified.[128] The "inglorious" nature of the British withdrawal not only led to Arab opprobrium, but also to the Shah's portrayal of the British as a humiliated former colonial power.[129]

The protection treaties were replaced on December 2 by a new treaty of friendship between Britain and the newly established United Arab Emirates, as well as a treaty of friendship between Britain and Ras al-Khaimah. Political Resident Arthur signed the new treaties with Shaikh Zayed and Shaikh Saqr respectively. Britain's first Ambassador to the UAE, Charles Treadwell, presented his credentials to Zayed on December 6 and Julian Walker became British Consul General to Ras al-Khaimah.[130] The British handed over the RAF base in Sharjah to Shaikh Khalid on December 20 and turned over the Trucial Oman Scouts as the nucleus of the UAE Defense Forces in late December. Britain would maintain a small number of military advisers inside the country, make periodic visits with its navy, army and air force, which included overflight and staging rights for the RAF and training facilities for British troops, and provide assistance to UAE police forces.[131] The United States also quickly recognized the new UAE and began to plan for its diplomatic representation there. On February 6, it was reported that William Stoltzfus, US Ambassador to Bahrain, Kuwait and Qatar would also be Ambassador to the UAE and Oman.[132]

The US reaction to the events of November 30 was mostly quiet. On December 4, the State Department prepared the preliminary text of the US remarks planned for the December 9 Security Council meeting on the islands. This text placed the islands issue in the overall context of the British voluntary withdrawal from the Gulf, the emergence of the states of the Gulf into independence, and the need to resolve a number of problems, including Iran's claim to Bahrain, the establishment of a federation of Arab states and other territorial disputes. The text said the United States had not been directly involved in the dispute over the ownership of the islands and had not taken any position on sovereignty over them, but had urged an amicable resolution on all the parties to the dispute. As such, they thought the arrangement on Abu Musa reflected the spirit of cooperation necessary in the Gulf and should be approved by the UN.

The United States regretted the unfortunate loss of life "which resulted from an apparent misunderstanding when the Iranian forces landed on Greater Tunb on November 30," but hoped that Iran and Ras al-Khaimah would try to resolve their differences and cooperate for their mutual interests and those of the area. According to the prepared text, it was a time for cooperation, not recrimination, and certainly not for outside interference. However, the United States would abstain from any motion.[133] Interestingly, none of the above remarks were presented when the Security Council met on December 9. Instead, throughout the debate, the US representative remained silent.[134]

The British naturally had more to say than the Americans, but they were not entirely clear, consistent and forthcoming in their statements. Foreign Secretary Douglas-Home accurately told the House of Commons on December 6 that under the MoU on Abu Musa, "no party has given up any of its claims, or recognized the sovereignty of the other party."[135] However, later in his remarks he said: "As for the Tunbs and Abu Musa, their sovereignty is left open." When questioned further, he replied: "The view of the government of Iran, as I understand it, is that the sovereignty issue has not been raised by either side."[136] It was a technically accurate reading of the MoU on Abu Musa to say that it left the issue of sovereignty open, but it was not accurate that the issue of sovereignty had not been raised regarding Abu Musa and the Tunbs. Indeed, Iranian Prime Minister Hoveyda had claimed to the Majlis on November 30 that Iranian sovereignty over the islands "had been restored following long negotiations with the British government" and that Iran had "in no conceivable way relinquished or will relinquish its incontestable sovereignty and right of control over the whole of Abu Musa island."[137]

Arthur expressed concern about Hoveyda's remarks, and British Ambassador Peter Ramsbotham also conveyed his concerns about these remarks to Alam, Foreign Minister Khalatbari and the Shah. Hoveyda's remark on Abu Musa was only the Iranian interpretation of the MoU. As for his remark about the Tunbs, however, Luce had given a pledge to the Shah during a meeting on November 11, 1971 that "Later, HMG would accept the incorporation of the Tunbs as part of Iran."[138] Thus, Douglas-Home was not acknowledging the whole story.

British Ambassador to the UN Colin Crowe also spoke on December 9, 1971 and developed many of the points Douglas-Home had made to the House of Commons. Crowe said that the British had considered the establishment of a federation and the resolution of territorial disputes to be essential prerequisites to stability in the Gulf after the British withdrawal, and pointed to successes in achieving both prerequisites. He noted that Bahrain and Qatar were now members of the UN, that the UAE had been established and had become a UN member, and expressed the hope that Ras al-Khaimah would also join.

Crowe called Bahrain "by far the most important" of the Gulf islands in dispute and noted that the Shah had renounced Iran's claim with the result that the island was now independent. He referred to Abu Musa as being "second in size and importance though in no way comparable to Bahrain" and called the MoU "a sensible compromise agreement." Regarding the Tunbs, Crowe said: "It is a matter of great regret to the British Government that it was not possible to reach a negotiated settlement." Overall, however, "In the view of my Government this outcome represents a reasonable and acceptable basis for the future security of the area, which should in turn be based on co-operation between all the States of the Gulf, Arab and non-Arab."[139]

While the above remarks were honest, Crowe was less than fully forthcoming in some of his other remarks. He referred to Abu Musa only as "an island administered by the Ruler of Sharjah," and did not acknowledge that Britain had long recognized Sharjah as sovereign over the island. He said that the Tunbs "have long been claimed by Iran" and that "for many years the British Government has been trying to bring about an agreed solution between Iran and the Ruler," but did not concede that Britain had long recognized Ras al-Khaimah as sovereign over the islands and had long rejected the Iranian claim to them.[140]

The decision of the UN Security Council to take no action on this dispute was influenced by the attitude of Britain and the United States. Either of them could have vetoed a resolution, although the United States intended to abstain. Britain wanted to promote security and stability before withdrawing from the Gulf in order to protect its access to oil, its investments in the region, its participation in the economic development of the region and its reputation.

In addition to these regional commercial and political interests, Britain was especially keen on relations with the Shah because it hoped he would serve as a regional policeman and bulwark against Arab radicalism and Soviet penetration and that Britain could promote British arms sales to Iran. Britain also wanted good relations with Saudi Arabia for commercial reasons and because Britain hoped Saudi Arabia would also be a guarantor of the *status quo* and a market for British arms. In the end, Britain considered the outcome of its efforts on Bahrain, the islands and the federation to be reasonably successful in promoting all these objectives.

The United States supported British efforts to promote security and stability for similar commercial and political reasons. Viewing Iran and Saudi Arabia in a similar way was also consistent with the 1969 Nixon Doctrine, which intended to provide military and economic aid to regional powers to protect their own and US interests. For both Britain and the United States, this commercial and strategic thinking took precedence over the historical and legal record on the islands, the rights of Ras al-Khaimah, Sharjah and later the UAE, and the responsibilities of the UN. Moreover, Britain and the US realized that the Gulf Arab states, particularly Saudi Arabia, were not willing to confront Iran or Britain or the US over the islands issue when they also viewed Iran as a bulwark against Arab radicalism and the Soviet Union.[141]

After the British withdrawal, the United States followed developments in the region closely and attempted to promote cooperation and stability there. The United States took special note of regional tensions, although it did not always gauge them accurately and sometimes relied on the British for its information. It also provided support to Iran and Saudi Arabia and urged them to cooperate more closely, particularly in supporting Oman and the Yemen Arab Republic (YAR) against challenges from the People's Democratic Republic of Yemen (PDRY).

From the US perspective, it quickly became apparent that Saudi Arabia's reluctance to cooperate with Iran was rooted in concerns about Iran's domination of the Gulf, including Saudi resentment over the Iranian occupation of Abu Musa and the Tunbs. Thus, it was important that Saudi Arabia take responsibility for normalizing relations with the UAE and also that the UAE support both Oman and the YAR. The British generally promoted the same policies and worked with the United States to do so. The British urged the UAE to normalize relations with Iran.[142]

As early as mid-December 1971, Deputy Assistant Secretary Davies visited the Gulf and in his meetings with Gulf Rulers stressed the importance of cooperation among all Gulf states, including their need to support the Sultan of Oman because of the importance of stability in Oman. Davies reported back to the State Department that he had found the Gulf Rulers to be appreciative of the need for cooperation, including cooperation with Iran.[143] An important example of this kind of cooperation during the following years was that the small British-officered Omani navy shared responsibility with the larger Iranian navy for joint patrols of the Strait of Hormuz.[144]

In late May 1972, President Nixon visited Tehran on his way home from his summit meeting in Moscow. Nixon agreed to the Shah's request for F-14 and F-15 aircraft and also agreed to approve future Iranian requests. Indeed, a joint communiqué issued at the end of this visit on May 31 said that the littoral states had primary responsibility for the security of the Gulf and the United States would continue to cooperate with Iran in strengthening its defenses.[145] Meanwhile, on July 15, a French company beat British, American and Soviet competitors to sell twelve fighter aircraft to the UAE.[146] Despite the US military sales to Iran and Saudi Arabia, and despite US competition for UAE contracts, the United States generally adopted a policy of restraint and made only modest sales of defensive military equipment to the UAE after 1973, lagging behind France, Britain and West Germany.[147]

Nevertheless, the US saw the UAE as a partner in promoting stability in the region. On August 22, the State Department provided background for a briefing for UAE Foreign Minister Ahmed Khalifa Al-Suwaidi on the PDRY and subversive activities in the Gulf. It noted that US policy had been to strengthen Oman and the YAR because they were more vulnerable to the PDRY than Saudi Arabia and urged the UAE to do the same.

> We believe that in [the] long-run progressive popular and prosperous regimes in these countries can resist PDRY-inspired subversion. We do not rpt not seek any direct involvement in efforts to topple [the] PDRY and believe security in [the] Arabian peninsula is [a] matter exclusively for regional cooperation. Best role for [the] UAE is generous aid to regimes in Sanaa and Muscat at [a] time they [are] under pressure from [a] fanatic and well-armed PDRY.[148]

Besides the discussion on the PDRY, however, no mention was made of the islands case.

The United States also urged Saudi Arabia to cooperate with Iran and to normalize relations with the UAE. On January 8, 1973, the US

Embassy in Jeddah reported on Saudi diplomat Al-Saqqaf's statement to Ambassador Thacher that Saudi Arabia would not let the islands dispute interfere with Saudi-Iranian cooperation. Thacher pressed him for some further estimation of what tangible steps for Saudi-Iranian cooperation were possible but Al-Saqqaf expressed some skepticism regarding cooperation between the intelligence services of the two countries. Ambassador Thacher also pointed to improved Iranian relations with Kuwait and the UAE, and called for a resolution of the Saudi-UAE border dispute, arguing that the "burden should continue to rest with [the] more powerful of [the] two neighbors to get [the] present, undesirable situation off dead center."[149]

The United States viewed Iranian military power, however, as centrally important. On January 9, 1973, the US Embassy in Tehran reviewed Iran's military power and foreign relations for the State Department. It stated as follows:

> The...Gulf sheikhdoms and Saudi Arabia pose no threat to Iran, but are seen in Tehran as fertile centers for the growth of radical Arab nationalism of the Iraqi or South Yemeni brand. Should the conservative rulers be replaced by hostile adventurers, Iran fears its strategic access through the Gulf would be threatened. Accordingly, the GOI is already involved to some extent in aiding the harassed North Yemeni and Oman governments, including some military assistance. We would expect this pattern of assistance against radical subversion or invasion to continue.

The report predicted the "possibility" of Iranian military intervention and went on to suggest:

> It is possible that we might wish quietly to endorse a particular GOI military 'police action' or program of assistance. It is also possible, but more unlikely, that an Iranian action could seriously damage other US interests in the area and conceivable that we would seek to use our advice/supply leverage to influence the Shah's decisions.

In the end, the report noted that despite the Shah's personal reservations, "he has agreed to the normalization of relations through an exchange of Ambassadors."[150]

On April 13, 1973, the State Department expressed concern that Saudi Arabia seemed reluctant to discuss peninsular security affairs with

Iran, noted that Saudi Arabia seemed to be disturbed about the presence of Iranian special forces and helicopters in Oman and also about Iranian hesitation to provide military support to the YAR, and argued for "early and frank discussions between Riyadh and Tehran about their respective roles and activities in supporting peninsula states threatened by PDRY aggression/subversion." It stressed that US policy was "to continue [to] encourage both Saudis and Iranians to assume primary responsibility for regional security." The United States should not be a middleman because this "vitiates our policy of stimulating greater regional cooperation and self-reliance." Thus, US efforts should be geared to "pressing both sides, and especially Saudis, in getting on with developing [the] kind of dialogue with each other that would genuinely facilitate meaningful coordinated planning of assistance to other peninsular states."[151]

Another report four months later on August 3, 1973 continued to argue for Saudi-Iranian cooperation in the Gulf, but also noted that the issue of Abu Musa and the Tunbs remained a problem. When Iranian Foreign Minister Khalatbari visited Riyadh in July 1973, King Faisal "raised the Gulf islands issue, which he insisted should be settled in a manner acceptable to the Arab shaykhdoms." Khalatbari said Iran would not permit anyone to lay claim to "her lands." The Shah then wrote to Faisal, saying that no Iranian "would cede an inch of national territory." The report concluded: "As a result of mutual suspicions and nationalistic pride, Saudi-Iranian cooperation in the Gulf has never reached the point of policy coordination, even with US and UK prodding."[152]

By the mid-1970s, Iranian military assistance and Saudi financial assistance helped to put down the Dhofar rebellion and shore up the regime in Oman. This was matched by far-sighted domestic reforms introduced by Sultan Qaboos of Oman, which further strengthened the stability of Oman. Iran's presence on the islands, however, was not important to this outcome. Ironically, Iran's destabilization later in the decade, juxtaposed with the stability and prosperity of the UAE, and taking into account the behavior of the new Iranian regime on the islands in the 1980s and 1990s, demonstrates the risks of minimizing principles of international law for the sake of geopolitical calculations on a seemingly minor matter, particularly in the deliberations of a United Nations body.

The International Community and the Islands Dispute since 1979

Following the British withdrawal from the Gulf region, the United States gradually assumed the leading role of providing security and stability to the region. Confronted with the Iranian moves and the situation on the ground, however, the United States advised the UAE not to consider the use of force in an attempt to regain control of Abu Musa and the Tunbs. Instead, the United States has consistently supported the UAE's determination to seek a peaceful resolution of the dispute. Like Britain, the United States has not considered using force against Iran to resolve the islands issue. It is in this context that this chapter also looks into the determinants of the international community's responses to regional conflicts and offers an evaluation of international guarantees that purport to ensure the territorial integrity of small states.

The Record Toward the Islamic Republic of Iran

The Iranian revolution of 1978 and 1979, which toppled the Shah and ushered in the Islamic Republic of Iran, ended the US policy of relying upon a strong and friendly Iran to play an important role in safeguarding Western interests in the Gulf. This was followed by the Soviet invasion of Afghanistan in December 1979, which brought the Soviets closer to the Gulf. President Jimmy Carter thus warned in his January 1980 enunciation of the Carter Doctrine that the United States had vital interests in the Gulf and would use all necessary means, including force, to defend them from outside threats. As a result, a US Rapid Deployment Force (RDF) for possible military intervention in the Gulf was established, the US reached agreement with Oman that provided access for the US military to Omani air bases and naval ports, and US military sales to Saudi Arabia continued.[1]

The region was thrown into further turmoil with the outbreak of the Iran–Iraq War in September 1980. From the outset, the United States and Britain tried to prevent the islands issue from complicating and widening the war in its initial stage. When the British discovered by early October 1980 that the Iraqis were planning to occupy the islands from bases in Oman, the British and the Americans dissuaded Oman from supporting this operation while the Saudis dissuaded Iraq.[2] Britain and the United States clearly did not want to see the geographical scope of the war expanded to the Lower Gulf, where passage through the Strait of Hormuz and the sea-lanes leading to and from the Strait could be jeopardized.

From the outset of this war, the United States and the European Community warned that freedom of navigation in the Gulf as well as to and from the Gulf must not be infringed by the belligerents. The United States, Britain and France also quickly augmented their naval forces in and near the Gulf, with US access to facilities in Bahrain and Oman being important in this effort.[3] Indeed, the Carter administration had already deployed airborne warning and control system (AWACS) aircraft to the Eastern Province of Saudi Arabia in the fall of 1980 to provide protection against Iran. The new Reagan administration would approve the sale of AWACS and F-15 fighter bombers to Saudi Arabia in 1981, as well as military sales to the UAE and other members of the newly formed GCC during the remainder of the war.[4]

In October 1983, after Iran threatened to close the Strait of Hormuz and began reinforcing its garrisons on Larak, Sirri and Farsi Islands and increasing its artillery emplacements on Qishm and the Greater Tunb, President Ronald Reagan warned that the West would not tolerate such a closure and that the United States did not rule out taking action to stop it.[5] However, Iran did not act on its threat and the United States, which continued to develop the Rapid Deployment Force and established the Central Command in 1983, confined itself to diplomatic calls for adherence to the principle of freedom of navigation, such as the one made on October 31 in UN Security Council Resolution 540.[6]

The major powers continued to rely primarily on diplomatic rhetoric rather than action in the following two years, with President

Reagan, Vice-President George H.W. Bush, Secretary of State George Shultz, and Assistant Secretary of State Richard Murphy stressing the importance of freedom of navigation and the flow of oil, although the US Navy also did begin to escort the small number of US-flagged merchant vessels in the Gulf in 1986.[7] One major effort led by the United States and Britain was UN Security Council Resolution 598 of July 20, 1987, which demanded an end to the fighting and to attacks on neutral shipping, specified conditions for the Secretary General to negotiate peace, and invoked Articles 39 and 40 of Chapter VII of the UN Charter calling for further action, including the use of force, against either party refusing to accept the resolution.

When Iran did not accept the resolution, despite UN Secretary General Javier Perez de Cuellar's September 1987 visit to Tehran, the United States and its Western allies pushed for UN sanctions against Iran, with the Soviet Union and the People's Republic of China (PRC), however, reluctant to support this.[8] In the end, these resolutions and other actions did not deter Iran from attacking neutral shipping in the Gulf and in the Strait of Hormuz. In fact, attacks beginning in 1986 also spread to Kuwaiti and Saudi shipping off the UAE coast. In this context, it is clear that a UN Security Council Resolution on Abu Musa and the Tunbs would not have deterred Iran from using these islands as bases for helicopter and small boat attacks against shipping during these years.

In January 1987, National Security Advisor Frank Carlucci announced that the United States would not tolerate any Iranian interference with Gulf shipping. He soon presented President Reagan with a plan to re-flag and escort Kuwaiti vessels. Despite a CIA assessment on Iranian capabilities that reported that there was no way to stop Iran from harassing shipping, the decision to re-flag and escort Kuwaiti vessels was made in March.[9] In announcing this operation on May 19, 1987, Reagan said: "The use of the sea lanes will not be dictated by the Iranians. These lanes will not be allowed to come under the control of the Soviet Union. The Persian Gulf will remain open to navigation by the nations of the world."[10]

The traffic lanes through the Strait of Hormuz lie primarily in the deep navigable channels on the southern side of the Strait, in the territorial waters of Oman. Merchant vessels and warships, including

US-led convoys, were generally able to use these lanes during the tanker war, although there were incidents, such as the Iranian attacks against the *Diamond Marine* and the *Petroship B*, which were attacked in the Strait by Iranian forces from the Tunbs.[11] Inside the Gulf, the traffic lanes lie north and south of the Tunbs and to the north of Abu Musa. Iran had early in the war declared the waters from its coast to a line running 12 nautical miles south of Abu Musa, Sirri and Farsi to be a maritime war zone, a zone that thus encompassed the traffic lanes.[12]

Much shipping, including US-escorted convoys, avoided this maritime war zone and thus the traffic lanes, but Iran also attacked many ships outside of the zone off the coast of the UAE by helicopters and small boats from Abu Musa.[13] This means that despite the US insistence on freedom of navigation, the Iranian occupation of the Tunbs and Abu Musa and its claim to a twelve mile belt of territorial water around each of these islands enabled Iran to force US-escorted convoys inside the Gulf to forego use of the normal west and eastbound shipping lanes. However, the United States did fire on Iranian vessels inside Iran's maritime war zone on numerous occasions in retaliation for Iranian attacks against shipping outside of that zone.

During the first US-escorted convoy into the Gulf, the re-flagged *Bridgeton* tanker, formerly *Al-Rekkah*, was hit on July 24, 1987 by a moored mine in the main shipping channel 19 nautical miles (nmi) west of Farsi island, i.e. outside of Iran's maritime war zone, perhaps laid during small boat activity detected by AWACS on the previous night. The United States announced it would attack anyone laying mines in international waterways.[14] British, French, Italian and even Soviet naval vessels were deployed to the Gulf to either increase or begin their own escort convoys after Iranian attacks on their shipping. British, French, Italian, Dutch, Belgian and Soviet minesweepers were also deployed to the Gulf to lend assistance in clearing mines.

British Secretary of Defence George Younger warned that British warships in the Gulf could fire back if they or British-registered merchant ships were attacked, but the British *Armilla Patrol* only escorted convoys to a point 40 nmi west of Dubai and did not encounter many incidents. On the night of September 20/21, the United States intercepted, attacked and captured the *Iran Ajr* while it was in the act of laying mines.[15] On October 8, four small Revolutionary Guard boats were surprised by US Army MH-6 helicopters 15 nmi southwest of Farsi, i.e. outside Iran's maritime war zone, and when the Iranians opened fire, the helicopters sank one boat and damaged two others, which were then captured.[16]

On October 16, the re-flagged tanker *Sea Isle City* was hit while anchored at the Mina al-Ahmadi port in Kuwait by a Silkworm missile fired by the Revolutionary Guard from a missile base on the Fao peninsula. A US National Security Planning Group under Deputy National Security Adviser General Colin Powell rejected an attack against the Silkworm missile battery because it would suggest US support for Iraq. The Joint Chiefs of Staff (JCS) and the armed services favored an attack against the Revolutionary Guard base at Farsi Island or against a frigate that had been engaged in harassing shipping, but the State Department argued against this. Instead, US navy destroyers shelled the Reshadat (formerly Rostam) and the Resalat (formerly Rakhsh) oil platforms, which served as bases for the Revolutionary Guard and which had fired at a US helicopter eleven days earlier.[17]

On October 28, the United States announced a ban on imports from Iran and exports to Iran and tried to promote a world-wide embargo of Iran.[18] On November 6, Revolutionary Guard speedboats from Abu Musa attacked the US-operated tanker the *Grand Wisdom* 20 nautical miles west of Dubai's port of Jebel Ali.[19] On April 14, 1988 the missile frigate USS *Samuel B. Roberts* was severely damaged by a mine on its way from Kuwait to Bahrain after having escorted a tanker convoy to Kuwait. The Revolutionary Guard had laid this minefield one day earlier, once again outside Iran's maritime war zone.

In an Oval Office meeting, Admiral William J. Crowe, Jr., Chairman of the Joint Chiefs of Staff, wanted to retaliate against an Iranian warship and Carlucci, who was now Secretary of Defense, was inclined to agree with this. However. they were opposed by everyone else in the meeting. In the end, President Reagan authorized attacks not only against offshore oil platforms used by the Revolutionary Guards as observation and tracking platforms, but also against any approaching Iranian vessels.[20]

Thus, on April 18 the United States attacked the Sassan (now Salman) platform as well as the Nasr platform near Sirri island and sank an Iranian missile patrol boat after it fired a missile at the USS

411

Wainwright. The United States then detected the Iranian frigate *Zahan* as well as a squadron of Iranian Boghammer patrol boats heading toward a group of UAE offshore oil platforms. The Iranian Boghammers attacked a US helicopter, a US supply ship, a British tanker and an oil platform operated by the US firm Crescent Petroleum in the Mubarak oil field offshore of Abu Musa. After President Reagan's personal authorization, US Navy A-6s from the aircraft carrier USS *Enterprise* attacked and sank the *Zahan* and two of the Boghammers. Crowe writes that the rest of the Boghammers "just managed to race back to their base at Abu Musa in front of the pursuing warplanes."[21] Notably, however, the A-6s did not attack the rest of the Boghammers when they reached their Abu Musa base and did not attack the base of Abu Musa itself.

Later, after the Iranian frigate *Zabalon* fired a missile at the frigate USS *Jack Williams* and another missile at US Navy jets, US A-6s and A-7s badly damaged the *Zabalon*, but Carlucci and Crowe allowed it to return to port without sinking it. Crowe writes:

> I wanted the Iranians to understand that any time we felt like it we could start picking off their ships, and there wasn't a thing they could do about it. April 18 had gotten that message across loud and clear. The only options they had left were the Silkworm missiles, but they knew that using those against us would elicit a devastating response.[22]

Indeed, the United States had warned Iran in the summer of 1987 that it would destroy Iranian Silkworms in the area of the Strait of Hormuz, on Qishm and at Kuhestak, if they were used to attack US-escorted convoys. Five missiles, possibly Silkworms, were fired at the frigate USS *Jack Williams* late in the day on April 18, but missed.[23] Had the frigate been hit, and had the missiles been identified as Silkworms, the US threat would have been tested and may have been carried out.

On July 3, 1988, the USS *Vincennes* shot down an Iran Air Airbus, mistaking it for an Iranian F-14, and killing its 290 civilian passengers. This tragedy occurred while the *Vincennes* was in the midst of an engagement with Iranian Boghammers in the western reaches of the Strait of Hormuz. The Boghammers had fired on a reconnaissance helicopter sent by the *Vincennes* to investigate Boghammer action against a neutral Pakistani merchant vessel.[24] Inasmuch as Abu Musa was a base for the Iranian Boghammer fleet and this engagement occurred in the western reaches of the Strait of Hormuz, it may be that the Boghammers that were involved in this incident and that contributed to the making of this tragedy were operating out of Abu Musa.

Iran finally accepted UN Security Council Resolution 598 in July 1988 and the UN Secretary General negotiated the terms of the cease-fire by August 1988. The Revolutionary Guard was withdrawn from its base at Abu Musa in October 1988 and Operation Earnest Will came to an end in January 1989.[25]

It should be noted here that US targeting decisions during Operation Earnest Will took into account military, political and legal considerations. Carlucci recalled later that the United States considered Iranian actions from Abu Musa and the Tunbs to be threats to shipping, but the islands were not discussed as targets for retaliation by a group including himself, Weinberger, Shultz, Crowe, Powell and White House Chief of Staff James Baker.[26] One State Department official stationed in Abu Dhabi at the time says that the islands could have been neutralized fairly readily, but it was not judged to be militarily necessary to hit the islands and there was no political reason to take action. The US Navy tracked Iran's activities from the islands closely and consulted with the UAE. While Iranian behavior was considered ominous, at no time did US officials think they could not deal with Iran.[27]

Another US official in Abu Dhabi at the time argues that it did not make sense to hit the islands as the United States was only seeking retaliation and deterrence. The United States could not neutralize the islands permanently unless US forces were stationed on the islands; and garrisoning the islands would have created complications both for the United States and the UAE.[28]

Crowe writes that whenever US retaliation was discussed, State Department officials argued that it must be "proportionate" and "not in any sense an escalation."[29] An official at the Department of State Legal Department also argues that a general rule guided US targeting decisions during the tanker war—the desire not to escalate the conflict and not to endanger the perception of US neutrality. Any US retaliation against Iran's land territory, even disputed territory such as the islands, would have run that risk. Iran's oil platforms on the other hand, although they were Iranian property, were in international waters, so retaliation against them did not run the same risk.[30]

In November 1992, Iran lodged a complaint against the United States at the International Court of Justice (ICJ) for firing at the Iranian offshore oil platforms during the tanker war. Iran claimed that the US had violated the terms of the 1955 Treaty of Amity, Economic Relations and Consular Rights between Iran and the US, which ensured freedom of commerce and navigation between the two parties. In its Counter-Memorial and Counter-Claim submitted to the ICJ in June 1997, the United States rebutted Iran's arguments. The United States documented Iran's use of these oil platforms to attack US and other neutral shipping with numerous pieces of evidence, including captured Iranian military communications, eye-witness and official reports, photographs and missile fragments. The US argued that its actions were "necessary to protect its essential security interests" and thus exempt from coverage by the treaty. The United States argued that its actions were taken in legitimate self-defense against unlawful armed attacks by Iran against US ships and nationals, arguing that they were "necessary and appropriate to restore their security and prevent continuing attacks," that they were "proportional to the antecedent attacks," were "deliberately limited in scope and duration," were "planned and conducted so as to avoid unnecessary suffering and collateral damage," and were not, as Iran argued, "reprisals intended to inflict economic damage."

According to an official with the Legal Department of the State Department, the US response also documents the use of Abu Musa and the Tunbs for attacking shipping. In that case, similar legal considerations of self-defense could have been taken into account in considering these islands as possible targets. It is possible that an attack against the Boghammers docked at Abu Musa and harbor facilities at the island could have been considered "necessary and proportionate" inasmuch as the Boghammers that attacked shipping near the Mubarak oil fields on April 18 were based at Abu Musa. Even if this legal argument had been made, however, the political and military rationale for not escalating the conflict by attacking territory claimed by Iran may have taken precedence.[31]

US policy in the future may be influenced by the accuracy or inaccuracy of the recollections of decision-makers during the tanker war, as well as the accuracy or inaccuracy of the information possessed by current decision-makers. It is thus worth noting that some key US officials during Operation Earnest Will do not recall the role that Abu Musa and the Tunbs played in the tanker war and that some more recent and current US officials with responsibility for the Gulf are not fully aware of the role that these islands played. One State Department official says that the islands could have been used to launch raids, but he does not remember.[32]

More significant is that a former Commander of US Central Command during the 1990s says that when he ran CENTCOM he never heard of Abu Musa having been used as a platform to launch attacks during the tanker war.[33] It is also a fact that a number of former and current US officials do not have very deep knowledge about the UAE's historic possession and legal right to the islands. One current State Department official who was at the US Embassy in Abu Dhabi during the tanker war says that he was never perfectly persuaded whether the UAE claim or the Iranian claim to the islands was stronger, that not many of his colleagues paid any attention to the issue, and that the United States did not take an official position on the issue during the war.[34] More accurate historical information about the way Iran used these islands during the tanker war and more knowledge about the strength of the UAE's historical and legal claim to the islands would help US decision-makers in the future.

A former American diplomat notes that the United States did not pay much attention to the islands until after Iran's 1992 violations of the MoU on Abu Musa. The United States deferred to and very much approved of the UAE intention to seek a peaceful resolution of the dispute. It also had a preference for a bilateral negotiated settlement with Iran and understood that the UAE was raising this issue in international fora, e.g. the GCC and the Arab League, in order to encourage Iran to engage in bilateral negotiations. However, the United States did not want to take a position on the contending legal claims to the islands. Neither was US military action considered as an option in response to the events of 1992.[35]

During the 1992-1993 timeframe, the United States and the UAE talked about but decided not to press for a Security Council resolution on the islands. If there were less than a very strong majority in the Security Council, such a move could have been counterproductive. Issues such as the change of membership of the Security Council over time and the views of some members due to their own parallel situations, e.g. Turkey and Greece thinking about their dispute over Cyprus and worries over possible precedents, prevented the United States and the UAE from moving forward. The United States also did not want to cause a further hardening of the Iranian position on the islands, which it suspected would happen if a new resolution was tabled.[36]

It may be added here that while post-Soviet Russia and the PRC have both valued their diplomatic and commercial relations with the UAE, Russia and China have both given priority to their diplomatic and commercial relations with Iran and would probably have been reluctant to support the UAE on the islands issue.[37] However, in September 1992 the Arab League did ask the UN Secretary General to use his good offices to take up the matter. On January 2, 1994, UN Secretary General Boutros Boutros Ghali said the UN would play any appropriate role to resolve the dispute. He sought a meeting, but Tehran would not receive him.[38]

The United States took further interest in Abu Musa and the Tunbs, beginning in 1994 and 1995. A communiqué released after an April 27, 1994 meeting between US Secretary of State Warren Christopher and the six GCC foreign ministers stated that the US Secretary of State and the GCC foreign ministers appreciated the UAE's efforts to resolve the issue of the three islands and called on Iran to enter into serious discussions with the UAE to resolve the dispute.[39] A press release issued after a September 30, 1994 meeting between the GCC foreign ministers and the Secretary of State said: "The GCC Ministers noted, with appreciation, the support of the United States for the GCC's call to refer the dispute between Iran and the United Arab Emirates over the three Emirate islands to the International Court of Justice."[40] Then, after a meeting on March 12, 1995, Christopher and the GCC foreign ministers issued a joint communiqué, which read as follows:

> The Ministers expressed their deep appreciation for the United Arab Emirates' efforts to peacefully resolve the issue of the Iranian occupation of the three islands – the Greater Tomb, the Lesser Tomb and Abu Musa, which belong to [the] UAE. The Ministers urged the Islamic Republic of Iran to respond positively to the initiative of the United Arab Emirates and to agree to refer this dispute to the International Court of Justice.[41]

Richard Schofield has written that when Christopher "added his name" to this March 12, 1995 communiqué, "the USA took the unusual step of departing from its position of neutrality in the territorial disputes of the region."[42] Indeed, the document asserted unequivocally that the islands "belong to the UAE." State Department officials in Washington and Abu Dhabi, however, have noted only that Christopher made a statement that "the UAE has a strong claim to the islands." While they acknowledge that this added a new element to the official US position on the history of and legal claims to the islands, they also argue that "Department of State policy is not to engage in the merits of the issue." The United States is not anxious to get into the ownership question, i.e. not anxious to take Iran on over territorial disputes, they say. There will be no unilateral US action to settle the legal dispute over the islands. The United States does not find the legal dispute to be a cause to provoke fighting for, although US officials do not concede the Iranian view.[43]

US support at the end of September 1994 came at a time when Washington appreciated UAE and GCC support for the Arab-Israeli peace process, particularly pledges to end their secondary and tertiary boycott of foreign firms doing business with Israel. Christopher's willingness to take an additional step in March 1995 came at a time when the United States was seeking UAE and GCC influence with other Arab League members to end these boycotts and when it was seeking UAE and GCC financial support for the Palestinian National Authority and the Middle East Development Bank.[44]

Christopher's announcement in March 1995 also coincided with growing US concern that the Iranian military buildup on and around the islands was a potential threat. On February 28, 1995, Chairman of the Joint Chiefs of Staff General John Shalikashvili noted that Iran had deployed Hawk anti-aircraft missiles on an island in the Strait of Hormuz, had loaded missiles into launchers and had deployed artillery in forward positions. "All of that could lead me to lots of conclusions," Shalikashvili said. "One of them is that they want to have the capability to interdict the traffic in the Straits of Hormuz." At the same time, other Pentagon officials observed that Iran had increased its troops on Abu Musa and the Tunbs from 700 to 4,000 and had deployed tanks, SA-6 surface-to-air missiles and 155-millimeter artillery on the islands. Coupled with Chinese-made Seersucker anti-ship missiles on the Iranian mainland and on other islands in the area, the deployment "gives them surface-to-surface missile and artillery coverage of waterways." However, another Pentagon official said "there's no indication of hostile intent. The real concern is the possibility for an inadvertent incident where ships pass too close and some trigger-happy guy lets loose a round." President Bill Clinton added that while "we think there is no undue cause for concern at this moment…It's a situation that we're monitoring very closely."[45]

After Iran complained about Shalikashvili's remarks, Defense Department spokesman Kenneth Bacon said on March 2 that the Iranian deployments on Abu Musa and neighboring islands had been taking place since mid-October 1994, when the United States had increased its military presence in the Gulf to thwart any move against Kuwait by Iraq, and observed:

> We see it as primarily defensive. We don't see it as something that is designed to threaten international or U.S. shipping in the area. The deployments do, however, increase the possibility of miscalculation and mistakes. They are worrisome from that standpoint.[46]

Nevertheless, in testimony before the Senate on the same day, Assistant Secretary of Defense Joseph Nye argued:

> Whatever the specific Iranian motivation for fortifying the islands, the creation by a hostile power of bases sitting astride the western approaches to the Straits of Hormuz is obviously a matter of serious concern for commercial traffic, our own naval presence, and the security of our Arab friends.[47]

Moreover, Secretary of Defense William J. Perry spoke publicly about these Iranian deployments in the Strait of Hormuz on March 22, 1995, during a tour of the six GCC states, arguing: "It's a deployment of force beyond any reasonable defensive requirement and can only be regarded as a threat to shipping in the area." When administration officials explained that they had seen evidence that chemical weapons had been deployed on Abu Musa, White House spokesman Michael McCurry said there was "a high degree of concern" in the administration about Iran's intentions. Those officials who had earlier considered the Iranian deployments to be a defensive reaction to the US deployments to the Gulf in October 1994 were now questioning their original analysis in light of the fact that the Iranian deployments were continuing and increasing in the spring of 1995.[48]

Later, in a May 1995 publication entitled *United States Security Strategy for the Middle East*, the US Department of Defense cited Iran's acquisition of conventional weapons and its military build-up on the disputed islands as evidence that Iran "is actively seeking the capability to menace merchant ships moving in and out of the Gulf" and "is assertively flexing its muscles vis-à-vis its smaller Gulf neighbors." The Department of Defense also warned in this publication that Iran's WMD programs could have "serious repercussions for regional stability and perhaps for our [US] ability to protect our interests in the area."[49] In the summer of 1995, the United States reactivated the Fifth Fleet as part of the Central Command with responsibility for naval operations in the Gulf and the Indian Ocean.[50] In January 1996, the commander of the US Fifth Fleet, based in Bahrain, noted that Iran had test-launched a Chinese-made ship-launched anti-ship missile near the Strait of Hormuz.[51] A year later, during a mid-June 1997 tour of the Gulf, US Secretary of Defense William Cohen noted that Iran had just test launched a new air-launched Chinese-made anti-ship missile and said, "Iran's words and actions suggest that it wants to be able to intimidate its neighbors and to interrupt commerce in the Gulf," warning, "The United States will not allow this to happen."[52]

Christopher's announcement in March 1995 also came at a time when the United States was considering legislation to prohibit US trade with Iran, particularly after the American oil company Conoco announced a deal with Iran in which the company would develop two Iranian oil and gas fields off shore of Sirri in the Gulf. President Clinton issued an Executive Order banning such oil and gas development deals on March 14, 1995. This was followed on May 6, 1995 by an Executive Order banning all US trade, trade financing, loans and financial services to Iran. In August 1996, Clinton signed the Iran and Libya Sanctions

Act, which authorized the President to impose sanctions on foreign firms investing in the development of Iran's oil and gas resources.[53]

The US Department of State issued an official statement in October 1997 that expressed the view that the UAE has a strong claim to the islands and supported the UAE's diplomatic efforts to achieve a peaceful resolution of the dispute with Iran and that also expressed concern about Iran's militarization of the islands. The statement read as follows:

> The United States supports the UAE's efforts to achieve a peaceful resolution of its dispute with Iran over three islands in the Gulf, Abu Musa and Greater and Lesser Tunb.
>
> We have watched with concern as Iran has built up a military presence on all three islands. Regrettably, Iran continues to heat up the dispute by taking more and more provocative actions, such as increasing its military presence and creating facts on the ground. Tehran should refrain from any further provocative or destabilizing action.
>
> The United States believes the UAE has a strong claim to the islands. We encourage the parties to find a peaceful solution, whether by direct negotiation, by referring the matter to the International Court of Justice in the Hague, or by some other mutually agreeable mechanism.
>
> We note that the GCC, the Arab League and the European Union have all expressed support for the UAE's diplomatic campaign to resolve the islands dispute peacefully. The world will be watching to see how Tehran responds.[54]

This can be seen as a definite statement of US policy toward the islands issue during the 1990s.

Britain also expressed support for the UAE from 1992 onwards. During meetings with UAE Minister of State for Foreign Affairs Shaikh Hamdan bin Zayed Al-Nahyan in London in October 1994, British Foreign Secretary Douglas Hurd and other British officials expressed British support for the UAE's demand that the issue of the three islands be referred to the International Court of Justice.[55] Hurd also said on a mid-March 1995 visit to the UAE, "The UAE approach in handling the matter is resolute and cautious and we strongly support their move to resolve it at the International Court of Justice."[56] The European Union, while under the presidency of Britain in April 1998, also reiterated its support for a peaceful resolution of the islands dispute in accordance with international law, either through direct negotiations or the ICJ.[57]

Iran's subsequent behavior also elicited new statements from US and British officials visiting the Gulf in March of 1999. British Minister of State for Foreign and Commonwealth Affairs Derek Fatchett said on March 4, "We want to see a peaceful solution to the conflict. That's why we have always said the issue should be resolved through the international legal system."[58] US Central Command Commander General Anthony Zinni also expressed US support for a peaceful resolution of the islands dispute on March 14.[59] The US Ambassador to the UAE, Theodore Kattouf, said in June, "We would like to see the islands' issue resolved through serious negotiations between Iran and the UAE," or through the ICJ, adding, "We are disturbed by the Iranian approach towards the islands' issue. The issue should be resolved amicably."[60]

British Foreign and Commonwealth Minister Peter Hain, addressing the islands issue, said in October, "The UAE is understandably concerned about its security and I have conveyed this to the Iranian government. We will stand rock solid behind the UAE protecting its security." Hain also noted, "We want to see Iran at peace with its neighbors. The UK feels that through positive diplomatic engagement with President Khatami and his reform programme – which we want to see fulfilled – this can be achieved."[61] Tarja Halonen, Finland's Minister of Foreign Affairs and the President of a EU-GCC meeting, reiterated that the EU supports a peaceful resolution of the islands dispute, either through direct negotiation or through the ICJ.[62]

In January 2000, the People's Republic of China reaffirmed its support for the UAE's efforts to resolve the islands issue peacefully when Deputy Foreign Minister A.J.B. Deng said in Abu Dhabi, "The UAE approach is wise and consistent with the international accords and norms."[63] In March, US Assistant Secretary of State Edward (Ned) Walker said that recent US overtures to Iran did "not mean any change in its policy towards the UAE islands issue." He noted, "The U.S. stands firmly behind the Gulf Cooperation Council initiative which calls for resolving the issue through peaceful negotiations," adding that the US overtures to Iran might enable the United States to persuade Iran's moderate leaders and new parliament to be more responsive to negotiations on the issue.[64]

In April, General Zinni said, "I think if they (Iranian officials) want good relations in the Gulf, they will have to come to grips with the issue and engage the UAE in resolving the issue." When asked specifically if the United States supported the UAE view that Iran must vacate the islands, Zinni said only, "I think the best position for us (the United States) to take is to encourage them (UAE and Iran) to sit down and resolve the issue."[65] In late October, Peter Hain said, "We are establishing good diplomatic relations with the Iranians and in that we represent the concerns of the Emirates and ask for the dispute to be resolved as peacefully as possible." He added, however, that "I don't think Britain can either take responsibility for this situation or play an up front role in resolving it," noting that Britain was waiting to see the outcome of the GCC's effort to resolve the dispute.[66]

Moreover, in April 2001, former US President Jimmy Carter, who would win the Nobel Peace Prize in 2002, noting GCC support for the UAE's position, said: "All the countries are cooperating with the UAE for the recovery of the islands and Iran will realise it is not just a lonely call, but others have joined in for the peaceful resolution of this issue."[67]

UAE Needs, UN Responsibilities and US Policy

An official from the UAE Ministry of Foreign Affairs noted in 1997 that the UAE has received support for its call for a peaceful resolution of the islands issue not only from the GCC, the Arab League, the Non-Aligned Movement and the European Union, but also from the General Assembly and from major foreign powers on the Security Council, particularly the United States and Britain. The UAE is making progress in developing international support, he said. It is patient. It does not want a crisis. It thinks Iran will come to its senses and is counting on the international community to persuade Iran regarding the cost of its occupation, namely that Iran cannot emerge from its isolation and improve its economy until it resolves this issue.[68]

In the meantime, however, Iran refuses to negotiate on all three islands, rebuffs the good offices of the UN Secretary General, and refuses to refer the dispute to the ICJ. Moreover, there is some concern in the UAE that even if both parties agreed to take the dispute to the ICJ, the Court would not reach a judgment until it thought that there was a mutual understanding between the parties and that the decision of the Court would be implemented by the parties. The Court generally does not want to have to enlist the Security Council to implement a binding Court judgment against the will of one of the parties to a dispute, and the UAE and the United States also do not want a Court decision that would be rejected by Iran and put the Court and the Security Council in this position.[69]

Another potential option for the UAE may be found in the ICJ's 1975 opinion on the *Western Sahara* case, which indicated that the Court may render advisory opinions even if one party has refused to submit the matter to the Court.[70] If the Court rendered an advisory opinion favorable to the UAE, there could be an initiative in the General Assembly to adopt the recommendation of the Court. The General Assembly cannot impose a decision on member states, but a Court opinion can influence the General Assembly's own activities. The General Assembly can also take the results to the Security Council for a binding or non-binding resolution adopting the Court decision. This could make it easier eventually to advocate and secure measures against Iran such as UN censure, economic sanctions or the use of force, although such measures are not now favored by the UAE.[71]

Under Article 96 of the UN Charter, the United States or Britain could ask the Security Council or the General Assembly to ask the ICJ for an advisory opinion on the islands, or they could ask the General Assembly to authorize a specialized agency to ask for such an opinion, perhaps asking whether Iran's presence on the Tunbs is legal in light of its use of force to acquire them and whether Iran's MoU on Abu Musa is legal in light of its use of duress to obtain it. It appears from conversations with State Department officials that the US has given little thought to this, and that it would be concerned that this would harden Iran's position. It is even more unlikely that Britain would pursue this option. Moreover, UAE officials think that the Court would be very reluctant to render such an opinion. Nevertheless, it remains an option for the future.[72]

One line of legal questioning that is of considerable interest to the US, is also one that the International Maritime Commission might be able to ask of the ICJ. It emerges from the tension between US support for a right of innocent passage of warships through territorial waters in peacetime without prior authorization or notification, and Iran's national legislation requiring prior authorization for the innocent passage of warships through Iran's territorial waters in peacetime.[73]

What are the implications of Iran's unresolved dispute with the UAE regarding sovereignty over these islands and over a twelve-mile belt of territorial sea around each of them? Does it mean that Iran cannot demand prior authorization to foreign warships seeking to exercise the right of innocent passage through the sea-lanes in the territorial waters of these islands during peacetime under the 1982 Convention of the Law of the Sea? Does the fact that Iran acquired the Tunbs by force and Abu Musa by duress mean that Iran has no right to make this demand? Other legal questions arise. Does the dispute over sovereignty and Iran's violations of international law in acquiring these islands mean that Iran cannot decide that the passage of foreign warships past the islands in peacetime is not innocent, and thus that Iran cannot prohibit their passage past the islands under the 1982 Convention on the Law of the Sea? Does the dispute over sovereignty and Iran's violations of international law in acquiring the islands mean that Iran cannot include these islands and their territorial waters in a maritime war zone, and thus that Iran cannot interfere with the passage of non-belligerent merchant ships and non-belligerent warships, e.g. neutral oil tankers, US Navy vessels and US-led convoys, past these islands during wartime?

Regarding the role of the United States, US officials have agreed with UAE thinking that the country can probably count on a broad US-led coalition including European states and Japan, as in the case of Desert Shield and Desert Storm, if an overt attack against and occupation of the UAE ever occurred. In the case of an imminent threat to international peace and security in the Gulf concerning the UAE or shipping in the Gulf, the US would want a Security Council resolution to back up any possible military action. However, this would not be an absolute necessity. During the second Gulf War, for example, US President George H.W. Bush indicated that the US would have engaged Iraq with or without a relevant Security Council Resolution.[74] In 2003, the United States and Britain undertook military operations against Iraq despite the opposition of the other permanent members of the Security Council, a subject that will be returned to in the coming pages.

Some UAE officials have noted, however, that Iran's occupation and militarization of the three islands has not triggered much US reaction beyond expressions of concern about the military buildup on the islands, which are basically US warnings to Iran not to think about interfering with shipping in the Gulf.[75] Interviews with former US officials indicate why there has not been more of a US response to the Iranian occupation and militarization of the islands, why the US response to any potential Iranian covert operations against the UAE is undefined, and why mobilizing a US and UN response to Iran's violation of international law since its 1971 occupation of the islands will continue to be difficult for the UAE. These interviews clearly do not bear out the Iranian charge that the UAE has been encouraged by the United States to expand this dispute with Iran, a charge that has even been made by a legal adviser to the Sharjah Ruler.[76]

US officials have noted that the UAE has not asked the United States for any specific action to resolve the islands dispute, such as the forcible eviction of Iran from the islands.[77] Neither has the UAE wanted the United States to employ military force for this. The UAE does not need or seek a confrontation with Iran and does not even want the islands issue to figure prominently in US-Iranian relations.[78] Even if the UAE asked, however, US officials have stressed that the United States faces constraints in playing an activist role in resolving regional disputes like the islands question.

In 1997, State Department officials stressed that in international law the theoretical possibility of attack does not justify the use of force. The Israeli attack on the Osirak nuclear reactor in Iraq in 1981 was therefore not lawful. Iran's military assets on Abu Musa and the Tunbs and the potential this gives Iran for attacking the UAE or its oil fields or even international shipping in the Gulf do not come close to justifying the use of force by the United States, these officials argued. A threat must be in the form of an armed attack or an immediate apparent threat of sufficient gravity to justify an act of self-defense. Furthermore, the use of force must be necessary and proportionate.[79] According to these arguments, US force would not be considered for the purpose of resolving the islands dispute. However, US force could possibly be applied against Iranian positions on the islands in the context of a larger military action against Iran, if that is ever considered necessary.

Moreover, US officials have argued that the islands issue is not primarily a US responsibility and that the United States has no political interest in escalating the conflict. Any US military action against Iran on the islands has been considered highly unlikely unless Iran were to launch an attack or become a greater threat. While there probably exists a contingency plan for the islands at the Pentagon, one former US diplomat assumes, the fact is that this has not been a subject of political discussion.[80] In theory, however, Defense Department officials list the following potential US courses of action:

1. Direct attack on the islands by air interdiction and sea bombardment for total destruction of Iranian military assets.

2. Direct attack on the islands for partial destruction of assets and then allow Iran to withdraw from the islands.

3. Direct attack on the islands to eliminate an immediate threat and then blockade the islands.

4. Bypass the islands and isolate them through a blockade.

Nevertheless, the United States does not outline specific responses to specific situations. The Iranians assume there is some arrangement between the UAE and the United States. If Iran uses the islands to attack the UAE or to fire on US ships or to interfere with other shipping, the United States will respond. However, if the islands are used for more covert operations, US retaliation is less likely because this would be harder to pin on Iran. Also, it is doubtful whether the sabotage of UAE oil fields would be considered a threshold for US action.[81]

Asked if the United States is waiting for an Iranian provocation to justify US military action on the islands, one official at the Joint Staff answered in 1997 that the United States really supports legal, peaceful ways of resolving the dispute. There is a tremendous downside to participation in military conflict—the financial cost and the military cost of taking on Iran. While the United States would consider military options if the UAE and the GCC asked for help regarding Iranian commando operations from the islands, these cannot be pinned down in terms of when or why or how. Moreover, any action specifically against the islands would have to follow through against the Iranian mainland and would be a very serious step. The islands are thus more of a political problem than a military problem. Therefore, the Defense Department has factored the island issue into Pentagon operational plans, but they have not thought of actively ejecting Iran from the islands.[82]

If anything, as another official at the Joint Staff said in 1997, there has been a concern that any military actions by the UAE or other GCC actors regarding the islands might complicate US access to oil. In order to avoid any such interruption of international commerce, the United States has continued to support a peaceful resolution of this dispute as a way to avoid more dangerous circumstances.[83] This reluctance to consider UAE or US military actions regarding the islands was also confirmed by interviews at the Defense Intelligence Agency. However, the islands are in the category of "indications and warnings" and are watched on a regular basis throughout the entire US intelligence community, e.g. or especially by US Naval Forces Central Command (NAVCENT), more than once a day.[84]

In the event of Iran again using the islands to interfere with traffic through the Gulf and the Strait of Hormuz, the United States could decide, as it did during Operation Earnest Will, to have the US Navy and merchant shipping travel along the UAE coast in an effort to avoid Iranian-claimed territorial waters and Iranian attacks. At present, US aircraft carriers transit south of Abu Musa, but smaller US naval craft transit north of the island. Moreover, the United States could decide to attack only those Iranian vessels operating from Abu Musa and the Tunbs, rather than attacking the islands themselves.

If, however, Iranian attacks were so widespread and effective as to threaten to actually interrupt traffic through the Gulf and the Strait, effectively closing them, then the military and political constraints of not escalating the conflict might no longer be relevant and US retaliation against the islands might meet the legal standard that retaliation must be necessary and proportionate. An overt Iranian attack against the UAE would seem to justify US retaliation against the islands for the same reasons, but it might not be true in the case of an overt Iranian attack against UAE oilfields or in the case of a covert and deniable Iranian attack against UAE oilfields or the UAE itself.

A former CENTCOM commander from the early 1990s adds that he cannot conceive of wanting or needing to eject Iran from the islands or to preemptively attack its military capabilities on the islands because the United States could neutralize the islands in short order if they figured in any Iranian military action.[85] An official with the Northern Gulf Affairs bureau adds that while the islands are a military threat, this has not translated into any necessity for a policy change because the United States is capable of dealing with the military threat.[86]

One important element of the US policy of containment of Iran, namely the US policy of economic sanctions against Iran, including the possibility of US secondary sanctions on foreign firms participating in Iran's oil and gas industry, may have limited utility in resolving the islands dispute and may even harden Iran's position on the issue. Although the sanctions are restricting US commercial interests, it is argued that this policy is designed to pressure Iran into changing its objectionable foreign policies. UAE officials are not convinced that such an approach, which serves to slow Iran's oil and gas development, is a good one.

Indeed, Iran is seen as attempting to intimidate and pressure the UAE into investing in Iran's troubled oil and gas industry. Thus, US sanctions may actually make Iran's motivation to pressure the UAE more acute. It also intensifies Iran's motivation to hold on to its stake in the Mubarak oil field production offshore of Abu Musa, as well as its stake in potential production offshore of the Tunbs.

An officer of Crescent Oil argues that the wording of the 1995 US Executive Order signed by President Clinton actually lent credence to Iran's position on the islands by saying it applied to "the land territory claimed by Iran and any other area over which Iran claims sovereignty, sovereign rights or jurisdiction, including the territorial sea, exclusive economic zone, and continental shelf claimed by Iran." The State Department has declined to clarify this and did not respond to a letter from UAE Minister of Finance and Industry HH Shaikh Hamdan bin Rashid Al-Maktoum to Warren Christopher on the issue, although it is said that the US advised the UAE verbally.[87]

An official with the State Department insisted in 1997 that it is not US policy to engage in the legal merits of the dispute. The Department of State thought about how to word the geographical scope clause of the Executive Order prohibiting the Conoco deal and restricting US participation in Iranian oil and gas projects without being misconstrued as making any statement about Iranian sovereignty. Thus, the wording was intended to avoid any US position on the relative merits of the claims of the respective parties. Nevertheless, Crescent Oil had to restructure its concession agreement for the Mubarak offshore oil field to fall in line with the Executive Order.[88] Meanwhile, the other major world powers do not want to cooperate with the United States on this sanctions policy. They continue to engage in trade with Iran, and argue that their policy of "constructive engagement" and "critical dialogue" is more likely to produce change in Iranian policies than the US policy of containment. This includes Britain, which restored diplomatic relations with Iran in 1999.[89]

With the emergence of reformist President Mohammed Khatami in 1997, signs for a possible easing of tensions in US-Iranian relations increased. In December 1997, President Clinton responded to President Khatami's call for a "thoughtful dialogue" to resolve differences with the United States by saying "I would like nothing better than to have a dialogue with Iran."[90] However, interviews with Clinton administration officials during the same time period indicated that dialogue was not a likely medium-term development. Many simply thought that Iran was not ready and that there was no visible change in standing Iranian policies. Others argued that US action is constrained by the US Congress, which has continued to take a largely negative view of developments in Iran. Even if a dialogue of sorts were to begin, officials said, the islands would not figure prominently at the top of any agenda.[91]

When reformists won Iran's parliamentary elections in early 2000, US Secretary of State Madeleine Albright announced the lifting of the US ban on Iranian pistachios, carpets and caviar, Iran's largest exports after oil and gas, acknowledged Iran's grievances against the United States, said that the United States had been shortsighted in restoring the Shah in 1953 and supporting him thereafter and also shortsighted in supporting Iraq during the Iran–Iraq War, and called for a new relationship with Iran. However, Iran did not respond positively and the US Congress also had reservations.[92]

Indeed, it should be noted that President Khatami said soon after his election in 1997 that the islands belong to Iran. Moreover, while he called for dialogue with the UAE on the issue, he said, "intervention of other governments and powers would not be in the interest of either of us."[93] These statements and Iran's attitude and behavior since 1997 suggest that Iran might not be willing to discuss this issue in any dialogue with the United States. The US position, however, has been that both parties should be able to bring up any issue in an authoritative dialogue. If such a dialogue can ever be arranged, the United States could certainly try to raise this issue.

In the aftermath of the terrorist attacks on New York and Washington, DC on September 11, 2001, the administration of President George W. Bush, the son of former President George H.W. Bush, expressed a willingness to engage in unilateral pre-emption against terrorists and their state sponsors. The Bush administration articulated this doctrine in *The National Security Strategy of the United States of America* in September 2002 and warned that it was prepared to apply this doctrine against Saddam Hussein's Iraq.[94]

In the light of the fact that President Bush included Iran in the "axis of evil" of terrorists and their state sponsors in his *State of the Union* speech in January 2002, there may be a greater willingness to engage in pre-emptive military action against Iran in the future. Iran was accused of shipping arms to Palestinian terrorists in January 2002 and was also accused of sheltering al-Qaeda terrorists fleeing from US military operations in Afghanistan in that same month. Iran successfully test-launched the intermediate range Shahab-3 ballistic missile in May 2002 and announced a whole series of developments in its nuclear energy program in 2002 and 2003, developments that persuaded many in the Bush administration that Iran was seeking nuclear weapons. In July 2002, Bush warned Iran to abandon its "uncompromising and destructive" policies and to embrace reform. The Bush administration also abandoned attempts to establish any dialogue with Iran in that same month.[95]

The Bush administration may be more likely to consider pre-emptive military action against Iran if the US campaign in Iraq is successful and if Iran does not change its policies. While pre-emptive military action would presumably target Iran's suspected weapons of mass destruction capabilities, the United States would have to consider the potential for Iran to retaliate against US military assets and allies in the Gulf. Thus, the United States would have to be prepared to attack Iran's conventional military capabilities in the Gulf, as well as Iran's weapons of mass destruction facilities. Under these circumstances, previous US military, political and legal concerns about attacking Iranian military assets on Abu Musa and the Tunbs would no longer apply. The UAE could possibly recover its islands in such a scenario. The UAE would then have a capability to defend the islands, but holding the islands would also depend upon a continuing commitment from the United States.

When thinking about US policy on bilateral negotiations between the UAE and Iran, an ICJ judgment or advisory opinion, US economic sanctions, US dialogue with Iran or the use of US force, the general lack of knowledge about the islands possessed by US policy-makers must be considered. While there are a few officials who are aware that the UAE has a much stronger legal claim to the islands than Iran, due to their exposure to the case, almost no one in the US Government could give an informed answer about the historical and legal claims of the UAE and contending claims by Iran. Interviews with numerous US officials have confirmed this.[96] Indeed, while the State Department recommends what the US position on the islands should be, this has not been based on an examination of the merits of the legal case, since the United States has favored a negotiated settlement of the issue.[97]

Clearly, the United States and Britain have viewed the Islamic Republic of Iran in an entirely different light from Iran under the Shah. This might have been reflected in a somewhat more serious effort to resolve the dispute over Abu Musa and the Tunbs following the two Gulf wars and after Iran became more aggressive on Abu Musa. Even so, due to the constraints and considerations mentioned above, the United States and Britain have confined themselves to diplomatic statements on the matter. The United States, which has had no diplomatic relations with Iran since the hostage crisis of 1979, has been concerned first and foremost with the containment of Iran. It has been thought that the islands problem can be "managed" in the intermediate time frame without hardening Iran's position and escalating the conflict. From 1989 until 1999, there was also a rupture in diplomatic relations between Britain and Iran over the Salman Rushdie affair, although Britain has had contacts with Iran through a Chargé d'Affaires in Tehran since 1997. Since 1999, diplomatic relations have been restored and Britain has discussed the islands issue with Iran. By 2002, however, the United States was warning Iran to change its objectionable policies or face pre-emptive military action.

This raises a question. If in the future Iran changes its behavior on issues of the most concern to the United States and Britain, namely on weapons of mass destruction and terrorism, would the United States and Britain continue to tolerate the occupation of these islands by an Iran that is no longer seen as so threatening? Or would a resolution of the dispute be made a precondition for the full reintegration of Iran into the regional and international fold? As it now stands, US officials are not well-informed about the history of the islands and the merits of the legal claims of the UAE and contending claims by Iran, although British officials are more so. The more US and British officials learn about the historical and legal documentation of the UAE's claim and the more seriously they take UN responsibilities, the more likely are the prospects that they will understand the importance of resolving this dispute.

Conclusion

The Gulf region hosts a number of Arab states that have emerged in the twentieth century to achieve prosperity and stability. These states are evolving in ways that will preserve important elements of their traditional government with increasing opportunities for popular participation. Moreover, the Arabian peninsula is also home to some of Islam's holiest sites and richest history. It is not surprising therefore that the Gulf region is viewed with importance, not only by the Gulf states themselves but also by the larger Arab world and by the world's 1 billion Muslims.

The Gulf is also vitally important to the rest of the world. The Gulf states possess two-thirds of the world's proven reserves of crude oil and 30% of the world's proven reserves of natural gas. They supply 30% of the world's daily consumption of oil, a level that will increase into the 21st century. Moreover, the Gulf region also has about three-quarters of the world's excess oil-production capacity. Thus, these states can respond to any shortage of supply in world oil markets by increasing production, thereby keeping prices down. While some of the Gulf's oil is shipped via pipelines, most of it is transported through the sea-lanes of the Gulf, which pass by Abu Musa and the Tunbs, and through the Strait of Hormuz, a narrow and vulnerable chokepoint.[1]

The United States, as the world's leading power, has national interests in the Gulf that need to be protected. These include maintaining access to the energy of the region at a reasonable price, maintaining access to the region's export markets for itself and its major allies and friends, maintaining the security of Western financial investments, protecting the well-being and security of friendly states in the region against external threats, and containing states and movements that threaten the United States and its friends and allies in the region. Europe and Asia rely to a greater extent than the United States on Gulf oil and their need is likely to grow.

However, despite their higher dependence, these countries are less capable of projecting and maintaining the military power in the Gulf that would be necessary to defend their interests. Thus, despite the normal commercial competition in the Gulf between the United States and these countries, the US military must play the leading role in protecting the basic interests of its allies if it wishes to prevent the economic dislocations these allies and trading partners would experience if their access to the Gulf were interrupted and if it wishes to avoid the resulting repercussions on the US economy.

The UAE and the other GCC states have entered into mutually beneficial security relationships with the United States, Britain and France, and have developed a military capability and strategy that is an effective deterrent against a major overt and attributable attack by Iran or Iraq against any GCC state. This is also intended as a credible deterrent against more limited forms of aggression against and intimidation of GCC states, such as attacks on the UAE's offshore oil fields, sabotage against the UAE or unreasonable political and economic demands against the UAE. It is certainly meant as a deterrent against any Iranian or Iraqi effort to interfere with maritime traffic through the sea-lanes of the Gulf and the Strait of Hormuz.

The first tier of the deterrent is the capability of each GCC state, in this case the UAE, to undertake the primary responsibility for its own defense. The second tier is the combined capability of the GCC to engage in "collective defense." The third tier is the capability of the United States and other extra-regional allies to assist regional states in deterring conflict and defending common interests.[2] For the United States, this three-tiered approach underlies a theatre strategy made up of five central pillars: power projection, forward presence, combined exercises, security assistance and the readiness to fight.[3]

It is too late to deter Iran from occupying Abu Musa and the Tunbs: that is a *fait accompli*. However, since the tanker war of 1986-88 Iran has not used its position on the islands to interfere with shipping or to engage in any action against the UAE. Thus, one can argue that the three-tiered deterrent has been effective in neutralizing Iran's position on the islands. On the other hand, the UAE, the GCC and the United States and its allies have not deterred Iran from its militarization of the islands, its military exercises on and around the islands, and its violations of the MOU on Abu Musa. Indeed, US efforts to stem the flow of conventional weapons to Iran, such as Chinese anti-ship missiles that may now be based at Abu Musa, have not succeeded. Furthermore, efforts to advance diplomatic or legal means to resolve the contending claims to the islands have not yet yielded results.

Consequently, Iran's future use of the islands in action against shipping and the UAE cannot be dismissed, despite US warnings, despite ongoing UAE and GCC military modernization, and despite the fact that there is a much greater US military presence in the Gulf than there was in 1986-1988. Nevertheless, a strategy of compellence, i.e. a strategy to compel Iran to quit the islands or halt its militarization of the islands, has not been favored either by the UAE, the GCC, major European powers or the United States. The United States has not been willing to initiate military action for the purpose of resolving the dispute, and neither have Britain or France. Indeed, both US and UAE officials have argued that this would only lead to Iranian retaliation against the UAE.

The US Department of Defense noted in 1995:

> A paradoxical risk posed by the United States' position as premier arbiter of Middle Eastern security is the high value Middle Eastern states now place on getting us involved in local conflicts. Meanwhile, the disappearance of the prospect that intervention in regional disputes could provoke a global confrontation with the Soviets may make us more susceptible to such efforts.[4]

This language suggests a reluctance to intervene because even in the post-Cold War, post-bipolar world, the United States must still weigh the potential costs of using force, for example, to compel Iran to quit the islands. Iran could conceivably strike at the United States or its friends in the region in some other way, such as terrorism. Indeed, a US effort at compellence could be more dangerous in the post-bipolar world than it would have been during the Soviet-American bipolar rivalry. With two competing nuclear superpowers, both had to exercise tremendous caution about confronting each other over a regional issue like the islands. In the post-bipolar world, the United States confronts a potential regional hegemon that possibly may not make the same rational calculations about gains and losses that the Soviet Union would have made. Thus, the United States may want to avoid action that leads to possibly irrational Iranian reaction, regardless of the degree of punishment that Iran would ultimately suffer. Such an Iranian reaction could entail damage to US, UAE and GCC assets. Moreover, the UAE has not sought to get the United States involved in resolving the islands dispute, and certainly not through military means.

After September 11, 2001, however, the United States has expressed a willingness to take pre-emptive military action against potential threats, and to do so unilaterally or with "coalitions of the willing" if necessary, as in the case of Iraq.[5] Iran, as a member of the "axis of evil" identified by the Bush administration, is a potential target for such pre-emptive action, particularly because it is thought to be developing weapons of mass destruction, has supported terrorism and has supported opponents of the Arab-Israeli "Oslo" peace process. The possibility of US pre-emptive action against Iran is something that the UAE and the other GCC states must consider very carefully.

The Need for a New Strategy

The existing potential for Iran to challenge the basic interests of the UAE, the United States and their friends in the Gulf, to destabilize the region and produce unforeseen scenarios, and for Iran to employ its positions on the islands in all of this, cannot be easily dismissed. One foreseeable scenario is another Iranian attempt to interfere with maritime traffic, for example, as a response to US pre-emptive attacks on suspected Iranian weapons of mass destruction facilities, despite the certain response by US forces. Indeed, Iran is developing the capability to interfere with this traffic more effectively than it did during 1986-1988.

Another scenario is Iranian demands and probes, and covert and overt operations against the UAE. Thus, key challenges should be to strengthen deterrence, to refine war-fighting capabilities and to develop a set of strategies for restoring UAE sovereignty over the islands and, indeed, for resolving other major outstanding differences between Iran and its neighbors and the West. One element of this study should be to consider some policy prescriptions on these matters.

The United States has explicitly warned Iran not to think of interfering with maritime traffic in the Gulf and the Strait of Hormuz. It may be suggested, therefore, that it could also be advantageous to warn Iran that the use of the islands to interfere with this traffic, to engage in any low-intensity or high-intensity conflict against the UAE or to pressure the UAE for any political or economic purpose will not be tolerated. It may also be sensible to provide the UAE with explicit answers about how the United States would respond to various Iranian actions and threats against UAE interests, specifically involving use of the islands, in order to reassure the UAE about US policy.

It should also be considered that there may be some future justification and requirement for militarily ejecting Iran from the islands, for example, if in some future crisis Iran does again use the islands to attack international merchant shipping in the Gulf, GCC or Western military assets in the Gulf, or the offshore oil fields or ports of the UAE and other GCC states. This may not be rational behavior for Iran, given the greater US force that could now be deployed against it. However, there are elements in Iran that may not be rational bargainers. Moreover, there may be scenarios in which even rational Iranian planners think that the country's self-defense requires such moves. If the United States takes pre-emptive action against suspected Iranian weapons of mass destruction facilities, rational Iranian planners may think that the United States also plans attacks against Iranian conventional forces in the Gulf, and they may take their own pre-emptive action in the Gulf.

The military forces of the UAE, the United States and their friends must be prepared for this possibility. Reacting to such a development, not only by neutralizing Iran on the islands, but by actually destroying its military assets located there, driving Iranian military forces off the islands, restoring UAE authority on the islands and protecting the UAE presence on the islands against Iranian counter-attack would be a departure from US decision-making during Operation Earnest Will, when the United States attacked Iranian offshore oil platforms and naval vessels, but did not attack the islands. This may be a scenario, however, in which the United States may argue that removing Iran from the islands is necessary and proportionate and does not escalate the conflict. There may also be a limit to the number of times that the regional states and the international community should be willing to deal with the Iranian threat from these islands.

However, if US pre-emptive action against Iran is not likely, perhaps because the operation in Iraq is not successful in some respect or because there is tremendous international pressure against repeating the policy in Iran, the United States may be expected to continue its previous policy of containment. As noted earlier, this policy has deterred Iranian aggression in the Gulf, but it has not deterred Iran from fortifying the islands and may even have heightened Iran's interest in known and potential oil and gas fields offshore of these islands. It has not deterred Iran from developing nuclear facilities that arouse US concerns or from opposing US Arab-Israeli policy.

Moreover, US economic sanctions have not deterred firms from other countries, such as France's TOTAL, from developing Iranian offshore oil and gas fields or, indeed, from wider trade and financial interactions with Iran. It may be that the United States should eventually re-think this aspect of its containment policy and particularly to permit US firms to purchase and develop Iranian oil and gas. This may even open the door for eventual US-Iranian political dialogue, as Iranian officials repeatedly claim that they must see good deeds by the United States before they would consent to any dialogue.

On the other hand, if US pre-emptive military action against Iran is deemed not necessary, perhaps because Iran seeks to avoid such military action by changing the foreign and domestic policies that are most objectionable to the United States, then the prospects for dialogue and the lifting of sanctions are even better. The new policy of pre-emption could conceivably be more successful in this regard than the previous policy of containment, including its wide range of economic sanctions. This could open the door to diplomacy on a wide range of other issues, including the islands.

Certainly, US officials have approved of the UAE's intention to seek a peaceful resolution of the islands dispute through bilateral diplomacy, regional mediation or the ICJ. Indeed, the United States has preferred a bilateral negotiated settlement of the issue and has thought that the UAE policy of raising the issue in international fora may eventually motivate Iran to agree to negotiation, if not immediately then perhaps if and when the evolution of Iran's domestic politics produces greater pragmatism and reform in Iran. The UAE can be expected to continue this patient policy whether US pre-emption is unlikely or unnecessary, whether US containment of Iran is tightened or loosened, or whether the US has or does not have a dialogue with Iran.

If there were to be an opportunity for dialogue between the United States and Iran, however, discussion about security and cooperation in the Gulf could perhaps be tackled early. In this discussion, the United States could offer to listen to Iranian arguments about what they view as their legitimate interests and defensive considerations in their own neighborhood, particularly vis-à-vis Iraq and the United States. The United States could test its concerns that Iran seeks hegemony in the Gulf, poses threats to the survival of US friends in the region, and jeopardizes US and allied access to the energy resources of the region.

Iran would presumably seek assurances that neither the United States nor any US ally intends to initiate military conflict against Iran, and particularly not to resolve the islands issue. The United States could argue that such a scenario would be considerably less likely if Iranian WMD programs, support for terror abroad and opposition to US-led Arab-Israeli peace efforts were no longer concerns. Indeed, if the United States were to follow through on its promise to help create a viable Palestinian state in the aftermath of its military action in disarming Iraq, Iran could accept the compromises the Palestinians accept. Iran's concerns regarding Israel and Iraq would be eased, and its motivations for WMD and terror could be defused somewhat. In the end, however, it will be up to Tehran to convince the GCC states and the United States that they need not fear Iran, if that is in fact the truth.

A dialogue should put forward an attractive picture of the future of GCC-Iranian relations and US-Iranian relations if Iranian policies in the Gulf, and particularly on the islands, change and if Iran addresses other important US concerns. To reach this future, Iran should at the very least be persuaded to implement a significant reduction of its military assets on Abu Musa and the Tunbs. More ambitiously, Iran needs to be convinced that it could relinquish its positions on the islands without jeopardizing its ability to ship its oil and gas through the Gulf. If Iran's interests in security and prosperity can be addressed in such a dialogue, this may set the stage for Tehran to consider bilateral negotiations regarding all three of the islands or even recourse to the ICJ.

If Iran's concerns are national pride and popular opinion regarding the islands, any dialogue could be discreet enough to avoid embarrassing the regime and to give them an opportunity to prepare the public for bilateral diplomacy or recourse to the ICJ. This would avoid the drawbacks of a Security Council resolution or ICJ advisory opinion that could possibly harden Iran's position. If Iran cannot be convinced to follow such a path, and that is a definite possibility, the major allies of the United States should be pressed to use their "constructive engagement" with Iran to take up the UAE cause on the islands. The British, in particular, know the historical record and the legal case very well and would not be easily misled by insupportable Iranian claims. France and Germany and Japan could, given their commercial relations with Iran, also press the UAE case.

Given the strategic significance of the UAE islands to the stability and security of the Gulf region, and beyond, it is unfortunate that not many policymakers are able to give an informed answer about the historical and legal claims of the UAE and contending claims by Iran. It is hoped that this book will bridge this knowledge gap by shedding more light on this significant issue, enhancing the awareness of leaders and decision makers, and guiding them to take appropriate measures in resolving this dispute, which threatens the peace and security of the strategic Gulf region.

ABOUT THE AUTHOR

Dr. Thomas R. Mattair is a consultant on international affairs to governments and business firms in the United States and the Middle East. He graduated with honors from Harvard University and earned his M.A. and Ph.D degrees from the University of California at Berkeley.

Dr. Mattair began his career as an Assistant Professor and Visiting Assistant Professor at several major American universities, including Kent State University, the University of Southern California and Cornell University. He then served as Director of Research and Analysis at the Middle East Policy Council, a non-profit educational organization in Washington, DC from 1992 through 1995.

In addition to this book, Dr. Mattair has authored several journal, magazine and newspaper articles and has lectured widely in the United States and the Middle East.

NOTES

INTRODUCTION

1 For general histories, see George Hourani, *Arab Seafaring in the Indian Ocean in Ancient and Medieval Times* (Princeton, NJ: Princeton University Press, 1951) and Sir Arnold Wilson, *The Persian Gulf: An Historical Sketch from the Earliest Times to the Beginning of the Twentieth Century* (Oxford: The Clarendon Press, 1928). The Portuguese explorer Duarte Barbosa reported in 1518 that the Greater Tunb was part of the Kingdom of Hormuz. He was very likely describing the situation that existed even before the arrival of the Portuguese, i.e. in the 1400s or perhaps earlier. See Mansel Longworth Dames (translator and editor), *The Book of Duarte Barbosa: An Account of the Countries bordering on the Indian Ocean and their inhabitants, circa 1518* (London: Hakluyt Society, 1918) vol. I, 68-82, especially 73-4 and 79-81. Barbosa's spelling for Tunb was "Fomon." The late Dr. Muhammad Morsy Abdullah, the ex-Director of the Centre for Documentation and Research in Abu Dhabi and a leading authority on the history of the emirates, said in an interview that Portuguese archival material indicates that these islands were part of the Kingdom of Hormuz before the arrival of the Portuguese.

2 For a detailed history of the rise of the Qawasim, see B.J. Slot, *The Arabs of the Gulf, 1602-1784* (Leidschendam, The Netherlands: 1993). Dr. Slot is the archivist responsible for the Dutch East India Company archives at the General State Archives in The Hague.

3 M.E. Bathurst, Northcutt Ely and Coward Chance, *Sharjah's Title to the Island of Abu Musa* (London: An unpublished study for the Ruler of Sharjah, September 1971), vol. 1, 25 and vol. 2, 241-2.

4 See Muhammad Morsy Abdullah, *The United Arab Emirates: A Modern History* (London: Hurtwood Press, 1978 and 1994), 233.

5 India Office Records, R/15/1/14/8, Arab Coast, Sultan bin Saqr to Political Resident, December 28, 1864. See also Abdullah, op. cit., 233.

6 P.L. Toye (ed.), *The Lower Gulf Islands: Abu Musa and the Tunbs* (London: Archive Editions, 1993), vol. 1, 563-707; Abdullah, op. cit., 234-8.

7 Toye, op. cit., vol. 1, 717-41 and vol. II, 3-111; Abdullah, op. cit., 238-43.

8 Toye, op. cit., vol. 2, 341-533; Abdullah, op. cit., 244-5.

9 Toye, op. cit., vol. 3, 439-64; vol. 4, 3-10, 19-21, 25-34, 37-120, 303-8, 331-3, 370, 389-90; and vol. 5, 24-6; Abdullah, op. cit., 255-73.

10 This period is covered in Toye, op. cit., vol. 6 in Richard Schofield (ed.), *Arabian Boundaries: New Documents*, 1961 to 1965, ten volumes (London: Archive Editions, 1993 through 1997), in recently declassified US Department of State documents from the National Archives in Bethesda, Maryland, and in recently declassified British Foreign Office records from the Public Record Office in London.

11 Husain Albaharna, *The Arabian Gulf States: Their Legal and Political Status and their International Problems* (Beirut: Librairie Du Liban, 1975), 339-48; *The Lower Gulf Islands*, op. cit., vol. 6, 489-504.

12 Albaharna, op. cit., 339-48; Brig. Gen. Mohamad Al-Kaabi, *The Iranian Occupation of the Islands, Greater Tunb, Lesser Tunb and Abu Musa Belonging to the United Arab Emirates* (Carlisle Barracks, PA: US Army War College, 1994), 62-6; *Provisional Verbatim Record of the Sixteen Hundred and Tenth Meeting of the United Nations Security Council* (S/10436, 9 December 1971).

13   Martin S. Navias and E.R. Hooton, *Tanker Wars: The Assault on Merchant Shipping During the Iran-Iraq Crisis, 1980-1988* (London: I.B. Tauris and Company Ltd., 1996), 111-5, 121, 151-2, 174 and confidential interviews with current and former officials of the British Foreign Office, the US State and Defense Department, and the UAE Ministry of Foreign Affairs.

14   Al Kaabi, op. cit., 73-7, Mohamed Abdullah Al-Roken, "Historical and Legal Dimensions of the United Arab Emirates-Iran Dispute Over Three Gulf Islands," in Edmund Ghareeb and Ibrahim Al Abed (eds), *Perspectives on the United Arab Emirates* (London: Trident Press Ltd., 1998), 153 and William Rugh, "UAE Foreign Policy," in Ghareeb and Al Abed, op. cit., 169.

15   See *The United Arab Emirates Yearbook 1996* (London: Trident Press, 1996) for a summary of the UAE positions.

16   Legal arguments supporting the claims of the UAE have been developed by Bathurst, Ely and Chance, op. cit. and Vinson and Elkins, *Territorial Sovereignty over the Tunb Islands* (an unpublished report for the Ruler of Ras al-Khaimah, 1980), chapter 3. Albaharna, op. cit., analyzes legal arguments on 339-48. Legal arguments advancing Iran's claims are made in Hooshang Amirahmadi (ed.) *Small Islands, Big Politics: The Tonbs and Abu Musa in the Gulf* (London: Macmillan Press Ltd., 1996). The basic legal principles and cases relevant in this case may be found in Louis Henkin, Richard Crawford Pugh, Oscar Schachter and Hans Smit, *International Law: Cases and Materials*, Third Edition (St. Paul, MN: West Publishing Company, 1993), especially 308-23.

17   Bathurst, Ely and Chance, op. cit., vol. I, 15-8.

18   For the text of the UN Charter, see Henkin et al., op. cit., especially 1-3 and 8.

19   For the text of the 1969 Vienna Convention, see Henkin, op. cit., especially 98.

20   The British had erroneously believed that the Lingeh Qawasim had a claim to the island, but even so, the British considered that the Lingeh Qawasim claim was based on their being Qawasim, not on their being Persian vassals or officials. More importantly, the British did not know about this correspondence from the Lingeh Qawasim acknowledging the title of the Qawasim of the Arab coast until the 1880s. There was one piece of evidence of taxes paid by Sirri, but the British did not think this supported a Persian claim or undermined the Qawasim claim. See Bathurst, Ely and Chance, op. cit., vol. 2, 32.

21   See Anthony Cordesman, "Threats and Non-Threats from Iran" and Kenneth Katzman, "The Politico-Military Threat from Iran" in Jamal S. Al-Suwaidi (ed.) *Iran and the Gulf: A Search for Stability* (Abu Dhabi: Emirates Center for Strategic Studies and Research, 1997).

22   This part and the following discussion on the debates concerning Iran's motivations for holding the islands is based on interviews with current and former officials of the US Department of State and Department of Defense, the British Foreign Office and the UAE Ministry of Foreign Affairs.

23   See numerous statements of Iranian officials quoted in Part Three.

24   Cordesman, "Threats and Non-Threats from Iran" in Al-Suwaidi, op. cit.

25   Some analysts argue that Iran would probably only interfere with international shipping for defensive reasons during a war, especially now that the US naval presence is so much larger than in the 1980s. However, Iran may provoke a war that leads to its "defensive" interference with shipping, particularly if the US military presence is eventually reduced. Based on interviews conducted in London, Washington DC, and Abu Dhabi (see note 22).

26 Cordesman in Al-Suwaidi, op. cit., 283-4 and interviews in London, Washington DC and Abu Dhabi.

27 See Jamal S. Al-Suwaidi, "The Gulf Security Dilemma: The Arab Gulf States, the United States, and Iran," in Al-Suwaidi, op. cit., 339 for Iran's general strategy to intimidate the UAE on economic issues.

28 Interviews in Abu Dhabi (see note 22).

29 This part and the following brief account of the Arab world's reaction to Iran's occupation of the islands in 1971 is drawn in part from Abdullah, op. cit., 283-4, Albaharna, op. cit., 339-41 and Ahmed Jalal Al-Tadmori, *The Three Arabian Islands: A Documentary Study* (Ras al-Khaimah: Ras al-Khaimah National Printing Press, 2000), 168-79, 196-7.

30 See Arab League documents cited in Part Four and also Abdullah Omran Taryam, *The Establishment of the United Arab Emirates, 1950-1985* (London: Croom Helm, 1987), 188-9.

31 Abdullah, op. cit., 280, 284.

32 *Closing Statements of the Sessions of the Supreme Council: Sessions 1-18* (Riyadh: The Secretariat General of The Cooperation Council for the Arab States of the Gulf, 1998) and Muhammad Jenab Tutunji, "The United Arab Emirates and International Organizations," in Ghareeb and Al Abed, op. cit., 189-90.

33 Interviews with current and former officials of the British Foreign Office and recently declassified British Foreign Office and US State Department documents cited in Part Four of this study.

34 This part and the analysis of the role of the United Nations and the United States is based in part on interviews with current and former officials of the UAE Ministry of Foreign Affairs and the US Department of State.

35 For an official discussion of US interests and military strategy in the Gulf, see *United States Security Strategy for the Middle East* (Department of Defense, Office of International Security Affairs, May 1995).

CHAPTER 1

1 George F. Hourani, *Arab Seafaring in the Indian Ocean in Ancient and Medieval Times* (Princeton, NJ: Princeton University Press, 1951; revised and expanded by John Carswell, 1995), 3-6. Donald Hawley, *The Trucial States* (London: Allen and Unwin, 1970), 25-9. Archaeological work carried out by the Abu Dhabi Islands Archaeological Survey in 1999 discovered pottery on Abu Dhabi island indicating that this area, along with sites along the coast of Ras al-Khaimah where the same pottery had previously been found, may have been involved in trade with the Mesopotamian city of Ubaid in 5000 BC or two thousand years before the first written records of Sumerian trade. See *Gulf News*, May 23, 1999. Hawley, op. cit., 38 suggests that red ochre imported by the Sumerians from Magan circa 3000 BC may have come from Abu Musa.

2 Hourani, *Arab Seafaring*, op. cit., 10-7, 36-50, 143 and Hawley, *The Trucial States*, op. cit., 29-41. Hawley writes on page 31 that the journals of Nearchus indicate that there was seaborne trade between the Assyrian port of Teredon in Mesopotamia and Cape Musandum circa 323 BC. Nearchus referred to an island off Qishm in 325 BC and several maps, entitled *The Eastern Part of the Ancient Persian Empire* and published in London in 1831 by the Society for the Diffusion

of Useful Knowledge, suggest that Nearchus may have anchored off the Greater Tunb. See Sultan bin Muhammad Al-Qasimi (ed.) *The Gulf in Historic Maps: 1478-1861*, Second Edition (Leicester: Streamline Press Limited, 1999), 270, 271, 273. The Roman Claudius Ptolemaeus (or Ptolemy) (d. 168 AD) made highly inaccurate descriptions of the Gulf and its islands that may have been meant to refer to Abu Musa and the Tunbs. For medieval European versions of his work, see Sultan bin Muhammad Al-Qasimi (ed.) *The Gulf in Historic Maps, 1493-1931* (Leicester, UK: Thinkprint Limited, 1996), 10-11. Other recent archaeological work carried out by the Department of Antiquities and Museums in Ras al-Khaimah, the University of Durham and the British Museum indicates that there was a settlement in Julfar near Ras al-Khaimah during the late Sasanian period and the early Islamic period. Excavations have unearthed a Sasanian Persian military fort built to protect its colonists from local inhabitants in the surrounding mountains and sands, the al-Azd of Oman, a fort that was then destroyed in the seventh century AD at the time of the rise of Islam. See *Gulf News: Friday Magazine*, January 8-14, 1999. Geoffrey R. King, "The History of the UAE: The Eve of Islam and the Islamic Period," in Edmund Ghareeb and Ibrahim Al Abed (eds) *Perspectives on the United Arab Emirates* (London: Trident Press Ltd., 1997) writes on pages 77-8 and 83 that there was a Sasanian Persian presence in the Gulf of Oman, which was also overrun by Muslim Al-Azd armies in the 7th century. He mentions that the Al-Azd engaged in fishing and used islands off the Arab and Persian coasts. Persian Sasanian settlers in Julfar or the Gulf of Oman and/or Al-Azd fishermen circa 600 AD may have known of or used Abu Musa and the Tunbs, but there are no ancient ruins on the islands to indicate that this was the case. These settlers may not have been the first or the only ones to know of or use the islands, given the seafaring trade that had already been going on in the Gulf for thousands of years. It should also be noted about the rulers of Persia in pre-Islamic history that while the Achaemenids were Persians, they were followed by Alexander and the Seleucids and the Parthians, who were not Persians, who were then followed by the Sasanids, who were Persians.

3   Hourani, op. cit., 52.

4   W.B. Fisher (ed.) *The Cambridge History of Iran*, volume I, *The Land of Iran* (Cambridge: Cambridge University Press, 1968), especially chapter 13, 433-5 and chapter 14, 469-70, 474. Regarding the rulers of Persia after the Islamic conquests, it should also be noted that the Ummayid and Abbasid caliphs were Arabs, the Buwayhids were Persians and the Seljuks were Turks. Following various Mongol and Turk rulers, it was the Safavids who finally re-established Persian rule.

5   Geoffrey King's note in Hourani, op. cit., 142-3; Hawley, op. cit., 50-3. Also, Geoffrey King in Ghareeb and Al Abed, op. cit., 85-9 writes that the Al-Julanda leaders of the Muslim Al-Azd were forced to take refuge in the mountains and islands during a rebellion soon after the death of the Prophet Mohammed (Peace Be Upon Him) and during the rule of the first Caliph Abu Bakr. He suggests that these were the islands off the coast of the emirates. He notes that the Abbasid Caliph Al-Saffah sent a fleet from Basra to Qays to Oman, probably to Julfar, soon after 750 AD and also that Buwayhid emirs sent a fleet from Siraf to Julfar in 965 AD. These fleets may have sailed near Abu Musa and the Tunbs.

6   Hourani, op. cit., 52-3, 61-84 and Sir Arnold Wilson, *The Persian Gulf: A Historical Sketch from the Earliest Times to the Beginning of the Twentieth Century* (Oxford: The Clarendon Press, 1928), 112.

7 Wilson, op. cit., 92-104; Hawley, op. cit., 47, 51-9.

8 Hawley, op. cit., 56 cites Al-Maqdisi, who wrote in 985/986 AD about his personal voyages.

9 Wilson, op. cit., 96-100 and Geoffrey R. King in Ghareeb and Al Abed, op. cit., 76.

10 Guive Mirfendereski, "The Ownership of the Tonb Islands: A Legal Analysis," in Hooshang Amirahmadi (ed.), *Small Islands, Big Politics: The Tonbs and Abu Musa in the Gulf* (London: Macmillan Press Ltd, 1996) writes that Ibn Al-Balkhis's *Farsnama* (1111 AD) referred to an island of Dam or Zam as belonging to a district of the province of Fars. Mirfendereski, op. cit., 121 concludes that this refers to the Tunbs and writes that "The Tonbs at this time pertained to Fars and in all likelihood were administered for the Seljuk by the Banu Qaysar rulers of Kish Island." However, the Banu Qaysar rulers of Qays, which is called Kish in Persian, were Arabs and the Seljuk governors (1055 AD to 1194 AD) who wielded authority under the Abbasid caliphate were Turks. Moreover, Ibn Al-Balkhi himself wrote that the rulers of Fars did not control Qays. See Wilson, op. cit., 95. Wilson, op. cit., 99 quotes Yakut Al-Rumi in 1224, i.e. after the fall of the Seljuks in 1194 and after the Turco-Mongol invasion of Persia in 1217, as writing that "Qais...is the residence of the sovereign of Oman, whose authority extends all over this sea and is the stopping-place of ships which cross between India and Fars. The king of this country is held in respect by the sovereigns of India on account of his naval forces and riches. I have seen him several times; his features are Persian and he dresses similarly to the Daylam; he has a numerous suite, much property and magnificent Arab horses. In these parts the pearl fishery is carried on; all the neighboring islands belong to the ruler of Qais." The neighboring islands are not named. The ruler's features may have been Persian, but he was of the Arab Banu Qaysar. Davoud H. Bavand, "The Legal Basis of Iran's Sovereignty over Abu Musa Island," in Amirahmadi, op. cit., 79 provides a version of this passage, which does not call Qays "the residence of the sovereign of Oman," but rather "the residence of the ruler of this Sea." He argues that the island was then "a dependency of Iran" and that "The presumed geographical situation of Abu Musa – it being in the middle of the waters bound by Kish and Oman – argues rather persuasively in favor of inclusion of the island among those under the authority of Kish." However, again, when Yakut Al-Rumi made his observations, the Arab Banu Qaysar ruled Qays, the Seljuk Turks had fallen, and the Turco-Mongol invasion of Persia had begun, ushering in another era of alien rule of Persia under a succession of various Mongol and Turk authorities. Moreover, Qays was soon replaced by Old Hormuz as the major trade emporium in the Gulf.

11 V. Fiorani Piacentini, "Siraf and Hormuz Between East and West: Merchants and Merchandise in the Gulf," paper presented at the Symposium on External Interests in the Arab Gulf, University of Exeter, Centre for Arab Gulf Studies, July 11-13, 1990, 11-8. See also Wilson, op. cit., 105-9.

12 Piacentini, op. cit., 19. Hawley, op. cit., 58-9 writes that the King of Hormuz was suzerain of the Arab coast. Wilson, op. cit., 117-21 notes that the King of Hormuz paid annual tribute to Shah Ismail of Persia until the Portuguese first seized the Kingdom in 1507 and that the King of Hormuz recognized the suzerainty of Shah Ismail until the Persians signed an agreement recognizing Portuguese suzerainty over Hormuz in 1515. B.J. Slot, *The Arabs of the Gulf: 1602-1784* (Leidschendam, The Netherlands, 1993) writes that Persia claimed

sovereignty over Hormuz but recognized the sovereignty of Hormuz and later Portugal over Qishm (55-6). However, as Piacentini notes, the Kings of Hormuz only began paying tribute to Shah Ismail Safavi beginning in 1503, after the death of the last great King. This was an era of petty kings and the decline of the Kingdom, crises of succession and institutions, and the extension of Safavid authority to Fars and its capital Shiraz. Indeed, Shah Ismail only founded the Safavid dynasty in 1501. Thus, the tribute was only paid for four years prior to the arrival of the Portuguese and during the ten years it took for the Portuguese to finally subdue the Kingdom.

13 King in Ghareeb and Al Abed, op. cit., 77, 90. See also King's note in Hourani, op. cit., 143 and John Hansman, *Julfar, An Arabian Port: Its Settlement and Far Eastern Ceramic Trade from the 14th to the 18th Centuries* (London: The Royal Asiatic Society of Great Britain and Ireland, 1985) and Jean Aubin, "Le Royaume d'Ormuz au debut du XVI siecle," *Mare Luso-Indicum*, vol. 2 (Geneve: Librarie Droz and Paris: Librarie Minard, 1973). Hawley, op. cit., 69 writes that the famous navigator Ahmad ibn Majid who guided the Portuguese navigator Vasco de Gama from East Africa to India in 1498 was from Julfar. See also Hourani, op. cit., 83-4.

14 See Wilson, op. cit., 105-9 for descriptions of the scarcity of fresh water, the importance of fish and the pearl trade in New Hormuz, written by visitors from the 1300s to the 1500s. Among these writers was the Portuguese explorer Duarte Barbosa (see below), who reported in 1518 that the Greater Tunb was part of the Kingdom of Hormuz. He was very likely describing the situation that existed even before the arrival of the Portuguese, i.e. in the 1400s or perhaps earlier. Mirfendereski, op. cit., 121-2 writes that Hamdallah Mustawfi Al-Kazvini's *Nuzhat al-Qulub* (1340 AD) referred to Kand, Kond, Gand or Gond as one of the islands "which are known, inhabited and belong to Iran." He concludes that this refers to the Tunbs and argues that "it may be surmised that the rulers of Hormuz in all likelihood gained directly or vicariously control over the Tonbs" and that "Iranian dominion in the Persian Gulf qua the local rulers of Hormuz remained unabated." Again, the local rulers of New Hormuz were Arabs. Moreover, Persia at the time had been overrun by the Turco-Mongol invaders and the rulers of New Hormuz were not under any Mongol or Turk rule. Persia was not re-established as an independent state and was not ruled by Persians until the Safavids came to power in 1501.

15 Wilson, op. cit., 112-27.

16 Mansel Longworth Dames (transl. and ed.), *The Book of Duarte Barbosa: An Account of the Countries Bordering on the Indian Ocean and their Inhabitants, circa 1518* (London: Hakluyt Society, 1918), vol. I, 68-82, especially 73-4 and 79-81. Barbosa's spelling for the Greater Tunb was "Fomon." See also King in Ghareeb and Al Abed, op. cit., 77, 90-1.

17 Muhammad Morsy Abdullah, in an interview in March 1998, noted that official Portuguese archival records of Portugal's Viceroy regarding the income of the Kingdom of Hormuz showed that the Greater Tunb provided water and food and paid taxes to the Kingdom of Hormuz.

18 Slot, *The Arabs of the Gulf*, op. cit., 36-9. Slot cites Gasparo Balbi, *Viaggi delle Indie Orientali* (Venezia: 1590).

19 King in Ghareeb and Al Abed, op. cit., 77. See also W.F. Sinclair and D. Ferguson (translators and editors) *The Travels of Pedro Teixeira* (London: Hakluyt Society, 1902).

20 Wilson, op. cit., 140-52, especially 151.

21 Slot, *The Arabs of the Gulf*, op. cit., 44-5, 65 6, 110 2, 126 9, 132-5, 217. Slot cites Jean de Thevenot, *Suite du Voyage du Levant* (Paris: 1674), 354 for this reference to the Greater Tunb.

22 See Slot, *The Arabs of the Gulf*, op. cit., chapters 2 and 3 for a history of Portuguese involvement in the Gulf.

23 Slot, *The Arabs of the Gulf*, op. cit., especially chapters 4, 5 and 10; Wilson, op. cit., chapters IX to XII, Hawley, op. cit., 68-79.

24 Slot, *The Arabs of the Gulf*, op. cit., 44-5. See also Jean de Thevenot, *Suite du Voyage*, op. cit., 354.

25 B.J. Slot, *The Oldest Historical Sources About Sirri, Abu Musa and the Tunbs* (Abu Dhabi: The Cultural Foundation, 1992), 2-3.

26 Interview with Muhammad Morsy Abdullah, Abu Dhabi, March 1998. Slot, *The Arabs of the Gulf*, op. cit., 158-9, writes that the Dutch knew that Julfar was engaged in some trade with Basra in 1646. Slot, *The Oldest Historical Sources*, op. cit., notes that the Dutch gave these islands Dutch names on the charts of the seventeenth century and that the Arabic names of these islands were not used on European maps and charts until the French maps of the early eighteenth century. Julian Walker notes that there are no Portuguese, Dutch, French or British forts or remains on the islands. The local pilot who said that snakes made access to the Greater Tunb's water impossible may have wished to discourage the Dutch from using the island during an era of European competition and fighting at sea, particularly when Portuguese warships had been using the island to collect tribute in previous years.

27 Interview with Muhammad Morsy Abdullah, March 1998.

28 Slot, *The Arabs of the Gulf*, op. cit., 21, 22, 46, 56.

29 Morsy Abdullah suggested in a 1998 interview that one of the Yarubi military leaders who drove the Portuguese from Julfar in 1632 was from the Qawasim tribe. Sirhan ibn Sa'id ibn Sirhan's *Annals of Oman* (Cambridge: The Oleander Press, 1964), 51-2, identifies the commander of this force as Ali bin Ahmed and notes that he left another leader of the army there as a governor. Slot's argument in *The Arabs of the Gulf*, op. cit., 160 and 251, of Sayf bin Ali bin Salih Al-Qasimi as the Shaikh of Sir would support the suggestion that he had earlier participated in driving the Portuguese from Julfar in 1632 and remained there as governor. Thus, this Qawasim leader may have ruled Julfar and exercised authority over its trade and its use of Abu Musa and the Tunbs from the mid-1600s, and perhaps from as early as 1632.

30 Slot, *The Arabs of the Gulf*, op. cit., 158-9, 170, 190, 255. The Dutch reported that in 1646 a ship from Julfar carried a cargo of sugar to Basra. At this time, Julfar may have been sending ships out of the Gulf to pick up such cargos, for example from the port of Muscat. The French explorer Thevenot also reported that ships from India were visiting Julfar in the 1650s/1660s. The Dutch further reported on trade between India and Julfar in 1701.

31 Slot, *The Arabs of the Gulf*, op. cit., 170, 190.

32 Ibid., 235-47, 249-52.

33 Ibid., 18-9, 22-5, 235-47, 249-52, 261-2, 266, 282-3, 296. Rahma bin Matar was also strong enough to make another bid for control of Hormuz in 1728. This time it was a diplomatic bid, but he recognized the greater strength of the Dutch and acquiesced to their control of Hormuz. Wilson, op. cit., 175 writes, "During the

Afghan occupation of Persia (1722-9) affairs in the neighbourhood of Bandar Abbas were again very unsettled. The Qasimi shaikh of Ras al Khaima obtained possession of Basidu, on Qishm Island, and created a situation detrimental to the trade of Bandar Abbas, until proceeded against, in 1727, by a small squadron composed of the frigate Britannia and some smaller vessels." Wilson does not identify the shaikh by name, or indicate whether his possession of Basidu was direct or indirect, but makes it clear that the British considered him a commercial rival. Slot argues, however, that this ruler of Basidu, Shaikh Rashid, was not a Qasimi shaikh himself, but rather an ally of the Qawasim Shaikh Rahma.

34 Slot, *The Arabs of the Gulf,* op. cit., 284-5, 295-320; Hawley, op. cit., 84-7.

35 Slot, *The Arabs of the Gulf,* op. cit., 327-30. See also *The Kniphausen Report* (Dutch General State Archives: Algemeen Rijksarchief in The Hague, referred to as ARA, Aanw.1e Afd. 1889, 23b, folio 12; English translation courtesy of Centre for Documentation and Research in Abu Dhabi, Dutch archives division). Slot notes that in 1740, while the Persian garrison at Julfar was blockaded by an Arab navy, and before the Arab sailors of the Persian navy mutinied, leaving the Persian garrison at Julfar isolated, Nadir Shah appointed his prisoner Rahma bin Matar Governor of Julfar for life. When Bin Matar actually reasserted his authority in Julfar in 1749, however, he ruled independently of Persia.

36 Slot, *The Arabs of the Gulf,* op. cit., 23-5, 331-9, 342-9. Rahma bin Matar began to support Mulla Ali Shah after marrying his daughter circa 1751.

37 *The Kniphausen Report* (ARA, Aanw. 1889, 23b, folio 3a, folio 5).

38 Carsten Niebuhr (translated into Dutch by S.J. Baalde) *Description of Arabia* (Utrecht: J. Van Schoonhoven and Company, 1774), 293, 298, 312; English translation courtesy of the Centre for Documentation and Research, Abu Dhabi, Dutch archives division.

39 Slot, *The Arabs of the Gulf,* op. cit., 381-91; See also Mohamed Al Roken, "Historical and Legal Dimensions of the United Arab Emirates-Iran Dispute Over the Gulf Islands," in *Perspectives on the United Arab Emirates*, op. cit., 140. The Al Ali, Banu Na'im and Bani Qatb also moved north to settle on the island of Qishm. Al Roken writes that the Qawasim settled in the area of Lingeh in 1750 upon an invitation from the Arab Ruler of Hormuz. While the Qawasim did initially settle in Lingeh circa 1755, this was not upon an invitation from the Arab Ruler of Hormuz. The Qawasim re-settled in Lingeh upon the invitation of the Arab Ruler of Hormuz in 1777. Al Roken also notes that after settling at Lingeh, the Qawasim "sought to extend their influence to the islands and coastal areas of the Gulf." Here, he may be referring to the many other islands of the Gulf inasmuch as the Qawasim must have been using Abu Musa and the Tunbs since at least the 1720s, long before settling in Lingeh. Shaikh Dr. Sultan bin Muhammad Al-Qasimi adds more information in the second edition of *The Myth of Arab Piracy in the Gulf* (London: Routledge, 1988), although he attributes to Rashid bin Matar many of the actions of his brother and predecessor Rahma bin Matar. The same mistaken attribution can be found in Hawley, op. cit. Niebuhr reported in his geographical manual that the Tunbs were uninhabited. The manual was published in 1772 and based on his travels from 1761 to 1765, although it is thought that he got much of his information from the Kniphausen Report of 1756 and other Dutch and British sources. Wilson, op. cit., 201 writes that the Qawasim were expelled from Qishm, Lingeh and Shinas by Karim Khan Zand in 1763, but does not indicate that they returned to Lingeh in the 1770s. One scholar has suggested

that the Qawasim were initially invited to Lingeh by the Banu Ma'in ruler of Hormuz, after the marriage between his daughter and Saqr bin Rashid in 1777. This invitation would explain their return after their expulsion in 1763. However, the presence of the Marazik in Lingeh in the 1750s and the reporting of Kniphausen and Niebuhr suggest that Lingeh was initially controlled by the Qawasim from as early as the 1750s onwards. As for Karim Khan Zand, he installed a Safavid prince, Ismail III, as Shah, and ruled Persia from his base in Shiraz, never taking the position of Shah for himself.

40 M.E. Bathurst, Northcutt Ely and Coward Chance, *Sharjah's Title to the Island of Abu Musa* (London: Unpublished study for the Ruler of Sharjah, September 1971), vol. I, 25. British officials of the 1800s, commenting on the historical practices of the Qawasim, i.e. in the 1700s, noted many of these uses of the islands.

41 Al-Qasimi, *The Myth of Arab Piracy*, op. cit., 27, 31, 38-9; Muhammad Morsy Abdullah, *The United Arab Emirates: A Modern History* (London: Hurtwood Press, Ltd., 1978 and 1994), 223.

42 Al-Qasimi, *The Myth of Arab Piracy*, op. cit., xiii-xvi, 31-2, 39-40. Dr. Shaikh Sultan makes excellent use of the Bombay Archive records. See also Charles E. Davies, *The Blood-Red Arab Flag* (Exeter: Exeter University Press, 1997).

43 J.B. Kelly, *Britain and the Persian Gulf: 1795-1880* (Oxford: The Clarendon Press, 1968), 19-20.

44 Al-Qasimi, op. cit., 32-8, 43-9. Wilson, op. cit., 199-208 in his account of the Qawasim blames them, and in particular Sultan bin Saqr and later the Wahhabis, for every encounter with the British.

45 Sultan Muhammad Al-Qasimi (ed.) *The Journals of David Seton in the Gulf: 1800-1809* (Exeter: University of Exeter Press, 1995), 19-20, 29.

46 P.L. Toye (ed.) *The Lower Gulf Islands: Abu Musa and the Tunbs* (London: Archive Editions, 1993), vol. 1, 3; R. Hughes Thomas (ed.) *Arabian Gulf Intelligence: Selections from the Records of the Bombay Government* (Cambridge: Oleander Press, 1985), 18.

47 Al-Qasimi, *The Myth of Arab Piracy*, op. cit., 41-61; *The Journals of David Seton in the Gulf: 1800-1809*, 31-45; Kelly, op. cit., 105-8; Davies, op. cit., 94-7.

48 Kelly, *Britain and the Persian Gulf*, op. cit., 42.

49 Al-Qasimi, *The Myth of Arab Piracy*, op. cit., 62-82; *The Journals of David Seton*, op. cit., 48-67.

50 *The Journals of David Seton*, op. cit., 53, 67-9, Al-Qasimi, *The Myth of Arab Piracy*, op. cit., 81-2 and Penelope Tuson (ed.), *Records of the Emirates: 1820-1958* (London: Archive Editions, 1990), vol. I, 5.

51 Al-Qasimi, *The Myth of Arab Piracy*, op. cit., 84-118; *The Journals of David Seton*, op. cit., 79-86; Kelly, op. cit., 108-16; Davies, op. cit., 98-107.

52 Al-Qasimi, *The Myth of Arab Piracy*, op. cit., 119-36; Kelly, op. cit., 116-7.

53 Al-Qasimi, *The Myth of Arab Piracy*, op. cit., 136-48; Kelly, op. cit., 118-24; Davies, op. cit., 135, 188-90. Shaikh Dr. Sultan notes that whereas the British used force against the Qawasim, their major commercial competitor, they used diplomatic correspondence to try to persuade Rahma bin Jabir to cease piracy and to persuade the Wahabbi leader Saud bin Abdul Aziz to restrain his subjects from piracy. Both agreed to comply, only reserving the right to make war on those who deviated from the Islamic faith. The account of the Bombay Marine first expedition against the Qawasim, commanded by Captain J. Wainwright, shows that Bombay and Delhi were concerned about the French. The British did not

want the islands in the hands of the French and thus set out to ensure that the French got no base on the other side of the Musandam peninsula.

54 Al-Qasimi, *The Myth of Arab Piracy*, op. cit., 161-7; Davies, op. cit., 191.

55 Al-Qasimi, *The Myth of Arab Piracy*, op. cit., 168-83, 185-219; Kelly, op. cit., 130-5, 137-49; Davies, op. cit., 82, 107-23, 145-50. Captain R. Taylor of the Third Regiment of the Bombay Naval Infantry and the Assistant Political Resident in Turkish Arabia, surveying "pirate" ports in 1818 in preparation for this expedition, reported that Abu Musa and the Tunbs were uninhabited, although he did not actually land on them. At the same time, he pointed to the report made by Captain Seton before 1809 that the islands were "frequented by the inhabitants of the opposite coasts, who are left undisturbed in their possession." Captain Taylor also referred to the importance of the pearl fishery and of commerce to these ports prior to their resort to "piracy." While he mentioned that other tribes along the coast remained engaged in pearl fishing in 1818, he did not name the Qawasim among these tribes. See *Records of the Emirates*, op. cit., vol. 1, 229-36; Toye, op. cit., vol. 1, 3-5; *Arabian Gulf Intelligence*, op. cit., 1-40, especially 18, 20, 36, 38-40. It is quite possible and even probable that the British expedition of 1809 and the fighting at sea since then had interrupted the pearl fishing, the normal commerce and the traditional uses of the islands by the Qawasim during these years.

56 Al-Qasimi, op. cit. 221. This reference places the meeting in August 1818, but the context of the narrative and the date of the citation indicate that this is a typographical error. Davies, op. cit., 203-4 also puts the meeting in August 1818.

57 For a discussion of these relations from 1809 until 1818, see Davies, op. cit., 193-203. Shaikh Sultan bin Saqr ruled Lingeh in 1814-1815, probably after the death of its ruler and before the succession to power of Shaikh Muhammad bin Qadhib.

58 Al-Qasimi, op. cit., 216, 222.

59 Toye, op. cit., 1, 29-37, 45-58, 62-98; Kelly, op. cit., 149, 159-62; *Records of the Emirates*, 1, 478. Davies, op. cit., 135-6, 202-3 indicates that in the winter of 1817-1818, Persian forces had marched against Mughu on the Persian coast, where they were supported by forces from Lingeh and Charak. According to the Prince of Shiraz, Persia defeated forces sent from Ras al-Khaimah to assist Mughu.

60 Kelly, op. cit., 159-62.

61 *The Lower Gulf Islands*, vol. 1, 6; *Records of the Emirates*, op. cit., vol. 1, 371.

62 Al-Qasimi, op. cit., 219-29; Kelly, op. cit., 151-9; Davies, op. cit., 210-5. For the text of the Treaty of 1820, see Toye, op. cit., vol. 1, 131-40 and *Records of the Emirates*, op. cit., vol. 1, 9-20.

63 Kelly, op. cit., 159, 166, 171, 196-7.

64 Kelly, op. cit., 166, 201, 205-6, 215, 227, 330-1, 354, 405, 573-4. See also *Records of the Emirates*, op. cit., vol. 1, 241-299 for the reporting of successive British officials who conveyed their distrust of Sultan bin Saqr. Clearly, the British did not favor the Qawasim of the Arab coast before or after the expeditions of 1809 and 1819 for many reasons. The British would not have been disposed to give Abu Musa and the Tunb islands to the Qawasim or to quickly recognize Qawasim claims to them as would later be alleged by Iranian officials and scholars. Moreover, there is no evidence of the British doing so. However, the evidence that is available, shows that the British, who were actively suppressing and restricting the Qawasim, only gradually developed an imperfect understanding about the use

of these islands and the contending claims to these islands by various Qawasim shaikhs and their neighbors. This imperfect understanding was influenced by the nature of British relations with these various shaikhs and by the reporting of the British Residency Agents.

65 Toye, op. cit., vol. 1, 6-13; *Records of the Emirates*, vol. 1, 371-2, 374-5, 412-4.

66 *Records of the Emirates*, vol. 1, 351-3, 357-8.

67 *Records of the Emirates*, vol. 1, 521-5, 545-9; Kelly, op. cit., 247, 366, 376.

68 Al-Roken, op. cit., 140; Bathurst, Ely, and Chance, op. cit., vol. I, 2-4, and vol. II, 82d, 242; Abdullah, op. cit., 233-4. Al Roken lists Hengam as belonging to the Lingeh Qawasim, but Shaikh Sultan bin Saqr said it belonged to Oman in an 1864 letter to the British. Al Roken also lists the Lesser Tunb as belonging to the Qawasim of Ras al-Khaimah and Sharjah, but Shaikh Sultan did not mention this in his 1864 letter. Shaikh Humaid bin Abdullah said it belonged to the Lingeh Qawasim in an 1873 letter to the British. In 1875, the British Native Agent in Lingeh told the British Assistant Resident that forty years earlier Abu Musa had been allocated to the Qawasim of the "Pirate Coast" and that the Greater Tunb had been allocated to the Lingeh Qawasim, but this oral representation about the Greater Tunb did not accord with the written representations made by the Rulers of Sharjah, Ras al-Khaimah and Lingeh during the late 1800s. Even the Rulers of Lingeh acknowledged that the Greater Tunb belonged to the Qawasim of Ras al-Khaimah. However, Shaikh Humaid of Ras al-Khaimah wrote in 1873 that the Lesser Tunb had been allocated to the Lingeh Qawasim and this may have led to the mistaken view about the Greater Tunb expressed by the British Native Agent in Lingeh and the British Assistant Resident in 1875.

69 Toye, op. cit., vol. 1, 14-5.

70 Op. cit., vol. 1, 16. See also *Records of the Emirates*, op. cit., vol. 2, 235-248 for Whitelock's 1836 publication on the Arab coast.

71 *Records of the Emirates*, op. cit., vol. 3, 565-6.

72 *Records of the Emirates*, op. cit., vol. 1, 253-99; vol. 2, 5-18, 151-64; vol. 3, 75-117, 121-33, 631-75. There is also no mention of this agreement by Kelly.

73 Abdullah, op. cit., 23; Kelly, op. cit., 354-409. For the texts of these truces and treaty, see Toye, vol. 1, 235, 245, 290-3. Kelly writes that "the treaty [of 1853]… made no provision for the defence of the Trucial Shaikhdoms against aggression from an outside power by sea. On the other hand, it had by now become an accepted fact that responsibility to defend the Trucial Shaikhdoms from such aggression devolved upon the British Government from the Trucial System." Indeed, British Political Resident Kemball assured the Shaikh of Dubai of this on the conclusion of the treaty in 1853. See Kelly, op. cit., 408 and 380, 527, 722, 804, 812, 836-7.

74 Toye, op. cit., vol. 1, 233-5; 239-42; Kelly, op. cit., 363-4.

75 Toye, op. cit., vol. 1, 236-7; *Records of the Emirates*, op. cit., vol. 1, 27-30. Kelly, op. cit., 358-9.

76 For excerpts from the *Persian Gulf Pilot*, see Toye, op. cit., vol. 1, 23-5. Some secondary sources mistakenly indicate that the first edition of the *Persian Gulf Pilot* appeared in 1870.

77 Ibid.

78 Another intriguing possibility for this British Admiralty view stems from the fact that the 1864 *Persian Gulf Pilot* was based on work done in the late 1850s and early 1860s. Shaikh Sultan bin Saqr resided in Lingeh in early 1855 after the death of

Lingeh's Ruler, his cousin Said bin Qadhib. Indeed, Shaikh Sultan bin Saqr, with his son Khalid bin Sultan, who married the widow of Said bin Qadhib, presided over the affairs of Lingeh until the young Shaikh Khalifa bin Said came of age and could rule Lingeh himself. Shaikh Khalid bin Sultan stayed in Lingeh until 1859. The British Admiralty view that the Chief of Lingeh had authority over Abu Musa and the Tunbs was based on work done when Shaikh Sultan bin Saqr, through his son Khalid bin Sultan, was either running the affairs of Lingeh for the young Khalifa bin Said of Lingeh or shortly thereafter. On the other hand, the British recognized the young Khalifa bin Said as the Ruler of Lingeh by July 1855. See Vinson and Elkins, *Territorial Sovereignty Over the Tunb Islands* (Houston: an unpublished study for the Ruler of Ras al-Khaimah, 1980) chapter 3, 17; Bathurst, Ely and Chance, op. cit., vol. I, 20-1; *The Lower Gulf Islands*, op. cit., vol. 1, 539-49, and vol. 2, 12; *Records of the Emirates*, op. cit., vol. 3, 84.

79 Bathurst, Ely and Chance, op. cit., vol. I, 22-3.

80 *Records of the Emirates*, op. cit., vol. 3, 77-8 and Toye, op. cit., vol. 1, 494-5 and Kelly, op. cit., 375-7, 604-13.

81 This despite the fact that in 1840, the Persian Prime Minister, Hajji Mirza Agasi, had made a sweeping declaration to the British that all of the Arabian Gulf and all of the islands in it belonged to Persia. See Pirouz Mojtahed-Zadeh, "Perspectives on the Territorial History of the Tonb and Abu Musa Islands," in Amirahmadi, *Small Islands, Big Politics*, op. cit., 40. Richard Schofield, "Border Disputes in the Gulf: Past, Present, and Future," in Gary G. Sick and Lawrence G. Potter (eds) *The Persian Gulf at the Millennium: Essays in Politics, Economy, Security, and Religion* (New York, NY: St. Martin's Press, 1997), 144 states that this declaration was made in the mid-1840s.

82 Kelly, op. cit., 375-7.

83 Ibid., 607-10.

84 Ibid., 611-3.

85 Abdullah, op. cit., 23, 229-30.

86 Bathurst, Ely and Chance, op. cit., I, 22-3.

87 Toye, op. cit., vol. 1, 494-5. Persia made successful efforts in 1856 and 1868, with some reluctant British help, to receive higher rents from Oman for renewing the lease over Bandar Abbas and Larak, and now also over Hormuz and Qishm. Persia terminated this lease in 1871. Bathurst, Ely and Chance wrote that when the lease was renewed in 1868, it mistakenly included Henjam, but this is not correct. Henjam, which was inhabited by the Al Bu Flasa from Dubai and ruled by the uncle of the Ruler of Dubai, was not included in the original lease or in its renewal. See also Kelly, op. cit., 530-3 and 659-61, 684-5.

88 India Office Records, R/15/1/246 bound along with file 14/88 I, Arab Coast, Sultan bin Saqr to Political Resident, 28 December 1864. English translations of this letter may also be found in Bathurst, Ely and Chance, op. cit., vol. II, 180; Vinson and Elkins, op. cit., vol. II, Doc. no. 3, 11; and Abdullah, *The United Arab Emirates*, op. cit., 233. Morsy Abdullah cites this as India Office Records, R/15/1/14/8. He provides a shorter excerpt, but his transliteration is more authoritative. He uses the term Tanb, which refers to the Greater Tunb. Shaikh Sultan made no reference to Tanb Sughra or Nabiyu Tanb, terms that referred to the Lesser Tunb.

89 Abdullah, op. cit., 233.

90 Toye, op. cit., vol. 1, 559-61; Abdullah, op. cit., 234.

91 See Toye, op. cit., vol. 1, 565-9 and 570-80, 586-95; Bathurst, Ely and Chance, op. cit., vol. I, 26 and vol. II, 50 attribute this letter to Shaikh Salim of Sharjah, as does Abdullah, op. cit., 234. However, the original documents seem to show that Shaikh Humaid, the Ruler of Ras al-Khaimah, was the writer. Vinson and Elkins, op. cit., 3, 21 also attribute this letter to Shaikh Humaid. The British Native Agent sent letters to the Shaikh of Ajman in 1869 and earlier, telling him not to use Abu Musa. Al Roken, op. cit., 140-1 writes that Abu Musa was used for agriculture and as a resort by the Ruler of Sharjah in the 1870s, that in 1879 he exiled his political opponents to the island, and that when he was overthrown in 1883, he took up residence on the island.

92 This led the Native Agent and the new Political Resident Ross to demand that this behavior not be repeated. See *The Lower Gulf Islands*, op. cit., vol. 1, 583-5 and 621-44; Bathurst, Ely and Chance, op. cit., vol. II, 53, 61-2, 65-6; Abdullah, op. cit., 234; Faleh Hanzal, *Al Mufassal and the History of the UAE* (Abu Dhabi, 1983), vol. II, 637.

93 Toye, op. cit., vol. 1, 651-6; 659-66 and Bathurst, Ely, and Chance, op. cit., vol. II, 67-71. See Abdullah, op. cit., 234 for text.

94 Toye, op. cit., vol. 3, 124-9. Shaikh Salim may have been the first permanent inhabitant of Abu Musa.

95 Toye, op. cit., vol. 1, 565-9; Vinson and Elkins, op. cit., 3, 21.

96 See Vinson and Elkins, op. cit., List of Photocopied Documents, 71 for the Arabic text of this letter, which is dated 1872. The Ruler's Court in Ras al-Khaimah indicates that this is a photocopy of the original letter in Arabic. See also Toye, op. cit., vol. 4, 207-8 for a translation which was prepared in 1928 from the original Arabic letter and which is also dated 1872, as is the original Arabic letter. There is one mistake in this translation, when "Oman" is substituted for Ajman. Many accounts, including that of Abdullah, op. cit., 235, indicate that this letter was written in November 1871, but they are based on an excerpt translated in 1881.

97 Toye, op. cit., vol. 1, 599-608.

98 Toye, op. cit., vol. 1, 610-7.

99 Toye, op. cit., vol. 1, 609; Abdullah, op. cit., 235-6 provides a narrative; see also 229-30.

100 See Toye, op. cit., vol. 1, 689-97, especially 696 for the Arabic text of this letter. See also Vinson and Elkins, op. cit., chapter 3, 25-8; Bathurst, Ely and Chance, op. cit., vol. II, 78-9; Abdullah, op. cit., 236.

101 Toye, op. cit., vol. 1, 659-66; Vinson and Elkins, op. cit., chapter 3, 28-9; Abdullah, op. cit., 236.

102 Toye, op. cit., vol. 1, 683-99; Vinson and Elkins, op. cit., chapter 3, 29-30; Bathurst, Ely and Chance, op. cit., II, 77-80; and Abdullah, op. cit., 237. The English language version of the letter from Shaikh Khalifa conveyed by Hajji Abu Al-Qasim in 1882 read only "regarding your second letter, in which you mentioned about the going on of the Boo Samey to Tumb, oh brother (know) that the Samey are your followers and obedient to you but you should prohibit such (people) as the Chiefs of Debaye, Ajman, and Umm al Kawain and the men of Basaidooh, as all of them go to that place, otherwise the Boo Samey as mentioned are in obedience (to you)." There are several possible explanations for this. First, this may have been an early letter from Shaikh Khalifa from 1871 or from November 15, 1872. Second, this may have been an excerpt, an incomplete translation of the November 22, 1872 letter from Shaikh Khalifa. If the latter,

then Hajji Abu Al-Qasim did not convey the full acknowledgement of the Shaikh of Lingeh of the rights of Shaikh Humaid. Referring to the letters written to Ras al-Khaimah Shaikh Humaid from Shaikh Khalifa in 1872, from Shaikh Ali in 1877 and from Shaikh Yusuf in 1884, Guive Mirfendereski has written, "The originals of these letters do not seem to exist." Elsewhere, he uses the word letters in quotation marks [as "letters"] suggesting that they are questionable in some way. Mirfendereski further writes that: "In 1881, the residency agent in Sharjah procured 'letters' seemingly written in 1872 and 1877 by the governor of Lingeh to the Sheikh of Ras al-Khaimah about Great Tonb." His use of the words "procured" and "seemingly" along with his use of the word letters in quotation marks all seem to suggest that he questions the legitimacy or authenticity of these letters. See Guive Mirfendereski, "The Ownership of the Tonb Islands: A Legal Analysis," in *Small Islands, Big Politics*, op. cit., 124-5, 127-8. Thus, the 1882 letter from Hajji Abu Al-Qasim is very important because he writes that he saw the originals of these letters from Shaikh Khalifa and Shaikh Ali. Also, in 1888, the Residency Agent in Sharjah informed the Political Resident that he had seen three letters from Shaikh Khalifa, Shaikh Ali and Shaikh Yusuf and sent copies to the Political Resident. Vinson and Elkins, op. cit., chapter 3, 26-8 notes that in 1928 a search of the Ras al-Khaimah archives yielded only the original Arabic letter from Shaikh Khalifa, but an affadavit was taken from a clerk who testified that he had taken dictation from Shaikh Ali and written his 1877 letter.

103 Vinson and Elkins, op. cit., chapter 3, 31-2; Bathurst, Ely and Chance, op. cit., II, 102; Abdullah, op. cit., 237. The Residency Agent saw this letter, along with the earlier letters from Shaikh Khalifa and Shaikh Ali, and sent them to the Political Resident in 1888.

CHAPTER 2

1 Muhammad Morsy Abdullah, *The United Arab Emirates: A Modern History* (London: Hurtwood Press, Ltd., 1978 and 1994), 224, 229-30. British officials often referred to both father and son only as Amin-es-Sultan or Court Favorite. Unlike his father, Mirza Ali Asghar Khan became Prime Minister, and was sometimes referred to as the Sadr Azam or Prime Minister by British officials. See W.B. Fisher (ed.) *The Cambridge History of Iran* vol. 7 *From Nadir Shah to the Islamic Republic* (Cambridge: Cambridge University Press, 1968), 190-4 for the distinction between these two Persian officials.

2 P.L. Toye (ed.), *The Lower Gulf Islands: Abu Musa and the Tunbs* (London: Archive Editions, 1993), vol. 1, 717, 721-41; Abdullah, op. cit., 23-5, 238-40, and J.B. Kelly, *Britain and the Persian Gulf: 1795-1880* (Oxford: The Clarendon Press, 1968), 834-5.

3 Toye, op. cit., vol. 1, 721-9. See also Vinson and Elkins, *Territorial Sovereignty Over the Tunb Islands* (Houston: Unpublished study for the Ruler of Ras al-Khaimah, 1980), especially chapter 3, 34-5; M.E. Bathurst, Northcutt Ely and Coward Chance, *Sharjah's Title to the Island of Abu Musa* (London: Unpublished study for the Ruler of Sharjah, September 1971), especially I, 29-30. Abdullah, op. cit., 238-9, writes that Persia "intended to encroach" on Sirri, the Greater Tunb, the Lesser Tunb and Abu Musa. Ross did not forward a copy of the letter from Shaikh Yusuf, suggesting that he may not yet have known about this third letter.

4   Toye, op. cit., vol. 1, 730-2. Abdullah, op. cit., 240 writes that Shaikh Humaid of Ras al-Khaimah also made the same protest and appeal.

5   Bathurst, Ely and Chance, op. cit., especially I, 30-1.

6   Toye, op. cit., vol. 1, 729-41 and Vinson and Elkins, op. cit., chapter 3, 35-7.

7   Toye, op. cit., vol. 2, 3-11. See also Vinson and Elkins, op. cit., especially chapter 3, 37-8; Bathurst, Ely and Chance, op. cit., II, 103-4.

8   Toye, op. cit., vol. 2, 12-19. See also Vinson and Elkins, op. cit., especially chapter 3, 38-9; Bathurst Ely and Chance, op. cit., II, 105-6 and Abdullah, op. cit., 240-1. While Shaikh Saqr sent his message to Ross before the latter wrote his memo of 23 January, it appears that Ross did not receive the message by January 23.

9   Toye, op. cit., vol. 2, 20-1, 89-111; Abdullah, op. cit., 241.

10   Toye, op. cit., vol. 4, 101; vol. 2, 22.

11   Vinson and Elkins, op. cit., especially chapter 3, 39-41; Bathurst Ely and Chance, op. cit., II, 105-6.

12   Bathurst Ely and Chance, op. cit., II, 106; and Abdullah, op. cit., 241-2.

13   Toye, op. cit., vol. 2, 28-29.

14   Toye, op. cit., vol. 2, 21-2; Bathurst, Ely and Chance, op. cit., I, 7 and 37 and II, 114-5 and 120. Hajji Ahmed Khan reported that the Qawasim leaving Lingeh had taken refuge on Abu Musa and that he considered it their base. They did not remain long, however, as they were not among the permanent inhabitants of the island in the early 1900s.

15   Toye, op. cit., vol. 2, 120-2.

16   Toye, op. cit., vol. 2, 79-85, 120-2; Abdullah, op. cit., 237-8, 242-3; Husain Albaharna, *The Arabian Gulf States: Their Legal and Political Status and Their International Problems* (Beirut: Librairie Du Liban, 1978), 342. Churchill said "The Arab tribes who claim these islands as theirs are within the radius of our jurisdiction and influence, and have appealed to us against the action of the local authorities in the Gulf in hoisting a flag on their island. We, on our part, have communicated this complaint to the proper quarter and have simply asked for an answer to be given to the Arabs. We have never said that this or that island belongs to this or that tribe. We are simply the proper channel for the transmission of their complaints…it has never been desired that this question should assume an official aspect, nor that it should become the subject of official correspondence between us." However, Nicolson had indeed asserted the Qawasim claims in official correspondence with Persia.

17   Abdullah, op. cit., 25-6, 243; J.B. Kelly, op. cit., 834-5. For the text, see Toye, op. cit., vol. 2, 137. While it is not in the text, it is argued that the British recognized the sovereignty of the rulers within the borders of their emirates in treaties and promised them protection. (One British legal source quarrels with the idea that the British promised protection, but see Lord Curzon's speeches to the shaikhs.)

18   Toye, op. cit., vol. 2, 163-97. See also Vinson and Elkins, op. cit., chapter 3, 42-3.

19   Toye, op. cit., vol. 2, 274-5, 329-37; Bathurst, Ely and Chance, op. cit., I, 5.

20   Toye, op. cit., vol. 2, 247-55; Bathurst, Ely and Chance, op. cit., II, 159-78; Abdullah, op. cit., 243. Abdullah writes that Meade repeated the mistake common among British officials at the time of not distinguishing among the islands and not understanding that Abu Musa and the Tunb had not been ruled by the Lingeh Qawasim. However, he was really only addressing the issue of Sirri and he did note that the Ruler of Ras al-Khaimah had argued conclusively that the Greater Tunb belonged to his section of the Qawasim.

21 See Abdullah, op. cit., 243-4. The Qawasim ejected from Lingeh had already briefly retaken Lingeh from the summer of 1898 to the spring of 1899.

22 Toye, op. cit., vol. 2, 341-92, especially 344-50, 364-9, 625-32. Also, Bathurst, Ely and Chance, op. cit., I, 43 and II, 189-94; Vinson and Elkins, op. cit., Chapter 3, 44-5; and Abdullah, op. cit., 231-2 and 244. By this time, Abu Musa had a permanent population of more than twenty families from the Sudan tribe from Sharjah, who were engaged in fishing and pearling and tending to their flocks and herds. There were also laborers in the red oxide mines who, together with their families, numbered about 100. Lorimer called these laborers Persians, but he also mistakenly called the contractor from Lingeh Persian, when he was in fact Arab. Furthermore, they were there only by virtue of a concession granted by the Qawasim Shaikh Salim. The Greater Tunb had a smaller permanent population, consisting of two Bani Yas families from Dubai, a Persian family from Lingeh who were employees of the Shaikh of Sharjah, and the Shaikh's representative on the island, who was responsible for the flag. These people were also engaged in fishing and pearling and tending to their animals. The Lesser Tunb did not have a permanent population. Pirouz Mojtahed-Zadeh writes that "the government of India ordered the occupation of Great Tonb and Abu Musa by and in the name of the Sheikh of Sharjah." Noting that Lord Curzon had produced a map in 1892 showing the islands as belonging to Persia, Mojtahed-Zadeh notes "That the sheikh had to be ordered to occupy the islands, which the British government previously had maintained consistently as belonging to Iran, contradicts and defeats the subsequent British attempts at revising history in order to rationalize and justify the sheikh's actions." See Pirouz Mojtahed-Zadeh, "Perspectives on the Territorial History of the Tonb and Abu Musa Islands," in Amirahmadi, *Small Islands, Big Politics*, op. cit., 44-5. This analysis does not take into account the previous use and possession of the islands by the Qawasim of Sharjah and Ras al-Khaimah, and misrepresents the position of the British government on ownership of the islands.

23 Toye, op. cit., vol. 2, 415-533, especially 442, 455, 473, 482-5, 508-17, 528. See also Vinson and Elkins, op. cit., chapter 3, 45-7; Bathurst, Ely and Chance, op. cit., I, 43-5; and Abdullah, op. cit., 244-5. Mojtahed-Zadeh, op. cit., 47 claims that "The withdrawal of the Iranian flag from the islands in 1904 was effected in part by the promise of the British government to negotiate the controversy while no action be taken to prejudice Iran's sovereignty over the islands." However, the British did not recognize Persia as sovereign and did not consent to the Persian request that the Qawasim flags not be re-hoisted. In 1928, an India Office memo by J.G. Laithwaite noted that "The Persian flag was stated to have been hoisted on Little Tamb in 1904 at the time of the Persian aggression on Tamb and Abu Musa. It was presumably removed at the same time as it was removed from those islands." The memo cited an April 15, 1904 telegram from the Political Resident to the Government of India, although this telegram does not make this assertion. An April 4, 1904 letter from the Residency Agent in Lingeh to the Political Resident suggests that the Persians had raised their flag on the Little Tunb, but this appears to be a mistake and there is no other reference or evidence to support this in the official records. See Toye, op. cit., vol. 4, 123.

24 Toye, op. cit., vol. 2, 490-1, 537-54. See also Abdullah, op. cit., 245-6.

25 The British were concerned about the visits to the Gulf of Russian and French warships in 1901, 1902 and 1903, and that these countries, along with Germany, sought naval bases in the Gulf.

26 The firm British policy regarding the islands may also be seen as consistent with the Lansdowne Declaration of May 1903, in which Foreign Secretary Lansdowne stated that Britain would resist the establishment of a naval base or fortified port in the Arabian Gulf by any other power. Furthermore, it was connected to the show of naval force and the statements made to the Trucial Chiefs by Lord Curzon on his late 1903 cruise through the Gulf, particularly his commitment to the British "policy of guardianship and protection which has given you peace and guaranteed your rights for the best part of a century." Abdullah, op. cit., 26-32, 225, 231, 244-5. For the text of the Lansdowne Declaration and documents regarding Lord Curzon's tour of the Gulf, see Toye, op. cit., vol. 2, 395-404, 407-11, 581-4.

27 Toye, op. cit., vol. 3, 3-14, 17-26. From 1907 to 1914, Germany and Britain argued the case on commercial and legal grounds, with Germany arguing that Shaikh Salim had granted the concession as the owner of Abu Musa and Britain arguing that Shaikh Salim had granted the concession on behalf of the Ruler of Sharjah, Shaikh Saqr, who ultimately had the right to terminate it. The outbreak of war in 1914 ended the argument. See Toye, op. cit., vol. 3, pp. 37-112, 114-53, 157-77, 181-258; 261-396; 399-436.

28 Bathurst, Ely and Chance, op. cit., I, 46-8.

29 Toye, op. cit., vol. 3, 541-3, 546-7; Vinson and Elkins, op. cit., chapter 3, 48; Bathurst, Ely and Chance, op. cit. I, 48-9 and II, 296 and 326.

30 Some of the other issues included the forced submission of the Arab shaikh of Arabistan, the granting of oil concessions to American companies in areas claimed by the Anglo-Persian Oil Company (APOC), the challenge to the legality of APOC's concession (the William Knox D'Arcy concession), leading to the eventual cancellation of that concession and negotiation of a new one, the smuggling of tea and sugar into Persia, which Persia blamed on Arabs and Britain blamed on Persians themselves, British tolerance of the waves of migration from Persia's southern coast to the Trucial States, Bahrain and Qatar, and the Dubai dhow incident. See Abdullah, op. cit., 246-62 and George Lenczowski, *The Middle East in World Affairs* (Ithaca: Cornell University Press, 1980), 170-8.

31 Frauke Heard-Bey, *From Trucial States to United Arab Emirates: A Society in Transition* (London: Longman Group, 1996), 84; Abdullah, op.cit., 255; Bathurst, Ely and Chance, op. cit., I, 49.

32 Toye, op. cit., vol. 3, 443-64 and vol. 4, 3-10; Bathurst, Ely and Chance, op. cit., I, 49-50 and II, 297-302; Vinson and Elkins, op. cit., chapter 3, 48-9. Abdullah, op. cit., 255 indicates that these events took place in 1921, but in fact they took place in late 1922 and 1923.

33 Toye, op. cit., vol. 4, 19-21 and 25-34. Bathurst, Ely and Chance, op cit., I, 50 and Abdullah, op. cit., 256, argue that British protests resulted in the withdrawal of the Persian note claiming sovereignty. However, no evidence of this in the documents could be located.

34 Toye, op. cit., vol. 4, 37-120, especially 76-7, 98, 103 and 110-20; Vinson and Elkins, op. cit., chapter 3, 49-50 and Documents 3.18, 211-3 as well as Abdullah, op. cit., 257-62.

35 Toye, op. cit., vol. 4, 123-30. Al-Roken, op. cit., 142 states that this memorandum "stated that the islands of Greater and Lesser Tunbs had belonged to Ras al-

Khaimah since its emergence as a separate entity independent of Sharjah, while Abu Musa belonged to Sharjah..." However, the memo actually argued inaccurately that all three islands belonged to the Shaikh of Sharjah and that the Shaikh of Ras al-Khaimah was dependent on him. Al Roken also asserts that the memo was issued after a verbal understanding between the Persian and British Governments that the islands were Arab. The Persian government, however, was energetically asserting its claims to the islands at this time and only agreeing to negotiate the issue rather than occupying them outright.

36   Toye, op. cit., vol. 4, 182-6 and 199-219; Bathurst, Ely and Chance, op. cit., vol. I 52-3.

37   Toye, op. cit., vol. 4, 237-41, 247-8. For the text of the draft treaty, in French, see 255-8. Abdullah, op. cit., 262 writes that it was Taimurtash who "proposed" the trade-off between Abu Musa and the Greater Tunb. Vinson and Elkins, op. cit., state in chapter 3, 50-1 that he "favored" such a trade-off. Clive, however, actually wrote that it was his "impression" that Taimurtash wanted this. Al Roken, op. cit., 142 writes that the draft treaty recognized Sirri as Persian and the Tunbs and Abu Musa as Arab, but there was no treaty actually concluded and these were not the positions taken by Persia.

38   Toye, op. cit., vol. 4, 303-8, 331-3. Abdullah, op. cit., 263 writes that Taimurtash "suggested" the trade-off between Bahrain and Abu Musa on the one hand and the Greater Tunb on the other, but Clive wrote that it was his "impression" that Taimurtash would yield on Abu Musa for the sake of the Greater Tunb.

39   Toye, op. cit., vol. 4, 370, 384, 389-90, 393-4, 397-408. Clive wrote in his first telegram on his late October 1930 meeting with Taimurtash that Taimurtash had proposed to lease both the Greater Tunb and Abu Musa, but in his subsequent and more complete report he referred only to a proposal to lease the Greater Tunb.

40   Toye, op. cit., vol. 4, 409-14, 439-41 and vol. 5, 24-6. See also Abdullah, op. cit., 264-6. In the 1950s, the British Foreign Office view was that Iran had withdrawn its offer and that the negotiations had been suspended. See Toye, op. cit., vol. 6, 344-5.

41   Toye, op. cit., vol. 4, 498, 500-1, 526-7, 546-54. A representative of the Ruler of Ras al-Khaimah administered the island, but the British actually operated the lighthouse.

42   Toye, op. cit., vol. 5, 45-59, 389-92. Abdullah, op. cit., 267 reports the alleged March 1934 visit as a fact.

43   Abullah, op. cit., 267.

44   Toye, op. cit., vol. 5, 60-9, 70, 141-52 and Abdullah, op cit., 267-8.

45   Toye, op. cit., vol. 5, 70-129, especially 109-15, 121, 124-5; 393 and 403-10. In addition, see 191-203, 317-48 and 373-85 for the British strategy if Persia raised its claims at the League of Nations. See also Abdullah, op. cit., 268-9.

46   Toye, op. cit., vol. 5, 415-563, especially 436-525.

47   Ibid., vol. 5, 526-8, 531, 540-1; Abdullah, op. cit., 124, 270-1.

48   The company would do so until 1968.

49   Toye, op. cit., vol. 5, 173-4, 187, 613-64, especially 616-9, 630-1, 639, 647-8.

50   Ibid., vol. 5, 529-30, 536-8, 548-57, 567-609, especially 603; Abdullah, op. cit., 271-3.

51   Toye, op. cit., vol. 6, 39-59, 63-74, 107-20, 131-50, 328-30.

52   Lenczowski, op. cit., 178-9.

53 Abdullah, op. cit., 78, 273. A very prominent member of the Qawasim tribe argues that the British deposed the Ruler of Ras al-Khaimah, Shaikh Sultan bin Salim, in 1948. Shaikh Sultan's nephew, Shaikh Saqr bin Mohammed, has ruled since 1948. Hawley writes on page 344 that the British recognized Shaikh Saqr following the suggestion of intrigue by Shaikh Sultan. When Shaikh Sultan resisted after being summoned to the British Residency at Sharjah, he was subsequently exiled to Muscat for a year. See also *Records of the Emirates*, vol. 9, 20-1.

54 Toye, op. cit., vol. 6, 180-4, 196-204.

55 Ibid., vol. 6, 210-1, 216-31, 236-50.

56 Ibid., vol. 6, 313-4; Richard Schofield (ed.) *Arabian Boundaries 1963* (London: Archive Editions, 1994), vol. 2, 445-8.

57 Toye, op. cit., vol. 6, 253-64, especially 260.

58 The Shah also reluctantly named Mossadegh Prime Minister on April 28. See Lenczowski, op. cit., 190-8.

59 See the following declassified US Department of State documents from the National Archives in Bethesda, Maryland: *Baghdad to Secretary of State, March 25, 1953*, filed at 788.022/3-2553; *Tehran to the Department of State, April 3, 1953*, filed at 788.022/4-353.

60 Toye, op. cit., vol. 6, 273-6, 285-8.

61 Ibid, 322.

62 Ibid, 349-50, 357-59.

63 Ibid., 315-50, 357-67.

64 Al Roken, op. cit., 143.

65 Toye, op. cit., vol. 6, 368-76.

66 Ibid., vol. 6, 379-88. See also the following declassified U.S. Department of State documents: *Tehran to Secretary of State, October 1, 1956* and *Department of State to Tehran, October 4, 1956*, filed at 788.022/10-156; *Tehran to Secretary of State, October 13, 1956*, and *Dhahran to Secretary of State, October 20, 1956*, filed at 788.022/10-1356; also *Tehran to Secretary of State, October 24, 1956*, filed at 788.022/10-2456.

67 *Department of State to Tehran*, October 31, 1956, declassified US Department of State document filed at 788.022/10-2456.

68 Toye, op. cit., vol. 6, 391-401, 405-7. The British naval party took photographs of this ceremony.

69 See declassified US Department of State documents, especially *Lampton Berry to Loftus Becker, July 22, 1957*, and *Lampton Berry through Loftus Becker to Hugh S. Cuming, Jr., July 22, 1957*, filed at 788.022/7-1057; *Forthcoming U.S.-U.K. Seabed Talks*, October 8, 1957, filed at 788.022/10-857; and *US-UK Persian Gulf Seabed Talks*, October 14, 1957, filed at 788.022/10-1457.

70 Schofield, *Arabian Boundaries: New Documents 1964*, op. cit., vol. 1, 569-70 and vol. 2, 474. In a January 1958 meeting between US Secretary of State Dulles and the Shah in Tehran, the Shah stated that he needed missiles to defend the oil fields of Iran. The Department of Defense official traveling with Dulles expected that because of the Pan-Arab movement led by Nasser's Egypt, which referred to the Gulf as the Arabian Gulf, and because of Bahrain, which the Shah had claimed again in 1957, the Shah would ask for naval support. The United States was prepared to offer the Shah coastal mine-sweeping and anti-submarine patrol capabilities, but neither side raised the issue. Furthermore, Dulles did not encourage the Shah on the availability of appropriate missiles. See *Audience with*

H.I.M. The Shah, January 25, 1958, a declassified US Department of State document filed at "Subject files relating to Iran 1951-1958," RG 59, Lot File 60D 533, Box 2 of 3.

71 *Tehran to Secretary of State, December 20, 1958*, filed at 788.022/12-2053, and *Department of State to Tehran, December 22, 1958*, filed at 788.022/12-2058, both declassified U.S. Department of State documents.

72 Ahmad Razavi, *Continental Shelf Delimitation and Related Maritime Issues in the Persian Gulf* (The Hague: Martinus Nijhoff Publishers, 1997), 26.

73 Toye, op. cit., vol. 6, 411-7.

74 Ibid., 421-5, 458, 465.

75 Ibid., 429-73, especially 454-5, 467 and 473. See also Schofield, *Arabian Boundaries 1961*, vol. 2, 555-93 for a duplicate set of documents. The British briefly wondered if the helicopter that landed on the Greater Tunb in May 1961 had been a US Navy helicopter, but they were assured by the US Navy that it had not been. It was also learned at this time that Iranian boats had been patrolling around the island to discourage the islanders from smuggling goods from Dubai to the south of Iran.

76 Toye, op. cit., vol. 6, 458-61. See also Schofield, *Arabian Boundaries 1961*, vol. 2, 584-7. The following year, in June 1962, while delegations from the Trucial States were in Kuwait to celebrate Kuwait's National Day, the Iranian Embassy in Kuwait distributed a magazine article in Arabic in which the Iranian claim to the Greater and Lesser Tunbs, Abu Musa and Bahrain was asserted. After determining that the article had not been drafted or approved by the Ministry of Foreign Affairs, the British decided to lodge only an oral and informal protest. See Toye, op. cit., vol. 6, 477-86 and Schofield, *Arabian Boundaries 1961*, vol. 2, 709-18 for a duplicate set of documents.

77 Rouhollah K. Ramazani, *Iran's Foreign Policy 1941-1973: A Study of Foreign Policy in Modernizing Nations* (Charlottesville, VA: University Press of Virginia, 1975), 315-21.

78 *Tehran to Secretary of State, May 20, 1963*, declassified US Department of State document, filed at Pol 7 Iran. See also Abdullah, op cit., 277-8, for a brief discussion of the Shah's view of Nasser's role in the Gulf. A previous union between Egypt and Syria had lasted from 1958 to 1961.

79 Schofield, *Arabian Boundaries 1963*, op. cit., vol. 1, 611-3.

80 Ibid., 614-8.

81 Ibid., 619-22.

82 Ibid., 611-20.

83 Ibid., 623-7.

84 Ibid., vol. 1, 628-37. Bathurst, Ely and Chance, op. cit., vol. 1, 6-7 wrote that "there were no reports of any Iranian inquiry or protest about the concession area" granted to American independent oil producer John Mecom in 1962. However, British government documents released since the Bathurst, Ely and Chance report show that Iranian protests were lodged in 1963 (in 1969, the Ruler of Sharjah granted oil exploration concessions in Abu Musa and its territorial waters, extending 12 miles, to the Buttes Gas and Oil Company). It should also be noted here that the dispute between Iran on the one hand and Sharjah and Ras al-Khaimah on the other hand was not the only dispute Britain had to consider. In early 1961, the British had begun to consider how to delimit the territorial sea and the seabed beyond the territorial sea between and among the seven Trucial States

themselves. It was recognized that this would depend on a final agreement regarding the delimitation of the land boundaries between and among these states, the delimitation of a median line through the Gulf, and the determination of the sovereignty of the islands in the Gulf and how these islands would be treated in determining the other boundaries. In the case of Ras al-Khaimah, settlement would depend on the delimitation of the land boundaries with her neighbors Umm al-Qawain and Oman. In the case of Sharjah, it would depend on the land boundaries with Dubai and Umm al-Qawain, as well as with Ajman, which is an enclave within Sharjah and would therefore divide the Sharjah territorial sea and the seabed beyond it.

The Hydrographic Department of the British Admiralty began to generate charts and maps in 1961 and 1962. As this was being done, it seemed in July 1962 to the Political Agent for the Trucial States in Dubai, James Craig, that "these islands [Abu Musa and the Tunbs] would seem from the lines drawn on chart 2888…to belong to Umm al Qaiwain." As for the disputed islands in general and their influence on the drawing of these boundaries, the Foreign Office agreed with the following recommendation contained in a British study that was submitted to the 1958 Conference on the Law of the Sea: "It might seem reasonable under such circumstances not to permit these islands to have any influence on a boundary but to allow them only their own belts of territorial sea for the purposes of exploration and exploitation. If this doctrine is accepted, neither a decision on sovereignty over Abu Musa or Sir Abu Nuair or any other islands will effect the sea-bed boundaries between the Trucial States nor vice versa." See Schofield, *Arabian Boundaries 1961*, op. cit., vol. 2, 55-7, 71-3 and Schofield, *Arabian Boundaries 1962*, op. cit., vol. 2, 102-10, 115-29, 152-5, 727-32. British efforts to secure agreements from the Trucial Shaikhs on their land and maritime boundaries took place in 1963. The seabed boundary between Sharjah and Dubai was now of particular concern inasmuch as Mecomoil wished to drill in the area. Mecom also wanted to drill in an area off Abu Musa, which was considered to be in the seabed area of Sharjah, but which could extend into the seabed areas of Umm al-Qaiwain and Ajman, depending on how the boundaries were drawn. The principles under consideration were the formal principle of equidistance and the less complicated principle of a base-line drawn from one end of the coast to the other. The Hydrographic Department wrote that "Abu Musa belongs to Sharjah, the Sharjah/Umm al-Qawain sea boundary should skirt the island territorial sea boundary." These efforts continued in 1964 and 1965. In September 1964, British Political Agent Craig reported that Sharjah and Umm al-Qawain had agreed on their seabed boundary. He also reported that Sharjah had offered to settle its seabed boundaries with Ajman, but that Ajman would not agree to the proposals. The Ras al-Khaimah boundaries with Umm al-Qawain and Oman took on more importance as Ras al-Khaimah granted oil concessions, but agreements proved elusive in 1964, as did any agreement between Sharjah and Dubai. See Schofield, *Arabian Boundaries 1964*, op. cit., vol. 1, 127-62, 181-205, and *Arabian Boundaries 1965*, op. cit., vol. 1, 269-73 and 304-6.

85 Schofield, *Arabian Boundaries 1963*, op. cit., vol. 1, 637-9.

86 *Tehran to Secretary of State, September 15, 1963*, declassified US Department of State document, filed at Def 19 US-Iran.

87 Schofield, *Arabian Boundaries 1963*, vol. 2, 529-31. One Foreign Office official wrote at this bottom of this memo that "Normally, I should have thought, islands such as the Tunbs would generate territorial sea <u>and</u> cause the median line to move over to half way between them and the Iranian shore." However, such a median line arrangement would have deprived Iran of significant continental shelf. In early September, the British Admiralty had made a similar argument to the Foreign Office that "[T]he sovereignty of these islands affects the drawing of the median line of the Arabian Gulf. If Sirri, Abu Musa and Tunb belong to Iran rather than to the Trucial States, then the median line would be drawn midway between the islands and the Trucial Coast; the Trucial States would thereby lose ownership of the sea bed resources of a large area of the Gulf, quite apart from the territory and territorial sea of the islands themselves," an area which the Admiralty estimated "could amount to about 2500 square nautical miles." It concluded therefore that "[i]t may well be this aspect of the islands suzerainty that has stimulated the Iranian interest." It was not likely that a median line could have been drawn and accepted on such a principle, although it might have been an Iranian hope. See Schofield, *Arabian Boundaries 1963*, op. cit., vol. 1, 626.

88 Schofield, *Arabian Boundaries 1963*, op. cit., vol. 1, 640-1. The Foreign Office continued its deliberations on the question of future negotiations over the median line throughout 1964. On February 4, the Foreign Office wrote to James Craig, the Political Agent in Dubai: "Though it should be recalled that, as a result of our reservation we do not regard it as applying in the Persian Gulf, the 1958 Geneva Convention on the Continental Shelf provides that, if there is no special agreement or special circumstances, states with opposite coast lines draw their common median line so that it is 'equidistant from the nearest points of the base lines from which the territorial sea of each state is measured' (Article 6). The base lines would be on the two opposite mainlands and islands (Article 1) but could be based also on low tide elevations situated wholly or partly at a distance not exceeding the breadth of the territorial sea from the mainland or island. (See article 11 of the Convention on the Territorial Sea and Contiguous Zone.) If the provision in the Convention was rigidly adhered to and baselines were drawn with the benefit of Article 11 of the Territorial Sea Convention, which is unlikely as long as we adhere to our reservation, it is true, that the breadth of the territorial sea would have some affect on the location of the median line; but the Gulf Rulers are not bound by the Convention because of our reservation, and the Iranians, as well as they, are much more likely to go for a special agreement rather than rely on the general provisions." Indeed, Iran had not ratified any of the 1958 Law of the Sea Conventions.

Continuing, the Foreign Office stated: "In fact, given Ras al-Khaimah's sovereignty over the two Tunb Islands, the Iranians could not afford to accept the recommendation no matter what extent of territorial waters they claimed. We can be certain therefore that the negotiation of a common median line with the Iranians will have to depend on a mutually agreed basis of settlement such as base lines drawn on the mainland coast or on the coasts of islands within three miles (or six miles) of the mainland. The breadth of territorial waters could not affect or would be merely coincidental to a settlement of this kind, which would be based solely on bargaining..." See Schofield, *Arabian Boundaries 1964*, op. cit., vol. 1, 227-8.

One issue that the British had to deal with as they were deliberating about negotiations on a median line, was the limits of the off-shore concession areas granted by the Trucial States and Iran. Prior to reaching agreements with Ras al-Khaimah in March, the Union Oil Exploration and Production Company and the Southern Natural Gas Company had refused to continue negotiating with Ras al-Khaimah if they were not allowed to explore beyond a safe operating limit five miles southeast of the British concept of a median line. The Foreign Office had decided to permit the companies to explore to the median line after a two-year moratorium. In September, the Foreign Office also agreed that the companies holding concessions from Dubai should be permitted to explore up to the British concept of the median line. In reaching this decision, the Foreign Office reasoned that if the companies were not permitted to do so, Iran "might take it as an indication of lack of resolution about a median line" and "would accordingly be all the more intransigent over any median line negotiation with them." Moreover, the Foreign Office believed that Iran had commissioned seismic surveys up to and over the median line and the Foreign Office did not know if Iran had imposed any safe operating limits on any companies to which they had granted concessions. Finally, the Foreign Office noted: "Hostile Arab propaganda has recently made much of our alleged support for Iranian claims and pretensions in the Persian Gulf. Refusal by us in this case could effectively be used as further evidence against us." See Schofield, *Arabian Boundaries 1964*, op. cit., vol. 1, 209-47, especially 243-7.

It is worth mentioning that the Foreign Office also wrote: "[t]he median line to which our safe operating limits are related is one constructed from the mainland shore without taking into consideration the various islands in the Gulf. The Department have once more consulted the Admiralty Hydrographer about the extent to which these islands, if taken into account, might deflect the median line in this part of the Gulf. The key island is Sirri, which H.M.G. regard as *de jure* Sharjah's but *de facto* Iranian. Sirri, if regarded as Iranian for median line purposes, would take that line so far to the south as to be manifestly unjust to the States on the Arabian littoral and almost certainly unnegotiable with the latter. It is not likely that H.M.G., while still responsible for the external affairs of the Trucial States, could ever in the future acquiesce in such a line. Use of the islands closer in shore (Abu Musa on the Arabian side and Forur and Bani Forur on the Persian side) would produce a line close to the present median line. However, if we were to agree to take these islands into consideration it would be difficult to exclude Sirri, or for that matter the Tunbs, which might take the line too far north to be negotiable with Iran. It is for these reasons our view and that of the Admiralty Hydrographer that no median line which could in the future be accepted by H.M.G. would differ appreciably from the present line. Thus to accede to the Companies' request now would not mean transgressing any median line likely to be established later by agreement."

Throughout the year, various departments of the Foreign Office considered whether the initiation of discussions on a median line with Iran would be portrayed by Egypt (formally the United Arab Republic) as evidence of Anglo-Iranian collusion. They also considered whether the failure to initiate discussions would result in charges that Britain had failed to protect the interests of the Trucial States if Iranian oil exploration crossed over British notions of a reasonable median line (as Britain thought it might opposite Bahrain and Qatar). In October, however, the Foreign Office learned from the Union Oil Company, which was about to bid for Iranian offshore concessions, that this particular concession area, Area II (opposite Bahrain, Qatar and Abu Dhabi), extended from Iran's "three mile territorial line" to "the median line of the Gulf," and that the NIOC map "appears to indicate that the median line referred to is one drawn without reference to any off-shore islands." The Foreign Office noted that this was "far less unreasonable than in Area 1 where large chunks of Iraqi and Kuwaiti offshore areas are claimed." See Schofield, *Arabian Boundaries 1964*, op. cit., vol. 1, 551-8, 564-5. It is worth noting that there was some consideration as to whether it "would be better to defer any move until there was some prospect of a settlement between Iran and the fully independent Gulf territories, which would provide cover for our negotiations…"

CHAPTER 3

1 Richard Schofield (ed.) *Arabian Boundaries: New Documents* (London: Archive Editions, 1993 to 1997), *vol.* 2, 471-85.

2 Schofield, *Arabian Boundaries: New Documents 1964*, op. cit., vol. 2, 486-90.

3 Ibid., 491-2.

4 Ibid., 493-5.

5 Ibid., 251-63.

6 Ibid., 259-60.

7 Ibid., 568-71.

8 Ibid., 252, 264-361. One Arab scholar writing in 1987 and citing an Iraqi Ministry of Information publication from 1973, repeated some of these same assertions when he wrote: "…in 1964 Iranian armed forces staged maritime manoeuvres within an area which included Abu Musa island, as well as other Arab islands. A contingent was landed on the uninhabited part of Abu Musa, and installations to aid navigation were erected in the territory. However, in the face of the ensuing protests, the Iranian Foreign Minister apologized, alleging that the act was merely part of the manoeuvres, and that no offence had been meant. The installations were dismantled and withdrawn, but of course the whole episode was intended to explore the British reaction in a similar situation and to remind the Arab people in the emirates that the Iranian dragon was always there and ready to act at any time." See Abdullah Omran Taryam, *The Establishment of the United Arab Emirates, 1950-1985* (London: Croom Helm Ltd., 1987), 46.

9 Schofield, *Arabian Boundaries: New Documents 1964*, op. cit., vol. 2, 524-5.

10 Ibid., vol. 2, 526.

11 Ibid., vol. 1, 568-79, 583-4, 586-90 and vol. 2, 529.

12 Ibid., vol. 2 352-62.

13 Schofield, *Arabian Boundaries: New Documents 1965*, op. cit., vol. 2, 363-71, 410.

14 Ibid., vol. 2, 372-93, 454. In response to a question, the British reported "that the Ruler of Sharjah was the only one who seemed basically well disposed towards Nasser, though he usually managed to drag his kinsman, the Ruler of Ras al-Khaimah, along with him. The Ruler of Sharjah's motives were probably a mixture

of genuine Arab nationalism and a mistaken belief that it was in his own interest to flirt with the Arab League." Soon after these meetings, in June, the British deposed and exiled Sharjah's Ruler, who had welcomed the involvement of an Arab League-created fund in the social and economic development of the Trucial States, which the British considered a threat to their own position. Shaikh Saqr was succeeded as Sharjah's Ruler by Shaikh Khalid bin Muhammad al-Qasimi. See Muhammad Morsy Abdullah, *The United Arab Emirates: A Modern History* (London: Hurtwood Press Ltd., 1978 and 1994), 75-6, 137; Taryam, op. cit., 48-52 and Donald Hawley, *The Trucial States* (London: Allen and Unwin, 1970), 226-9.

15 Schofield, *Arabian Boundaries: New Documents 1965*, op. cit., vol. 2, 380.

16 Ibid., 398-412, 418-21. The British also reasoned that any anti-British reaction in Iran would at least help to defuse charges of Anglo-Iranian collusion in the Gulf. On another note, Iran's Foreign Minister also began to object to the use of the term "Arabian Gulf" by the BBC and the Arab Rulers in the Gulf region, particularly on the new currency decided upon at their meeting in Dubai. The British Embassy replied that the official British Government terminology was 'the Persian Gulf' and that the BBC had made a mistake. As far as the currency was concerned, Luce agreed that the Rulers should be advised against such a use as this would offend the Iranians and damage their trade with Iran. The Rulers of Bahrain, Qatar, Abu Dhabi and Dubai were advised on this point. However, the British soon learned that the Shaikh of Bahrain and the Deputy Ruler of Qatar refused to drop the term "Arab Gulf" from currency and that Abu Dhabi and Dubai, while amenable to a name change, would not oppose them on this issue. A proposal by the Ruler of Dubai to visit the Shah to try to reconcile him to the currency agreement and to maintain trade between the two was accepted. The British also considered asking Saudi Arabia's King Faisal to ask the Shah to drop his claim to Bahrain, but decided not to do so, reasoning that the Shah was not in the right frame of mind, particularly while the questions of "Arabian Gulf" currency and Bahrain's inclusion in a federation were being discussed. Ibid., 436-66, 469-70. See also Taryam, op. cit., 58 for a brief discussion of this July 1965 meeting.

17 Schofield, *Arabian Boundaries: New Documents 1965*, op. cit., vol. 2, 413-7,424-5.

18 Ibid., 426-7, 432-7, 450-3.

19 Ibid., 467-8.

20 In December 1965, Iran and Saudi Arabia initialed an agreement on a median line, which also related to Farsi and Arabi. The revised agreement would not be signed until 1968. In 1966, Britain began negotiations on behalf of Qatar and the Trucial States with Iran over maritime boundaries. Iran insisted on using Qishm island as her baseline while the Arabs insisted on the Persian coastline as Iran's baseline. Iran also laid claim to Abu Musa and the Tunb. See Abdullah, op. cit., 278.

21 FCO/8/53, February 11, 1966; FCO/8/52, March 7, 1967.

22 FCO/8/2, January 27, 1967.

23 FCO/8/52, January 4, 1967.

24 FCO/8/52, February 22 and 28, March 2, 7, 10, 17, and 22, 1967.

25 FCO/8/52, March 17, 20, April 6, 1967. Iran also protested against the Mecomoil drilling 4 miles off-shore from Abu Musa. Britain promptly replied that the Mecomoil operations would continue.

26 FCO/8/52, April 12 and 14, 1967.

27 FCO/8/52, February 1, March 7, 14 and 23, 1967.

28 FCO/8/53, June 21, 1967.

29 FCO/8/53, July 18, 1967.

30 FCO/8/53, August 2, 16, 1967.

31 FCO/8/53, October 6, 18, 1967.

32 FCO/8/53, October 18 and 31, November 1, 22 and 30, as well as December 9, 1967; also FCO/8/54, December 21, 1967.

33 FCO/8/53, December 21, 1967; FCO/8/54, February 2 and 14, 1968.

34 FCO/8/53, January 8, 1968; FCO/8/53 and FCO/8/54, January 9, 1968. See also February 9 memo.

35 FCO 8/54, January 15, 1968.

36 Shahram Chubin and Sepehr Zabih, *The Foreign Relations of Iran: A Developing State in a Zone of Great-Power Conflict* (Berkeley, CA: University of California Press, 1974), 218 quote *The Times*, June 10, 1969.

37 James Noyes, *The Clouded Lens: Persian Gulf Security and U.S. Policy* (Stanford, CA: Hoover Institution Press, 1982), 31.

38 Interview with Shaikh Saqr, Ruler of Ras al-Khaimah, at Ras al-Khaimah Ruler's Court, April 14, 1998.

39 FCO/960/1, October 14, 15, 17, 24, 30 and 31, 1968, December 18, 1968, and Richard Weston's December 26, 1968 letter to Shaikh Saqr; interview at Ras al-Khaimah Ruler's Court, April 14, 1998.

40 Asadollah Alam in Alinaghi Alikhani (ed.) *The Shah and I: The Confidential Diary of Iran's Royal Court, 1969-1977* (London: I.B. Tauris and Company, Ltd., 1991) 113. See also Alam's entries for 23 December, 1969, 114 and 18 January 1970, 125.

41 FCO/8/962, December 24, 1969.

42 FCO/8/962, December 29, 1969.

43 FCO/960/1, April 2, 1969.

44 See the letter from Shaikh Khalid, Ruler of Sharjah, to Arab heads of state, August 23, 1971 in *Middle East Economic Survey* (MEES), XV, no. 6, December 3, 1971, 6-7.

45 Alam, op. cit., 125.

46 Chubin and Zabih, op. cit., 218. See also J.B. Kelly, *Arabia, the Gulf, and the West* (London: George Weidenfeld and Nicolson Limited, 1980 and USA: Basic Books, 1980) 55, 58-9. See also Ruhollah Ramazani, *The Persian Gulf and the Strait of Hormuz* (Alphen aan den Rijn, The Netherlands: Sijthoff and Noordhoff, 1979) 102 for text.

47 Interview with Julian Walker, London, October 1997. Walker was the British Political Agent in Dubai and a member of the British mediation team under Sir William Luce in 1971. See also Abdullah, op. cit., 281.

48 Chubin and Zabih, op. cit., 222-5; Abdullah, op. cit., 282. The latter refers to Occidental as working for Sharjah.

49 Abdullah, op. cit., 282. See Schofield, *Arabian Boundaries: New Documents 1963*, op. cit., vol. 2, 249-56 and successive volumes for the views of Luce in 1963, 1964 and 1965. Recently de-classified US Department of State documents at the National Archives in Bethesda, Maryland contain US reports of briefings given by British officials on Luce's diplomacy. These are cited in chapter eight.

50 Interview with Julian Walker, London, October 1997. Videotaped deposition of Northcutt Ely at the ICJ at The Hague, 1992. Also Taryam, op. cit., 170-1.

51 Saeed M. Badeeb, *Saudi-Iranian Relations: 1932-1982* (London: Center for Arab and Iranian Studies, 1993), 120 and recollections of the Kuwaiti representative in the *Provisional Verbatim Record of the Sixteen Hundred and Tenth Meeting of the United Nations Security Council* (S/10436, 9 December 1971).

52 Husain Albaharna, *The Arabian Gulf States: Their Legal and Political Status and Their International Problems* (Beirut: Librairie Du Liban, 1978), 341.

53 FCO 8/1316, "Record of a conversation between the Foreign and Commonwealth Secretary and the Shah of Iran, at the Iranian Embassy in Brussels at 10:00 a.m. on Friday, 10 July [1970]."

54 FCO 8/1320, "Record of Audience with the Shah of Iran in Tehran on 19 September, 1970."

55 FCO 8/1557, "Record of Conversation at the Niavaran Palace Tehran on 4 May, 1971." In the farewell audience with Ambassador Wright in April 1971, the Shah had already indicated that the sovereignty issue would only be delayed by two or three years if his other demands were met. See FCO 8/1556, Tel. No. 261 of 18 April, 1971 from Tehran to FCO. See also FCO 8/1554 entitled "Gulf Islands and the Union of Arab Emirates" referring to a conversation with the Shah from February 1971.

56 Kelly, op. cit., 94. Iranian Foreign Minister Zahedi has indicated in July that "the Shah was prepared to go to war to secure his interests." See FCO 8/1561, Telno. 539 of 22 July 1971 Tehran to FCO. The Kuwaiti press reported the Shah's demand on September 29, calling this more of a threat against the Arab states of the Gulf than against Britain, and warning that hasty military action by the Shah would cause the whole framework of Iranian-Arab cooperation and friendship in the Gulf to collapse. Iranian Foreign Minister Khalatbari had said that guerillas in the southern Arabian peninsula were the only threat to the Gulf after the British withdrawal and that Iran's forces could protect the Gulf against this threat, and the Kuwaiti press had responded that the interests of all the states of the Gulf rested on mutual cooperation and understanding. See declassified US State Department document, September 30, 1971, filed at Politics 33/Persian Gulf.

57 See FCO 8/1297, Tel. No 286, Bullard, Dubai to Political Residency Bahrain, in which Shaikh Saqr argues that a compromise with Iran followed by them taking the islands would leave him open to more criticism than no compromise and Iranian occupation as in the latter scenario Iran would be accused of using naked force.

58 Ahmad Jalal al Tadmori, *The Three Arabian Islands: A Documentary Study* (Ras al-Khaimah: 2000), 93, 96, 101, 103, 110; Kelly, op. cit., 93; Chubin and Zabih, op. cit., 225-6; Frauke Heard-Bey, *From Trucial States to United Arab Emirates: A Society in Transition* (London and New York: Longman, 1996), 368-9.

59 Declassified US Department of State documents, September 24 and 29, 1971, filed at Politics, Trucial States-US/XR Defense 15, Trucial States-US.

60 Tadmori, op. cit., 115-6; *Al-Khaleej*, 1 November 1971. Taryam, op. cit., 181 refers to Shaikh Saqr's rejection of Luce's proposals on October 30. He also presents a set of Luce's proposals and indicates that after rejecting these proposals Shaikh Saqr was accused in the Kuwaiti press of having agreed to sell the Tunbs to Iran, prompting Kuwait to demand an explanation, and prompting Ras al-Khaimah's Crown Prince Khalid bin Saqr to go to Kuwait, where he denied the

rumors. However, this set of proposals and sequence of events took place during the summer of 1971, not at the end of October 1971. *Al-Khaleej*, which was licensed in Sharjah, but published in Kuwait, began reporting stories on the negotiations regarding the islands in early June 1971. Taryam, op. cit., 182 also writes that "Ras al-Khaimah faced less pressure [than Sharjah] because first, its ruler rejected negotiations in principle and, second, Iran itself was not persistent in its claims, partly because it was convinced that its claim to the two islands belonging to Ras al-Khaimah had a legitimate basis, and partly because the islands themselves had relatively fewer inhabitants." Ras al-Khaimah only faced less pressure in November, after it rejected the Shah's proposals and no compromise was under consideration. Ras al-Khaimah only rejected negotiations on sovereignty, not negotiations on leasing. Iran was very persistent in its claims to the Tunbs. Kelly, op. cit., 93 writes that "Muhammad Reza Shah refused to treat with Ras al-Khaimah over the Tunbs, since the islands, he maintained, were Persia's by incontrovertible right." However, in fact the Shah did offer financial compensation to Ras al-Khaimah in exchange for sovereignty over the islands.

61 Tadmori, op. cit., 204.

62 Interview with Julian Walker, London, October 1997. There was no more red oxide to share. On November 3, 1971 the State Department received a British briefing which noted that the Sharjah paper *Al-Khaleej* had reported that Britain was pressuring the Ruler of Sharjah to make concessions on Abu Musa, apparently due to a leak by a Sharjah notable with whom Khalid had consulted and who had been encouraged by Iraq. The paper reported Khalid as saying that he was "subject to fearful pressure" and was "appealing to Arab countries to move quickly to coordinate their position and take [a] United Arab stand on [the] Islands question." Upon Luce's suggestion, Khalid sent a telegram to the Shah, assuring the Shah that the statements attributed to him were false and reaffirming his desire for a peaceful settlement of the islands problem. See declassified US State Department document, November 3, 1971, filed at Politics 33/Persian Gulf.

63 Tadmori, op. cit., 115-6, 204.

64 For the text of this MoU, along with the map and the financial agreement and the relevant correspondence, see P.L. Toye (ed.) *The Lower Gulf Islands: Abu Musa and the Tunbs* (London: Archive Editions, 1993), vol. 6, 489-504. Albaharna, op. cit., 345 and appendices provides the text.

65 Brigadier General Al-Kaabi has written that Iran stopped transferring Sharjah's share of the oil revenues in 1984. See Brigadier General Mohamed Hilal Al-Kaabi, *The Question of Iranian Occupation of the Islands, Greater Tunb, Lesser Tunb and Abu Musa Belonging to the United Arab Emirates* (Carlisle Barracks, Pennsylvania: US Army War College, 1994), 72. Both Iran and Sharjah, however, were paid regularly by the Buttes Gas and Oil Company International and later by the Crescent Oil Company, which bought the concession from Buttes. Iran evidently never transferred any revenues to Umm al-Qawain.

66 See the remarks of Shaikh Khalid, quoted by Mohammed Al Roken in "Historical and Legal Dimensions of the United Arab Emirates-Iran Dispute over Three Gulf Islands," in Edmund Ghareeb and Ibrahim Al Abed (eds.) *Perspectives on the United Arab Emirates* (London: Trident Press Ltd., 1997), 152.

67 Interview with Julian Walker, London, October 1997.

68 Videotaped deposition of Northcutt Ely at the ICJ at The Hague, 1992. See *Middle East Economic Survey* (MEES) XV, no. 6, December 3, 1971, 4-8, for the text of Shaikh Khalid 's letter.

69 Interview with Julian Walker, London, October 1997. Walker says that Iran gave the villagers a choice to remain or to leave and that they chose to evacuate to Ras al-Khaimah. Luce told Kuwait's Ambassador to London on December 3, 1971 that it was not true that Iran had evicted the inhabitants. See *Records of the Emirates, 1966-1971*, op. cit., vol. 6, 1971, 596. Some residents of the island later recalled that they had been given a choice to stay or to leave, but that all but two of the 450 residents of the island feared for their safety in case they decided to remain on the island. See *Gulf News*, July 10, 1999. Brigadier General Mohamed Hilal Al-Kaabi, 62, suggests that Iran forced the inhabitants to leave. Affidavits taken by the Ras al-Khaimah Ruler's Court from some of those arriving in Ras al-Khaimah after the Iranian landing testify that the inhabitants of the Greater Tunb were forcibly evicted.

70 He should not be confused with the Ruler of Ras al-Khaimah. See Heard-Bey, op. cit., 366.

71 Kelly, op. cit., 96-7.

CHAPTER 4

1 *The United Arab Emirates Yearbook 1996* (London: Trident Press, 1996), 46. Husain Albaharna, *The Arabian Gulf States: Their Legal and Political Status and Their International Problems* (Beirut: Librairie Du Liban, 1978), 346 provides a slightly different text.

2 Vinson and Elkins, *Territorial Sovereignty Over the Tunb Islands* (Houston: Unpublished study for the Ruler of Ras al-Khaimah, 1980), 60.

3 Ahmad Jalal al Tadmori, *The Three Arabian Islands: A Documentary Study* (Ras al-Khaimah: 2000), 148-50.

4 The Iraqi News Agency reported on December 3 that it had learned from reliable sources in Ras al-Khaimah that when a UAE delegation headed by Ahmad Khalifa Al-Suwaidi met with Shaikh Saqr on December 2, Shaikh Saqr stated as conditions for joining the UAE that "The Union should undertake the defence of the Arab islands in the Gulf, that no diplomatic relations should be established with Iran and that all Iranian citizens must be expelled from the federal state in retaliation for the expulsion of the islands' inhabitants by the Iranian forces." (See BBC *Survey of World Broadcasting*, ME/3857/A/1, December 6, 1971). The December 4 issue of *Al-Khaleej* also reported that an informed source had told the paper the same story. The same issue stated that the Iraqi News Agency had reported that Shaikh Saqr declared that he was ready to receive any Arab force to defend the islands, whether this force came from one Arab country or several Arab countries through the Arab League. It reported that Shaikh Saqr had made a statement to the press calling on all the Arab states "to liberate the islands by an armed Arab force." The December 3 issue of *An-Nahar* published an interview with Shaikh Saqr and quoted him as calling for the expulsion of Iranian communities from Arab Gulf states and for a campaign against British and Iranian commercial interests throughout the Arab world. The Iraqi News Agency also reported on December 10 that an unnamed Ras al-Khaimah spokesman had stated

that Ras al-Khaimah's conditions for joining the UAE were that the UAE should boycott Iran "economically and culturally," refrain from establishing diplomatic relations with Iran, and deport all Iranians entering the UAE illegally. The spokesman was also quoted as saying that "The UAE authorities' acceptance and implementation of these demands will mean Ras al-Khaimah's immediate accession, and cancellation of its previous condition that the UAE should liberate the three islands from Iranian occupation by armed force." (See *Arab Report and Record*, December 1-15, 1971, 623-4.)

Ras al-Khaimah did call for members of the Arab League to break diplomatic, commercial and cultural relations with Iran on December 7, and the UAE was now a member of the Arab League. These calls were explicitly contained in the letter that Shaikh Saqr wrote to the rulers of the other six emirates on December 3, but were not acknowledged by Shaikh Zayed in his December 5 statement on the issue. The Ras al-Khaimah Ruler's Court asserted in April 1999 that these were not "conditions" for joining the federation. Indeed, the Ruler's Court denied in April 1999 that Ras al-Khaimah had called for the use of force. In fact, Ras al-Khaimah did not expel all Iranians from its emirate. However, Shaikh Saqr's letter and the weight of evidence seems to suggest that these were the kinds of "effective measures" and the "kinds of means" that Ras al-Khaimah had in mind for its "one condition" of defending the islands. Iraq, meanwhile, broke diplomatic relations with Iran; demanded that the UAE refrain from establishing relations with Iran as a condition for admission to the Arab League; and later expelled 60,000 Iranians from Iraq. Libyan Major Jalloud also called for the expulsion of Iranians during his early December visit to the emirates.

5 *Al-Khaleej*, December 6, 1971; BBC *Survey of World Broadcasting*, ME/3859/E/4, December 8, 1971.

6 Jenab Tutunji, "The United Arab Emirates and International Organizations" in Edmund Ghareeb and Ibrahim Al Abed (eds.), *Perspectives on the United Arab Emirates* (London: Trident Press Ltd., 1997), 188-9. See also the text of Arab League Council Resolution 2865, December 7, 1971, in Arabic, courtesy of the Arab League Archives.

7 For the full text of these deliberations, see *Provisional Verbatim Record of the Sixteen Hundred and Tenth Meeting of the United Nations Security Council* (S/10436, December 9, 1971).

8 Vinson and Elkins, op. cit., 60. The English translation in this source is slightly garbled; the correct translation has been provided by the Ras al-Khaimah Ruler's Court.

9 Tadmori, op. cit., 150-1. The English translation of the original Arabic document was also provided by the Ras al-Khaimah Ruler's Court.

10 Taryam, op. cit., 191-2.

11 Muhammad Morsy Abdullah, *The United Arab Emirates: A Modern History* (London: Hurtwood Press, Ltd., 1978 and 1994), 75-6; Abdullah Omran Taryam, *The Establishment of the United Arab Emirates, 1950-1985* (London: Croom Helm Ltd., 1987), 191; George Lenczowski, *The Middle East in World Affairs*, 4th Edition (Ithaca: Cornell University Press, 1980), 679; Richard Schofield (ed.), *Arabian Boundaries: New Documents 1965* vol. 2 (London: Archive Editions, 1994), 347-471.

12 *Arab Record and Report*, 1972, 40, cites *Al-Rai Al-Am*, January 29, 1972. See also John Duke Anthony, *Arab States of the Lower Gulf: People, Politics, Petroleum* (Washington, DC: The Middle East Institute, 1975), 186.

13 J.B. Kelly, *Arabia, the Gulf and the West* (London: George Weidenfeld and Nicolson Ltd, 1980), 96-7.

14 Interview with Julian Walker, London, October 1997; R.K. Ramazani, *The Persian Gulf and the Strait of Hormuz* (Alphen aan den Rijn,: Sijthoff and Noordhoff, 1979) 74; Taryam, op. cit., 191.

15 Abdullah, op. cit., 284.

16 Al Roken in "Historical and Legal Dimensions of the United Arab Emirates-Iran Dispute over Three Gulf Islands," in Ghareeb and Al Abed, op. cit., 152.

17 Again in June 1972, Shaikh Zayed stressed that the UAE had referred the issue to the Arab League and expressed the "hope that the friendly and fraternal countries will attain a resolution that will satisfy both parties." See Shaikh Zayed's interview with *Al-Amal*, reprinted in *Al-Ittihad*, June 7, 1972. In November 1972, Shaikh Zayed said that "this question is not just a local one; it is an Arab issue in the first place." He stressed again that the subject had been submitted to and considered by the Arab League and that Arab states with friendly relations with Iran had been "commissioned…to mediate the issue and put an end to it by calm diplomacy." See Shaikh Zayed interview with *Rus Al-Yusuf*, reprinted in *Al-Ittihad*, November 27, 1972.

18 Shaikh Zayed interview with *Al-Amal*, reprinted in *Al-Ittihad*, June 7, 1972.

19 Anwar Gargash, "Iran, the GCC States, and the UAE: Prospects and Challenges in the Coming Decade," in Jamal S. Al-Suwaidi (ed.) *Iran and The Gulf: A Search for Stability* (Abu Dhabi: The Emirates Center for Strategic Studies and Research, 1996), 149.

20 Gargash, op. cit., 149-50, 152 and an interview with Julian Walker, London, October 1997.

21 Taryam, op. cit., 219-20, 227.

22 Gargash, op. cit., 149-52.

23 Ibid., 150. Ali Mohammed Khalifa, *The United Arab Emirates: Unity in Fragmentation* (Boulder: Westview Press, 1979), 161-4. See also "Joint Communiqué of the Result of the Visit of H.H. Sheikh Zayed to Iran," Documentation Department of the Center for Documentation and Research, Cultural Foundation, Abu Dhabi, 1975, 442-4 (in Arabic).

24 Abdullah, op. cit., 280, 284.

25 Lenczowski, op. cit., 731.

26 Interview with the Crown Prince of Ras al-Khaimah, March 1999.

27 Vinson and Elkins, op. cit., 3.7 and document 3.8.

28 *Al-Ittihad*, November 1 and 2, 1977.

29 Gargash, op. cit., 150-51; MEED XXIII, no. 2, January 12, 1979, 46 and no. 3, January 19, 1979, 24.

30 Taryam, op. cit., 239-48.

31 Gargash, op. cit., 150.

32 *Al-Ittihad*, February 25, 1979.

33 *Al-Ittihad*, May 29, 1979.

34 Jasim M. Abdulghani, *Iraq and Iran: The Years of Crisis* (Baltimore, MD: The Johns Hopkins University Press, 1984), 184, 199; *Arab Report*, no. 11, 20 June 1979, 31-2; BBC *Survey of World Broadcasting*, ME/6147/A/6, June 21, 1979.

35 This letter was provided by the Ras al-Khaimah Ruler's Court in Arabic. See also Tadmori, op. cit., 152-4 for an English text of this letter.

36 *Al-Ittihad*, April 7, 1980; Abdulghani, op. cit., 199; Dilip Hiro, *The Longest War: The Iran-Iraq Military Conflict* (London: Paladin Grafton Books, 1990), 35.

37 See Dr. Ali Humaidan, "From the Shah's Empire to the Islamic Republic: The UAE, Iran and the Three Islands," Part IV, *Al-Ittihad*, July 13, 1997 (in Arabic).

38 Jenab Tutunji, "The United Arab Emirates and International Organizations" in Ghareeb and Al Abed, op. cit., 189.

39 Tutunji, op. cit., 190; Vinson and Elkins, op. cit., 3.59-3.60. Elsewhere Vinson and Elkins cite the *New York Times*, September 24, 1980, 10. Gargash, op. cit, 152 writes that the UAE "raised the issue at its annual UN speech to the General Assembly," suggesting that the UAE did so throughout the years of the Iran-Iraq war.

40 See Shaikh Zayed's interview with *Al-Anwar*, January 3, 1981, also quoted by *Al-Ittihad*, January 4, 1981.

41 BBC *Survey of World Broadcasting*, ME/6731/A/1 and 2, May 23, 1981.

42 Al Roken, op. cit., 152 and William Rugh, "UAE Foreign Policy," 165-6 in Ghareeb and Al Abed, op. cit.

43 Brig. Gen. Al-Kaabi wrote in 1994 that "Some reports suggest that it [Abu Musa] was used as a base for boat attacks against shipping during the tanker war of 1987-88, though this is not completely clear from the record." Brigadier General Mohamed Hilal Al-Kaabi, *The Question of Iranian Occupation of the Islands, Greater Tunb, Lesser Tunb and Abu Musa Belonging to the United Arab Emirates* (Carlisle Barracks, Pennsylvania: US Army War College, 1994). US Department of State sources are more convinced that this is true. For documentation, see Martin S. Navias and E.R. Hooton, *Tanker Wars: The Assault on Merchant Shipping During the Iran-Iraq Crisis, 1980-1988* (London: I.B. Tauris, 1996), 111-5, 121, 151-2 and 174. Jasim Abdulghani of the UAE Ministry of Foreign Affairs says that Iran began steadily encroaching on the southern zone of Abu Musa from about 1983.

44 Richard Schofield, "Border Disputes in the Gulf: Past, Present, and Future" in Gary G. Sick and Lawrence G. Potter (eds.) *The Persian Gulf at the Millenium: Essays in Politics, Economy, Security, and Religion* (New York, NY: St. Martin's Press, 1997), 149-50.

45 Navias and Hooton, op. cit., 174; Tutunji, op. cit., 177, 179-83; See also Joseph Twinam, *The Gulf, Cooperation and the Council: An American Perspective* (Washington, DC: The Middle East Policy Council, 1992), 140-2.

46 Rugh in Ghareeb and Al Abed, op. cit., 166-9.

47 The move may be tied to the suspicious visit by a Dutch vessel and Iranian concerns about espionage in advance of Iran's planned amphibious exercises in the region in April 1992.

48 Schofield in Sick and Potter, op. cit., 149-50; Al Roken in Ghareeb and Al Abed, op. cit., 153; Rugh in Ghareeb and Al Abed, op. cit., 169; Gargash in Al-Suwaidi, op. cit., 153; Anthony H. Cordesman, *Iran and Iraq: The Threat from the Northern Gulf* (Boulder, CO: Westview Press, 1994), 32; and "Iran is Said to Expel Arabs from Gulf Island," *The New York Times*, April 16, 1992, A7.

49 Cordesman, *Iran and Iraq*, op. cit., 32. See also Michael Eisenstadt, *Iranian Military Power: Capabilities and Intentions* (Washington, DC: The Washington Institute for Near East Policy, 1996), 49-50.

50 Al-Kaabi, op. cit., 76-7. He provides statements by people who were on the ship.

51 *The United Arab Emirates Yearbook 1996*, op. cit., 46.

52 Al-Kaabi, op. cit., 78-9, cites the Islamic Republic News Agency, September 8, 1992 quoted in Foreign Broadcasting Information Service (FBIS), September 9, 1992, 19 and Agence France Presse (AFP), September 10, 1992, quoted in *FBIS*, September 11, 1992, 20.

53 For the texts of the GCC and Damascus Declaration Group's resolutions, see Shaikh Khaled bin Mohammed Al-Qasimi, *The Three Islands Between Arab Sovereignty and Iranian Occupation* (Alexandria: Modern University Office, 1997), 248-9 and 259, in Arabic. For the text of the Arab League resolution, see Tutunji in Ghareeb, op. cit., 190.

54 *The United Arab Emirates Yearbook 1996*, op. cit., 47 for a summary of the UAE position and the UAE statement at the end of the meeting. Also see Tadmori for the UAE summary and statement and also for the statement of the Iranian Embassy in Abu Dhabi, 222-6. On September 24, 1992, days before these talks began, Iran had reportedly declared its full sovereignty over the islands.

55 Interview with a member of the UAE delegation, Abu Dhabi, March 1999.

56 *The United Arab Emirates Yearbook 1996*, op. cit., 46-7. See also Al-Kaabi, op. cit., 74 6 for a UAE Foreign Ministry 1992 memo citing Iran's various violations of the MoU, as well as a September 1997 interview with Jasim Abdulghani of the UAE Foreign Ministry.

57 Cordesman, op. cit., 32-3; Al-Kaabi, op. cit., 79-80.

58 Al-Kaabi, op. cit., 81; interview with Dr. Jamal S. Al-Suwaidi, Director of the Emirates Center for Strategic Studies and Research, August 1997; interview at the UAE Foreign Ministry, September 1997; interview with UAE military source, May 1999; interviews with current and former US State and Defense Department officials, September and October 1997.

59 See *Closing Statements of the Sessions of the Supreme Council: Sessions 1-18* (Riyadh: The Secretariat General of The Cooperation Council for the Arab States of the Gulf, 1998), 133-4, 141-2.

60 "Iran Asserts Claims to 3 Disputed Islands in Gulf," *New York Times*, December 27, 1992, 8.

61 See Foreign Broadcasting Information Service (FBIS-NES), 95-237 (IIXII 95), 84-5; Cordesman, op. cit., 33 reports that Iran said it had been willing to fight for eight years, but Iran said eighty.

62 Al Roken, op. cit., 153. Saleh Al-Mani, "The Ideological Dimension in Saudi-Iranian Relations" in Al-Suwaidi, op. cit., 171 writes that Iran annexed the Tunbs in April 1993.

63 For excerpts from Shaikh Zayed's remarks, see *The United Arab Emirates Yearbook 1996*, op. cit., 48.

64 Rugh, op. cit., 169; Al Roken, op. cit., 155.

65 *Al Hayat*, March 20, 1994. UAE Minister of State for Foreign Affairs Shaikh Hamdan bin Zayed Al-Nahyan had also called for referring the issue to the ICJ in a June 1994 interview. For excerpts, see Tadmori, op. cit., 233-4.

66 Al Roken, op. cit., 153, 157.

67 For excerpts from Shaikh Zayed's remarks, see *The United Arab Emirates Yearbook 1996*, op. cit., 48.

68 Anthony Cordesman, "Threats and Non-Threats from Iran," in Jamal S. Al-Suwaidi (ed.) *Iran and the Gulf: A Search for Stability* (Abu Dhabi: Emirates Center for Strategic Studies and Research, 1996); Anthony Cordesman, *Bahrain, Oman,*

Qatar, and the UAE: Challenges of Security, op. cit., 301-3; interviews with UAE, US and British officials.

69 Al Roken, op. cit., 153-4; Cordesman, *Bahrain, Oman, Qatar, and the UAE*, op. cit., 302.

70 The *New York Times*, March 1, 1995, A11; the *Washington Post*, March 1, 1995.

71 The *New York Times*, March 23, 1995, A9; the *Christian Science Monitor*, March 23, 1995, 1 and 8; Cordesman, *Bahrain, Oman, Qatar, and the UAE*, op. cit., 303.

72 Ibid., op. cit., 378. See also Rosemary Hollis, "Europe and Gulf Security: A Competitive Business," in David E. Long and Christian Koch (eds.) *Gulf Security in the Twenty-First Century* (Abu Dhabi: The Emirates Center for Strategic Studies and Research, 1997), 82.

73 Interview, UAE Ministry of Foreign Affairs, Abu Dhabi, 1997.

74 For excerpts from this speech, see *The United Arab Emirates Yearbook 1996*, op. cit., 49.

75 *Chronicle of Progress*, op. cit., 399.

76 Interview, US Department of State Legal Department, Washington DC, October 1997.

77 *The United Arab Emirates Yearbook* 1996, op. cit., 48-9; interview with Khalifa Shahin Al-Marri, UAE Foreign Ministry, September 1997.

78 Schofield, op. cit., 157; *The United Arab Emirates Yearbook 1996*, op. cit., 48-9; *Chronicle of Progress*, op. cit., 401.

79 Interview at the UAE Ministry of Foreign Affairs, September 1997.

80 See *Closing Statements of the Sessions of the Supreme Council: Sessions 1-18* (Riyadh: The Secretariat General of The Cooperation Council for the Arab States of the Gulf, 1998), 170.

81 *The United Arab Emirates Yearbook 1996*, op. cit., 50.

82 For excerpts from this communiqué, see *The United Arab Emirates Yearbook 1996*, op. cit., 51-2.

83 See *Closing Statements of the Sessions of the Supreme Council*, op. cit., 183-5. At the same time, US officials continued to pay close attention to Iranian military developments. In mid-June 1997, while on a visit to Bahrain, US Secretary of Defense William Cohen disclosed that the Iranian air force had conducted test launches of a new Chinese anti-ship cruise missile. He said that Iran was seeking the ability to intimidate its neighbors and to interrupt commerce, and warned Iran not to consider disrupting traffic in the sea-lanes of the Arabian Gulf. See *The Washington Post*, June 18, 1997.

84 Tutunji, op. cit., 190.

85 Interview, UAE Ministry of Foreign Affairs, Abu Dhabi, 1997.

86 The text of Shaikh Saqr's letter was provided by the Ras al-Khaimah Ruler's Court; see *Gulf News*, May 28, 1997 for Khatami's public statement.

87 *Gulf News*, June 27, 1997, 1; September 16, 21 and 22, 1997, 1. Arab League Secretary General Esmat Abdel Meguid noted Iran's calls for improved relations, but called on Iran to end its occupation of the islands peacefully.

88 *Emirates News*, November 14, 1997, 1; interview at the UAE Ministry of Foreign Affairs, November 1997.

89 This included calls by Arab League Secretary General Esmet Abdel Meguid and UAE Foreign Minister Rashid Abdullah. See *Gulf News*, December 7, 1997 as well as *Emirates News*, December 11, 1997, 4 for the text of Rashid Abdullah's speech.

90 *Emirates News*, December 24, 1997.

91 *Emirates News*, December 23, 1997.

92 *Emirates News*, December 24, 1997; *Gulf News*, December 24, 1997.

93 Interview at the UAE Ministry of Foreign Affairs, May 1998.

94 *Gulf News*, May 23, 1998.

95 *Gulf News*, December 10, 1998.

96 *Gulf News*, February 21, 27 and 28, 1999; March 1, 2, 3, 4, 5, 16, 19, 25 and 31, 1999; *Al-Ittihad*, March 4, 16 and 19, 1999; *Khaleej Times*, March 18, 1999; *Al-Hayat*, March 5, 18 and 19, 1999; *Al-Sharq Al-Awsat*, March 5, 1999 as well as *Al-Shorouq Magazine*, March 8-14, 1999.

97 *Gulf News*, February 21, 1999.

98 *Gulf News*, March 5, 1999; *Al-Shorouq Magazine*, March 8-14, 1999.

99 *Gulf News*, December 8, 1998, 1.

100 *Gulf News*, December 10, 1.

101 *Gulf News*, March 25, 1999.

102 *Gulf News* and *Al-Ittihad*, April to June 1999.

103 *Gulf News*, July 18, 1999, 1 and 7 for the full text of Shaikh Hamdan's interview with the Qatari paper *Al-Watan*.

104 *Gulf News*, July 19, 1999.

105 *Gulf News*, September 19, 1999.

106 *Gulf News*, September 23, 1999.

107 *Gulf News*, September 26 and 27, 1999.

108 *Gulf News*, October 2 and 3, 1999.

109 *Gulf News*, January 31, 2000.

110 *Gulf News*, February 26 and 28, 2000.

111 *Gulf News*, February 28, 2000.

112 *Gulf News*, March 1, 2000.

113 *Gulf News*, March 9, 2000. For Shaikh Sultan's remarks on the islands, see Shaikh Sultan bin Zayed bin Sultan Al-Nahyan, "Gulf Security: The View from Abu Dhabi," in *A Century in Thirty Years: Shaykh Zayed and the United Arab Emirates*, edited by Joseph A. Kechichian (Washington, DC: Middle East Policy Council, 2000), 275.

114 Text from Manama, Bahrain Television in Arabic, December 31, 2000.

115 *Gulf News*, March 20, April 3, 2001; *Khaleej Times*, March 20, 2001.

116 *Gulf News*, May 27, 2001.

117 www.defensenews.com, August 20-26, 2001.

118 *Gulf News*, December 2, 3, 2001.

119 *Gulf News*, January 1, 2002.

120 *Gulf News*, February 26, 2002.

121 *Gulf News*, May 27, 28, 2002.

122 *Al-Sharq Al-Awsat*, June 10, 2002. Abdulhaq also reported that Iran had agreed to abide by the 1971 MoU on Abu Musa, agreed that sovereignty over the islands is still in dispute, and agreed to reverse its unilateral steps, i.e. to reverse its appointment of a military governor of the islands, transfer the military airfield on Abu Musa to joint use, reduce its military presence and to stop holding military exercises on or around Abu Musa. However, the Saudi paper *Al-Watan* reported Iranian sources as indicating that any agreement would be based only on the Abu Musa MoU, with the Tunbs remaining under Iranian control.

123 *Gulf News*, September 6, 2002.

124 *Gulf News*, September 21, 2002.
125 *Gulf News*, October 7, 2002.
126 *Gulf News*, December 4, 2002.
127 *Gulf News*, January 20, 2003.

CHAPTER 5

1   In reference to the legal question and its supporting evidence, the relevant source materials have not been repeatedly cited, as they have already been listed as part of the historical evidence in chapters 1 to 4. In those instances where the evidence needed to be repeated or emphasized, or where additional references were thought to be necessary, the appropriate citation has been made. In all other instances, the reader should refer back to the relevant sections in the historical chapters and its corresponding reference.

2   Ibrahim Al Abed, "Historical Background and Constitutional Basis to the Federation" in Edmund Ghareeb and Ibrahim Al Abed (eds) *Perspectives on the United Arab Emirates* (London: Trident Press Ltd., 1997), 117-8.

3   Martin Dixon and Robert McCorquodale, *Cases and Materials on International Law* (London, Blackstone Press Limited, 1995), 282.

4   M.E. Bathurst, Northcutt Ely and Coward Chance, *Sharjah's Title to the Island of Abu Musa* (Unpublished report for the Ruler of Sharjah, September 1971); Vinson and Elkins, *Territorial Sovereignty over the Tunb Islands* (an unpublished report for the Ruler of Ras al-Khaimah, 1980); P.L. Toye (ed.) *The Lower Gulf Islands: Abu Musa and the Tunbs* (London: Archive Editions, 1993). These documents have naturally been cited and quoted in the previous chapter and will be mentioned again in this chapter. The legal opinions expressed in the two legal studies prepared for the Ruler of Sharjah and the Ruler of Ras al-Khaimah will sometimes be quoted in this chapter. One reason for quoting this material is that the studies themselves are, due to attorney-client privilege, generally unavailable without permission from the Rulers' Courts. Another reason is that the studies will presumably be considered important and be submitted by the UAE in any legal proceeding to resolve this dispute.

5   J.L. Brierly, *The Law of Nations* (Oxford: The Clarendon Press, 1963). For excerpts from Brierly, see Louis Henkin, Richard Crawford Pugh, Oscar Schachter and Hans Smit, *International Law: Cases and Materials*, Third Edition (St. Paul, MN: West Publishing Company, 1993), 322-33.

6   The Lesser Tunb may have been apportioned for the use of the Lingeh Qawasim, circa 1835.

7   Coward Chance and Associates, *Interim Report to His Highness the Ruler of Sharjah* (Swithin's House, London, Unpublished, July 23, 1971), quoted in Husain Albaharna, *The Arabian Gulf States: Their Legal and Political Status and their International Problems* (Beirut: Librarie du Liban, 1974), 344.

8   Guive Mirfendereski seems to question the authenticity of these letters. See Guive Mirfendereski, "The Ownership of the Tonb Islands: A Legal Analysis," in Hooshang Amirahmadi (ed.) *Small Islands, Big Politics: The Tonbs and Abu Musa in the Persian Gulf* (New York, NY: St. Martin's Press, 1996), 124-8. However, these letters were actually seen by British Native Agents in Sharjah in 1881 and 1888. One of them, a letter from Shaikh Khalifa, was still in the archives of the Ruler of

478

Ras al-Khaimah's Court in 1928, and again in 1980, when the study by Vinson and Elkins was prepared, and is reportedly there today.

9   Vinson and Elkins, op. cit., chapter 3, 75.

10   Henkin, Pugh, Schachter and Smit, op. cit., provide the quotation from Brierly on page 322, the quotation from the Island of Palmas case on page 313 and the quotation from the Eastern Greenland case on page 317.

11   See a UAE Ministry of Foreign Affairs document from 1992 entitled "The Question of the Iranian Occupation of the Islands of Greater Tunb, Lesser Tunb, and Abu Musa Belonging to the United Arab Emirates," cited by Brigadier General Mohamed Hilal Al-Kaabi, "The Question of Iranian Occupation of the Islands, Greater Tunb, Lesser Tunb and Abu Musa Belonging to the United Arab Emirates" (Carlisle Barracks, Pennsylvania: US Army War College, 1994), 67-8, 86-7. The Qawasim Ruler Rahma bin Matar and his successors earned much of their wealth from the pearl banks from the 1720s onwards. David Seton noted in 1801 that the pearlers from Julfar or Ras al-Khaimah lived on the Great Tunb during the summer pearling season. In his 1818 report, Captain Robert Taylor described how rulers on the Gulf coasts had traditionally collected fees from pearlers during the years that had preceded piracy, i.e. the early 1800s and almost certainly the 1700s. Captain Brucks, Lieutenant Guy and Lieutenant Houghton also reported that in the 1820s pearlers from Sharjah and Ras al-Khaimah paid taxes to the Qawasim Ruler of Sharjah. See their reports in P.L. Toye (ed.) *Records of the Emirates, Primary Documents, 1820-1958* (London: Archive Editions, 1990), vol. 1, 236, 352-3, 358, 374, and Toye, *The Lower Gulf Islands*, vol. 1, 8. Charles E. Davies, *The Blood-Red Arab Flag* (Exeter: Exeter University Press, 1997), 221 writes that the Sharjah's Ruler's income from pearling in 1822 was from 2,000 to 3,000 Spanish dollars or 450 to 700 British pounds. Frauke Heard-Bey, *From Trucial States to United Arab Emirates: A Society in Transition* (London: Longman, 1996), 113 notes that Ibn Batuta described a similar system of taxation on the pearling industry in the Gulf in the latter half of the fourteenth century.

12   Persian authorities landed on the Greater Tunb in 1933 to inspect the lighthouse, landed again in April 1934 and anchored off the island in August and September 1934. It is unclear, however, whether these acts were intended to establish Persia's claim.

13   Persian activity on Abu Musa included a landing to take a red oxide sample in 1925 and the visit of a naval party in 1951. Just as in the case on the Greater Tunb, one cannot say that these acts were carried out with the intent to underscore an Iranian claim.

14   Vinson and Elkins, op. cit., chapter 3, 99.

15   Vinson and Elkins, op. cit., chapter 3, 101-2. Pirouz Mojtahed-Zadeh claims that "in 1929, Iran offered to refer the parties' irreconcilable differences over the issue of the islands to international arbitration. The British government turned down the offer." However, reference to the footnote of this claim, which is drawn from British Minister to Tehran Sir Robert Clive's correspondence, shows that Mojtahed-Zadeh's use of the words "offered" and "turned down" seem overstated: "The [Persian] Court Minister said in that case there is no other way but to refer the matter to an international arbitration. Replying to His Excellency I expressed hopes that the two sides could settle the differences without having to refer the case to international arbitration." There is a considerable difference between a remark such as that made by the Court Minister and an actual offer, and probably

a considerable difference between an actual offer and an official act of submitting a matter to arbitration. There is also a considerable difference between a remark like that made by Clive and turning down a serious proposal. See Pirouz Mojtahed-Zadeh, "Perspectives on the Territorial History of the Tonb and Abu Musa Islands," in Hooshang Amirahmadi (ed.), *Small Islands, Big Politics*, op. cit., 50, 69-70.

16 In January 1929, Persian Minister of Court Taimurtash said arbitration might be the only way to resolve the issue of Abu Musa and the Tunbs, and British Minister Clive said he hoped the matter could be settled without arbitration. However, Persia did not formally seek arbitration and Britain did not formally reject it.

17 Private audience with the Ruler of Ras al-Khaimah, April 14, 1998.

18 For a discussion of estoppel, see Ian Brownlie, *Principles of Public International Law*, 4th edition (Oxford: Clarendon Press, 1990), 161-2, 640-2. Brownlie notes that Professor Bowett argues that for estoppel to apply there must be reliance on the statement, either to the disadvantage of the party relying on the statement or to the advantage of the party making the statement.

19 Y.Z. Blum, *Historic Titles in International Law*, 1965, 335, quoted in Bathurst, Ely and Chance, op. cit., I, 15.

20 Robert Jennings, *The Acquisition of Territory in International Law*, 1963, 25-6, quoted in Henkin, Pugh, Schachter and Smit, op. cit., 323-4.

21 Charles de Visscher (translated from French by Percy E. Corbett) *Theory and Reality in Public International Law* (Princeton, NJ: Princeton University Press, 1957), 200-1, is quoted in Bathurst, Ely and Chance, op. cit., I, 15-6. De Visscher's revised edition, 1968, translated by Corbett, is quoted in Henkin et. al., op. cit., 323.

22 Bathurst, Ely and Chance, op. cit., I, 16. The British, as a colonial power with responsibility for the foreign relations of Sharjah, asserted, exercised and defended Sharjah's title during the earlier period. In the Island of Palmas case, Judge Huber wrote: "It is quite natural that the establishment of sovereignty may be the outcome of a slow evolution, of a progressive intensification of State control. This is particularly the case, if sovereignty is acquired by the establishment of suzerainty of a colonial Power over a native State, and in regard to outlying possessions of such a vassal State."

23 Bathurst, Ely and Chance, op. cit., I, 17.

24 Ibid., 17.

25 Henkin et. al., op. cit., 310, 312-3. Some portions are also quoted in Bathurst, Ely and Chance, op. cit., 18.

26 Henkin et. al., op. cit., 318, also quoted in Bathurst, Ely and Chance, op. cit., I, 17-8.

27 Bathurst, Ely and Chance, op. cit., I, 17. See also the quotation from Sir Humphrey Waldock, "Disputed Sovereignty in the Falkland Islands Dependencies," in *British Yearbook of International Law*, Volume XXV (Oxford: Oxford University Press, 1948), 336.

28 Bathurst, Ely and Chance, op. cit., I, 18, quotation from Hall, *International Law*, op. cit., 6th edition, 103.

29 As the UAE Ministry of Foreign Affairs has noted, "Iran's claims to sovereignty, as we have seen, have been based on rather flimsy grounds: either the argument that the Islands were once Iranian (though clearly since the 18th century they have been Arab), or the evidence of the 1886 British map, which uses a non-

authoritative source and relies on the evidence of a power which by Iran's own argument had no right to determine sovereignty." For quotations from this UAE Ministry of Foreign Affairs report, see Al-Kaabi, op. cit., 68-9.

30 Robert Jennings, *The Acquisition of Territory in International Law*, op. cit., 25-6 quoted in Henkin et.al., op. cit., 324.

31 For the text of the United Nations Charter, see Henkin, Pugh, Schachter and Smit, *Basic Documents*, op. cit., especially 1-3 and 8.

32 Al-Kaabi has pointed this out.

33 For the text of UN General Assembly Resolution 2625, see Henkin et al., *Basic Documents Supplement*, op. cit., 133-40.

34 For the text of UN General Assembly Resolution 3314, see ibid., 333-5.

35 For the text of the Geneva Convention, see Henkin et.al., *Basic Documents*, op. cit., 366-74, especially 372.

36 Affidavits on file at the Ras al-Khaimah Ruler's Court.

37 For the numbers of Iranians on Abu Musa, see Pirouz Mojtahed-Zadeh, "Perspectives on the Territorial History of the Tonb and Abu Musa Islands," in Amirahmadi, op. cit., 33-4.

38 Ministry of Foreign Affairs study quoted by al-Kaabi, op. cit., 84-5.

39 For the text of the MoU, see *The Lower Gulf Islands*, op. cit., vol. 6, 490. See also Albaharna, op. cit., 345 and appendices.

40 Muhammad Morsy Abdullah, *The United Arab Emirates: A Modern History* (London: Hurtwood Press Limited, 1978 and 1994), 282; Abdullah Omran Taryam, *The Establishment of the United Arab Emirates 1950-1985* (London: Croom Helm Ltd., 1987), 170-2; J.B. Kelly, *Arabia, the Gulf and the West* (Basic Books, 1980), 93-4; interview with Julian Walker, London, October 1997.

41 *Middle East Economic Survey (MEES)* 15, no. 6, December 3, 1971; Albaharna, op. cit., 342-5; Taryam, op. cit., 170, 180-1.

42 Quoted by Mohamed Al Roken in "Historical and Legal Dimensions of the United Arab Emirates-Iran Dispute over Three Gulf Islands," in Ghareeb and Al Abed, op. cit., 152.

43 Al Roken, op. cit., 150-2.

44 Henkin et. al., *Basic Documents Supplement*, op. cit., 98. In customary international law, treaties provide for succession, i.e. rights and obligations are passed from the predecessor state to the successor state. This has been codified in the 1969 Vienna Convention on the Law of Treaties, although this convention did not enter into force until 1980 and the UAE was not a party to it in 1993. Its provisions are binding only on parties to the convention; its provisions are applicable only to treaties entered into subsequent to entry into force in 1980. However, Article 18 expects parties not to undermine the convention prior to its coming into force. Moreover, the convention is codifying customary international law, which is applicable to all treaties, even if the states concerned are not parties to the convention.

45 For the text of the declaration, see the *Official Gazette*, no. 240, July 1992, cited in Al Roken, op. cit., 148.

46 *The United Arab Emirates Yearbook 1996* (London: Trident Press, 1996), 46-7.

47 Interview with UAE constitutional law scholar Mohamed Al Roken, Abu Dhabi, May 1998.

48 Albaharna, op. cit., 347-8.

49 Interview with Husain Albaharna, Bahrain, December 1997.

50 Ibid.

51 Albaharna, op. cit., 348.

52 See *Provisional Verbatim Record of the Sixteen Hundred and Tenth Meeting of the United Nations Security Council*, December 9, 1971, 23, 41-2.

53 For the text of the Exclusive Agreements, see Toye, op. cit., vol. 2, 137. See also *Records of the Emirates*, vol. 4, 243-4.

54 See *Provisional Verbatim Record of the Sixteen Hundred and Tenth Meeting of the United Nations Security Council*, December 9, 1971, 23, 41-2. Pirouz Mojtahed Zadeh has also argued that the MoU is not legally binding, because Sharjah did not have the right to enter into correspondence with any country other than Britain according to what he inaccurately refers to as its special treaty of 1864. In making this point, Mojtahed Zadeh argues that "Of course both Iran and the United Arab Emirates have a moral obligation to the memorandum, but in the long term, it is the privilege of the Iranian government to adhere to it or otherwise." See *Round Table Discussion On "The Dispute Over The Gulf Islands"* (London: Arab Research Centre, 1992), 40.

55 Northcutt Ely testified in his videotaped deposition at the International Court of Justice at The Hague in 1992 that during the November 1971 negotiations over the Buttes Gas and Oil concession off Abu Musa, William Luce said that Ras al-Khaimah had refused to negotiate over the Tunbs and that Iran would take them by force.

56 Interview with confidential legal source, London, October 1997.

57 Interview with Julian Walker, London, October 1997.

58 Interview with confidential legal source, London, October 1997.

59 See *Provisional Verbatim Record of the Sixteen Hundred and Tenth Meeting of the United Nations Security Council*, December 9, 1971.

60 J.B. Kelly, *Britain and the Persian Gulf: 1795-1880* (Oxford: The Clarendon Press, 1968), 408.

61 For the text of Lord Curzon's address to the Trucial Shaikhs, see Toye, op. cit., vol. 2, 581-4.

62 See the Ministry of Foreign Affairs study cited by Al-Kaabi, op. cit., 74-6.

63 For this correspondence, see Toye, op. cit., vol. 6, 489-504.

64 *Kayhan International*, October 23, 1971. See also the remarks of the Iranian representative at the UN Security Council deliberations on December 9, 1971.

65 As quoted by Dr. Ali Humaidan, "From the Shah's Empire to the Islamic Republic: The UAE, Iran, and the Three Islands," Part IV, *Al-Ittihad*, July 13, 1997.

66 Mojtahed-Zadeh, op. cit., 34-42; Bavand, op. cit., 78-80; Mirfendereski, op. cit., 119-23 in *Small Islands, Big Politics*, op. cit. These authors reach general conclusions without offering specific evidence about these specific islands and without distinguishing between periods of native and alien rule of Persia. Mirfendereski writes on page 120 that "in ancient and medieval times the Tunbs would have had to belong to Iran." After referring to the Achaemenid, Seleucid, Parthian and Sassanian periods of power in the Gulf in pre-Islamic times, he states on pages 120-1 that "in pre-Islamic times the Tunbs most likely belonged to Iran." However, it should be remembered that the Seleucids were Greeks and the Parthians were Arsacids. Moreover, Hourani writes on pages 13-4 of *Arab Seafaring* (Princeton: Princeton University Press, 1951) that "the Greeks of the Seleucid Empire never showed much activity on the Persian Gulf," continuing

"But it is possible that there was a sea trade which is simply not recorded in our fragmentary sources for Seleucid history." Hourani also writes on page 14 that "The Parthian emperors could draw a fine revenue from the land routes across their realm to India and China, and gave no facilities to Western enterprise, Greek or Roman, to establish a rival sea route." On page 38, Hourani notes that "The Sassanids seem to have encouraged native Persian seafaring, which had never flourished before," and suggests that Persians were trading with Africa, India and China during this period. Regarding the period after the emergence of Islam, Mirfendereski writes on page 121 that "in Buyid times (945-1055 AD) the Tonbs in all likelihood belonged to Iran." However, the Buyids, who were Persian, legitimized their *de facto* power under the *de jure* authority of the Abbasid caliphate in Baghdad. He states on the same page that Ibn Al-Balkhi's *Farsnama* (1111 AD) refers to the Tunbs as belonging to Fars and argues that "The Tonbs...in all likelihood were administered for the Seljuk by the Banu Qaysar rulers of Kish Island." While Kish is the Persian name for Qays, the Banu Qaysar rulers were Arabs and the Seljuks (1055-1194 AD) were Turks also ruling under the *de jure* authority of the Abbasid caliphate in Baghdad. The Seljuks and their tributaries in Fars did not control Qays. Bavand makes similar arguments about Abu Musa, writing on page 79 that during successive historical periods "the island...would have been in all likelihood a part of Iranian territory." In addition to arguing that Yakut Al-Rumi wrote (in 1224 A.D.) that Qays owned all the neighboring islands, Bavand writes that Kish or Qays was a dependency of Iran and that Abu Musa probably belonged to the ruler of Kish. By this time, however, the Seljuk Turks had fallen and Persia was overrun by the Turco-Mongol invasion, which led to an era of alien rule under a succession of Turk and Mongol rulers. Moreover, Qays was succeeded by Old Hormuz as an important trade emporium at this time. Mirfendereski, op. cit., 121 says that after the fall of the Seljuks, the Salghurid rulers of Fars drove the Banu Qaysar from Kish and incorporated Kish, Hormuz and all their dependencies. After 1260 AD, there was conflict among Kish, Hormuz and Fars, and "it is difficult to say what effect these developments would have had on the status of the Tonbs." The Salghurids were also Turks and served as governors for the Seljuks, the Khwarazm, who were also Turks, and the Mongols, in that order. See also footnote 69 below.

67 Henkin et. al., op. cit., 314.

68 Brierly quoted in Henkin et. al., op. cit., 322.

69 Bavand, op. cit., 79-80 argues that the Kingdom of Hormuz was a dependency of Iran when the Portuguese came to the Gulf in 1507, and notes that in 1518 the Portuguese navigator Duarte Barbosa listed the Tunbs as possessions of Hormuz. Bavand writes that Abu Musa's proximity to the Tunbs "argues rather persuasively in favor of inclusion of the island in the roster of Hormuzi territories." Mirfendereski, op. cit., 121-2 writes that "...it may be surmised that the rulers of Hormuz in all likelihood gained directly or vicariously control over the Tonbs..." after 1329. He cites Hamdallah Mustawfi Al-Kazvini's *Nuzhat al-Qulub* (1340) as indicating that the Tunbs belonged to Iran, and argues that "Iranian dominion in the Persian Gulf qua the local rulers of Hormuz remained unabated" until the arrival of the Portuguese in the early 1500s. Mirfendereski also notes that Duarte Barbosa listed the islands as possessions of Hormuz. However, these attempts to establish an Iranian claim to the islands ignore the fact that the Kingdom of Hormuz was ruled by Arabs and was independent for 200 years while Persia was

ruled by Turks and Mongols before the Kingdom of Hormuz briefly paid tribute to the new Persian Safavid dynasty from 1503 to 1515. It also does not take into consideration that Persia recognized Portuguese sovereignty over the Kingdom of Hormuz in 1515. Mirfendereski continues: "Following the expulsion of the Portuguese from the Iranian littoral in 1622-1625, Iran regained the coastal possessions formerly under Hormuz/Portuguese control, including the garrison in Ras al-Khaimah. Under these conditions, it is likely that the Tonbs too reverted to Iranian possession or control." Bavand also claims that Persia must have reestablished control over Abu Musa at this time. Again, these attempts to establish an Iranian claim ignore the fact that the small garrisons Persia established on the Arab coast beginning in 1619 were already routed by the Portuguese by 1623, so that any Iranian control or possession of the islands would have lasted only about four years. While Mirfendereski writes that "It is also likely that in the course of the ascendancy of the Al-Yaariba rule in Oman the Tonbs may have passed temporarily under their control in 1679-1711," the fact is that the Al-Yaariba were Arabs.

70   Kuwait's representative to the UN Security Council deliberations on December 9, 1971 said that Iranian officials made this argument in conversations with Kuwaiti officials in 1970 and 1971. See *Provisional Verbatim Record*, op. cit., 56. Albaharna, op. cit., 341-2 develops this Iranian argument. Bavand, op. cit., 80 suggests that Persia must have had sovereignty over Abu Musa during the reign of Shah Nadir Afshar from 1737 to 1747 when "Iranian mastery of the Persian Gulf was reinstated in full, inclusive of Ras al-Khaimah on the opposite shore." Mirfendereski, op. cit., 122-3 writes that "it would appear unlikely for the Iranian government to have permitted control by the Qawasim over strategic islands such as the Tonbs" at this time. Bavand in particular ignores the fact that the Persian garrison at Julfar was blockaded by Arab naval forces in 1738, isolated after a mutiny in 1740 and abandoned in 1747, so that it would have been difficult to establish any Persian control over these islands during this ten year period of time. He also hints at Persian sovereignty over Abu Musa later in the 1700s, by claiming that the Qawasim of Ras al-Khaimah were in a position of "servitute" to Mulla Ali Shah, who he refers to as "the Persian governor of Bandar Abbas." This misstates the relationship of Mulla Ali Shah and the Qawasim, who were allies in the 1750s, and ignores the fact that Mulla Ali Shah was an Arab and was often fighting against the Persians for control of the Persian coast.

71   Interview with the Shah, *Blitz*, June 24, 1971, reprinted in *Kayhan International*, June 26, 1971 and quoted by Mirfendereski, op. cit., 119. J.G. Laithwaite's India Office memorandum in August 1928 noted that Persia had not exercised dominion in Abu Musa or the Tunbs between 1750 and 1887, and that it was not clear that Iran had exercised dominion in these islands prior to 1750. D.W. Lascelles of the Foreign Office prepared a memorandum in September 1934, also noting that Persia had not exercised dominion in Abu Musa and Tanb for at least 184 years and that it was doubtful that she had exercised dominion in these islands even before 1750.

72   Persian officials made this argument in 1887 and 1888. See also Mirfendereski, op. cit., 123-4 and Bavand, op. cit., 81-2.

73   This is noted in Chapter One, footnote 102. Mirfendereski, op. cit., 125 and 127-8 questions the authenticity of these letters, suggesting that the originals do not exist and that the translations from the Arabic are suspect. However, the original

of the 1872 letter was in the archives of the Ras al-Khaimah Ruler's Court in 1928 and according to the Court it is still there today. An affidavit was taken in 1928 from the secretary who took dictation and wrote out the original 1877 letter. These two letters were first seen by the Residency Agent in Sharjah in 1882, and then along with the 1884 letter in Sharjah in 1888. Moreover, Mirfendereski provides no evidence that these letters are not authentic.

74 Persian officials made this claim in 1887 and 1888. See Mirfendereski, op. cit., 125-6. What Mirfendereski fails to mention is that Persia did not actually produce any evidence of any taxes paid by the Greater Tunb.

75 Bathurst, Ely and Chance, op. cit., vol. I, 7.

76 See remarks of Shah Mohammed Reza Pahlavi to Associated Press, reported in *Kayhan*, February 20, 1971, cited in Taryam, op. cit., 167. See also the Iranian Ambassador to the United Nations in *Provisional Verbatim Record of the Sixteen Hundred and Tenth Meeting of the Security Council*, December 9, 1971, 86; Pirouz Mojtahed-Zadeh, op. cit., 42, 46 and 66 and footnote 36; Davoud H. Bavand, op. cit., 88-9 and Mirfendereski, op. cit., 127-34. Reissued without revision in 1891, the [1886] *Map of Persia* later formed the basis for Lord Curzon's *Map of Persia, Afghanistan, and Baluchistan* (1891) and the Government of India's *Map of Persia* (1897). On all these, the Tonbs continued to be depicted as Iranian territory. Mirfendereski, op. cit., 128-9.

77 G. Weissberg, "Maps as Evidence in International Boundary Disputes: A Reappraisal," *American Journal of International Law* 57 (1963), 781 quoted in Bathurst, Ely and Chance, op. cit., I, 11.

78 Cited in Bathurst, Ely and Chance, op. cit., I, 12.

79 Ibid. Since Weissberg, *Minquiers and Ecrehos*, and the *Island of Palmas* case, maps have continued to play a fairly misleading role in land boundary cases (particularly Chad/Libya in ICJ in 1994), although the law has not significantly changed. For arguments in favor of giving more weight to maps and charts, particularly modern ones, see the series of articles by Dennis Rushworth on "Mapping in Support of Frontier Arbitration," prepared for the University of Durham conference on *Preparing for Boundary Litigation and Arbitration*, Durham, England, March 25-26, 1998.

80 Bathurst, Ely and Chance made a comprehensive study of maps and charts dating from the sixteenth to the nineteenth century. Their findings are summarized in Bathurst, Ely and Chance, op. cit., vol. I, 62-95 and vol. III, 1-end. Some of these maps have been reproduced in Sultan bin Muhammad Al-Qasimi, *The Gulf in Historic Maps, 1493-1931* (Leicester, UK: Thinkprint Limited, 1996) and Sultan bin Muhammad Al Qasimi (ed.) *The Gulf in Historic Maps, 1478-1861*, Second Edition (Leicester, UK: Streamline Press Limited, 1999). See also B.J. Slot, *The Arabs of the Gulf: 1602-1784* (Leidschendam, The Netherlands: 1993), 3-6, for a discussion of the inaccuracies and unreliability of European nautical charts and maps of the sixteenth through the eighteenth centuries.

81 Bathurst, Ely and Chance, op. cit., vol. I, 13 and vol. III, Section B, map 72, 54; Vinson and Elkins, op. cit., chapter 3, 106-7.

82 Interview with confidential legal source, London, October 1997. Mojtahed-Zadeh, op. cit., 42 claims that these 1835 and 1836 maps were intended to distinguish between Arab and Persian possessions and thus recognized Persian sovereignty over the islands. However, Hennell and Morrison did not indicate that this was their intention or conclusion.

83 Bathurst, Ely and Chance, op. cit., vol. I, 24-5, 70; vol. III, 37-9, 40-1 and Al-Qasimi, *The Gulf in Historic Maps 1493-1931*, op. cit. and *The Gulf in Historic Maps 1478-1861*, op. cit. Another example of errors in earlier maps can be found in two maps by the German cartographer Carsten Niebuhr in 1772. One of them colors Lingeh and the islands in the same color as Persia, while the other does not clearly designate the islands as Persian or Arab. Niebuhr, however, had written earlier that Lingeh belonged to the Qawasim Shaikh of Ras al-Khaimah and that the Tunbs were uninhabited. In addition, his source, Van Kniphausen, had written that the Tunbs belonged to the Marazik of Lingeh, who were dependents of the Qawasim Shaikh of Ras al-Khaimah.

84 Bathurst, Ely and Chance, op. cit., vol. I, 62-95 and vol. III, 1-end. See also Al-Qasimi, *The Gulf in Historic Maps, 1493-1931* and *The Gulf in Historic Maps, 1478-1861*, op. cit.

85 Toye, op. cit., vol. 4, 93-5, 101-2, 129. Coward Chance and Associates, *Interim Report to His Highness the Ruler of Sharjah* (unpublished), (Swithin's House, London, July 23, 1971), cited in Albaharna, op. cit., 344, also noted that the British Government view was that "the error (in the colouring of the map) in no way prejudiced the case of the Trucial Rulers whose consent had not been obtained." Indeed, the 1928 Laithwaite memorandum noted: While the error in question is extremely regrettable from the standpoint of His Majesty's Government, it cannot be taken as a formal declaration by His Majesty's Government of their view of the status of the islands, nor, it is suggested, can it be regarded as of substantial importance in view of the consistent repudiation, before and after the dates mentioned, of the Persian claim. Mirfendereski, op. cit., argues that these maps are part of a pattern of British recognition. He writes on page 128: "In October 1887, the Shaikh of Sharjah complained to the political resident about Iran's actions in the previous month on Sirri Island and asked that the British government prevent such actions at Great Tonb." He continued that then "The British government decided, however, to confine their representations solely to Iran's actions on Sirri Island." Iran, however, had said and done nothing at that point regarding the Greater Tunb. When Iran then claimed the Greater Tunb and provided documents that purportedly supported its claim, the British Chargé in Tehran told the Persian Prime Minister in March 1888 that the Persian documents on Sirri and the Greater Tunb did not support the Persian claim. Mirfendereski does not mention this March 1888 communication. Mirfenderski also claims that British officials "did not object to the contents" of Hajji Ahmed Khan's 1888 report claiming Persian ownership of Sirri, the Tunbs and Abu Musa, and that "In communicating a copy of the report to the British minister in Tehran, the political resident observed that the report did not contain anything new other than a claim to Abu Musa Island." However, the Political Resident wrote: "The claim now put forward to the Island of Abu Musa has no justification whatsoever. Any attempt to assert Persian authority there in a practical form would probably lead to disturbances." Moreover, Persia did not assert any official claim to Abu Musa to which the British would need to object. Mirfendereski claims that these versions of the historical record, which are incomplete and inaccurate, along with the maps, which are also inaccurate, are all part of a pattern of British recognition of or at least acquiescence to the Iranian claim. He argues that Britain should therefore have been subsequently *estopped* from claiming the islands for Sharjah and Ras al-Khaimah. On page 129, he writes: "the inaction or lack of protest on

the part of the British government regarding the Sheikh of Ras al-Khaimah's concern about Great Tonb, Iran's statement of claim to the Tonbs, and the depiction of the Tonbs as Iranian territory on the map all were consistent with and necessary consequences of Britain's recognition of or acquiescence to Iran's ownership of the Tonbs." However, again Iran took no action on the Tunbs other than to claim them, and the British did reply in March 1888 that the Persian documentation did not support the Persian claim. Mirfendereski also states on page 130: The agreement that existed at the time between the Iranian and British views about the status of the Tunbs, as evidenced by official British conduct and statements, obviated the need by the Iranian government to do anything more with respect to the Tonbs in 1887-1888. To that extent, Iran relied upon Britain's conduct and in so doing may have acted in detriment of its interest by not erecting a flag or garrison on the Tonbs as she had done on Sirri, therefore leaving that form of display of sovereignty to a later time (1903) when doing so received vociferous and militant opposition by the British due to change in Britain's political attitude.

However, the British Chargé's letter in March 1888 made it clear that Britain was not in agreement with Persia on either Sirri or the Greater Tunb. Thus, in not attempting to exercise sovereignty over the Tunbs, Persia could not have relied on any agreement, and Britain could not be estopped from later challenging the Persian claims. The argument on page 131 reads: At no time during the period from 1870 through 1896 did the British government communicate to the Iranian government a view other than the plain and simple meaning of the depictions and descriptions contained in these two official British government documents [the 1864 *Persian Gulf Pilot*, which he misdates 1870, and the 1886 *Map of Persia*] consistent with the political resident's considered opinion that the Tonbs were Iranian territory.

This argument is inaccurate because Iran was making no claim to the Tunbs in the 1870s, the Political Resident was misinformed in the 1870s and changed his views in the 1880s as he acquired better information on the subject, Britain did indeed communicate a different view to Persia in 1888 and Britain also challenged Persian arguments about Sirri in 1894. On page 131, Mirfenderski writes that "Research indicates that the depiction of the Tonbs on the *Map of Persia* (1886) as Iranian was not and could not have been a mistake. The depiction was wholly consistent with the Iranian and longstanding British political views at the time that the Tonbs belonged to Iran." Where this argument falls short is in the fact that it does not acknowledge the British Chargé's March 1888 letter or reflect the changed view of the British Political Resident in 1888. Mirfenderski's states as follows: "in view of the Shah's open, categorical, and adversarial reliance on the *Map of Persia* (1886) in 1888 and the Marquis of Salisbury's subsequent admonition [that maps should not be gifts in the future] it is unlikely that no one in the British Empire at the time would deny, correct, or otherwise rectify the 'mistake.'" This statement does not take into account the fact that the Shah cited the map as a bar to Qawasim claims to Sirri, not the Tunbs, and that he only mentioned that the Tunbs were in Persia's color. Britain did acquiesce to the Persian occupation of Sirri in 1888 because Britain placed a higher priority on concluding the Persian-Afghan border negotiations. However, Britain did not acquiesce to any Persian action on the Tunbs. As Mirfendereski notes on page 132, the British War Office did re-issue the *Map of Persia* without revision in 1891 and Lord Curzon did issue his unofficial *Map of Persia, Afghanistan, and Baluchistan* in 1892, which was based in part on the 1886 and 1891 British War Office maps. However, Curzon's map was an unofficial map. Moreover, Britain re-opened the issue of Sirri in 1894, re-asserting the Qawasim claim to it, and asking Persia to remove its flag, thus challenging the entire foundation of Persia's prior claim to the Tunbs. This must have constituted an indication about the British reaction to any future claims to the Tunbs and Abu Musa. Mirfendereski does not mention this British challenge to Persia's claim to Sirri in 1894. Furthermore, while he does note that the British Government of India re-issued the *Map of Persia* in 1897 without revision, he fails to point out that the *Persian Gulf Pilot* was revised in 1890 and did not designate the islands as belonging to Lingeh or Persia. Mirfendereski claims on pages 133-4 that the information in the 1886 map "must be presumed to have been accurate," that "there were no differing views" on this information between Britain and Iran, that the re-issue of subsequent maps with the same information "must be presumed to have verified and ratified the information," that the maps were "official and semi-official British maps" and that according to Judge Huber's criteria "these maps indicate in law the proof of an existence of Iranian sovereignty over the Tonbs." This statement simply ignores the fact that the information in the 1886 map was inaccurate. Not only were there differing views on the information between Britain and Persia, but the re-issue of the maps occurred along with a British diplomatic challenge to the basis of the Persian claim in 1894, and official and semi-official maps are treated with reserve in international law.

86 Toye, op. cit., vol. 2, 120-2.

87 Al Roken, op. cit., 145-6 specifies the conditions for acquisitive prescription. He cites Ian Brownlie, *Principles of Public International Law* (Oxford: Clarendon Press, 1990), 153-9.

88 Vinson and Elkins, op. cit., chapter 3, 97.

89 Ibid., chapter 3, 97-8.

90 Ibid., chapter 3, 96.

91 See remarks of the Iranian Ambassador to the United Nations in *Provisional Verbatim Record of the Sixteen Hundred and Tenth Meeting of the Security Council*, December 9, 1971, 86-7.

92 Vinson and Elkins, op. cit., chapter 3, 112-3.

93 Henkin et. al., op. cit., 311-2.

94 Northcutt Ely deposition at the ICJ, The Hague, 1992. Ely noted that this was not consistent with a 75-year history of British insistence that the Tunbs belonged to Ras al-Khaimah, but he thought "so be it."

95 *Kayhan International*, October 23, 1971 and January 22, 1972.

96 See, for example, the remarks of the Iraqi Ambassador in the *Provisional Verbatim Record of the Sixteen Hundred and Tenth Meeting of the Security Council*, December 9, 1971, 33-6.

97 Vinson and Elkins, op. cit., chapter 3, 86-7, 101-2. The Persian Minister of Court Taimurtash did say during a 1929 meeting with British Minister Robert Clive that arbitration might be the only way to resolve the issue of the islands, to which Clive replied that he hoped arbitration would not be necessary. However, this cannot be considered a formal Persian proposal or a formal British rejection.

98 Ibid., chapter 3, 101-2.

99 Interview with Shaikh Fahim Al-Qasimi, Abu Dhabi, September 1997.

100 Henkin et. al., op. cit., 242, citing the Restatement (Third) of the Foreign Relations Law of the United States, 1986.

101 The borders of these emirates had been defined through the assistance of British arbitrator Julian Walker during the 1950s and 1960s.

102 Henkin et. al., op. cit., 249-50.

103 Kelly, *Britain and the Persian Gulf: 1795-1880*, op. cit., 131.

104 Henkin et. al., op. cit., 244-5.

105 Interview with Khalifa Shahin Al-Marri, UAE Ministry of Foreign Affairs, Abu Dhabi, September 1997.

106 Dixon and McCorquodale, op. cit., 288.

107 Ibid., op. cit., 292.

108 Henkin et. al., op. cit., 310.

109 Ibid., op. cit., 311.

110 Ibid., 805-64. See also D. W. Bowett et. al., *The International Court of Justice: Process, Practice, and Procedure* (London: British Institute of International and Comparative Law, 1997); Arthur Eyffinger, *The International Court of Justice: 1946-1996* (Kluwer Law International, 1996); Shabtai Rosenne, *The Law and Practice of the International Court* (Leiden: W.Λ. Sijthoff, 1985). The *Eastern Greenland* case was decided in 1933 by the Permanent Court of Justice, the predecessor to the ICJ. The ICJ ruled in 1994 that it had jurisdiction to hear the Bahrain-Qatar dispute on the basis of a unilateral application to the Court by Qatar and despite Bahrain's protests, because Qatar and Bahrain had earlier agreed that they would take the case to the ICJ if bilateral negotiations failed.

111 Interview with Khalifa Shahin Al-Marri at the UAE Ministry of Foreign Affairs, September, 1997.

112 See Henkin et. al., op. cit., 788-805. Eritrea occupied the Hanish islands in the Red Sea in December 1995. Eritrea accepted the 1998 arbitral decision awarding most of the Hanish islands archipelago to Yemen.

113 Interview with Husain Albaharna in Bahrain, December 1997.

114 Bathurst, Ely and Chance, op. cit., vol. I, 15.

115 Shabtai Rosenne, "Introduction to International Litigation," an address to the University of Durham conference on *Preparing for Boundary Litigation and Arbitration*, Durham, England, March 25-26, 1998.

116 Henkin et. al., op. cit., 805, 856. For the text, see Henkin et. al., *Basic Documents Supplement*, op. cit., 20.

117 Henkin et. al., op. cit., 862-3.

CHAPTER 6

1   For a discussion of these traffic lanes, see Brigadier General Mohammad Hilal Al-Kaabi, *The Question of Iranian Occupation of the Islands, Greater Tunb, Lesser Tunb and Abu Musa Belonging to the United Arab Emirates* (Carlisle Barracks, PA: US Army War College, 1994), 1-6.

2   George Lenczowski, *The Middle East in World Affairs* (Ithaca, NY: Cornell University Press, 1980), 657, 728, 816.

3   For example, Saudi Arabia's Petroline pipeline from Jubail in the Eastern Province to Yanbu on the Red Sea has had the increased capacity to export 4.8 mbpd of oil from the Gulf to the Red Sea since 1993. Iraq has exported oil via a 1.6 mbpd

capacity pipeline through Turkey since 1996. See *The Middle East and North Africa 1997* (London: Europa Publications Limited, 1996), 518, 522, 529, 868-70. For a brief discussion of the Middle East's pipelines, see George Lenczowski, "Major Pipelines in the Middle East: Problems and Prospects," *Middle East Policy* 3, no. 4 (April 1995), 40-6. For the location of these pipelines, see *Energy Map of Arab Oil Producers* (London: Petroleum Economist Ltd., September 1996).

4   See "World Oil Transit Chokepoints," United States Energy Information Administration (http://www.eia.doe.gov). See *BP Amoco Statistical Review of World Energy*, June 2002 (http://www.bpamoco.com) for production figures. Production by Oman, Yemen and Syria has not been included in the figure of Gulf production of 20.2 mbpd.

5   See *BP Amoco Statistical Review of World Energy*, June 2001 for production and export figures. The UAE and Qatar accounted for this 21 billion cubic meters of gas exports by tanker in 2000. The UAE Offsets Group's Dolphin Project plans a pipeline to export Qatar gas to Abu Dhabi, Dubai, Oman and on to Pakistan. Saudi Arabia has a natural gas pipeline from Abqaiq on the Gulf to Yanbu on the Red Sea, although currently Saudi Arabia consumes virtually all of its natural gas production domestically.

6   Martin S. Navias and E.R. Hooton, *Tanker Wars: The Assault on Merchant Shipping During The Iran-Iraq Crisis, 1980-1988* (London: I.B. Tauris Publishers, 1996), 4, 14. The 40 million tonnes constituted virtually all of the UAE's imports, with only 500,000 tons imported through the UAE's airports. See "Shipping Industry Shapes Up For Expansion Plans," *Gulf Business* 3, no. 9 (January 1999).

7   For the location of these oil and gas fields, see *Energy Map of Arab Oil Producers*, op.cit.

8   See Navias and Hooton, *Tanker Wars*, op. cit., for a detailed study of the Iranian attacks from these islands during the tanker war.

9   Interview with UAE military source, Abu Dhabi, May 1999.

10 Hooshang Amirahmadi, "The Colonial-Political Dimension of the Iran-UAE Dispute," in Hooshang Amirahmadi (ed.) *Small Islands, Big Politics* (London: Macmillan Press Ltd., 1996), 15-8.

11 Ibid., 18-9.

12 Thomas R. Mattair, "Interview with U.N. Ambassador Kamal Kharazi of Iran," *Middle East Policy* (Fall 1994), 125.

13 Interview at US National Security Council, Washington, DC, December 1994; interview at US Department of Defense, Arlington, Virginia, October 1997. See David Menashri, *Revolution at a Crossroads: Iran's Domestic Politics and Regional Ambitions* (Washington, DC: The Washington Institute for Near East Policy, 1997) for a discussion of pragmatic, radical and conservative forces in Iran.

14 Cordesman has raised this possibility, although he thinks that Iran would be deterred by the probable outcome of such a major conflict. See Anthony Cordesman, *Iran and Iraq: The Threat from the Northern Gulf* (Boulder, CO: Westview Press, 1994), 1-6, 282-3.

15 See Kenneth Katzman, "The Politico-Military Threat from Iran" in Jamal S. Al-Suwaidi (ed.) *Iran and the Gulf: A Search for Stability* (Abu Dhabi: The Emirates Center for Strategic Studies and Research, 1996), especially 206-7. Katzman suggests that the Revolutionary Guard could lash out against GCC states as part of an internal power struggle if its patron, the clerical regime, were overthrown. He

also argues that if the radical faction with which it identifies loses political power, then the Revolutionary Guard could become more aggressive by undertaking military or political actions designed to embarrass the moderates and set them back politically. See also Kenneth Katzman, *Warriors of Islam: Iran's Revolutionary Guard* (Boulder, CO: Westview Press, 1993) for a more thorough discussion of the Guards.

16   For an overview of the Iranian political system, see Wilfried Buchta, *Who Rules Iran? The Structure of Power in the Islamic Republic* (Washington DC: The Washington Institute for Near East Policy and the Konrad Adenauer Stiftung, 2000).

17   Interview at the UAE Ministry of Foreign Affairs, Abu Dhabi, Fall 1997.

18   Interviews at the US Joint Staff and the US Defense Intelligence Agency, Arlington, Virginia, September 1997. See Shahram Chubin, *Iran's National Security Policy: Capabilities, Intentions and Impact* (Washington, DC: The Carnegie Endowment for International Peace, 1994), 69 and 72 for the organizational structure of the Iranian security apparatus and the Revolutionary Guard.

19   Interview, Abu Dhabi, November 1997.

20   Interview, British Embassy, Abu Dhabi, August 1997.

21   Interview, Washington, DC, October 1997.

22   Cordesman, *Iran and Iraq*, op. cit., 3-4.

23   Interview, US Department of Defense, Office of International Security Affairs, Arlington, Virginia, September 1997.

24   Interview, US Department of State, Washington, DC, January 1998. As was pointed out, in those cases where national existence is not at stake, Iran has in fact acted rationally. It is cautious in Central Asia and ideological in Lebanon and was statist in Afghanistan.

25   See for example Lenczowski, *The Middle East in World Affairs*, op. cit., 181-2, 187-90, 200-1, 214-9.

26   Shah Mohammed Reza Pahlavi, in an interview with the editor of *Blitz* (New Delhi), June 24, 1971, reprinted in the English edition of *Kayhan International* (Tehran) June 26, 1971, quoted in Amirahmadi, op. cit., 18.

27   This history includes the US embargo of Iranian oil after Iran's nationalization of the Anglo Iranian Oil Company in 1951; opposition to Prime Minister Mohammed Mossadegh in the early 1950s; involvement in the coup that overthrew Mossadegh and restored the Shah to the throne in 1953; continuing support to the Shah throughout the following decades; use of Iran's oil resources; arms sales to and military advisers in Iran; opposition to the 1978-1979 revolution; and opposition to the Islamic Republic since the revolution, including alleged instigation of the UAE to make an issue of Iran's presence on Abu Musa and the Tunbs.

28   Hamid Algar (translator and annotator) *Islam and Revolution: Writings and Declarations of Imam Khomeini* (Berkeley, CA: Mizan Press, 1981), 258.

29   See George Lenczowski, *American Presidents and the Middle East* (Durham: Duke University Press, 1990), 243-54 for a concise summary of the US role in the Iran-Iraq war. See R.K. Ramazani, *Revolutionary Iran: Challenge and Response in the Middle East* (Baltimore, MD: The Johns Hopkins University Press, 1986) for a more detailed study of Iran in the early years of revolution and war. Former US Deputy Assistant Secretary of State Joseph Twinam cites the figure of $50 billion in *The Gulf, Cooperation and the Council: An American Perspective* (Washington,

DC: The Middle East Policy Council, 1992), 133. Former US Ambassador to Saudi Arabia James Akins has provided the $60 billion figure.

30 Ramazani, *Revolutionary Iran*, op. cit., 275-81 provides extensive excerpts from the text of this sermon. He cites Foreign Broadcast Information Service, *Daily Report, South Asia*, October 17, 1983, vol. 8, no. 201, 11-3.

31 Ramazani, *Revolutionary Iran*, op. cit., 139 cites *The Washington Post*, June 9, 1984.

32 Anthony H. Cordesman, *Bahrain, Oman, Qatar, and the UAE: Challenges of Security* (Boulder, CO: Westview Press, 1997), 298.

33 See Navias and Hooton, *Tanker Wars*, op. cit. for a detailed study of the tanker war.

34 R.K. Ramazani, "Iran's Resistance to the US Intervention in the Persian Gulf" in Nikki R. Keddie and Mark J. Gasiorowski (ed.) *Neither East Nor West: Iran, the Soviet Union, and the United States* (New Haven, CT: Yale University Press, 1990), 38 cites Foreign Broadcast Information Service, *Daily Report, South Asia* (FBIS-SA), May 8, 1987.

35 Lenczowski, *American Presidents and the Middle East*, op. cit.; Navias and Hooton, *Tanker Wars*; Ramazani, "Iran's Resistance to the US Intervention in the Persian Gulf," in *Neither East Nor West* op. cit.

36 See Anthony H. Cordesman and Abraham R. Wagner, *The Lessons of Modern War, Volume II: The Iran-Iraq War* (Boulder, CO: Westview Press, 1990), 394 for these and other quotations of Iran's leaders. Iran sought reparations from the United States at the International Court of Justice.

37 President Hashemi Rafsanjani's "Informal Talk to the Participants in the Seminar on *Horizons for Cooperation in the Persian Gulf and the Oman Sea*," Tehran, December 19-20, 1994, sponsored by the Institute for Political and International Studies, a research institution affiliated with the Ministry of Foreign Affairs, and published in its journal, *The Iranian Journal of International Affairs* 7, no. 3 (Fall 1995), 698.

38 Mattair, "Interview," op. cit., 128-9.

39 Author's notes from attendance at Iranian Foreign Minister Velayati's speech to the seminar on *Horizons for Cooperation in the Persian Gulf and the Oman Sea*, sponsored by the Institute for Political and International Studies, Tehran, December 19-20, 1994.

40 *Kayhan International*, February 4, 1993.

41 Mattair, "Interview," op. cit., 128-9.

42 George Nader, "Interview with President Ali Akbar Hashemi Rafsanjani," *Middle East Insight* XI, no. 5 (July-August 1995) 13.

43 Ramazani, *Revolutionary Iran*, op. cit., 106, 142.

44 Ramazani, "Iran's Resistance to the US Intervention in the Persian Gulf" in *Neither East Nor West*, 48 cites FBIS-NES, June 24, 1987.

45 Speech delivered by Ayatollah Seyyed Ali Khamenei, Iran's Spiritual Leader, at the Opening Ceremony of the 8th Organization of the Islamic Conference Summit Meeting, Tehran, December 9, 1997 in *The Iranian Journal of International Affairs* IX, no. 4 (Winter 1997/98), 594, 597.

46 Statement by HE Seyyed Mohammad Khatami, President of the Islamic Republic of Iran and Chairman of the Eighth Session of the Islamic Summit Conference, Tehran, December 9, 1997 in *The Iranian Journal of International Affairs* IX, no. 4 (Winter 1997/98), 605, 607, 609.

47 R.K. Ramazani, "The Shifting Premise of Iran's Foreign Policy: Towards a Democratic Peace?" *The Middle East Journal* 52, no. 2 (Spring 1998) 179. Iran also blames Israel and the pro-Israeli lobby in the United States for advocating the "dual containment" policy. Soon after President Clinton's May 8, 1995 Executive Order banning trade with and investment in Iran, Rafsanjani said this was "partly because of the pressure that is exerted by Zionist circles." See Nader, "Interview with President Ali Akbar Rafsanjani," *Middle East Insight*, 9.

48 Nader, op. cit., 9-10.

49 *The Wall Street Journal*, December 16, 1997 and *Transcript of Interview with Iranian President Mohammad Khatami*, CNN interactive, January 7, 1998.

50 *Gulf News*, January 17, 1998.

51 Khatami interview with *Al-Jazeera*, cited in *Al-Bayan*, May 24, 1999.

52 Cordesman, *Iran and Iraq*, op. cit., 32-3.

53 Quoted by Anwar Gargash, "Iran, the GCC States, and the UAE: Prospects and Challenges in the Coming Decade," in Al-Suwaidi, op. cit., 154. Gargash cites *Al-Safir*, September 16, 1992 and *Al-Siyasah*, December 19, 1992.

54 Nader, op. cit., 13. Iranian officials in Tehran told the author in 1994 that they also blame Israel for "inciting" the United States and the UAE on this issue. Interviews at the Institute for International Political Studies, Tehran, Iran, December 1994.

55 *The New York Times*, December 27, 1992.

56 See Foreign Broadcasting Information Service (FBIS)-NES, 95-237 (IIXII 95), 84-5. Cordesman reports that Iran said it had been willing to fight for eight years, but Iran said eighty. See Cordesman, *Iran and Iraq*, op. cit., 33.

57 *Gulf News*, May 28, 1997.

58 *Gulf News*, May 23, 1998.

59 For a summary of the various purchases and acquisitions, including jet fighters, surface-to-air missiles, tanks, amphibious craft, patrol craft, fast attack craft, frigates, destroyers, surface-to-surface missiles, maritime patrol aircraft and helicopters, see Alvin J. Cottrell, "Iran's Armed Forces Under the Pahlavi Dynasty," in George Lenczowski (ed.) *Iran Under the Pahlavis* (Stanford, CA: Hoover Institution Press, 1978), 403, 407-13, 418-29.

60 See Cordesman, "Threats and Non-Threats from Iran," in Al-Suwaidi, op. cit., 223-4, 243-6, 248-51; Paul Jackson (ed.) *Jane's All the World's Aircraft, 1998-1999* (London: Jane's Information Group Limited, 1999), 344-5, 352-4, 381-8, 417-9, 441-2. These sources also note that Islamic Iran has acquired Russian-made MiG-29 deep-penetration air-to-air combat fighters, Chinese-made versions of MiG 21 fighters (the Chengdu F-7M Airguard) and the Russian-made Tupolev-22M Backfire bombers with a maximum range of 2,500 miles and equipped with long-range anti-ship missiles, and has sought many other systems. Iran has also reported that it has begun production of its own fighters, the Azarakhsh (Lightning) and the Owj (Zenith). See also Michael Eisenstadt, *Iranian Military Power: Capabilities and Intentions* for another overview and assessment of Iranian military programs.

61 Cordesman, "Threats and Non-Threats from Iran," op. cit., 246-51, 276-7. US Defense Intelligence Agency and Navy Intelligence analysts report that Iran has surface-to-air missiles (SAMs) on the mainland with ranges sufficient to hit aircraft over the GCC states, and Iran is known to have Russian-made long-range SA-5 SAMs with a range of 250 km at ports and oil facilities such as Bandar

Abbas. Interview at US Department of Defense, Arlington, Virginia, September 1997. Cordesman and Pentagon analysts note that Iran's aircraft and surface-to-air systems would not have these offensive and defensive capabilities in the face of US opposition and perhaps not in the face of the opposition of the Saudi airforce.

62 *Jane's Sentinel Security Assessment: The Gulf States*, January 13, 2003 (www4.janes.com)

63 Reuters, July 7, 2003.

64 Cordesman, "Threats and Non-Threats from Iran," op. cit., 271-4; *Jane's Strategic Weapons Systems*, Issue 24, May 1997 and Issue 25, September 1997; Andrew Rathmell with Paul Beaver (ed.), *Jane's Sentinel: The Gulf States* (London: Jane's Information Group Limited, 1996), 98-9, 132. These sources also note that Iran may be trying to acquire the North Korean-made Tapeo Dong 1 and Tapeo Dong 2, intermediate range ballistic missiles with a range of 2,000 km and 4,000 km respectively. North Korea's testing of a three stage Tapeo Dong missile in August 1998 led to concerns that Iran could acquire such a missile and that it could have a range of 4,000 to 6,000 km, thus capable of targeting Western Europe. Due to these developments, the US Central Intelligence Agency concluded that Iran is among the countries that could have an intercontinental ballistic missile capable of hitting the United States by 2015. The Revolutionary Guard displayed a new surface-to-surface missile, the Zelzal, which reportedly has both short and long-range versions, at a military parade in September 1999, but no details of its range or payload have been reported. For reporting about Iran's initial tests of the Shahab-3 missile, see *Gulf News*, July 25 and August 3, 1998 and also July 16, 2000.

65 Cordesman, "Threats and Non-Threats from Iran," op. cit., 275-6. Iranian ballistic missile attacks against area targets along the southern coast of the Gulf would be similar to the Iraqi Scud attacks against Iran during the 'war of the cities' or against Saudi Arabia and Israel during the Gulf War. Incoming Iranian missiles would be vulnerable to point defense by the improved Patriot anti-missile systems, although US Secretary of Defense William Cohen noted in October 1998 that developments such as the Shahab-3 test make continued research and development of an effective theatre anti-missile system important. Iranian missile launching facilities would also be vulnerable to offensive attacks by US air power, but, as during the Gulf war, the US could not hunt out and destroy enough of Iran's missile capabilities to stop all attacks. Thus, the United States might have to escalate its offensive attacks against other high-value Iranian targets in order to deter Iranian missile attacks. See *Gulf News*, October 12, 1998 for Secretary Cohen's remarks.

66 Cordesman wrote in his 1996 essay that "Although Iran already has a significant capability to wage chemical warfare, this capability is not large or lethal enough to pose a major threat to the southern Gulf if the southern Gulf states have the support of US forces." He argued that Iran could use chemical weapons in artillery or multiple rocket launchers (and in bombs) at line-of-sight ranges, but had problems loading chemical weapons into warheads and delivering them to beyond-visual range targets by aircraft, ballistic missiles or cruise missiles. Iran would also have the same problems if it were to produce or acquire biological and/or nuclear weapons. However, he argued that Iran's acquisition of the North Korean-made Scud-C could significantly change Iran's capability to deliver WMDs, because North Korea normally deploys the Scud-C with a chemical warhead and may have

tested biological warheads. See Cordesman, "Threats and Non-Threats from Iran," op. cit., 268-9, 272-3, 276-7. Al-Suwaidi has also written in a 1996 essay that Iran is producing chemical toxins "in conjunction with medium-range missiles superior to those fielded by Iraq," which he later identified as the Shahab-3. See Jamal S. Al-Suwaidi, "The Gulf Security Dilemma," in Al-Suwaidi, op. cit., 338 and an interview with Jamal S. Al-Suwaidi, September 1997. Again, it should be pointed out that no anti-missile defense system is foolproof and no offensive attacks can root out all launching facilities, although an Iranian WMD attack would make the escalation of US counter-attacks all the more likely.

67 Cordesman, "Threats," op. cit., 237, 276, 278, 282.

68 Ibid., 277-8; *Jane's Sentinel: The Gulf States*, op. cit., 101-2.

69 Cordesman, "Threats," op. cit., 277-9; *Jane's Sentinel: The Gulf States*, op. cit., 101.

70 This includes reports of Iranian attempts to acquire enriched uranium from Kazakhstan, the People's Republic of China's (PRC's) agreement to construct one or two 300-megawatt nuclear reactors near Tehran, the Russian agreement to augment the power of a Chinese-built gas centrifuge in Iran capable of producing weapons-grade uranium, and Chinese delivery to Iran of rocket components to improve the accuracy, payload and range of Iran's No-Dong (or perhaps Iran's Shahab 3) missile. See Cordesman, "Threats," op. cit., 279-83; Al-Suwaidi, "The Gulf Security Dilemma," 337; *Jane's Sentinel: The Gulf States*, op. cit., 99-101. This last source indicates that subsequent reports claimed that China might not go forward with its agreement to build the two reactors, that Russia would not sell gas-centrifuge uranium-enrichment technology, and that Iran had offered to return any spent fuel from Russian reactors back to Russia.

71 *Jane's Sentinel Security Assessment: The Gulf States* (www4.janes.com); *Gulf News*, November 23, 2002; February 17, 25, 2003.

72 Cordesman, "Threats and Non-Threats from Iran," op. cit., 283. Given the nuclear cooperation agreement between Iran and Pakistan, Pakistan's underground nuclear tests in May 1998 may benefit Iran's nuclear program. Iran's tests of its intermediate-range Shahab-3 ballistic missile from July 1998 to May 2002 may take Iran one step closer to a workable nuclear delivery system. See *Jane's Sentinel: The Gulf States*, op. cit., 101.

73 Cordesman, "Threats and Non-Threats from Iran," op. cit., 253, 255-6, 261-2, 274-5; *Jane's Strategic Weapons Systems*, Issue 24, May 1997 and Issue 25, September 1997; Duncan Lennox (ed.) *Jane's Air-Launched Weapons* (London: Jane's Information Group Limited, 1997), Issue 25, November 1996; *Washington Post*, May 31, 1997; June 18, 1997; interview at the US Department of Defense, Office of the Assistant Secretary for International Security Affairs, October 1997; *Jane's Sentinel: The Gulf States*, op. cit., 112, 118; Captain Richard Sharpe, RN (ed.) *Jane's Fighting Ships, 2000-2001* (UK: Jane's Information Group Limited, 2000), 325. These sources also indicate that Iran has sought longer-range anti-ship cruise missiles, such as an upgraded version of the Chinese-made C-802 and the Tupolov-22M bomber's missiles, and that Iran may be trying to extend the range of its Silkworm missiles to 400 km and seeking to produce its own cruise missiles with an even longer range.

74 Cordesman, "Threats and Non Threats from Iran," op. cit., 255-6, 263; "Troubled Waters," in *Gulf States Newsletter*, May 1997, 9; *Jane's Fighting Ships, 2000-2001*, 326-8.

75 *Jane's Fighting Ships, 2000-2001*, 328. See also *Jane's Intelligence Review* 8, no. 9 (September 1996), 414; *Jane's Defence Weekly*, April 30, 1997, 6.

76 Cordesman, "Threats and Non-Threats from Iran," op. cit., 256, 261-2; *Jane's Fighting Ships, 2000-2001*, op. cit., 329-30.

77 There are also reports that Iran may acquire additional submarines from China.

78 Interview, US Embassy, Abu Dhabi, UAE, Fall 1997.

79 *Jane's Fighting Ships, 2000-2001*, op. cit., 325. A military attaché at the US Embassy in Abu Dhabi argued in 1997 that these submarines do not constitute a short-term threat, because the Iranians do not yet have the training or the logistical support necessary to carry out effective tactics. US submarine commanders, for example, have fifteen years of experience before they are given command of a submarine and there are no Iranians in the regular navy or the naval branch of the IRGC, both of which operate these submarines, who have this kind of experience. Particularly inside the Gulf, he argued, these submarines would be far from their base at Bandar Abbas and its support. The commanders and the crews especially do not yet have the training and the confidence to operate for long periods underwater. The Iranian submarines are very quiet when they switch off their diesel engines and go on electric mode, but they can only operate this way for one or two days before they have to come up to take in air and then they are relatively noisy and easier to find. Their submerged cruise range is 400 nautical miles. Moreover, he argued, the Iranian submarines would have a hard time finding their targets inside the Gulf. Indeed, Cordesman writes that the heat patterns of the Gulf disturb submarine sonars. Cordesman adds that much of the Gulf is so shallow, particularly along the southern coast, that hiding and diving and protecting against anti-submarine warfare (ASW) is difficult. He also notes that the Strait of Hormuz has only two deep navigable channels with a maximum depth of 80 meters and that each is only two km wide, so that ASW detection of these submarines in the strait would be possible, although underwater currents would complicate both the detection of the submarines as well as the operations of the submarines. Cordesman's assessment is that "If they did not face the US or the UK, the Iranian Kilos could operate in or near the Gulf with considerable impunity. If they did face US and British forces, they might be able to attack a few tankers or conduct some mining operations, but are unlikely to survive extended combat. This makes the Kilos a weapon that may be more effective as a threat than in actual combat." The US military attaché also argues that it is not necessary to use the submarines to lay mines inside the Gulf when they have surface vessels that can do that; neither are submarines needed to position commandos in a GCC state inasmuch as the dhow traffic across the Gulf is so heavy that commandos could be hidden and positioned that way. Interview at US Embassy, Abu Dhabi, UAE, Fall 1997; Cordesman, "Threats," op. cit., 258-260.

80 *Jane's Sentinel: The Gulf Region*, op. cit., 117.

81 Interview at US Embassy, Abu Dhabi, UAE, Fall 1997. Indeed, Iran's submarine exercises have generally taken place in the Gulf of Oman rather than inside the Arabian Gulf, and there are plans to move its home base from Bandar Abbas to Chah Bahar on the northern Gulf of Oman. See *Jane's Sentinel: The Gulf States*, op. cit., 118; *Jane's Fighting Ships, 2000-2001*, op. cit., 325. However, even in the Gulf of Oman where there is enough noise to make ASW more difficult,

Cordesman argues that Iran's submarines would be vulnerable to US and British nuclear attack submarines. Cordesman, "Threats," op. cit., 260.

82 It is not clear, however, that Iran can yet provide the training and support for successful operation of these vessels. See Cordesman, "Threats," op. cit., 252, 258; *Jane's Fighting Ships, 2000-2001*, op. cit., 326.

83 *Jane's Fighting Ships, 2000-2001*, op. cit., 325.

84 Anthony J. Watts (ed.), *Jane's Underwater Weapons Systems, 1998-1999* (London: Jane's Information Group Limited, 1998) 380-2.

85 Cordesman, "Threats and Non-Threats from Iran," op. cit., 263; *Jane's Underwater Warfare Systems*, 1998-1999, op. cit., 13-14, 285.

86 Cordesman, "Threats and Non-Threats from Iran," op. cit., 240, 256-7, 264-5. He argues that Iran could not successfully conduct an overt amphibious movement across the Gulf in the face of significant air and sea defenses, particularly US and British. See also *Jane's Fighting Ships, 2000-2001*, op. cit., 330-1.

87 Thus, for example, Revolutionary Guard divers/frogmen may be able to attach explosives to the underwater foundations of off-shore oil and gas rigs, pipelines, ship's hulls and ports in the Gulf, particularly if Iran's midget submarine vessels become operational and if Iran's swimmer delivery vehicles are employed. See Cordesman, "Threats and Non-Threats from Iran," op. cit., 239-40, 262. Intelligence forces, including the Ministry of Intelligence and Security, or VEVAK, and other intelligence services associated with the Revolutionary Guard, the regular armed forces, the Foreign Ministry, the Islamic Culture and Guidance Ministry, and the *bonyads* or charitable foundations, independently or in cooperation with extremist groups in other countries, may engage in unconventional warfare or terrorism against GCC forces or US forces in the Gulf similar in nature to the bombing of the Khobar Towers complex housing US military personnel in Dhahran, Saudi Arabia in 1996 and the bombing of the *USS Cole* in the harbor at Aden, South Yemen in 2000. See Cordesman, "Threats," op. cit., 266-8.

88 Eisenstadt, op. cit., 49-50. See also Cordesman, *Iran and Iraq*, op. cit., 32. In the spring of 1993, Iran conducted the Victory 4 exercise, a multi-service exercise that practiced amphibious and heliborne assaults intended to project power across the Gulf. This exercise and similar ones in the same year demonstrated that Iran did not yet have the amphibious and heliborne capability to do more than launch limited attacks against or to seize small islands and oil facilities in the Gulf, or to deploy battalion-sized forces to support some coup attempt in an exposed country like Bahrain, and that it could not do so in the face of US or British opposition. See Cordesman, "Threats," op. cit., 239.

89 *Jane's Defence Weekly*, Special Report, "Iran Steps Up Gulf Exercises," January 1, 1996 (jdw.janes.com) *Jane's Intelligence Review* 8, no. 9 (September 1996), 412-3. It has been reported that Iranian helicopters equipped with spray tanks simulated chemical or biological weapons attacks against shipping during a late 1995 exercise. This last capability could enable Iran to temporarily close the Strait of Hormuz. Eisenstadt, op. cit., 59, cites *Helicopter News* 21, no. 2, 27 October 1995, 4. Iran test-launched a shore-based C-802 anti-ship missile during a December 1995 exercise and a ship-based C-802 missile from a Houdong-class fast attack boat during a January 1996 exercise. *Jane's Defence Weekly*, Special Report, "Iranian Manoeuvres Keep West On Alert," April 1, 1996 (jdw.janes.com). In February 1997, Iran conducted naval exercises including the use of at least one of its

submarines off the Chah Bahar naval base in the Gulf of Oman and the Indian Ocean, where an effort could be made to deny access to the Strait of Hormuz. See *Jane's Defence Weekly*, Special Report, "Iranian Exercises Move To Deeper Water," May 1, 1997 (jdw.janes.com). An American intelligence analyst noted that during a major exercise in the spring of 1997, Iran practiced mine laying and amphibious landings just off Bandar Abbas. This exercise, like the earlier ones, "was crude in terms of power projection." As far as the analyst was concerned, the United States watches for capabilities that Iran does and does not demonstrate during exercises like this and Iran has over-publicized what they have been doing in these exercises, compared to what the United States has actually observed. She also mentioned, however, that part of another Iranian naval exercise at this time practiced re-taking Abu Musa and that there must therefore be some thinking that this may be necessary. Interview, US Defense Department Office of the Assistant Secretary for International Security Affairs, October 1997. See also *Gulf News*, September 26 and 27, 1999.

90 Interview with UAE military source, Abu Dhabi, May 1999.

91 *Gulf News*, February 28, 1999.

92 Interview with UAE military source, Abu Dhabi, May 1999. Back in 1996, Cordesman wrote that: "It is…impossible to rule out a sudden or surprise Iranian attack in support of an uprising against a southern Gulf regime that produced success out of all proportion to the size and effectiveness of the Iranian forces deployed. Iran has a number of land units that should perform well in unconventional warfare missions in support of any popular uprising. It could deploy brigade-sized forces relatively rapidly across the Gulf, if it were allowed to make an unopposed amphibious and air assault. It could intervene in a civil war in Bahrain, or another of the smaller Gulf states, under these conditions." See Cordesman, "Threats," op. cit., 239.

93 *United States Security Strategy for the Middle East* (Washington, DC: Office of the Assistant Secretary of Defense for International Security Affairs, Middle East and North African Affairs, May 1995), 16.

94 *The Washington Post*, June 18, 1997.

95 Cordesman, "Threats," op. cit., 260-1.

96 Interview with US Navy intelligence analyst at the US Defense Intelligence Agency, the Pentagon, September 1997.

97 Interview with UAE military source, Abu Dhabi, May 1999.

98 Interview at US Defense Intelligence Agency, the Pentagon, September 1997; interview at US Embassy, Abu Dhabi, August 1997.

99 Cordesman, *Bahrain, Oman, Qatar, and the UAE*, op. cit., 302-3. Cordesman indicates that the SA-6s have a range of "under 100 miles," but a UAE military source indicated in a May 1999 interview that their range is only 40 km. Their range is only 24 km according to *Jane's Land-Based Air Defence, 1998-1999*, op. cit., 123-6, 351. The UAE military source stated that the Improved Hawks (IHawks) deployed to Abu Musa in 1995 are of an older vintage, namely the Phase 1 and Phase 2 Hawks, with a range of 40 km, some of which were supplied to Iran by the United States during the Iran-Contra affair in 1985 and 1986, and that they do not include the more modern Phase III Hawks. See also *Jane's Land-Based Air Defence*, 1998-1999, op. cit., 303-9.

100 Interview with UAE military source, Abu Dhabi, May 1999. While Iran's land-based air defense systems on the islands, like its systems on the mainland, would

have some capability against a regional air force without sophisticated jammers and anti-radiation missiles, it would not have this capability in the face of the US Air Force. Even the SA-6 is vulnerable to active and passive countermeasures and the IHawk is not comparable to the Patriot in performance capability. See Cordesman, "Threats," op. cit., 250-1. Thus, while Iran may currently be able to stop UAE aircraft from attacking the islands, they cannot stop US aircraft from doing so. As analysts from the Joint Staff put it, anything deployed on the islands can be "kissed off" when the United States decides to neutralize them by electronic disabling of their assets (jamming their radars and communications), or shooting or intimidation of their military by telling them they are doomed. Interview at the Joint Staff, the Pentagon, September 1997. However, the US may decide, as in the 1980s, that for political and legal reasons it should not attack Iranian positions on the islands. The UAE's acquisition of US-made F-16s and its insistence on acquiring the planes with their electronic counter-measure technology should also eventually render Iran's land-based air defense system on the islands vulnerable, although the involvement of the Iranian airforce could complicate matters.

101 Al-Kaabi, *The Question of Iranian Occupation*, op. cit., 3.

102 Cordesman, *Bahrain, Oman, Qatar and the UAE*, op. cit., 302-3. This reference to the SA-6 calls it an air-to-surface missile, but this must be a typographical or editing error.

103 Al-Kaabi, *The Question of Iranian Occupation*, op. cit., 3.

104 Ibid., 3.

105 Clifford Beal, "Uncovered: Iran's [*sic*] Abu Musa island," *Jane's Defence Weekly* 33, no. 10, March 8, 2000, 28-9.

106 Ibid., 28-9.

107 In any case, Iran may be more likely to deploy these systems outside where they would be visible during times of tension rather than all the time.

108 Interview with UAE military source, Abu Dhabi, May 1999. Richard Schofield has written that "Iran's mobilization has, of course, altered the status quo on Abu Musa. Whether it has contravened the express terms of the MOU must be open to considerably more doubt. Only by demonstrating that the territorial reality introduced by the MOU has been deliberately altered to its own advantage by Iran could one claim that more than the spirit of the agreement has been broken. Despite frequent claims to the contrary, there is simply no evidence that Iran has brought areas of the southern, Sharjah-administered part of Abu Musa under its aegis." See Richard N. Schofield, "Border Disputes in the Gulf: Past, Present, and Future" in Gary G. Sick and Lawrence G. Potter (eds.) *The Persian Gulf in the Millennium: Essays in Politics, Economy, Security, and Religion* (New York, NY: St. Martin's Press, 1997) 152-3. In fact, however, Iran's militarization and fortification of Abu Musa has definitely included the southern zone allocated to Sharjah. The image published in *Jane's Defence Weekly* shows fortifications in Sharjah's zone and the UAE military evidence shows substantially more of the same.

109 Al-Kaabi, *The Iranian Occupation*, op. cit., 81.

110 Interview at the UAE Ministry of Foreign Affairs, September 1997.

111 A US diplomat also argues that while the Scuds are mobile, they could not be deployed in a hidden mode on the islands. They are too vulnerable to be deployed on the island, as they could easily be taken out by the United States military. This was also the opinion of a leading UAE analyst. Interviews at the US Defense

Intelligence Agency, Arlington, Virginia; Washington, DC; the US Embassy in Abu Dhabi; and the Emirates Center for Strategic Studies and Research, Abu Dhabi. August to October 1997. The same reasoning could be applied to the issue of some of the surface-to-surface missiles discussed below. Interview at the US Embassy, Abu Dhabi, August 1997.

112 Interview, UAE military source, Abu Dhabi, May 1999.

113 Cordesman, *Bahrain, Oman, Qatar, and the UAE*, op. cit., 303.

114 Interview, UAE military source, Abu Dhabi, May 1999.

115 Cordesman, "Threats and Non-Threats from Iran," op. cit., 260-1; Cordesman, *Bahrain, Oman, Qatar, and the UAE*, op. cit., 302-3, 415; Cordesman also writes that Iran may be deploying a surface-to-surface modification of the SA-6 on Abu Musa in order to pose a "token" threat to the UAE's cities. However, he calls these reports "very uncertain," simply due to the short range of the SA-6.

116 Interview, UAE military source, Abu Dhabi, May 1999. See also Eisenstadt, op. cit., 56-7.

117 Interview at US Department of State, Washington, DC, January 1998; see also Cordesman, *Bahrain, Oman, Qatar and the UAE*, op. cit., 300 for published confirmation that during the Iran-Iraq war Iran "constructed secure storage sites it could use to hold Silkworm and surface-to-air missiles." Another US official stationed in the region at the same time recalls that he saw reports of Silkworms as well as Scuds on Abu Musa, but he did not regard them as credible reports. Interview in Washington, DC, October 1997.

118 Interview at the US Defense Intelligence Agency, the Pentagon, Arlington, Virginia, 1997. A UAE military source said in May 1999 that Silkworm and Seersucker missiles are heavy and require more vehicles for transportation to their launching site, in addition to the fact that they require liquid fuel. These two factors mean they take longer to deploy and give the United States and the UAE more time to discover them. He added, however, that there are ready launching sites for C-801s on Abu Musa and the Greater Tunb, that the C-801s can be brought to the islands in six hours and that they are solid-fuel missiles and are lighter and more easily transportable to the launching sites. Interview with UAE military source, Abu Dhabi, May 1999.

119 Interview, Abu Dhabi, May 1999.

120 Interview in Washington, DC, October 1997.

121 Interview at the US Embassy, Abu Dhabi, September 1997.

122 Interview in Washington, DC, October 1997.

123 Interview with UAE military source, Abu Dhabi, May 1999.

124 Interview at the US Defense Intelligence Agency, Arlington, Virginia, September 1997. Another analyst goes so far as to argue that the islands would only provide Iran with a forward staging advantage if there were no US military presence. With the US military presence, the islands provide no significant military advantage to the Iranians, primarily because Iranian military assets on the islands are so exposed to US counterattack. She also argues that if the Chinese did not provide over-the-horizon capabilities with its C-802 anti-ship missiles, Iran would have to fire its shore-based C-802s within line of sight, i.e. 20 to 25 kms, a sufficient range to hit shipping at the narrowest point of the Strait of Hormuz, but not sufficient to attack shipping to the west of the strait. Thus, if the shore-based C-802s lacked over-the-horizon capability, anti-ship missiles on the islands would enhance Iran's capability to hit shipping to the west of the strait. However, she argues, Iran would

only get off one shot before losing its anti-ship missile launchers on the islands because the islands are so small and exposed. Interview at the US Department of Defense Office of International Security Affairs, October 1997. In Iran's Victory–7 exercises in early 1996, early in Iran's program to deploy this missile, the C-802 missile was test-launched from a Hudong fast attack craft with a range of only 22 to 24 km. See *Jane's Defence Weekly* 27, no. 15, April 16, 1997, 26-7.

125 Mattair, "Interview," op. cit., 127-8.

126 Interview, London, October 1997. See also Shahram Chubin and Sepehr Zabih, *The Foreign Relations of Iran: A Developing State in a Zone of Great-Power Conflict* (Berkeley: University of California Press, 1974), 219-20, 226.

127 Rouhollah K. Ramazani, *Iran's Foreign Policy, 1941-1973* (Charlottesville, VA: University Press of Virginia, 1975), 411, 414-16.

128 R.K. Ramazani, *The Persian Gulf and the Strait of Hormuz* (Alphen aan den Rijn: Sijthoff and Noordhoff, 1979), 72.

129 See Unpublished FCO 8/1557 *Record of conversation at the Niavaran Palace Tehran on 4 May, 1971.*

130 *Kayhan International*, January 29, 1972.

131 See for example J.B. Kelly, *Arabia, the Gulf and the West* (USA: Basic Books, 1980), 89.

132 See Chapter 2.

133 Muhammad Morsy Abdullah, *The United Arab Emirates: A Modern History* (London: Hurtwood Press, 1994), 275.

134 See for example Chubin and Zabih, *The Foreign Relations of Iran*, chapter 7.

135 See for example Rouhollah K. Ramazani, *The Persian Gulf: Iran's Role* (Charlottesville, VA: University Press of Virginia, 1972), 89; Ramazani, *Iran's Foreign Policy*, op. cit., especially 427; Ramazani, *The Persian Gulf*, op. cit., 72-5; Lenczowski, *The Middle East in World Affairs*, op. cit., 657; James Noyes, *The Clouded Lens: Persian Gulf Security and US Policy* (Stanford, CA: Hoover Institution Press, 1982), 18.

136 *Kayhan International*, October 23, 1971.

137 *Kayhan International*, January 29, 1972.

138 Ramazani, *Iran's Foreign Policy*, op. cit., 404-6, 420-3; Abdullah, op. cit., 277-8.

139 For the Shah's quote, see *Middle East Monitor*, op. cit., July 15, 1971. See also Lenczowski, *The Middle East in World Affairs*, op. cit., 221-2.

140 This also included the signing of a Soviet-Iraqi cooperation treaty in April 1972, and Soviet and Iraqi support to the PFLOAG and the PDRY. See Ramazani, *Iran's Foreign Policy*, op. cit., 348-52, 427-30, 435-8.

141 *Provisional Verbatim Record of the Sixteen Hundred and Tenth Meeting of the United Nations Security Council* (S/10436, December 9, 1971). The official views of Arab states and organizations are discussed at length in chapter 7 of this manuscript.

142 Kelly, *Arabia, the Gulf and the West*, op. cit., 89.

143 Ramazani, *The Persian Gulf*, op. cit., 57.

144 Interview at the UAE Ministry of Foreign Affairs, Abu Dhabi, September, 1997. See also Keith McLachlan (ed.) *The Boundaries of Modern Iran* (London: University College London Press, 1994).

145 These resentments have been exacerbated by the GCC redressing the regional military imbalance after Iraq's defeat in Desert Storm by drawing closer to the United States and the West; by the US launching of the Madrid conference for

Arab-Israeli negotiations, which was opposed by Iran but supported by most Arab states; and by the development of the US "dual containment" policy. The feeling of isolation became even more acute with Syria's participation in the Damascus Declaration and in the Madrid peace process.

146 Interviews at the UAE Ministry of Foreign Affairs, Abu Dhabi, September 1997.

147 Mattair, "Interview with U.N. Ambassador Kamal Kharazi of Iran," *Middle East Policy*, 128.

148 Interviews at the Institute for Political and International Studies, Tehran, Iran, December 1994. See also comments by Richard Cottam in "Symposium: US Policy Toward Iran: From Containment to Relentless Pursuit?" in *Middle East Policy* IV, no. 1 and 2 (September 1995), 11, 18. Numerous US officials agree with the assessment that the islands are important to the Iranian people and the regime is legitimizing itself by defending a nationalistic issue. One former Ambassador argues that it would be difficult for the Islamic Republic to withdraw its claim to sovereignty because it was made by the Shah and the revolutionary regime can be no less supportive of the claim to sovereignty. Interviews in Washington, DC, October 1997 and January 1998. Another analyst says Iran views losing the islands as a loss of "face" since they think they have a valid claim. Interview at the US Defense Intelligence Agency, Arlington, Virginia, September 1997.

149 See for example Geoffrey Kemp, "The Impact of Iranian Foreign Policy on Regional Security: An External Perspective," in Al-Suwaidi, op. cit., 130.

150 Interview with a former US Ambassador to the UAE. Washington, DC, October 1997. CIA and Defense and Naval intelligence analysts agree that it is a possible motive. Interviews in Washington, DC, September and October 1997.

151 Pirouz Mojtahed-Zahedi, "Iran's Maritime Boundaries in the Persian Gulf: The Case of Abu Musa Island," in McLachlan (ed.) *The Boundaries of Modern Iran*, op. cit., 109.

152 Cordesman, *Bahrain, Oman, Qatar, and the UAE*, op. cit., 301.

153 Interview in London, October 1997.

154 Some Pentagon analysts have suggested that Iran may want the islands as a prelude to claiming other UAE offshore oil fields, although they think this is unlikely. The former British official agrees that this is unlikely, noting that Iran has median line agreements with Abu Dhabi and Dubai, and that this is where most of the UAE's other offshore oil fields lie, far from Abu Musa and the Tunbs and their territorial waters. Interviews at the US Defense Department, September and October 1997 and in London, October 1997. For a concise discussion of these median lines, see Rodman Bundy, "Maritime Delimitation in the Gulf," in Richard Schofield (ed.) *Territorial Foundations of the Gulf States* (London: University College London Press, 1994), 178, 182-3.

155 Interview, UAE Ministry of Foreign Affairs, Abu Dhabi, September 1997.

156 Interview, Washington, DC, October 1997.

157 Interview, Abu Dhabi, November 1997.

158 Eisenstadt, op. cit., 57. See 57-8 for his review of other possible intentions.

159 Interviews at the US Department of Defense and US Department of State, the British Embassy in Abu Dhabi, and with former British officials in London, September and October 1997.

160 Navias and Hooton, *Tanker Wars*, op. cit., 62.

161 Interview, US Department of Defense, October 1997.

162 Interviews at US Department of Defense and US Department of State in London and in Abu Dhabi. For suggestions of this, see Zalmay Khalilzad, "The United States and the Persian Gulf: Preventing Regional Hegemony," *Survival* 37, no. 2 (Summer 1995), 100-1, and Patrick Clawson, *US Sanctions on Iran* (Abu Dhabi: The Emirates Center for Strategic Studies and Research, 1997), 14.

163 Interview at the US Department of State, Washington, DC, October 1997. The use of Abu Musa was also corroborated in January 1998 by a US official based at the US Embassy in Abu Dhabi at that time, who recalls that Abu Musa was used as an observation post and that Boghammers and other vessels, while not permanently based there, were dispatched from Abu Musa. See also Navias and Hooton, *Tanker Wars*, op. cit., 151-2, for specific operations launched from Abu Musa and the Tunbs. A former US CENTCOM commander argues that Iran has onshore assets for this purpose, but that the islands also could be useful for interdiction of traffic in the future if Iranian military commanders want flexibility and as many options as possible. Interview, Abu Dhabi, November 1997.

164 Interview, Washington DC, October 1997. See also Shahram Chubin, "Arms Build-Up and Regional Military Balance," in Hooshang Amirahmadi and Eric Hooglund (eds.) *US-Iran Relations: Areas of Tension and Mutual Interest* (Washington, DC: The Middle East Institute, 1994), 45-6.

165 Interview, UAE Ministry of Foreign Affairs, Abu Dhabi, September 1997.

166 Interview with Martin Indyk, US National Security Council, Washington, DC, December 1994.

167 Interview at the Office of the US Assistant Secretary of Defense for International Security Affairs, Arlington, Virginia, October 1997. See also Cordesman, *Bahrain, Oman, Qatar, and the UAE*, op. cit., 302-3, Eisenstadt, op. cit., 57-8, and Khalilzad, op. cit., 100-1 for somewhat similar views. A British diplomat also says Iran wants to be able to prevent the UAE air force from attacking the islands. Iranian officials also say they fear that Israel may attack Iranian nuclear facilities and Iranian positions on these three islands. For Iranian views of Israeli threats, see Thomas R. Mattair, "Containment or Collision?" *Middle East Insight* XI, no. 5 (July-August, 1995) 27-8.

168 *Gulf News*, February 8, 12, 18, 2003.

169 Interviews at the Intercontinental Hotel, the British Embassy and the UAE Ministry of Foreign Affairs, Abu Dhabi, September and November 1997.

170 Interview at the US Defense Intelligence Agency, Arlington, Virginia, September 1997.

171 Interviews, US Embassy, Abu Dhabi, September 1997. See also S.H. Amin, *International and Legal Problems of the Gulf* (London: Middle Eastern and North African Studies Press Ltd., 1981), 20; Ahmad Razavi, *Continental Shelf Delimitation and Related Maritime Issues in the Persian Gulf* (The Hague: Marthinus Nijhoff Publishers, 1997). This US official, concerned that this is the Iranian motivation, has asked: If the Iranian legal claim were successful, what difference would it make for the US Navy? Would Iran have a legal right to deny the territorial waters around these islands to the US Navy? Would they then have the ability to establish open military bases, real fortresses that could cause real problems? These issues and questions will be taken up at greater length in the chapter on big power policies. For the definition of "innocent passage," see Henkin, Pugh, Schachter and Smit (eds.) *International Law: Cases and Materials*, Third Edition (St. Paul, MN: West Publishing Company, 1993) 1254-5.

172 Al-Suwaidi, "The Gulf Security Dilemma," op. cit., 340-2; see also 342-7 for more on Iran's economic needs. Most British and US officials and analysts agree with Al-Suwaidi and UAE officials that an overt and attributable Iranian attack against the UAE is deterred for now. To be sure, there would be a Western reaction to such an event. Indeed, given the US presence in the area, any Iranian preparations on the islands for such an attack would advertise their intentions in advance and risk US preemption. While Iran could use Abu Musa and the Tunbs in an overt and attributable attack, the official view is that Iran would not want to do so in the near term. Interviews at the British Embassy in Abu Dhabi; the US Department of Defense and the US Department of State in Washington, DC; and London, September and October 1997.

173 Interview at UAE Ministry of Foreign Affairs, August 1997.

174 Interviews at the British Embassy in Abu Dhabi; the US Department of Defense and the US Department of State in Washington, DC and London, September and October 1997.

175 Al-Suwaidi, "The Gulf Security Dilemma," op. cit., 340-2. He argues that GCC cooperation and the GCC–Western coalition foils this Iranian intention to intimidate GCC states into appeasing Iran.

176 Interviews at the US Department of Defense and the US Department of State, Washington, DC, September and October 1997. US officials think that this may be an Iranian motivation. A former CENTCOM commander says Iran's leverage on the islands may well enable it to intimidate the UAE in these ways.

177 Interview in London, October 1997.

178 Interview, Washington DC, October 1997.

179 *Gulf News*, March 30, 2000.

180 Cordesman, *Iran and Iraq*, op. cit., 282-3. See also Cordesman, "Threats," 283-4.

181 *Jane's Sentinel* claimed in 1996: "The threat of an Iranian-backed coup has been regarded by the UAE as the most likely challenge to its national security." See *Jane's Sentinel: The Gulf States*, 7. Such an assessment is supported by US officials who see the possibility of Iran acting through Iranians in the UAE and through infiltration. Interviews at the US Embassy in Abu Dhabi, and the Office of the US Assistant Secretary of Defense for International Security Affairs in Washington, DC, September and October 1997. Currently, there are 100,000 Iranians in the UAE and the direct ferry traffic between Bandar Abbas and Sharjah carries 400,000 passengers a year, mainly Iranian shoppers to the UAE. The UAE has since July 1, 1994 been restricting all boat traffic between the two countries, stopping, boarding and detaining all vessels that do not have valid documents. Still, as one British official has pointed out, Iran could easily infiltrate agents into the Iranian merchant community in Dubai and the northern emirates. Regular UAE round-ups of Iranian economic migrants suspected of illegal activities confirm this possibility. Interview, British Embassy, Abu Dhabi, September 1997.

182 Interviews in Abu Dhabi and Washington, DC, September and October 1997.

183 Interview, UAE Ministry of Foreign Affairs, Abu Dhabi, September 1997.

184 See Cordesman, *Bahrain, Oman, Qatar, and the UAE*, op. cit., 341-74; *Jane's Sentinel Security Assessment, May–October 2001*, op. cit., 484-98.

185 Reuters, July 2, 2001. As of early 2003, plans to increase the Peninsula Shield Force from 6,000 to 22,000 had not yet been implemented.

186 *Defense News*, May 22, 2001.

187 Interviews at UAE Ministry of Foreign Affairs, Abu Dhabi, September and October 1997.

188 Ibid.

189 Interview with confidential legal adviser to the Ruler of Sharjah, London, October 1997.

190 The UAE has conducted numerous joint military exercises with the United States and France in May 1996 and February 2000. See *Jane's Sentinel Security Assessment*, May-October 2000, 473, 475, 482.

191 Cordesman, *Bahrain, Oman, Qatar, and the UAE*, op. cit., 377-8; interviews, US Embassy, Abu Dhabi, September 1997 and March 2000.

192 *Jane's Sentinel Security Assessment*, May-October 2000, op. cit., 474-5; United Arab Emirates, Country Profile (London: Economist Intelligence Unit, 1999-2000), 5. Jane's indicates that France has made explicit promises of support in a crisis, whereas Britain has not. Jane's even indicates that Britain has no formal defense agreement with the UAE, but the British Embassy in Abu Dhabi indicates that they do, and Britain did sign a MoU with the UAE in 1996.

193 *Gulf News*, May 17, 1998.

194 *Jane's Sentinel Security Assessment*, May-October 2000, 485, 496.

195 *Gulf News*, March 6, 2000.

196 *Jane's Sentinel Security Assessment*, May-October 2000, 479, 496.

197 Ibid., 457, 471, 476, 485. *Defense News*, June 23, 2003.

198 Ibid., 486, 495-6.

199 Ibid., 490, 497-8.

200 *Jane's Sentinel Security Assessment: The Gulf States 2003* (www4.janes.com); *Gulf News*, February 26, 2003.

201 *Jane's Sentinel Security Assessment*, May-October 2000, 457, 474, 495.

202 Ibid., 479-80, 496-7.

203 Interview, UAE Ministry of Foreign Affairs, Abu Dhabi, September 1997.

204 Interviews in Washington, DC, September and October 1997. A British official in the UAE noted that the UAE was worried that if the United States lashed out at Iran for the Khobar Towers bombing, Iran would lash out at soft targets such as the UAE, and that the UAE had approached Britain to ask the United States to respond cautiously on this issue. Interviews in Abu Dhabi, September and October 1997.

205 Interviews in Abu Dhabi and Washington, D.C., September and October 1997.

206 Ibid.

CHAPTER 7

1 Declassified British Foreign Office records, FCO/8/960/1 (hereinafter referred to simply as FCO), October 30, 31, November 2, 3, 4, 9, 12, 1968, January 7, 1969. These records also show that British officials reported that King Faisal's adviser, Rashad Pharaon, said such a median line was consistent with Saudi thinking and that US officials told British officials that Saudi Arabia at that time hoped that the Shah could be persuaded to accept a median line leaving the Tunbs and Sirri to Iran and leaving Abu Musa to the Arabs. The British Political Resident in Bahrain, Sir Stewart Crawford, interpreted this to mean that King Faisal might attempt to persuade the Shah of this during their November 1968 summit. These

records do not provide any evidence that King Faisal actually made such an effort. Additional British records indicate that the idea of one Tunb going to Iran and one Tunb going to Ras al-Khaimah was mentioned to British officials by Saudi Chief of Intelligence Kamal Adham as early as May 1968. See FCO/8/56, May 1968. Prior to his December 1969 visit to Tehran, Shaikh Saqr asked British Political Agent Bullard for his reaction to the idea of an Iranian garrison on the Tunb closer to Iran while Saqr kept the Tunb closer to Ras al-Khaimah. Bullard answered that the Lesser Tunb to Iran and the Greater Tunb to Ras al-Khaimah would not be acceptable to Iran. See FCO/8/962, December 14, 1969.

2 FCO/8/1310, March 16, July 29, 1970; FCO/8/1319, August 23, 1970.
3 FCO/8/56, April 8, 1968; FCO/8/57, July 30, 1968. British Ambassador to Kuwait Geoffrey Arthur referred in April 1968 to "Shaikh Sa'ad" and "Shaikh Jabir al Ali." Shaikh Saad must refer to Defense Minister Shaikh Saad al Abdullah al Salem Al-Sabah. Shaikh Jabir al Ali must be a mistaken reference to Shaikh Jaber al Ahmad al Jaber Al-Sabah.
4 FCO/8/1310, July 23, 1970.
5 FCO/8/1319, September 12, 1970.
6 Asadollah Alam (Alinaghi Alikhani) *The Shah and I: The Confidential Diary of Iran's Royal Court, 1969-1977* (London: I.B. Tauris and Company, Ltd., 1991), 159-60.
7 FCO/8/1543, July 6, 1970.
8 A.L.P. Burdett (ed.) *Records of the Emirates, 1966-1971* (London: Archive Editions, 2002), vol. 6 (1971), 639.
9 Ibid., 644-5, 646-7.
10 Shahram Chubin and Sepehr Zabih, *The Foreign Relations of Iran* (Berkeley, CA: University of California Press, 1974), 228. Saudi Arabia made the suggestion that there be a joint garrison during an April 1970 visit to the Kingdom by Iranian Foreign Minister Zahedi, according to Saeed M. Badeeb, *Saudi-Iranian Relations: 1932-1982* (London: Centre for Arab and Iranian Studies, 1993), 120. Saudi Acting Foreign Minister Omar Al-Saqqaf may have made the suggestion. He did meet with Zahedi and the Shah in Tehran on April 11, 1970. See Chubin and Zabih, op. cit., 239 and Alam, op. cit., 144. Ras al-Khaimah had already considered agreeing to an Iranian garrison on the Tunbs in 1968. Later, an adviser to Ras al-Khaimah Shaikh Saqr, Tawfiq Abu Khader, speaking in the presence of Ras al-Khaimah's Crown Prince Khalid bin Saqr, told US State Department official Joseph Sisco on November 8, 1971 that "Ras al-Khaimah has no problem with presence of Iranian troops on islands so long as Ras al-Khaimah's sovereignty is acknowledged." See declassified US State Department document, November 8, 1971, filed at Politics, Trucial States-U.S./XR Politics 19, Trucial States/XR Politics 33/Persian Gulf. Sharjah's Shaikh Khalid ultimately agreed to an Iranian garrison on the northern half of Abu Musa in the November 1971 MoU.
11 FCO/8/1310, July 28, 1970.
12 FCO/8/1319, August 22, 1970. Earlier in the month, Kamal Adham and Rashad Pharaon told the British that they were prepared to consider Saudi participation in the garrisoning of Abu Musa and the Tunbs. See FCO/8/1310, August 8, 1970 and FCO/8/1319, August 20, 1970.
13 Declassified US Department of State documents, October 26, 1970, filed at Politics 33/Persian Gulf/Politics 1, Saud-US; November 3, 1970, filed at Politics 33/Persian Gulf/Politics 1, Iran-Saud; See also Badeeb, op. cit., 62.

14 Chubin and Zabih, *The Foreign Relations of Iran*, op. cit., 228. Nadav Safran, *Saudi Arabia: The Ceaseless Quest for Security* (Ithaca, NY: Cornell University Press, 1988), 236 says that in July 1973 Saudi Defense Minister Sultan ibn Abd Al-Aziz "revealed that Saudi Arabia had tried to arrange for Iran to lease the islands from their owners, but that the outcry of the radical Arab countries against Iran's demand to control the islands caused the Iranians to annex them instead." It seems from this quote that Saudi Arabia made this effort before the occupation, but it also seems reasonable that Saudi Arabia may have done so both before and after the occupation. A member of the Kuwaiti team attempting to mediate between Iran and the emirates recalled in a December 1998 interview that Kuwait may also have made the suggestion that Iran lease the islands. An adviser to Sharjah's Shaikh Khalid, Mustafa Zayn, on the eve of his April 1971 meetings with Iranian officials in Tehran, told the US Consul in Dhahran that the Shah could have a ninety-nine year lease to Abu Musa, and Zayn may have repeated this in Tehran. See declassified US Department of State document from the National Archives at College Park, Maryland, April 1971, filed at Politics, Iran-Trucial States. Ras al-Khaimah was also willing to consider a leasing arrangement, as noted for example by Khalid bin Mohammed al Qasimi, *The Three Islands Between Arab Sovereignty and Iranian Occupation* (Alexandria: Modern University Office, 1997), in Arabic, 136-8. (This author is not to be confused with Shaikh Khalid, the Ruler of Sharjah, who was assassinated in 1972, or with Khalid bin Saqr, the Crown Prince of Ras al-Khaimah.) A close adviser to Ras al-Khaimah Ruler Shaikh Saqr in 1971 said in an interview in December 1998 that Ras al-Khaimah considered leasing to be an acknowledgment of Ras al-Khaimah's sovereignty, but that they were not willing to make a 99-year arrangement. Shaikh Saqr told Sir William Luce in September 1970 that he had offered Iran an arrangement for up to fifty years and that Iran had rejected this. See FCO/8/1319. Husain Albaharna, *The Arabian Gulf States: Their Legal and Political Status and their International Problems* (Beirut: Librarie du Liban, 1974), 341 writes that on November 10, 1971 Iran's new Foreign Minister Khalatbari said that Iran "had rejected Arab suggestions that Abu Musa and the Tunbs should be leased to Iran when Britain left the area."

15 Ahmad Jalal Al-Tadmori, *The Three Arabian Islands: A Documentary Study* (Ras al-Khaimah: 2000), 94 quotes Sir William Luce in conversation with Ras al-Khaimah Ruler Shaikh Saqr.

16 FCO/8/1319, August 26, 1970.

17 FCO/8/1310, November 17, 1970. See also FCO 8/1297, Tel. No. 445, Wilton, Political Agency Kuwait to FCO, London, dated December 9, 1970 in which the Kuwaiti Foreign Minister is said to have stated that the grabbing of the islands by Iran was a possibility but it would be an outcome less damaging than one in which the regional states such as Kuwait and Saudi Arabia would seek a compromise formula before a federation had come into being.

18 FCO/8/1310, November 26, 1970. This document also shows that Kuwait's Ambassador in Tehran had discussed the islands with Zahedi and found him to be inflexible. Kamal Adham had earlier suggested this idea about no military forces on the islands to the British in July 1970. See FC0/8/1310, July 29, 1970.

19 See recollections of the Kuwaiti representative in the *Provisional Verbatim Record of the Sixteen Hundred and Tenth Meeting of the United Nations Security Council:*

Discussion and Record of the Security Council On Two Islands in the Arabian Gulf, December 9, 1971.

20 *Middle East Economic Survey (MEES)*, 15, no. 6, December 3, 1971. See also Abdullah Omran Taryam, *The Establishment of the United Arab Emirates: 1950-85* (London: Croom Helm Ltd., 1987), 170, 180-1 and Albaharna, op. cit., 342-5.

21 For the complete text of this memorandum, see *MEES*, vol. 15, no. 6, December 3, 1971. See also Tadmori, op. cit., 201-2, Frauke Heard-Bey, *From Trucial States to United Arab Emirates* (London: Longman Group, 1996), 365-6 for the excerpt, and Taryam, op. cit., 180 for the excerpt.

22 Interview with member of Luce's mediation team, London, October 1997 and declassified US Department of State document, September 28, 1971, filed at Politics 33/Persian Gulf. See also Chubin and Zabih, op. cit., 225-6.

23 See recollections of the Legal Adviser to Sharjah in the "Confidential Minutes of the Extraordinary Meeting of the Arab League to Discuss the Three Arab Islands of the United Arab Emirates," Cairo, December 6, 1971, in Arabic, courtesy of the Arab League's archives.

24 See recollections of the Legal Adviser to Sharjah in the "Confidential Minutes of the Extraordinary Meeting of the Arab League to Discuss the Subject of the Three Arab Islands of the United Arab Emirates," Cairo, December 6, 1971, in Arabic; *MEES*, December 3, 1971, 4, citing the Beirut daily *Al-Anwar*, November 30, 1971; Heard-Bey, op. cit., 496, also citing this issue of *Al-Anwar*, Taryam, op. cit., 180. The American attorney Northcutt Ely, who advised Shaikh Khalid at this time, said in his deposition at the ICJ in 1992 that Shaikh Khalid had written in advance to other Arab rulers saying that he intended to negotiate a MoU on Abu Musa, that the alternative was that the island would be taken by force and asking if the other rulers had any advice. Ely recollects that only two rulers answered, both supporting him, and that the others raised no objections. Ely's recollection may have been slightly imprecise. The memo shows a readiness to compromise, although the terms of the eventual MoU had not yet been devised. The memo was answered by four governments, not two. The Ruler of Sharjah also said in a December 8 interview with *An-Nahar* that Iraq did not answer his letter.

25 See interview with *Al-Anwar*, December 8, 1971.

26 See Shaikh Khalid press conference in *Al-Khaleej*, December 4, 1971; Shaikh Khalid interview in *Al-Anwar*, December 8, 1971. See also Mohammed Al Roken, "Historical and Legal Dimensions of the United Arab Emirates-Iran Dispute Over Three Gulf Islands," in Edmund Ghareeb and Ibrahim Al Abed (eds.) *Perspectives on the United Arab Emirates* (London: Trident Press Ltd., 1997), 152 for the English translation of an excerpt from the interview in *Al-Anwar*. See also J.B. Kelly, *Arabia, the Gulf, and the West* (USA: Basic Books, 1980), 93 and Taryam, op. cit., 182-3.

27 *Records of the Emirates, 1966-1971*, vol. 6 (1971), 498.

28 Declassified US Department of State documents, September 21, 28, November 2, 1971, filed at Politics 33/Persian Gulf.

29 Shaikh Khalid bin Mohammed Al-Qasimi, *The Three Islands Between Arab Sovereignty and Iranian Occupation*, in Arabic, op. cit., 138-43.

30 Tadmori, op. cit., 115-6; *Al-Khaleej*, November 1, 1971. Taryam refers to Shaikh Saqr's rejection of Luce's proposals on October 30 on page 181. He also presents a set of Luce's proposals and indicates that after rejecting these proposals, Shaikh

Saqr was accused in the Kuwaiti press of having agreed to sell the Tunbs to Iran, prompting Kuwait to demand an explanation, and prompting Ras al-Khaimah's Crown Prince Khalid bin Saqr to go to Kuwait, where he denied the rumors. However, this set of proposals and sequence of events took place during the summer of 1971, not at the end of October 1971. *Al-Khaleej*, which was licensed in Sharjah, but published in Kuwait, began reporting stories on the negotiations regarding the islands in early June 1971. Taryam, op. cit., 182 says that "Ras al-Khaimah faced less pressure [than Sharjah] because first, its ruler rejected negotiations in principle and, second, Iran itself was not persistent in its claims, partly because it was convinced that its claim to the two islands belonging to Ras al-Khaimah had a legitimate basis, and partly because the islands themselves had relatively fewer inhabitants." Ras al-Khaimah only rejected negotiations on sovereignty, not negotiations on leasing. Iran was very persistent in its claims to the Tunbs. Kelly, op. cit., 93 writes that "Muhammad Reza Shah refused to treat with Ras al-Khaimah over the Tunbs, since the islands, he maintained, were Persia's by incontrovertible right." In fact, the Shah did offer financial compensation to Ras al-Khaimah in exchange for sovereignty over the islands.

31 Tadmori, op. cit., 204.

32 Taryam, op. cit., 182.

33 *Al-Khaleej*, November 8, 1971.

34 See recollections of the Iraqi representative in the "Confidential Minutes of the Extraordinary Meeting of the Arab League to Discuss the Subject of the Three Arab Islands of the United Arab Emirates," Cairo, December 7, 1971, in Arabic. The Iraqi representative referred to this meeting as taking place in September, but this seems to be a simple case of him misspeaking. There are no other references to a September meeting and numerous references to the November meeting. See for example Khalid bin Mohammed Al-Qasimi, *The Three Islands Between Arab Sovereignty and Iranian Occupation*, in Arabic, op. cit., 111-3, 150.

35 See recollections of the Assistant Secretary General in the "Confidential Minutes of the Extraordinary Meeting of the Arab League to Discuss the Three Arab Islands of the United Arab Emirates," Cairo, December 6, 1971, in Arabic.

36 Tadmori, op. cit., 180-2.

37 See recollections of the Assistant Secretary General in the "Confidential Minutes of the Extraordinary Meeting of the Arab League to Discuss the Three Arab Islands of the United Arab Emirates," Cairo, December 6, 1971, in Arabic. See also Tadmori, op. cit., 189-91.

38 See the recollections of the Tunisian representative in the "Confidential Minutes of the Extraordinary Meeting," Cairo, December 7, 1971, in Arabic.

39 Taryam, op. cit., 181-2.

40 Ibid., 183.

41 Ruhollah K. Ramazani, *The Persian Gulf: Iran's Role* (Charlottesville, VA: University Press of Virginia, 1972), 67 and 140, provides excerpts from Shaikh Khalid's public announcement of the MoU.

42 "Memorandum Respecting the Claim of Iran of its Ownership of Abu Musa Island which Belongs to Sharjah," the Arab League Secretariat General Legal Department, November 28, 1971, in Arabic. Albaharna, op. cit., 347 indicates that there were two memoranda, dates these memoranda December 28, 1971, and argues that the memoranda questioned the legal validity of the MoU on Abu Musa

on the basis that it had been obtained by pressure and threat. This argument is not contained in the November 28 memorandum, which was written prior to the MoU, although this argument is contained in an undated 'Complementary Memorandum' released later.

43 Tadmori, op. cit., 182-4.

44 Ibid., 116-7.

45 Vinson and Elkins, *Territorial Sovereignty over the Tunb Islands* (Unpublished report for the Ruler of Ras al-Khaimah, 1980), 3.4 cites document 3.2 as having been written on November 30, 1971. A translation of this letter provided by the Ras al-Khaimah Ruler's Court is, however, dated November 26, 1971. The text makes it clear that this letter was written prior to Iran's forcible occupation of the islands. Libya's Premier and Vice-Chairman of the Revolutionary Command Council, Major Abd-al Salam Jaloud, later stated that Libya had intended to deploy Libyan airborne forces on the Tunbs and Abu Musa by November 28 in order to defend the islands. Libya had asked for and received permission from Iraq to land these forces at Basra on their way to the islands, but called its action off due to the lack of adequate staging bases while the area was still under British control. See *Arab Report and Record*, December 1-15, 1971, 623. On the subject of the letter to U Thant, Vinson and Elkins, op. cit., 3.5 indicate that this letter was written after Iran's forcible occupation of the Tunbs, but the text of the letter, found in document 3.3. makes it clear that it was written prior to the occupation.

46 Vinson and Elkins, op. cit., 3.4–3.5 and document 3.3 note in particular that this cable was sent to Iraq. Tadmori, op. cit., 137-8 makes it clear that it was sent to all Arab leaders.

47 Tadmori, op. cit., 138-9.

48 Ibid., 141; Taryam, op. cit., 184; interview, Ras al-Khaimah Ruler's Court, February 1, 1999.

49 Vinson and Elkins, op. cit., 3.5. and document 3.3; Tadmori, op. cit., 139-40.

50 Tadmori, op. cit., 140.

51 "Reports Respecting the Iranian Occupation of Abu Musa, Tonb Al Kubra, and Tonb Al Sughra," Directorate-General of Political Affairs of the Arab League, Cairo, December 1 through 5, 1971, in Arabic; Tadmori, op. cit., 127-33, 168-9; Heard-Bey, op. cit., 366.

52 "Reports Respecting the Iranian Occupation of Abu Musa, Tonb Al Kubra, and Tonb Al Sughra," Tadmori, op. cit., 169-77.

53 "Reports Respecting the Iranian Occupation of Abu Musa, Tonb Al Kubra, and Tonb Al Sughra," Tadmori, op. cit., 169-77, Albaharna, op. cit., 346, citing only the Third and Fourth Reports of the Political Department of the Arab League on December 2, 1971, claims that "all" Arab countries "condemned" Iran, but not all Arab states used this language in their private and public comments. See also *Arab Report and Record*, December 1-15, 1971, 627.

54 "Reports Respecting the Iranian Occupation of Abu Musa, Tonb Al Kubra, and Tonb Al Sughra," Tadmori, 169-77. Taryam, op. cit., 186 claims that Egypt, Jordan and Lebanon issued "denunciations," but they did not actually use this language in their remarks. See also *Arab Report and Record*, December 1-15, 1971, 627.

55 "Reports Respecting the Iranian Occupation of Abu Musa, Tonb Al Kubra and Tonb Al Sughra," Tadmori, op. cit., 170-7; Albaharna, op. cit., 346. Part of the Iraqi statement can be found in *MEES* XV, no. 6 (December 3, 1971). Part of the

Libyan statement can be found in *MEES*, Supplement to vol. XV, no. 7 (December 10, 1971), 1.

56 Tadmori, op. cit., 184-9. See also the report of the Assistant Secretary General in the "Confidential Minutes of the Extraordinary Meeting of the Arab League to Discuss the Subject of the Three Arab Islands of the United Arab Emirates," Cairo, December 6, 1971 and December 7, 1971, in Arabic. Vinson and Elkins, op. cit., document 3.8 contains an account of this meeting by the Ruler of Ras al-Khaimah in his April 1976 letter to Ahmad Al-Suwaidi. This account appears to suggest that the Arab League foreign ministers instructed the Secretary General to make these contacts and arguments after the occupation, but they instructed him to do so before the occupation.

57 See report of the Assistant Secretary General in the "Confidential Minutes of the Extraordinary Meeting of the Arab League to Discuss the Subject of the Three Arab Islands of the United Arab Emirates," Cairo, December 6, 1971 and December 7, 1971 in Arabic.

58 Tadmori, op. cit., 190-2. See also report of the Assistant Secretary General in the "Confidential Minutes of the Extraordinary Meeting of the Arab League to Discuss the Subject of the Three Arab Islands of the United Arab Emirates," Cairo, December 6, 1971 and December 7, 1971, in Arabic. Alyafi told Iran's Ambassador in Cairo of the Arab states' "condemnation of the Iranian aggression and denunciation of that action," noting again that he was "surprised and astonished at the invasion of those islands," calling upon Iran to withdraw from the islands, and saying that the Arab League would work with Iran to create the atmosphere for a peaceful agreement.

59 "Confidential Minutes of the Extraordinary Meeting of the Arab League to Discuss the Subject of the Three Arab Islands of the United Arab Emirates," December 6, 1971 in Arabic.

60 "Complementary Memorandum Respecting the Extent of Legality of Iran's Occupation of the Arab Islands at the Entrance of the Arab Gulf," Directorate General of Legal Affairs of the Arab League, Cairo, undated, in Arabic. See also Albaharna, op. cit., 347, who refers inaccurately to two memoranda dated December 28, 1971.

61 "Confidential Minutes of the Extraordinary Meeting of the Arab League to Discuss the Subject of the Three Arab Islands of the United Arab Emirates," Cairo, December 6, 1971, in Arabic; *MEES* XV, no. 7, December 10, 1971, 10 provides an incomplete but accurate list of conditions.

62 "Confidential Minutes of the Extraordinary Meeting of the Arab League to Discuss the Subject of the Three Arab Islands of the United Arab Emirates," Cairo, December 6, 1971, in Arabic. Albaharna, op. cit., 342-3; Tadmori, op. cit., 144-7, 192 indicates that Saif Saeed Ghabbash, who would later become UAE Minister of State for Foreign Affairs, spoke on behalf of Ras al-Khaimah and provides an English translation. He indicates on 147-8 that Shaikh Abdul Aziz bin Hameed Al-Qasimi, the Director of the Ras al-Khaimah Ruler's Court, delivered a letter for an expected meeting of Arab League foreign ministers. However, the Arab League records themselves indicate that it was Shaikh Abdul Aziz who spoke on behalf of Ras al-Khaimah. It appears from the transcript of the meeting, from Albaharna's citations, and from the files of the Ras al-Khaimah Ruler's Court that Ras al-Khaimah did not submit its historical documents to the Arab League until the December 6, 1971 meeting. Thus, the "Complementary

Memorandum" prepared by the Arab League prior to this December 6 meeting did not benefit from these documents. Indeed, a close reading of this "Complementary Memorandum" indicates that this was the case. These and many other relevant documents may be found in Vinson and Elkins, op. cit.

63 "Confidential Minutes of the Extraordinary Meeting of the Arab League to Discuss the Subject of the Three Arab Islands of the United Arab Emirates," Cairo, December 7, 1971, in Arabic. Muhammad Morsy Abdullah, *The United Arab Emirates: A Modern History* (UK: Hurtwood Press Limited, 1994) writes that Egypt and Saudi Arabia "condemned" the Iranian behavior at the Arab League. It is more accurate to say that they allowed a resolution denouncing the occupation to pass. Morsy Abdullah cites Chubin and Zabih, op. cit., 228-31, but these authors do not actually write that Egypt and Saudi Arabia "condemned" Iran. They do write about Saudi Arabia on page 229 that "its silence by no means indicated its consent" to the occupation. In fact, however, Saudi Arabia was by no means "silent" during the Arab League deliberations. George Lenczowski, *The Middle East in World Affairs* (Ithaca, NY: Cornell University Press, 1980), 730 notes the moderating role played by Egypt.

64 Text of Arab League Council Resolution 2865, December 7, 1971, Arab League archives, in Arabic; Tadmori, op. cit., 193. Taryam, op. cit., 188-9 notes that the Secretary General was instructed to initiate communications; Ramazani, op. cit. suggests inaccurately that the resolution called upon Iran to evacuate the islands. See Tadmori, op. cit., 147-8 for a written statement submitted by Ras al-Khaimah for consideration by the proposed meeting of the Arab League foreign ministers.

65 "Confidential Minutes of the Extraordinary Meeting of the Arab League to Discuss the Three Arab Islands of the United Arab Emirates," Cairo, December 7, 1971 in Arabic; Tadmori, op. cit., 194. A Kuwaiti official involved in Kuwait's mediation efforts said in a December 1998 interview that Kuwait thought that it had fulfilled its duty in discussions with Iran and did not think it could make progress in further discussions. It should also be noted that Kuwait was facing domestic calls to break relations with Iran and Kuwait had just refused to accept the credentials of the new Iranian Ambassador.

66 *MEES*, Supplement to vol. XV, no. 7, December 10, 1971, 1-2; *Arab Report and Record*, December 1-15, 1971, 628; Taryam, op. cit., 186.

67 For the text of the letter to the Security Council, see *Records of the Emirates, 1966-1971* vol. 6 (1971), 583. All the statements from the debate may be found in the *Provisional Verbatim Record of the Sixteen Hundred and Tenth Meeting of the United Nations Security Council: Discussion and Record of the Security Council On Two Islands in the Arabian Gulf*, December 9, 1971. See also Albaharna, op. cit., 340-1 and 346, for excerpts. Tadmori, op. cit., 196-7 provides a brief summary.

68 Ibid.

69 Ibid.

70 Ibid.

71 Ibid.

72 Ibid.

73 Ibid.

74 *Al-Hawadith*, December 23, 1971; Tadmori, op. cit., 177-9.

75 Tadmori, op. cit., 152; *Records of the Emirates, 1966-1971*, vol. 6 (1971), 249.

76 Khalid bin Mohammed Al-Qasimi, *The Three Islands Between Arab Sovereignty and Iranian Occupation*, in Arabic, op. cit., 134-5.

77 *MEES* XV, no. 8, December 17, 1971, 5-6. For a summary of the Kuwaiti parliamentary debate, see *Records of the Emirates, 1966-1971*, vol. 6 (1971), 573-5.

78 Taryam, op. cit., 189. The Assistant Secretary-General's characterization of Ras al-Khaimah's opinions may have been an accurate report of those opinions at the end of his visit, but during his visit Shaikh Saqr had reportedly expressed some different opinions. In a statement published in the December 23, 1971 issue of the Kuwaiti weekly *Al-Hadaf*, during the tour of the League's Assistant Secretary General, Shaikh Saqr of Ras al-Khaimah said that he intended to ask the Arab League to provide a military force to free the Tunbs and Abu Musa from Iran's occupation and that "I might conclude a bilateral agreement with an Arab state in this respect." The Lebanese newspaper *Al-Hawadith* also reported on December 23, 1971 that Ras al-Khaimah had agreed to Libyan Major Jaloud's proposal to organize commando groups to disturb Iran's presence on the Tunbs. Certainly, Shaikh Saqr would not have received a positive response from the Arab League and Libya's proposal may not have been reliable. Thus, Shaikh Saqr may have abandoned any hope for the use of force. Shaikh Saqr was also quoted in *Al-Hawadith* as saying that "I have never thought of compromise solutions. If we are unable to fight now, we must not give our enemies official recognition of their right to our land and the land of our forefathers." The Ras al-Khaimah Ruler's Court argued in an April 1998 interview that they were not willing to lease the Tunbs after the Iranian occupation. However, Ras al-Khaimah had been willing to lease the islands from 1968 through 1971, believing that this would constitute Iranian recognition of Ras al-Khaimah sovereignty, and thus Shaikh Saqr would not have thought of leasing as a compromise solution. Tadmori, op. cit., 166-7 has written that Shaikh Saqr rejected an offer of compensation to the inhabitants of the Tunbs from the Shah.

79 Indeed, Saudi Arabia's moderate response had made it a reluctant but potential mediator, while Kuwait's criticism of Iran, its refusal to accept the credentials of the new Iranian Ambassador, and the parliamentary and public outcry had no doubt ended its value as a mediator.

80 Tadmori, op. cit., 194; Shaikh Khalid, op. cit., 154.

81 Vinson and Elkins, op. cit., 3.6. and documents 3.5 and 3.6.; Tadmori, op. cit., 194-5; *Arab Report and Record*, January 1-15, 1972, 17; "Confidential Minutes of the Extraordinary Meeting of the Arab League to Discuss the Three Arab Islands of the United Arab Emirates," Cairo, December 7, 1971, in Arabic; Text of Arab League Resolution 2865, December 7, 1971, Arab League archives, in Arabic. Shaikh Khalid, op. cit., 154 that Tunisia and Morocco did not initially respond to appeals from the Secretary General.

82 *Arab Report and Record*, December 16-31, 1971, 647; Lenczowski, op. cit., 308-10.

83 The signatories were Algeria, Bahrain, Egypt, Iraq, Kuwait, Lebanon, Libya, Morocco, Oman, the People's Democratic Republic of Yemen, Sudan, Syrian Arab Republic, Tunisia, United Arab Emirates and Yemen. Text of UN Document S/10740, in the original English, from the Arab League archives; Vinson and Elkins, op. cit., 3.6.; Ramazani, op. cit., 75; Chubin and Zabih, op. cit., 231.

84 Ali Humaidan, "From the Shah's Empire to the Islamic Republic: The UAE, Iran and the Three Islands," Part III of a six-part series in *Al-Ittihad*, June 6, 1997, in Arabic. He indicates that the letter was signed by only fourteen states.

85 Declassified US State Department documents, September 2, 1972, filed at Politics, Saud/XR Politics, Iran-Saud; January 9, 1973, filed at Politics 1, Iran.

86 Interview with the Ruler of Ras al-Khaimah, March 1998. In early January 1973, following a trip to Iran, Saudi Arabia's Acting Foreign Minister Saqqaf told US Ambassador Thacher that "he had been quite frank reiterating Saudi concern with Iranian occupation of Arab islands but both sides had understood this problem was not to come in [the] way of cooperation in more important matters." See declassified US Department of State document, January 8, 1973, filed at Politics, Iran-Saud/XR Politics, Saud-UAE.

87 Declassified US Department of State document, August 3, 1973, filed at Politics, Iran-Saud/XR Politics 32-6/Persian Gulf.

88 The Egyptian forces soon withdrew, along with the Syrian forces, not long after the United Arab Republic split into its component parts of Egypt and Syria.

89 William Quandt, *Saudi Arabia in the 1980s: Foreign Policy, Security, and Oil* (Washington, DC: The Brookings Institution, 1981), 38; Lenczowski, op. cit., 604, 667, 747; Kelly, op. cit., 277, 282-4; Safran, op. cit., 138.

90 Ali Mohammed Khalifa, *The United Arab Emirates: Unity in Fragmentation* (Boulder, CO: Westview Press, 1979), 144; Joseph Twinam, *The Gulf, Cooperation and the Council: An American Perspective* (Washington, DC: The Middle East Policy Council, 1992), 9-10; interview with former US Ambassador to the UAE, Washington, DC, January 1998.

91 Kelly, op. cit., 134-8, 141-9, 158; Khalifa, op. cit., 164-9; Lenczowski, op. cit., 605-7; F. Gregory Gause, III, *Saudi-Yemeni Relations: Domestic Structures and Foreign Influence* (New York, NY: Columbia University Press, 1990), 112-4.

92 Abdullah, op. cit., 278; Badeeb, op. cit., 129.

93 Lenczowski, op. cit., 605-7, 730. Safran, op. cit., 126.

94 Declassified US State Department document, December 4, 1971, filed at Politics 16 UAE/XR Politics 32-6/Persian Gulf/Politics 33/Persian Gulf.

95 Abdullah, op. cit., 280-1; Badeeb, op. cit., 58, 119-20, 121-2; Lenczowski, op. cit., 604 and 671.

96 Badeeb, op. cit., 63-4; Lenczowski, op. cit., 607.

97 Taryam, op. cit., 93-4; Khalifa, op. cit., 10, 142-3; Twinam, op. cit., 68; Abdullah, op. cit., 280; Quandt, op. cit., 23-4; interview with member of Luce's mediating team, London, October 1997.

98 Chubin and Zabih, op. cit., 216, cite the *New York Times*, May 16, 1968.

99 Kelly, op. cit., 59, 74-5, 210.

100 Khalifa, op. cit., 10, 142-3, 174; Lenczowski, op. cit., 604, 680, 785; Kelly, op. cit., 210; *Arab Report and Record*, February 16-29, 1972, 96, April 16-30, 1972, 218 and July 16-31, 1974, 307; Richard Schofield, "Boundaries, Territorial Disputes and the GCC States," in David E. Long and Christian Koch (eds.) *Gulf Security in the Twenty-First Century* (Abu Dhabi: The Emirates Center for Strategic Studies and Research, 1997), 139, 144, 151-2. It should be briefly noted here that Saudi Arabia wanted influence over any federation in order to satisfy its territorial claims against Abu Dhabi, to ensure that any federation would be a bulwark against radicalism, and to maintain its traditional influence in the area. When Bahrain and Qatar chose independence rather than federation, Saudi hopes

of exercising influence over a nine-member federation through these two traditional clients were dashed and it became clear that Abu Dhabi would dominate a federation of only six or seven. Thus, Saudi Arabia worked to strengthen its traditional relations with the other individual emirates in order to preserve Saudi Arabia's patterns of influence with these emirates as well as pressuring Abu Dhabi, even when not recognizing or establishing diplomatic relations with the federation. This was true in the case of Ras al-Khaimah, even though Saudi Arabia was not heeding Ras al-Khaimah's call for support over the islands. Saudi Arabia successfully pressured the new UAE to suspend its February 1972 agreement to establish diplomatic relations with the Soviet Union because Saudi Arabia feared that a Soviet diplomatic presence would spread radicalism to the UAE and the Gulf. Taryam, op. cit., 216, 219-1, Lenczowski, op. cit., 680 and an interview with a member of Luce's mediating team, London, October 1997.

101 Lenczowski, op. cit., 671-3, 675-6, 683-5; Joseph H. Kechichian, *Oman and the World: The Emergence of an Independent Foreign Policy* (Santa Monica, CA: The Rand Corporation, 1995), 8-11, 48, 99-100, 108.

102 Chubin and Zabih, op. cit., 230-1. These authors note that the Ruler of Qatar was deposed during a February 1972 vacation in Iran and that informed sources at the time believed that this vacation, at a time of Arab resentment over Iran's behavior regarding the islands, "may have been the direct cause of the coup." However, Lenczowski, op. cit., 674 points out that this Ruler had a history of long vacations and of neglecting affairs of state, and that this may have been the more general reason for the coup. It should also be pointed out that under the new Ruler, Qatar did not sign the July 17, 1972 letter affirming that the islands were an integral part of the UAE and of the Arab world, whereas Bahrain and Oman did sign, an indication that this issue may not have been so important as to explain the coup.

103 Kechichian, op. cit., 8.

104 For discussions about these border disputes, see Abdullah, op. cit., 212-3 and chapter 5, and Kechichian, op. cit, 100.

105 Lenczowski, op. cit., 671-6; Kechichian, op. cit., 70-3.

106 Lenczowski, op. cit., 666-9.

107 Chubin and Zabih, op. cit., 230.

108 Khalifa, op. cit., 162.

109 Ibid., 152; *Provisional Verbatim Record of the Sixteen Hundred and Tenth Meeting of the UN Security Council*; December 1998 interview with Abdullah Bishara, who was the private secretary to Kuwait's foreign minister during Kuwait's diplomatic efforts regarding Bahrain, Abu Musa and the Tunbs and who served as Kuwait's representative at the December 9, 1971 Security Council discussion on Abu Musa and the Tunbs.

110 Abdullah, op. cit., 277-8, 281. Saudi Arabia and Jordan, as well as Kuwait, Bahrain, Qatar and Oman, also welcomed the new Iranian position on Israel, and this may also have influenced their stance on the islands.

111 Interview with member of the Kuwaiti team mediating between the emirates and Iran, Abu Dhabi, December 8, 1998. Indeed, in 1974, in the aftermath of the October 1973 war with Israel, Egypt would receive $1 billion in economic assistance from Iran. See Lenczowski, op. cit., 219.

112 Chubin and Zabih, op. cit., 167-8, 225; Ramazani, op. cit., 421-23; Lenczowski, op. cit., 730.

113 Lenczowski, op. cit., 564.

114 Ali Humaidan, "From the Shah's Empire to the Islamic Republic: The UAE, Iran and the Three Islands," Part III, *Al-Ittihad,* June 6, 1997, in Arabic.

115 Anwar Gargash, "Iran, the GCC States, and the UAE: Prospects and Challenges in the Coming Decade," in Jamal S. Al-Suwaidi (ed.) *Iran and the Gulf: A Search for Stability* (Abu Dhabi: The Emirates Center for Strategic Studies and Research, 1996), 152 and Khalifa, op. cit., 145-7.

116 Gargash, op. cit., 152.

117 *Al-Wahdah,* April 7, 1975.

118 *Al-Ittihad,* September 22, 1976 and October 15, 1976; Taryam, op. cit., 239-48; *Arab Report and Record,* 1976, 642.

119 Quandt, op. cit., 23-4.

120 As Keith McLachlan has written, "The Iraqi government, exhausted by its protracted and unsuccessful war in Kurdistan, was forced to concede Iranian claims over the Shatt al-Arab boundary in the Algiers Agreement. Iraqis, however, saw the agreement as a betrayal in which the Iranians had stolen sovereign Iraqi rights…The government in Baghdad never abandoned its determination eventually to redress the situation over the control over the Shatt al-Arab." See Keith McLachlan, "Territoriality and the Iran-Iraq war," in Keith McLachlan (ed.) *The Boundaries of Modern Iran* (London: University College London Press, 1994), 60.

121 Jasim M. Abdulghani, *Iraq and Iran: The Years of Crisis* (Baltimore, MD: The Johns Hopkins University Press, 1984), 158.

122 *Al-Azminah Al-Arabiah,* October 8, 1980, 4-6.

123 For succinct discussions about the distinctions between "radical" and "conservative" Arab states in the 1960s and 1970s, see for example Michael Hudson, *Arab Politics: The Search for Legitimacy* (New Haven, NJ: Yale University Press, 1977), 24-30; and Lenczowski, *The Middle East in World Affairs,* op. cit., chapter 19.

CHAPTER 8

1   Keith McLachlan (ed.), *The Boundaries of Modern Iran* (London: University College London Press, 1994), 61-2.

2   *Al-Ittihad,* April 7, 1980; Jasim M. Abdulghani, *Iraq and Iran: The Years of Crisis* (Baltimore, MD: The Johns Hopkins University Press, 1984), 199; Dilip Hiro, *The Longest War: The Iran-Iraq Military Conflict* (London: Paladin Grafton Books, 1990), 35.

3   Abdulghani, op. cit., 191-2; Qotbzadeh quoted by Dr. Ali Humaidan, "From the Shah's Empire to the Islamic Republic: The UAE, Iran and the Three Islands," Part IV, *Al-Ittihad,* July 13, 1997.

4   *Al-Ittihad,* June 12, 1980.

5   Martin S. Navias and E.R. Hooton, *Tanker Wars: The Assault On Merchant Shipping During The Iran-Iraq Crisis, 1980-1988* (London: I.B. Tauris and Company Ltd., 1996), 21, 38-39; Abdulghani, op. cit., 206.

6   Dilip Hiro argues that the Iraqis were planning to occupy the islands from bases in Oman and that the British and Americans dissuaded Oman while the Saudis dissuaded Iraq. Former Deputy Assistant Secretary of the US Department of Defense James Noyes reports this as well. Thus, despite Saudi Arabia's unequivocal

support for Iraq in the war and despite Saudi support for the UAE demand to recover the islands, even the Saudis did not support the use of force to recover the islands. See the *Financial Times*, October 2, 1980; the *Daily Telegraph*, October 3, 1980; Vinson and Elkins, *Territorial Sovereignty Over the Tunb Islands* (Houston: unpublished study for the Ruler of Ras al-Khaimah, 1980), 3.7 and 3.8; Hiro, op. cit., 40-70, especially 77-8; James Noyes, *The Clouded Lens: Persian Gulf Security and U.S. Policy* (Stanford, CA: Hoover Institution Press, 1982), 114. See also R.K. Ramazani, *Revolutionary Iran: Challenge and Response in the Middle East* (Baltimore, MD: The Johns Hopkins University Press, 1986), 102. Anthony H. Cordesman and Abraham R. Wagner, *The Lessons of Modern War, Volume II: The Iran-Iraq War* (Boulder, CO: Westview Press, 1990), 38 write that "Experts dispute the extent to which Oman and the UAE prepared at the start of the war to support an Iraqi invasion of the Tunb Islands in the Straits of Hormuz and the Abu Musas [*sic*]...Similarly, it is far from clear that any element of the UAE had the slightest desire to become involved in a war over any of the islands in the Gulf. Nevertheless, some authorities on the Gulf feel that Oman and Abu Dhabi did agree to allow such Iraqi action and were stopped from granting such support only after quiet British intervention." This reference to "the Abu Musas" [*sic*] is unfortunate, because there is only one island of Abu Musa. This passage also contains the very seriously inaccurate statement that "It is important to note that the Shah did not seize the islands in the Straits of Hormuz when the British left; they had been in Iranian hands for years [*sic*]."

7   *Al-Ittihad*, October 2, 1980; *BBC Survey of World Broadcasting*, ME/6541/A October 4, 5 and 6, 1980; Hiro, op. cit., 38.

8   *Chronicle of Progress: Twenty-Five Years of Progress in the United Arab Emirates* (London: Trident Press Ltd., 1996), 164. There were rumors that the UAE's official silence on the islands and its opposition to the use of force to regain the islands during these early months of the war provoked Ras al-Khaimah in November to threaten to secede from the federation unless the UAE took a strong stand. However, the Ruler of Ras al-Khaimah acknowledged at the time that the UAE federal government had called for the return of the islands, as indeed it had in August 1980, and as it would again in December 1980. Ras al-Khaimah's Crown Prince Khalid also said in a March 21, 1999 interview that Iraq proposed to Ras al-Khaimah that it was now time to take the islands back by force, but that Ras al-Khaimah deferred to and agreed with the UAE policy of opposing this. The Ruler's Court also asserted in an April 1999 interview that Ras al-Khaimah never threatened to secede from the UAE.

9   Mohamed Al Roken, "Historical and Legal Dimensions of the United Arab Emirates-Iran Dispute Over Three Gulf Islands" and William Rugh, "UAE Foreign Policy" in Edmund Ghareeb and Ibrahim Al Abed (eds) *Perspectives on the United Arab Emirates* (London: Trident Press Ltd., 1997), 152 and 165; Joseph Twinam, *The Gulf, Cooperation and the Council: An American Perspective* (Washington, DC: The Middle East Policy Council, 1992), 8-9, 10, 132-3; Martin S. Navias and E.R. Hooton, *Tanker Wars: The Assault on Merchant Shipping During the Iran-Iraq Crisis, 1980-1988* (London: I.B. Tauris and Company Ltd., 1996), 40-1.

10   Abdulghani, op. cit., 193-200; Saeed M. Badeeb, *Saudi-Iranian Relations: 1932-1982* (London: Centre for Arab and Iranian Studies, 1993), 90-2, 113, 125-6, 131-2; William Quandt, *Saudi Arabia in the 1980s: Foreign Policy, Security and Oil*

(Washington, DC: The Brookings Institution, 1981), 39-40; Twinam, op. cit., 132-3; Hiro, op. cit., 75-7.

11 Anthony H. Cordesman, *Bahrain, Oman, Qatar, and the UAE: Challenges of Security* (Boulder, CO: Westview Press, 1997), 298-9.

12 Anwar Gargash, "Iran, the GCC States, and the UAE: Prospects and Challenges in the Coming Decade" in Jamal S. Al-Suwaidi (ed.), *Iran and the Gulf: A Search for Stability* (Abu Dhabi: The Emirates Center for Strategic Studies and Research, 1996), 151.

13 Ibid., 143.

14 Hameed, op. cit., 85.

15 *Middle East Economic Digest (MEED)* 26, no. 24, June 11, 1982, 32; *Al-Ittihad*, June 9, 1982.

16 McLachlan, op. cit., 65.

17 Tutunji in Ghareeb and Abed, op. cit., 179.

18 Cordesman and Wagner, op. cit., 174; Navias and Hooton, op. cit., 56-64.

19 Twinam, op. cit., 135-7; Twinam cites Ramazani, *The GCC*, op. cit., chapter five, for a discussion of GCC mediation efforts; Tutunji, op. cit., 186.

20 Twinam, op. cit., 135-7; see Navias and Hooton, op. cit., 112-5, 121, 132-8, 151-6 for a discussion of the escalation of the tanker war in 1986 and 1987.

21 Navias and Hooton, op. cit., 111-5, 121; Cordesman and Wagner, op. cit., 230-1, 334.

22 Navias and Hooton, op. cit., 151-2; Cordesman and Wagner, op. cit., 285-8, 300, 334.

23 David L. Mack, "In A Tough Neighborhood," *Middle East Insight*, Special UAE Issue, vol. XII, no. 6 (September-December 1996), 34. Mack was US Ambassador to the UAE during these years. Cordesman and Wagner, op. cit., 171, write that the UAE allowed E3A airborne warning and control aircraft (AWACS) to overfly UAE territory. Navias and Hooton, op. cit., 174 write that the UAE denied permission for E3A overflights in the summer of 1988.

24 Tutunji, op. cit., 177, 179-83; Twinam, op. cit., 140-2.

25 Tutunji, op. cit., 190-1; Twinam, op. cit., 141. The Arab summit also authorized the resumption of relations with Egypt, and the GCC states did so as a means of restoring the Egyptian counterweight in the Gulf.

26 To be sure, the GCC states were not convinced that that they could or should count on a continuing Egyptian and Syrian military presence in Saudi Arabia and Kuwait. Indeed, Egypt withdrew its 38,000-man army from the Gulf theatre in May 1992 and Syria withdrew its troops in June 1992, due in part to these GCC reservations.

27 Twinam, op. cit., 177-82, 228-33; Gargash, op. cit., 142.

28 Gargash, op. cit., 139, 141-2.

29 Rugh, op. cit., 166-7.

30 Twinam, op. cit., 182-5; Gargash, op. cit., 139, 142-3. Iran also condemned Iraq, remained neutral during Desert Shield and Desert Storm, opposed the partition of Iraq and did not take undue advantage of the Shi'a uprising in southern Iraq in the aftermath of the war. Iran generally adhered to some aspects of the UN embargo against Iraq, although it also condemned the GCC for welcoming Western military powers into the Gulf during and after the war.

31 For the full text, see *Closing Statements of the Sessions of the Supreme Council: Sessions 1-18* (Riyadh: The Secretariat General of The Cooperation Council for the Arab States of the Gulf, 1998), 108; see also Foreign Broadcasting Information Service (FBIS)-NES-90-248, December 26, 1990, 13; see also Twinam, op. cit., 184. *Closing Statements* is an official GCC collection of all of the Supreme Council's Closing Statements from 1981 to 1998. *FBIS* is another source for all of these statements.

32 Gargash, op. cit., 145; Saleh Al-Mani, "The Ideological Dimension in Saudi-Iranian Relations" in Al-Suwaidi, op. cit., 169-70 and Twinam, op. cit., 222.

33 Twinam, op. cit., 222-3. See *Closing Statements of the Sessions of the Supreme Council*, op. cit., 124 for the full text of the GCC summit's closing statement in 1991.

34 *The United Arab Emirates Yearbook 1996* (London: Trident Press, 1996), 46.

35 Khalid bin Mohammed Al-Qasimi, *The Three Islands Between Arab Sovereignty and Iranian Occupation*, 247 cites *Al-Khaleej*, September 1, 1992.

36 For the text, see Shaikh Khalid, op. cit., 248-9 and *Al-Khaleej*, September 10, 1992.

37 For the text, see Shaikh Khalid, op. cit., 259 and Ahmad Jalal Tadmori, *The Three Arabian Islands: A Documentary Study* (Ras-al-Khaimah: 2000), 255-6. Rugh, op. cit., 169 and 176 cites the Manama Wakh News Agency, September 11, 1992.

38 For the text of the Arab League resolution, see Tutunji in Ghareeb and al Abed, op. cit., 189-90.

39 *New York Times*, September 20, 1992, p. A10.

40 Shaikh Khalid, op. cit., 260 cites *Al-Khaleej*, September 17, 1992.

41 Ibid., 263, cites *Sout Al-Kuwait*, September 27, 1992.

42 Mohsen M. Milani, "Iran's Gulf Policy: From Idealism and Confrontation to Pragmatism and Moderation" in Al-Suwaidi, op. cit., 97.

43 Gargash, op. cit., 142-4; Richard Schofield (ed.) *Territorial Foundations of the Gulf States* (London: University College London Press Limited, 1994), 145.

44 Cordesman, op. cit., 301, cites Reuters, September 19, 1992.

45 Tadmori, op. cit., 259. Shaikh Khalid, op. cit., 251, cites *Al-'Ta'awen*, the magazine of the General-Secretariat of the GCC, December 28, 1992, 39.

46 Shahram Chubin and Charles Tripp, *Iran-Saudi Arabia Relations and Regional Order*, Adelphi Paper 304 (London: Oxford University Press, 1996), 30.

47 Tadmori, op. cit., 258. On September 12, Oman's Minister of State for Foreign Affairs had stated publicly that "Oman is a member of the GCC Council and it endorsed the statement issued by the GCC meeting which affirmed the UAE sovereignty over the island of Abu Musa." See Shaikh Khalid, op. cit., 254, who cites *Al-Khaleej*, September 13, 1992.

48 Gargash, op. cit., 146. This willingness may also be attributed to the fact that Oman and the UAE were moving toward agreement about their borders between May 1991 and April 1993, agreement that would be reached and signed in May 1999. Oman and Saudi Arabia had already delimited their border in March 1990, although they did not sign detailed maps until July 1995. See Schofield, op. cit., 144, and *Gulf News*, May 2, 1999, for the UAE-Oman border agreement.

49 Tadmori, op. cit., 257, 259.

50 Twinam, op. cit., 223.

51 Most of this field is situated on Qatar's side of its maritime boundary with Iran, but some of the field is situated on Iran's side. Iran had not developed its side of

the field, but was disturbed that Qatar had developed its side. Qatar also may have been reluctant because of its unresolved disputes with Bahrain over the Hawar islands, the Dibal and Jarada shoals, and the coastal settlement of Zubara. See Schofield, op. cit., 144-5, 154-6.

52 Tadmori, op. cit., 258-60.

53 Tadmori, op. cit., 257-8.

54 Shaikh Khalid, op. cit., 265-6 and 268-9, cites *Al-Khaleej*, October 3, 1992 and November 18, 1992.

55 Shaikh Khalid, op. cit., 260-1, cites *Al-Khaleej*, October 2, 1992. On September 9, after the GCC Council of Ministers issued its statement and just before the Damascus Declaration states were to meet and issue their statement, Egypt's Foreign Minister Amr Moussa expressed Egypt's support for the UAE in its dispute with Iran over Abu Musa and explained that "Our attitude supporting the UAE stems from Egypt's prime concern with Arab security." Shaikh Khalid, 260, cites *Al-Bayan*, September 10, 1992.

56 For the full text, see *Closing Statements of the Sessions of the Supreme Council*, 141-2; for excerpts, see Schofield, op. cit., 148. The second clause of the Abu Dhabi Declaration stressed that "the regional and international dealings of the Council's states [are] based on the respect for the principle of good neighbourliness as a basic and legitimate rule and commitment to respect the independence and sovereignty of states on their lands and non-interference in the internal affairs and respecting the sovereignty of every state over its resources." The third clause stressed their "adoption of the principle of dialogue and negotiation as a basic means of solving disputes among states in accordance and harmony with the United Nations Charter and international laws and customs and the rejection of the principle of the use of force or the threat of using it in relations between states and the inadmissibility of acquiring land by force. Within this framework the leaders of the Council's states stress the sovereignty of the State of the United Arab Emirates on the islands of Tonb al-Kubra and Tonb al-Sughra and Abu Musa and consider them an integral part of the State of the United Arab Emirates. They also stress their complete rejection of the continuing occupation by the Islamic Republic of Iran of these islands belong[ing] to the State of the United Arab Emirates."

57 For the full text, see *Closing Statements of the Sessions of the Supreme Council*, op. cit., 133-4; see also Tadmori, op. cit., 254-5; for excerpts, see Schofield, op. cit., 161.

58 *New York Times*, December 27, 1992 (International Edition), 8; Schofield cites *MEES*, January 11, 1993, C3. Tadmori, op. cit., 159, notes that in the course of meetings with Ras al-Khaimah's Ruler, Shaikh Saqr, on December 9, Iran's Ambassador to the UAE, Hassan Ameenian, asked that the upcoming GCC summit not "condemn and malign Iran." See Tadmori, op. cit., 154-160 for the transcripts of these meetings, which also indicate that Ameenian offered money for Ras al-Khaimah and the UAE to abandon the islands issue and that Shaikh Saqr refused.

59 See *FBIS-NES*, 95-237 (IIXII 95), 84-5; Anthony H. Cordesman, *Iran and Iraq: the Threat from the Northern Gulf* (Boulder, CO: Westview Press, 1994) 33, reports that Iran said it had been willing to fight for eight years, but Iran said eighty. Despite this aggressive reaction, Kuwait's Foreign Minister Shaikh Sabah al Ahmed al Jabir Al-Sabah, after discussing with the Iranian Ambassador to Kuwait the decisions of the recent GCC Summit and Kuwait's hope that the dispute could

be resolved by peaceful means, said that he found that Iran was understanding. See Shaikh Khalid, op. cit., 252, citing *Al-Khaleej*, January 10, 1993.

60   Tadmori, op. cit., 248, 252.

61   Gargash, op. cit., 143-4 cites *Al-Hayat*, April 2, 1993 and *Al-Sharq Al-Awsat*, May 18, 1993.

62   Al-Mani, op. cit., 170-2. Al-Mani writes that "The abrupt decision of the Iranian government not to discuss the 'islands' issue in the planned round of negotiations in Tehran in early October between the UAE and Iran soured relations further. Thus negotiations were damaged on the eve of the proposed meeting." However, Iran had earlier refused to issue a communiqué saying that the negotiation would discuss all three islands, leading the UAE to cancel the trip and the negotiation on September 10, 1993. See *Chronicle of Progress*, op. cit., 368.

63   Tadmori, op. cit., 261-7.

64   Gargash, op. cit., 156, cites *Kayhan International*, October 7, 1993.

65   Schofield, op. cit., 149-50.

66   For the full text, see *Closing Statements of the Sessions of the Supreme Council*, op. cit., 146-7; for excerpts, see Shaikh Khalid, op. cit., 250-1, which cites *Okaz*, December 24, 1993; see also Tutunji, op. cit., 190. For excerpts from Shaikh Zayed's remarks on December 2, 1993, see Tadmori, op. cit., 214-5.

67   Schofield, op. cit., 162.

68   Chubin and Tripp, op. cit., 30, cite *SWB*/ME/1963 MED/9, April 5, 1994.

69   Chubin and Tripp, op. cit., 32; Schofield, op. cit., 162.

70   Shaikh Khalid, op. cit., 252, cites *Al-Hawadeth*, no. 1967, July 15, 1994, 16.

71   Schofield, op. cit., 162.

72   Gargash, op. cit., 155 cites *Al-Hayat*, September 19, 1994. Saudi Foreign Minister Prince Saud Al-Faisal also made this call in his speech to the General Assembly. See Cordesman, *Bahrain, Oman, Qatar, and the UAE*, op. cit., 302; *Middle East Economic Digest (MEED)*, December 23, 1994, 10.

73   Gargash, 155 cites *Al-Hayat*, November 22, 1994. Cordesman, *Bahrain, Oman, Qatar, and the UAE*, op. cit., 301 writes that Syria attempted to mediate between the UAE and Iran in 1993 and 1994, but without success. Chubin and Tripp, op. cit., 32 write that Saudi Arabia attempted to use Syria as a mediator between the UAE and Iran in early 1995, but again without success.

74   For the full text, see *Closing Statements of the Sessions of the Supreme Council*, 156-7; see also Tutunji, op. cit., 190.

75   For the text, see Schofield, op. cit., 163.

76   Ibid., 163-4.

77   Ibid., 149 50, 156, 163 4, 166.

78   Interview, UAE Ministry of Foreign Affairs, Abu Dhabi, September 1997; interview with former US ambassador to the UAE, Washington, DC, December 1997. Schofield, op. cit., 156 notes a tendency in territorial cases, and especially in maritime delimitation cases, for the ICJ "to arrive at an arrangement with which both states will not be entirely dissatisfied." However, on page 167 he refers to GCC "enthusiasm" for an ICJ decision on the islands and indicates that it "stems from a genuine belief that, certainly as far as Abu Musa is concerned, the UAE would stand an excellent chance of having its title confirmed by the courts." UAE officials, however, express reservations about the ICJ, expressing concern that it might try to make an arrangement with which Iran would not be entirely dissatisfied by giving Iran the Tunbs.

79 Chubin and Tripp, op. cit., 31; *Chronicle of Progress*, op. cit., 397.

80 Schofield, op. cit., 164.

81 For the full text, see *Closing Statements of the Sessions of the Supreme Council*, op. cit., 170.

82 *The United Arab Emirates Yearbook, 1996*, op. cit., 50. The GCC Council of Ministers had also issued a statement of support for the UAE on March 17, 1996. See *Chronicle of Progress*, op. cit., 408.

83 *Chronicle of Progress*, op. cit., 412.

84 For excerpts from this communiqué, see *The United Arab Emirates Yearbook*, 1996, op. cit., 51-2.

85 For the full text, see *Closing Statements of the Sessions of the Supreme Council*, op. cit., 183-5.

86 *Gulf News*, June 27, 1997.

87 *Gulf News*, August 6, 1997.

88 Iran's new foreign minister, Kamal Kharrazi, also called for improved relations with Iran's neighbors. See *Gulf News*, September 16, 1997.

89 "Address of H.E. Dr. Ahmed Esmat Abdel Meguid to the 108th Session of the Arab League Council, Cairo, September 20, 1997," transcript from the Arab League, Office of the Secretary General, in Arabic; *Gulf News*, September 21 and 22, 1997.

90 *Emirates News*, November 14, 1997.

91 *Al Hayat*, December 5, 1997; *Gulf News*, December 7, 1997.

92 "Address of H.E. Dr. Ahmed Esmet Abdel Meguid, Secretary General of the Arab League, to the Islamic Summit, Tehran, December 9, 1997," transcript from the Arab League, Office of the Secretary General, in Arabic.

93 *Gulf News*, December 8, 1998. See also R.K. Ramazani, "The Shifting Premise of Iran's Foreign Policy: Towards a Democratic Peace?" in *The Middle East Journal* 52, no. 2 (Spring 1998), 184-5.

94 *Emirates News*, December 24, 1997.

95 *Emirates News*, December 21, 1997. See Cordesman, *Bahrain, Oman, Qatar, and the UAE*, op. cit., 40-5, for a discussion of Bahrain's accusations.

96 For the full text, see *Closing Statements of the Sessions of the Supreme Council*, op. cit., 198-9; see also *Emirates News*, December 23, 1997.

97 *Al Ittihad*, February 28, 1998.

98 *Al-Sharq Al-Awsat*, March 7, 1998.

99 *Gulf News*, March 9, 1998.

100 Interview, UAE Ministry of Foreign Affairs, May 1998.

101 *Gulf News*, November 28, 1998.

102 *Gulf News*, December 7, 1998.

103 *Gulf News*, December 5, 1998.

104 *Gulf News*, February 2, 1999; *Al-Ittihad*, March 1999.

105 *Gulf News*, December 8, 1998.

106 *Gulf News*, December 8, 1998.

107 *Gulf News*, December 10, 1998.

108 For the full text of the communiqué, see *Gulf News*, December 10, 1998.

109 *Al-Hayat*, February 11, 1999.

110 *Gulf News*, February 28, 1999.

111 *Gulf News*, February 28, 1999.

112 *Gulf News*, March 1, 1999.

113 *Gulf News*, March 2, 1999.

114 *Gulf News*, March 3, 1999.

115 *Gulf News*, March 3, 1999.

116 *Gulf News*, March 4 and 5, 1999; *Al-Shoroouq Magazine*, March 8-14, 1999.

117 *Gulf News*, March 5, 1999; *Al-Hayat*, March 5, 1999; *Al-Sharq Al-Awsat*, March 5, 1999; *Al-Sharouq Magazine*, March 8-14, 1999.

118 *Gulf News*, March 5, 1999; *Al-Hayat*, March 5, 1999; *Al-Sharq Al-Awsat*, March 5, 1999; *Al-Shorouq Magazine*, March 8-14, 1999.

119 These considerations may explain why a lower level official was sent to the emergency meeting. In addition, however, UAE observers noted that Kuwait may not have been satisfied with a recent statement by UAE Minister of Information Shaikh Abdullah bin Zayed about Iraq's threat to the Gulf, and may have decided not to send its foreign minister for this reason as well. Shaikh Abdullah had said at the end of December 1998, after two weeks of intense US and British air strikes against Iraq, that "Iraq poses a threat to some extent, but there is a greater threat to the GCC countries than the Iraqi threat. Iran still occupies the islands of the Emirates and Israel possesses the capabilities to develop non-traditional missiles and Iran as well has the desire to produce nuclear weapons. Israel and Iran represent more danger than Iraq at present." This statement had elicited strong protests from Iran's Foreign Ministry and semi-official media, and these protests were answered forcefully by the UAE's semi-official media. See *Al-Ittihad*, December 31, 1998. Thus, Shaikh Abdullah's statement, Iran's protest and the ensuing media commentary, all taking place during the crisis over Iraq, when Kuwait would have been keen to have Iran's support, also may have concerned Kuwait enough to show some dissatisfaction by sending a lower level official to the emergency meeting.

120 UAE observers noted, however, that UAE relations with Qatar had been strained, since Qatar's Shaikh Hamad bin Khalifa Al-Thani had walked out of the 1995 GCC Summit in protest over the appointment of Saudi Arabia's Jamil Al-Hujailan as Secretary General and especially in the middle of an effort by the UAE's Shaikh Zayed to mediate between Qatar and Saudi Arabia on the disagreement. See Cordesman, *Bahrain, Oman, Qatar, and the UAE*, op. cit., 305, for an account of the walkout and the suspected coup. Qatar also perceived the UAE as favoring Bahrain in its dispute with Qatar over the Hawar islands issue, a dispute so serious that Bahrain boycotted the 1996 GCC Summit in Doha.

121 *Gulf News*, March 6, 1999; *Al-Hayat*, March 6, 1999.

122 *Al-Ittihad*, March 16, 1999; *Gulf News*, March 16, 1999.

123 *Khaleej Times*, March 18, 1999.

124 *Al-Hayat*, March 18 and 19, 1999.

125 *Al-Ittihad*, March 19, 1999; *Gulf News*, March 19, 1999.

126 *Al-Ittihad*, March 19, 1999; *Gulf News*, March 19, 1999.

127 *Gulf News*, March 25 and 31, 1999.

128 *Gulf News*, March 19, 24 and 31, 1999.

129 *Gulf News*, March 31, 1999.

130 *Gulf News*, April 14, 1999.

131 *Gulf News*, May 3, 4 and 6, 1999.

132 *Gulf News*, May 3 and 4, 1999.

133 *Gulf News*, May 11 and 16, 1999.

134 *Gulf News*, May 17, 18 and 20, 1999.

135 *Al-Ittihad*, May 24, 1999.

136 *Akhbar Al-Sa'ah*, May 24, 1999.

137 *Gulf News*, June 2, 1999.

138 *Gulf News*, June 6, 1999.

139 *Gulf News*, June 7, 1999.

140 *Gulf News*, June 9, 1999.

141 *Gulf News*, June 13, 1999.

142 *Gulf News*, June 10, 1999.

143 *Gulf News*, June 15 and 16, 1999; *United Arab Emirates, Country Profile, 1999-2000* (London: The Economist Intelligence Unit, 1999), 10.

144 *Gulf News*, June 15, 1999.

145 *Gulf News*, June 20, 21 and 22, 1999.

146 *Gulf News*, May 5, 1999.

147 *Gulf News*, June 24, 25 and 30, 1999, July 2, 1999.

148 *Gulf News*, July 4, 1999.

149 *Gulf News*, July 4, 1999.

150 *Gulf News*, July 6, 1999.

151 *Gulf News*, July 8, 1999.

152 *Gulf News*, July 11, 1999; *Khaleej Times*, July 11, 1999.

153 *Gulf News*, September 13 and 14, 1999.

154 *Gulf News*, November 8, 1999.

155 *Gulf News*, January 22 and 26, 2000.

156 *Gulf News*, April 9 and 10, 2000.

157 *Gulf News*, April 21, 2000.

158 *Gulf News*, April 23, 2000.

159 *Gulf News*, April 26, May 3, 2000.

160 *Gulf News*, April 30, 2000.

161 *Gulf News*, June 5, 2000.

162 *Khaleej Times*, June 6, 2000.

163 *Gulf News*, April 30, 2000.

164 *Gulf News*, September 2000.

165 *Khaleej Times*, September 7, 2000; *Gulf News*, September 8, 2000.

166 *Gulf News*, January 2, 9, 2001; *Al-Hayat*, January 18, 2001.

167 *Khaleej Times*, February 27, 2001.

168 *Gulf News*, March 15, 19, 2001.

169 For the text, see www.al-bab.com/arab/docs/league/summit

170 *Al-Watan*, (Saudi Arabia), April 18, 2001.

171 For the text, see "Press communiqué issued by the Ministerial Council of the Gulf Cooperation Council at its seventy-ninth session, held in Jeddah on 2 June 2001," at www.gcc-sc.org

172 For the text, see "Final communiqué adopted by the Supreme Council of the Gulf Cooperation Council at its twenty-second session, held in Muscat, Oman, on 30 and 31 December 2001," at www.gcc-sc.org

173 *Gulf News*, January 20, 2002.

174 *Gulf News*, March 11, 12, 2002.

175 *Gulf News*, March 29, 2002. For the full text, see www.al-bab.com/arab/docs/league/communique

176 For the text, see "Press communiqué issued by the Ministerial Council of the Gulf Cooperation Council at its eighty-third session, held in Jeddah, Saudi Arabia, on 8 June 2002," at www.gcc-sg.org

177 *Al-Sharq Al-Awsat*, June 10, 2002.

178 *Al-Watan*, July 2, 2002.

179 See chapter four of this book for these remarks.

180 For the text, see "Communiqué issued on 3 September 2002 by the Ministerial Council of the Gulf Cooperation Council at its eighty-fourth session held in Jeddah," at www.gcc-sc.org

181 *Gulf News*, September 6, 2002.

182 *Gulf News*, December 23, 2002.

183 Interview with the Ruler of Ras al-Khaimah, March 1998.

184 Interview, Abu Dhabi, September 1997.

185 Interview at UAE Ministry of Foreign Affairs, August 1997.

186 Interview at UAE Ministry of Foreign Affairs, September 1997.

187 Gargash, op. cit., 146.

188 Interview at UAE Foreign Ministry, August 1997.

189 Interview, Abu Dhabi, December 1998.

CHAPTER 9

1 Interview with former British Ambassador to the UAE, Abu Dhabi, September 1997.

2 See Chapter 2, especially pgs. 84-85.

3 See Chapter 3 of this study for a review of the 1950s and 1960s.

4 FCO/8/54, January 15 and 29, 1968.

5 FCO/8/58, May 21, 1968.

6 FCO/8/54, January 29; FCO/8/58, May 21, 1968.

7 FCO/8/54, February 2 and 14, 1968.

8 FCO/8/54, December 21, 1967.

9 FCO/8/54, January 29, 1968.

10 See the various correspondence contained in FCO 8/53, FCO 8/54 and FCO 8/55.

11 FCO/8/49, January 7, 1968. See also Rouhollah K. Ramazani, *Iran's Foreign Policy, 1941-1973: A Study of Foreign Policy in Modernizing Nations* (Charlottesville, VA: University Press of Virginia, 1975), 409; Shahram Chubin and Sepehr Zabih, *The Foreign Relations of Iran* (Berkeley, CA: University of California Press, 1974). *Arab Report and Record*, January 1-15, 1968, 2 reported that Roberts proposed a regional defense pact including Iran, Saudi Arabia, Kuwait and the Trucial States. The British Foreign Office documents do not indicate this. Duncan Slater said in an interview in London in July 1999 that Brenchley's remarks on the Tunbs greatly angered the Shah, who long afterwards still complained about them. Slater was a Foreign Office official who accompanied and assisted Luce on his visits to the Gulf in 1970 and 1971. See also the FCO files cited below for this trip.

12 FCO/8/47, January 8, 9, 10, 11, 1968. See also J.B. Kelly, *Arabia, the Gulf, and the West* (USA: Basic Books, 1980), 49-51, 53; interview with former Foreign Office official M.S. Weir, London, July 1999; FCO/8/1322, December 4, 1970. See also FCO/8/48, especially January 23, 1968, for some disparaging remarks made by the British Defence Secretary, Denis Healey, regarding the Rulers' offers of financial assistance for British military forces in the Gulf and for his subsequent apology. This source also shows that among the numerous reasons for not accepting the Rulers' offer was that "There would be a problem of command and control; for example, the Rulers might demand a more active reaction by our forces in the event of a flare-up of the islands dispute with Iran than we would necessarily consider justified or wise." Britain welcomed the February 18 agreement of Abu Dhabi's Shaikh Zayed and Dubai's Shaikh Rashid to form a federation, but urged formation of a wider federation. See A.O. Taryam, *The Establishment of the United Arab Emirates, 1950-1985* (London: Croom Helm Ltd., 1987) 89-92. Britain and the United States also welcomed the February 27 agreement of Bahrain, Qatar and the seven Trucial Shaikhdoms to form a United Arab Emirates federation by March 30, 1968. Taryam, op. cit., 91-3. Taryam suggests that by May and September Britain may have started favoring a seven-member federation.

13 FCO/8/47, January 10, 1968. What Faisal actually said was somewhat cryptic, namely, that the issue of the Tunbs could be resolved through international procedures: if the Tunbs were in Iran's territorial waters they belonged to Iran; if they were not, he did not think it important.

14 F. Gregory Gause, "British and American Policies in the Persian Gulf, 1968-1973," in *Review of International Studies* (Cambridge: Cambridge University Press, 1985) 11, iv, 253, cites an interview with former US Ambassador to Saudi Arabia Herman Eilts; see also FCO/8/47, January 17, 1968.

15 Taryam, op. cit., 61, 68-71; Joseph Twinam, *The Gulf, Cooperation, and the Council: An American Perspective* (Washington, DC: The Middle East Policy Council, 1992), 87; Gause, op. cit., 258-9.

16 James Noyes, *The Clouded Lens: Persian Gulf Security and U.S. Policy* (Stanford, CA: Hoover Institution Press, 1982), 55, 57-9; Twinam, op. cit., 92-6. This consisted of a transport flagship and a C-131 transport aircraft based in Bahrain as well as rotational visits by two destroyers from the Atlantic fleet.

17 Noyes, op. cit., 56-7; Twinam, op. cit., 88 and footnote; Ramazani, *Iran's Foreign Policy*, 409-10; Chubin and Zabih, op. cit., 237. Iran, Turkey and Pakistan, along with Britain, were members of the US-sponsored Central Treaty Organization (CENTO). This suggestion of outside involvement prompted Iranian Prime Minister Amir Abbas Hoveyda on January 27 to reject any regional security role for outside forces, including Britain and the United States. See Kelly, op. cit., 54; Taryam, op. cit., 74.

18 Twinam, op. cit., 89; FCO/8/58, May 21, 1968.

19 Taryam, op. cit., 83; *Arab Report and Record*, January 1-15, 1968, 2 and March 1-15, 1968. Rouhollah K. Ramazani, *The Persian Gulf: Iran's Role* (Charlottesville, VA: University Press of Virginia, 1972), 105 provides excerpts from the March 3, 1968 Tass statement.

20 Taryam, op. cit., 74.

21 Chubin and Zabih, op. cit., 72-4, 262-6. See also Mark N. Katz, *Russia and Arabia: Soviet Foreign Policy toward the Arabian Peninsula* (Baltimore, MD: The Johns Hopkins University Press, 1986), 178. In early March 1971, for example,

Pravda wrote that the British efforts to establish a federation were intended "as a kind of fig-leaf to cover up the British presence" and argued that these efforts were like "building a house of cards on the shifting Arabian sands." See *Arabian Report and Record*, March 1-15, 1971, 135.

22   FCO/8/53, January 8, 1968; FCO/8/53 and FCO/8/54, January 9, 1968. See also February 9 memo. See also FCO/8/47, January 7, 1968.

23   FCO/8/54, January 10, 12, 13, 24, 1968. On January 24, the Political Agent in Dubai provided an eyewitness account of his visit to the Greater Tunb during the crisis.

24   FCO/8/53, January 12, 13, 1968; FCO/8/54, January 15, 17, 24, February 12, 1968. The Iranian Foreign Ministry also reiterated its protest against the flying of the Ras al-Khaimah flag on the Tunbs on January 16. FCO/8/53, January 17, 1968.

25   FCO/8/54, January 15, 1968.

26   FCO/8/54, January 15, 1968; FCO/8/53, January 15, 1968. In the light of this discussion, the Foreign Office decided to send an anodyne note in reply to the Iranian Embassy's protest of January 15 and not to respond to the Iranian Foreign Ministry's January 16 protest. See FCO/8/54, January 24, 1968. On January 30, the Iranian Embassy in London issued a statement that rejected the January 15 British protest and repeated Iranian claims. It also protested against Ras al-Khaimah actions on the Greater Tunb, called for an end to these actions before resuming discussion on the Tunbs, and reserved the right to take action. FCO/8/54, January 30, 1968. A February 12 Foreign Office memo on how to respond to the Iranian protest recommended simply repeating that Britain's position was clear so as to put the exchange of protests to an end. FCO/8/55, February 12, 1968. Also in mid-February, the Foreign Office had very technical draft proposals for Iran regarding a median line between the Trucial States and Iran without prejudice to the islands, proposals that the Foreign Office had said it would draft at its late November 1967 meeting with Aram in London. At the time, the Foreign Office made a decision not to submit them to Iran in anticipation of Iranian rejection.

27   FCO/8/53, January 12, 13, 15, 17, 1968; FCO/8/54, January 17, 1968.

28   FCO/8/54, January 18, 1968.

29   FCO/8/54, January 23, 1968.

30   FCO/8/54, January 25, 1968. On February 14, 1968 the Embassy in Jeddah advised the Foreign Office that its briefing points regarding the islands were too technical for the Saudis and proposed alternative points. The alternative points presented a questionable history of the islands in stating they had been under the administration of Lingeh in the early nineteenth century. See FCO/8/55, February 14, 1968.

31   FCO/8/54, January 29, 1968. The British Embassy in Tehran advised the Foreign Office on January 29 that Saudi Arabia should not divulge to Iran that the Saudis were receiving a British briefing on the islands.

32   FCO/8/54, February 1, 1968.

33   There were several reasons for this. On the same day an Iranian gunboat arrested the crew of an Aramco oil rig and ordered the removal of the rig in an oil field on the Saudi side of a provisional median line, a line based on an agreement that Iran had previously initialed but not ratified. The discovery of oil on the Saudi side of this median line in early January had changed the Iranian view of this agreement.

In subsequent weeks, Iran began drilling in this field. See *The Guardian*, February 18, 1968; FCO/8/49, January 7, 1968; Muhammad Morsy Abdullah, *The United Arab Emirates: A Modern History* (UK: Hurtwood Press Limited, 1994) 280. Another reason was the Iranian objection to the January 17 communiqué issued at the end of the Ruler of Bahrain's visit to Saudi Arabia saying that Saudi Arabia pledged to "fully endorse and effectively support the Bahrayn government in all circumstances." See Chubin and Zabih, op. cit., 215-6. The Shah also objected to King Faisal's public advice to the Bahrain Ruler that he should join a federation of emirates. Taryam, op. cit., 72-3, 83-4.

34 FCO/8/54, February 1, 1968.

35 FCO/8/54, February 7, 1968.

36 FCO/8/54, February 3, 1968.

37 FCO/8/55, February 3, 1968.

38 FCO/8/54, February 5, 1968.

39 FCO/8/54, February 7, 1968.

40 FCO/8/55, February 9, 1968.

41 FCO/8/55, February 14, 1968.

42 FCO/8/55, February 17, 1968. On February 21, Bahrain Political Agent Anthony Parsons warned that failure to deter Iran or to dislodge Iran from the islands would influence Bahrain and Arab opinion against Britain. See FCO/8/55, February 21, 1968.

43 FCO/8/55, February 22, 1968. Iran may have understood the British hint that it would not resist an Iranian military move against the islands after British withdrawal. As a Foreign Office memo of May 21 later noted, "The Iranian Prime Minister, Mr. Hoveyda, suggested in early 1968 that we and the Iranians might agree to the continuance of the status quo, on the firm understanding that in 1971 we should wash our hands of the dispute and acquiesce in an Iranian seizure of the islands." See FCO/8/56, May 21, 1968.

44 Sir Denis Wright, unpublished memoirs, 418.

45 FCO/8/56, May 30, 1968. By April 4, the Foreign Office was considering options of mediation, conciliation, arbitration, and the International Court of Justice as methods of resolving the islands issue. A comprehensive memo on such possible solutions was produced on May 21. FCO/8/56, April 4, 1968; May 21, 1968.

46 FCO/8/56, April 4, 1968; Sir Denis Wright said in a July 1999 interview that he does not believe that he was ever provided with such documentation.

47 FCO/8/56, May 21, 1968.

48 Ibid. It may be added here that Ambassador Wright also met with Iranian Deputy Foreign Minister Amir Khosrow Afshar on April 9. Despite what the Shah had hinted to Wright on April 6, Afshar gave Wright the impression that he regarded Abu Musa as expendable, although not the Tunbs. Afshar agreed with Wright that Saudi Arabia would have to be a party to a package deal. In an April 10 conversation with banker Roger Stevens, the Shah expressed commitment to the islands based on considerations of prestige and history, not strategic considerations, and spoke of compensating the people but not the Rulers. The Shah's reference to the Rulers indicated once again that whatever Afshar's personal thoughts, the Shah wanted to acquire not only the Tunbs, but also Abu Musa. See FCO/8/56, April 11, 1968.

49 FCO/8/56, April 5, 1968.

50 FCO/8/56, April 5, 1968.

51 FCO/8/56, April 9, 10, 11, 1968.

52 FCO/8/56, April 18, 1968.

53 FCO/8/56, April 8, 1968.

54 FCO/8/56, April 29, May 1, 1968. Arthur also noted that the American lawyer, banker and official John J. (Mack) McCloy had visited Kuwait after talking with the Shah and had brought the seriousness of the Shah's claims to the attention of the Kuwaiti officials. See also FCO/8/56, April 15, 1968.

55 FCO/8/56, April 29, 1968.

56 FCO/8/56, May 1, 1968. After this conversation, Allen proposed to the Foreign Office that it consider naming an arbitrator to consider the median line in the Lower Gulf and the disputed islands.

57 Taryam, op. cit., 82 cites *The Times*, April 26, 1968.

58 Taryam, op. cit., 74.

59 Ramazani, *Iran's Foreign Policy*, op. cit., 363-5 and Alvin J. Cottrell, "Iran's Armed Forces Under the Pahlavi Dynasty," in George Lenczowski (ed.) *Iran Under the Pahlavis* (Stanford, CA: Hoover Institution Press, 1978).

60 FCO/8/56, May 21, 1968.

61 Ibid.

62 Ibid.

63 Ibid.

64 Ibid.

65 FCO/8/56, May 30, 1968.

66 Ibid.

67 Ibid. Finally, Wright was advised that Crawford had been asked to comment on these instructions before Wright's next meeting with the Shah. Wright was also encouraged to have his meeting in time for the British to communicate the results to the Americans before the Shah's June visit to the United States.

68 FCO/8/57, June 3, 1968.

69 FCO/8/57, June 3 and 4, 1968.

70 FCO/8/57, June 6, 7, 1968.

71 FCO/8/57, June 18, 19, 1968.

72 FCO/8/57, June 20, 21, 1968.

73 FCO/8/57, June 19, 21, 24, 25, 1968. Chargé d'Affaires Craig expressed similar concern that Crown Prince Shaikh Khalid of Ras al-Khaimah would receive an inaccurate version of Craig's conversation with Saqqaf when he met with Prince Fahd in Saudi Arabia. There is, however, no evidence that the Saudis briefed Ras al-Khaimah on this. See FCO/8/57, June 23, 1968. During an early July visit to London, the Ruler of Dubai was told of a proposal to trade-off Abu Musa and the Tunbs for Bahrain. The British suspected that the inaccurate leak may have come from the Saudi or Kuwaiti ambassadors. See FCO/8/57, July 11, 15, 1968.

74 FCO/8/57, June 7, 8, 1968.

75 Ramazani, *Iran's Foreign Policy*, op. cit., 413; Chubin and Zabih, op. cit., 217. See FCO/8/57, June 7, 8, 1968.

76 Chubin and Zabih, op. cit., 216-7.

77 FCO/8/57, June 11, 1968.

78 Ramazani, *Iran's Foreign Policy*, op. cit., 414-5.

79 FCO/8/56.

80 Ibid.

81 FCO/8/57, July 1, 11, 1968; FCO/8/58, July 1, 1968. Brenchley told Aram that King Faisal had shown interest in the package deals, but thought that any of them would be best arranged after a federation. Wright also told Afshar that King Faisal "had not rejected out of hand" the idea of surrendering the Tunbs to Iran, but thought any package must be reached with a nine-member federation. On July 17, Iran protested "constructional operations" on the Greater Tunb, but Britain answered later that it had discovered no evidence of this. See FCO/8/57, July 18, August 1, 2, 4, 1968; FCO/8/58, August 16, 21, September 6, 19, 1968.

82 *The Times*, June 26, 1968; FCO/8/57, July 25, 26, 1968. The British learned that this story originated from a leak by Aram and suspected that the Saudi Ambassador might have been another source.

83 FCO/8/57, July 26, 1968. The Ambassador also told Alam that he would like to ask the Shah if Iran would refrain from condemning a federation of nine if it came into being before a plebiscite could be arranged for Bahrain, or how Iran would react if Bahrain chose to become an independent state and member of the UN.

84 FCO/8/57, July 29, 1968.

85 FCO/8/57, July 30, 1968.

86 FCO/8/57, July 31, 1968.

87 Sir Denis Wright, unpublished memoirs.

88 FCO/8/58, August 15, 27, 1968.

89 See FCO/8/960/1, letter from Richard Weston to Shaikh Saqr, December 20, 1968. This letter, which summarizes Weston's meetings with Savak officials in December 1968, notes that Weston, who was representing Shaikh Saqr, asked for 525,000 pounds sterling and the Savak officials recalled that they had offered only 300,000 pounds sterling in August 1968.

90 The memo also noted that Shaikh Saqr had asked the Shah for arms and argued that this would endanger stability in the Trucial States. As such, it advised that Wright should encourage the Shah to offer only humanitarian aid to Ras al-Khaimah as compensation for the Tunbs. See FCO/8/58, August 29, 31, September 10, 1968. Richard Schofield, "Borders and Territoriality in the Gulf and the Arabian Peninsula during the Twentieth Century," in Richard Schofield (ed.) *Territorial Foundations of the Gulf States* (London: University College London Press Limited, 1994), 38-9 writes that "Iran was apparently prepared to supply the shaikhdom with military and humanitarian support by way of compensation. Though the Ruler of Ras al-Khaimah initially seemed disposed to accept Iran's offer of Western-built guns and armoured vehicles plus the unspecified 'humanitarian' component, he apparently later changed his mind, demanding a significant sum of money instead. Iran continues to maintain that it could not possibly have entertained paying a huge amount of money for features that possessed no economic value. The value of the Tunbs was and remains purely strategic to Iran." The Foreign Office records, which were not declassified until 1999 and 2000, indicate that it was Savak officials who offered money and Shaikh Saqr who asked for arms during this August visit. Shaikh Saqr said in a 1998 interview that it was the Shah who initially offered money for the Tunbs but that specific sums were not discussed with the Shah. Moreover, there was some reason for Iran to believe that the Tunbs might have economic value inasmuch as Shaikh Saqr had granted concessions for oil exploration in the territorial waters around the Tunbs. Hoveyda and Zahedi told Saqr he could have the mineral wealth around

the islands. Moreover, *Arab Report and Record*, August 16-31, 1968, 238, wrote at the time that "The proximity of Ras al-Khaimah's offshore oil-drilling operations to Iranian waters is understood to have been discussed." Ras al-Khaimah had granted concessions to explore for oil up to a hypothetical median line that would divide Ras al-Khaimah's continental shelf from Iran's, as well as to explore in the territorial waters around the Tunbs, which were on the Iranian side of the hypothetical median line. The Foreign Office record indicates that Shaikh Saqr and the Shah did not engage in discussions about a median line during this visit. Chubin and Zabih, op. cit., cite the Iranian press on the visit.

91 Interview with Sir Denis Wright, England, July 1999; FCO/8/58, September 11, 1968. In the meantime, after the fall of President Aref and the rise of President Bakr and the Baath Party in Iraq in July, the Foreign Office advised against having any detailed conversations with Iraq about the Gulf, particularly while Iran and a number of Arab states were engaged in discussions, and noted King Faisal's view that Iraq should be kept at arms length. See FCO/8/46, August 30, 1968. In August, the Iraqi press had denounced British imperialism for fostering foreign immigration to the Gulf in an attempt to undermine the Arabism of the Gulf and the tide of Arab revolution and for working with the Americans to replace British imperialism in the Gulf with American imperialism. See FCO/8/46, August 29, 1968. A September cable from the British Embassy in Baghdad said, however, that the anti-colonial statements were "just show" and noted that the Iraqi attitude toward a Gulf federation was favorable. The Embassy expressed concern about Saudi Arabia, Kuwait, and the UAE being no match for the Iranians, noted that Iraq was concerned about Iran dominating the Gulf and controlling the Strait of Hormuz, argued that Iraq might be useful in balancing Iran, and argued in favor of discussing Gulf plans with the Iraqis. See FCO/8/46, September 21, 1968.

92 FCO/8/960/1, October 17, 18, 1968. Some of the records in FCO/8/960/1, as well as FCO/8/961/1 and FCO/8/962, which were declassified in January 2000, were reproduced in a twelve-part series in *The Gulf Today*, running from January 16 to February 5, 2000. Unfortunately, the documents are not presented and analyzed in a sensible chronological order; indeed, the series even presents and analyzes documents from 1969 before presenting and analyzing documents from 1968. One of the most notable errors of analysis in this series is the repeated reference to "the Iranian intention to take over Bahrain and the three islands." Actually, Iran was looking for a face-saving way to relinquish its claim to Bahrain.

93 FCO/8/960/1, October 14, 15, 22, 23, 24, 30, 31, November 2, 1968.

94 FCO/8/960/1, October 30, 31, November 2, 3, 4, 9, 12, 1968. The British Embassy reported that Saudi official Rashad Pharaon had replied that such a median line was consistent with Saudi thinking. The Embassy also indicated that the US Embassy had reported that the Saudi hope was that the Shah would agree to a median line leaving the Tunbs to Iran and Abu Musa to the Arabs. Crawford interpreted this to mean that King Faisal might attempt to persuade the Shah of this at their November 1968 summit, but there is no record that Faisal did so. See also FCO/8/956/1, October 24, 28, November 14, 1968 for a discussion touching on package deals between British Ambassador Willie Morris and Saudi official Rashad Pharaon. Britain generally stayed in the background when Shaikh Saqr's legal adviser Richard Weston travelled to Iran in mid-December in an unsuccessful effort to negotiate an arrangement on the Tunbs. Crawford and Bullard had

recommended, however, that Saqr get a clear agreement on issues like the flying of flags, thinking that Ras al-Khaimah might later call upon Britain to defend the emirate's rights if there was no clear agreement and Iran pulled Ras al-Khaimah's flag down. See FCO/8/960/1, December 16, 24, 1968.

95 Sir Denis Wright, unpublished memoirs; interview with Sir Denis Wright, England, July 1999; Chubin and Zabih, op. cit., 217, 219. See also Ramazani, *The Persian Gulf*, op. cit., 101-2 for excerpt; *Arab Report and Record*, 1969, 2 for more excerpts. The Shah had already told this to the British seven months earlier, but he had done so in private and now he was stating it in public.

96 Ramazani, *Iran's Foreign Policy*, op. cit., 414-5; Asadollah Alam (ed. Alinaghi Alikhani) *The Shah and I: The Confidential Diary of Iran's Royal Court, 1969-1977* (London: I.B. Tauris and Company Ltd., 1991), 44.

97 FCO/8/960/1, January 31, February 5, 14, 1969. The British Embassy also asked the State Department to discourage Ras al-Khaimah from thinking it would have any special US support if a union failed, and asked that any US aid to Ras al-Khaimah be channeled through the Trucial States Development Fund.

98 FCO/8/960/1, January 29, 1969. This record also shows that Foreign Minister Zahedi had "sounded off" on Abu Musa to British Conservative MP Sir Tufton Beamish.

99 FCO/8/960/1, February 4, 1969; FCO/8/955/1.

100 FCO/8/960/1, February 13, May 5, 12, 1969; FCO/8/961/1, June 5, 11, 25, 1969. *The Gulf Today* on January 19, 2000 mistakenly wrote that the February memo was from the British Foreign Office and the June reply was from the Iranians.

101 Alam, *The Shah and I*, op. cit., 33-4. Pirouz Mojtahed-Zadeh, "Perspectives on the Territorial History of the Tonb and Abu Musa Islands," in Hooshang Amirahmadi (ed.) *Small Islands, Big Politics: The Tonbs and Abu Musa in the Gulf* (London: MacMillan Press Ltd., 1996) says this was February 18, 1970, but he is mistaken. Alam and the Shah were vacationing in Switzerland on February 18, 1970.

102 Interview with Sir Denis Wright, England, July 1999.

103 Alam, op. cit., 43.

104 Interview with Sir Denis Wright, England, July 1999.

105 Sir Denis Wright, unpublished memoirs, 424.

106 Sir Denis Wright, "Ten Years in Iran: Some Highlights," in *Asian Affairs*, XXII (III) October 1991, 269; also quoted by Mojtahed-Zadeh in Amirahmadi, op. cit., 53.

107 Alam, op. cit., 44.

108 Alam, op. cit., 44-5; See also Mojtahed-Zadeh in Amirahmadi, op. cit., who cuts the quote before Wright's reference to the Shaikh of Sharjah, but resumes part of it later.

109 FCO/8/960/1, April 2, 5, 9, 10, 11, 15, 1969. See also Kelly, op. cit., 57-8, and Taryam, op. cit., 117.

110 Alam, op. cit., 58; See also Mojtahed-Zadeh, op. cit., 54.

111 Alam, op. cit., 70.

112 Sir Denis Wright, unpublished memoirs.

113 FCO/8/961/1, June 13, 1969.

114 Alam, op. cit., 71.

115 FCO/8/961/1, June 5, 1969.

116 FCO/8/961/1, May 31, 1969.

117 FCO/8/961/1, June 5, 1969.

118 FCO/8/961/1, June 13, 1969.

119 FCO/8/961/1, June 19, 20, 26, 1969. In its series of articles covering the British Foreign Office records released in January 2000, *The Gulf Today* on January 18, 2000 mistakenly wrote that Crawford's appeal for a delay had come from the Arabian Department at the Foreign Office in London, but in fact it had come from the Bahrain Residency.

120 FCO/8/961/1, July 3, 5, 9, 15, August 28, September 11, 1969.

121 Alam, op. cit., 83; see also Alam's entries for August 12 and 13, 85-6, and October 2, 93-4.

122 FCO/8/961/1, September 12, 15, 1969. Also in mid-September, Wright was pressed on the islands by Dr. Manuchehr Zelli of Iran's Foreign Ministry. Wright repeated the messages he had conveyed to Afshar, namely, that Britain had urged the Rulers to reach a compromise agreement with Iran. FCO/8/961/1, September 11, 13, 1969. On January 20, 2000, *The Gulf Today* wrote that in his telegram on this conversation, Wright said that "The Iranians regarded the islands as theirs, and they must be recognized as such." Wright was only quoting Zelli. It was not Wright's view that the islands must be recognized as Iran's. It should also be noted that as Iran was signaling the urgency of its interest in the islands in September, British officials considered a report that Sharjah's Shaikh Khalid intended to establish a police post on Abu Musa. While there was some concern that Iran would react badly to such a development, the Foreign Office decided that it would turn a blind eye, particularly because Shaikh Khalid had not informed them and they could plausibly argue to Iran that they had not heard about it. If Shaikh Khalid mentioned it, however, Bullard was to say that the British recognized Sharjah's rights on the island and the decision was his, but to ask if his interest in a few police outweighed his interest in an agreement with Iran and to indicate that the British view was that it would be unwise to irritate Iran at this time. FCO/8/961/1, September 23, 26, 27, 30, October 4, 8, 1969. Since late 1968, British officials had many similar concerns about Iran's reactions to developments concerning the islands. British officials expressed concern about a news item reporting that the British had dropped off a new Sharjah flag on Abu Musa. British officials requested that a new air chart of the Gulf should show the islands without any indication of sovereignty. British officials prevailed upon Shaikh Saqr not to visit the Tunbs after visiting an offshore oil rig. British officials expressed a preference that a new offshore oil concession by Sharjah should include Abu Musa, but not specifically mention Abu Musa by name. British officials also took careful note of information that Sharjah might develop a tanker servicing station on Abu Musa and that it was planning a school and clinic on the island. British officials also withheld permission for the Trucial Oman Scouts to make occasional visits to the island. On the other hand, concern for Ras al-Khaimah's reaction led British officials to thwart a plan by a British journalist to visit the Tunbs from Iran's port at Bandar Abbas. See for example FCO/8/960/1, October 25, November 7, 13, 25, 1968, January 6, 7, February 18, March 11, April 23, May 12, 13, 1969; and FCO/8/961/1, September 27, 1969.

123 Ramazani, *Iran's Foreign Policy*, op. cit., 415; Ramazani, *The Persian Gulf*, op. cit., 51.

124 George Lenczowski, *American Presidents and the Middle East* (London: Duke University Press, 1990), 116-9, 184; Noyes, op. cit., 120-1.

125 Ramazani, *Iran's Foreign Policy*, op. cit., 365-7.

126 Alam, op. cit., 101.

127 FCO/8/961/1, November 19, 1969.

128 FCO/8/961/1, November 19, 20, 21, 22, 1969.

129 FCO/8/961/1, November 22, 24, 26, 27, 1969.

130 FCO/8/962, December 9, 14, 16, 19, 1969.

131 FCO/8/962, December 24, 1969. Letter from Shaikh Khalid to Arab heads of state, August 23, 1971 in *Middle East Economic Survey (MEES)* XV, no. 6, December 3, 1971, 6-7; FCO/8/1543, April 23, 1970.

132 FCO/8/1543, April 29, 1970.

133 FCO/8/1543, May 5, 1970.

134 FCO/8/1543, May 6, 13, 1970.

135 Alam, op. cit., 147.

136 Alam, op. cit., 119; see also 129, 140-4, 152.

137 FCO/8/1304, April 23, 1970. See also FCO 8/1354 "Visit E. Luard M.P. to Arabia" Speaking Notes and Backround Brief on the Islands, 24 April to 7 May 1970 which provices and overview and summary of the British position at the time.

138 Alam, op. cit., 153; see also Alam's entry for June 1, 155-6.

139 Interview with Sir Denis Wright, July 1999. An executive with Buttes Gas and Oil, which had a concession from Sharjah to drill in a twelve-mile territorial sea around Abu Musa, argued during a December 1997 interview at the Crescent Oil Company in Sharjah that the British wanted to keep the Shah happy, and that the United States supported the British for geopolitical reasons, with Ambassador MacArthur lecturing him about Iran's role in stopping the Soviet Union from reaching the warm waters of the Gulf.

140 FCO/8/1224, May 28, 1970.

141 Alam, op. cit., 154-5; interview with Sir Denis Wright, July 1999.

142 FCO/8/1543, June 7, 9, 10, 11, 13, 15, 17, 26, July 6, 1970. On May 6, when Shaikh Saqr told Hayman of an Iraqi offer to help in road construction in Ras al-Khaimah, Hayman had advised him against accepting this offer. See FCO/8/1543, May 6, 1970.

143 Alam, op. cit., 159-60.

144 On June 19, the British deliberately sought to avoid more Iranian pressure on the islands when they decided not to request training facilities for British tank forces in Iran out of a concern that the Shah would use this request as a lever on the islands. See FCO/8/1224, June 19, 1970.

145 Alam, op. cit., 161. Saudi Arabia had proposed to Iran in April 1970 that a joint Iranian-Arab garrison stationed on the islands could satisfy Iran's security concerns. See Chapter Four of this study.

146 Chubin and Zabih, op. cit., 222. It is not clear from this quote whether the authors believed that the islands once belonged to Iran or whether they were simply paraphrasing Iranian officials.

147 Interview with Sir Denis Wright, July 1999.

148 Sir Denis Wright, unpublished memoirs.

CHAPTER 10

1   A. O. Taryam, *The Establishment of the United Arab Emirates, 1950-1985* (London: Croom Helm, 1987), 150 and J.B. Kelly, *Arabia, the Gulf, and the West* (USA: Basic Books, 1980), 78-9.

2   Kelly, op. cit., 79.

3   Asadollah Alam (ed. Alinaghi Alikhani), *The Shah and I: The Confidential Diary of Iran's Royal Court, 1969-1977* (London: I.B. Tauris, 1991), 163. See also Alam's entry for July 13, 163-4.

4   Sir Denis Wright, unpublished memoirs, 433.

5   Kelly, op. cit., 82; Balfour-Paul, op. cit., 124, 128.

6   See Taryam, op. cit., 150-1; Kelly, op. cit., 79-80.

7   Britain's new Conservative Government decided in July that France could not be counted on to provide support and should not be told details of Britain's efforts in the Gulf, primarily because they were commercial competitors in the Gulf. See FCO/8/1319, July 15, 1970; FCO/8/1324, December 18 and 23, 1970.

8   Kelly, op. cit., 80-2; see Alam entries on August 21, 165, and September 22, 170.

9   *Arab Report and Record*, August 16-31, 1970, 467 and September 1-15, 1970, 491.

10   Interview with Duncan Slater, London, July 1999.

11   FCO/8/1319, August 22, 1970. Luce also met with Rashad Pharaon, Kamal Adham and Omar Saqqaf. See FCO/8/1319, August 20 and 22, 1970. As he explained the "without prejudice" formula to Pharaon and Adham on August 20, "Iran would continue to believe, as she had for more than a hundred years, that the islands were hers, whilst Ras al-Khaimah and H.M.G. and the rest of the world could continue to say that the islands belonged to Ras al-Khaimah. Furthermore the inhabitants of the islands would continue to be subjects of Ras al-Khaimah and the Ras al-Khaimah flag would fly over the civil institutions on the islands, although of course the Iranian military camp would be under the Iranian flag." The ideas and reactions expressed to Luce by officials in Saudi Arabia, Kuwait, Sharjah and Ras al-Khaimah have been discussed in the previous chapter.

12   FCO/8/1319, August 23-27, September 3, 5, 6, 7, 8, 1970. Luce also cautioned Shaikh Saqr about his relations with Iraq, as Bullard and Coles had recommended. FCO/8/1543, July 6, August 24, September 9, 1970.

13   *Arab Report and Record*, September 16-30, 1970, p. 515. However, Alam wrote on September 22 that Luce "asked me to explain a comment of HIM's. What did he mean when he said that Iran would have no objection to a British presence in the Persian Gulf provided that it came on the basis of a bilateral agreement with the Sheikhs? 'Firstly,' said HIM, 'the Emirates must become independent; only then can they negotiate any sort of agreement. A pre-condition of their gaining independence is a complete withdrawal by foreign powers from the Persian Gulf. If the newly formed Federation of Emirates was subsequently to invite the British to return, that would be quite another matter'..." See Alam, op. cit., 170.

14   Interview with Duncan Slater, July 1999.

15   *Arab Report and Record*, September 16-30, 1970, 515.

16   Kelly, op. cit., 82.

17   FCO/8/1224, September 25, 1970. Douglas-Home also asked if Iran would need large defense installations on the islands. Zahedi said he did not see why but that this could be kept quiet.

18 FCO/8/1224, October 16, 1970. On the same day, Sir Philip Adams of the Foreign Office met with Massoudi and told him that "It might be harmful if Iran, a great power, appeared to be acting too drastically towards small states like the Sheikhdoms."

19 FCO/8/1304, October 20, 1970. At the same time, Douglas-Home hoped that Bahrain's Shaikh Isa might be able to influence the Shah on the questions of the UAE and the islands on Isa's scheduled visit to Iran. See FCO/8/1373, October 27, 1970.

20 FCO/8/1224, October 15, 1970. On the other hand, British Ambassador to Saudi Arabia William Morris wrote that "I share Political Resident's view that all we are likely to achieve in continuing to press the Saudis for help on the islands is to make them feel uncomfortable. I also agree that it is tactically desirable to do this (as also on the U.A.E.) since it could help to stifle Saudi grouses about our Gulf policy generally and our inability to get a better offer from Zaid on the Abu Dhabi frontier." See FCO/8/1310, November 1, 1970. Heath and Douglas-Home both indicated an interest in the Shah's request to purchase Chieftain tanks in their conversations with Iranian officials.

21 Interview with Duncan Slater, July 1999.

22 Taryam, op. cit., 155-6.

23 Taryam, op. cit., 153-4; Kelly, op. cit., 89; Shahram Chubin and Sepehr Zabih, *The Foreign Relations of Iran* (Berkeley, CA: University of California Press, 1974), 224. See also Alam's entry for October 20–November 21, 174. *Arab Report and Record,* October 1-15, 1970, 548. The Shah had already said this to Luce in September although the *Financial Times* did not report this until October 15. The *Financial Times* also said the Arabs had rejected an Iranian proposal to rent the islands, but this was mistaken.

24 Declassified US State Department document, October 28, 1970, filed at Politics 2/Trucial States.

25 Declassified US State Department document, October 2, 1970, filed at Politics 33/Persian Gulf. The two American companies, Occidental Petroleum and Buttes Gas and Oil, had taken their dispute to a California court, which had heard the case in September but had reached no decision. In early October, the State Department declined an appeal from Occidental to urge the UK to permit Occidental to drill in Abu Musa's waters inasmuch as the company claimed it had obtained permission from Iran. State argued that the American companies should first settle their legal dispute to facilitate UK mediation so that the UK ban on drilling could be lifted. Soon afterward, on October 15, Sharjah's Ruler Shaikh Khalid wrote to the Political Agent in Dubai, Julian Bullard, protesting that the British had given the Occidental Petroleum Company a map that showed Abu Musa lying within Iran's rather than Sharjah's jurisdiction. Shaikh Khalid expressed concern that Occidental had shared this map with Iran in its discussions and that Iran might use this map against Sharjah in their dispute over the island. He requested an immediate clarification of Britain's position. On the same date, John Boreta, the president of the Buttes Gas and Oil Company, which had a concession from Sharjah, wrote to British Minister of State Joseph Godber expressing concern about reports that the Foreign Office would not object to Occidental's deal with Iran. He also asked for official clarification. See declassified US State Department documents, November 18, 1970, filed at Politics 33/Persian Gulf. On October 28, 1970, Minister of State Godber replied to Buttes President

Boreta that Britain had reminded Occidental that the dispute was not yet resolved and that the British government favored continued mediation. Britain would also consider the interests of all the concerned shaikhdoms. Godber wrote "As you know, the fact that Iran claims sovereignty over Abu Musa is a factor which has had to be taken into account in this whole problem, notwithstanding the fact that, in the view of Her Majesty's Government and the Trucial States involved, sovereignty rests with Sharjah." See declassified US State Department document, November 18, 1970, filed at Politics 33/Persian Gulf; see also the Ruler of Sharjah's letter in *MEES*, December 3, 1971, 5.

26 Declassified US State Department document, October 27, 1970, filed at Politics 33/Persian Gulf. Buttes sought arbitration, arguing that the UK mediation of its contending claims with Occidental had been "inequitable" and had not recognized Sharjah's rights to drill in the continental shelf beyond its twelve-mile territorial sea. While the State Department did not know how oil concessions would be granted if Iran got sovereignty, they doubted Occidental's claim that Iran no longer objected to drilling as long as the proceeds were placed in escrow pending a decision on the distribution of revenues.

27 Declassified US State Department documents, April 30, 1971, filed at Politics 33/Persian Gulf. In late February, Bell had proposed a new oil revenue sharing formula raising Sharjah's proposed share from 20 to 25%, but Sharjah had rejected it. These documents provided by the Buttes Gas and Oil Company to the US Embassy in London also include correspondence from Buttes President Boreta to Shaikh Zayed of Abu Dhabi complaining of Abu Dhabi's drilling for oil within the concession area granted to Buttes by Sharjah in the twelve-mile territorial sea offshore of the island of Sir Abu Nu'air. Sir Abu Nu'air had long been claimed by the Qawasim but lies offshore of Abu Dhabi.

28 Declassified US State Department document, October 23, 1970, filed at Politics 33/Persian Gulf.

29 Declassified US State Department document, November 3, 1970, filed at Politics 33/Persian Gulf. The November 3 telegram summarizing a briefing by Iranian Foreign Minister Zahedi referred to Zahedi saying that Iran would make generous financial arrangements with Sharjah and Ras al-Khaimah over the islands, but that he warned Faisal that Iran would occupy the islands if satisfactory arrangements were not reached. Zahedi referred to King Faisal's "refusal to intercede in islands dispute."

30 Declassified US State Department document, November 6, 1970, filed at Politics 33/Persian Gulf. See also FCO 8/1296, Tel. No. 3236, Freeman, Washington to FCO, London dated 3 November 1970 which stated that HMG "has now decided to lean heavily on the rulers of Ras al-Khaimah and Sharjah to reach an agreement with Iran."

31 *Arab Report and Record*, November 1-15, 1970, 605.

32 From the Ruler of Sharjah's letter in *MEES*, December 3, 1971, 5.

33 From the Ruler of Sharjah's letter in *MEES*, December 3, 1971, 5. Taryam, op. cit., 179 provides a very seriously mistaken version of this quotation from the Ruler of Sharjah's letter: "The British government did seize [*sic*] Abu Musa from the Iranians and hand it over to Sharjah at the time of its entry into the Gulf." He then quotes correctly: "The British government has since its entry into the Gulf

considered Abu Musa to be Arab, and according to old documents in possession of the British government, the island was Arab."

34 Kelly, op. cit., 83; *Arab Report and Record*, November 1-15, 1970, 605. There were also Anglo-American discussions in December about the growing involvement of the Soviet Union and the People's Republic of China in the Indian Ocean, Arabian Gulf, Red Sea and Mediterranean Sea. See FCO/8/1322, November 23, 24, 26, 27, 1970.

35 Noyes, op. cit., 59.

36 Alvin J. Cottrell, "Iran's Armed Forces Under the Pahlavi Dynasty," in George Lenczowski (ed.), *Iran Under the Pahlavis* (Standford, CA: Hoover Institution Press, 1978), 403.

37 FCO/8/1304, November 18, 1970.

38 FCO/8/1304, November 18, 1970; FCO/8/1322, November 18, 1970.

39 FCO/8/1310, November 17, 1970.

40 FCO/8/1310, November 16, 1970.

41 FCO/8/1310, November 18, 1970. Prime Minister Heath also met briefly with Prince Fahd and said that Britain continued to work for a union of nine, but did not address other Gulf issues. FCO/8/1310, November 24, December 7, 1970. Se FCO 8/1311 "Brief II (b) Anglo-Saudi talks – Gulf Islands" for a summary of the British position and the questions as how to get Saudi assistance on the matter.

42 FCO/8/1310, November 26, 1970.

43 FCO/8/1310, December 3, 1970.

44 Kelly, op. cit., 85-8. British Ambassador to Saudi Arabia Morris had warned on November 18 that in this meeting "I suspect that one may be in for more talk about Saudi Arabia's willingness to look after our interests in the Gulf and provide us with commercial benefits (e.g. arms contracts) if we will cooperate in (so far unspecified) ways." See FCO/8/1310, November 18, 1970.

45 FCO/8/1322, December 4, 1970. Luce had expressed a similar view about the islands in his August 17, 1970 memo outlining his understanding of his assignment. "We hope to be able to resolve the two local disputes which might be considered a threat to peace, i.e. the islands problem and the Saudi/Abu Dhabi border dispute. But should one or both of these disputes remain unresolved when our Exclusive Agreements are terminated, could it conceivably be in the British interest to undertake a new defense commitment to the Union which might involve us in conflict with either Iran or Saudi Arabia or both?" See FCO/8/1319, August 17, 1970. Luce had also rejected arguments advanced by the Israelis that the British could take advantage of the disarray in the Arab world after the death of Nasser and therefore remain in the Gulf, arguing that Egypt and Iraq would still oppose a reversal of the withdrawal decision. Luce wrote: "We do not consider the Israelis to be particularly reliable judges of Arab attitudes and actions. Moreover in this particular case they may have been acting for reasons of their own in suggesting this idea since they may have concluded that a decision by us to reverse our withdrawal policy would lead to hostility between us and the Arabs; this might both take some of the Arab pressure off Israel and also cause us to be more pro-Israel." See FCO/8/1322, November 11, 12, 19, 20, 1970 and FCO/8/1324, December 22, 1970.

46 FCO/8/1322, November 12, 15, 16, 26, 1970; FCO/8/1324, December 3, 11, 15, 18, 21, 22, 28, 1970.

47 *Arab Report and Record*, December 1-15, 1970, 670.

48 FCO/8/1324, December 17, 1970. On December 16, Israeli Foreign Minister Abba Eban told Douglas-Home that the Shah had told Eban that he would take the islands by force if necessary. See FCO/8/1324, December 18, 1970.

49 FCO/8/1324, December 18, 1970.

50 *Arab Report and Record*, December 16-31, 1970, 684.

51 A.L.P. Burdett (ed.), *Records of the Emirates, 1966-1971* (London: Archive Editions, 2002), volume 6 (1971), 667-8.

52 Alam, op. cit., 182. See also Alam's entries for January 3, 1971, 187 and January 7, 1971, 189.

53 Sir Denis Wright, unpublished memoirs.

54 *Arab Report and Record*, January 16-31, 1971, 54.

55 Kelly, op. cit., 90; Interview with Duncan Slater, July 1999.

56 *Arab Report and Record*, February 1-14, 1971, 83; Taryam, op. cit., 164.

57 Sir Denis Wright, unpublished memoirs.

58 Interview with Duncan Slater, July 1999.

59 Taryam, op. cit., 167, for text.

60 Sir Denis Wright, unpublished memoirs, 435.

61 Declassified US State Department document, February 19, 1971, filed at Politics 33/Persian Gulf.

62 Ibid. On the same issue see FCO 8/1554, Tel. No 690 of 25 February [1971] Washington to FCO.

63 Kelly, op. cit., 90-1; *Arab Report and Record*, March 1-15, 1971, 135. Britain offered to turn over control of the Trucial Oman Scouts to form the core of the federation's army; it also offered British officers and British equipment for this force. Britain also offered the continued stationing of some British forces and other personnel for training of and liaison with the federation's defense forces as well as regular calls at Gulf ports by the British navy. Britain expected to retain its staging and overflying rights for its military aircraft.

64 *Arab Report and Record*, March 1-15, 1971, 135.

65 Ibid.

66 Twinam, op. cit., 87-8; Noyes, 55-8.

67 Ramazani, *Iran's Foreign Policy*, op. cit., 367-9; Lenczowski, *The Middle East in World Affairs*, op. cit., 218; Cottrell, op. cit., 418-27.

68 William Quandt, *Saudi Arabia in the 1980s* (Washington, DC: Brookings Institution Press, 1981), 51-3, 163.

69 Declassified US State Department document, April 1971, filed at Politics/Iran-Trucial States.

70 The British documents indicate that the attitude of US officials was that Great Britain should impose a solution which was possible if they "have the will to do so." See FCO 8/1573 Moberly, British Embassy in Washington to Acland, Arabian Department, FCO, London, 6 May 1971. Another letter dated March 11, 1971 mentioned the fact that Richard Murphy, the State Department Arabian Peninsula Country Director had inquired of William Luce during a meeting in London "whether it was really impossible to hope to solve the islands problem through deposing the Rulers concerned" and "whether our [British] interests and objectives would really be jeopardized by simply handing over the Islands to Iran." See FCO 8/1573 Egerton, Arabian Department, FCO, London to Moberly, British Embassy, Washington, 11 March, 1971.

71 Declassified US State Department document, September 8, 1971, filed at Politics 33/Persian Gulf.

72 Interview with Duncan Slater, July 1999. Tadmori, op. cit., 202-3 writes that Luce presented this 99-year lease proposal to Shaikh Khalid and that Shaikh Khalid rejected it. This is not consistent with what Zayn told the US Consul General. Moreover, Tadmori writes that this 99-year lease proposal was only one element of a larger draft agreement, which had as its other element a division of Abu Musa between Sharjah and Iran, a deferral of the issue of sovereignty for two years, and a determination of sovereignty after these two years. These two elements seem somewhat contradictory, inasmuch as a 99-year lease would not make sense if Iran insisted on and obtained sovereignty after two years. Tadmori may have been inadvertently mixing elements of different draft proposals. The lease proposal was evidently made by Sharjah, as noted by Zayn. The other proposal was evidently made or considered by Iran, as noted in the State Department's telegram of February 19, 1971.

73 Declassified US State Department document, May 6, 1971, filed at Politics 33/Persian Gulf.

74 Sir Denis Wright, unpublished memoirs.

75 Ibid.

76 Declassified US State Department document, May 6, 1971, filed at Politics 33/Persian Gulf.

77 See Chubin and Zabih, op. cit., 225; Taryam, op. cit., 171. Taryam suggests on 171-2 that there may have been some Iranian-British thought of a "pre-engineered" conflict during which Iran would take the islands.

78 *Records of the Emirates*, op. cit., vol. 6 (1971), 352-8.

79 Kelly, op. cit., 92-93, has written that this contract gave the British reasons "to pander to his [the Shah's] whims in May 1971..." Certainly the British regarded this as an important export contract, but it was only one of many reasons for accommodating the Shah. Britain began to deliver on Iran's order of 760 Chieftains in 1973 and Iran ordered another 1200 in 1975. See Alvin Cottrel, op. cit., 419 in George Lenczowski, op. cit.

80 The Ruler of Sharjah's August 23, 1971 letter to Arab leaders in *MEES*, December 3, 1971, 7, provides an excerpt from Luce's statement of the Shah's proposals to Shaikh Khalid.

81 Declassified US State Department document, May 12, 1971, filed at Politics 33/Persian Gulf.

82 Ahmed Jalal Al-Tadmori, *The Three Arabian Islands: A Documentary Study* (Ras al-Khaimah: 2000), 90-1 provides a brief extract from minutes of the meeting between Luce and Ras al-Khaimah Shaikh Saqr and Crown Prince Shaikh Khalid bin Saqr. This extract indicates that the Ras al-Khaimah police could remain on the Tunbs for two years after the Iranian occupation. However, the Sharjah Ruler's August 23, 1971 letter indicates that Sharjah's police were to withdraw "when the Iranian forces have landed," which is more consistent with the period of two or three weeks cited in the Department of State records.

83 Declassified US State Department document, dated June 18, 1971, filed at Politics 33/Persian Gulf. This is dated as a June 18 telegram, but it refers to a May 16 meeting with British officials and refers to the May 6 telegram concerning the Shah's proposals (telegram 2359). It is possible that Twinam waited until June 18 to write a telegram on the May 16 meeting, or that the June 18 telegram should

have been dated May 18, or that the meeting actually took place on June 16 rather than May 16.

84 Taryam, op. cit., 170-1 and 194 cites minutes from the meeting in Dubai on June 3. See also Kelly, op. cit., 93.

85 See *Arab Report and Record*, June 1-15, 1971, 287, which cites *Al-Khaleej*, June 5, 1971. See also the Ruler of Sharjah's letter in *MEES*, December 3, 1971, 7, which Taryam, op. cit., 180-181 cites.

86 Kelly, op. cit., 93. For recently declassified British Foreign Office records, see *Records of the Emirates*, op. cit., vol. 6 (1971), 371.

87 *Records of the Emirates, 1966-1971*, vol 6 (1971), 157-8.

88 Taryam, op. cit., 182.

89 Interview with Duncan Slater, July 1999.

90 *Chronicles*, op. cit., 12; Ramazani, *Iran's Foreign Policy*, op. cit., 424; Taryam, op. cit., 172. These sources indicate that Hoveyda and Zahedi also threatened force and opposition to the federation if the islands were not "restored."

91 Noyes, op. cit., 59.

92 Taryam, op. cit., 175-6; Twinam, op. cit., 89.

93 This is despite the fact that during this time Douglas-Home argued that Iran should not have a veto over the establishment of a UAE federation even if negotiations over the islands do not succeed. See FCO 8/1561 Tel No. 382 of 20 July 1971, FCO to Tehran.

94 Chubin and Zabih, op. cit., 227, 232.

95 Declassified US State Department document, July 29, 1971, filed at Politics 3/Trucial States.

96 See Chapter 5 of this study.

97 Declassified US State Department documents, filed at Politics 33/Persian Gulf, September 8 and 13, 1971. Rogers also conveyed the Shah's message that if the shaikhs refused to accept the terms to which the UK and Iran had agreed, Anglo-Iranian relations would be seriously jeopardized, Iran would denounce the proposed Federation of Arab Emirates, and Iran reserved the right to take whatever action it deemed necessary to protect its national interests. Rogers wrote that he understood that the Shah had already conveyed a similar message to the British. He also wrote that the United States and the UK were in agreement that an amicable settlement of the issue was essential for cooperation and security in the Gulf, and that he did not think the United States could add to British efforts to influence the shaikhs at that time.

98 Interview with Duncan Slater, July 1999. This letter itself was based on a September 9 memo from Assistant Secretary Sisco to Rogers, in which Sisco said he agreed with MacArthur that "'the Islands' dispute has now reached a crucial stage in which the British must persuade the shaykhs to accept the arrangement negotiated with Iran if there is to be stability and cooperation in the Gulf after British withdrawal." Sisco wrote: "I think we should be on record as encouraging this British effort. I believe the proposed letter...is the best way to assure that the British appreciate the seriousness with which we regard this problem." See declassified US State Department document, September 9, 1971, filed at Politics 33/Persian Gulf.

99 Tadmori, op. cit., 90-100, provides lengthy excerpts from transcripts of these meetings.

100 Ibid., 100-8 provides lengthy excerpts from the transcript of this meeting.

101 Declassified US State Department document, September 21, 1971, filed at Politics 33/Persian Gulf. The counterproposals put forward by Sharjah's Ruler indicated that he would agree to Iranian troops on Abu Musa and the flying of the Iranian flag and the exercise of Iranian jurisdiction within a garrison area, but insisted that all mineral rights on the island and within its territorial waters would remain Sharjah's; that Sharjah's administration and manifestation of authority would continue in those areas outside of the garrison area; and that the issue of sovereignty would be moot in perpetuity. He also proposed that Iran pay rent for the use of the island by its garrison. Luce answered that this would be unacceptable to Iran because it would tend to confirm Sharjah's sovereignty, and Sharjah's legal advisor Ely agreed with Luce.

102 Declassified US State Department document, September 28, 1971, filed at Politics 33/Persian Gulf. Slater told the author that Parsons was not central in the negotiations, that his information was second-hand, and that the American reporting is third-hand. This may explain the confusion over the attitudes of the two Rulers. Interview with Duncan Slater, London, July 1999. Parsons also noted that the British thought the Buttes/Occidental dispute complicated an Abu Musa settlement and did not agree to Sharjah's claim of a twelve-mile territorial sea around Abu Musa because it favored Sharjah at the expense of the other emirates and caused a row between the companies. British Embassy officials had asked Deputy Assistant Secretary Davies one day earlier about the prospects for agreement between the companies and were told that while company lawyers were talking to each other there was no indication of agreement.

103 Declassified US State Department document, October 8, 1971, filed at Politics 33/Persian Gulf. Boreta, Ely and Kuchel also said during this October 6 meeting at the State Department that Khalid demanded that the ban on drilling offshore of Abu Musa be re-imposed for Occidental, that Buttes be permitted to drill and that Luce had said he could make no commitment on this. This account supports Taryam's version of strong British pressure on Sharjah and supports the UAE argument that the MoU was obtained under British duress as well as Iranian duress. See Taryam, op. cit., 182-3. However, Slater again said that Boreta, Ely and Kuchel were not present at the meeting between Luce and Shaikh Khalid, and argued that this quoted language was not used. Interview with Duncan Slater, London, July 1999. During their meeting at the State Department, Boreta, Ely and Kuchel warned that the Sharjah Ruler might turn to Libya or Iraq for support if abandoned by Britain and if the United States did not influence the Shah. They referred to the 750-page Coward Chance report on "Sharjah's Title to the Island of Abu Musa," dated September 1971, which had been submitted to the Foreign Office and the State Department and had concluded that "the title of Sharjah to the island is unassailable under international law." Boreta asked if the report should be submitted to Iran and the State Department said "they'd have to make own judgment." See declassified State Department document, October 8, 1971, filed at Politics 33/Persian Gulf.

104 Kelly, op. cit., 94.

105 Declassified US State Department document, September 29, 1971, filed at Politics 33/Persian Gulf.

106 Declassified US State Department document, October 8, 1971, filed at Politics 33/Persian Gulf. During their October 6 meeting at the State Department, Ely and Kuchel asked the United States to help persuade the Shah to go to arbitration rather than to use force if negotiations broke down, but the State Department said it had already urged compromise on the Shah, most recently on October 5, and could not suggest other means of resolving the dispute while negotiations were ongoing.

107 Declassified US State Department document, November 2, 1971, filed at Politics 33/Persian Gulf. Shaikh Khalid's demand regarding a twelve-mile territorial sea was viewed as a ploy to involve the British in recognizing Sharjah's decree on the subject, which applied not only to Abu Musa but also to Sir Abu Nu'air. Luce did not agree to this. Northcutt Ely said in his 1992 deposition at the Hague that Iran wanted the concession granted to Buttes by Sharjah to be replaced by a concession to Buttes from Iran and that Ely proposed instead a protocol to Sharjah's concession to Buttes which would share the revenue equally between Sharjah and Iran. Shaikh Khalid also agreed to the Shah's demand that the Buttes concession be modified to conform with "standard OPEC terms." See declassified State Department document, November 3, 1971 for a report that the Sharjah newspaper *Al-Khaleej* had written that Britain was pressuring Shaikh Khalid, that he had said that he was "subject to fearful pressure" and was "appealing to Arab countries to move quickly to coordinate their position and take [a] United Arab stand on [the] Islands question." Upon Luce's suggestion, Khalid sent a telegram to the Shah, assuring the Shah that the statements attributed to him were false and reaffirming his desire for a peaceful settlement of the islands problem.

108 Tadmori, op. cit., 108-15 provides excerpts from the minutes of this meeting. See also declassified US State Department document, November 2, 1971, filed at Politics 33/Persian Gulf. After describing the terms of the MoU on Abu Musa, Chubin and Zabih, op. cit., 227 writes that "The Shaykh of Ras al-Khaymah refused a similar agreement." Glen Balfour-Paul, *The End of Empire in the Middle East: Britain's Relinquishment of Power in her Last Three Arab Dependencies* (Cambridge: Cambridge University Press, 1991), 133-4 also describes the Abu Musa MoU and then writes that the Ruler of Ras al-Khaimah "maintained his adamant rejection of a similar agreement over the Tunbs." The version of Vinson and Elkins, op. cit., 3.59-3.61 also claims that a similar deal was offered to Ras al-Khaimah. In fact, the only deal on the table for Ras al-Khaimah at this time was to cede sovereignty over both the Tunbs for financial compensation, whereas the MoU on Abu Musa did not require Sharjah to cede sovereignty and did permit Sharjah to continue its administration over half of the island. Thus the deals were not similar.

109 Declassified US State Department document, November 8, 1971, filed at Politics 33/Persian Gulf. On November 9, the State Department advised the US Embassy in Kuwait that Ely was upset regarding continuing stories in *Al-Khaleej*, which was licensed in Sharjah, but published in Kuwait, and had asked whether the Government of Kuwait could stop these stories. The State Department had then learned that at the urging of the British, Sharjah's Ruler had suspended publication of the paper. The Department recommended that if Kuwaiti papers picked up the story then the US Embassy in Kuwait, after consulting with the British Embassy there, should urge the Government of Kuwait "to prevent publication of articles

undermining promising prospects for Abu Musa settlement." See declassified US State Department even document, November 9, 1971, filed at Politics 33/Persian Gulf.

110 Declassified US State Department document, November 12, 1971, filed at Politics 33/Persian Gulf.

111 Declassified US State Department document, November 8, 1971, filed at Politics 33/Persian Gulf. Later, congressional staff member Michael Van Dusen told the Crown Prince that there was congressional opposition to any extension of US foreign commitments. Many of these requests by Ras al-Khaimah had already been conveyed to the State Department on September 24 by American businessman Robert Sheridan, who said that the emirate sought US support for an independent Ras al-Khaimah and its admission to the UN, and that Ras al-Khaimah was offering the United States a military base. Sheridan said he had been told that Ras al-Khaimah had been approached three times by the Soviets for a refueling facility and that Ras al-Khaimah did not intend to join a federation. Consul General Dinsmore was instructed to advise Ras al-Khaimah that a US military presence in the emirate would be offensive to its neighbors and could stimulate pressure against Shaikh Saqr and his family, and that Ras al-Khaimah should join a larger grouping for its future security and prosperity. The State Department advised Dinsmore that "we view Saqr's approach as attempted end-run to avoid facing problems with Iran on islands issue and sacrificing his 'sovereignty' in federation context." See declassified US State Department document, September 24, 1971, filed at Politics/Trucial States-United States. Dinsmore reported that he had followed his instructions on September 27. Despite promising Shaikh Saqr that he would keep this a secret, he informed British Political Agent Walker, knowing that the State Department intended to inform the British. Walker was not surprised and knew that Saqr had been contacting Arab governments and having no luck in this endeavor. Walker also thought that Saqr would go into the federation. Dinsmore advised Washington that Saqr had no choice but to join the federation, that the Soviets would offend local and wider Arab opinion if they supported Ras al-Khaimah, and that Saqr would isolate himself if he invited the Soviets in. See declassified US State Department document, September 29, 1971, filed at Politics/Trucial States-United States.

112 Declassified US State Department document, November 11, 1971, filed at Politics/Trucial States-United States.

113 Ibid.

114 Declassified US State Department document, November 17, 1971, filed at Politics/Trucial States-United States.

115 *The Times*, November 18, 1971.

116 The MoU even permitted Buttes to begin drilling offshore of Abu Musa. Interview, Crescent Oil, Sharjah, December 1997.

117 Kelly, op. cit., 95; Cordesman, *The Gulf and the Search for Strategic Stability* (Boulder, CO: Westview Press, 1980), 417, also indicates that there was such an agreement. Recently declassified documents published in *Records of the Emirates, 1966-1971*, vol. 6 (1971), 569, indicate that British official Wilton in Kuwait, referring to "events in the Tunbs," wrote on December 1: "The action Sir W. Luce agreed on 11 November could be so described was [sic] occupation with return of the police to the mainland." Tadmori, op. cit., 85, 126 indicates that refugees from the Tunbs said after Iran's November 30 invasion of the island that three foreign television jounalists had visited the Greater Tunb one week before the invasion

and had taken footage of the Ras al-Khaimah policemen and their weapons, and that one of these journalists accompanied Iranian paratroopers who landed on the islands on November 30. According to Tadmori, the refugees reported that the journalists had come to the island before the invasion with the knowledge and cooperation of the British Commander of the Ras al-Khaimah police in Ras al-Khaimah. They argued that the purpose of this British-sponsored visit was to gather information on the strength of the police force on the island and to pass this information on to the Iranians before the invasion.

118 Ramazani, *Iran's Foreign Policy*, op. cit., 424. Ramazani notes, however, that Luce did not confirm the Masudi account. One Washington analyst said in a March 1999 interview in Abu Dhabi that Sir Peter Ramsbotham and Sir William Luce both personally swore to him that the Shah was making up the story of a side agreement with Britain regarding the islands. According to them, the Shah felt that he had to tell this story that he had a deal with the British in order to save face. The official Foreign Office documents show that the British had proposed such a package deal to the Shah, but had not promised to deliver it. They had tried to negotiate a reasonable deal for the emirates and had tried to discourage the Shah from the use of force. However, in the face of the Shah's threats to use force, and in the interest of achieving a federation, the British did press the Rulers to satisfy the Shah on the islands.

119 Chubin and Zabih, op. cit., 226-7.

120 Julian Walker, "The Historical Background to the Dispute over the Gulf Islands up to 1971," lecture notes, courtesy of Julian Walker.

121 Glen Balfour-Paul, *The End of Empire in the Middle East,* op. cit., 134. As for the motivation for the Shah's timing, Balfour-Paul suggests on 134 that "possibly he wanted as much of the resulting Arab odium as possible to fall on Britain's head."

122 Declassified US State Department document, November 27, 1971, filed at Politics/Trucial States-United States.

123 Ibid.

124 Declassified US State Department document, November 30, 1971, filed at Politics/Trucial States-United States.

125 *MEES*, December 3, 1971.

126 Kelly, op. cit., 97 reports on the British naval presence in the Gulf of Oman; Tadmori, op. cit., 118-21, reports on the Iranian military assets deployed in its operation against the Tunbs.

127 Tadmori, op. cit., 141-4, 161-2, 166, provides the texts of the statements made by Douglas-Home, Arthur, and Walker. See also Taryam, op. cit., 184.

128 See *Arab Report and Record*, December 1-15, 1971, 623, 625 and 628. A word may be added here about Libya, which did not go as far as breaking diplomatic relations with Britain. The British Treasury announced on December 14 that it was expelling Libya from the Sterling Area and that Libya's currency would be considered as a foreign currency for exchange purposes after Libya withdrew its funds from British banks.

129 Kelly, op. cit., 95. A recent British Ambassador to the UAE said in a July 1997 interview that the Shah occupied the islands one day before the termination of the British treaty with the emirates and days before the establishment of the UAE, so that the occupation would not be seen as an overt attack against an independent Arab state and because it would enable Iran to claim British connivance. Also, Tehran was happy to embarrass Britain for pressuring Iran to drop its claim to

Bahrain. British and US documents do not, however, support the assertion by Taryam that "It was the influence and the short-term interests of the United States that made Britain condone and, in fact, concur in the occupation of the islands while its presence in the region still had to be officially terminated." See Taryam, op. cit., 186.

130 *Arab Report and Record*, 1-15 December 1971, 622; Tadmori, op. cit., 161-6.

131 A maritime patrol of five British frigates and destroyers, as well as reconnaissance aircraft, would be maintained "East of Suez" and the RAF base on Oman's Masireh Island would be expanded. The Political Residency in Bahrain was terminated in March 1972. See Alec Douglas-Home speech to the House of Commons, December 6, 1971, quoted in Tadmori, op. cit., 142; Balfour-Paul, op. cit., 135; Gause, op. cit., 255; *Arab Report and Record*, December 16-31, 1971, 646-7.

132 *Arab Report and Record*, February 1-14, 1972, 67.

133 Declassified US State Department document, December 4, 1971, filed at Politics 16/UAE. The US view was also expressed in Joseph Twinam's 1991 book, in which he wrote of the Sharjah Ruler's "statesmanship in resolving this potentially explosive problem" and also wrote that the Ras al-Khaimah Ruler "refused to cooperate with British efforts to strike some bargain with Iran over ownership of the virtually uninhabited Tunbs..." 54.

134 US Ambassador MacArthur cabled the State Department on December 5 to say that Iran's Foreign Minister Khalatbari had informed him that Iranian troops landing on the Tunbs had found Yemenis among those who had opposed the Iranian landings, that they had found small arms of Baathist origin and that Iran thought this was why there had been resistance to the landings. MacArthur seemed to accept the Iranian argument that it was a radical Arab presence on the islands rather than an indigenous Ras al-Khaimah presence that accounted for resistance to Iranian occupation. See declassified US State Department document, December 5, 1971, filed at Politics 32-6/Persian Gulf.

135 Alec Douglas-Home to the House of Commons, December 6, 1971, quoted in Tadmori, op. cit., 142.

136 Kelly, op. cit., 95.

137 Ibid., 96.

138 *Records of the Emirates, 1966-1971*, vol. 6 (1971), 588-9, 599-602.

139 *Provisional Verbatim Record of the Sixteen Hundred and Tenth Meeting of the UN Security Council: Discussion and Record of the Security Council on Two Islands in the Arabian Gulf*, December 9, 1971; Taryam, op. cit., 188. Tadmori, op. cit., 181-9, provides the transcripts of several conversations in late November and early December between the British Ambassador in Cairo, Richard Beaumont, and the Assistant Secretary General of the Arab League, during which Beaumont made many of the same arguments made on 9 December by Crowe and earlier in December by Arthur, Walker and Douglas-Home.

140 *Provisional Verbatim Record*, op. cit.

141 The Soviet Union also remained silent during the Security Council discussions. The Soviets did not want to jeopardize their improving relations with Iran by confronting the Iranians on this issue. Furthermore, such a confrontation was unnecessary in order to continue building relations with both radical and

conservative Arab states. The People's Republic of China and France also remained silent.

142 On September 2, 1972 the US Embassy in Amman reported to the State Department that British and Jordanian officials, as well as the Arab League Secretary General, were coordinating to press Shaikh Zayed into meeting the Shah's terms for rapprochement. See declassified US State Department document, September 2, 1972, filed at Politics/Saud.

143 Declassified US Department of State document, January 26, 1972, filed at Politics/UAE-US.

144 Twinam, op. cit., 98.

145 Ramazani, *Iran's Foreign Policy*, 356, 370.

146 *Arab Report and Record*, July 1-15, 1972, 337.

147 Twinam, op. cit., 96.

148 Declassified US State Department document, August 22, 1972, filed at Politics/South Yemen-UAE. On December 30, the US Embassy in Sanaa reported to the State Department that the Ambassador told YAR officials that YAR defense needs would be taken under review by the United States and its friends and allies in the region. See declassified US State Department document, December 30, 1972, filed at Politics 15/Yemen.

149 Declassified US State Department document, January 8, 1973, filed at Politics/Iran-Saud.

150 Declassified US State Department document, January 9, 1973, filed at Politics 1/Iran.

151 Declassified US State Department document, April 13, 1973, filed at Politics/Iran-Saud.

152 Declassified US State Department document, August 3, 1973, filed at Politics/Iran-Saud.

CHAPTER 11

1 George Lenczowski, *American Presidents and the Middle East* (Durham: Duke University Press, 1990), 203-8 and Joseph Twinam, *The Gulf, Cooperation and the Council: An American Perspective* (Washington, DC: The Middle East Policy Council, 1992), 73, 98. The UAE condemned the Soviet invasion of Afghanistan, but was uneasy about the US reaction, fearing this would lead to superpower conflict in the area.

2 Dilip Hiro, *The Longest War: The Iran-Iraq Military Conflict* (London: Paladin Grafton Books, 1990), 40-70, 77-8; James Noyes, *The Clouded Lens: Persian Gulf Security and U.S. Policy* (Stanford, CA: Hoover Institution Press, 1982), 114-5. The *Financial Times*, October 2, 1980, wrote that Iraq intended to occupy the islands from bases in the UAE.

3 Martin S. Navias and E.R. Hooton, *Tanker Wars: The Assault on Merchant Shipping During The Iran-Iraq Crisis, 1980-1988* (London: I.B. Tauris and Company Ltd., 1996), 39-40.

4 Twinam, op. cit., 145-7, 159-62.

5 Navias and Hooton, op. cit., 62-3, 68.

6   Ibid., 68-9.

7   Ibid., 77-9, 92-6, 123-5.

8   Twinam, op. cit., 140-2; Tutunji, op. cit., 178-81. Two other UN Security Council resolutions should be noted. When Iran answered Iraqi air attacks against Iranian oil installations and shipping with Iranian attacks on neutral shipping to and from Kuwaiti and Saudi ports, mainly in the northern Gulf, UNSC Resolution 552 of June 1, 1984 condemned all attacks against neutral shipping and demanded an end to them, insisting on freedom of navigation, but did not mention Iran by name. The UN Security Council also passed a number of cease-fire resolutions during 1986 and 1987, including UNSC Resolution 582 of February 24, 1986, which again deplored attacks on neutral shipping.

9   Interview with Frank Carlucci, Washington, DC, October 1997. The US logic for undertaking this mission, named Operation Earnest Will, has been explained by a number of the decision-makers who were involved. Former Chairman of the Joint Chiefs of Staff Admiral William Crowe writes that he supported the re-flagging and escorting as a way of improving ties with Saudi Arabia, Kuwait, the UAE, Oman and Jordan, noting in particular that Saudi Arabia was dismayed by US congressional rejection of a number of Saudi requests for US arms sales. See Admiral William J. Crowe, Jr., with David Chanoff, *The Line of Fire* (New York, NY: Simon and Schuster, 1993), 181-2. While Crowe does not say so, these countries were also deeply concerned about the reliability of the United States in the wake of the November 1986 "Iran-Contra" revelations that the United States had worked with Israel since August 1985 to supply TOW anti-tank missiles and Hawk surface-to-air missiles to Iran, in an effort to secure the release of US hostages held in Lebanon. See Lenczowski, *American Presidents and the Middle East*, op. cit., 233-42 for an account of this episode. It was later learned that the United States had also transferred 23 F-4E fighter jets to Iran in 1984, as well as aircraft spare parts and TOW missiles in 1982. See *Jane's Sentinel Security Assessment: The Gulf States* (UK: Jane's Information Group, Ltd., 2000), 112. Former US Secretary of Defense Weinberger writes "...it seemed immaterial to me whether Kuwaiti ships were re-flagged or not. To my mind the main thing was for us to protect the right of innocent, non-belligerent and extremely important commerce to move freely in international open waters – and by our offering protection, to avoid conceding the mission to the Soviets." Caspar Weinberger, *'Fighting for Peace': Seven Critical Years in the Pentagon* (New York, NY: Warner Books, 1990), 397. The May 17, 1987 Iraqi Mirage jet and Exocet missile attack on the *USS Stark* was viewed as an accident, but raised the possibility that Iran might think it could harass US naval forces in the Gulf. See Lenczowski, *American Presidents and the Middle East*, op. cit., 246.

10 Navias and Hooton, op. cit., 140.

11 Razavi, op. cit., 62-3; Navias and Hooton, op. cit., 8, 64, 122, 152.

12 Navias and Hooton, op. cit., 31.

13 Ibid., 112-5, 121, 135-8, 141, 170, 183; interview, Joint Staff, Pentagon, Arlington, Virginia, 1997. Also see Anthony H. Cordesman and Abraham R. Wagner, *The Lessons of Modern War, Volume II: The Iran–Iraq War* (Boulder, CA: 1990), 298 and 563.

14 Crowe, op. cit., 192-7; Navias and Hooton, op. cit., 143-4.

15 Crowe, op. cit., 197-9. See also Navias and Hooton, op. cit., 141, 143-6, 155-6, 169, 173-4 and Weinberger statement. Crowe suggests that this took place in the Strait of Hormuz, but Cordesman and Wagner, op. cit., 318-9, and Navias and Hooton, op. cit., 146, indicate that it took place 50 nautical miles northeast of Bahrain. The United States later returned the surviving crew and destroyed the vessel.

16 Navias and Hooton, op. cit., 153.

17 Ibid., 154.

18 Ibid., 155.

19 Cordesman and Wagner, op. cit., 334.

20 Crowe, op. cit., 200-1; Cordesman and Wagner, op. cit., 375-6; Navias and Hooton, op. cit., 170-1.

21 Crowe, op. cit., 201-2; Cordesman and Wagner, op. cit., 378; Navias and Hooton, op. cit., 171. Crowe writes that the Iranian frigate, the *Zahan*, was operating with the Boghammers and was sunk with them. However, the other two sources state that the *Zahan* came out later in the afternoon and was sunk off Qeshm island and Larak island.

22 Crowe, op. cit., 202-3; Cordesman and Wagner, op. cit., 378; Navias and Hooton, op. cit., 170-3.

23 Cordesman and Wagner, op. cit., 379; Navias and Hooton, op. cit., 143, 173.

24 Crowe, op. cit., 203-9; Cordesman and Wagner, op. cit., 390-4; Navias and Hooton, op. cit., 174-5.

25 Navias and Hooton, op. cit., 177-81.

26 Interview with Frank Carlucci, Washington, DC, October 1997. Navias and Hooton, op. cit., 154, write that Farsi was discussed and rejected as a target in October 1987.

27 Interview, Washington, DC, October 1997.

28 Interview, US State Department, Washington, DC, December 1997.

29 Crowe, op. cit., 200-1.

30 Interview, US State Department, Washington, DC, 1997. Several other officials with the Arabian Peninsula Affairs bureau of the State Department, the Northern Gulf Affairs bureau of the State Department, and the Joint Staff also make this argument. Interviews, US State Department, Washington, DC, and the Pentagon, Arlington, Virginia, 1997.

31 Iran's argument was that the United States violated the *1955 Treaty of Amity, Economic Relations and Consular Rights between the United States and Iran* when the United States took combat action against the Iranian platforms. The Counter-Memorial and Counter-Claim of the United States of America, filed at the International Court of Justice in June 1997, also argues that the oil platforms were not producing oil that could have been sold to the US, noting that *Rostam* was not producing at all when the US fired on it in October 1987, and that the US had already prohibited US imports of Iranian oil before firing on *Sirri* and *Sassan* (now *Salman*) in April 1988. The US also argues that Iran itself had violated the treaty by its attacks on US shipping and that this precluded Iran from seeking relief. The ICJ held its first hearing on this case in February 2003.

32 Interview, Washington, October 1997.

33 Interview, Abu Dhabi, November 1997.

34 Interview, US State Department, Washington, DC, 1997.

35 Interview, Washington, DC, 1997.

36 Interview, Washington, DC, 1997.

37 For a general discussion of Russian policy in the Gulf, see Robert V. Barylski, "The Collapse of the Soviet Union and Gulf Security" in David E. Long and Christian Koch (eds.) *Gulf Security in the Twenty-First Century* (Abu Dhabi: The Emirates Center for Strategic Studies and Research, 1997), especially 106-17. For a general discussion of Chinese policy in the Gulf, see John Calabrese, "China and the Persian Gulf," *Middle East Journal* 52, no. 3 (Summer 1998), 351-66.

38 Tutunji, op. cit., 189; Al Roken, op. cit., 155; Rugh, op. cit., 169.

39 Tadmori, op. cit., 256.

40 "Warren Christopher Has Productive Meeting with GCC." Press release regarding Secretary of State Warren Christopher's meeting with Gulf Cooperation Council Foreign Ministers, September 30, 1994. Text of press release courtesy of US Information Agency.

41 "Christopher, Gulf Cooperation Council Issue Joint Communiqué." Remarks by Secretary of State Warren Christopher and Bahraini Foreign Minister Mohammed bin Mubarak Al-Khalifa regarding a joint communiqué released by the US and the Gulf Cooperation Council, March 13, 1995. Text of the communiqué and press conference courtesy of the US State Department.

42 Richard Schofield, "Boundaries, Territorial Disputes and the GCC States," in *Gulf Security in the Twenty-First Century*, 162-3. See also Richard Schofield, "Border Disputes in the Gulf: Past, Present, and Future," in Gary G. Sick and Lawrence G. Potter (eds) *The Persian Gulf at the Millennium: Essays in Politics, Economy, Security, and Religion* (New York, NY: St. Martin's Press, 1997), 152. These articles also provide excerpts from the text of the joint communiqué.

43 Interview, US. Embassy, Abu Dhabi, UAE, September 1997 and interview, US Department of State, Washington, DC, October, 1997.

44 Interview, US Embassy, Abu Dhabi, 1999.

45 *New York Times*, March 1, 1995, A11; *Washington Post*, March 1, 1995. Cordesman, *Bahrain, Oman, Qatar, and the UAE*, op. cit., 303, writes that Iran had deployed Improved Hawks on Abu Musa, had also built a CSSC-3 Seersucker anti-ship missile site on the south side of Abu Musa, thus enabling Iran to hit UAE ports, and that Iran may have also deployed a surface-to-surface modification of the SA-6 surface-to-air missile in order to pose a threat to UAE cities. He also writes that Iran had lengthened the runway on Abu Musa to accept larger military cargo aircraft and had built a new pier, a new command bunker and a new desalination plant on the island. He also noted that the other islands on which Iran had deployed CSSC-3 Seersucker anti-ship missiles were Qeshm and Sirri. The US was also concerned at this time about Iran's acquisition of three Russian-built diesel electric submarines, long-range missiles, and nuclear reactors, as well as about Iranian terror and Iranian opposition to the Arab-Israeli peace process. For a brief analysis of US objections to Iran's foreign policy in general, including in the Gulf, see, for example, Thomas R. Mattair, "Horizons for Cooperation in the [Persian] Gulf: The View from Washington," in *The Iranian Journal of International Affairs*, VII, no. 3 (Fall 1995), 576-84.

46 *Washington Post*, March 3, 1995.

47 Testimony of Joseph Nye, Assistant Secretary of Defense for International Security Affairs, before the Senate Foreign Relations Committee Subcommittee on Near Eastern and South Asian Affairs, March 2, 1995.

48 Another administration official indicated that Perry had called renewed attention to the Iranian deployments in part because of his efforts to convince the UAE and the other GCC states to increase military cooperation and defense spending and to allow the US to pre-position military equipment in these states for possible use in a future conflict in the Gulf. See *New York Times*, March 23, 1995, A9; *Christian Science Monitor*, March 23, 1995, 1 and 8. It should be noted here that some US military officers claimed that Iranian troops on the islands numbered only 3,700 and that Perry had provided "inflated" numbers. Furthermore, some said Iran's real purpose for the deployments was for defense against the US military deployments that had taken place in October 1994 and against the US interception of two Iranian tankers attempting to smuggle Iraqi oil in violation of the UN sanctions against Iraq. As a result, the administration was accused of "manufacturing a crisis." Indeed, one army officer argued that the Iranian troops should be ignored, asking "What offensive action could they launch from an island?" and also asking "Why would they [Iran] want to close the Strait of Hormuz? The only money they make is from oil, and every drop of it comes through the Strait of Hormuz." It did not appear from the interview that this army officer was aware that Iran had used Abu Musa and the Tunbs as platforms to attack neutral shipping in the Gulf and the Strait of Hormuz during the 1980s. See *Washington Times*, March 27, 1999, A1, A22. Cordesman writes that some US experts also thought that Secretary Perry confused the deployment of poison gas with the deployment of non-lethal agents, but that Iran did seem to have deployed small stocks of CS gas on Abu Musa. Cordesman, *Bahrain, Oman, Qatar, and the UAE*, op. cit., 303.

49 *United States Security Strategy for the Middle East* (Washington, DC: Office of the Assistant Secretary of Defense for International Security Affairs, Middle East and North African Affairs, May 1995), 16. Schofield, op. cit., 163 writes: "The United States' overt support for the position of the UAE in the islands dispute was consistent with condemnation of Iran a month earlier for having significantly remilitarized the northern half of Abu Musa island and the Lower Gulf more generally. Chief among American concerns were the periodically large number of Iranian ground forces stationed on the island and the movement by the Iranian military of air defense capabilities to Abu Musa and other Lower Gulf islands." Iran had not only remilitarized the northern half of the island, but had also militarized the southern half of the island, which was allocated to the jurisdiction of Sharjah. Moreover, Iran had not only increased its troops and air defense capabilities on the island, but had also increased its anti-ship missile capabilities on the island, and particularly on the southern half of the island.

50 Navias and Hooton, op. cit., 201-2.

51 *Middle East Insight* XII, no. 2 (January-February 1996), 4.

52 *Washington Post*, June 18, 1997.

53 See for example Patrick Clawson, "US Sanctions on Iran," *The Emirates Occasional Papers*, no. 8 (Abu Dhabi: The Emirates Center for Strategic Studies and Research, 1997).

54 Text provided to the author by the US Department of State, Near East Agency, Arabian Peninsula Affairs.

55 Tadmori, op. cit., 253-4.

56 *United Press International*, March 13, 1995.

57 *Gulf News*, April 30, 1998. In April 1996, the German Minister of State for Foreign Affairs, Helmut Schieffer, met with Shaikh Zayed and expressed Germany's support for the UAE's efforts to seek a peaceful resolution of the issue of the three islands. See *Chronicle of Progress*, op. cit., 410.

58 *Gulf News*, March 4, 1999, 5.

59 *Al-Ittihad*, March 14, 1999, 1.

60 *Gulf News*, June 13, 1999.

61 *Gulf News*, October 27, 1999.

62 *Gulf News*, November 3, 1999.

63 *Gulf News*, January 25, 2000.

64 *Gulf News*, March 23, 2000.

65 *Gulf News*, April 19, 2000.

66 *Gulf News*, November 1, 2000.

67 *Gulf News*, April 25, 2001.

68 Interview, UAE Ministry of Foreign Affairs, Abu Dhabi, 1997.

69 Ibid.

70 Louis Henkin, Richard Crawford Pugh, Oscar Schachter and Hans Smit, *International Law: Cases and Materials*, Third Edition (St. Paul, MN: West Publishing Company, 1993), 862-3. The Court may render an advisory opinion if it has sufficient evidence and if it does not violate the propriety of the Court.

71 Interview, US State Department, Washington, DC, 1997. For example, the ICJ issued an advisory opinion in 1950 indicating that the supervisory functions provided for in the League of Nations mandate over South West Africa were to be exercised by the UN. The General Assembly then passed Resolution 2145 in 1966, declaring that South Africa's mandate over South West Africa was terminated and that it now came under the responsibility of the UN. The Security Council declared South Africa's continued presence in South West Africa, now Namibia, to be in violation of General Assembly Resolution 2145 in a number of Security Council Resolutions, including Security Council Resolution 276 of 1970, which declared South Africa's presence in Namibia to be illegal. The Security Council asked the ICJ to render an advisory opinion as to the legal consequences for states of South Africa's continued presence in Namibia notwithstanding Security Council Resolution 276. The ICJ then issued an advisory opinion that South Africa was under an obligation to end its administration over Namibia and that other states were under an obligation not to recognize the acts of South Africa's administration in Namibia. Both the General Assembly and the Security Council then passed resolutions welcoming this opinion. In 1974, the UN Council for Namibia issued a decree requesting that all states refrain from exploiting Namibia's mineral resources as long as South Africa maintained its administration of Namibia, and in 1985, the UN Council for Namibia instituted legal proceedings against the Netherlands for violating the 1974 decree. See Henkin, Pugh, Schachter and Smit, op. cit., 1088; Dixon and McCorquodale, op. cit., 101-2.

72 Interviews, US Department of State, Washington, DC, 1997; British Embassy in Abu Dhabi, 1997, UAE Ministry of Foreign Affairs, Abu Dhabi, 1997. A request by the Security Council may be blocked by a single veto, but it only takes a simple majority in the General Assembly to make a request. There are agreements between the General Assembly and various organs and agencies as to whether they can or cannot request an advisory opinion in generic rather than specific kinds of cases within the scope of their concerns. The General Assembly can also authorize

an organ or agency to request an advisory opinion in a specific case. The ICJ can accept or reject a request from a UN organ or agency after finding that it is or is not within the scope of the organ or agency.

73 For discussions of the right of innocent passage, see Henkin, Pugh, Schachter and Smit, op. cit., 1254-7 and Rezai, op. cit., 37-49. For discussions of the right of transit passage, which applies to international straits such as the Strait of Hormuz, see Henkin et. al., op. cit., 1261-3 and Rezai, op. cit., 56-71.

74 Interviews, US Department of State, Washington, DC and the US Department of Defense, Arlington, Virginia, 1997.

75 Interviews, UAE Ministry of Foreign Affairs, Abu Dhabi, 1997.

76 In an interview in London in October 1997, this adviser claimed that the UAE federal government is concerned about the manifestations of Iranian influence in the emirates, that the federal government would like battles with Iran, and that the federal government is encouraged by "outside parties" to expand its disputes with Iran.

77 Interviews, US Department of Defense, Arlington, Virginia, 1997.

78 Interviews, UAE Ministry of Foreign Affairs, Abu Dhabi, 1997. Carlucci adds that the islands are a problem for the UAE and Iran to solve; that the Arab world is not prepared to tolerate a US military initiative on the islands; that the US would have to put troops on the islands to hold them; and that if the US could not explain a compelling security interest for US involvement in Bosnia it could not do so for involvement on the islands. The US can train the UAE's internal security, he says, but the US cannot carry out their internal security for them. It would undermine their domestic legitimacy and be exploited by Iran. Moreover, it is not possible for the US to act as a mediator when it has no relations with Iran. Interview with Frank Carlucci, Washington, D.C., 1997.

79 Interviews, US State Department, Washington, DC, 1997. There can be a long time lag between an attack and a defensive measure. See Ian Brownlie, *International Law and the Use of Force by States* (Oxford: Clarendon Press, 1963). Europe takes a more restrictive view of self-defense. The United States takes a less restrictive view on self-defense and on the time lag before self-defense. See Louise Doswald-Beck, *The San Remo Manual on Armed Conflict at Sea*. See the Caroline case for the concept of anticipatory self-defense, when the "necessity of self-defence is instant, overwhelming, and leaving no choice of means, and no moment for deliberation." Henkin, Pugh, Schachter and Smit, op. cit., 872.

80 Interview, US Department of State, Washington, DC, 1997 and interview, Washington, DC, 1997.

81 Interviews, the Pentagon, Arlington, Virginia, 1997.

82 Interview, the Pentagon, Arlington, Virginia, 1997.

83 Interview, the Pentagon, Arlington, Virginia, 1997. One example of a peaceful resolution to this type of dispute occurred in October 1998, when the Permanent Court of Arbitration ruled unanimously that Yemen has the right to sovereignty over the Hanish islands. Eritrea, which had occupied the islands in 1995 and agreed to international arbitration in 1996, accepted the ruling. See *Gulf News*, October 11, 13, 1998.

84 Interview, the Pentagon, Arlington, Virginia, 1997.

85 Interview, Abu Dhabi, November 1997.

86 Interview, US Department of State, Washington, DC, 1997.

87 Interview, Crescent Oil, Sharjah, December 1997. See *Executive Order #12957 Prohibiting Certain Transactions With Respect to the Development of Iranian*

Petroleum Resources, March 15, 1995. See also *Executive Order #12959 Prohibiting Certain Transactions With Respect To Iran*, May 6, 1995, which refers to "the territory of Iran and any other territory or marine area, including the exclusive economic zone and continental shelf, over which the Government of Iran claims sovereignty, sovereign rights or jurisdiction, provided that the Government of Iran exercises partial or total de facto control over the area or derives a benefit from economic activity in the area pursuant to international arrangements."

88 Interview, US Department of State, Washington, DC, 1997. Crescent consulted with the Office of Foreign Assets Control at the US Treasury Department in restructuring this agreement.

89 It should be noted that there have been some voices in the US calling for improving relations and a dialogue with Iran, and particularly after the election of the reform-minded President Khatami in 1997. See for example the article by Zbigniew Brzezinski, Brent Scowcroft and Richard Murphy, "Differentiated Containment" in *Foreign Affairs* 76, no. 3 (May/June 1997). Former Defense Secretary Frank Carlucci said in October 1997 that the US gains nothing by blinding itself, so a dialogue is necessary. However, this should only be pursued if it can be done without sanctioning Iran's expansionist activities, particularly its use of terror, and if it spells out the corrective action Iran must take in order to have more normal relations with the United States. Interview, Washington DC, October 1997.

90 *Wall Street Journal*, December 16, 1997.

91 Interviews, US Department of State, Washington DC and US Department of Defense, Arlington, Virginia, 1997.

92 *Gulf News*, March 26, 2000, April 6, 2000 and May 6, 2000.

93 *Gulf News*, May 28, 1997.

94 *The National Security Strategy of the United States of America* (Washington, DC: the White House, September 2002).

95 For a brief review of these developments, see *Jane's Sentinel Security Assessment: The Gulf States, 2003* at www4.janes.com.

96 Interviews, Washington, DC, 1997.

97 Interview, US Department of State, Washington, DC, 1997. If the State Department wanted a brief on the merits of the case, the Legal Department would be asked to provide a confidential opinion.

CONCLUSION

1 For an official discussion of the strategic significance of the Gulf and of US interests and military strategy in the Gulf, see *United States Security Strategy for the Middle East* (Department of Defense, Office of International Security Affairs, May 1995).

2 Ibid., 21-3.

3 General J.H. Binford Peay, III, Commander-in-Chief, U.S. Central Command, "Five Pillars of Peace: A Blueprint for Achieving Peace and Stability in the Central Region," US-GCC Corporate Cooperation Committee Inc. *Occasional Paper Series*, no. 5, September 1995, 4-7.

4 *United States Security Strategy*, op. cit., 18.

5 *The National Security Strategy of the United States of America* (Washington, DC: White House, September 2002).

BIBLIOGRAPHY

Abdulghani, Jasim M. *Iraq and Iran: The Years of Crisis* (Baltimore, MD: The Johns Hopkins University Press, 1984).

Abdullah, Muhammad Morsy. *The United Arab Emirates: A Modern History* (London: Hurtwood Press, Ltd., 1978 and 1994).

Address of H.E. Dr. Ahmed Esmet Abdel Meguid, Secretary General of the Arab League, to the Islamic Summit, Tehran, December 9, 1997 in Arabic (Arab League, Cairo, 1997).

Al-Kaabi, Brigadier General Mohamed Hilal. *The Question of Iranian Occupation of the Islands, Greater Tunb, Lesser Tunb and Abu Musa Belonging to the United Arab Emirates* (Carlisle Barracks, Pennsylvania: US Army War College, 1994).

Al-Qasimi, Shaikh Dr. Sultan bin Muhammad. *The Myth of Arab Piracy in the Gulf* (London: Routledge, 1988).

—— (ed.) *The Gulf in Historic Maps, 1478-1861* (Leicester: Streamline Press Limited, 1999).

—— (ed.) *The Gulf in Historic Maps, 1493-1931* (Leicester: Thinkprint Limited, 1996).

—— (ed.) *The Journals of David Seton in the Gulf: 1800-1809* (Exeter: University of Exeter Press, 1995).

Al-Qasimi, Khalid bin Mohammed. *The Three Islands: Between Arab Sovereignty and Iranian Occupation* (in Arabic) (Alexandria: Modern University Office, 1997).

Al-Suwaidi, Jamal S. (ed.) *Iran and the Gulf: A Search for Stability* (Abu Dhabi: The Emirates Center for Strategic Studies and Research, 1996).

Al-Tadmori, Ahmad Jalal. *The Three Arabian Islands: A Documentary Study* (Ras al-Khaimah: RAK National Printing Press, 2000).

Alam, Asadollah (Alinaghi Alikhani ed.) *The Shah and I: The Confidential Diary of Iran's Royal Court, 1969-1977* (London: I.B. Tauris and Company, Ltd., 1991).

Albaharna, Husain. *The Arabian Gulf States: Their Legal and Political Status and Their International Problems* (Beirut: Librairie Du Liban, 1978).

Algar, Hamid (translator and annotator) *Islam and Revolution: Writings and Declarations of Imam Khomeini* (Berkeley, CA: Mizan Press, 1981).

Amirahmadi, Hooshang (ed.) *Small Islands, Big Politics: The Tonbs and Abu Musa in the Gulf* (London: Palgrave Macmillan Press Ltd., 1996).

—— and Eric Hooglund (eds.) *US-Iran Relations: Areas of Tension and Mutual Interest* (Washington, DC: The Middle East Institute, 1994).

Anthony, John Duke. *Arab States of the Lower Gulf: People, Politics, Petroleum* (Washington, DC: The Middle East Institute, 1975).

Aubin, Jean. "Le Royaume d'Ormuz au debut du XVI siecle." *Mare Luso-Indicum*, vol. 2 (Geneve: Librarie Droz, and Paris: Librarie Minard, 1973).

Badeeb, Saeed M. *Saudi-Iranian Relations: 1932-1982* (London: Centre for Arab and Iranian Studies, 1993).

Balfour-Paul, Glen. *The End of Empire in the Middle East: Britain's Relinquishment of Power in her Last Three Arab Dependencies* (Cambridge: Cambridge University Press, 1991).

Bathurst, M.E., Northcutt Ely and Coward Chance. *Sharjah's Title to the Island of Abu Musa* (London: Unpublished study for the Ruler of Sharjah, September 1971).

Beal, Clifford. "Uncovered: Iran's Abu Musa island." *Jane's Defence Weekly* 33, no. 10, March 8, 2000.

Bowett, D. W. *The International Court of Justice: Process, Practice, and Procedure* (London: British Institute of International and Comparative Law, 1997).

BP Amoco Statistical Review of World Energy, June 2002.

Brierly, J.L. *The Law of Nations* (Oxford: The Clarendon Press, 1963).

British Yearbook of International Law, Volume XXV (Oxford: Oxford University Press, 1948).

Brownlie, Ian. *Principles of Public International Law*, 4th edition (Oxford: Clarendon Press, 1990).

—— *International Law and the Use of Force by States* (Oxford: Clarendon Press, 1963).

Brzezinski, Zbigniew, Brent Scowcroft and Richard Murphy. "Differentiated Containment." *Foreign Affairs* 76, no. 3 (May/June 1997).

Buchta, Wilfried. *Who Rules Iran? The Structure of Power in the Islamic Republic* (Washington DC: The Washington Institute for Near East Policy and the Konrad Adenauer Stiftung, 2000).

Burdett, A.L.P. (ed.) *Records of the Emirates, 1966-1971* (London: Archive Editions, 2002).

Calabrese, John. "China and the Persian Gulf." *Middle East Journal* 52, no. 3 (Summer 1998).

Chronicle of Progress: Twenty-Five Years of Progress in the United Arab Emirates (London: Trident Press Ltd., 1996).

Chubin, Shahram and Charles Tripp. *Iran-Saudi Arabia Relations and Regional Order*. Adelphi Paper 304 (London: Oxford University Press, 1996).

—— *Iran's National Security Policy: Capabilities, Intentions and Impact* (Washington, DC: The Carnegie Endowment for International Peace, 1994).

—— and Sepehr Zabih. *The Foreign Relations of Iran* (Berkeley, CA: University of California Press, 1974).

Clawson, Patrick. *US Sanctions on Iran*. The Emirates Occasional Papers no. 8 (Abu Dhabi: The Emirates Center for Strategic Studies and Research, 1997).

Closing Statements of the Sessions of the Supreme Council: Sessions 1-18 (Riyadh: The Secretariat General of The Cooperation Council for the Arab States of the Gulf, 1998).

Cordesman, Anthony H. *Bahrain, Oman, Qatar, and the UAE: Challenges of Security* (Boulder, CO: Westview Press, 1997).

—— *Iran and Iraq: The Threat from the Northern Gulf* (Boulder, CO: Westview Press, 1994).

—— *The Gulf and the Search for Strategic Stability* (Boulder, CO: Westview Press, 1980).

—— and Abraham R. Wagner, *The Lessons of Modern War, Volume II: The Iran-Iraq War* (Boulder, CO: Westview Press, 1990).

Cottam, Richard. "Symposium: US Policy Toward Iran: From Containment to Relentless Pursuit?" *Middle East Policy* IV, no. 1 and 2 (September 1995).

Coward Chance and Associates, *Interim Report to His Highness the Ruler of Sharjah* (unpublished) (Swithin's House, London, July 23, 1971).

Crowe, Admiral William J. with David Chanoff. *The Line of Fire* (New York, NY: Simon and Schuster, 1993).

Dames, Mansel Longworth (trans. and ed.) *The Book of Duarte Barbosa: An Account of the Countries Bordering on the Indian Ocean and their Inhabitants, circa 1518* (London: Hakluyt Society, 1918).

Davies, Charles E. *The Blood-Red Arab Flag* (Exeter: Exeter University Press, 1997).

De Visscher, Charles (translated from French by Percy E. Corbett) *Theory and Reality in Public International Law* (Princeton, NJ: Princeton University Press, 1957).

Dixon, Martin and Robert McCorquodale. *Cases and Materials on International Law* (London: Blackstone Press Limited, 1995).

Eisenstadt, Michael. *Iranian Military Power: Capabilities and Intentions* (Washington, DC: The Washington Institute for Near East Policy, 1996).

Ely, Northcutt. Videotaped deposition at the ICJ at The Hague, 1992.

Energy Map of Arab Oil Producers, 2nd edition (London: Petroleum Economist Ltd., September 1996).

Eyffinger, Arthur. *The International Court of Justice: 1946-1996* (Leiden: Kluwer Law International, 1996).

"Final communiqué adopted by the Supreme Council of the Gulf Cooperation Council at its twenty-second session, held in Muscat, Oman, on 30 and 31 December 2001" (www.gcc-sc.org).

Fisher, W.B. (ed.) *The Cambridge History of Iran*, vol. I (Cambridge: Cambridge University Press, 1968).

Foreign Office (Great Britain) up to 1968, FO 371, General Correspondence (Cited as Unpublished FO).

Foreign and Commonwealth Office after 1968, FCO 8 (Cited as Unpublished FCO).

Gause, F. Gregory. *Saudi-Yemeni Relations: Domestic Structures and Foreign Influence* (New York, NY: Columbia University Press, 1990).

—— "British and American Policies in the Persian Gulf, 1968-1973." *Review of International Studies* (Cambridge: Cambridge University Press, 1985).

Ghareeb, Edmund and Ibrahim Al Abed (eds) *Perspectives on the United Arab Emirates* (London: Trident Press Ltd., 1997).

Hansman, John. *Julfar, An Arabian Port: Its Settlement and Far Eastern Ceramic Trade from the 14th to the 18th Centuries* (London: The Royal Asiatic Society of Great Britain and Ireland, 1985).

Hanzal, Faleh. *Al Mufassal and the History of the UAE* (in Arabic) (Abu Dhabi: The Heritage and History Committee, 1983).

Hawley, Donald. *The Trucial States* (London: Allen and Unwin, 1970).

Heard-Bey, Frauke. *From Trucial States to United Arab Emirates: A Society in Transition* (London: Longman Group, 1996).

Henkin, Louis, Richard Crawford Pugh, Oscar Schachter and Hans Smit. *International Law: Cases and Materials* (St. Paul, MN: West Publishing Company, 1993).

Hiro, Dilip. *The Longest War: The Iran-Iraq Military Conflict* (London: Paladin Grafton Books, 1990).

Hourani, George F. *Arab Seafaring in the Indian Ocean in Ancient and Medieval Times* (Princeton, NJ: Princeton University Press, 1951, revised and expanded by John Carswell, 1995).

Hudson, Michael. *Arab Politics: The Search for Legitimacy* (New Haven, NJ: Yale University Press, 1977).

Humaidan, Ali. "From the Shah's Empire to the Islamic Republic: The UAE, Iran and the Three Islands." (in Arabic) Part III and IV, *Al-Ittihad,* June 6 and July 13, 1997.

Jackson, Paul (ed.) *Jane's All the World's Aircraft, 1998-1999* (London: Jane's Information Group Limited, 1999).

Jane's Sentinel Security Assessment: The Gulf States (UK: Jane's Information Group, Ltd., 2000).

Katz, Mark N. *Russia and Arabia: Soviet Foreign Policy toward the Arabian Peninsula* (Baltimore, MD: The Johns Hopkins University Press, 1986).

Katzman, Kenneth. *Warriors of Islam: Iran's Revolutionary Guard* (Boulder, CO: Westview Press, 1993).

Kechichian, Joseph. *Oman and the World: The Emergence of an Independent Foreign Policy* (Santa Monica, CA: The Rand Corporation, 1995).

—— (ed.) *A Century in Thirty Years: Shaykh Zayed and the United Arab Emirates* (Washington, DC: Middle East Policy Council, 2000).

Keddie, Nikki R. and Mark J. Gasiorowski (eds.) *Neither East Nor West: Iran, the Soviet Union, and the United States* (New Haven, NJ: Yale University Press, 1990).

Kelly, J.B. *Arabia, the Gulf and the West* (London: George Weidenfeld and Nicolson Ltd, 1980).

—— *Britain and the Persian Gulf: 1795-1880* (Oxford: The Clarendon Press, 1968).

Khalifa, Ali Mohammed. *The United Arab Emirates: Unity in Fragmentation* (Boulder, CO: Westview Press, 1979).

Khalilzad, Zalmay. "The United States and the Persian Gulf: Preventing Regional Hegemony." *Survival* 37, no. 2 (Summer 1995).

Kniphausen Report (Dutch General State Archives: Algemeen Rijksarchief in The Hague, referred to as ARA, Aanw.1e Afd. 1889, 23b, folio 12; English translation courtesy of Centre for Documentation and Research in Abu Dhabi, Dutch archives division).

Lenczowski, George. *American Presidents and the Middle East* (Durham: Duke University Press, 1990).

—— *The Middle East in World Affairs* (Ithaca: Cornell University Press, 1980).

—— (ed.) *Iran Under the Pahlavis* (Stanford, CA: Hoover Institution Press, 1978).

—— "Major Pipelines in the Middle East: Problems and Prospects," *Middle East Policy* 3, no. 4 (April 1995).

Lennox, Duncan (ed.) *Jane's Air-Launched Weapons* (London: Jane's Information Group Limited, 1997), Issue 25, November 1996.

Long, David E. and Christian Koch (eds.) *Gulf Security in the Twenty-First Century* (Abu Dhabi: The Emirates Center for Strategic Studies and Research, 1997).

Mack, David L. "In a Tough Neighborhood," *Middle East Insight*, Special UAE Issue, vol. XII, no. 6 (September-December 1996).

Mattair, Thomas R. "Horizons for Cooperation in the [Persian] Gulf: The View from Washington." *The Iranian Journal of International Affairs* VII, no. 3 (Fall 1995).

—— "Containment or Collision?" *Middle East Insight* 11, no. 5 (July-August, 1995).

—— "Interview with U.N. Ambassador Kamal Kharazi of Iran." *Middle East Policy* (Fall 1994).

McLachlan, Keith (ed.) *The Boundaries of Modern Iran* (London: University College London Press, 1994).

Menashri, David. *Revolution at a Crossroads: Iran's Domestic Politics and Regional Ambitions* (Washington, DC: The Washington Institute for Near East Policy, 1997).

Middle East and North Africa 1997 (London: Europa Publications Limited, 1996).

Nader, George. "Interview with President Ali Akbar Hashemi Rafsanjani." *Middle East Insight* XI, no. 5 (July-August 1995).

National Archives and Records Administration, College Park, Maryland (United States) Department of State Record Group 250 to 1963 (Listed as Unpublished NARA) Record Group 59 after 1963 (Listed as Unpublished NARA)

National Security Strategy of the United States of America (Washington, DC: The White House, September 2002).

Navias, Martin S. and E.R. Hooton. *Tanker Wars: The Assault on Merchant Shipping During The Iran-Iraq Crisis, 1980-1988* (London: I.B. Tauris and Company Ltd., 1996).

Niebuhr, Carsten (translated into Dutch by S.J. Baalde) *Description of Arabia* (Utrecht: J. Van Schoonhoven and Company, 1774). English translation courtesy of the Centre for Documentation and Research, Abu Dhabi, Dutch archives division.

Noyes, James. *The Clouded Lens: Persian Gulf Security and U.S. Policy* (Stanford, CA: Hoover Institution Press, 1982).

Piacentini, V. Fiorani. "Siraf and Hormuz Between East and West: Merchants and Merchandise in the Gulf," paper presented at the Symposium on External Interests in the Arab Gulf, University of Exeter, Centre for Arab Gulf Studies, July 11-13, 1990.

"Press communiqué issued by the Ministerial Council of the Gulf Cooperation Council at its seventy-ninth session, held in Jeddah on 2 June 2001" (www.gcc-sc.org).

Quandt, William. *Saudi Arabia in the 1980s: Foreign Policy, Security, and Oil* (Washington, DC: The Brookings Institution, 1981).

Ramazani, R.K. *Revolutionary Iran: Challenge and Response in the Middle East* (Baltimore, MD: The Johns Hopkins University Press, 1986).

—— *The Persian Gulf and the Strait of Hormuz* (Alphen aan den Rijn: Sijthoff and Noordhoff, 1979).

—— *Iran's Foreign Policy 1941-1973: A Study of Foreign Policy in Modernizing Nations* (Charlottesville, VA: University Press of Virginia, 1975).

—— *The Persian Gulf: Iran's Role* (Charlottesville, VA: University Press of Virginia, 1972).

—— "The Shifting Premise of Iran's Foreign Policy: Towards a Democratic Peace?" *The Middle East Journal* 52, no. 2 (Spring 1998).

Razavi, Ahmad. *Continental Shelf Delimitation and Related Maritime Issues in the Persian Gulf* (The Hague: Martinus Nijhoff Publishers, 1997).

Reports Respecting the Iranian Occupation of Abu Musa, Tonb Al Kubra, and Tonb Al Sughra (Arab League, Cairo, 1971).

Rosenne, Shabtai. *The Law and Practice of the International Court* (Leiden: W.A. Sijthoff, 1985).

—— "Introduction to International Litigation," an address to the University of Durham conference on *Preparing for Boundary Litigation and Arbitration*, Durham, England, March 25-26, 1998.

Round Table Discussion on "The Dispute Over The Gulf Islands" (London: Arab Research Centre, 1992).

Safran, Nadav. *Saudi Arabia: The Ceaseless Quest for Security* (Ithaca, NY: Cornell University Press, 1988).

Schofield, Richard (ed.) *Territorial Foundations of the Gulf States* (London: University College London Press Limited, 1994).

—— (ed.) *Arabian Boundaries: New Documents* (London: Archive Editions, 1993 to 1997).

—— (ed.) *Arabian Boundaries: New Documents 1965* vol. 2 (London: Archive Editions, 1994).

Sharpe, Captain Richard, RN (ed.) *Jane's Fighting Ships, 2000-2001* (London: Jane's Information Group Limited, 2000).

Sick, Gary G. and Lawrence G. Potter (eds) *The Persian Gulf at the Millennium: Essays in Politics, Economy, Security, and Religion* (New York, NY: St. Martin's Press, 1997).

Sinclair, W.F. and D. Ferguson (trans. and eds.) *The Travels of Pedro Teixeira* (London: Hakluyt Society, 1902).

Sirhan ibn Sa'id ibn Sirhan. *Annals of Oman* (Cambridge: The Oleander Press, 1964).

Slot, B.J. *The Arabs of the Gulf: 1602-1784* (Leidschendam: 1993).

—— *The Oldest Historical Sources About Sirri, Abu Musa and the Tunbs* (Abu Dhabi: The Cultural Foundation, 1992).

Taryam, Abdullah Omran. *The Establishment of the United Arab Emirates, 1950-1985* (London: Croom Helm, 1987).

Thomas, R. Hughes (ed.) *Arabian Gulf Intelligence: Selections from the Records of the Bombay Government* (Cambridge: Oleander Press, 1985).

Toye, P.L. (ed.) *The Lower Gulf Islands: Abu Musa and the Tunbs* (London: Archive Editions, 1993).

—— (ed.) *Records of the Emirates, Primary Documents, 1820-1958* (London: Archive Editions, 1990).

Tuson, Penelope (ed.) *Records of the Emirates: 1820-1958* (London: Archive Editions, 1990).

Twinam, Joseph. *The Gulf, Cooperation and the Council: An American Perspective* (Washington, DC: The Middle East Policy Council, 1992).

United Arab Emirates, Country Profile, 1999-2000 (London: The Economist Intelligence Unit, 1999).

United Arab Emirates Yearbook 1996 (London: Trident Press, 1996).

United States Security Strategy for the Middle East (Washington, DC: Office of the Assistant Secretary of Defense for International Security Affairs, Middle East and North African Affairs, May 1995).

Vinson and Elkins. *Territorial Sovereignty Over the Tunb Islands* (Houston: An unpublished study for the Ruler of Ras al-Khaimah, 1980).

Watts, Anthony J. (ed.), *Jane's Underwater Weapons Systems, 1998-1999* (London: Jane's Information Group Limited, 1998).

Weinberger, Caspar. *'Fighting for Peace': Seven Critical Years in the Pentagon* (New York, NY: Warner Books, 1990).

Weissberg, G. "Maps as Evidence in International Boundary Disputes: A Reappraisal," *American Journal of International Law* 57 (1963).

Wilson, Sir Arnold. *The Persian Gulf: A Historical Sketch from the Earliest Times to the Beginning of the Twentieth Century* (Oxford: The Clarendon Press, 1928).

Wright, Sir Denis. "Ten Years in Iran: Some Highlights." *Asian Affairs*, XXII (III) October 1991.

Wright, Sir Denis. Unpublished memoirs.

Newspapers, Journals, Magazines and News Agencies

Akhbar Al Sa'ah (ECSSR analytical bulletin)
Al-Anwar (Lebanon)
Al-Azmina al-Arabiah (UAE)
Al-Bayan (UAE)
Al-Hadaf (Kuwait)
Al-Hawadith (Lebanon)
Al-Hayat (UK)
Al-Ittihad (UAE)
Al-Khaleej (UAE)
Al-Sharouq Magazine (Sharjah)
Al-Sharq Al-Awsat (UK)
Al-Wahdah (UAE)
Al-Watan (Saudi Arabia)
An-Nahar (Lebanon)
Christian Science Monitor (USA)
Emirates News (UAE)
Financial Times (UK)
Foreign Broadcast Information Service (FBIS) (USA)
Gulf News (UAE)
Gulf Today (UAE)
Iraqi News Agency
Kayhan International (Iran)
Khaleej Times (UAE)
Jane's Defence Weekly (UK)
Jane's Intelligence Review (UK)
Jane's Sentinel (UK)
Middle East Economic Digest (MEED) (UK)
Middle East Economic Survey (MEES) (Cyprus)
Middle East Monitor (UK)
New York Times (USA)
Reuters
The Daily Telegraph (UK)
The Guardian (UK)
The Iranian Journal of International Affairs (Iran)
The Times (UK)
Wall Street Journal (USA)
Washington Post (USA)

Personal Interviews

Dr. Muhammad Morsy Abdullah (Former Director of the Centre for Documentation and
  Research, Abu Dhabi)

Husain M. Albaharna (Legal scholar, Bahrain)

H.E. Ambassador Khalifa Shahin Al-Marri (Former Director of the GCC Affairs
  Department, UAE Foreign Ministry and Currently UAE Ambassador to Iran)

Dr. Jamal S. Al-Suwaidi (Director General, The Emirates Center for Strategic Studies
  and Research)

H.H. Shaikh Saqr bin Muhammad Al-Qasimi (Member of the Supreme Council and
  Ruler of Ras al-Khaimah)

H.H. Shaikh Khalid bin Saqr Al-Qasimi (Former Crown Prince and Deputy Ruler of
  Ras al-Khaimah)

Shaikh Fahim bin Sultan Al-Qasimi (Former GCC Secretary-General and currently
  Minister of Supreme Council and GCC Affairs)

Dr. Mohamed Abdullah Al Roken (Constitutional law scholar)

Abdullah Bishara (Former GCC Secretary-General)

Frank Carlucci (Former US National Security Advisor and Defense Secretary)

Martin Indyk (US National Security Council)

Duncan Slater (Former aide to British Political Resident Sir William Luce)

Julian Walker (Former British Consul General to Ras al-Khaimah and British Political
  Agent in Dubai)

Michael S. Weir (Former Foreign Office Official)

Sir Denis Wright (Former British Ambassador to Tehran)

Interviews with Officials

British Embassy, Abu Dhabi

Institute for International Political Studies, Tehran, Iran

Joint Staff–The Pentagon

UAE Foreign Ministry

US Defense Intelligence Agency

US Department of Defense, Office of the Assistant Secretary for International Security
  Affairs

US Department of Defense, Office of International Security Affairs

US Department of State

US Embassy, Abu Dhabi

US National Security Council

INDEX

The Emirates Center for Strategic Studies and Research

The Emirates Center for Strategic Studies and Research (ECSSR) is an independent research institution dedicated to the promotion of professional studies and educational excellence in the UAE, the Gulf and the Arab world. Since its establishment in Abu Dhabi in 1994, ECSSR has served as a focal point for scholarship on political, economic and social matters. Indeed, ECSSR is at the forefront of analysis and commentary on Arab affairs.

The Center provides a forum for the scholarly exchange of ideas by hosting conferences and symposia, organizing workshops, sponsoring a lecture series and publishing original and translated books and research papers. ECSSR also has an active fellowship and grant program for the writing of scholarly books and for the translation into Arabic of works relevant to the Center's mission. Moreover, ECSSR has a large library including rare and specialized holdings and a state-of-the-art technology center, which has developed an award-winning website that is a unique and comprehensive source of information on the Gulf.

Through these and other activities, ECSSR aspires to engage in mutually beneficial professional endeavors with comparable institutions worldwide, and to contribute to the general educational and scientific development of the UAE.